DATE DUE

AN

LOPMENT

RT 2003

ium Development

compact among

to end human

UNDP

Published
for the United Nations
Development Programme
(UNDP)

New York   Oxford
Oxford University Press
2003

Oxford University Press
Oxford   New York
Athens   Auckland   Bangkok   Calcutta
Cape Town   Chennai   Dar es Salaam   Delhi
Florence   Hong Kong   Istanbul   Karachi
Kuala Lumpur   Madrid   Melbourne
Mexico City   Mumbai   Nairobi   Paris
Singapore   Taipei   Tokyo   Toronto

and associated companies in
Berlin   Ibadan

ISBN 0-19-521915-5

9 8 7 6 5 4 3 2 1
Printed by Phønix-Trykkeriet A/S, Aarhus, Denmark on acid-free, recycled paper. ISO 14001 certified and EMAS-approved.

Cover and design: Gerald Quinn, Quinn Information Design, Cabin John, Maryland

Editing, desktop composition and production management: Communications Development Incorporated,
Washington, DC

TEAM FOR THE PREPARATION OF
Human Development Report 2003

Director and Editor-in-Chief
Sakiko Fukuda-Parr

Special Adviser
Nancy Birdsall

Guest Contributing Editor
Jeffrey Sachs

Core team

Silva Bonacito, Emmanuel Boudard, Carla De Gregorio, Haishan Fu (Chief of Statistics), Claes Johansson, Christopher Kuonqui, Santosh Mehrotra, Tanni Mukhopadhyay, Omar Noman (Deputy Director), Stefano Pettinato, David Stewart, Aisha Talib, Nena Terrell and Emily White

Principal consultants

Nancy Birdsall, Fernando Calderón, Isidoro P. David, Angus Deaton, Diane Elson, Richard Jolly, James Manor, Ann Pettifor, Sanjay Reddy and Frances Stewart

Statistical adviser: Tom Griffin

Editors: Charis Gresser and Bruce Ross-Larson
Design: Gerald Quinn

The team benefited from close collaboration with
The Millennium Project team

John McArthur (Manager), Chandrika Bahadur, Michael Faye, Margaret Kruk, Guido Schmidt-Traub and Thomas Snow

The Millennium Project Task Force coordinators and principal contributors

Jhoney Barcarolo, Nancy Birdsall, Kwesi Botchwey, Mushtaque Chowdhury, Prarthna Dayal, Lynn Freedman, Pietro Garau, Caren Grown, Amina Ibrahim, Calestous Juma, Yolanda Kakabadse Navarro, Alec Irwin, Zahia Khan, Jim Kim, Yee-Cheong Lee, Roberto Lenton, Ruth Levine, Don Melnick, Patrick Messerlin, Eva Ombaka, Joan Paluzzi, Mari Pangestu, Geeta Rao Gupta, Allan Rosenfield, Josh Ruxin, Pedro Sanchez, Sara Scherr, Elliott Sclar, Burton Singer, Smita Srinivas, M.S. Swaminathan, Paulo Teixeira, Awash Teklahaimanot, Ron Waldman, Paul Wilson, Meg Wirth, Albert Wright and Ernesto Zedillo

Foreword

This Report is about a simple idea whose time has come: the Millennium Development Goals.

Born of the historic Millennium Declaration adopted by 189 countries at the UN Millennium Summit in September 2000, these eight Goals—ranging from halving extreme poverty to halting the spread of HIV/AIDS to enrolling all boys and girls everywhere in primary school by 2015—are transforming development. Governments, aid agencies and civil society organizations everywhere are re-orienting their work around the Goals.

But despite these welcome commitments in principle to reducing poverty and advancing other areas of human development, in practice—as this Report makes very clear—the world is already falling short. For some of the Goals much of the world is on track. But when progress is broken down by region and country and within countries, it is clear that a huge amount of work remains. More than 50 nations grew poorer over the past decade. Many are seeing life expectancy plummet due to HIV/AIDS. Some of the worst performers—often torn by conflict—are seeing school enrolments shrink and access to basic health care fall. And nearly everywhere the environment is deteriorating.

The central part of this Report is devoted to assessing where the greatest problems are, analysing what needs to be done to reverse these setbacks and offering concrete proposals on how to accelerate progress everywhere towards achieving all the Goals. In doing so, it provides a persuasive argument for why, even in the poorest countries, there is still hope that the Goals can be met. But though the Goals provide a new framework for development that demands results and increases accountability, they are not a programmatic instrument. The political will and good policy ideas underpinning any attempt to meet the Goals can work only if they are translated into nationally owned, nationally driven development strategies guided by sound science, good economics and transparent, accountable governance.

That is why this Report also sets out a Millennium Development Compact. Building on the commitment that world leaders made at the 2002 Monterrey Conference on Financing for Development to forge a "new partnership between developed and developing countries"—a partnership aimed squarely at implementing the Millennium Declaration—the Compact provides a broad framework for how national development strategies and international support from donors, international agencies and others can be both better aligned and commensurate with the scale of the challenge of the Goals. And the Compact puts responsibilities squarely on both sides: requiring bold reforms from poor countries and obliging donor countries to step forward and support those efforts.

The aim is not to propose yet another new vision or one-size-fits-all solution to the problems of the developing world; the past 50 years have been littered with the skeletons of far too many of those. Rather, the Compact seeks to highlight the key areas of intervention—from democratic governance to economic stability to commitments to health and education—that should guide national efforts and international support for the Goals. In middle-income countries these interventions should be integrated with regular budget processes and long-term development strategies. In the poorest countries Poverty Reduction Strategy Papers will likely be the most appropriate instrument. The point is not to provide something new or place additional burdens on over-stretched governments, but to offer concrete ideas on how to ensure that the fine words of the Millennium Declaration—elevating poverty to the top of the global agenda—are matched by real, country-owned action plans that make those words a reality.

There are good technocratic reasons for taking this approach. As this Report makes clear, the Goals not only support human development, they are also achievable with the right policies and sufficient resources. But the real power of the Goals is political. They are the first global development vision that combines a global political endorsement with a clear focus on, and means to engage directly with, the world's poor people.

Poor people care about what happens to their income levels. Poor people care about whether their children get into school. Poor people care about whether their daughters are discriminated against in terms of access to education. Poor people care enormously about pandemics and about infectious diseases such as HIV/AIDS, which are devastating communities in Africa. And poor people care a lot about their environment, and whether they have access to clean water and sanitation. Now, with democracy spreading across the developing world, poor people can finally do more than care.

In a very real sense the Goals are a development manifesto for ordinary citizens around the world: time-bound, measurable, pocketbook issues that they can immediately understand—and more important, with adequate data, the Goals seek to hold their governments and the wider international community accountable for their achievement.

That is important. Because while the main focus of the Millennium Development Compact is the first seven Goals and how they apply to developing countries, it is no exaggeration to say that the overall success or failure of the new global partnership the world is trying to build will hinge on achieving the eighth Goal: the one that sets outs the commitments of rich countries to help poor ones who are undertaking good faith economic, political and social reforms.

A key conclusion of this Report is that while reallocating and mobilizing more domestic resources towards targets related to the Goals, strengthening governance and institutions and adopting sound social and economic policies are all necessary to achieve the Goals, they are far from sufficient. The Report is full of examples of countries that are model reformers—but that have not achieved strong growth because geographic isolation, hostile environments or other handicaps mean that sustained external support at well above existing levels is critical to advance their development.

Long-term initiatives to halve hunger and poverty will fail without fundamental restructuring of the global trade system—particularly in agriculture—that includes rich countries dismantling subsidies, lowering tariffs and levelling the playing field. The fight against HIV/AIDS, malaria and other diseases will be lost without effective supplies of affordable, essential drugs to poor countries. Stable, long-term fiscal planning will be impossible for some of the poorest countries without more systematic, sustained debt relief. And last but by no means least, it is important to remember that estimates of an additional $50 billion a year in development assistance to meet the Goals are a minimum—and assume large-scale reallocations of and better access to domestic resources and other sources of finance.

If the fundamental vision of the Goals as a means of better managing globalization on behalf of poor people is to be met, the Goals need to be seen as an indivisible package. It is a package that holds unprecedented promise for improving human development around the world—and a promise that every country has pledged to keep. The challenge is to hold countries to their promises and help them reach the Goals.

Every Human Development Report is a collaborative effort that relies on the help and expertise of not only a dedicated core team but also a wide range of friends and advisers. This year that pool has been broader than usual because UNDP has been able to draw on the preliminary work of The Millennium Project—a network of more than 300 policy-makers, practitioners and experts from around the world who are providing their time, knowledge and energy to a three-year effort to map out exciting new strategies to help countries meet the Goals.

As with previous Reports, this is an independent analysis seeking to advance the debate on human development, not a formal statement of UN or UNDP policy. Nevertheless, as an outline of the central development obstacles and opportunities over the next decade, we believe that it helps frame an ambitious agenda for UNDP and our development partners in the months and years to come.

Mark Malloch Brown

Mark Malloch Brown
Administrator, UNDP

The analysis and policy recommendations of this Report do not necessarily reflect the views of the United Nations Development Programme, its Executive Board or its Member States. The Report is an independent publication commissioned by UNDP. It is the fruit of a collaborative effort by a team of eminent consultants and advisers and the *Human Development Report* team. Sakiko Fukuda-Parr, Director of the Human Development Report Office, led the effort.

Acknowledgements

This Report could not have been prepared without the generous contributions of many individuals and organizations.

The team is particularly grateful for close collaborations with the Millennium Campaign, directed by Eveline Herfkens; the Millennium Project, directed by Jeffrey Sachs; and the Millennium Development Goal Country Reporting Initiative, led by Jan Vandemoortele.

CONTRIBUTORS

Background research commissioned for the Report was contributed by Nancy Birdsall and Michael Clemens, Fernando Calderón and Christopher Pinc, Isadoro P. David, Angus Deaton, Richard Jolly, James Manor, Ann Pettifor and Romilly Greenhill, Sanjay Reddy and Camelia Miniou, and Frances Stewart.

Country studies on selected themes commissioned for the Report were contributed by Halis Akder, Gustavo Arriola, Prosper Backiny-Yetna, Nirupam Bajpay, Edgar Balsells, Shuming Bao, Siaka Coulibaly, Michael Faye, Juan Alberto Fuentes, Ricardo Fuentes, Carlos Alonso Malaver, John McArthur, Rosane Mendonça, Solita T. Monsod, Toby T. Monsod, Andrés Montes, Marc Raffinot, Lucía Mina Rosero, Jeffrey Sachs, Alfredo Sarmiento, Thomas Snow, Irena Topinska, Sandra Álvarez Toro, Wing Woo and Natalia Zubarevich.

The Report also drew on research contributed by members of the Millennium Project's task forces, as listed at http://www.unmillenniumproject.org/html/task_force.shtm.

The UNDP Bureau for Development Policy's Environmentally Sustainable Development Group made special contributions to the chapter on the environment, especially Peter Hazelwood, Susan McDade, Charles McNeill, Alvaro Umana and Jake Werksman, with editor Karen Holmes.

Several organizations generously shared their data and other research materials: the Carbon Dioxide Information Analysis Center, Center for International Comparisons (University of Pennsylvania), Food and Agriculture Organization, International Institute for Strategic Studies, Inter-Parliamentary Union, International Labour Organization, International Telecommunication Union, Joint United Nations Programme on HIV/AIDS, Luxembourg Income Study, Organisation for Economic Co-operation and Development, Statistics Canada, Stockholm International Peace Research Institute, Treaty Section of the Office of Legal Affairs of the United Nations, United Nations Children's Fund, United Nations Conference on Trade and Development, United Nations Department of Economic and Social Affairs, United Nations Educational, Scientific and Cultural Organization Institute for Statistics, United Nations Environment Programme, United Nations High Commission for Human Rights, United Nations High Commissioner for Refugees, United Nations Human Settlements Programme, United Nations Interregional Crime and Justice Research Institute, United Nations Population Division, United Nations Population Fund, United Nations Statistics Division, World Bank, World Health Organization, World Intellectual Property Organization and World Trade Organization.

Chapter 2 benefited from the country maps created by the Center for International Earth Science Information Network (CIESIN), especially the work of Deborah Balk, Gregory Booma, Melanie Brickman and Marc Levy.

ADVISORY PANELS

The Report benefited greatly from intellectual advice and guidance provided by an external advisory panel of eminent experts including Sudhir Anand, Per Pinstrup-Anderson, Peggy Antrobus, Roberto Bissio, Shahid Javed Burki, Angus Deaton, Geoffrey Heal, Ellen t'Hoen, Danuta Hübner, Nicolas Imboden, Richard Jolly, K.S. Jomo, Stephen Lewis, Nora Lustig, James Manor, Solita Monsod, Emmanuel Tumisimi Mutebile, Ann Pettifor, Surin Pitsuwan, Jorge F. Quiroga, Steve Radelet, Gustav Ranis, Kate Raworth, Sanjay Reddy, Mary Robinson, Iyer Saradha, Arjun Sengupta, George Soros, Frances Stewart, Joseph Stiglitz, Paul Streeten, Miguel Szekely, Robert Wade and Ngaire Woods. An advisory panel on statistics included Sudhir Anand, Paul Cheung, Willem DeVries, Lamine Diop, Carmen Feijo, Andrew Flatt, Paolo Garonna, Robert Johnston, Irena Krizman, Nora Lustig, Ian Macredie, Marion McEwin, Wolf Scott, Tim Smeeding and Michael Ward.

CONSULTATIONS

During the preparation of the Report many individuals provided invaluable advice, information and material. The Report team thanks Carla Abouzahr, Masood Ahmed, Claude Akpabie, Diana Alkaron, Sahin Alpay, Philip Alston, Brian Ames, Shaida Badiee, Christian Barry, Grace Bediako, Misha Belkindas, Julia Benn, Anna Betran, Surjit Bhalla, Yonas Biru, Ties Boerma, Virginia Braunstein, Heinrich Brüngger, Edelisa Carandang, Gabriella Carolini, Marion Cheatle, Nicholas Chipperfield, David Cieslikowski, Patrick Cornu, Andrew Creese, Gloria Cuaycong, Sufian Daghra, Alberto Pedro D'Alotto, Shantayanan Devarajan, Volodymyr Demkine, Michael Doyle, Elizabeth Drake, Jean Drèze, Graham Eele, Simon Ellis, Kareen Fabre, Neil Fantom, Shahrokh Fardoust, Kayode Fayemi, Karen Fogg, Phillip Fox, Marta Gacic-Dobo, Gourishankar Ghosh, Alexandre Goubarev, Stefanie Grant, Isabelle Guillet, Emmanuel Guindon, Messaoud Hammouya, Sufian Abu Harb, Ines Havet, Eveline Herfkens, Harvey Herr, Nadia Hijab, John Hilary, Masako Hiraga, Karen Holmes, John Hough, Béla Hovy, José Augusto Hueb, Roslyn Jackson, Daniel Janzen, Jens Johansen, Lawrence Jeff Johnson, Robert Johnston, Karen Judd, Kei Kawabata, Taro Komatsu, Eline L. Korenromp, Aki Kuwahara, Olivier Labe, Mark Lattimer, Henri Laurencin, Sophia Lawrence, Haeduck Lee, Richard Leete, Corinne Lennox, Denise Lievesley, Rolf Luyendijk, Nyein Nyein Lwin, Doug Lynd, Esperanza C. Magpantay, Mary Mahy, Kamal Malhotra, Stephen Marks, Gordon McCord, Jeff McNeely, Pratibha Mehta, José Antonio Mejia, Clare Menozzi, Jorge Mernies, Camelia Minouiu, Franco Modigliani, Roland Monasch, Sufian Mushasha, Maryann Neill, Aimée Nichols, Ann Orr, Jude Padyachy, François Pelletier, Francesca Perucci, Rudolphe Petras, Marina Ponti, William Prince, Agnes Puymoyen, Tatiana Rosito, William Ryan, Sudhir Shetty, Antoine Simonpietri, Anuja Singh, Armin Sirco, Anatoly Smyshlyaev, Abigail Spring, Petter Stålenheim, Eric Swanson, Sirageldin Suliman, Minoru Takada, Gordon Telesford, Javier Teran, Benedicte Terryn, Nyi Nyi Thaung, Michel Thieren, Irene Tinker, Zineb Touimi-Benjelloun, Pierre Varly, Neff Walker, Tessa Wardlaw, Catherine Watt, Simon Wezemon, Caitlin Wiesen, Robertson Work, Nuri Yildirim, A. Sylvester Young, Zohra Yusuf, Elizabeth Zaniewski and Hania Zlotnik.

Consultations were held with diverse groups at workshops on the Millennium Development Goals in Dhaka (Bangladesh) and Bratislava (Slovakia), with civil society groups at the World Social Forum in Porto Alegre (Brazil) and during panel discussions at the Asia Social Forum in Hyderabad (India). The team is particularly grateful to Roberto Bissio, Marina Ponti and Caitlin Wiesin for facilitating these consultations.

An informal statistical consultation provided the team with helpful comments and suggestions. The statistical team thanks Simon Ellis, Brian Hammond, Robert Johnston, Gareth Jones, Denise Lievesley, Laila Manji, Robert Mayo, Abdelhay Mechbal, Sulekha Patel, Francesca Perucci, José Pessoa, Eric Swanson, Michel Thieren, Abiodun Williams and A. Sylvester Young.

The Report team also held several informal consultations with the executive board of UNDP and members of the programme.

UNDP READERS

A Readers Group, made up of colleagues in UNDP, provided extremely useful comments, suggestions and inputs during the writing of the Report. The Report team is especially grateful to Anne-Birgitte Albrectsen, Zéphrin Diabre, Djibril Diallo, Moez Doraid, Enrique Ganuza, Ameerah Haq, Nicola Harrington, Rima Khalaf Hunaidi, Selim Jahan, Zahir Jamal, Abdoulie Janneh, Bruce Jenks, Deborah Landey, Khalid Malik, Elena Martinez, Kalman Miszei, Shoji Nishimoto, Hafiz Pasha, Monica Sharma, Mark Suzman, Julia Taft, Alvaro Umana, Jan Vandemoortele, Gita Welch and Jake Werksman.

STAFF SUPPORT

Administrative support for the Report's preparation was provided by Oscar Bernal, Renuka Corea-Lloyd, Mamaye Gebretsadik, Maria Leon, Myriame Montrose and Bhagirathi Savage. Other colleagues from the Human Development Report Office provided invaluable inputs: Sarah Burd-Sharps, Ana Cutter, Carolina Den Baas, Sharmila Kurukulasuriya, Juan Pablo Mejia, Mary Ann Mwangi, and Frédéric Teboul. The Report also benefited from the dedicated work of interns: Nicola Baroncini, Bethany Donithorn, Abdoulie Abrar Janneh, Barcai M. Karim, Alia Malik, Julia Wanjiru Schwarz, Wilatluk Sinswat and Lara Weisstaub. Nebi Ayele, Gilberto de Jesus and Stephanie Meade made valuable contributions to the outreach and statistical teams.

Invaluable organizational and administrative support was provided by Jennifer Copeland of the Millennium Project, Debbie Creque, Dan Nienhauser and Martha Synnott of the Earth Institute at Columbia University, and Rana Barar, Lisa Dreier, Evelyn Luciano, Alissa Schmelz, Brian Torpy, Christie Walkuski and Haynie Wheeler of the Millennium Project's task forces.

Liliana Izquierdo, Juan Luís Larrabure, Natalia Palgova and Gerardo Nuñez of the United Nations Office for Project Services provided critical administrative support and management services.

EDITING, PRODUCTION AND TRANSLATION

As in previous years, the Report benefited from the editors at Communications Development Incorporated: Meta de Coquereaumont, Paul Holtz, Elizabeth McCrocklin, Bruce Ross-Larson and Alison Strong. The Report was designed by Gerald Quinn and laid out by Elaine Wilson and Wendy Guyette.

The Report also benefited from the translation, design, promotion and distribution work of the Communications Office of the Administrator, especially Maureen Lynch, William Orme, Hilda Paqui, Pia Reunala and Erin Trowbridge. Translations were reviewed by Alia Al-Dalli, Jean Barut, Ghaith Faliz, Enrique Ganuza, Yolaine Michaud, Cielo Morales and Vladimir Scherbov.

* * *

The team expresses sincere appreciation to the Report's peer reviewers—Richard Jolly, Solita Monsod and Jorge F. Quiroga—who carefully reviewed drafts and shared their most recent research and insights. The team is also grateful to Ian Macredie, Lene Mikkelsen and Darryl Rhoades, the statistical peer reviewers who scrutinized the use of data in the Report and lent their statistical expertise.

Finally, the authors are especially grateful to Mark Malloch Brown, UNDP's Administrator, for his leadership and vision. And although thankful for all the support they have received, the authors assume full responsibility for the opinions expressed in the Report.

Sakiko Fukuda-Parr
Director
Human Development Report 2003

Contents

Note on statistics in the Human Development Report   190

MILLENNIUM DEVELOPMENT GOAL INDICATORS

HUMAN DEVELOPMENT INDICATORS

MONITORING HUMAN DEVELOPMENT: ENLARGING PEOPLE'S CHOICES. . .

. . . TO LEAD A LONG AND HEALTHY LIFE. . .

Millennium Development Goals: A compact among nations to end human poverty

The new century opened with an unprecedented declaration of solidarity and determination to rid the world of poverty. In 2000 the UN Millennium Declaration, adopted at the largest-ever gathering of heads of state, committed countries—rich and poor—to doing all they can to eradicate poverty, promote human dignity and equality and achieve peace, democracy and environmental sustainability. World leaders promised to work together to meet concrete targets for advancing development and reducing poverty by 2015 or earlier.

Emanating from the Millennium Declaration, the Millennium Development Goals bind countries to do more in the attack on inadequate incomes, widespread hunger, gender inequality, environmental deterioration and lack of education, health care and clean water (box 1). They also include actions to reduce debt and increase aid, trade and technology transfers to poor countries. The March 2002 Monterrey Consensus—reaffirmed in the September 2002 Johannesburg Declaration on Sustainable Development and the Johannesburg Plan of Implementation—provides a framework for this partnership between rich and poor countries.

It is hard to think of a more propitious time to mobilize support for such a global partnership. In 2003 the world has seen even more violent conflict, accompanied by heightened international tension and fear of terrorism. Some might argue that the war on poverty must take a backseat until the war on terrorism has been won. But they would be wrong. The need to eradicate poverty does not compete with the need to make the world more secure. On the contrary, eradicating poverty should contribute to a safer world—the vision of the Millennium Declaration.

Addressing poverty requires understanding its causes. This Report adds to that understanding by analysing the root causes of failed development. During the 1990s debates about

development focused on three sets of issues. The first was the need for economic reforms to establish macroeconomic stability. The second was the need for strong institutions and governance—to enforce the rule of law and control corruption. The third was the need for social justice and involving people in decisions that affect them and their communities and countries—an issue that this Report continues to champion.

These issues are all crucial for sustainable human development, and they continue to deserve priority attention in policy-making. But they overlook a fourth factor, explored here: the structural constraints that impede economic growth and human development. The Millennium Development Compact presented in this Report proposes a policy approach to achieving the Millennium Development Goals that starts by addressing these constraints.

National ownership—by governments and communities—is key to achieving the Millennium Development Goals. Indeed, the Goals can foster democratic debate, and leaders are more likely to take the actions required for the Goals when there is pressure from engaged populations

The Goals will succeed only if they mean something to the billions of individuals for whom they are intended. The Goals must become a national reality, embraced by their main stakeholders—people and governments. They are a set of benchmarks for assessing progress—and for enabling poor people to hold political leaders accountable. They help people fight for the kinds of policies and actions that will create decent jobs, improve access to schools and root out corruption. They are also commitments by national leaders, who must be held accountable for their fulfilment by their electorates.

continued on next page

BOX 1

Millennium Development Goals and targets

Goal 1: Eradicate extreme poverty and hunger

Target 1: Halve, between 1990 and 2015, the proportion of people whose income is less than $1 a day

Target 2: Halve, between 1990 and 2015, the proportion of people who suffer from hunger

Goal 2: Achieve universal primary education

Target 3: Ensure that, by 2015, children everywhere, boys and girls alike, will be able to complete a full course of primary schooling

Goal 3: Promote gender equality and empower women

Target 4: Eliminate gender disparity in primary and secondary education, preferably by 2005 and in all levels of education no later than 2015

Goal 4: Reduce child mortality

Target 5: Reduce by two-thirds, between 1990 and 2015, the under-five mortality rate

BOX 1 (continued)

Millennium Development Goals and targets

Goal 5: Improve maternal health

Target 6: Reduce by three-quarters, between 1990 and 2015, the maternal mortality ratio

Goal 6: Combat HIV/AIDS, malaria and other diseases

Target 7: Have halted by 2015 and begun to reverse the spread of HIV/AIDS

Target 8: Have halted by 2015 and begun to reverse the incidence of malaria and other major diseases

Goal 7: Ensure environmental sustainability

Target 9: Integrate the principles of sustainable development into country policies and programmes and reverse the loss of environmental resources

Target 10: Halve by 2015 the proportion of people without sustainable access to safe drinking water

Target 11: Have achieved by 2020 a significant improvement in the lives of at least 100 million slum dwellers

Goal 8: Develop a global partnership for development

Target 12: Develop further an open, rule-based, predictable, non-discriminatory trading and financial system (includes a commitment to good governance, development, and poverty reduction—both

continued on next page

When adopted by communities, the Goals can spur democratic debates about government performance, especially when impartial data are made available—posted on the door of every village hall. They can also become campaign platforms for politicians, as with Brazilian President Luis Inacio "Lula" da Silva's Fome Zero (Zero Hunger) campaign to eliminate hunger, part of the manifesto for his presidential bid.

Civil society groups—from community organizations to professional associations to women's groups to networks of non-governmental organizations (NGOs)—have an important role in helping to implement and monitor progress towards the Goals. But the Goals also require capable, effective states able to deliver on their development commitments. And they require popular mobilization to sustain the political will for achieving them. This popular mobilization requires open, participatory political cultures.

Political reforms, such as decentralizing budgets and responsibilities for the delivery of basic services, put decision-making closer to the people and reinforce popular pressure for implementing the Goals. Where decentralization has worked—as in parts of Brazil, Jordan, Mozambique and the Indian states of Kerala, Madya Pradesh and West Bengal—it has brought significant improvements. It can lead to government services that respond faster to people's needs, expose corruption and reduce absenteeism.

But decentralization is difficult. To succeed, it requires a capable central authority, committed and financially empowered local authorities and engaged citizens in a well-organized civil society. In Mozambique committed local authorities with financing authority increased vaccination coverage and prenatal consultations by 80%, overcoming capacity constraints by contracting NGOs and private providers at the municipal level.

Recent experiences have also shown how social movements can lead to more participatory decision-making, as in the public monitoring of local budgets. In Porto Alegre, Brazil, public monitoring of local budgets has brought huge improvements in services. In 1989 just under half of city residents had access to safe water. Seven years later, nearly all did. Primary school enrolments also doubled during that time, and public transportation expanded to outlying areas.

Such collective action improves basic services and helps spur and sustain political will. Ordinary citizens have pressured their leaders to deliver on their political commitments. And the Goals provide citizens with a tool to hold their governments accountable.

Because the Millennium Development Goals will not be realized with a business as usual approach, the pace of progress must be dramatically accelerated

The past 30 years saw dramatic improvements in the developing world. Life expectancy increased by eight years. Illiteracy was cut nearly in half, to 25%. And in East Asia the number of people surviving on less than $1 a day was almost halved just in the 1990s.

Still, human development is proceeding too slowly. For many countries the 1990s were a decade of despair. Some 54 countries are poorer now than in 1990. In 21 a larger proportion of people is going hungry. In 14, more children are dying before age five. In 12, primary school enrolments are shrinking. In 34, life expectancy has fallen. Such reversals in survival were previously rare.

A further sign of a development crisis is the decline in 21 countries in the human development index (HDI, a summary measure of three dimensions of human development—living a long and healthy life, being educated and having a decent standard of living). This too was rare until the late 1980s, because the capabilities captured by the HDI are not easily lost.

If global progress continues at the same pace as in the 1990s, only the Millennium Development Goals of halving income poverty and halving the proportion of people without access to safe water stand a realistic chance of being met, thanks mainly to China and India. Regionally, at the current pace Sub-Saharan Africa would not reach the Goals for poverty until 2147 and for child mortality until 2165. And for HIV/AIDS and hunger, trends in the region are heading up—not down.

That so many countries around the world will fall far short of the Millennium Development Goals in the 12 years to 2015 points to an urgent need to change course. But past development successes show what is possible even in very poor countries. Sri Lanka managed to increase life expectancy by 12 years between 1945 and 1953. Botswana provides another inspiring example: gross enrolments in primary school jumped from 40% in 1960 to almost 91% in 1980.

Today's world has greater resources and know-how than ever before to tackle the challenges of infectious disease, low productivity, lack of clean energy and transport and lack of basic services such as clean water, sanitation, schools and health care. The issue is how best to apply these resources and know-how to benefit the poorest people.

Two groups of countries require urgent changes in course. First are countries that combine low human development and poor performance towards the Goals—the top priority and high priority countries. Second are countries progressing well towards the Goals but with deep pockets of poor people being left behind

There are 59 top priority and high priority countries, where failed progress and terribly low starting levels undermine many of the Goals. It is on these countries that the world's attention and resources must be focused.

In the 1990s these countries faced many types of crises:
- *Income poverty:* poverty rates, already high, increased in 37 of 67 countries with data.
- *Hunger:* in 19 countries more than one person in four is going hungry, and the situation is failing to improve or getting worse. In 21 countries the hunger rate has increased.
- *Survival:* in 14 countries under-five mortality rates increased in the 1990s, and in 7 countries almost one in four children will not see their fifth birthdays.
- *Water:* in 9 countries more than one person in four does not have access to safe water, and the situation is failing to improve or getting worse.
- *Sanitation:* in 15 countries more than one person in four does not have access to adequate sanitation, and the situation is failing to improve or getting worse.

Underlying all these crises is an economic crisis. Not only are these countries already extremely poor, but their growth rates are appallingly slow as well.

In the 1990s average per capita income growth was less than 3% in 125 developing and transition countries, and in 54 of them average per capita income fell. Of the 54 countries with declining incomes, 20 are from Sub-Saharan Africa, 17 from Eastern Europe and the Commonwealth of Independent States (CIS), 6 from Latin America and the Caribbean, 6 from East Asia and the Pacific and 5 from the Arab States. They include many priority countries but also some countries with medium human development.

Countries less often in the public eye are those progressing well but excluding or leaving behind certain groups and areas. All countries should address significant disparities between groups—between men and women, between ethnic groups, between races and between urban and rural areas. Doing so requires looking behind country averages.

Many countries with national averages indicating adequate progress towards the Goals by the target dates have deep pockets of entrenched poverty. China's spectacular achievement of lifting 150 million people out of income poverty in the 1990s was concentrated in coastal regions. Elsewhere, deep pockets of poverty persist. In some inland regions economic progress has been much slower than in the rest of the country.

In a number of countries the Goals could be met more easily simply by improving the circumstances of people already better off. Evidence suggests that this is happening in health. But while this approach may fit the letter of the Goals, it does not fit their spirit. Women, rural inhabitants, ethnic minorities and other poor people are typically progressing slower than national averages—or showing no progress—even where countries as a whole are moving towards the Goals.

Of 24 developing countries with subnational data on child mortality between the mid-1980s and the mid-1990s, only 3 have narrowed the gap in under-five mortality rates between the richest and poorest groups. Similar patterns can be found in immunization coverage and school enrolment and completion rates, where urban-rural gaps and ethnic gaps appear to be persisting or worsening. Women in poor areas also tend to be excluded from overall progress towards the Goals.

The Millennium Development Compact is a plan of action aimed primarily at the top priority and high priority countries most in need of support

Global policy attention needs to focus on countries facing the steepest development challenges

Global policy attention needs to focus on countries facing the steepest development challenges. Without an immediate change in course, they will certainly not meet the Goals. With that in mind, this Report offers a new plan of action aimed primarily at these countries: the Millennium Development Compact.

To achieve sustainable growth, countries must attain basic thresholds in several key areas: governance, health, education, infrastructure and access to markets. If a country falls below the threshold in any of these areas, it can fall into a "poverty trap".

Most of the top and high priority countries are trying to attain these basic thresholds. Yet they face deep-seated structural obstacles that will be difficult to overcome on their own. The obstacles include barriers to international markets and high debt levels—well over what they can service given their limited export capacity. Another important obstacle is a country's size and location. Other structural constraints linked to a country's geography include low soil fertility, vulnerability to climatic shocks or natural disasters and rampant diseases such as malaria. But geography is not destiny. With proper policies, these challenges can be overcome. Better roads and communications and deeper integration with neighbouring countries can increase access to markets. Prevention and treatment policies can greatly mitigate the impact of pandemic diseases.

The same structural conditions that contribute to an entire country's poverty trap can also affect large population groups in countries that are otherwise relatively prosperous. China's remote inland regions, for instance, face much longer distances to ports, much poorer infrastructure and much tougher biophysical conditions than the country's coastal regions—which in recent years have enjoyed the fastest economic growth in history. Reducing poverty in poorer regions requires national policies that reallocate resources to them. The top policy priority here is increasing equity, not just economic growth.

Policy responses to structural constraints require simultaneous interventions on several fronts—along with stepped-up external support. Six policy clusters can help countries break out of their poverty traps:
- Invest early and ambitiously in basic education and health while fostering gender equity. These are preconditions to sustained economic growth. Growth, in turn, can generate employment and raise incomes—feeding back into further gains in education and health gains.
- Increase the productivity of small farmers in unfavourable environments—that is, the majority of the world's hungry people. A reliable estimate is that 70% of the world's poorest people live in rural areas and depend on agriculture.
- Improve basic infrastructure—such as ports, roads, power and communications—to reduce the costs of doing business and overcome geographic barriers.
- Develop an industrial development policy that nurtures entrepreneurial activity and helps diversify the economy away from dependence on primary commodity exports—with an active role for small and medium-size enterprises.
- Promote democratic governance and human rights to remove discrimination, secure social justice and promote the well-being of all people.
- Ensure environmental sustainability and sound urban management so that development improvements are long term.

The thinking behind these policies is that for economies to function better, other things must fall into place first. It is impossible to reduce dependence on primary commodity exports, for instance, if the workforce cannot move into manufacturing because of low skills.

The job facing top and high priority countries is too big for them to do alone—especially the poorest countries, which face uncommonly high hurdles with very limited resources. In this the Millennium Development Compact is unapologetic. The poorest countries require significant external resources to achieve essential levels of human development. But this is not a demand for open-ended financing from rich countries—because the Compact is also unapologetic on the need for poor countries to mobilize domestic resources, strengthen policies and institutions, combat corruption and improve governance, essential steps on the path to sustainable development.

Unless countries adopt far more ambitious plans for development, they will not meet the Goals. Here the Compact argues that a new principle should apply. Governments of poor and rich countries, as well as international institutions, should start by asking what resources are needed to meet the Goals, rather than allowing the pace of development to be set by the limited resources currently allocated.

Every country—especially the top and high priority ones—needs to systematically diagnose what it will take to achieve the Goals. This diagnosis should include initiatives that governments of poor countries can take, such as mobilizing domestic fiscal resources, reallocating spending towards basic services, drawing on private financing and expertise and introducing reforms to economic governance. All this will still leave a large resource gap, which governments should identify. Filling this gap will require additional financial and technical cooperation from rich countries, including financing for recurrent costs, more extensive debt relief, better market access and increased technology transfers.

There is broad consensus on the need for a single framework to coordinate development efforts, based on country-owned development strategies and public investment programmes. For low-income countries this framework occurs through Poverty Reduction Strategy Papers, in place in some two dozen countries and under way in two dozen more. Poverty Reduction Strategy Papers, in taking on the challenges of the Millennium Development Goals in a more systematic way, need to start asking what it will take to achieve them—and assess the resource gaps and policy reforms that need to be addressed.

Halving the proportion of people in extreme poverty (Goal 1) will require far stronger economic growth in the top priority and high priority countries where growth has been failing. But growth alone will not be enough. Policies also need to strengthen the links between stronger growth and higher incomes in the poorest households

More than 1.2 billion people—one in every five on Earth—survive on less than $1 a day. During the 1990s the share of people suffering from extreme income poverty fell from 30% to 23%. But with a growing world population, the number fell by just 123 million—a small fraction of the progress needed to eliminate poverty. And excluding China, the number of extremely poor people actually increased by 28 million.

South and East Asia contain the largest numbers of people in income poverty, though both regions have recently made impressive gains. As noted, in the 1990s China lifted 150 million people—12% of the population—out of poverty, halving its incidence. But in Latin America and the Caribbean, the Arab States, Central and Eastern Europe and Sub-Saharan Africa the number of people surviving on less than $1 a day increased.

A lack of sustained poverty-reducing growth has been a major obstacle to reducing poverty. In the 1990s only 30 of 155 developing and transition countries with data—about one in five—achieved per capita income growth of more than 3% a year. As noted, in 54 of these countries average incomes actually fell.

But economic growth alone is not enough. Growth can be ruthless or it can be poverty reducing—depending on its pattern, on structural aspects of the economy and on public policies. Poverty has increased even in some countries that have achieved overall economic growth, and over the past two decades income inequality worsened in 33 of 66 developing countries with data. All countries—especially those doing well on average but with entrenched pockets of poverty—should implement policies that strengthen the links between economic growth and poverty reduction.

Growth is more likely to benefit poor people if it is broadly based rather than concentrated in

Unless countries adopt far more ambitious plans for development, they will not meet the Goals

Import tariffs protect markets in rich countries and reduce incentives for farmers in poor countries to invest in agriculture, which would contribute to more sustainable food security

a few sectors or regions, if it is labour intensive (as in agriculture or apparel) rather than capital intensive (as in oil) and if government revenues are invested in human development (as in basic health, education, nutrition and water and sanitation services). Growth is less likely to benefit poor people if it is narrowly based, if it neglects human development or if it discriminates in the provision of public services against rural areas, certain regions, ethnic groups or women.

Public policies that can strengthen the links between growth and poverty reduction include:
• Increasing the level, efficiency and equity of investments in basic health, education and water and sanitation.
• Expanding poor people's access to land, credit, skills and other economic assets.
• Increasing small farmers' productivity and diversification.
• Promoting labour-intensive industrial growth involving small and medium-size enterprises.

Halving the proportion of hungry people (Goal 1) presents two challenges: ensuring access to food now plentiful and increasing the productivity of farmers now hungry—especially in Africa

The number of hungry people fell by nearly 20 million in the 1990s. But excluding China, the number of hungry people increased. South Asia and Sub-Saharan Africa are home to the largest concentrations of hungry people. In South Asia the challenge is improving the distribution of plentifully available food. In Sub-Saharan Africa the challenge also involves increasing agricultural productivity.

Many public actions can be used to reduce hunger. Buffer stocks, especially at the local level, can release food into the market during food emergencies—reducing the volatility of prices. Many countries, such as China and India, have such systems. Food stocks can be particularly important for landlocked countries susceptible to droughts.

In addition, many hungry people are landless or lack secure tenure. Agrarian reform is needed to provide rural poor people with secure

access to land. Women produce much of the food in Sub Saharan Africa and South Asia yet do not have secure access to land.

Low agricultural productivity also needs to be addressed, particularly in marginal ecological regions with poor soils and high climatic variability. The dramatic gains of the green revolution have bypassed these areas. A doubly green revolution is needed—one that increases productivity and improves environmental sustainability. Increased investments are needed to research and develop better technologies and disseminate them through extension services. So are investments in infrastructure, such as roads and storage systems. Yet public investments and donor support for agriculture have fallen in recent decades.

Import tariffs protect markets in rich countries and reduce incentives for farmers in poor countries to invest in agriculture, which would contribute to more sustainable food security. Enormous subsidies in rich countries also reduce incentives to invest in long-term food security and depress world market prices—though they can benefit net food importers.

Achieving universal primary education and eliminating gender disparities in primary and secondary education (Goals 2–3) require addressing efficiency, equity and resource levels as related problems

Across developing regions, more than 80% of children are enrolled in primary school. Yet some 115 million children do not attend primary school, and enrolments are woefully low in Sub-Saharan Africa (57%) and South Asia (84%). Once enrolled, there is a pitiful one in three chance that a child in Africa will complete primary school. In addition, one in six of the world's adults is illiterate. And gaping gender gaps remain: three-fifths of the 115 million children out of school are girls, and two-thirds of the 876 million illiterate adults are women.

Lack of education robs an individual of a full life. It also robs society of a foundation for sustainable development because education is critical to improving health, nutrition and productivity. The education Goal is thus central to meeting the other Goals.

In most poor countries the provision of basic education is highly inequitable, with the poorest 20% of people receiving much less than 20% of public spending—while the richest 20% capture much more. In addition, primary education receives much less financing per student than secondary and higher education. This pattern also discriminates against poor people because they benefit much more from basic education.

Household costs for education, such as user fees and uniforms, also discourage enrolment—especially from the poorest families. Enrolments increased sharply when uniforms and fees were eliminated in Kenya, Malawi and Uganda. An equitable system also leads to better outcomes: countries that perform well in education tend to spend more on the poorest households and more on primary education.

Countries that have eliminated gender disparities in education show how parents can be encouraged to send their daughters to school: locating schools close to home, minimizing out-of-pocket costs, scheduling school hours to accommodate household chores and recruiting female teachers (giving parents a sense of security). High-achieving countries that have eliminated gender disparities have shares of female teachers much larger than regional averages.

Many school systems suffer from operational inefficiencies, with too many children repeating classes and dropping out of school. In countries where several languages are spoken, teaching in the mother tongue in the early years dramatically improves the learning experience. School feeding programmes also help bring children to school and keep them there; hungry children cannot learn. Early childhood programmes help prepare children entering school, especially children from the first generation of learners in their families.

A daunting challenge in countries with low enrolments is managing recurrent costs to strike a better balance between teacher wage bills—which typically eat up 90% or more of recurrent spending—and other costs, such as textbooks. Low spending hurts poor people in particular because elites and powerful groups tend to capture disproportionate shares of small budgets. Small budgets also make it difficult to implement reforms. Increasing equity or efficiency is easier when education resources are growing.

Compounding the resource problem is the decline in donor support for education. In the 1990s such support fell 30% in real terms, to $4.7 billion—with just $1.5 billion for basic education. Donors also typically fund equipment and other capital costs rather than textbooks, teacher salaries and other operating costs. But that is where the real bottlenecks lie.

In both provision and finance, the private sector must do more in secondary and tertiary education. Governments need to encourage NGOs and the private sector to expand supply while maintaining control over standards and centralizing data on the number and quality of private schools. In resource-constrained environments, equity and efficiency require that public subsidies for private primary schooling not be at the expense of basic education for poor people.

Countries can usually spend more on education as their economies grow. But the poorest countries need to spend more on education to escape their poverty traps—and do not have enough resources to make such basic investments.

Countries can usually spend more on education as their economies grow. But the poorest countries need to spend more on education to escape their poverty traps

---

Promoting gender equality and empowering women (Goal 3), valuable in themselves, are also central to achieving all the other Goals

Promoting gender equality and women's empowerment in its broader scope is a key objective of the Millennium Declaration, though eliminating disparities in primary and secondary education is the only quantitative target set. Education contributes to better health, and better education and health increase the productivity that leads to economic growth. Growth then generates resources that finance improvements in people's health and education, further raising productivity. Gender equality is central in these synergies because women are agents of development.

Women are the primary caregivers in almost all societies. Thus their education contributes more to the health and education of the next generation than does that of men—even more so when women also have a strong say in family decisions. As they get older, educated girls have fewer and healthier children, hastening the transition to lower fertility rates. Better-educated, healthier women also contribute to higher productivity—for example, by adopting farming innovations—and thus to higher household incomes. In addition, such women often work outside the home and earn independent incomes, enhancing their autonomy. These beneficial processes have more force when women have a voice in household decisions. And when women can take collective action to demand more rights—to education, health care, equal employment—these positive synergies are even more likely.

Governments in poor countries must rank health spending higher than other types of spending, such as defence

----

Reducing child mortality, improving maternal health and combating HIV/AIDS, malaria and other diseases (Goals 4–6) require a dramatic increase in access to health care

Every year more than 10 million children die of preventable illnesses—30,000 a day. More than 500,000 women a year die in pregnancy and childbirth, with such deaths 100 times more likely in Sub-Saharan Africa than in high-income OECD countries. Around the world 42 million people are living with HIV/AIDS, 39 million of them in developing countries. Tuberculosis remains (along with AIDS) the leading infectious killer of adults, causing up to 2 million deaths a year. Malaria deaths, now 1 million a year, could double in the next 20 years.

Without much faster progress, the Millennium Development Goals in these areas (Goals 4–6) will not be met. Even for the child mortality Goal, where progress has been steady, at the current pace Sub-Saharan Africa will not reduce child mortality by two-thirds until 150 years later than the date set by the Goal.

Such statistics are shameful given that many of these deaths could be avoided with more widespread use of bednets, midwives, affordable antibiotics, basic hygiene and the treatment approach known as DOTS (Directly Observed Therapy Short Course) to combat tuberculosis—none a high-tech solution, yet together they could save millions of lives. But for too many countries they remain out of reach. Why? For broad systemic reasons. As with education,

there is a lack of resources for health systems (especially for basic health), a lack of equity in what systems provide and a lack of efficiency in how services are provided.

Health systems in poor countries are severely underfunded for meeting the Goals. No high-income OECD country spends less than 5% of GDP on public health services. But developing countries rarely exceed this share—most spend 2–3%. In 1997 average public spending on health was a mere $6 per capita in the least developed countries and $13 in other low-income countries—compared with $125 in upper-middle-income countries and $1,356 in high-income countries. The World Health Organization (WHO) estimates that $35–40 per capita is the bare minimum for basic health services. In poor countries it is basically impossible to pay international prices for life-saving medicines—and almost criminal to expect poor people to do so.

With small and inadequate budgets, poor people lose out. In most countries the poorest 20% of households benefit from much less than 20% of health spending. Yet more equitable spending leads to better outcomes: countries with higher allocations to poorer households have lower child mortality rates. Rural-urban disparities are another example of unfair spending. Rural areas usually get much less. In Cambodia 85% of people live in rural areas, but only 13% of government health workers are located there. In Angola 65% of people live in rural areas, but only 15% of health professionals work there.

The lack of resources has a corrosive effect on health systems because shortcomings in one area feed into others. When clinics have no drugs, patients are discouraged from going to them for treatment. That leads to high absenteeism among staff, further eroding effectiveness. Because the community is unlikely to find health services worthwhile, it does not monitor the system, and services becomes less (rather than more) responsive to their needs.

Public policy needs to respond to the issues of resource levels, equity and efficiency:
• *Mobilizing resources.* Governments in poor countries must rank health spending higher than other types of spending, such as defence. And within health budgets, priority must be

given to basic health. But in low-income countries this is unlikely to be enough.

• *Increasing external resources.* This includes aid, but debt relief, drug donations and price discounts from pharmaceutical companies would also help.

• *Achieving greater equity.* Governments must redress imbalances by focusing on rural areas, poor communities, women and children. But focusing on primary care alone will not help; public hospitals overwhelmed by AIDS or tuberculosis patients cannot cope with any other patients.

• *Making health systems work better.* Cash-strapped governments face a dilemma when setting priorities. The first priority is to maintain an integrated system. Vertical programmes focused on specific diseases have become popular, but they cannot be effective or sustainable without basic health infrastructure. Such programmes should be integrated with the overall health structure. Maternal and reproductive health care also cry out for integration. Many countries focus on family planning to the exclusion of child and maternal health. Focusing on essential interventions is not enough; equal focus is needed to ensure that every primary health centre has essential drugs.

Because private health care providers are the first port of call for many poor people, governments must bring them into the public domain through better regulation. Many measures can help: consumer protection legislation, accreditation to signal to consumers which providers are registered, having practitioners agree to restrict their practices to essential medicines. But where higher-level services have been privatized through the use of managed care services, as in many Latin American countries, the experience has been less than positive for the poorest people.

Halving the proportion of people without access to safe drinking water and improved sanitation (Goal 7) requires an integrated approach. Without sanitation and hygiene, safe water is much less useful for health

More than 1.0 billion people in developing countries—one person in five—lack access to safe water. And 2.4 billion lack access to improved sanitation. Both can be life and death issues. Diarrhoea is a major killer of young children: in the 1990s it killed more children than all the people lost to armed conflict since the Second World War. Most affected are poor people in rural areas and slums.

And as with the other health Goals, low-cost technical solutions for community access are well known: protected dug wells, public standpipes, protected springs, pour-flush latrines, simple pit latrines, ventilated pit latrines and connections to septic tanks or covered public sewers. Yet several factors undermine the effectiveness of these solutions. In addition, they are not fully adequate:

Water without sanitation. Access to safe water is far less useful without improved sanitation and better hygiene. Better health care is wasted on treating water-borne diseases that could have been prevented by safe water, improved sanitation and better hygiene. But while the demand for safe water is evident, the demand for safe sanitation depends far more on hygiene education. Poor households generally must take the initiative to install sanitation systems in their homes, and often have to finance the costs themselves. If not convinced that such investment is necessary, they are unlikely to pursue it.

Lack of resources to finance high-cost infrastructure. In urban and peri-urban areas, water supply requires source development, bulk transmission to the community to be served and a local distribution network. Sanitation requires public sewage collection and treatment systems. These investments entail significant costs far beyond the means of most local authorities. Even in middle-income countries such elements must be provided by national governments. The most expensive component of water and sanitation infrastructure is wastewater treatment to prevent raw sewage from entering rivers and contaminating groundwater. This also requires improved technologies. But municipal authorities lack the resources to invest in basic sanitation.

High charges and poor maintenance. Governments must ensure that poor people's access to water and sanitation services is not undermined by unfair charges that subsidize non-poor people. The well-off must shoulder more

Because private health care providers are the first port of call for many poor people, governments must bring them into the public domain through better regulation

of the financial costs of maintaining the infrastructure for these services. Spending on high-cost systems for the better-off parts of towns leave few resources for low-cost schemes—and often leave slums and peri-urban areas with no services. Moreover, water systems tend to be poorly maintained in rural and peri-urban areas. Community involvement has proven key to improving services in such areas.

Experiences with multinational private participation in water and sanitation have been mixed. There have been some private sector successes with increased water services for poor communities in large cities (such as Buenos Aires, Argentina, and metropolitan Manila, the Philippines). But these successes have sometimes been offset by large-scale corruption and backtracking on agreements with governments. Local entrepreneurship has to be promoted in the sector, with national development banks providing the finance.

Policies that promote environmental sustainability should stress the importance of involving local people in the solutions and altering policies in rich countries

---

Ensuring environmental sustainability (Goal 7) will require managing ecosystems so that they can provide services that sustain human livelihoods. It will also be an important part of reaching the other Goals

Soil degradation affects nearly 2 billion hectares, damaging the livelihoods of up to 1 billion people living on drylands. Around 70% of commercial fisheries are either fully or over-exploited, and 1.7 billion people—a third of the developing world's population—live in countries facing water stress.

There is an uneven geography of consumption, environmental damage and human impact. Rich countries generate most of the world's environmental pollution and deplete many of its natural resources. Key examples include depletion of the world's fisheries and emissions of greenhouse gases that cause climate change, both of which are tied to unsustainable consumption patterns by rich people and countries. In rich countries per capita carbon dioxide emissions are 12.4 tonnes—while in middle-income countries they are 3.2 tonnes and in low-income countries, 1.0 tonne. Poor people are most vulnerable to environmental shocks and stresses such as the anticipated impacts of global climate change.

Reversing these negative trends is an end in itself. But it would also contribute to the other Goals because the health, incomes and opportunities of poor people are heavily influenced by the depletion of natural resources. Some 900 million poor people living in rural areas depend on natural products for much of their livelihoods. Up to a fifth of the disease burden in poor countries may be linked to environmental risk factors. Climate change could damage agricultural productivity in poor countries and increase the risks, exposing them to such shocks as floods. These are just a few examples of the interactions between the environmental Goal and the other Goals.

Policies that promote environmental sustainability should stress the importance of involving local people in the solutions. They should also stress the importance of policy changes in rich countries. Among the policy priorities:
- *Improving institutions and governance.* Clearly define property and user rights, improve monitoring and compliance with environmental standards and involve communities in managing their environmental resources.
- *Addressing environmental protection and management* in each country's sector policies and other development strategies.
- *Improving the functioning of markets.* Remove subsidies, especially in rich countries, that damage the environment (such as subsidies for fossil fuels or large-scale commercial fishing fleets), and reflect environmental costs through pollution charges.
- *Strengthening international mechanisms.* Improve international management of global issues such as protecting international watersheds and reversing climate change, together with mechanisms to share these burdens equitably.
- *Investing in science and technology.* Invest more in renewable energy technologies and create an observatory to monitor the functioning and state of major ecosystems.
- *Conserving critical ecosystems.* Create protected areas with the involvement of local people.

A new partnership is needed between rich and poor countries for these policies to take root and bear fruit. For a fair division of responsibilities, large countries need to contribute more to mitigating environmental degradation and apply more resources to reversing it. In this, as in the other Goals, there is an urgent need to rectify some glaring imbalances.

Policy changes in rich countries for aid, debt, trade and technology transfers (Goal 8) are essential to achieving the Goals

It is hard to imagine the poorest countries achieving Goals 1–7 without the policy changes required in rich countries to achieve Goal 8. Poor countries cannot on their own tackle the structural constraints that keep them in poverty traps, including rich country tariffs and subsidies that restrict market access for their exports, patents that restrict access to technology that can save lives and unsustainable debt owed to rich country governments and multilateral institutions.

The poorest countries do not have the resources to finance the investments required to reach critical thresholds in infrastructure, education and health. They do not have the resources to invest in agriculture and small-scale manufacturing to improve worker productivity. These investments lay the groundwork for getting out of poverty traps—and cannot wait for economic growth to generate resources. Children cannot wait for growth to generate resources when they are faced with death from preventable causes.

The partnership framework of the Millennium Declaration and the Monterrey Consensus makes clear that the primary responsibility for achieving Goals 1–7 lies with developing countries. It commits those countries to mobilizing domestic resources to finance ambitious programmes, to implementing policy reforms to strengthen economic governance, to giving poor people a say in decision-making and to promoting democracy, human rights and social justice. But the consensus is also a compact that commits rich countries to doing more—though on the basis of performance rather than entitlement. The Millennium Development Compact makes clear the critical role of rich countries, as reflected in Goal 8.

Rich countries have pledged action on a number of fronts, not only at the Millennium Summit but also at the Monterrey International Conference on Financing for Development in March 2002 and at the Johannesburg World Summit on Sustainable Development in September 2002. And in Doha, Qatar, in November 2001, trade ministers pledged to make the interests of poor countries central to their future work on the multilateral trade system. Now is the time for rich countries to deliver on these promises.

The top priority countries are in greatest need of actions by rich countries. Having the farthest to go to achieve the Goals, economic growth has stagnated for a decade or more, leading to an accumulation of unsustainable debt levels. These countries depend on exports of primary commodities whose prices have steadily fallen. Aid also fell in the 1990s—by nearly a third on a per capita basis in Sub-Saharan Africa—and falls far short of what is needed to achieve the Goals.

More aid—and more effective aid. The tide of declining aid was turned with the pledges made at the Monterrey conference, promising some $16 billion a year in additional aid by 2006. Yet this increase would bring total official development assistance to just 0.26% of the gross national incomes of the 22 members of the OECD's Development Assistance Committee, falling far short of the 0.7% towards which rich countries promised to work in Monterrey and Johannesburg. It also falls short of the estimated need, for which the conservative low order of magnitude is about $100 billion a year—a doubling of aid that would come to about 0.5% of the gross national incomes of the Development Assistance Committee countries.

But more aid is not enough: it also has to be more effective. The Monterrey Consensus includes a commitment from donors to help only if developing countries make concerted efforts to improve economic and democratic governance and implement policies for effective poverty reduction. The Consensus also requires donors to improve their practices, especially to respect development priorities in recipient countries, to untie aid, to harmonize their practices and reduce administrative burdens for recipient countries and to decentralize.

It is hard to imagine the poorest countries achieving Goals 1–7 without the policy changes required in rich countries to achieve Goal 8

These important commitments were reiterated in the Rome Declaration on Harmonization, adopted by heads of multilateral and bilateral development institutions that gathered in Rome in February 2003.

New approaches to debt relief. Twenty-six countries have benefited from debt relief under the Heavily Indebted Poor Countries (HIPC) initiative, with eight of them having reached the completion point—meaning that they have had some debt cancelled. But much more needs to be done: not only for more countries to benefit, but also to ensure that countries' debt burdens are really sustainable. Uganda, for example, recently suffered from collapsing coffee prices and shrinking export earnings, so its debt levels have once again become unsustainable.

Expanding market access to help countries diversify and expand trade. Trade policies in rich countries remain highly discriminatory against developing country exports. Average OECD tariffs on manufactured goods from developing countries are more than four times those on manufactured goods from other OECD countries. Moreover, agricultural subsidies in rich countries lead to unfair competition. Cotton farmers in Benin, Burkina Faso, Chad, Mali and Togo have improved productivity and achieved lower production costs than their rich country competitors. Still, they can barely compete. Rich country agricultural subsidies total more than $300 billion a year—nearly six times official development assistance.

Better access to global technological progress. In recent decades technological breakthroughs have dramatically increased technology's potential to improve people's lives. There is enormous scope for rich countries to channel technological innovations in ways that advance human development, reversing the neglect of poor people's needs. Today, for example, only 10% of global spending on medical research and development is directed at the diseases of the poorest 90% of the world's people.

Rich countries can also help ensure that the World Trade Organization (WTO) agreement on Trade-Related Aspects of Intellectual Property Rights (TRIPS) protects the interests of developing countries. The agreement does not adequately protect the rights of indigenous communities to traditional knowledge sometimes patented by outsiders. And though the agreement contains provisions for technology transfers, the wording is vague—so no means of implementation are in place. The 2001 WTO ministerial conference in Doha, Qatar, reaffirmed that the TRIPS agreement should not prevent poor countries from making essential medicines accessible to their people. The conference resolved to reach an agreement by December 2002 on how countries without adequate manufacturing capacity could access medicines. But that deadline has come and gone, with no resolution in sight.

Following through on commitments—and setting new targets. Rich countries have made many commitments, but most without time-bound, quantitative targets. If developing countries are to achieve Goals 1–7 by 2015, rich countries need to make progress in some critical areas before then—with deadlines, so that progress can be monitored. This Report proposes that rich countries set targets to:

• Increase official development assistance to fill financing gaps (estimated to be at least $50 billion).

• Develop concrete measures for implementing the Rome Declaration on Harmonization.

• Remove tariffs and quotas on agricultural products, textiles and clothing exported by developing countries.

• Remove subsidies on agricultural exports from developing countries.

• Agree and finance, for HIPCs, a compensatory financing facility for external shocks—including collapses in commodity prices.

• Agree and finance deeper debt reduction for HIPCs having reached their completion points, to ensure sustainability.

• Introduce protection and remuneration of traditional knowledge in the TRIPS agreement.

• Agree on what countries without sufficient manufacturing capacity can do to protect public health under the TRIPS agreement.

Just as people can monitor actions by their governments to live up to their commitments, rich countries should monitor their progress in delivering on their commitments. They should prepare progress reports—contributing to a

Trade policies in rich countries remain highly discriminatory against developing country exports

global poverty reduction strategy—that set out their priorities for action.

* * *

The Millennium Development Goals present the world with daunting challenges. Unless there is radical improvement, too many countries will miss the targets—with disastrous consequences for the poorest and most vulnerable of their citizens. Yet today the world has an unprecedented opportunity to deliver on the commitment to eradicating poverty. For the first time there is genuine consensus among rich and poor countries that poverty is the world's problem. And it is together that the world must fight it. As this Report explains, many of the solutions to hunger, disease, poverty and lack of education are well known. What is needed is for efforts to be properly resourced, and for services to be distributed more fairly and efficiently. None of this will happen unless every country, rich and poor, assumes its responsibilities to the billions of poor people around the world.

The Millennium Development Compact

In September 2000 the world's leaders adopted the UN Millennium Declaration, committing their nations to stronger global efforts to reduce poverty, improve health and promote peace, human rights and environmental sustainability. The Millennium Development Goals that emerged from the Declaration are specific, measurable targets, including the one for reducing—by 2015—the extreme poverty that still grips more than 1 billion of the world's people. These Goals, and the commitments of rich and poor countries to achieve them, were affirmed in the Monterrey Consensus that emerged from the March 2002 UN Financing for Development conference, the September 2002 World Summit on Sustainable Development and the launch of the Doha Round on international trade.

World leaders from countries rich and poor described the Monterrey conference as marking a compact between them in support of shared development goals. That commitment forms the basis for the Millennium Development Compact proposed here—a Compact through which the world community can work together to help poor countries achieve the Millennium Development Goals. This Compact calls on all stakeholders to orient their efforts towards ensuring the success of the Goals, in a system of shared responsibilities. Poor countries can insist on increased donor assistance and better market access from rich countries. Poor people can hold their politicians accountable for achieving the poverty reduction targets within the specified timetable. And donors can insist on better governance in poor countries and greater accountability in the use of donor assistance.

Yet despite the admirable commitments at the Millennium Assembly and more recent international gatherings, dozens of countries are considered priority cases (differentiated as "top priority" and "high priority" in this Report)

because they are perilously off track to meet the Goals, making the Compact more crucial than ever. Global forces for development—expanding markets, advancing technology, spreading democracy—are benefiting large parts of the world. But they are also bypassing hundreds of millions of the world's poorest people. The target date for the Goals is just a dozen years away. And good governance and effective institutions in the poorest countries, though vital for success, will not be enough. Rich countries need to provide far more financing and better rules for the international system, as they have promised, to make the Goals attainable in the poorest countries.

Meeting the Goals should start with the recognition that each country must pursue a development strategy that meets its specific needs. National strategies should be based on solid evidence, good science and proper monitoring and evaluation. Within those bounds, poor countries require freedom of manoeuvre with donors to design locally appropriate policies. Without true ownership, national programmes will be neither appropriate to local conditions nor politically sustainable. National programmes must also respect human rights, support the rule of law and commit to honest and effective implementation. When these conditions are met, poor countries should be able to count on much more assistance from rich countries, both in finance and in fairer rules of the game for trade, finance and science and technology.

GIVING PRIORITY TO COUNTRIES LEFT BEHIND

The Millennium Development Compact must first focus on priority countries that face the greatest hurdles in achieving the Goals—countries with the lowest human development and that have made the least progress over the past decade (see chapter 2). For them, domestic policy reforms and far more development assistance are vital.

The Millennium Development Compact is a collaborative product of the Human Development Report team and The Millennium Project Task Force coordinators, with contributions from other Millennium Project participants.

But just as globalization has systematically benefited some of the world's regions, it has bypassed others as well as many groups within countries

In the 1980s and much of the 1990s many development efforts by international financial institutions and major donor countries were guided by the belief that market forces would lift all poor countries onto a path of self-sustaining economic growth. Globalization was seen as the great new motor of worldwide economic progress. Poor countries were assumed to be able to achieve economic growth as long as they pursued good economic governance, based on the precepts of macroeconomic stability, liberalization of markets and privatization of economic activity. Economic growth, in turn, was expected to bring widespread improvements in health, education, nutrition, housing and access to basic infrastructure, such as water and sanitation—enabling countries to break free of poverty.

Though this optimistic vision has proven hugely inadequate for hundreds of millions of poor people, it still has considerable merit for much of the world. Despite protests against globalization in recent years, world market forces have contributed to economic growth—and poverty reduction—in China, India and dozens of other developing countries. Billions of people are enjoying higher living standards and longer lives as a result of global market forces and national policies that help harness those forces.

But just as globalization has systematically benefited some of the world's regions, it has bypassed others as well as many groups within countries. In the 1990s most of East and South Asia saw living standards improve dramatically. But large parts of Sub-Saharan Africa, parts of Eastern Europe and the Commonwealth of Independent States (CIS) and many countries in Latin America and the Middle East did not. In addition, epidemic diseases, most dramatically HIV/AIDS, prey disproportionately on those left behind and push them back even further—trapping poor people in a vicious cycle of poverty and disease.

Even large and growing economies—Brazil, China, India, Mexico—contain regions of intense poverty relieved little by overall national growth. Economic and social progress often also bypasses ethnic and racial minorities, even majorities—especially girls and women, who suffer gender bias in access to schooling, public services, employment opportunities and private property.

Thus, despite the higher living standards that globalization (backed by good economic governance) has delivered in large parts of the world, hundreds of millions of people have experienced economic reversals rather than advances. And more than 1 billion fight for daily survival from the scourges of hunger and poor health.

There are many reasons economic development continues to bypass many of the world's poorest people and places. One common reason is poor governance. When governments are corrupt, incompetent or unaccountable to their citizens, national economies falter. When income inequality is very high, rich people often control the political system and simply neglect poor people, forestalling broadly based development. Similarly, if governments fail to invest adequately in the health and education of their people, economic growth will eventually peter out because of an insufficient number of healthy, skilled workers. Without sound governance—in terms of economic policies, human rights, well-functioning institutions and democratic political participation —no country with low human development can expect long-term success in its development efforts or expanded support from donor countries.

Though many observers would simply lecture poor people to do better on their own, most poor countries face severe structural problems far beyond their control. These problems often involve the international trade system— as when rich countries block agricultural exports from poor countries or heavily subsidize their own farmers, depressing world prices of these products. Poor countries also face trade barriers when exporting textiles and apparel, processed foods and beverages and other products in which they might be competitive. In addition, many governments are hamstrung by insurmountable external debts inherited from past administrations—while efforts at debt relief have been too little, too late.

Geography provides another important explanation for failed economic development. Many poor countries are simply too small and geographically isolated to attract investors, domestic or foreign. Landlocked Mali, with 11 million people and an annual per capita income of $240 ($800 when measured in purchasing power parity terms), is of little interest to most potential foreign investors. With a GNP of $2.6 billion, its economy is about that of a small city in a rich country where, say, 85,000 people live on an average of $30,000 a year. Facing very high transport costs, and with almost no interest from international firms to invest in production for small domestic markets, such countries are bypassed by globalization.

Poor, remote countries like Mali generally connect to the world economy by producing a few traditional primary commodities. But slow world market growth, unchanging technologies and often volatile and declining world prices for these commodities offer much too narrow a base for economic advance. Continued heavy dependence on a handful of primary commodity exports provides no chance for long-term success. This unfortunate situation afflicts much of Sub-Saharan Africa, the Andean region and Central Asia.

Exacerbating these structural problems is rapid population growth, which tends to be fastest in countries with the lowest human development. These challenges can seriously hinder the availability of farmland and increase environmental degradation (deforestation, soil degradation, fisheries depletion, reduced freshwater).

Moreover, geographic barriers, commodity dependence and demographic pressures are often compounded by a heavy burden of diseases such as HIV/AIDS, tuberculosis and malaria—or by biophysical constraints such as depleted soils and degraded ecosystems. Rich countries, and the economic institutions they control, may focus on good governance when determining aid allocations. But far too often they are oblivious to the other challenges facing many of the poorest countries—especially since rich countries have not experienced the onslaught of endemic tropical diseases such as malaria. Too many policy-makers in rich countries believe that poor countries are simply not trying hard enough to develop, failing to understand the deeper structural forces at work.

CRITICAL THRESHOLDS FOR ESCAPING POVERTY TRAPS

These structural impediments leave countries stuck in poverty traps. But even in such dire conditions there is reason for hope. Widespread disease, geographic isolation, fragile ecologies, overdependence on primary commodity exports and rapid population growth are amenable to practical, proven solutions. Those include policy changes by rich countries and much larger investments in infrastructure, disease control and environmental sustainability by poor countries, backed by more financial assistance from donor governments. Thus the need for the Millennium Development Compact: without it, poor countries will remain trapped in poverty, with low or negative economic growth.

Sustained economic growth helps break the shackles of poverty in two ways. First, it directly increases average household incomes. When households below the poverty line share in the average rise in national income, the extent of extreme income poverty (that is, the share of people surviving on $1 a day) is directly reduced. Economic growth has a powerful record of pulling poor people above the income poverty line.

But such gains are not automatic. They can be dissipated if income inequality widens and poor people do not share adequately in growth—a phenomenon observed in many countries in recent years. So, the Compact emphasizes actions to ensure that poor people share in overall growth, with a focus on expanding their access to critical assets—including by providing secure land tenure, making it easier to start small businesses, supporting labour-intensive exports and broadening access to microfinance. Note that economic growth reduces income poverty most when initial income inequality is narrow.

Economic growth also works indirectly, reducing non-income poverty by raising government revenues and enabling increased public investments in education, basic infrastructure, disease control and health (particularly maternal and child health). In addition to reducing non-income poverty, these investments expedite economic growth by raising worker skills and productivity —and thus poor people's market incomes.

Although economic growth is not an automatic remedy for non-income poverty, it makes a powerful contribution—as long as public policies ensure that its dividends reach poor people. Some poor countries have achieved impressive

Thus the need for the Millennium Development Compact: without it, poor countries will remain trapped in poverty, with low or negative economic growth

gains in education and health by making them high priorities. But only growth can sustain such gains, because sooner or later government budget deficits get the upper hand in a stagnant economy. In sum: public investments in poor people spur economic growth, while economic growth sustains such investments.

Gender equality plays a central role in all these areas. The powerful links between productivity and girls' and maternal health—including reproductive health—and girls' education are too often stymied by women's lack of empowerment. Better-educated girls marry later. They have fewer, better-educated, healthier children. And they earn higher incomes in the workforce. If girls are kept out of school or educated women are not allowed to fully participate in the labour market, these potential gains are squandered. If public investments in basic infrastructure (such as safe water) ignore women's needs, women may be condemned to spend hours a day fetching water when they could be participating more productively in society. When women have no say in household decision-making, the synergies between productivity, health and education are hobbled. Gender equality is thus more than social justice—it promotes development.

For countries stuck in poverty traps, growth will not come on its own, and domestic investments in human development will be inadequate. To break out of poverty traps, countries require greatly expanded donor financing to invest much more heavily in health, education, agriculture, water and sanitation and other key infrastructure even before economic growth occurs. Such investments are vital to create the conditions for sustained economic growth.

The message is simple: escaping poverty traps requires countries to reach certain critical thresholds—of health, education, infrastructure and governance—that will permit them to achieve takeoff to sustained economic growth. Dozens of poor countries fall below those thresholds, often through no fault of their own and for reasons utterly beyond their control. Here is where the Compact between rich and poor countries must come in. If a country pursues the right policies and commits to good governance

in implementing those policies, the world community—international agencies, bilateral donors, private actors, civil society organizations—must help the country reach the critical thresholds through increased assistance.

POLICY CLUSTERS FOR ESCAPING POVERTY TRAPS

Breaking out of poverty traps requires a multifaceted approach—one that goes beyond the usual sound commandments of good economic and political governance. For countries trapped in poverty, six policy clusters are crucial:
- Investing in human development—nutrition, health (including reproductive health), education, water and sanitation—to foster a productive labour force that can participate effectively in the world economy.
- Helping small farmers increase productivity and break out of subsistence farming and chronic hunger—especially in countries with predominantly rural populations.
- Investing in infrastructure—power, roads, ports, communications—to attract new investments in non-traditional areas.
- Developing industrial development policies that bolster non-traditional private sector activities, with special attention to small and medium-size enterprises. Such policies might include export processing zones, tax incentives and other initiatives to promote investment and public spending on research and development.
- Emphasizing human rights and social equity to promote the well-being of all people and to ensure that poor and marginalized people—including girls and women—have the freedom and voice to influence decisions that affect their lives.
- Promoting environmental sustainability and improving urban management. All countries, but especially the very poorest, need to protect the biodiversity and ecosystems that support life (clean water and air, soil nutrients, forests, fisheries, other key ecosystems) and ensure that their cities are well managed to provide livelihoods and safe environments.

The first cluster—investing in human development—needs to be bolstered by much larger donor contributions even before economic growth takes hold. Indeed, because better health

Public investments in poor people spur economic growth, while economic growth sustains such investments

and education are both goals of human development and precursors to sustained growth, investments in these areas are important for a later takeoff in private activities. Supported by additional donor resources, public investments can make major progress in health, population, nutrition, education and water and sanitation. The needed technologies are well known and well proven. Thus big gains in health and education can—and should—be achieved well before per capita incomes rise substantially.

The second cluster for breaking out of poverty traps involves raising the productivity of small poor farmers. Agricultural productivity can be raised by introducing improved technologies, including better seeds, tillage and crop rotation systems and pest and soil management. It can also be raised by improving rural infrastructure such as irrigation systems, storage and transport facilities and roads connecting villages to larger market centres. To raise long-term productivity, security in landholding can protect the rights of farmers and give them incentives to invest in land improvements. These steps require public-private partnerships to promote rural development, including through crucial investments in agricultural science and technology.

The third policy cluster involves achieving an adequate threshold of key infrastructure to support economic diversification. This will be easier in some locations, such as coastal port cities. But it will be much harder elsewhere, such as landlocked or mountainous countries facing high transport costs. Again, donor assistance will be pivotal in enabling poor countries to reach the takeoff threshold for infrastructure. Without outside help, countries will remain trapped—too poor to invest in infrastructure and too lacking in infrastructure to become internationally competitive in new exports.

The fourth policy cluster involves the use of special industrial development policies—including promoting science and technology—to create a sound investment environment for non-traditional business activities. Many development success stories, such as East Asia's tiger economies, have supported the development of non-traditional activities through tax holidays, export processing zones, special economic zones,

science parks, investment tax credits, targeted funding for research and development and public grants of infrastructure and land. Without such special inducements it is difficult for small poor countries to gain a foothold in non-traditional areas of the world economy. As a result, few succeed. Here microfinance institutions can help, providing special incentives at a much smaller scale to promote employment and income generation in micro, small and medium-size enterprises. As with rural landholdings, secure housing tenure for poor urban residents can enhance their productive investments.

The fifth policy cluster involves promoting human rights and empowering poor people through democratic governance. In dozens of countries poor people, ethnic minorities, women and other groups still lack access to public services and private opportunities—and so will not benefit even when growth begins to take off. Political institutions must allow poor people to participate in decisions that affect their lives and protect them from arbitrary, unaccountable decisions by governments and other forces.

National strategies for the Millennium Development Goals must include a commitment to women's rights to education, reproductive health services, property ownership, secure tenure and labour force participation. They must also address other forms of discrimination—by race, ethnicity or region—that can marginalize poor people within countries. Deepening democracy through reforms of governance structures, such as decentralization, can enhance poor people's voice in decision-making.

The sixth policy cluster calls for better environmental and urban management, especially to protect poor people. Not coincidentally, many of the world's poorest places suffer from enormous climatic variability and vulnerability—requiring sound ecological management. These include tropical and subtropical regions vulnerable to El Niño–driven fluctuations in rainfall and temperature. Such regions are also feeling the effects of long-term climate change. In addition, rapid population growth and indiscriminate business activities have stressed ecosystems in many countries with low incomes and low human development. These pressures are leading to loss of habitat through deforestation and encroachment

National strategies for the Millennium Development Goals must include a commitment to women's rights to education, reproductive health services, property ownership, secure tenure and labour force participation

by roads, cities and farmland—and to depletion of scarce resources such as freshwater aquifers and coastal fisheries. A related challenge involves managing rapid urbanization to safeguard public health and access to basic amenities such as land, housing, transportation, safe drinking water, sanitation and other infrastructure. Such efforts require careful urban planning and considerable public investments.

In sum, to achieve the Goals the poorest countries must escape their poverty traps. To do so, they must reach minimum thresholds in health, education, infrastructure and governance. They also need agricultural policies that enhance productivity, as well as industrial development policies that build a base for long-term economic growth led by the private sector. Finally, these policies should be implemented with respect for social equity, human rights and environmental sustainability. Increased donor financing is critical for the poorest countries to reach these thresholds—financing that must be matched by better governance and resource use. Over a generation or so, sustained economic growth will enable these countries to take over from donors the financing of basic public services and infrastructure.

IMPLEMENTING THE MILLENNIUM DEVELOPMENT COMPACT

The Millennium Development Compact is based on shared responsibilities among major stakeholders. It requires many combined and complementary efforts from rich and poor countries, international agencies, local authorities, private actors and civil society organizations. Some actions will occur at the level of governments and some at the level of the international system—such as international agreements to change the rules of the game for trade, for financing and for developing and managing science and technology.

COUNTRIES WITH LOW HUMAN DEVELOPMENT—ERADICATING POVERTY AND ADDRESSING BASIC NEEDS

Without question, countries with low human development—particularly those stuck in poverty

traps—have the most pressing needs. These countries must construct coherent strategies for achieving the Millennium Development Goals, building on the six policy clusters described above.

As part of these overall development strategies, the Monterrey Consensus (see above) emphasizes the importance of nationally owned strategies for reducing poverty. To that end more than two dozen poor countries have prepared Poverty Reduction Strategy Papers (PRSPs), which provide frameworks for financing, implementing and monitoring such strategies. The papers describe macroeconomic, structural and social policies and programmes to promote growth, reduce poverty and make progress in areas such as education and health, indicating external financing requirements. PRSPs are prepared by governments but emerge from participatory processes involving civil society and external partners, including the World Bank and International Monetary Fund (IMF).

Though far from perfect, PRSPs move poverty reduction closer to the centre of development strategies. They also provide a framework for donor coordination based on national priorities. But they do not yet adequately support the Millennium Development Goals. Though PRSPs increasingly mention the Goals, they should provide a basis for assessing country policies more systematically—and indicate the scale of needed donor assistance. When preparing PRSPs, governments are advised to be realistic. What that tends to mean is that they should accept existing levels of donor assistance and assume various constraints on economic growth (such as lack of access to foreign markets). As a result PRSPs fall short of identifying the resources required to meet the Goals.

For example, IMF and World Bank guidelines for preparing the papers—the *PRSP Sourcebook*—recommend a method for setting targets in the face of fiscal and technical constraints. The guidelines do not stress that such constraints can and should be eased (for example, through increased donor assistance) so that countries can achieve the Goals. Consider Malawi's PRSP, which does not aim high enough to achieve the Goals. In a joint staff assessment of the paper, the IMF and World Bank said that

The Millennium Development Compact is based on shared responsibilities among major stakeholders

"while most indicators are in line with the Millennium Development Goals (MDG), the PRSP's targets are less ambitious. Further work is required to develop longer-term targets that relate directly to the 2015 goals. However, extrapolating the targets set in the PRSP for 2005 suggests that Malawi will fall short of meeting the 2015 [Goals]. The staffs believe that these PRSP targets are more realistic and reflect Malawi's current socioeconomic conditions" (pp. 3–4, 23 August 2002, http://www.imf.org).

The IMF and World Bank's assessment of Malawi's PRSP risks undermining the Goals and the commitments made at the Monterrey conference. Malawi requires far more donor assistance—as do many other countries in similar circumstances. Rather than being told to lower their sights, they should be aided in achieving the Goals, with the IMF and World Bank helping to mobilize the needed additional assistance. The Millennium Development Compact provides the framework for that kind of international help.

Every national development strategy, including every PRSP, should ask two questions. First, what national policies—including mobilizing and reallocating domestic resources and focusing spending on reforms that increase efficiency and equity—are needed to achieve the Goals? Second, what international policies—including increased donor assistance, expanded market access, swifter debt relief and greater technology transfers—are needed?

The Compact calls on every developing country to align its development strategy (including its PRSP, if it has one) with the Millennium Development Goals, in the context of its national priorities and needs. Every national strategy should clearly define efforts within the country's reach—and those requiring more international support, such as increased debt relief, expanded donor assistance and better access to foreign markets. National strategies should also estimate medium-term budget needs for all critical sectors—health, education, infrastructure, environmental management. And they should specify the parts of budgets that can be covered by domestic resources and the parts to be covered by increased development assistance.

This process will highlight the gap between current official development assistance and the levels needed to achieve the Goals. Poor countries and their development partners can then work together, in good faith, to ensure that national strategies are backed by sound policies and adequate financing.

COUNTRIES WITH MEDIUM HUMAN DEVELOPMENT—ATTACKING POCKETS OF DEEP POVERTY

Most countries at medium levels of human development should be able to finance most or all of their development needs through domestic resources or non-concessional foreign resources (including private flows and official loans from multilateral development banks and bilateral agencies). Many are on track to achieve most of the Goals. But several still contain pockets of deep poverty. Thus they still require key forms of support from rich countries—especially better market access for exports and better international rules of the game for finance and technology transfers. They also need to mitigate domestic structural inequalities—targeting policy interventions at groups most vulnerable or marginalized, whether due to gender, ethnicity, religion or geography.

These countries can also help the top and high priority countries define objectives and determine the resources required to achieve the Goals. Countries with medium levels of human development are diverse—ranging from Brazil to Malaysia, from Mauritius to Mexico—and provide important lessons for countries still trapped in poverty because they have grappled with (and often still face) many of the same ecological, health and other challenges. Many middle-income countries have recently started to provide development advice and even financial assistance, a heartening trend that should be strongly encouraged.

INTERNATIONAL FINANCIAL INSTITUTIONS—PUTTING THE GOALS AT THE CENTRE OF COUNTRY STRATEGIES

International financial institutions should put the Millennium Development Goals at the centre of their analytical, advisory and financing efforts for every developing country. For each PRSP,

International financial institutions should put the Millennium Development Goals at the centre of their analytical, advisory and financing efforts for every developing country

for example, joint assessments by the IMF and World Bank should indicate whether the proposed strategy is likely to achieve the Goals—and if not, what changes are needed to do so. The PRSPs would then provide an occasion for these institutions to consider not only the domestic policy reforms needed to strengthen institutions, improve economic governance and increase government support, but also the steps needed from the international community: increased donor assistance (including more extensive debt relief), better access to foreign markets for the country's exports, greater technology transfers and related actions pursued in partnership with the country.

The IMF and World Bank should work with countries to agree on macroeconomic frameworks consistent with meeting the Goals, including adequate external financing. They can then help countries mobilize the needed increases in official development assistance—as well as help them accommodate those flows in macroeconomic terms. In some countries large increases in official development assistance will cause the real exchange rate to appreciate. But the net result will be beneficial—if the currency appreciation occurs in the context of an appropriate medium-term macroeconomic framework and if the donor assistance is invested in human capital, physical infrastructure and other development needs. Thus the IMF and World Bank should help countries—and their donors—use increased official development assistance most effectively in support of the Goals.

Regional development banks also have a major role in putting the Goals at the centre of their country strategies and in streamlining their lending operations and technical cooperation efforts. They are in a unique position to finance regional public goods and encourage regional integration and cooperation. The Inter-American Development Bank has started to move in this direction, but it and other regional banks need to do much more.

Bilateral donors — revising approaches and setting new targets

Bilateral development assistance must take a new approach. The guiding question should

no longer be, "What progress can be made towards the Goals within the bounds of current bilateral assistance?" Instead it should be, "What levels and types of donor assistance are needed to achieve the Goals, and will countries make effective use of that assistance?"

Bilateral donors know that they need to improve how they deliver official development assistance—especially as amounts of assistance increase. These improvements should be based on the following principles:
• Countries should design and own their strategies for meeting the Goals.
• Assistance should be results-oriented, based on expert reviews of country proposals and careful monitoring, evaluation and auditing of programmes.
• Bilateral donors should coordinate their support for country strategies—for example, through sector-wide approaches that emphasize budget rather than project financing.
• Bilateral donors should finally eliminate the flawed distinction between assistance for capital costs and for recurrent costs. Both outlays need ample support.

Because most donors have agreed, in principle, to align their programmes with PRSPs, it is even more important that these documents highlight the support needed to achieve the Goals—the additional donor resources and debt relief, the increased access to markets and technology, and so on.

All rich countries should set targets for their repeated commitments to improving aid, trade and debt relief for poor countries. They should also be encouraged to prepare their own world poverty reduction assessments and strategies, setting bold targets in line with these commitments.

UN agencies — providing expert assistance

UN agencies have a vital role in helping countries meet the Millennium Development Goals, especially through expert assistance in designing and implementing development programmes. The United Nations has extensive expertise in every focus area of the Goals, including education, health, development planning, technological development, the rule of

Because most donors have agreed to align their programmes with Poverty Reduction Strategy Papers, it is even more important that these documents highlight the support needed to achieve the Goals

law, agriculture and many others. Each of the main UN agencies should develop a strategy for helping low-income, low-human-development countries—especially the priority ones—implement their national strategies.

The UN system also has a global role to play. It is mobilizing to:
- Monitor progress globally.
- Track progress nationally.
- Identify key obstacles to the Goals—and solutions.
- Engage broad segments of society around the world through the Millennium Campaign.

REGIONAL ORGANIZATIONS AND DEVELOPMENT INSTITUTIONS—FOSTERING REGIONAL INTEGRATION AND COOPERATION

For poor countries with small markets—whether because of small populations or geographic impediments to accessing global markets—regional integration must be a policy priority. Regional cooperation, including shared investments in critical infrastructure, can expand trading opportunities across small economies and thus provide a central platform for sustained economic growth. Regional integration is particularly needed in Africa, where many countries have small or inland populations. As the leading initiatives for intergovernmental cooperation in Africa, the New Partnership for African Development and the African Union have important roles in fostering economic integration and political partnerships.

THE DOHA ROUND AND OTHER INTERNATIONAL TRADE NEGOTIATIONS—OPENING MARKETS AND REDUCING SUBSIDIES

Even if national policies are appropriate and donor financing is increased, the Millennium Development Goals will not necessarily be achieved if poor countries' non-traditional exports continue to be blocked, or lose value in world markets, due to rich country protectionism. Poor countries also require much more international support for technology transfers.

The Monterrey Consensus and the Johannesburg Plan of Implementation (from the 2002 World Summit on Sustainable Development)

reiterate the trade facilitation commitments made by rich countries at the UN Millennium Summit. Rich countries have pledged to help poor countries reach the Goals—especially the least developed countries, small island states and landlocked developing countries—by granting them full access to their markets. Still, though the Doha Round—the next round of international trade negotiations—has been dubbed a "development round", early attempts to put development at the fore have produced stalemate and frustration.

CIVIL SOCIETY—PLAYING A LARGER ROLE IN POLICIES AND POVERTY REDUCTION

One significant area of progress over the past decade has been the growing influence of local, national and global civil society organizations and networks in driving policy change, as with debt relief. Non-governmental organizations (NGOs), community organizations, professional associations and other civil society groups are regularly called on to help design and implement poverty reduction strategies. Their participation is also built into the efforts of the Global Fund to Fight AIDS, Tuberculosis and Malaria.

These new approaches reflect the three roles of civil society: as participants in the design of strategies, as service providers through community organizations and national NGOs and as watchdogs to ensure government fulfilment of commitments. But in many countries these roles are taking root only gradually, with governments continuing to dominate decision-making and implementation. By insisting on transparent processes to develop national strategies for the Millennium Development Goals, bilateral and multilateral institutions can help civil society gain a stronger foothold in policy-making and implementation.

PRIVATE ENTERPRISE—PARTICIPATING IN GLOBAL ACTION PLANS

The private sector plays a critical role in market-led growth, particularly in creating jobs and raising incomes. Private businesses, in addition to supporting anticorruption measures, should support the Millennium Development Goals in a variety of other ways: through corporate

Still, though the Doha Round has been dubbed a "development round", early attempts to put development at the fore have produced stalemate and frustration

philanthropy, technology transfers, greater foreign investment in countries at the margins of the international system and differential pricing of goods and services for countries with low incomes and low human development.

Companies can be most effective when operating under global action plans—as with the growing willingness of pharmaceutical companies to discount the prices of essential AIDS medicines when called on to do so by the United Nations. There should be similar cooperation in other crucial areas, including agriculture, environmental management and information and communications technology. Moreover, corporations must demonstrate ethical behaviour: respecting human rights, refraining from corruption and abiding by basic proscriptions against forced and child labour and environmental destruction.

SCIENTIFIC COMMUNITY—ADDRESSING THE NEEDS OF POOR PEOPLE

Many current technologies urgently need to be supplemented by technological breakthroughs, such as vaccines or new drugs for HIV/AIDS, tuberculosis and malaria. Because most international scientific efforts bypass the needs of poor people, it is crucial that the world scientific community—led by national laboratories, national science funding agencies and private foundations—work with scientific groups in poor countries to identify priority targets for research and development and greatly expand funding.

For that reason the Millennium Development Compact recommends the creation of several international forums for technological innovation. Some such forums already exist, but they must be supported with greater resources—and others must be created. These forums will help set priorities for research and development to meet the technological needs of poor countries. They will bring together international research institutions and scientific academies, multilateral and bilateral donors, country representatives and leading academic and private sector representatives in such key areas as health, agriculture, infrastructure, information and communications technology, energy systems, environment management and mitigation of and adaptation to climate fluctuations and long-term climate change.

Identifying scientific priorities and agreeing on ways to fund needed research and development, including through public-private partnerships, the forums will recommend plans for technological advance in each of these areas for the donor community's review.

GLOBAL SYSTEM FOR IMPROVING BENCHMARKING AND EVALUATING PROGRESS

By adopting specific, time-limited, quantified goals, the Millennium Development Goals provide a firm basis for benchmarking and for evaluating progress. But sound monitoring and evaluation will require the international community to dramatically increase investments in surveys and data collection. For too many Goals in too many countries, data are insufficient for proper quantitative assessments. Because joint commitments lie at the centre of every national programme, the actions of poor countries and their rich country partners need to be monitored much more closely than in the past.

New initiatives should be encouraged to monitor the performance of both rich and poor countries in their commitments under the Compact. For example, the size and quality of donor flows must be carefully monitored to ensure that they are consistent with achieving the Goals. The Doha Round negotiations should be closely monitored to ensure that they indeed constitute a "development round". Special care must also be taken to reduce corruption, and this too can and should be better monitored. The counterpart of greatly increased donor flows must be greatly increased transparency and accountability in their use.

CONCLUSION

The world has made tremendous progress in its knowledge and practice of development policies. The Millennium Development Compact aims to bring this knowledge and practice together in a coherent framework that recognizes the need for a multi-pronged approach to meeting the Millennium Development Goals, based on the promises of partnership in recent international declarations. The Compact provides a framework in which the poorest countries develop and own national plans that draw on sustained external assistance to break out of poverty traps and improve the well-being of their poorest citizens. In essence, the Compact provides a Goal-oriented development process in which all the main stakeholders have clear responsibilities—as well as obligations to other actors.

Escaping poverty traps requires that countries reach certain critical thresholds—for health, education, infrastructure and governance—in order to achieve a takeoff to sustained economic growth and development. Dozens of poor countries fall below such thresholds, often through no fault of their own and for reasons beyond their control. This is the most important area where the Compact between rich and poor countries and actors must come in. If a country pursues the right policies and commits to good governance in implementing those policies, the world community—international agencies, bilateral donors, private actors, civil society organizations—must help the country reach the critical thresholds through increased assistance.

In adopting this Millennium Development Compact, all countries are called on to reaffirm their commitments to the Millennium Development Goals and their readiness to accept the responsibilities that accompany those commitments. Bilateral donors, international financial institutions, UN specialized agencies, private actors and civil society organizations should step forward with bold, specific commitments and actions to ensure success in reaching the Goals.

CHAPTER 1

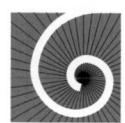 **The Millennium Development Goals**

We recognize that, in addition to our separate responsibilities to our individual societies, we have a collective responsibility to uphold the principles of human dignity, equality and equity at the global level. As leaders we have a duty therefore to all the world's people, especially the most vulnerable and, in particular, the children of the world, to whom the future belongs.

—UN Millennium Declaration[1]

In September 2000 the world's leaders gathered at the UN Millennium Summit to commit their nations to strengthening global efforts for peace, human rights, democracy, strong governance, environmental sustainability and poverty eradication, and to promoting principles of human dignity, equality and equity.[2]

The resulting Millennium Declaration, adopted by 189 countries, includes urgent, collective commitments to overcome the poverty that still grips most of the world's people. Global leaders did not settle for business as usual—because they knew that business as usual was not enough. Instead they committed themselves to ambitious targets with clearly defined deadlines.

At the 2000 summit the UN General Assembly also asked the UN Secretary-General to prepare a road map for achieving the Declaration's commitments—resulting in the Millennium Development Goals, made up of 8 Goals, 18 targets and 48 indicators.[3] The Goals are unique in their ambition, concreteness and scope. They are also unique in their explicit recognition that the Goals for eradicating poverty can be achieved only through stronger partnerships among development actors and through increased action by rich countries—expanding trade, relieving debt, transferring technology and providing aid.

AN AGENDA FOR ACCELERATING HUMAN DEVELOPMENT

The Millennium Development Goals address many of the most enduring failures of human development. Unlike the objectives of the first, second and third UN Development Decades (1960s, 1970s, 1980s), which mostly focused on economic growth, the Goals place human well-being and poverty reduction at the centre of global development objectives—an approach advocated by the *Human Development Report* since its inception.

The Goals and the promotion of human development share a common motivation and reflect a vital commitment to promoting human well-being that entails dignity, freedom and equality for all people. The Goals are benchmarks of progress towards the vision of the Millennium Declaration—guided by basic values of freedom, equality, solidarity, tolerance, respect for nature and shared responsibilities. These values have much in common with the conception of human well-being in the concept of human development. They also mirror the fundamental motivation for human rights. Thus the Goals, human development and human rights share the same motivation (box 1.1).

Every *Human Development Report* has argued that the purpose of development is to improve people's lives by expanding their choices, freedom and dignity. Poverty involves much more than the restrictions imposed by lack of income. It also entails lack of basic capabilities to lead full, creative lives—as when people suffer from poor health, are excluded from participating in the decisions that affect their communities or have no right to guide the course of their lives. Such deprivations distinguish human poverty from income poverty.

The Millennium Development Goals are intended to ease the constraints on people's ability to make choices. Still, the Goals do not

The Goals and the promotion of human development share a common motivation and reflect a vital commitment to promoting human well-being that entails dignity, freedom and equality for all people

BOX 1.1

The Millennium Development Goals, human development and human rights share a common motivation

Values guiding the UN Millennium Declaration and Millennium Development Goals

As articulated in the Millennium Declaration, the Millennium Development Goals are benchmarks for progress towards a vision of development, peace and human rights, guided by "certain fundamental values…essential to international relations in the twenty-first century. These include:

• *Freedom*. Men and women have the right to live their lives and raise their children in dignity, free from hunger and from the fear of violence, oppression or injustice. Democratic and participatory governance based on the will of the people best assures these rights.

• *Equality*. No individual and no nation must be denied the opportunity to benefit from development. The equal rights and opportunities of women and men must be assured.

• *Solidarity*. Global challenges must be managed in a way that distributes the costs and burdens fairly in accordance with basic principles of equity and social justice. Those who suffer or who benefit least deserve help from those who benefit most.

• *Tolerance*. Human beings must respect one another, in all their diversity of belief, culture and language. Differences within and between societies should be neither feared nor repressed, but cherished as a precious asset of humanity. A culture of peace and dialogue among all civilizations should be actively promoted.

• *Respect for nature*. Prudence must be shown in the management of all living species and natural resources, in accordance with the precepts of sustainable development. Only in this way can the immeasurable riches provided to us by nature be preserved and passed on to our descendants. The current unsustainable patterns of production and consumption must be changed in the interest of our future welfare and that of our descendants.

• *Shared responsibility*. Responsibility for managing worldwide economic and social development, as well as threats to international peace and security, must be shared among the nations of the world and should be exercised multilaterally. As the most universal and most representative organization in the world, the United Nations must play the central role." (UN 2000, p. 2.)

The Goals—building blocks for human development…

Human development is about people, about expanding their choices to live full, creative lives with freedom and dignity. Economic growth, increased trade and investment, technological advance—all are very important. But they are means, not ends. Fundamental to expanding human choices is building human capabilities:

Source: UN 2000a; Human Development Report Office; UN 1966; Marks 2003; UNDP 2000.

the range of things that people can be. The most basic capabilities for human development are living a long and healthy life, being educated, having a decent standard of living and enjoying political and civil freedoms to participate in the life of one's community.

The first three of these are incorporated in this Report's human development index (HDI). Though the Millennium Development Goals contribute to these capabilities, they do not reflect all the key dimensions of human development, which is a broader concept.

…and human rights

Achieving the Goals will advance human rights. Each Goal can be directly linked to economic, social and cultural rights enumerated in the Universal Declaration of Human Rights (articles 22, 24, 25, 26) and other human rights instruments.

Recognizing that the targets expressed in the Goals are not just development aspirations but also claimable rights has important implications.

• Viewing the Goals in this way means that taking action to achieve them is an obligation, not a form of charity. This approach creates a framework for holding various actors accountable, including governments, citizens, corporations and international organizations.

• Human rights carry counterpart obligations on the part of others—not just to refrain from violating them, but also to protect and promote their realization. Human rights conventions recognize the need for an international order that

ensures that these rights be secured (article 28 of the Universal Declaration of Human Rights, article 2 of the Covenant on Economic, Social and Cultural Rights) and that establishes the counterpart obligations of governments and other actors to contribute to their realization.

• Viewing the Goals through a human rights framework increases understanding of the policies and institutional reforms required to achieve them. Full realization of the human right to education, for example, requires more than achieving universal literacy and primary education. It also requires that people participate meaningfully in public decisions about education. And it requires that measures for achieving education-related goals be equitable—not disadvantaging vulnerable groups or entrenching gender discrimination.

The full realization of economic, social and cultural rights requires far more than achieving the Millennium Development Goals. But achieving the Goals is an important step towards that end. Because rights to education, health care and an adequate standard of living depend on long-term economic growth and institutional reform, these rights can be realized progressively. But the acceptable pace of "progressive realization" and the obligations to achieve it are rarely spelled out, left instead to each country to define and debate. The Millennium Development Goals more explicitly define what all countries agree can be demanded—benchmarks against which such commitments must be measured.

How do human development goals relate to the Millennium Development Goals?

Key capabilities for human development	Corresponding Millennium Development Goals
Living a long and healthy life	Goals 4, 5 and 6: reducing child mortality, improving maternal health and combating major diseases
Being educated	Goals 2 and 3: achieving universal primary education, promoting gender equality (especially in education) and empowering women
Having a decent standard of living	Goal 1: reducing poverty and hunger
Enjoying political and civil freedoms to participate in the life of one's community	Not a Goal but an important global objective included in the Millennium Declaration

Essential conditions for human development	Corresponding Millennium Development Goals
Environmental sustainability	Goal 7: ensuring environmental sustainability
Equity—especially gender equity	Goal 3: promoting gender equality and empowering women
Enabling global economic environment	Goal 8: strengthening partnership between rich and poor countries

cover all the crucial dimensions of human development. In particular, they do not mention expanding people's participation in the decisions that affect their lives or increasing their civil and political freedoms. Participation, democracy and human rights are, however, important elements of the Millennium Declaration.

The Goals provide building blocks for human development, with each relating to key dimensions of this process. The Goals also reflect a human rights agenda—rights to food, education, health care and decent living standards, as enumerated in the Universal Declaration of Human Rights. The need to ensure all these rights—economic, social and cultural—confers obligations on the governments of countries both rich and poor.

ORIGIN, EVOLUTION AND FOLLOWUP

The Millennium Development Goals reflect key aims of various UN development conferences in the 1990s. Thus they are the product of many national, regional and international consultations that involved millions of people and represented a wide range of interests, including those of governments, civil society organizations and private sector actors. These conferences emphasized the multidimensional nature of development—with human well-being as its end.

The Goals also build on the momentum created by the International Development Goals, devised in 1996 by the Development Assistance Committee (DAC) of the Organisation for Economic Co-operation and Development (OECD) to define how its 23 bilateral donors would work together to improve lives in developing countries in the 21st century. The OECD goals set an important precedent because they were time-bound and quantifiable, and so could be monitored and help mobilize support.

But because the International Development Goals originated in the donor community, they were never wholeheartedly adopted by developing countries or by civil society groups. A 2000 publication, *A Better World For All: Progress towards the International Development Goals,* was widely criticized by civil society groups for holding developing countries accountable for their progress without acknowledging the roles in the process of rich countries and multilateral institutions.[4]

So, although the Millennium Development Goals include all but one of the International Development Goals, they are seen not as the brainchild solely of rich countries. Instead they are truly global development goals that reaffirm the world's collective commitment to improving the lives of people in poor countries. The Goals also recognize the responsibility of developing countries for their development—while placing more concrete demands on rich countries.

Defining the responsibilities of all countries was crucial for developing countries. Goal 8, for a global partnership, has no time-bound, quantified indicator to monitor progress and hold actors to account, as Goals 1–7 do. But its inclusion in the Goals is a significant step towards "solidarity"—a basic principle of the Millennium Declaration.

The March 2002 International Conference on Financing for Development in Monterrey, Mexico, reaffirmed the world's commitment to the Millennium Declaration and its development targets. The conference advanced new terms for a global partnership based on mutual responsibilities between developing and rich countries. It also reaffirmed the primary responsibility of national governments for mobilizing domestic resources and improving governance—including sound economic policies and solid democratic institutions. And it reaffirmed commitments by rich countries to work towards a supportive international environment and increased financing for development.[5] These commitments received additional backing at the September 2002 World Summit on Sustainable Development in Johannesburg, South Africa (see chapter 8).

DO GLOBAL GOALS MAKE A DIFFERENCE?

The global community, often led by the United Nations, has set many development goals since the first Development Decade of the 1960s—and has a history of many failures. For example, in the Alma Ata Declaration of 1977 the world committed to health care for all people by the end of the century. Yet in 2000 millions of poor people died of pandemic and other diseases, many readily preventable and treatable. Similarly, at the 1990 Summit on Children the world committed to universal primary education by 2000.

The conference advanced new terms for a global partnership based on mutual responsibilities between developing and rich countries

But that target was also missed. And the failures should serve as reminders of past neglect to follow through on solemn global pledges.

But UN goals have also achieved many successes—some spectacular. An immunization goal dramatically increased coverage, from 10–20% in 1980 to more than 70% in 1990 in more than 70 countries. And even when quantitative targets have not been achieved by their target dates, they have accelerated progress. For example, by 2000 life expectancy had been raised to at least 60 years in 124 countries. In the 1990s child mortality was reduced by a third or more in only 63 countries—but in more than 100 it was cut by a fifth. Thus global goals can raise ambitions and spur efforts (box 1.2).

ADDRESSING THE CRITICS

The Millennium Development Goals have been widely acclaimed, inspiring new energy for action against poverty. But they have also been criticized for:

- Being too narrow, leaving out development priorities such as strong governance, increased employment, reproductive health care and institutional reform of global governance.
- Relying on narrow indicators—such as school enrolment gaps to track progress in gender equality, or numbers of telephones to measure access to technology.
- Being unrealistic and setting the stage for discouragement—and for being used to name and shame countries that do not achieve them.
- Distorting national priorities, possibly undermining local leadership by promoting a top-down, often donor-led agenda at the cost of participatory approaches in which communities and countries set their own priorities.[6]

These concerns point to what could go wrong if the Goals—particularly their numerical indicators—are taken out of context and seen as ends in themselves rather than as benchmarks of progress towards the broader goal of eradicating human poverty. Though the Goals reflect consensus on key global development objectives, they are not a new model for development. And while all are important, the priority placed on each should be determined by national development strategies.

The Goals are ambitious—reflecting the urgent need for much faster progress on development. They are intended to mobilize action, not name and shame. They place demands on all actors to identify new actions and resources so that they can be reached. The poorer the country is, the greater the challenge. Contrast what Mali will have to do to halve poverty by 2015, to 36%[7] and reduce under-five mortality by two-thirds, to 85 per 1,000 live births,[8] with Sri Lanka's task: cutting poverty to 3.3%[9] and under-five mortality to 8 per 1,000 live births.[10] That does not mean that Mali is destined to fail. Rather, it reveals the huge challenges facing the poorest countries—and the enormous efforts needed from the international community.

Moreover, success should not be judged simply by achieving the Goals on time. Halving poverty by 2015 is not the end of the road, because countries must continue to halve it again and again. And countries should not be condemned if they do not achieve the Goals on time.

GLOBAL GOALS MUST BE COUNTRY OWNED

Although the Millennium Development Goals originated in the United Nations, they are people's goals—and they can be achieved only if efforts are nationally owned and country driven.

STRONG NATIONAL OWNERSHIP

Developing countries have been pursuing the underlying objectives of the Millennium Development Goals for decades. But the Goals require new political momentum for faster progress on reducing human poverty—a process already under way in many countries. As governments begin to assess whether and how the Goals will be achieved by 2015, they also assess policy priorities and develop national strategies. Several countries have increased social spending and launched new programmes in support of the Goals. For example, Bolivia has aligned its social policies with the Goals. Proposals have been made to substantially increase spending on health and education, and two national programmes have been created towards that end. Cameroon has also boosted funding for education and health,

Failures should serve as reminders of past neglect to follow through on solemn global pledges

BOX 1.2

Do global goals make a difference?

Since the earliest days of the United Nations, its member governments have set global goals, with several recurring objectives. Ending colonialism was a major theme of the 1950s and 1960s. Accelerating economic growth and advancing other economic goals—such as employment, industrialization and international assistance—were major themes of the first, second and third development decades (1960s, 1970s, 1980s). Goals for literacy, schooling, health, survival and water and sanitation were set from the early 1960s into the 1990s, culminating in the 2000 Millennium Declaration.

UN goals are often dismissed as overly ambitious and rarely achieved. Yet many goals have been achieved:
• Eradicating smallpox (World Health Organization declaration, 1965)—achieved in 1977.
• Immunizing 80% of infants (before their first birthday) against major childhood diseases by 1990 (World Health Organization declaration, 1974, refined in 1984)—achieved in about 70 countries, though the achievements have not been maintained in Sub-Saharan Africa and South Asia.
• Reducing children's deaths from diarrhoea by half (World Summit for Children, 1990)—achieved in the 1990s.
• Cutting infant mortality to less than 120 per 1,000 live births by 2000 (World Summit for Children, 1990)—achieved in all but 12 developing countries.
• Eliminating polio by 2000 (World Summit for Children, 1990)—achieved in 110 countries. More than 175 countries are now polio free.
• Eliminating guinea-worm disease by 2000 (World Summit for Children, 1990)—by 2000 the number of reported cases had declined by 97%, and the disease has been eliminated in all but 14 countries.

Significant progress has been made on many other goals even though they were not fully achieved:
• Accelerating economic growth in developing countries to 5% a year by the end of the 1960s and to 6% in the 1970s (UN resolution, 1961)—during the 1960s, 32 countries exceeded 5%, and during the 1970s, 25 countries exceeded 6%. (Though the record in the 1980s and 1990s was far more disappointing; see chapters 2 and 4.)
• Increasing developing countries' share in global industrial production (United Nations Industrial Development Organization declaration, 1975)—the share rose from 7% in 1970 to 20% in 2000, though these gains were limited to a small number of countries.
• Raising life expectancy to 60 years by 2000 (UN General Assembly resolution, 1980)—achieved in 124 of the 173 countries that fell below this threshold (almost all of them among the least developed countries, with many in Sub-Saharan Africa).
• Reducing child mortality by at least one-third more during the 1990s (World Summit for Children, 1990)—63 countries achieved the goal, and in more than 100 countries child deaths were cut by 20%.
• Eliminating or reducing hunger and malnutrition by 2000 (Third Development Decade, 1980s; World Summit for Children, 1990)—in developing countries malnutrition dropped 17% between 1980 and 2000, but in Sub-Saharan Africa the number of undernourished people rose by 27 million in the 1990s.
• Achieving universal access to safe water by 1990, then by 2000 (Third Development Decade, 1980s; World Summit for Children, 1990)—access increased by 4.1 billion people, reaching 5 billion.

Still, some goals have failed almost entirely:
• Increasing official development assistance to 0.7% of rich countries' GNP starting in 1970 (UN General Assembly resolution, 1970; International Development Strategy for the 1970s)—assistance has actually fallen as a share of GNP, and in the 1990s only four countries achieved the 0.7% target (Denmark, the Netherlands, Norway and Sweden).
• Allocating 0.15% of GNP for official development assistance to the least developed countries in the 1980s and 1990s (UN Conference on the Least Developed Countries, 1981)—8 of 16 members of the OECD's Development Assistance Committee achieved the 0.15% target in the 1980s, but only 5 of 20 did so in the 1990s.
• Halving adult illiteracy by 2000 (World Summit for Children, 1990)—illiteracy fell from 25% in 1990 to just 21% in 2000.
• Eradicating malaria (World Health Organization declaration, 1965)—although there was success in Asia and Latin America, the "global" anti-malaria programme of the 1960s largely bypassed Africa (due to the perceived intractability of the disease there) even though it suffers the largest malaria burden. Over the next several decades the international community devoted little attention and scant resources to malaria, leading to fragmented interventions.

Whether the numerical target of a global goal was achieved is an important but inadequate measure of success, because it does not indicate whether setting the goal made a difference. In many cases enormous progress has been made even though numerical targets have not been reached—as with the International Drinking Water Supply and Sanitation Decade of the 1980s (UN General Assembly, 1980), during which hardly any developing country achieved universal coverage. But the setting of global goals drew attention to these needs, and in the 1980s access to safe water increased 130% and access to sanitation increased 266%, both much more than in the 1970s or 1990s. Yet the decade has often been viewed as a failure simply because the numerical targets were not met.

Once set, goals agreed to at the United Nations have been followed up in very different ways. At one extreme have been goals like accelerating economic growth, where there has been little mobilization for implementation by the international community. At the other extreme have been goals like eradicating smallpox, expanding immunizations and reducing child mortality, where the international community—led by the World Health Organization and the United Nations Children's Fund—have supported country action.

Source: Jolly 2003.

and politicians are using data on progress towards the Goals in their campaign debates.

National ownership is not just government ownership. Action must be driven not just by politicians and government agencies but also by communities, local authorities and civil society groups. The political momentum for policy change must come from a country's people, pressing for more schools, better health care, improved water supplies and other essential elements of development. The Goals provide an entry point for applying such pressure. They empower communities and people to hold authorities accountable. And they offer a scorecard for people to assess the performance of political leaders—from local to national government officials, to parliamentarians, to opposition parties (see chapter 7).

Civil society groups—from community organizations to global networks—are supportive allies, helping to build schools and mobilize research on neglected diseases. But they also have an essential role as watchdogs, monitoring those responsible for delivering results and shaping democratic debates on economic and social policies in poor communities. In newly democratizing states open debate on policy choices has often been absent or inadequate, leaving people vulnerable to populist rhetoric. Thus social mobilization around the Millennium Development Goals can help nurture and consolidate democratic processes, with the voices of ordinary people influencing policy-making. Though civil society groups have started to engage with the Goals, many are unaware or suspicious of them.[11]

COMMITMENT OF RICH COUNTRY PARTNERS AND THE INTERNATIONAL COMMUNITY

The Goals are a major step towards building a true partnership for development, and in defining what is meant by partnership. The agreements that emerged from the 2002 International Conference on Financing for Development and the World Summit on Sustainable Development advanced the consensus on the mutual responsibilities of developing and rich countries. Developing countries are to focus on improving governance, especially in mobilizing resources, allocating them equitably and ensuring their effective use. Rich countries are to increase concessional financing and debt relief and to foster trade and technology transfers (see chapter 8).

CLEAR DIAGNOSIS OF WHAT NEEDS TO BE DONE

The world needs a clear analysis of why global poverty endures, where and what the biggest obstacles are and what needs to be done to tackle them. Every poor country has to prepare a national strategy that addresses its circumstances.

The international community also needs to set priorities on how to achieve the Millennium Development Goals. These priorities need to be based on objective analysis of the biggest challenges and main obstacles, on evidence of what has worked (and what has not) and on ideas for new actions to accelerate progress.

For this analysis the UN Secretary-General has established the Millennium Project, a research initiative that brings together nearly 300 experts from academia, civil society, international organizations and the public and private sectors around the world. This project will issue its final report in 2005.

This *Human Development Report* also helps identify global priorities, provides data and analyses new ideas. This Report has been prepared in close collaboration with the Millennium Project, drawing on its work and on other in-house and commissioned research. It describes:
- Overall global progress towards the Goals—and identifies areas requiring the most attention (chapter 2).
- The structural constraints to economic growth and human development and the ways to overcome them (chapters 3).
- Policy options for achieving the Goals for education, hunger, health, gender equality and water and sanitation (chapter 4).
- Appropriate roles for the private and public sectors in expanding basic social services (chapter 5).
- Policy options for achieving the environment Goal (chapter 6).
- The role of people in building political momentum for policy change (chapter 7).
- New policies for trade, debt relief, technology transfers and aid needed to support the implementation of all the Goals (chapter 8).

The Millennium Development Compact, at the beginning of this Report, is its main policy plank. The Compact presents a new approach to help countries escape poverty traps and achieve the Goals, identifies the responsibilities of stakeholders and builds on the principles of the Monterrey Consensus (adopted at the International Conference on Financing for Development)—which takes a performance rather than an entitlement approach to development cooperation.

The Goals are a major step towards building a true partnership for development, and in defining what is meant by partnership

CHAPTER 2

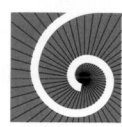 **Priority challenges in meeting the Goals**

Two groups of developing countries face especially difficult—and different—challenges in achieving the Millennium Development Goals. In the first group are top priority and high priority countries where entrenched human poverty and failed—or even reversing—progress have created crises, requiring the world's focused attention and resources. The second group is in the public eye less often, having made good progress overall. But that progress has been uneven, and gaps are widening because poor groups and regions are being left behind.

Since 1990 East Asia and the Pacific, led by China, has nearly halved extreme income poverty—and is making significant progress on the other Goals as well. For the Arab States and Latin America and the Caribbean, achieving the Goals by 2015 will be challenging but possible (figure 2.1). But for other developing regions achieving the Goals remains a huge challenge. Unless things improve, it will take Sub-Saharan Africa until 2129 to achieve universal primary education, until 2147 to halve extreme poverty and until 2165 to cut child mortality by two-thirds.

FIGURE 2.1
Timeline: when will the Millennium Development Goals be achieved if progress does not accelerate?

	Poverty	Hunger	Primary education	Gender equality	Child mortality	Access to water	Access to sanitation
ACHIEVED	Arab States[a] East Asia & the Pacific	Central & Eastern[a] Europe & the CIS	Latin America &[a] the Caribbean Central & Eastern[a] Europe & the CIS East Asia[a] & the Pacific	Latin America &[a] the Caribbean		Central & Eastern[a] Europe & the CIS	
2000	World South Asia	East Asia & the Pacific			Latin America & the Caribbean	South Asia **World** Latin America & the Caribbean	
2015					East Asia & the Pacific	East Asia & the Pacific	South Asia **World** Latin America & the Caribbean East Asia & the Pacific
2020		Latin America & the Caribbean		East Asia & the Pacific Arab States South Asia	South Asia Arab States **World**	Sub-Saharan Africa	
		World	South Asia				
2050			Arab States **World**				
2100	South Asia						
2200	Sub-Saharan Africa	Sub-Saharan Africa	Sub-Saharan Africa		Sub-Saharan Africa	Central & Eastern Europe & the CIS	
REVERSAL	Latin America & the Caribbean Sub-Saharan Africa Central & Eastern Europe & the CIS	Arab States					Sub-Saharan Africa

a. Region is considered to have achieved the Goal because it has low human poverty (below 10%) in the most recent year for the relevant Goal (see technical note 2).
Source: Human Development Report Office calculations based on feature 2.1.

For hunger no date can be set because the region's situation continues to worsen. Though South Asia has made faster progress, substantial improvements will be required in most areas if the Goals are to be met.

During the 1990s many developing countries saw reversals and stagnation in many areas essential to the Goals. Some 54 countries are poorer now than in 1990. In 21 countries a larger proportion of people are going hungry. In 14 countries more children are dying before age five. In 12 countries primary school enrolment rates have fallen. And in many countries things have simply stagnated—neither worsened nor improved.[1]

In the 1980s only 4 countries experienced reversals in the human development index (a summary measure based on the ability of a country's citizens to live a long and healthy life, be educated and enjoy a decent standard of living). In the 1990s that number jumped to 21. Behind these reversals were failed economic growth and the HIV/AIDS epidemic. The 1990s also saw declining development assistance from rich countries, increasing debt burdens in poor countries and continuing drops in the prices of primary commodities—which many poor countries depend on for the bulk of their export revenues (see chapter 8).

Many developing countries face huge challenges in one or two areas related to the Goals. But most worrisome are the 31 top priority countries facing failed progress and extremely low starting levels for many of the Goals. Though they come from all regions, most are in Sub-Saharan Africa. In another 28 high priority countries the situation is less desperate—though significant progress is still needed if the Goals are to be met.

Yet some of the world's poorest countries are making progress towards higher levels of development. Success stories are emerging in the fight against HIV/AIDS. Education is improving. And economies are beginning to grow. A key message of this Report is that much is known about how to achieve the Goals. But this knowledge must be applied quickly if struggling countries are to do so.

When measuring progress, it is vital to look beyond country averages. In many countries the letter of the Goals may be achieved if efforts focus on people already doing the best in society. But the spirit of the Goals is not met if countries that cross the finishing line leave behind many poor people. In Brazil, China, India and Mexico overall progress has been excellent. But some areas and groups are not benefiting enough, while wealthy segments of the population continue to surge ahead. And in countries doing badly, much of the burden is borne by marginalized groups—as in Burkina Faso, Mali and the Russian Federation.

This chapter assesses progress towards the Millennium Development Goals using a global perspective to identify areas most in need of policy attention (box 2.1 and feature 2.1 at the end of the chapter; see also the Millennium Development Goal indicator tables 1–10 in the statistical annex). The assessment shows:

- Stark contrasts between and within regions.
- Human development reversals in the 1990s.
- Struggles to achieve the Goals, with reversals, stagnation and countries in crisis.
- Good performance by some of the poorest countries.
- Widening gaps within countries: who is being left behind?

STARK CONTRASTS BETWEEN AND WITHIN REGIONS

Around the world, progress is being made on the Goals. But stark differences are emerging between regions, with some pulling ahead and reaching new levels of development—while others are left behind. The same pattern is occurring within regions: some countries are succeeding amid disappointing regional trends, while others are falling behind in regions making good overall progress:

- *South Asia—advancing from low levels.* South Asia remains one of the world's poorest regions. And because it is so heavily populated, it is home to the largest number of poor people. The task is enormous—with more than one-third of South Asians lacking access to improved sanitation, one-third in poverty, one-quarter hungry, one-fifth of children out of primary school and almost one-tenth of children dying before age five. But significant progress was made in all these areas in the 1990s, lifting the region

During the 1990s many developing countries saw reversals and stagnation in many areas essential to the Goals

BOX 2.1

Building statistical capacity—unprecedented demand, urgent opportunity

The Millennium Development Goals have made clear the need for relevant, reliable, timely statistics to set policies, hold decision-makers accountable, monitor progress and evaluate results. Yet despite considerable improvements in recent years, meeting the demand for basic data on human development remains a major global challenge.

Though the data situation varies across developing countries, the Millennium Indicators Database (see http://millenniumindicators.un.org) —based on national statistics compiled or estimated by international data agencies—is revealing. Not only are there significant gaps for almost every indicator, there are also extensive problems in relevance, accuracy, consistency and reliability. For example:

• Many of the indicators chosen for the Millennium Development Goals are based on available data—not necessarily the data most appropriate for the Goals. An example is the $1 a day indicator, the most debated measure of absolute poverty (see box 2.3). Another is the indicator of sustainable access to affordable essential drugs, where both access and affordability are difficult to assess accurately. Meanwhile, adequate indicators for the target on slum dwellers (part of Goal 7) have yet to be fully developed.

• For indicators on income poverty, health, gender inequality, employment and the environment, many countries have no data for 1990–2001—and few have data on trends over that time (see table).

• Some data—such as for maternal mortality and HIV/AIDS—are based on incomplete vital registrations or non-representative surveys and so are subject to enormous uncertainty. And even when data are available for multiple periods,

they often are not comparable due to changes in definitions, methods and coverage.

By creating long-term demand for data, the Goals are challenging national and international institutions to go beyond short-term responses and to build sound, sustainable national statistical capacity and systems. What needs to be done—or done differently—to achieve those objectives?

Building national demand

Lacking appreciation of the importance of statistics in supporting informed decision-making, too many countries are trapped in a circle of low demand and low resources for statistics, resulting in inadequate supply. Such countries do not routinely collect data—many have not conducted a population census in the past 10 years—and lag far behind in the adoption of up-to-date statistical standards and methods. They also have limited capacity to analyse and disseminate statistics, discouraging the use of data in national policy analysis.

Demand for data must increase if national statistical systems are to break this circle of underperformance and underfunding. Efforts to increase the supply of data must also strengthen the capacity of governments and the general public to use data effectively. Though country ownership and commitment are crucial to such efforts, the international community can help by:

• Advocating the importance of statistics and statistical systems in supporting effective governance and empowering people. Important opportunities include the processes for developing Poverty Reduction Strategy Papers, national human development reports and Millennium Development Goals country reports, which emphasize the need for monitoring and evaluation.

• Making better use of existing data to meet short-term demands for specific programmes, and making long-term investments in statistical systems.

• Training statistical analysts, managers of statistical systems and users of statistics; designing new tools for data collection; increasing access to data through support for data dissemination and analysis and encouraging the use of existing technology to lower costs and make national statistical programmes more effective.

Improving national strategies and systems

International agencies have conducted a variety of household surveys to narrow data gaps in developing countries, particularly for poverty, health and education. These surveys—including Demographic and Health Surveys, Multiple Indicator Cluster Surveys, Living Standards Measurement Surveys and Core Welfare Indicator Questionnaires—have provided essential data on socio-economic characteristics and trends, especially among poor people.

But when similar surveys are conducted in resource-constrained countries, they are sometimes driven by short-term external needs, distort local priorities and offer no sustainable improvements to local statistical infrastructure. Though administrative systems can provide detailed time-series and disaggregated data for national planning, they require long-term investments and are often neglected.

To foster the development of sustainable statistical systems and minimize distortions of priorities and outputs, data collection and analysis should be conducted in the framework of national statistical strategies. These strategies should be closely aligned with national policies and agreed priorities for statistical systems.

In recent years several African countries have significantly improved their statistical capacity by using national demands to guide their statistical development efforts. Uganda restructured its statistical agency, enabling it to better manage and meet user demands. In Malawi donor and government investments in household surveys and data analysis have increased understanding of poverty— resulting in poverty maps, an agreed poverty line and a comprehensive profile of poor people.

An international poverty survey

The Millennium Development Goals highlight areas where national statistical systems require dramatic improvements. Many countries, including the top and high priority countries identified in this Report, require extensive assistance to conduct regular surveys of income and

Large data gaps even in basic human development indicators: countries lacking data, 1990–2001
Percent

Indicator	Countries lacking trend data	Countries lacking any data
Children underweight for age	100	22
Net primary enrolment ratio	46	17
Children reaching grade five	96	46
Births attended by skilled health personnel	100	19
Female share of non-agricultural wage employment	51	41
HIV prevalence among pregnant women ages 15–24 in major urban areas	100	91
Population with sustainable access to an improved water source	62	18
Population living on less than $1 a day	100	55

Note: Data refer to developing countries and countries in Central and Eastern Europe and the CIS. A country is defined as having trend data if at least two data points are available—one in 1990–95 and one in 1996–2001—and the two points are at least three years apart.
Source: UN 2003c.

Continued on next page

BOX 2.1 (continued)

Building statistical capacity—unprecedented demand, urgent opportunity

consumption—especially to assess extreme poverty and basic living conditions. Such countries also need to develop or strengthen statistical programmes for other social indicators, particularly for health data singled out by the Goals.

An international poverty survey could be one way to respond to the new demand for statistical support created by the Goals. Although existing surveys (such as Demographic and Health Surveys) provide important data in many areas, none provides consistent, reliable data on extreme poverty and basic living conditions. Using new or improved international standards and methodologies, the international poverty survey could be modular, with some modules unchangeable and consistent over time and space—and others adapted to current or long-term country needs. Built within an integrated survey programme, such a survey could provide invaluable data for national and global analysis, and become a major tool for building national statistical capacity.

Securing more—and more effective use of—resources

Many poor countries lack all but the barest statistical infrastructure and training. Severely constrained by resources, they require significant financial support to start building statistical capacity. Other countries have well-developed programmes in certain areas but require support to strengthen overall statistical systems. They also need to adjust national priorities and invest in statistical activities to ensure sustainable capacity building.

Governments and donors should recognize that strengthening statistical systems is integral to achieving the Millennium Development Goals. Rather than focusing on short-term results and relying on expensive external experts, efforts should favour long-term planning and make more effective use of local resources and knowledge.

New financing instruments
Many donors are making efforts to finance statistical systems, both by increasing funding (such as including statistical components in projects) and by experimenting with new instruments. For example, the World Bank's new multidonor Trust Fund for Statistical Capacity Building provides grants to develop master plans and small-scale projects for statistical capacity building. In addition, new lending facilities—such as investment loans that gradually reduce support for recurrent costs (the bulk of expenses facing statistical offices) during implementation phases—will help developing countries increase investments and ease dependence on donor financing.

Cooperation among developing countries
Decades of technical cooperation and assistance from donors have fostered significant knowledge in developing countries. But while experts from rich countries have a vital role to play, so do practitioners within countries—and from other developing countries with similar problems and conditions. In the late 1980s, for example, the Philippines's National Statistical Coordination Board helped Indonesia's Central Bureau of Statistics compile national accounts data.

Several factors are key to the success of such efforts: ownership and commitment by recipient countries; similar economic, cultural and data systems in recipient and assisting countries, facilitating technology transfer; affordable consultation costs to enable long-term support; a sense of being peers; and willingness to cooperate fully.

Improving collaboration and coordination

Statistical capacity building must be coordinated effectively both within countries and among donors. Statistical programmes in most developing countries, even those with long statistical traditions, are often decentralized among various ministries beyond national statistical offices. The statistical offices of international agencies, such as those at UN headquarters and regional commissions, mainly work with national statistical offices. Other statistical units in specialized donor agencies—such as the International Labour Organization, Food and Agriculture Organization, United Nations Educational, Scientific and Cultural Organization and World Health Organization—generally work with their national counterparts in line ministries. Still other donors, mostly multilateral and bilateral, often manage technical cooperation through technical cooperation ministries or similar mechanisms.

This structure poses enormous challenges for coordination. Different donors inevitably duplicate similar projects, with overlapping and inconsistent objectives, competing for limited local resources and overloading national capacity. There is also severe incoherence within national systems and disconnection between national statistical offices and various ministries. The result? Enormous inefficiency, less valuable data from surveys that use different definitions and methods and discrepancies in national and international statistics.

The Millennium Development Goals offer a unique opportunity to establish clear, effective responsibilities both nationally and internationally.

For example, national statistical offices could play a more central role in coordinating national statistics for national and international needs. Practical mechanisms should be created to coordinate and monitor international assistance.

To coordinate statistical capacity building, the Partnership in Statistics for Development in the 21st Century (PARIS21) was established in 1999. This partnership links national and international statisticians and users of statistics in an effort to develop strategies for building statistical capacity and promote effective cooperation between poor and rich countries. Though relatively new, PARIS21 has addressed many challenges—advocating the need for better data, mobilizing resources, designing tools for assessing statistical capacity and identifying priorities and encouraging countries to develop long-term plans for statistical development.

Strengthening international data systems
The growing demand for coherent, consistent international statistics poses a serious challenge. Although stronger international statistics depend on stronger national statistics, changes are also needed in international statistical agencies. They must increase their capacity to respond to new measurement challenges and provide timely statistics, reduce data gaps and inconsistencies, improve collaboration with national statistical systems and strengthen coordination among themselves to enhance international standards and methods and to ensure consistency among international data series.

The international community plays an important role in statistical development by implementing internationally agreed standards, methods and frameworks for statistical activities. Significant milestones include the development and adoption of the System of National Accounts, General Data Dissemination Standards and Data Quality Assessment Framework. The Millennium Development Goals have generated new momentum for the development of international guidelines on appropriate concepts and methods for each country to build on—such as measures of extreme poverty and living conditions in urban slums. These needs are especially essential to meet the needs of top and high priority countries.

The Goals have mobilized the international community and inspired developing countries to assume responsibility for building statistical capacity. Closing enormous statistical gaps will require commitment and effort from donors and recipients alike. Capacity building is not something that can be done for countries: they must do it themselves. Still, external assistance is essential.

Source: Human Development Report Office based on David 2003; De Vries 2003; Johnston 2002, 2003; UNDP 2002a, 2003e; McEwin 2003; Simonpietri 2003; UN 2002g; World Bank 2002a, 2003d, 2003h.

from the basement of development. Moreover, country performance was more homogeneous than in any other region: except for Afghanistan, no country experienced reversals in the key indicators for the Millennium Development Goals. Still, there was some divergence: Bangladesh and Bhutan reduced their under-five mortality rates by more than 6 percentage points, and Nepal by more than 5 points. Now a smaller proportion of children die before age five in these countries than in Pakistan, where progress has been much slower. Moreover, India's performance varied enormously across states, with inequality increasing between several.

- *Sub-Saharan Africa—left behind.* Like South Asia, Sub-Saharan Africa faces enormous poverty. But unlike South Asia, it is being left behind. Almost across the board the story is one of stagnation. Economies have not grown, half of Africans live in extreme poverty and one-third in hunger, and about one-sixth of children die before age five—the same as a decade ago. And because of population growth, the number of people suffering increased considerably in the 1990s. Some progress was made in education, but the primary enrolment rate is still only 57%. And with low completion rates, only one in three children in the region finish primary school. Yet amid this dismal picture of stagnation and reversals, some countries achieved impressive progress in the 1990s. In Cape Verde, Mauritius, Mozambique and Uganda per capita income grew by more than 3% a year, and Ghana and Mozambique achieved some of the world's sharpest reductions in hunger. In Benin the primary enrolment rate increased by more than 20 percentage points. And in the face of HIV/AIDS, 10 countries reduced child mortality by 3 percentage points or more—Malawi by more than 5 points.

- *Latin American and the Caribbean—stalled progress.* At the other end of the spectrum of developing regions, Latin America and the Caribbean has human development indicators approaching levels in rich countries. But though progress continued in some areas (education, under-five mortality), the 1990s saw slow economic growth and slight increases in poverty. As a result East Asia is fast closing its income gap with Latin America and now has a lower proportion of hungry people. Although most Latin American and Caribbean countries had slow growth in per capita incomes in the 1990s, in five countries per capita growth was more than 3% a year—with Chile and Guyana seeing per capita growth of almost 5%. In hunger, too, there was great variation: the proportion of hungry people almost tripled in Cuba, from 5% to 13%, while Peru had the region's biggest reduction, from 40% to 11%. Under-five mortality rates fell in Bolivia (from 12% to 8%) and Ecuador (6% to 3%), while Barbados, Jamaica and Saint Vincent and the Grenadines experienced almost no improvement.

- *East Asia and the Pacific—performing well across the board.* East Asia's economy grew by almost 6% a year in the 1990s, while poverty fell by about 15 percentage points—and this despite the severe financial crisis that hit the region in 1997–98. The reduction in hunger was the fastest of any region, falling from 17% to 11%—now lower than in the Arab States or Latin America and the Caribbean. Universal primary education attendance and completion are within reach, and under-five mortality has fallen significantly. China has been pivotal to the region's success. With 1.2 billion people, it accounts for about 70% of East Asia's population. (China's success and its uneven distribution are discussed later in this chapter.) Other success stories include higher enrolment rates in Lao People's Democratic Republic and lower under-five mortality rates in Indonesia. Still, many countries in the region did not enjoy similar progress in the 1990s. Income growth was slow in the Philippines—and negative in Brunei Darussalam, Mongolia, the Solomon Islands and Vanuatu. And in Cambodia under-five mortality rates rose 2 percentage points.

- *Central and Eastern Europe and the Commonwealth of Independent States—increasing poverty and declining life expectancy.* People in Central and Eastern Europe and the Commonwealth of Independent States (CIS) ended the 1990s less healthy and with lower average incomes than people in Latin America and the Caribbean. These negative trends date to the 1980s, but data for the 1990s give an idea of the size of the decline: poverty more than tripled, to almost 100 million people—25% of the region's

In Cape Verde, Mauritius, Mozambique and Uganda per capita income grew by more than 3% a year, and Ghana and Mozambique achieved some of the world's sharpest reductions in hunger

population.[2] The experience in the transition to market economies has been a tale of two regions—Central and Eastern Europe on the one hand and the CIS on the other. Some countries in Central and Eastern Europe have made remarkable improvements since the late 1990s: the Czech Republic, Hungary, Poland, Slovakia and Slovenia are on the verge of joining the European Union. The challenge is to replicate these successes in CIS countries struggling to move forward. The CIS Seven—Armenia, Azerbaijan, Georgia, Kyrgyzstan, Moldova, Tajikistan and Uzbekistan—ended the 1990s with incomes close to those of the least developed countries.

• *Arab States—persistent gaps.* In the Arab States high incomes have improved many aspects of human development since 1970. Yet of all regions the Arab States has the widest gap between incomes and other aspects of human development. Despite narrowing gender gaps in enrolments, gender inequality remains an issue: in countries with parliaments, women hold only 5% of seats.[3] Political and civil rights pose the greatest challenge—in 1999 only 4 of the region's 17 countries with data had multiparty electoral systems.[4] Still, despite general economic stagnation, Lebanon, Sudan and Tunisia grew by more than 3% a year in the 1990s. Kuwait reduced its hungry population from 22% to 4%, and Egypt achieved the largest reduction in under-five mortality rates, from around 10% to 4%. But other countries are being left behind. In Iraq the under-five mortality rate almost tripled in the 1990s, to 13%. Countries facing less extreme circumstances have also struggled: in

Yemen the proportion of underweight children jumped from 30% in 1992 to 46% in 1997.[5]

GAPS BETWEEN RICH AND POOR COUNTRIES: MOVING BEYOND INCOME INEQUALITY ALONE

Questions about global income inequality inspire some of the most contentious debates on the international stage. The answers depend on how the questions are asked. And even when the questions seem the same, the answers can be very different (box 2.2). People look to data on income inequality as they might a stock market index to gauge how the world is doing. Are things on the right track? Is enough being done? Yet debates on global income inequality indicate little more than how economists and statisticians can find many answers to the seemingly same questions.

Nobel Prize winner Amartya Sen has suggested that careful consideration be given to what is meant by inequality.[6] Looking at income inequalities alone can mask inequalities in human lives and capabilities and how they are changing. But capturing how gaps between rich and poor people and regions are changing in areas other than income is often hard to do, because most basic human development indicators have a limit at the top. When nearly all children are in school, all adults are literate and life expectancy approaches its biological limit, countries can make little further progress. So while rich countries can get little better according to these indicators, any improvement in poor countries represents a reduction in inequality.

But even when a country can progress no further in a basic human development indicator, things can continue to improve. The quality of education can get better. Health care can dramatically improve people's lives in ways not reflected in life expectancy data. Hidden behind income levels can be more enjoyable employment and increased leisure time. Women can be empowered in the home and workplace. Such indicators are at the frontier of measurement in human development—and it is through them that many changes in non-income inequality will be identified.

Yet inequalities in basic human development indicators are not always falling. For example,

Questions about global income inequality inspire some of the most contentious debates on the international stage: the answers depend on how the questions are asked

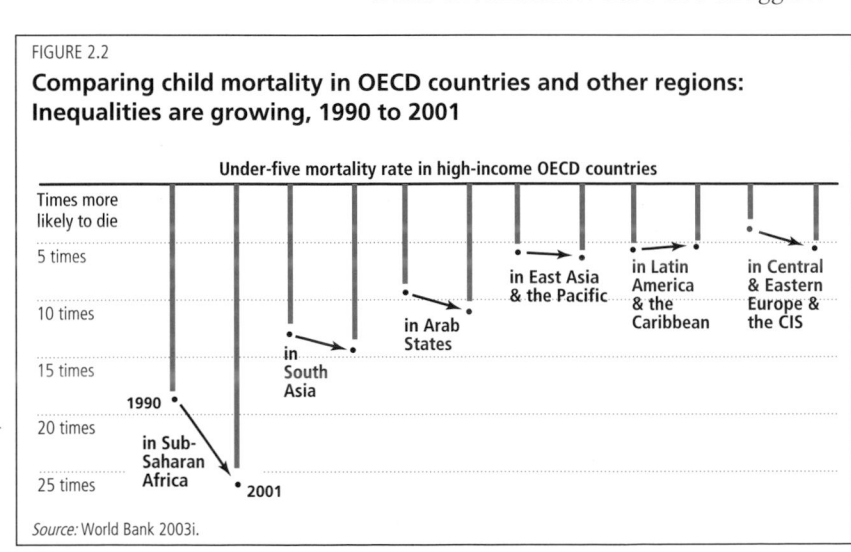

FIGURE 2.2

Comparing child mortality in OECD countries and other regions: Inequalities are growing, 1990 to 2001

Source: World Bank 2003i.

BOX 2.2

What is happening with global income inequality?
Grotesque levels, ambiguous trends

Human Development Report 2002 noted that while the definition of global income inequality is fuzzy and its trends ambiguous, there is widespread consensus on its grotesque levels. This has not changed. Incomes are distributed more unequally across the world's people (with a Gini coefficient of 0.66) than in the most unequal countries (Brazil, for example, has a Gini coefficient of 0.61). (The Gini coefficient is a measure of income inequality that ranges between 0, indicating perfect equality, and 1, indicating complete inequality.) The richest 5% of the world's people receive 114 times the income of the poorest 5%. The richest 1% receive as much as the poorest 57%. And the 25 million richest Americans have as much income as almost 2 billion of the world's poorest people (Milanovic 2002, pp. 51–92).

Monitoring and containing income inequality are essential not only to increase opportunities for as many people as possible, but also to reduce social friction in areas (usually urban) with high inequality. As globalization deepens and access to information becomes cheaper and more widely available, awareness of global inequality is increasing. People no longer compare themselves only to their fellow citizens: they are also aware of international gaps, making divergence across countries increasingly harmful—and dangerous. To reduce growing tensions, it is crucial that the tide of development lift all boats.

Findings on global inequality vary considerably depending on the approach used to analyse it. Inequality can be calculated across countries (using average national incomes), across the world's people (regardless of national boundaries) and across people within countries.

Inequality across countries
International inequality is generally measured by comparing national per capita incomes. Countries with the highest per capita incomes in the early 1800s are still today's richest countries, indicating persistence in the structure of international inequality.

In 1820 Western Europe's per capita income was 2.9 times Africa's—and in 1992, 13.2

times (Maddison 2001). In the 1990s per capita incomes increased slowly but steadily in high-income OECD countries, but many transition countries in Central and Eastern Europe, particularly the CIS, many parts of Sub-Saharan Africa and some countries in Latin America and the Caribbean experienced economic stagnation. At the same time, highly populated developing countries such as China and India achieved rapid growth.

As a result per capita incomes have been converging in rich countries, while in developing countries the pattern is mixed. But when income data are weighted by population—to capture the relative importance of each country's performance—average incomes across countries appear to be converging. Highly populated developing countries drive such trends: fast-growing China and India are catching up with parts of the industrialized world, such as North America and Western Europe.

Inequality across the world's people
Some studies have tried to capture trends in true global inequality—that is, the distribution of income across citizens of the world, regardless of national borders. Income surveys suggest that when measured this way, global inequality increased between 1987 and 1998. The main forces behind this divergence were:
• A widening income gap between the poorest and the richest people due to slow growth in rural incomes in populous Asian countries relative to rich OECD countries.
• Faster progress in urban China relative to rural China and to India.
• Shrinkage in the world's middle-income group (Milanovic 2002, pp. 51–92).

But these conclusions are not entirely robust due to the limited timeframe covered and the use of purchasing power parity (PPP) rates, which are often unsuitable and do not accurately reflect international price differences (see box 2.3).

Using alternative methodologies, other analysts have reached more optimistic conclusions suggesting convergence in global individual incomes: that after peaking in 1970, the gap in

1995 had returned to the level in 1950 (Dollar and Kraay 2002, pp. 120–33; Bhalla 2002; Sala-i-Martin 2002). A driving factor in this debate is the measure of inequality used to draw conclusions. When measured using single summary indicators such as the Gini coefficient, incomes appear to be converging. (Because of the Gini coefficient's construction, it gives more weight to middle-income groups and less to the extremes.) Still, in recent decades there has unquestionably been a widening gap between the incomes of the very richest and the very poorest.

Inequality across people within countries
National income inequality is the concept used for country-level analysis. This concept is suitable for analysing the correlation between a country's policies—typically economic openness or redistribution measures—and its distribution of income.

In many countries inequality in assets and especially income appears to be on the rise. Numerous studies have tried to capture trends in income distribution over time across large samples of countries. Cornia and Kiiski (2001) estimate that between the 1980s and the mid- to late 1990s inequality increased in 42 of 73 countries with complete and comparable data. Only 6 of the 33 developing countries (excluding transition countries) in the sample saw inequality decline, while 17 saw it increase. In other words, within national boundaries control over assets and resources is increasingly concentrated in the hands of a few people.

Though not the case for all these countries, in many inequality began increasing during the debt crisis of the early 1980s (Kanbur and Lustig 1999). Since then inequality has soared, particularly in the Commonwealth of Independent States (CIS) and south-eastern Europe. And in many Latin American countries inequality remains extremely high. If sharp increases in inequality persist, they may have dire effects on human development and social stability (including violence and crime rates; see Fajnzylber, Lederman and Loayza 1998 and Bourguignon 2001).

Source: Ravallion 2002; Schultz 1998, pp. 307–44; Korzeniewicz and Moran 1997, pp. 1000–39; Sprout and Weaver 1992, pp. 237–58; Maddison 2001; Milanovic 2002, pp. 51–92, 2003; Dollar and Kraay 2002, pp. 120–33; Kanbur and Lustig 1999; Bhalla 2002; Sala-i-Martin 2002; Cornia and Kiiski 2001; UNDP 2002e; Fajnzylber, Lederman and Loayza 1998; Bourguignon 2001.

while there is heated debate on whether income inequality is increasing between rich and poor countries, inequality in child mortality has gotten unambiguously worse. In the early 1990s children under five were 19 times more likely to

die in Sub-Saharan Africa than in rich countries—and today, 26 times more likely (figure 2.2). Among all developing regions only Latin America and the Caribbean saw no worsening in the past decade relative to rich countries, with children still about 5 times more likely to die before their fifth birthdays.

HUMAN DEVELOPMENT REVERSALS IN THE 1990S

For human development the 1990s were the best of years and the worst of years. Some regions and countries saw unprecedented progress, while others stagnated or reversed. What is most striking is the extent of the stagnation and reversals—not seen in previous decades.

This is apparent not just by looking at the targets for the Millennium Development Goals, but also from the human development index (HDI), the summary measure of key dimensions of human development (see feature 2.2). The index usually moves steadily upwards, though usually slowly because three of its key components—literacy, enrolment rates and life expectancy—take time to change. So when the HDI falls, it indicates crisis, with nations depleting their basis for development—people, their real wealth.

DECELERATING HUMAN DEVELOPMENT

Though average incomes have risen and fallen over time, human development has historically shown sustained improvement, especially when measured by the HDI. But as noted, the 1990s saw unprecedented stagnation and deterioration, with the HDI falling in 21 countries. Many of these countries have insufficient data to calculate the HDI before 1990, so there is no way of knowing if their HDIs also fell in the 1980s. Of the 114 countries with data since 1980, only 4 saw their HDIs decline in the 1980s—while 15 saw declines in the 1990s (table 2.1). Much of the decline in the 1990s can be traced to the spread of HIV/AIDS, which lowered life expectancies, and to a collapse in incomes, particularly in the CIS.

As a result, after a steady increase since the mid-1970s, there has been a deceleration in HDI progress. The slowdown, particularly in the late 1980s and first half of the 1990s, was led by countries in Central and Eastern Europe and the CIS. Many of these countries had already started

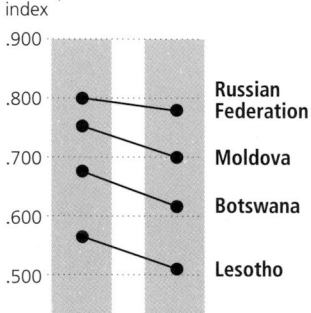
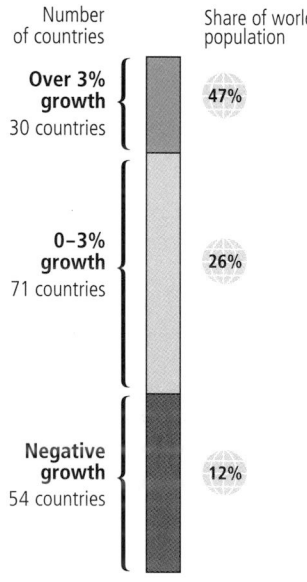
TABLE 2.1

Countries that saw a drop in the human development index, 1980s and 1990s

Period	Number	Countries
1980–90	4	Congo, Dem. Rep. of; Guyana; Rwanda; Zambia
1990–2001	21	Armenia[a]; Belarus[a]; Botswana; Burundi; Cameroon; Central African Republic; Congo; Congo, Dem. Rep. of; Côte d'Ivoire; Kazakhstan[a]; Kenya; Lesotho; Moldova; Russian Federation; South Africa; Swaziland; Tajikistan[a]; Tanzania[a]; Ukraine[a]; Zambia; Zimbabwe

Note: Based on a sample of 113 countries with complete data.
a. Country does not have HDI data for 1980–90, so fall in HDI may have begun before 1990.
Source: Indicator table 2.

on a downward spiral in the mid-1980s, and between 1990 and 1995 the region's average HDI declined. In Sub-Saharan Africa overall growth in the HDI merely slowed, though some countries suffered terrible declines (figure 2.3).

FAILING ECONOMIC GROWTH

Failed economic growth lies behind the faltering HDI and the inability of many countries and regions to reduce income and human poverty (figure 2.4). Seldom if ever is income poverty reduced in a stagnant economy, and the regions growing fastest economically are also the ones that have reduced income poverty most (table 2.2). That provides a clear message: economic growth is essential for reducing income poverty. But the link is far from automatic. In Indonesia, Poland and Sri Lanka income poverty rose in the 1990s despite economic growth (figure 2.5). (Chapter 3 considers pro-poor growth and how it can be achieved.)

At constant inequality levels, a country needs to grow by 3% or more a year to double incomes in a generation—say, from $1 to $2 a day. Yet of 155 countries with data, only 30 had annual per capita income growth rates above 3% in the 1990s. Among the rest, 54 countries saw average incomes fall, and in 71 countries annual income growth was less than 3%.

The consequences of this dismal growth performance? At the turn of the millennium more than 1.2 billion people were struggling to survive on less than $1 a day—and more than twice as many, 2.8 billion, on less than $2 a day. Living on $1 a day does not mean being able to afford what $1 would buy when converted into a local currency, but the equivalent of what $1 would buy in the United States: a newspaper, a local bus ride, a bag of rice.

Debate rages over the validity of $1 a day poverty data, which come from the World Bank, because calculating them is fraught with conceptual and practical problems. Some experts believe them to be rough but reasonable. Others believe that they reveal little about income poverty and its trends (box 2.3).

Whatever the case, the data show that globally the proportion of people living on less than $1 a day dropped from nearly 30% in 1990 to 23% in 1999 (table 2.3).[7] But the story is not one of good overall progress. Rather, it is one of some countries forging ahead while others see bad situations get even worse. Much of the impressive reduction in global poverty has been driven by China's incredible economic growth of more than 9% a year in the 1990s, lifting 150 million people out of poverty.[8]

Of 67 countries with data, 37 saw poverty rates increase in the 1990s.[9] But others achieved impressive reductions in poverty: Brazil, Chile, India, Uganda, Thailand, Viet Nam. Many of the countries where poverty rates soared were in Eastern Europe—particularly Central Asia—though other cases included Algeria, Mongolia, Nigeria, Pakistan, Venezuela and Zimbabwe.[10]

When populations grow, reductions in the proportion of poor people can still mean an increase in the number. Only in East Asia did the number of people in extreme poverty decline significantly in the 1990s. In South Asia, home to almost 500 million poor people, the number hardly changed. In all other regions the number of poor people rose—notably in Sub-Saharan Africa, where an additional 74 million people, the population of the Philippines, ended the decade in extreme poverty. And as noted, in Eastern Europe and the CIS the number of poor people more than tripled, from 31 million to almost 100 million (see table 2.3).[11]

TABLE 2.2
Economic growth and income poverty: strong links

Region	Growth in the 1990s (annual per capita income growth) (%)	Poverty reduction in the 1990s (percentage point reduction)
East Asia and the Pacific	6.4	14.9
South Asia	3.3	8.4
Latin America & the Caribbean	1.6	–0.1
Middle East & North Africa	1.0	–0.1
Sub-Saharan Africa	–0.4	–1.6
Central and Eastern Europe and the CIS	–1.9	–13.5[a]

a. Change measured using the $2 a day poverty line, which is considered a more appropriate extreme poverty line for Central & Eastern Europe & CIS.
Source: World Bank 2002f.

INCREASING SPREAD OF HIV/AIDS

In recent decades the greatest shock to development has been HIV/AIDS. The first cases were recognized in the early 1980s, and by 1990 some 10 million people were infected (figure 2.6). Since then that number has more than quadrupled, to about 42 million. Moreover, the disease has already killed 22 million people and left 13 million orphans in its wake.

The disease's impact on the HDI occurs through its devastating effect on life expectancy in the worst-affected countries (figure 2.7). But HIV/AIDS destroys more than lives. By killing and incapacitating adults in the prime of their lives, it can throw development off course.

HIV/AIDS is crippling parts of Africa—about 1 in 3 (or more) adults is infected in

FIGURE 2.5
Growth and income poverty: links not automatic

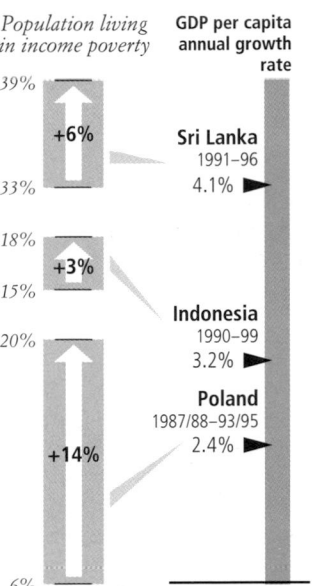

Source: Human Development Report Office calculations based on World Bank 2003i and World Bank 2000a.

TABLE 2.3
Changes in the share and number of people living on $1 a day have been uneven

Region	Percentage 1990	Percentage 1999	Number 1990	Number 1999
Sub-Saharan Africa	47.4	49.0	241	315
East Asia and the Pacific	30.5	15.6	486	279
Excluding China	24.2	10.6	110	57
South Asia	45.0	36.6	506	488
Latin America and the Caribbean	11.0	11.1	48	57
Central and Eastern Europe and the CIS[a]	6.8	20.3	31	97
Middle East and North Africa	2.1	2.2	5	6
Total[b]	29.6	23.2	1,292	1,169
Excluding China	28.5	25.0	917	945

a. Changes measured using the $2 a day poverty line, which is considered a more appropriate extreme poverty line for Central and Eastern Europe and the CIS.
b. Data are based on the $1 a day poverty line for all regions.
Source: World Bank 2002f.

BOX 2.3

Measuring income poverty: where to draw the line?

The animated debate on whether the Millennium Development Goal of halving poverty will be achieved is largely driven by the lack of agreement on the best way to measure poverty. (Among the main participants in this debate are Surjit Bhalla, Angus Deaton, Thomas Pogge, Sanjay Reddy, Martin Ravallion and Xavier Sala-i-Martin.) Thus conclusions on whether the poverty Goal will be met must be qualified in terms of definitions and, more important, methodologies.

Absolute poverty is the main indicator used to assess progress towards the Goal. This indicator measures the proportion of a population surviving on less than a specific amount of income per day. This specific amount is the poverty line—arguably the most contentious issue in the debate. Shifting the international poverty line by just a few cents can alter world poverty estimates immensely, "moving" millions of individuals in or out of poverty.

Poverty rates based on national poverty lines can capture the dynamics of poverty over time in a single country. National poverty lines are generally based on the amount needed for an individual in one country to live decently. Surviving in the Russian Federation requires different minimum survival goods than surviving in Haiti. Because the costs of the consumption bundles used to estimate poverty lines vary across countries, poverty lines vary as well. The concepts and criteria used to define poverty lines also differ across countries, making national poverty lines problematic when the analytical purpose is to make international poverty comparisons—as with the monitoring of regional and global progress towards the Millennium Development Goal for poverty.

An international poverty line—messy but necessary

To compare poverty rates across countries, poverty data based on an internationally defined poverty line would be more suitable, at least in theory. To that end the World Bank uses an extreme poverty line of about $1 a day (measured in purchasing power parity terms). Behind this approach is the assumption—based on national poverty lines from a sample of developing countries—that, after adjusting for cost of living differences, $1 a day is the average minimum consumption required for subsistence in the developing world. But this approach has been assailed as being conceptually and methodologically inaccurate in capturing minimum subsistence levels across developing countries.

Some analysts see poverty as a concept set by society—implying that people are considered poor relative to their fellow citizens (Oster, Lake and Oksman 1978). This view inevitably raises the poverty line as income rises, weakening the argument for a common poverty line across countries. Reddy and Pogge (2002) provide a similar argument against the $1 a day poverty line and propose one based on locally defined minimum capabilities. Ravallion (2000, pp. 3245–52), on the other hand, defends the $1 a day poverty line based on its simplicity. One of the main benefits of this line is as a rhetorical and advocacy tool: it is intuitively appealing because it suggests the degree of deprivation of poor people in developing countries. But because of enormous methodological and conceptual inconsistencies, poverty data calculated using international poverty lines are extremely problematic and can lead to misleading poverty rates.

Problems comparing prices across countries

One of the main problems with $1 a day poverty data derives from underlying adjustments of international price differences. Assuming that $1 a day is the correct average price of the subsistence consumption bundle in developing countries—a major assumption—the price of this bundle needs to be translated into national currencies. The World Bank does this using purchasing power parity (PPP) rates: price indices that compare the price of a bundle of goods in one country with the price in another.

But the process for obtaining these rates is not entirely transparent. Moreover, they produce inaccurate poverty lines because many of the prices they are based on are for goods that poor people do not consume (Reddy and Pogge 2002; Deaton 2003). Making matters worse, these conversions do not take into account the considerable price differences between countries' urban and rural areas. Moreover, poor people have to pay higher unit prices for many goods and services because they cannot afford to buy in bulk (Ward 2003).

Using national accounts instead of income surveys—better or biased?

The World Bank's $1 a day poverty line is based on income and budget surveys that provide information on the distribution and level of income (or consumption). Given a specific poverty line, these two indicators determine the income poverty rate. There is debate on whether the income levels from these surveys should be replaced with another consumption aggregate (Sala-i-Martin 2002; UNCTAD 2002a; Bhalla 2002). Advocates point out that, for various reasons, surveys grossly underestimate the incomes of very rich people in poor countries (Székely and Hilgert 1999). One way to avoid this problem is to retain the income distribution information from surveys but to calculate poverty rates based on (usually higher) national accounts data on average consumption.

But while the national accounts approach may be more consistent across countries, income levels based on surveys are not necessarily less accurate than those based on national accounts. National accounts data on consumption may be more complete than surveys because they include goods such as financial services, imputed rents and income from employer contributions to pension funds. But poor people do not consume these goods—so while surveys may underestimate average incomes, that does not mean that they overestimate poverty. Furthermore, as countries become richer, the items missed by surveys may overstate the growth of consumption of poor people.

The end result? Using national accounts instead of income surveys to derive poor people's income levels risks overestimating the rate of poverty decline. Furthermore, using national accounts may underestimate the number of poor people in all but the poorest countries—where, conversely, poverty levels may be overstated because national accounts miss significant informal activity. Using income levels from surveys avoids these problems by directly targeting income and consumption goods relevant to poor households (food, shelter, health, education).

Still, surveys are not free of severe problems in measurement and interpretation. Most important, surveys are not very common in the countries where they are needed most because of the high costs and considerable expertise required for their design and implementation. Moreover, using survey-based poverty rates to draw conclusions on poverty levels across countries—let alone changes in poverty across countries—may be misleading because definitions, methodologies, coverage and accuracy vary across countries and over time.

Because of these concerns, more efforts should be made internationally and nationally to perfect the price collection efforts behind purchasing power parities (the World Bank is currently engaged in such an effort and expects to release new rates in 2005), to harmonize design and collection methods for income and consumption surveys and to agree on local bundles of minimum capabilities on which to base poverty figures, for which feedback and guidance from countries and communities are crucial.

Source: Sala-i-Martin 2002; Ravallion 2000; Reddy and Pogge 2002; Deaton 2003; UNCTAD 2002a; Székely and Hilgert 1999; Bhalla 2002; Oster, Lake and Oksman 1978; Ward 2003.

Botswana, Lesotho, Swaziland and Zimbabwe, 1 in 5 in Namibia, South Africa and Zambia and more than 1 in 20 in 19 other countries. The disease kills both rich and poor people, including teachers, farmers, factory workers and civil servants. In 1998 Zambia lost 1,300 teachers to the disease—two-thirds of those trained each year.[12] By 2020 the hardest-hit African countries could lose more than a quarter of their workforces.[13]

The depth of this human tragedy is immeasurable. Uganda is the only Sub-Saharan country to have begun to reverse the epidemic once it reached crisis proportions. In Zambia HIV prevalence among young women fell 4 percentage points between 1996 and 1999, offering hope that it would become the second country in the region to begin to reverse the crisis. Senegal is another success story, having kept HIV/AIDS under control from the beginning through an immediate, concerted response.[14]

But elsewhere in Sub-Saharan Africa, signs are not good. In Cameroon and Nigeria infection rates were thought to be stable, yet are starting to increase. In a survey, half of the continent's teenage respondents did not realize that a healthy-looking person could have HIV/AIDS. And of people using contraception worldwide, just 7% use condoms—an effective barrier against HIV.[15]

Though Sub-Saharan Africa accounts for nearly 70% of HIV/AIDS cases, the epidemic is causing considerable damage in other regions. Almost 0.5 million people are infected in the Caribbean, 1.2 million in East Asia, 1.2 million in Eastern Europe and the CIS, 1.5 million in Latin America and 6.0 million in South Asia.[16]

China, India and the Russian Federation—all with large populations and at risk of seeing

HIV infection rates soar—are of particular concern. About 7 million people are infected in these countries, and in Sub-Saharan Africa 7 million cases exploded to 25 million in a decade.[17] The course of the epidemic depends on social characteristics and responses to the threat. But even in a moderate scenario, by 2025 almost 200 million people could be infected in these three countries alone (table 2.4).

STRUGGLES TO ACHIEVE THE GOALS

The drop in many countries' HDIs signals a problem; looking at key indicators of progress towards the Millennium Development Goals reveals its depth. Without significant changes, countries experiencing reversals or stagnation have little chance of achieving the Goals.

FOR EACH GOAL—TOP PRIORITY AND HIGH PRIORITY COUNTRIES

For each Goal there are countries where the situation is particularly urgent—where failed progress is combined with brutally low starting levels. These top priority countries are in greatest need of the world's attention, resources and commitments (box 2.4; technical note 2).[18]

In high priority countries the situation is less desperate but progress is still insufficient (see feature 2.1). These countries are either making progress from low levels of development or achieving slow (or negative) progress from higher levels.

- As noted, per capita incomes fell in 54 countries during the 1990s (see figure 2.5). Of these, 32 are top priority countries facing economic crises. Many are extremely poor, and most are in Sub-Saharan Africa. But there are also crisis countries in Central and Eastern Europe and the CIS, Latin America and the Caribbean and East Asia and the Pacific. Low per capita incomes are also a serious problem in 20 high priority countries.

- Hunger increased in 21 countries in the 1990s. In 19 top priority countries more than one-quarter of people are going hungry and things are failing to improve much—or are worsening. In 19 high priority countries the situation is better but hunger remains a serious challenge.

TABLE 2.4

Big countries face big threats from HIV/AIDS by 2025, even with a moderate epidemic

Country	Estimated HIV/AIDS cases by 2025	Estimated reduction in life expectancy (years)
China	70 million	8
India	110 million	13
Russia	13 million	16

Source: Eberstadt 2002.

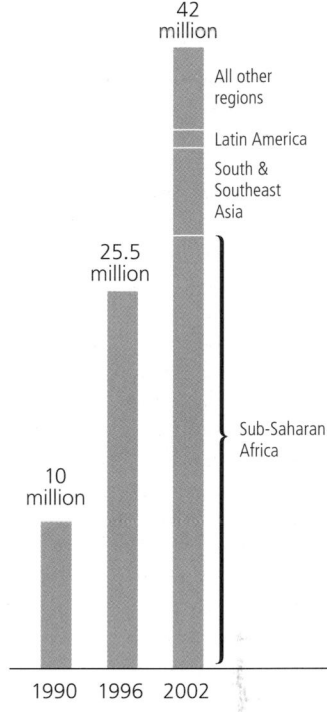

FIGURE 2.6

HIV/AIDS cases have skyrocketed

Number of HIV/AIDS cases

Source: UNAIDS 2002b.

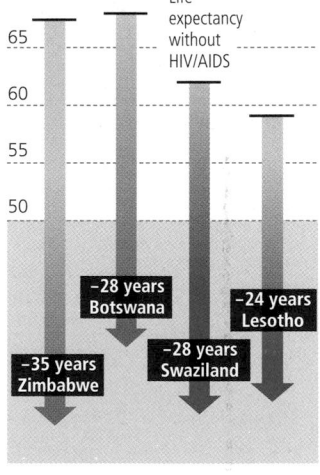

FIGURE 2.7

Loss of life expectancy due to HIV/AIDS

Decline in life expectancy by 2000–2005

Source: UNDP 2001c.

BOX 2.4

Struggling to meet the Goals—defining top priority and high priority countries

Priority countries for each Goal

This Report identifies top priority and high priority countries for each Millennium Development Goal (see feature 2.1). The aim is to identify countries where urgent action is needed to meet a Goal (top priority countries) and countries where the situation is less desperate but still demands significant improvements in progress (high priority countries; see technical note 2).

In top priority countries entrenched human poverty is combined with failing or even reversing progress (see matrix). These are the countries that are in crisis for each Goal, and these are the countries where the world's attention and resources must be focused.

In high priority countries the situation is less desperate—but great needs remain. These countries are either at medium starting levels but

facing failed or reversing progress, or they are suffering from extreme human poverty yet making moderate progress—but still moving far too slowly to meet the Goal.

Priority countries across the Goals

There are 31 top priority countries across the Goals, meaning that they are top priority countries for at least three Goals or for at least half of the Goals for which they have data, with a minimum of three data points. If data are available for only two Goals, they are top priority in both.

There are 28 high priority countries across the Goals. These countries do not fall into the top priority category but are top or high priority for at least three Goals, are top priority for two Goals, or are top or high priority for at least half of the Goals for which they have data, with a minimum

of three data points. If data are available for only two Goals, they are top or high priority in both.

Another 78 countries have sufficient data to be assessed and do not fall into the top priority or high priority categories. And for 32 other countries there are not sufficient data to make reliable assessments.

Grouping countries into top priority, high priority and other categories is useful, but such efforts should be viewed with caution. The classifications point out that the countries most at risk of failing to meet the Goals are in Sub-Saharan Africa and Central Asia. But the underlying data for individual Goals are often measured imprecisely, and some country classifications will change as data improve. Moreover, many countries are missing too much data for individual Goals to be given proper overall classifications. Thus some of the 32 countries in the "other" category would probably be top or high priority countries if the underlying data were more complete. (Examples include Kyrgyzstan and Pakistan.)

In addition, the classification criteria used here are plausible but only one among many reasonable choices. Some countries are on the border between categories, and would shift if slightly different classification criteria were used. Finally, many countries that are not top or high priority are often falling behind on one or more Goals and need considerable international attention and help.

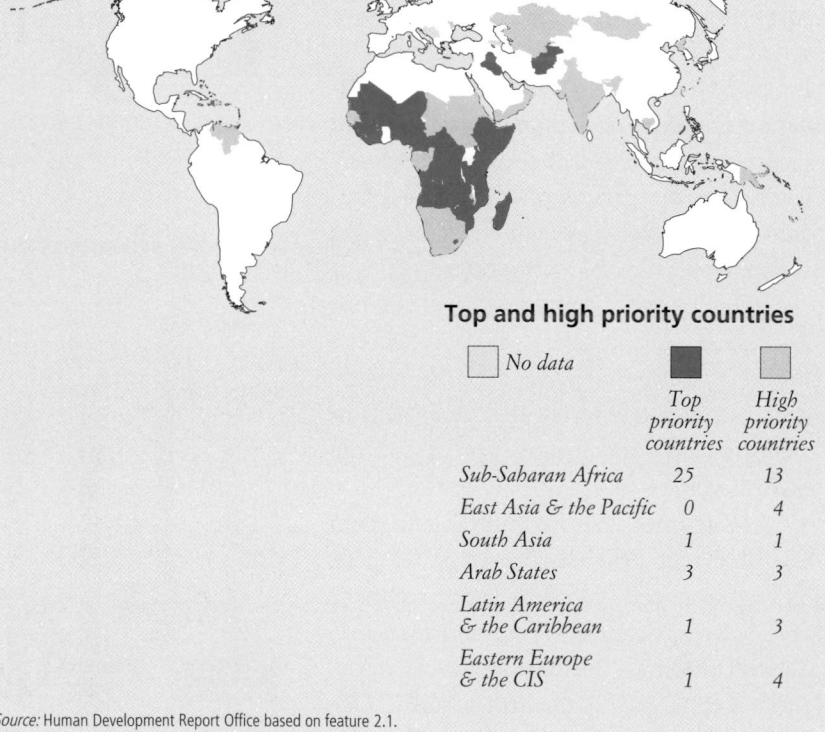

Top and high priority countries

	No data	Top priority countries	High priority countries
Sub-Saharan Africa		25	13
East Asia & the Pacific		0	4
South Asia		1	1
Arab States		3	3
Latin America & the Caribbean		1	3
Eastern Europe & the CIS		1	4

Level of human poverty (in Goal)

	Slow or reversing	Moderate	Fast
Low			
Medium	HIGH PRIORITY		
High	TOP PRIORITY	HIGH PRIORITY	

Progress towards the Goal

Source: Human Development Report Office based on feature 2.1.

• In 11 top priority countries at least one-quarter of children do not attend primary school, and little progress is being made towards the Goal of universal enrolment. Again, most are in Sub-Saharan Africa. But this is one development area where good data are sorely lacking. Low primary enrolments are also a concern in 13 high priority countries.

• Child mortality rates increased in the 1990s in a way not seen in previous decades, rising in 14 countries. Overall, bad situations are failing to improve in 32 top priority countries. In some of these countries almost one-third of children will not reach age five. All but 6 of these countries—Afghanistan, Cambodia, Iraq, Somalia, Sudan, Tajikistan—are in Sub-Saharan

Africa. Child mortality rates are also extremely worrisome in 24 high priority countries.

ACROSS THE GOALS—31 TOP PRIORITY COUNTRIES, 28 HIGH PRIORITY COUNTRIES

Data on top and high priority countries across the Goals are shown in box 2.4. There are 31 such countries: 25 from Sub-Saharan Africa, 3 from the Arab States and 1 each from South Asia, Latin America and the Caribbean and Central and Eastern Europe and the CIS. These countries are seeing development fail across the board— and require the world's attention and resources if the Goals are to be achieved.

Another 28 high priority countries face serious challenges across the Goals. Again, many are from Sub-Saharan Africa: 13. But 4 each are from Central and Eastern Europe and the CIS and East Asia and the Pacific, and 3 each are from the Arab States and Latin America and the Caribbean. One is from South Asia.

No single factor can explain the predicaments of the top and high priority countries. Still, the ones from Sub-Saharan Africa tend to share common features. Many are landlocked or have a large portion of their populations living far from a coast. In addition, most are small—only four contain more than 40 million people. Being far from world markets and having a small economy makes it much harder to diversify from primary commodities to less volatile exports with more value added. Indeed, primary commodities account for more than two-thirds of exports in 14 of the 17 top and high priority Sub-Saharan countries with data. Many of the region's priority countries also have other serious concerns: in 23 more than 5% of the population has HIV/AIDS, and in 9 violent conflicts occurred in the 1990s (box 2.5).[19]

In other regions top priority countries face very different challenges. Many countries in the CIS, for example—while also facing some of the structural issues affecting Sub-Saharan Africa—are trying to make the transition to market economies, a process that has been much more successful in Central and Eastern Europe. In the Arab States constraints are unrelated to income, and derive instead from a failure to convert income into human development and progress towards the Goals.

So what needs to be done to achieve the Millennium Development Goals? No matter how that question is answered, the top priority and high priority countries must be front and centre. The issues they face and ways to resolve them are considered in detail in the chapters that follow.

But poor countries failing to achieve progress are not the only concern. Later in this chapter another group of countries is examined: those where progress has been unevenly distributed, leaving vast numbers of people in terrible conditions.

GOOD PERFORMANCE BY SOME OF THE POOREST COUNTRIES

Many of the world's poorest countries are making good progress on most or all of the Goals. Indeed, for all the Goals the poorest countries have made some of the fastest progress. True, with low starting levels they have the most room for improvement. But that should not detract from achievements that countries have made in circumstances that have caused many of their development peers to stagnate or fall backwards. The success of Southern African countries is particularly fragile, because widespread HIV/AIDS and recent droughts seriously threaten continued progress.

BOX 2.5

Violent conflict and the Goals

Violent conflict is a key obstacle to achieving the Millennium Development Goals. During 1990–2001 there were 57 major armed conflicts in 45 locations. Sub-Saharan Africa has been hit the hardest, but no developing region has been unaffected.

Deaths from conflicts are hard to gauge, and estimates vary. But since 1990 conflicts have killed as many as 3.6 million people and injured many millions more. Particularly tragic is that civilians, not soldiers, are increasingly the victims—accounting for more than 90% of deaths and injuries. Shockingly, children account for at least half of civilian casualties.

Beyond these tragic direct effects, collapsing economies and infrastructure can take a further human toll. Among the top and high priority countries for achieving the Goals, 13 experienced serious conflict in the 1990s. Surprisingly, some countries—such as Indonesia and Sri Lanka—have experienced significant conflict yet continue to make good progress towards the Goals. Two reasons explain these seemingly unlikely successes.

First, good policies are vital: strong governments that continue to provide services for all people can make a huge difference in human outcomes. (Box 3.5 in chapter 3 examines government and donor policies that can mitigate the human costs of conflict.) Second, conflicts often do not involve entire countries, but are isolated to specific regions. Thus the impacts of war may not be reflected in national social indicators—but in areas where conflict rages, its effects can still be devastating. Box 2.8 examines countries where isolated areas are suffering from conflict.

Source: Stewart 2003; Marshall 2000; UNHCR 2000; UNICEF 1996; SIPRI 2002b.

Still, during the 1990s:

• Cape Verde, Mauritius, Mozambique and Uganda averaged per capita income growth of more than 3% a year.

• Countries in Sub-Saharan Africa achieved some of the world's sharpest reductions in hunger. Ghana reduced its hunger rate from 35% to 12%, and Mozambique from 69% to 55%.

• Benin increased its primary enrolment rate from 49% to 70%. Mali and Senegal increased primary enrolment rates by 15 percentage points or more. Primary completion rates also rose in some of the poorest countries—in Mali by more than 20 percentage points.

• Many of the poorest countries made good progress towards gender equality in primary and secondary education. Mauritania led the pack, increasing the ratio of girls to boys from 67% to 93% between 1990 and 1996. Mali and Nepal narrowed their gaps by 10 percentage points or more in the 1990s.

• Despite HIV/AIDS, there were some remarkable improvements in child survival in Sub-Saharan Africa. Guinea reduced its child mortality rate by 7 percentage points, and

Malawi and Niger by 5 percentage points or more. There were also dramatic reductions in some of the poorest countries in Asia. Bhutan and Lao People's Democratic Republic reduced under-five deaths from around 16% to 10%, and Bangladesh from 14% to 8%.

• Though HIV/AIDS has generally taken a crushing toll on Sub-Saharan Africa, there have been some notable exceptions. Uganda reduced infection rates for eight consecutive years in the 1990s, and Zambia may become the second country in the region to reverse the spread of HIV/AIDS from crisis levels. Senegal has also prevented the spread of the disease.[20]

• Côte d'Ivoire and Mali increased the proportion of people with access to safe water by 10 percentage points or more. In addition, Ghana and Senegal increased the proportion of people with access to improved sanitation by 10 percentage points or more.

These successes, along with rapid improvements in more developed countries, show that all countries can achieve the Millennium Development Goals (box 2.6). (Chapters 4 and 5 analyse what underpinned some of these successes.)

WIDENING GAPS WITHIN COUNTRIES: WHO IS BEING LEFT BEHIND?

While national performance indicators help convey what is happening to a country's inhabitants, progress often differs widely across regions of the same country. Many countries with good average performance on the Goals contain population groups—and sometimes entire areas—being left behind. What are the gaps in human development within countries, and how have they evolved over the past decade (see feature 2.3)?

National statistics are midpoints of internal differences or summaries of domestic idiosyncrasies that average out economic, social, cultural, gender and ethnic cleavages within borders. Thus indicators used to assess national progress towards the Goals may not adequately reflect the living conditions of many inhabitants (box 2.7).

Wide—and widening—gaps are cause for concern because of their likely negative effects

---

BOX 2.6

Great leaps forward are possible in years—not decades

The Millennium Development Goals aim to dramatically improve people's lives in the course of a generation. Such targets are ambitious but achievable: many countries have made great leaps forward in all aspects of human development in short periods.

In just seven years (1946–53) Sri Lanka increased average life expectancy by an incredible 12 years. Between 1970 and 1985 Botswana doubled the proportion of children in primary school, nearly achieving universal primary education. In the 1990s China almost halved the proportion of people living in poverty. And between 1994 and 2001 South Africa halved the number of people without access to safe water.

These successes resulted from appropriate policies in specific circumstances, and replicating them is not straightforward. But they show what can be done. Later chapters of this Report examine what works and what does not—identifying key policies for achieving the Goals.

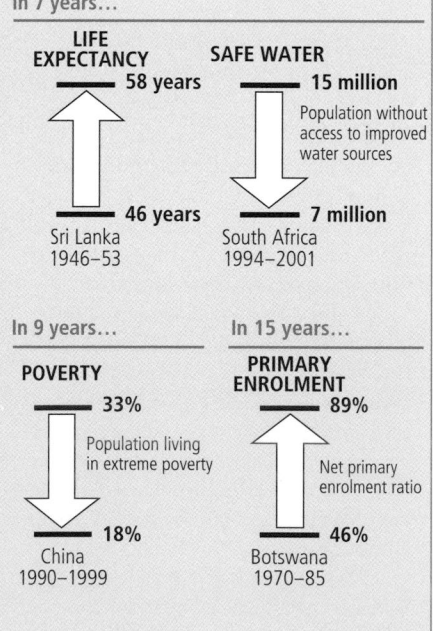

In 7 years…

LIFE EXPECTANCY
58 years
46 years
Sri Lanka
1946–53

SAFE WATER
15 million
Population without access to improved water sources
7 million
South Africa
1994–2001

In 9 years…

POVERTY
33%
Population living in extreme poverty
18%
China
1990–1999

In 15 years…

PRIMARY ENROLMENT
89%
Net primary enrolment ratio
46%
Botswana
1970–85

Source: Millennium Project Task Force 7 2003; WSP 2002b; Human Development Report Office calculations based on World Bank 2002f and 2003i; Caldwell 1986, pp. 171–220; World Bank 2003i.

---

on the pace of development. They also indicate uneven opportunities, with powerful people securing more of the benefits of development. As gaps worsen and reach high levels, they may destabilize human development as a result of social unrest, political disputes, biased resource allocations and violence and conflict (box 2.8).

For these reasons subnational trends deserve attention even among countries that appear to be performing well on the Goals. These countries may be advancing through a top-down approach, with policy efforts and resources initially focused on groups that are easier to reach, such as non-poor people or urban residents. This approach can raise national averages enough to declare the achievement of a Goal or some other target.

This is a particular concern for health because the health-related Goals and targets (such as reducing child mortality by two-thirds and maternal mortality by three-quarters) seek to lower average rates and so apply to the entire population—while those for nutrition, education and poverty focus on hungry, uneducated and poor people. Thus the health targets can be achieved by targeting any group, including better-off people. Some governments may be tempted to meet the health Goals by concen-trating efforts among the better off, only later targeting people who are harder to reach.[21] Some analysts argue that such a top-down approach has its merits because it will allow Goals to be met at the country level and will eventually benefit everyone. But that may not be true.

For progress to be sustained and inclusive, it should take a bottom-up approach, emphasizing equity and focusing first on people most in need of support. In pursuing the health Goals, the worst-off and hardest to reach people should not receive attention only at the last minute. For policy-makers, putting poor people at the end of the queue for social services is easier and less costly in the short and medium run.[22] But the false progress that results may prove unsustainable in the long run.

GAPS BETWEEN SOCIO-ECONOMIC GROUPS

Evidence from many countries suggests that some groups are receiving fewer benefits from national improvements in income, health and education. Income disparities appear to be increasing in several countries, indicating wider gaps between people at the top of the income distribution (generally middle and upper classes in urban areas) and people at the bottom (mostly

---

BOX 2.7

Disaggregated data within countries: national human development reports

Since 1992 some 135 countries have used country-owned processes to produce more than 450 national and regional human development reports. Many of these reports present data disaggregated along gender, ethnic, age, race, geographic or other lines, enabling deeper analysis of country-specific causes of inequality and poverty—and sometimes revealing systemic discrimination and serious deprivations. The reports have become crucial sources of the most recent disaggregated country data, contributing to policy strategies for advancing and tools for measuring progress on human development. The following examples show what the reports can help achieve:
• Since 1997 Brazil has calculated the human development index (HDI) annually for each of its more than 5,000 municipalities. In response the state of Minas Gerais introduced the Robin Hood Law, which allocates a proportion of tax revenues to municipalities that rank low on the HDI and other indicators.
• Nepal's 2001 human development report used extensive disaggregated data that revealed significant inequities in the distribution of resources and opportunities, leading the report to conclude that weak governance is at the root of disappointing outcomes in poverty reduction. The report found that life expectancy averaged 51 years in the most disadvantaged castes—and 63 years for the Newar ethnic group.
• Egypt's annual human development reports disaggregate socio-economic, environmental, demographic and other indicators for each of the nation's 26 governorates. These data and the reports' findings form the basis for yearly meetings of the country's governors to jointly examine disparities and identify policy responses.
• Lithuania's 2000 report analysed urban-rural disparities in human development. Disaggregated data for key indicators such as mortality, suicide, employment and education showed that rural Lithuanians are losing their ability to sustain themselves with traditional occupations—and no alternative, productive, sustainable livelihoods have emerged. The report warned that this trend could undermine social cohesion.
• Namibia's human development reports have examined human poverty by disaggregating the HDI across language groups. This disaggregation reveals high human development levels among predominantly European groups—people who speak Afrikaans, English or German—and very low levels among the San (bushmen). These findings have led to targeted investments in health, education and job creation.

Disaggregated data from the reports are available online at http://sedac.ciesin.columbia.edu/hdr/. (To view national human development reports online, see http://hdr.undp.org.)

Source: Human Development Report Office, National Human Development Report Unit.

BOX 2.8

Violent conflicts are often contained within certain areas of countries, driven by ethnic, linguistic and similar social fault lines. This tendency may explain the good overall performance on the Millennium Development Goals in countries—such as Indonesia and Sri Lanka—that experienced years of conflict in the 1990s. Human development is likely to be lower in areas that suffer from conflict than in areas not directly affected by it. (Sometimes neighbouring regions are also affected by nearby conflicts, experiencing refugee flows and humanitarian emergencies.)

The links between conflicts and poor development can go both ways. Economic and social hardships, especially when accompanied by sharp inequalities across groups and areas, can foment violence. At the same time, conflicts are often major causes of weak economic development, leading to (among other things) health crises and destruction of infrastructure. This relationship can be captured by comparing the spatial distribution of conflicts with subnational indicators of development. But due to data limitations, few countries allow for such analysis. This Report was able to obtain such data for four countries:

- *Indonesia.* Sharp regional disparities in the human poverty index (HPI) appear across and within the islands of Indonesia. Violent, separatist conflicts have occurred in areas with high poverty, with sharp divisions along religious, ethnic and social lines.

- *Colombia.* Violence runs high and medium throughout the parallel mountain chains that run from the north to south of Colombia, as well as in the areas linking these mountains to the Pacific coast. The mountains are largely rural, with little infrastructure, and often inhospitable. The human development index (HDI) is lowest in some of the areas where conflict has been most violent (see map).

- *Nepal.* The Maoist uprising that began in Nepal in 1996 is based in the country's most isolated, neglected, resource-poor areas—those lacking even the most basic social infrastructure. Among these are remote villages containing ethnic minorities, including low HDI areas in the northwest and some areas in the north.

- *Sri Lanka.* After nearly 20 years of civil conflict between the minority Tamil population and the majority Sinhalese, more than 65,000 Sri Lankans have been killed and nearly 1 million have been displaced. The map shows how the northern and north-eastern Tamil regions have been excluded from the country's infrastructure development.

Source: UNDP 2003a.

Conflicts within countries

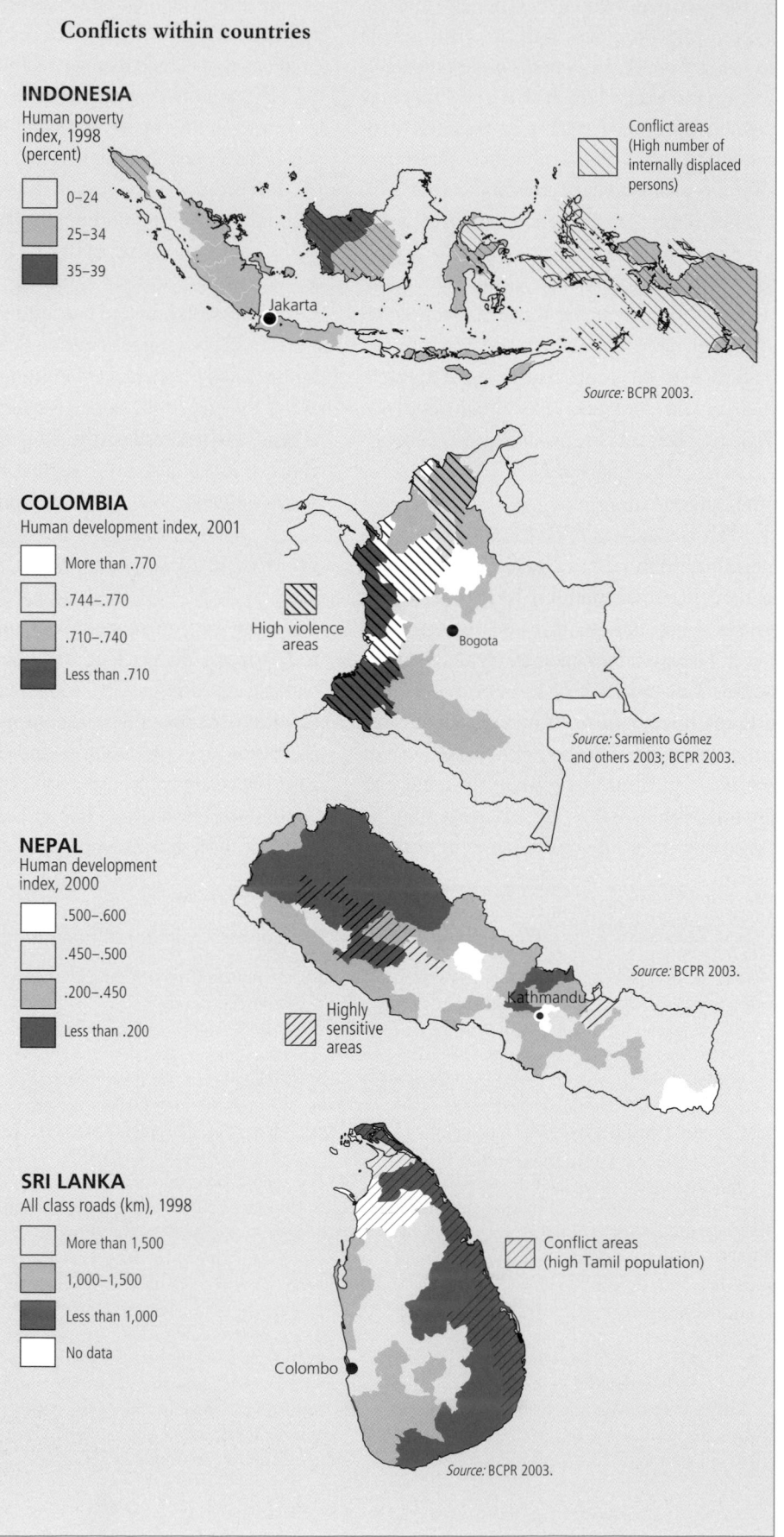

INDONESIA
Human poverty index, 1998 (percent)
- 0–24
- 25–34
- 35–39

Conflict areas (High number of internally displaced persons)

Jakarta

Source: BCPR 2003.

COLOMBIA
Human development index, 2001
- More than .770
- .744–.770
- .710–.740
- Less than .710

High violence areas

Bogota

Source: Sarmiento Gómez and others 2003; BCPR 2003.

NEPAL
Human development index, 2000
- .500–.600
- .450–.500
- .200–.450
- Less than .200

Highly sensitive areas

Kathmandu

Source: BCPR 2003.

SRI LANKA
All class roads (km), 1998
- More than 1,500
- 1,000–1,500
- Less than 1,000
- No data

Conflict areas (high Tamil population)

Colombo

Source: BCPR 2003.

TABLE 2.5

Child mortality rates: changes in levels and in wealth gaps, selected countries, 1980s and 1990s

		Relative gap (between rich and poor)		
		Narrowing	Constant	Widening
Average level	**Improving**	Guatemala	Egypt Mali Morocco Peru Senegal	Bangladesh Bolivia Brazil Colombia Dominican Rep. Ghana Indonesia Uganda
	Constant	Togo Zambia	Burkina Faso Cameroon Niger	Philippines Tanzania
	Worsening		Kenya	Kazakhstan Zimbabwe

Source: Minujin and Delamonica 2003.

rural, female-headed households of indigenous or ethnically marginal descent). Unless persistent income inequality is dealt with, it may limit the benefits of economic growth for poverty reduction (see box 2.2).

Wealth, probably even more than income, appears to be crucial in securing basic social services. (The studies cited in this section estimated wealth using surveys of household assets and characteristics.)[23] Between the mid-1980s and mid-1990s the gap in child mortality rates between the wealthiest and poorest quintiles narrowed in only 3 of 24 developing countries with data.[24] And in 13 countries considered good performers in reducing average child mortality rates, there is evidence of constant or increasing gaps between the richest and poorest groups (table 2.5).

Among the same sample of 24 countries, despite a substantial narrowing of wealth-related gaps in immunization coverage, by the late 1990s less than half the children from the poorest families had been immunized with DPT3 (three doses of diphtheria, pertussis and tetanus immunizations). In Burkina Faso, Cameroon, Mali and Niger less than 30% of poor children were covered. In many countries immunization coverage for the poorest fifth of the population showed no change or fell slightly in the 1990s.[25]

Disparities in education provide further evidence of inequality between wealthy and poor households. In many countries children from poor households are much less likely to attend school and are more likely to drop out if they

do. Enrolment rates are especially low for poor households, and dropout rates especially high, in Sub-Saharan Africa.[26]

South Asia shows a similar pattern, though dropout rates are concentrated after grade 5. In Latin America poor households are more likely to send children to school, resulting in higher enrolment rates, but dropout rates are just as high as in the other regions.[27] Even countries with low income inequality, such as Viet Nam, show wide variations in education across wealth quintiles. The data on wealth gaps in health and education support an undeniable conclusion: for the Goals to be met by as many countries and people as possible, policies should focus on closing the wealth divides within countries.

RURAL-URBAN GAPS

Widening gaps between urban and rural areas also indicate skewed development. In some African countries, despite satisfactory overall progress towards the Millennium Development Goals, urban-rural divides persist—or are widening—for most indicators.[28] In 8 of 11 countries with data, overall poverty rates have fallen—but rural poverty has fallen more slowly, particularly in Niger, Senegal and Tanzania.

As with wealth gaps, rural-urban divides are reflected in uneven progress on education and health. In 26 African, Latin American and Asian countries, rural areas are struggling on many of the Goals.[29] Usually this is relative to urban areas, but sometimes it is absolute (with

Gender equality is at the core of whether the Goals will be achieved—from improving health and fighting disease, to reducing poverty and mitigating hunger, to expanding education and lowering child mortality, to increasing access to safe water, to ensuring environmental sustainability

conditions in rural areas deteriorating and those in urban areas improving). Between the late 1980s and the mid- to late 1990s the gap in child mortality rates for rural and urban households widened in 14 of the 26 countries.

Similarly, children in urban areas are much more likely to receive a decent education. Parents in poor rural areas are often reluctant to send their children to school—and when they do, there are often not enough teachers, textbooks and classrooms. In the developing world a man living in a rural area is twice as likely to be illiterate as one in an urban area.[30] South Asia is home to the largest rural-urban education disparities.

GENDER GAPS

The Millennium Declaration calls for empowering women politically, socially and economically. To that end, the third Millennium Development Goal aims to reduce the gap between males and females in primary, secondary and eventually higher education. But gender gaps in education are only a small part of gender inequality. As this Report argues, gender equality is at the core of whether the Goals will be achieved—from improving health and fighting disease, to reducing poverty and mitigating hunger, to expanding education and lowering child mortality, to increasing access to safe water, to ensuring environmental sustainability.

One clear indicator of the gender crisis is the gap in mortality rates between men and women. Despite women's biological advantage, they have higher mortality rates in a number of countries, mainly in South and East Asia. The "missing women" phenomenon refers to females estimated to have died due to discrimination in access to health and nutrition. Census data indicate that missing women have increased in number but fallen as a share of women alive today. Improvements have occurred in Bangladesh, Pakistan and most Arab States, yet there have been only small improvements in India—and deterioration in

China.[31] Conversely, in some countries in the western CIS men are dying up to 15 years earlier than women.[32]

In most cases gender discrimination is accompanied by biases against other personal characteristics, including location (rural areas), ethnic background (indigenous minorities) and socio-economic status (poor households). Gender gaps in health and particularly education are important causes of gender discrimination. In many developing countries gender gaps in primary and secondary education are much higher among the poorest fifth of the population. Moreover, in most of these countries the situation did not change significantly in the 1990s—supporting evidence of discrimination against girls at the household level, particularly in poor households.[33]

Globally, women account for just under half of the adults living with HIV/AIDS. But in Sub-Saharan Africa, where the virus is spread mostly through heterosexual activity, more than 55% of infected adults are women.[34] Young women there are two to four times more likely than young men to become infected. In South and South-East Asia 60% of young people with HIV/AIDS are female.[35]

*   *   *

That all countries can meaningfully achieve the Millennium Development Goals is beyond doubt. Countries at all levels of development and from all regions have made dramatic progress. Countries have also progressed without incurring higher inequality. Chapters 3 through 7 consider what lessons lie behind these successes and how they can be applied to countries now failing. While many of the steps for success are known, ensuring that they are taken will require fundamental changes in development thinking. Traditional approaches of trying to do what is possible in the face of weak policies and severe resource constraints will not be enough. Chapter 8 considers cross-cutting actions needed to create the environment required to meet the Goals, with a focus on actions needed by rich countries.

That all countries can meaningfully achieve the Millennium Development Goals is beyond doubt

Feature 2.1 Progress towards the Millennium Development Goals

Millennium Development Goals regional summary

Poverty

Percentage of the population living below $1 a day

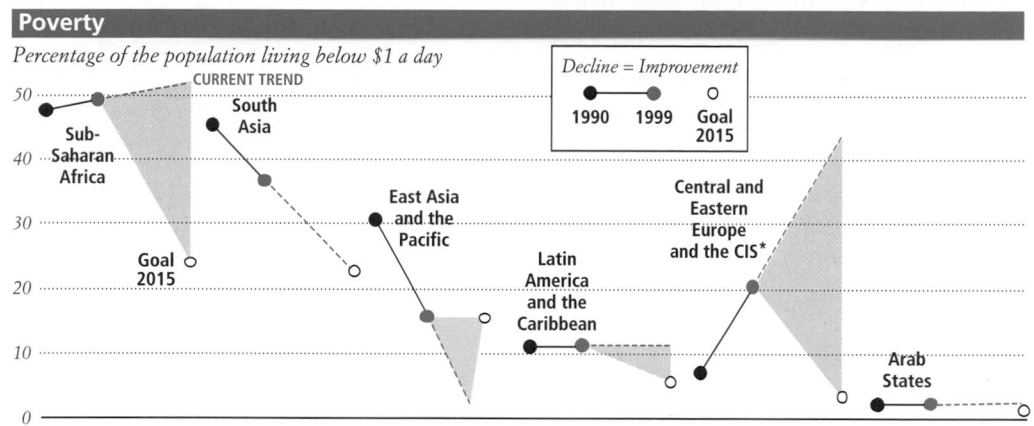

Hunger

Percentage of the population that is malnourished

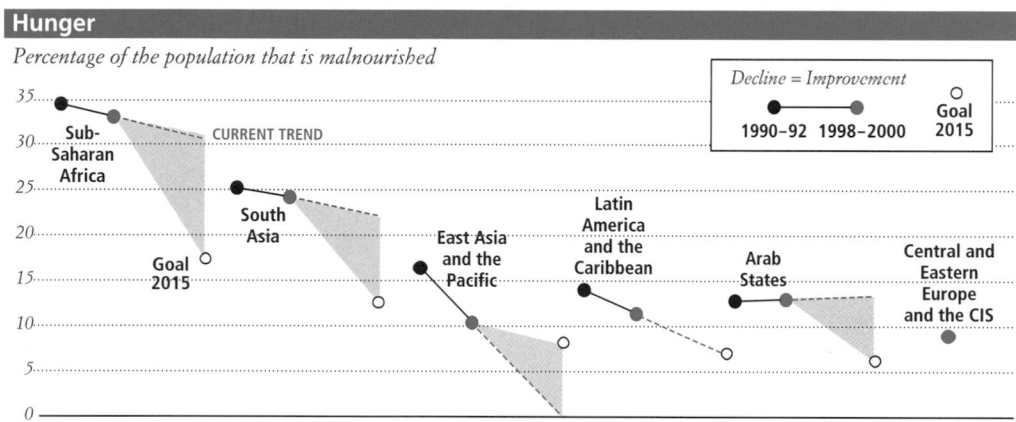

Primary education

Net primary enrolment ratio (percent)

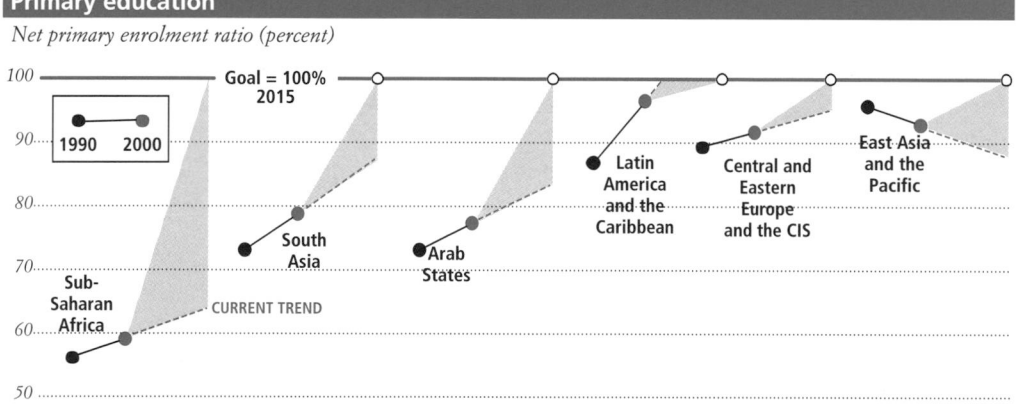

* refers to population living below $2 a day.

Gender equality

Ratio of girls to boys in primary and secondary education (percent)

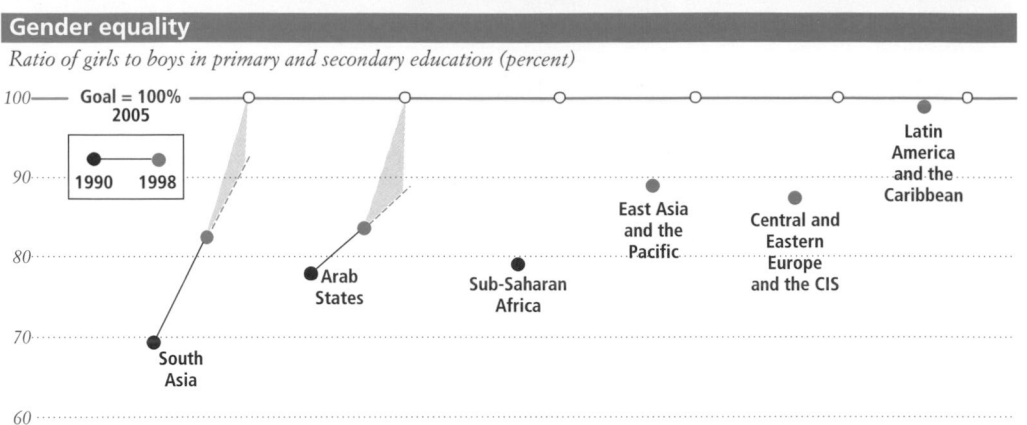

Child mortality

Under-five mortality rate per 1,000 live births

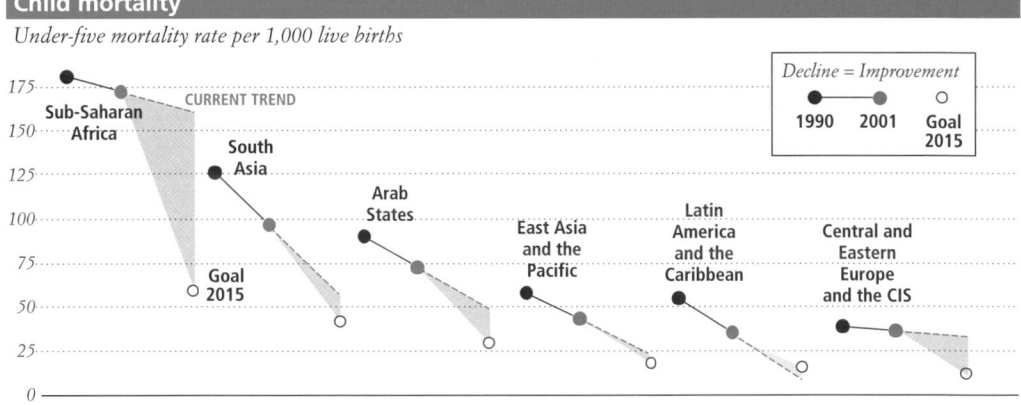

Access to water

Percentage of the population with access to safe drinking water

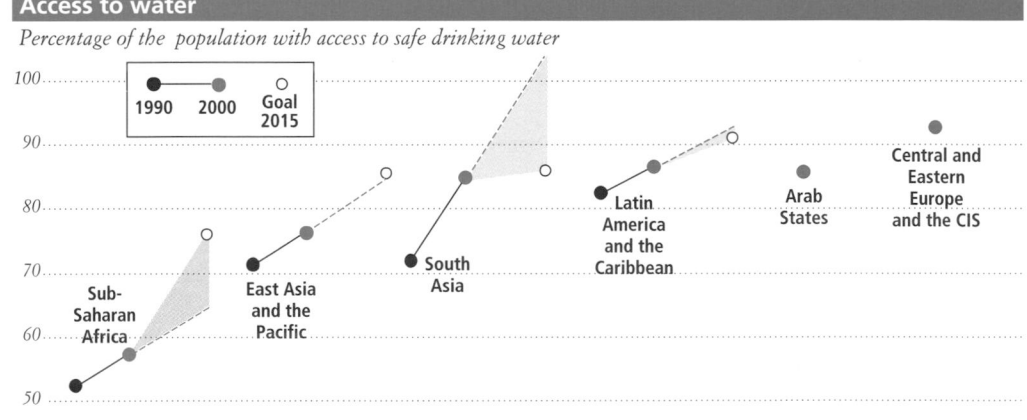

Access to sanitation

Percentage of the population with access to adequate sanitation

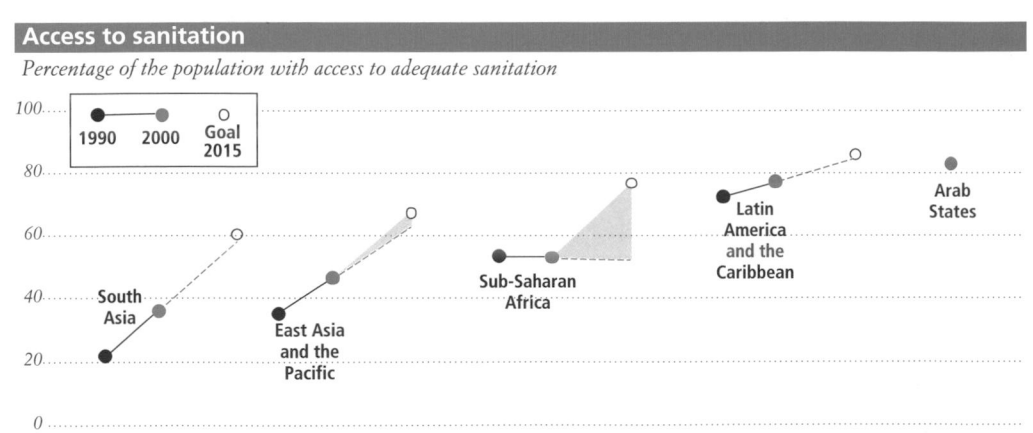

Income poverty

GDP per capita (PPP US$ thousands)

Countries with 1990 income of $10,000 or less

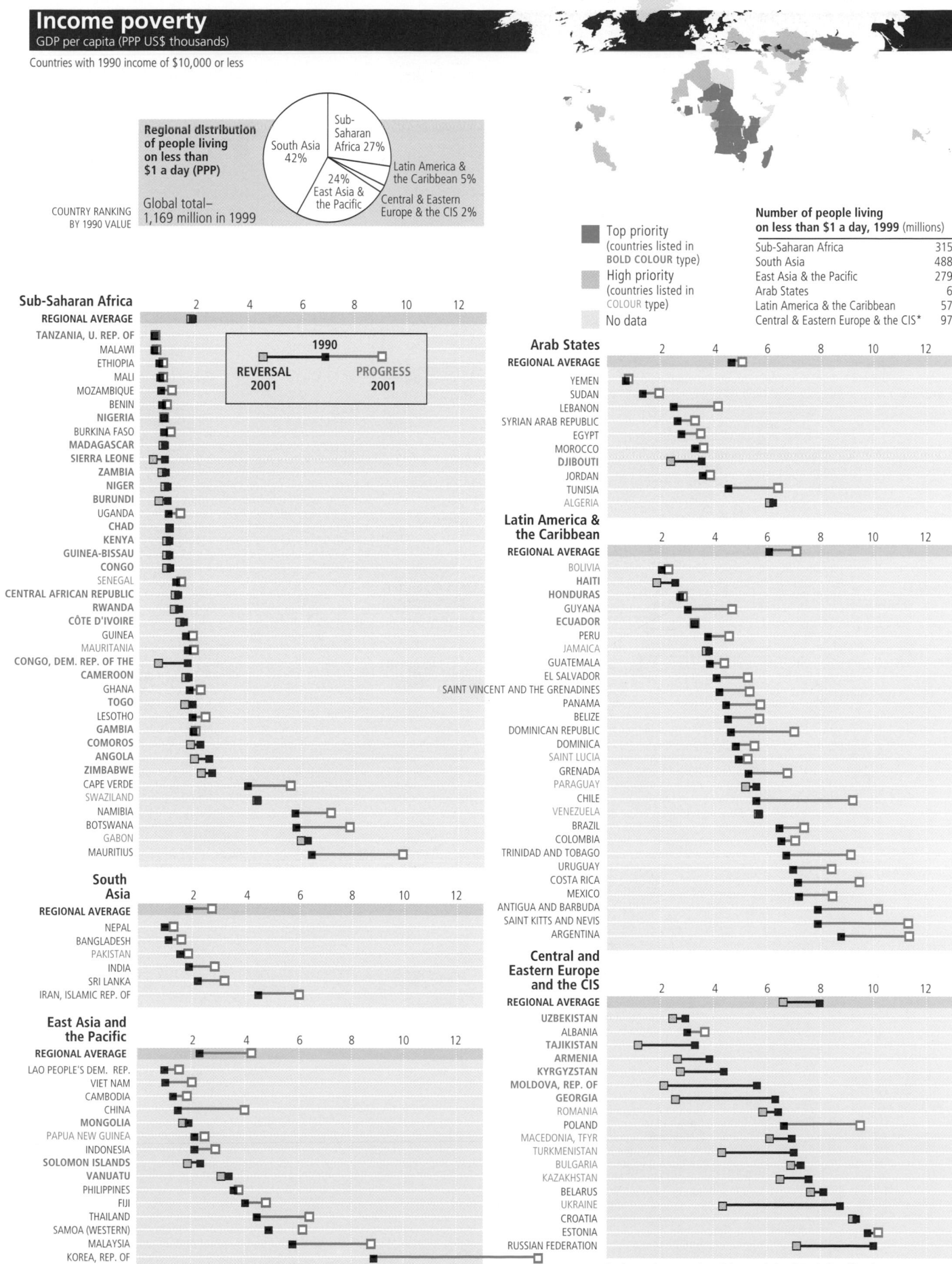

Regional distribution of people living on less than $1 a day (PPP)

South Asia 42%
Sub-Saharan Africa 27%
Latin America & the Caribbean 5%
24% East Asia & the Pacific
Central & Eastern Europe & the CIS 2%

Global total– 1,169 million in 1999

COUNTRY RANKING BY 1990 VALUE

Top priority (countries listed in BOLD COLOUR type)

High priority (countries listed in COLOUR type)

No data

Number of people living on less than $1 a day, 1999 (millions)

Sub-Saharan Africa	315
South Asia	488
East Asia & the Pacific	279
Arab States	6
Latin America & the Caribbean	57
Central & Eastern Europe & the CIS*	97

Sub-Saharan Africa
REGIONAL AVERAGE
TANZANIA, U. REP. OF
MALAWI
ETHIOPIA
MALI
MOZAMBIQUE
BENIN
NIGERIA
BURKINA FASO
MADAGASCAR
SIERRA LEONE
ZAMBIA
NIGER
BURUNDI
UGANDA
CHAD
KENYA
GUINEA-BISSAU
CONGO
SENEGAL
CENTRAL AFRICAN REPUBLIC
RWANDA
CÔTE D'IVOIRE
GUINEA
MAURITANIA
CONGO, DEM. REP. OF THE
CAMEROON
GHANA
TOGO
LESOTHO
GAMBIA
COMOROS
ANGOLA
ZIMBABWE
CAPE VERDE
SWAZILAND
NAMIBIA
BOTSWANA
GABON
MAURITIUS

1990
REVERSAL 2001
PROGRESS 2001

South Asia
REGIONAL AVERAGE
NEPAL
BANGLADESH
PAKISTAN
INDIA
SRI LANKA
IRAN, ISLAMIC REP. OF

East Asia and the Pacific
REGIONAL AVERAGE
LAO PEOPLE'S DEM. REP.
VIET NAM
CAMBODIA
CHINA
MONGOLIA
PAPUA NEW GUINEA
INDONESIA
SOLOMON ISLANDS
VANUATU
PHILIPPINES
FIJI
THAILAND
SAMOA (WESTERN)
MALAYSIA
KOREA, REP. OF

Arab States
REGIONAL AVERAGE
YEMEN
SUDAN
LEBANON
SYRIAN ARAB REPUBLIC
EGYPT
MOROCCO
DJIBOUTI
JORDAN
TUNISIA
ALGERIA

Latin America & the Caribbean
REGIONAL AVERAGE
BOLIVIA
HAITI
HONDURAS
GUYANA
ECUADOR
PERU
JAMAICA
GUATEMALA
EL SALVADOR
SAINT VINCENT AND THE GRENADINES
PANAMA
BELIZE
DOMINICAN REPUBLIC
DOMINICA
SAINT LUCIA
GRENADA
PARAGUAY
CHILE
VENEZUELA
BRAZIL
COLOMBIA
TRINIDAD AND TOBAGO
URUGUAY
COSTA RICA
MEXICO
ANTIGUA AND BARBUDA
SAINT KITTS AND NEVIS
ARGENTINA

Central and Eastern Europe and the CIS
REGIONAL AVERAGE
UZBEKISTAN
ALBANIA
TAJIKISTAN
ARMENIA
KYRGYZSTAN
MOLDOVA, REP. OF
GEORGIA
ROMANIA
POLAND
MACEDONIA, TFYR
TURKMENISTAN
BULGARIA
KAZAKHSTAN
BELARUS
UKRAINE
CROATIA
ESTONIA
RUSSIAN FEDERATION

* refers to the proportion of the population living below $2 a day.

PRIORITY CHALLENGES IN MEETING THE GOALS

53

Hunger
Undernourished people as a percentage of the total population

Regional distribution of undernourished people, 1998–2000

Total– 827.5 million people

Pie chart:
- South Asia 40%
- Sub-Saharan Africa 22%
- Arab States 4%
- Latin America & the Caribbean 7%
- Central & Eastern Europe & the CIS 4%
- East Asia & the Pacific 24%

COUNTRY RANKING BY 1990 VALUE

1990-92

REVERSAL 1998-2000 — PROGRESS 1998-2000 — GOAL 2015

■ Top priority (countries listed in **BOLD COLOUR** type)
■ High priority (countries listed in COLOUR type)
□ No data

Number of malnourished people 1998-2000 (millions)

Sub-Saharan Africa	183.3
South Asia	333.6
East Asia & the Pacific	193.3
Arab States	32.2
Latin America & the Caribbean	54.9
Central & Eastern Europe & the CIS	30.2

Sub-Saharan Africa
REGIONAL AVERAGE
MOZAMBIQUE
ANGOLA
CHAD
BURUNDI
CENTRAL AFRICAN REPUBLIC
MALAWI
KENYA
SIERRA LEONE
ZAMBIA
ZIMBABWE
NIGER
GUINEA
CONGO
TANZANIA, U. REP. OF
MADAGASCAR
GHANA
RWANDA
LIBERIA
CONGO, DEM. REP. OF THE
CAMEROON
TOGO
LESOTHO
MALI
SENEGAL
BURKINA FASO
UGANDA
GAMBIA
BENIN
CÔTE D'IVOIRE
BOTSWANA
NAMIBIA
MAURITANIA
NIGERIA
GABON
SWAZILAND
MAURITIUS

South Asia
REGIONAL AVERAGE
AFGHANISTAN
BANGLADESH
SRI LANKA
INDIA
PAKISTAN
NEPAL
IRAN, ISLAMIC REP. OF

East Asia and the Pacific
REGIONAL AVERAGE
CAMBODIA
MONGOLIA
LAO PEOPLE'S DEM. REP.
THAILAND
VIET NAM
PHILIPPINES
PAPUA NEW GUINEA
KOREA, DEM. REP.
CHINA
MYANMAR

Arab States
REGIONAL AVERAGE
SOMALIA
YEMEN
SUDAN
KUWAIT
IRAQ
MOROCCO
ALGERIA
EGYPT
SYRIAN ARAB REPUBLIC
JORDAN
SAUDI ARABIA

Latin America & the Caribbean
REGIONAL AVERAGE
HAITI
PERU
NICARAGUA
DOMINICAN REPUBLIC
BOLIVIA
HONDURAS
PANAMA
GUYANA
PARAGUAY
COLOMBIA
GUATEMALA
JAMAICA
TRINIDAD AND TOBAGO
BRAZIL
EL SALVADOR
SURINAME
VENEZUELA
ECUADOR
CHILE
COSTA RICA
URUGUAY
CUBA
MEXICO

Primary education
Net primary enrolment ratio (percent)

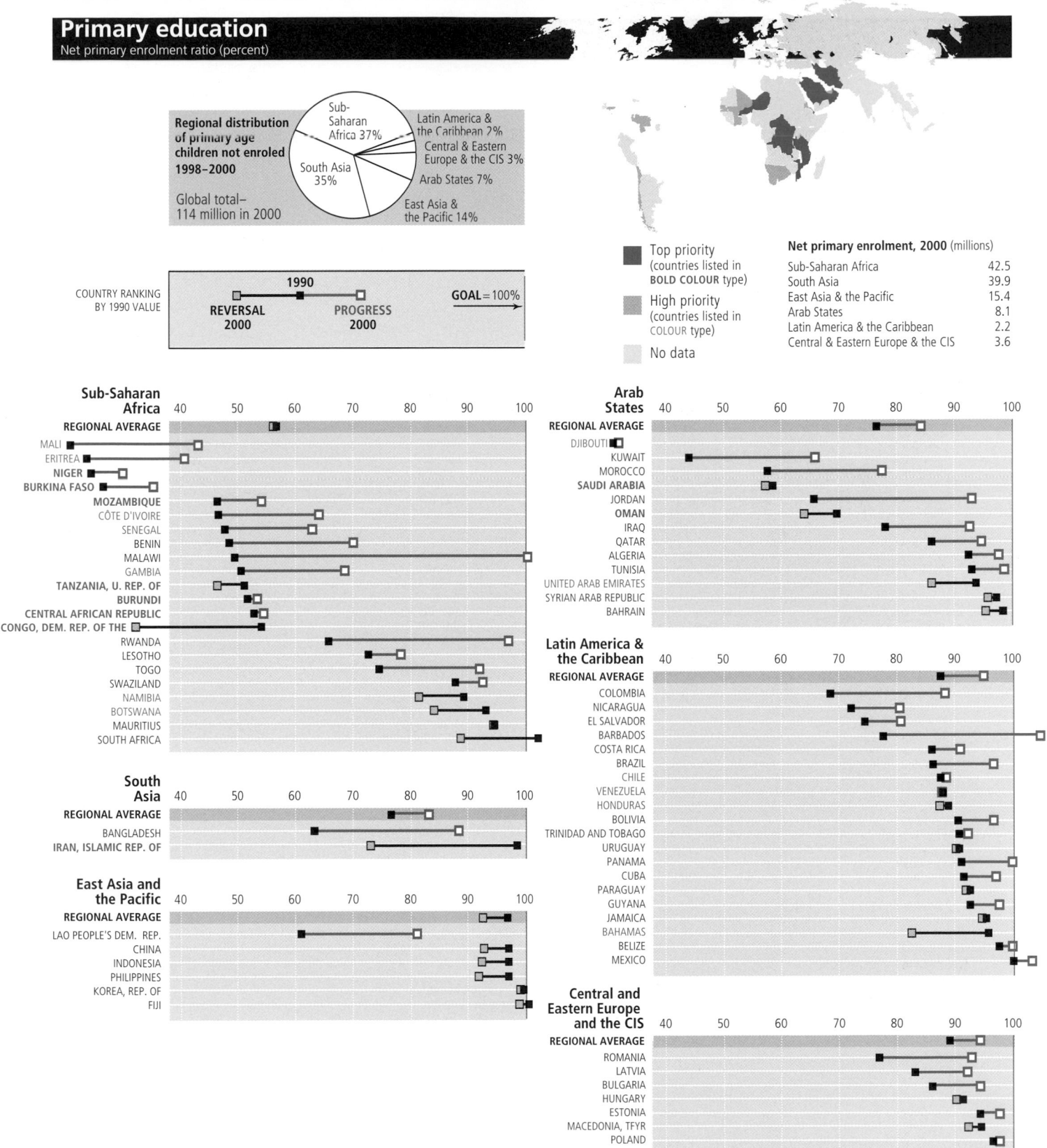

Regional distribution of primary age children not enroled 1998–2000

Global total– 114 million in 2000

- Sub-Saharan Africa 37%
- Latin America & the Caribbean 2%
- Central & Eastern Europe & the CIS 3%
- Arab States 7%
- East Asia & the Pacific 14%
- South Asia 35%

COUNTRY RANKING BY 1990 VALUE

1990

REVERSAL 2000 — PROGRESS 2000

GOAL = 100%

- Top priority (countries listed in **BOLD COLOUR** type)
- High priority (countries listed in COLOUR type)
- No data

Net primary enrolment, 2000 (millions)

Sub-Saharan Africa	42.5
South Asia	39.9
East Asia & the Pacific	15.4
Arab States	8.1
Latin America & the Caribbean	2.2
Central & Eastern Europe & the CIS	3.6

Sub-Saharan Africa
REGIONAL AVERAGE
MALI
ERITREA
NIGER
BURKINA FASO
MOZAMBIQUE
CÔTE D'IVOIRE
SENEGAL
BENIN
MALAWI
GAMBIA
TANZANIA, U. REP. OF
BURUNDI
CENTRAL AFRICAN REPUBLIC
CONGO, DEM. REP. OF THE
RWANDA
LESOTHO
TOGO
SWAZILAND
NAMIBIA
BOTSWANA
MAURITIUS
SOUTH AFRICA

South Asia
REGIONAL AVERAGE
BANGLADESH
IRAN, ISLAMIC REP. OF

East Asia and the Pacific
REGIONAL AVERAGE
LAO PEOPLE'S DEM. REP.
CHINA
INDONESIA
PHILIPPINES
KOREA, REP. OF
FIJI

Arab States
REGIONAL AVERAGE
DJIBOUTI
KUWAIT
MOROCCO
SAUDI ARABIA
JORDAN
OMAN
IRAQ
QATAR
ALGERIA
TUNISIA
UNITED ARAB EMIRATES
SYRIAN ARAB REPUBLIC
BAHRAIN

Latin America & the Caribbean
REGIONAL AVERAGE
COLOMBIA
NICARAGUA
EL SALVADOR
BARBADOS
COSTA RICA
BRAZIL
CHILE
VENEZUELA
HONDURAS
BOLIVIA
TRINIDAD AND TOBAGO
URUGUAY
PANAMA
CUBA
PARAGUAY
GUYANA
JAMAICA
BAHAMAS
BELIZE
MEXICO

Central and Eastern Europe and the CIS
REGIONAL AVERAGE
ROMANIA
LATVIA
BULGARIA
HUNGARY
ESTONIA
MACEDONIA, TFYR
POLAND

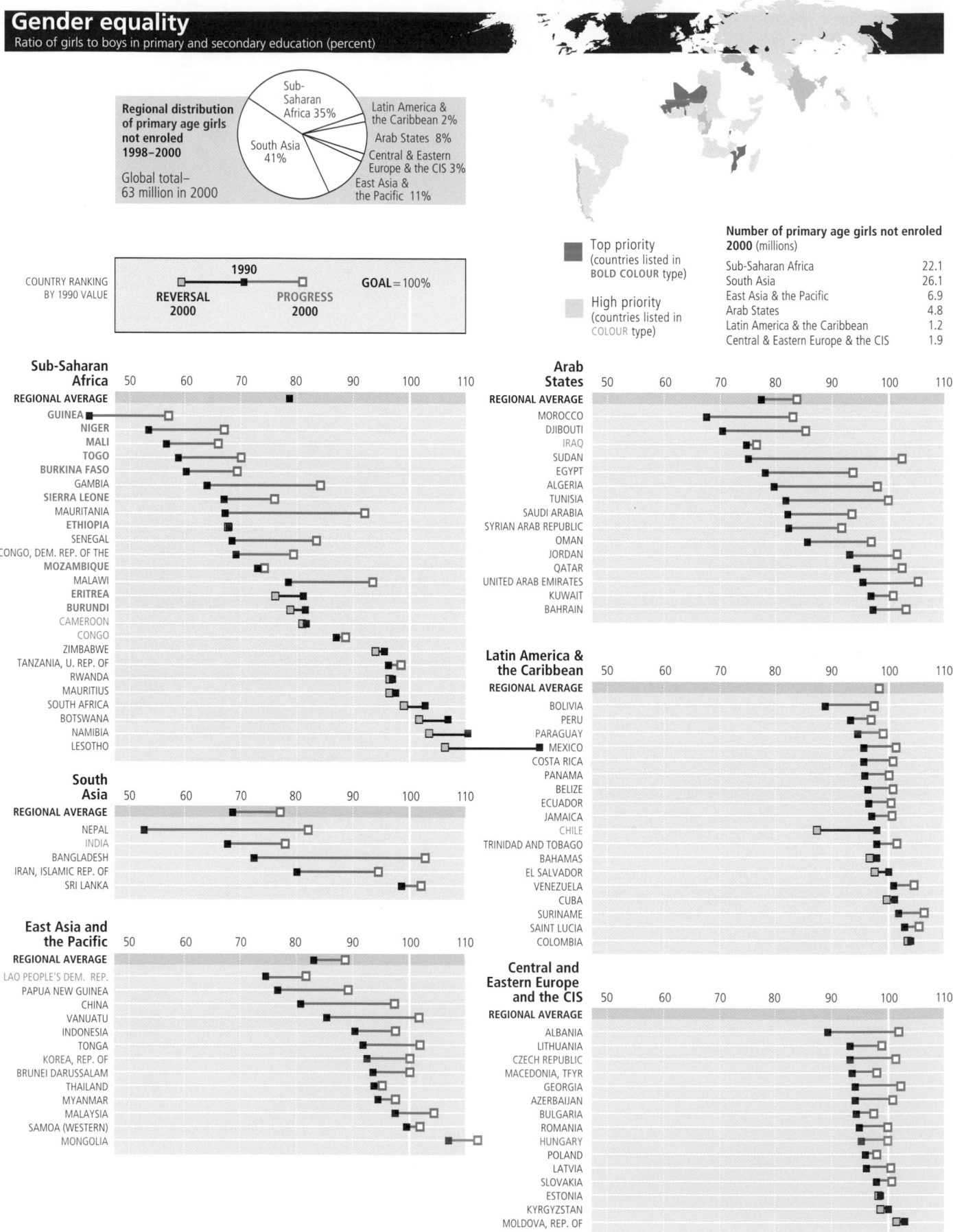

Gender equality

Ratio of girls to boys in primary and secondary education (percent)

Regional distribution of primary age girls not enroled 1998–2000

Global total– 63 million in 2000

Pie chart:
- Sub-Saharan Africa 35%
- South Asia 41%
- Latin America & the Caribbean 2%
- Arab States 8%
- Central & Eastern Europe & the CIS 3%
- East Asia & the Pacific 11%

COUNTRY RANKING BY 1990 VALUE

1990 · REVERSAL 2000 · PROGRESS 2000 · GOAL = 100%

■ Top priority (countries listed in **BOLD COLOUR** type)

□ High priority (countries listed in COLOUR type)

Number of primary age girls not enroled 2000 (millions)

Sub-Saharan Africa	22.1
South Asia	26.1
East Asia & the Pacific	6.9
Arab States	4.8
Latin America & the Caribbean	1.2
Central & Eastern Europe & the CIS	1.9

Sub-Saharan Africa

REGIONAL AVERAGE
GUINEA
NIGER
MALI
TOGO
BURKINA FASO
GAMBIA
SIERRA LEONE
MAURITANIA
ETHIOPIA
SENEGAL
CONGO, DEM. REP. OF THE
MOZAMBIQUE
MALAWI
ERITREA
BURUNDI
CAMEROON
CONGO
ZIMBABWE
TANZANIA, U. REP. OF
RWANDA
MAURITIUS
SOUTH AFRICA
BOTSWANA
NAMIBIA
LESOTHO

South Asia

REGIONAL AVERAGE
NEPAL
INDIA
BANGLADESH
IRAN, ISLAMIC REP. OF
SRI LANKA

East Asia and the Pacific

REGIONAL AVERAGE
LAO PEOPLE'S DEM. REP.
PAPUA NEW GUINEA
CHINA
VANUATU
INDONESIA
TONGA
KOREA, REP. OF
BRUNEI DARUSSALAM
THAILAND
MYANMAR
MALAYSIA
SAMOA (WESTERN)
MONGOLIA

Arab States

REGIONAL AVERAGE
MOROCCO
DJIBOUTI
IRAQ
SUDAN
EGYPT
ALGERIA
TUNISIA
SAUDI ARABIA
SYRIAN ARAB REPUBLIC
OMAN
JORDAN
QATAR
UNITED ARAB EMIRATES
KUWAIT
BAHRAIN

Latin America & the Caribbean

REGIONAL AVERAGE
BOLIVIA
PERU
PARAGUAY
MEXICO
COSTA RICA
PANAMA
BELIZE
ECUADOR
JAMAICA
CHILE
TRINIDAD AND TOBAGO
BAHAMAS
EL SALVADOR
VENEZUELA
CUBA
SURINAME
SAINT LUCIA
COLOMBIA

Central and Eastern Europe and the CIS

REGIONAL AVERAGE
ALBANIA
LITHUANIA
CZECH REPUBLIC
MACEDONIA, TFYR
GEORGIA
AZERBAIJAN
BULGARIA
ROMANIA
HUNGARY
POLAND
LATVIA
SLOVAKIA
ESTONIA
KYRGYZSTAN
MOLDOVA, REP. OF

Child mortality
Under-five mortality rate (per 1,000 live births)

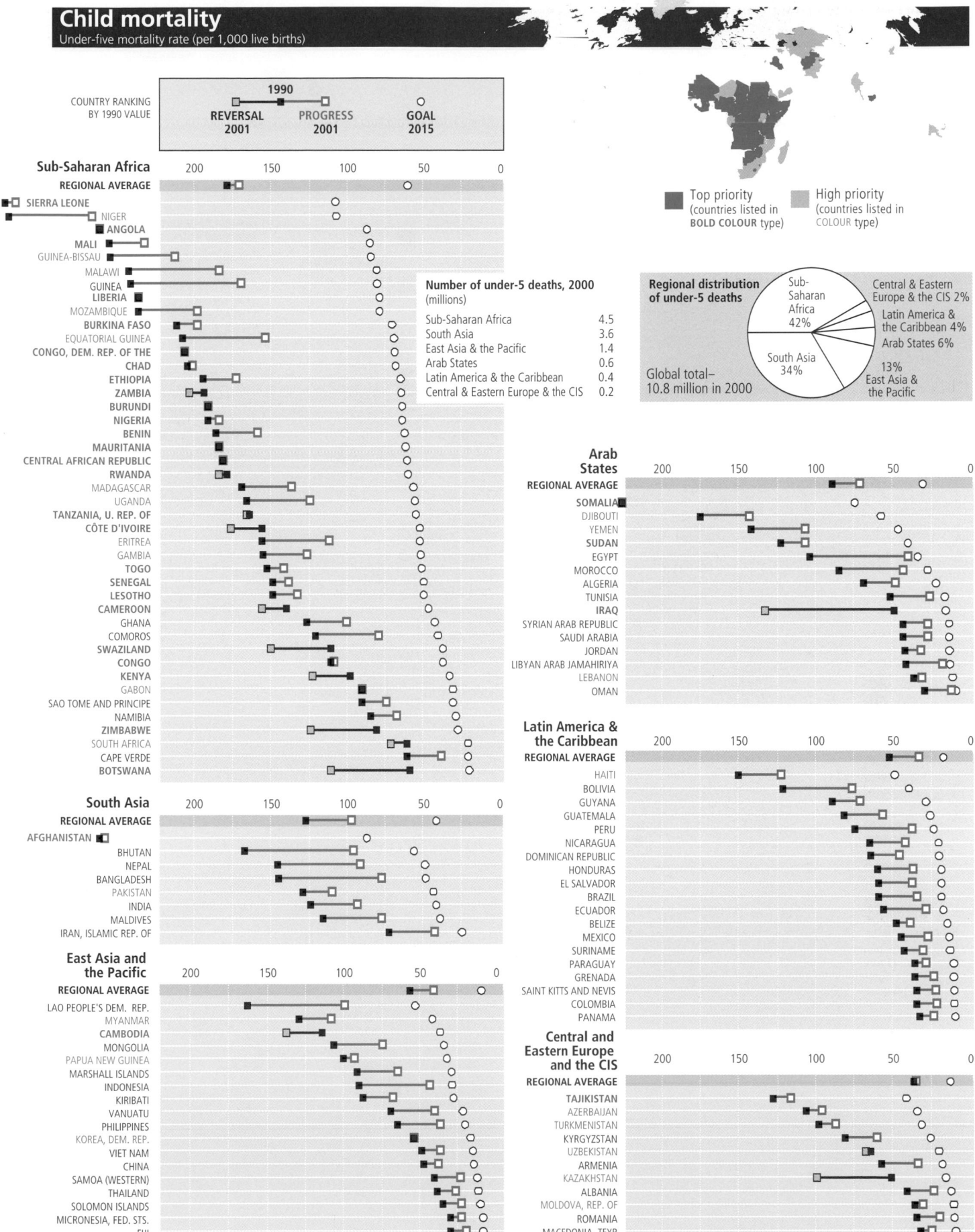

COUNTRY RANKING BY 1990 VALUE		1990		
	REVERSAL 2001		PROGRESS 2001	GOAL 2015

Top priority (countries listed in **BOLD COLOUR** type)
High priority (countries listed in COLOUR type)

Sub-Saharan Africa
200 150 100 50 0

REGIONAL AVERAGE
SIERRA LEONE
NIGER
ANGOLA
MALI
GUINEA-BISSAU
MALAWI
GUINEA
LIBERIA
MOZAMBIQUE
BURKINA FASO
EQUATORIAL GUINEA
CONGO, DEM. REP. OF THE
CHAD
ETHIOPIA
ZAMBIA
BURUNDI
NIGERIA
BENIN
MAURITANIA
CENTRAL AFRICAN REPUBLIC
RWANDA
MADAGASCAR
UGANDA
TANZANIA, U. REP. OF
CÔTE D'IVOIRE
ERITREA
GAMBIA
TOGO
SENEGAL
LESOTHO
CAMEROON
GHANA
COMOROS
SWAZILAND
CONGO
KENYA
GABON
SAO TOME AND PRINCIPE
NAMIBIA
ZIMBABWE
SOUTH AFRICA
CAPE VERDE
BOTSWANA

Number of under-5 deaths, 2000 (millions)

Sub-Saharan Africa	4.5
South Asia	3.6
East Asia & the Pacific	1.4
Arab States	0.6
Latin America & the Caribbean	0.4
Central & Eastern Europe & the CIS	0.2

Regional distribution of under-5 deaths

Sub-Saharan Africa 42%
South Asia 34%
East Asia & the Pacific 13%
Arab States 6%
Latin America & the Caribbean 4%
Central & Eastern Europe & the CIS 2%

Global total– 10.8 million in 2000

Arab States
200 150 100 50 0

REGIONAL AVERAGE
SOMALIA
DJIBOUTI
YEMEN
SUDAN
EGYPT
MOROCCO
ALGERIA
TUNISIA
IRAQ
SYRIAN ARAB REPUBLIC
SAUDI ARABIA
JORDAN
LIBYAN ARAB JAMAHIRIYA
LEBANON
OMAN

South Asia
200 150 100 50 0

REGIONAL AVERAGE
AFGHANISTAN
BHUTAN
NEPAL
BANGLADESH
PAKISTAN
INDIA
MALDIVES
IRAN, ISLAMIC REP. OF

Latin America & the Caribbean
200 150 100 50 0

REGIONAL AVERAGE
HAITI
BOLIVIA
GUYANA
GUATEMALA
PERU
NICARAGUA
DOMINICAN REPUBLIC
HONDURAS
EL SALVADOR
BRAZIL
ECUADOR
BELIZE
MEXICO
SURINAME
PARAGUAY
GRENADA
SAINT KITTS AND NEVIS
COLOMBIA
PANAMA

East Asia and the Pacific
200 150 100 50 0

REGIONAL AVERAGE
LAO PEOPLE'S DEM. REP.
MYANMAR
CAMBODIA
MONGOLIA
PAPUA NEW GUINEA
MARSHALL ISLANDS
INDONESIA
KIRIBATI
VANUATU
PHILIPPINES
KOREA, DEM. REP.
VIET NAM
CHINA
SAMOA (WESTERN)
THAILAND
SOLOMON ISLANDS
MICRONESIA, FED. STS.
FIJI

Central and Eastern Europe and the CIS
200 150 100 50 0

REGIONAL AVERAGE
TAJIKISTAN
AZERBAIJAN
TURKMENISTAN
KYRGYZSTAN
UZBEKISTAN
ARMENIA
KAZAKHSTAN
ALBANIA
MOLDOVA, REP. OF
ROMANIA
MACEDONIA, TFYR

Access to water

People with access to improved water sources (percent of the population)

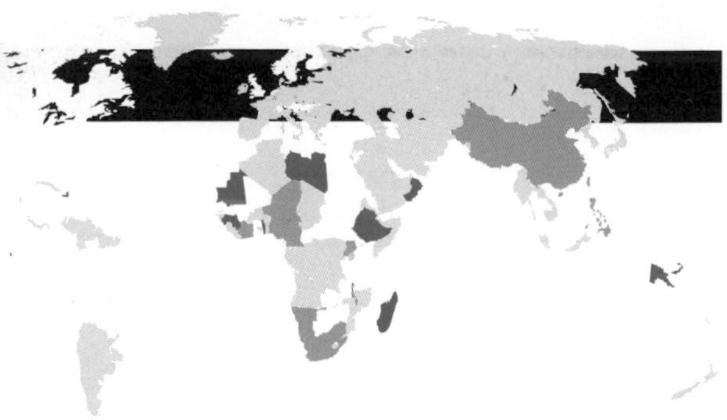

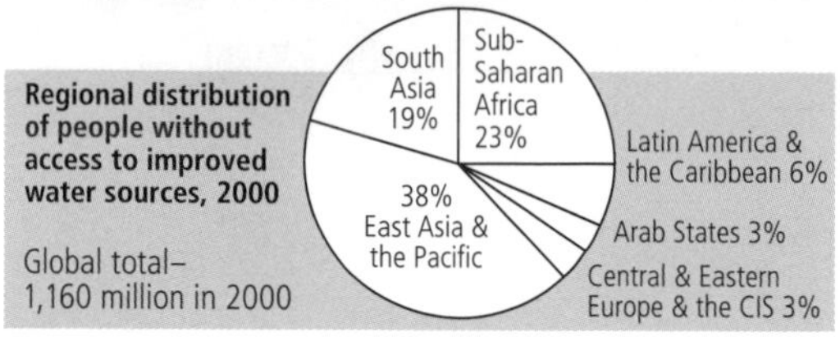

Regional distribution of people without access to improved water sources, 2000
Global total–
1,160 million in 2000
South Asia 19%
Sub-Saharan Africa 23%
Latin America & the Caribbean 6%
Arab States 3%
Central & Eastern Europe & the CIS 3%
38% East Asia & the Pacific

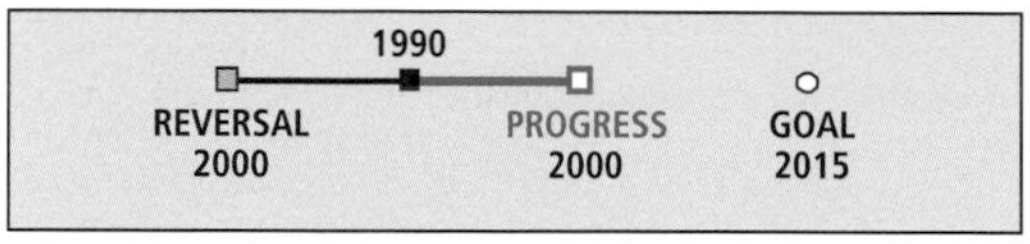

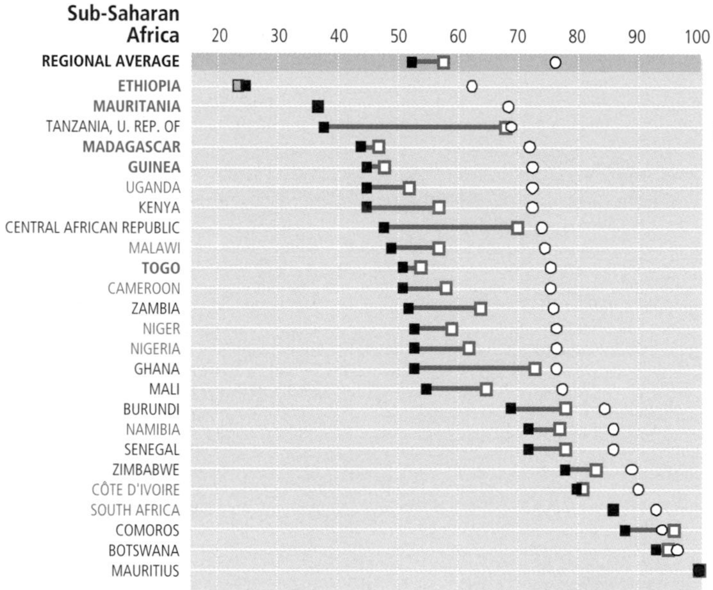

Top priority (countries listed in **BOLD COLOUR** type)

High priority (countries listed in COLOUR type)

No data

Number of people without access to improved water sources, 2000 (millions)

Sub-Saharan Africa	264.5
South Asia	215.8
East Asia & the Pacific	440.3
Arab States	39.6
Latin America & the Caribbean	69.4
Central & Eastern Europe & the CIS	29.6

COUNTRY RANKING BY 1990 VALUE

1990
REVERSAL 2000
PROGRESS 2000
GOAL 2015

Sub-Saharan Africa
20
30
40
50
60
70
80
90
100
REGIONAL AVERAGE
ETHIOPIA
MAURITANIA
TANZANIA, U. REP. OF
MADAGASCAR
GUINEA
UGANDA
KENYA
CENTRAL AFRICAN REPUBLIC
MALAWI
TOGO
CAMEROON
ZAMBIA
NIGER
NIGERIA
GHANA
MALI
BURUNDI
NAMIBIA
SENEGAL
ZIMBABWE
CÔTE D'IVOIRE
SOUTH AFRICA
COMOROS
BOTSWANA
MAURITIUS

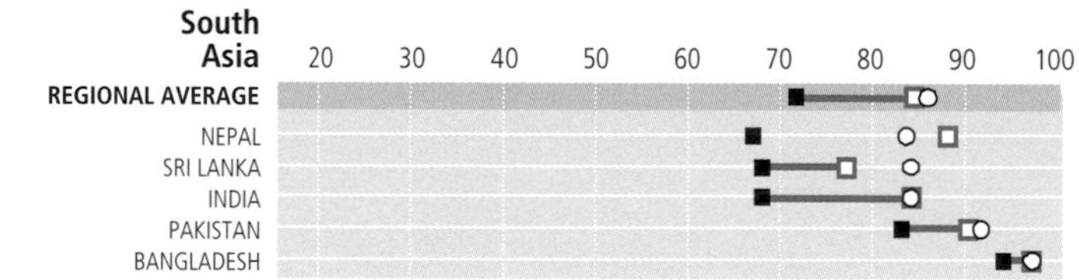

South Asia
20
30
40
50
60
70
80
90
100
REGIONAL AVERAGE
NEPAL
SRI LANKA
INDIA
PAKISTAN
BANGLADESH

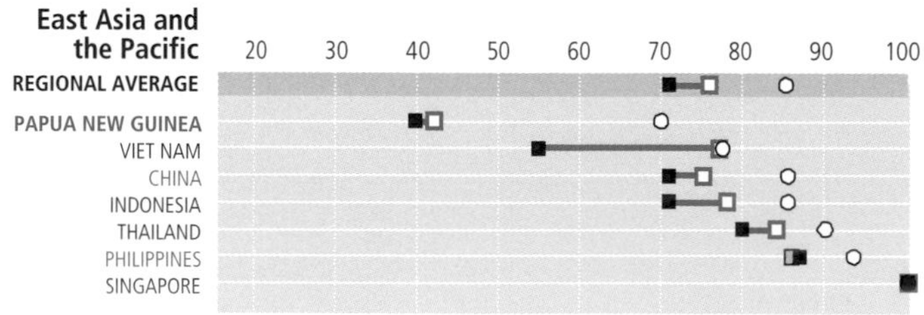

East Asia and the Pacific
20
30
40
50
60
70
80
90
100
REGIONAL AVERAGE
PAPUA NEW GUINEA
VIET NAM
CHINA
INDONESIA
THAILAND
PHILIPPINES
SINGAPORE

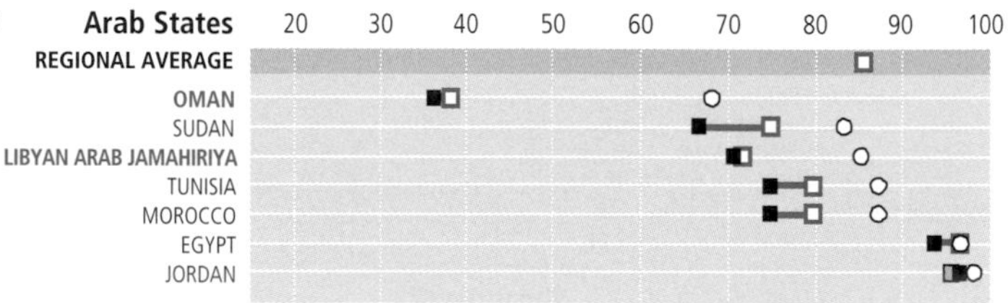

Arab States
20
30
40
50
60
70
80
90
100
REGIONAL AVERAGE
OMAN
SUDAN
LIBYAN ARAB JAMAHIRIYA
TUNISIA
MOROCCO
EGYPT
JORDAN

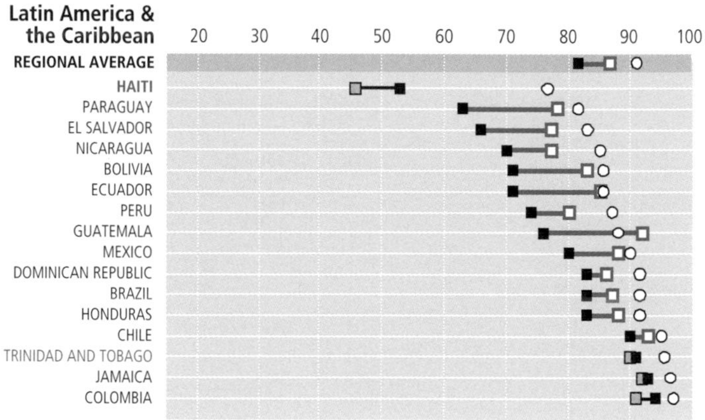

Latin America & the Caribbean
20
30
40
50
60
70
80
90
100
REGIONAL AVERAGE
HAITI
PARAGUAY
EL SALVADOR
NICARAGUA
BOLIVIA
ECUADOR
PERU
GUATEMALA
MEXICO
DOMINICAN REPUBLIC
BRAZIL
HONDURAS
CHILE
TRINIDAD AND TOBAGO
JAMAICA
COLOMBIA

Access to sanitation
People with access to adequate sanitation (percentage of the population)

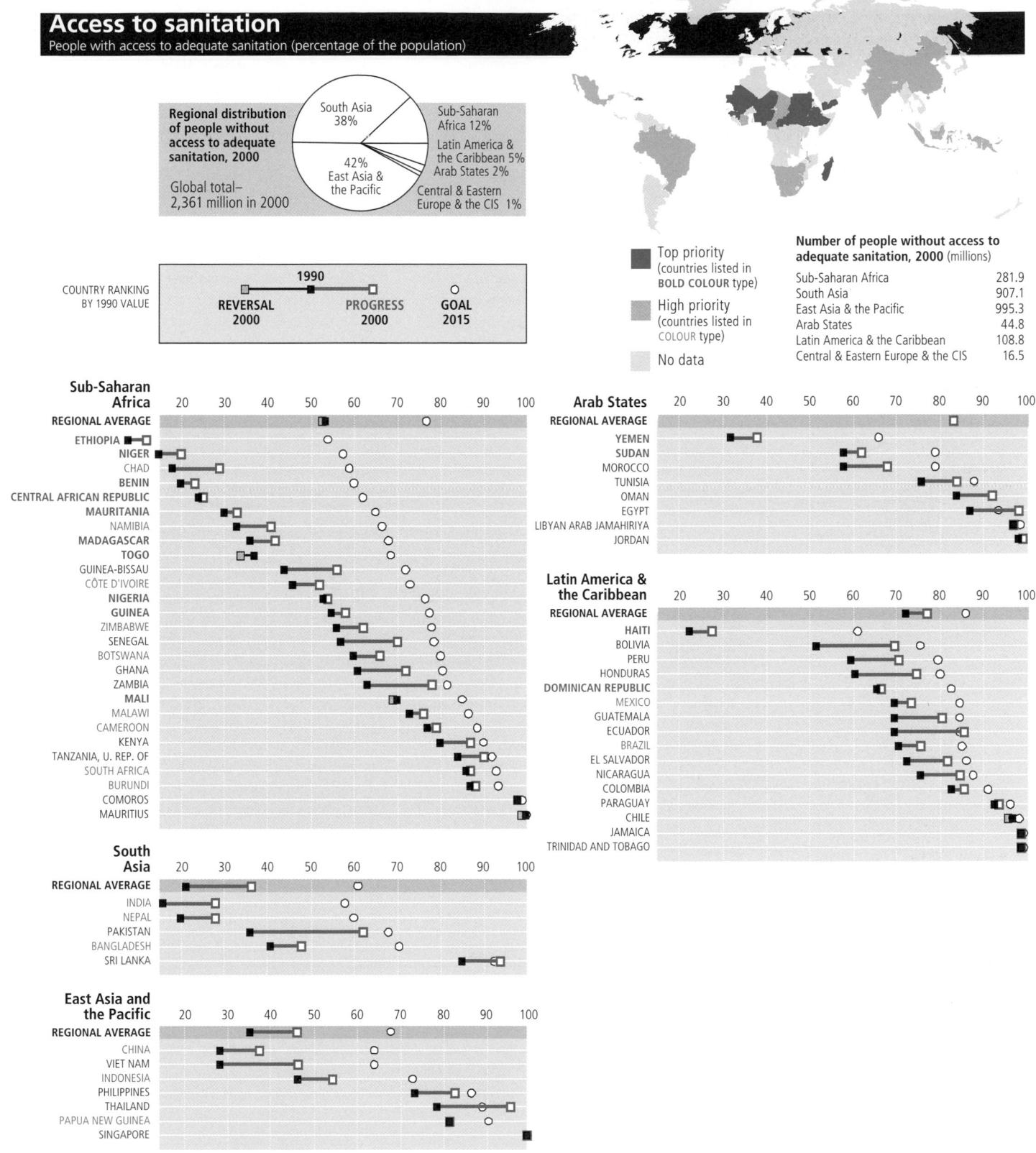

Regional distribution of people without access to adequate sanitation, 2000

Global total– 2,361 million in 2000

- South Asia 38%
- Sub-Saharan Africa 12%
- Latin America & the Caribbean 5%
- Arab States 2%
- 42% East Asia & the Pacific
- Central & Eastern Europe & the CIS 1%

COUNTRY RANKING BY 1990 VALUE

1990

REVERSAL 2000 | PROGRESS 2000 | GOAL 2015

■ Top priority (countries listed in **BOLD COLOUR** type)

■ High priority (countries listed in COLOUR type)

□ No data

Number of people without access to adequate sanitation, 2000 (millions)

Sub-Saharan Africa	281.9
South Asia	907.1
East Asia & the Pacific	995.3
Arab States	44.8
Latin America & the Caribbean	108.8
Central & Eastern Europe & the CIS	16.5

Source: **Income:** Human Development Report Office calculations based on data on GDP at market prices (constant 1995 US$), population and GDP per capita (PPP US$) from World Bank 2003i; World Bank 2002f. **Hunger:** MDG indicator table 1; FAO 2002b. **Primary education:** MDG indicator table 1; UNESCO 2002a. **Gender equality:** World Bank 2003i; aggregates calculated for the Human Development Report Office by the World Bank; UNESCO 2002a. **Child mortality:** World Bank 2003i; UNICEF 2003b. **Access to water:** UN 2003c; aggregates calculated for the Human Development Report Office by the World Bank; Human Development Report Office calculations based on UN 2003c, 2003h. **Access to sanitation:** UN 2003c; aggregates calculated for the Human Development Report Office by the World Bank; Human Development Report Office calculations based on UN 2003c, 2003h.

PRIORITY CHALLENGES IN MEETING THE GOALS

Human development index

The human development index (HDI) is a simple summary measure of three dimensions of the human development concept: living a long and healthy life, being educated and having a decent standard of living (see technical note). Thus it combines measures of life expectancy, school enrolment, literacy and income to allow a broader view of a country's development than using income alone—which is too often equated with well-being. Since the creation of the HDI in 1990 three supplementary indices have been developed to highlight particular aspects of human development: the human poverty index (HPI), gender-related development index (GDI) and gender empowerment measure (GEM).

The HDI can highlight the successes of some countries and the slower progress of others. Venezuela started with a higher HDI than Brazil in 1975, but Brazil has made much faster progress. Finland had a lower HDI than Switzerland in 1975 but today is slightly ahead. Rankings by HDI and by GDP per capita can also differ, showing that high levels of human development can be achieved without high incomes—and that high incomes do not guarantee high levels of human development (see indicator table 1). Pakistan and Viet Nam have similar incomes, but Viet Nam has done much more to translate that income into human development. Similarly, Jamaica has achieved a much better HDI than Morocco with about the same income.

Swaziland achieves the same HDI as Botswana with less than two-thirds of the income, and the same is true of the Philippines and Thailand. So with the right policies, countries can advance human development even with low incomes.

Most regions have seen steady progress in HDI over the past 20 years, with East Asia and the Pacific performing particularly well in the 1990s. Arab States have also seen substantial growth, exceeding the average increase for developing countries. Sub-Saharan Africa, by contrast, has been almost stagnant—on par with South Asia in 1985, it has fallen far behind. Two groups of countries have suffered such setbacks: CIS countries going through what has become for many a long, painful transition to market economies, and poor African countries whose development has been hindered or reversed for a variety of reasons—including HIV/AIDS and internal and external conflicts.

Although the HDI is a useful starting point, it omits vital aspects of human development, notably the ability to participate in the decisions that affect one's life. A person can be rich, healthy and well-educated, but without this ability human development is held back.

The omission of dimensions of freedoms from the HDI has been highlighted since the first *Human Development Reports*—and drove the creation of a human freedom index (HFI) in 1991 and a political freedom index (PFI) in 1992. Neither measure survived past its first year, testament to the difficulty of adequately capturing in a single index such complex aspects of human development. But that does not mean that indicators of political and civil freedoms can be ignored entirely in considering the state of a country's human development.

There are strong links between the Human Development Indices and the Millennium Development Goals. The three dimensions of human development captured in the HDI are very similar to goals 1–7 which also focus on issues of education, health and a decent standard of living (see also Box 1.2 in Chapter 1). Furthermore, the GDI and GEM which aim to capture, respectively, gender inequalities in human capabilities and in political and economic decision making focus very much on the aspirations of Goal 3 to promote gender equality and empower women.

Different paths in HDI

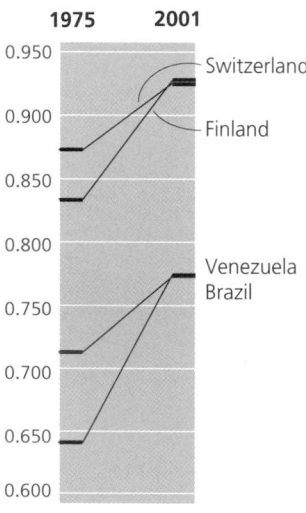

Source: Indicator table 2.

HDI, HPI-1, HPI-2, GDI—same components, different measurements

Index	Longevity	Knowledge	Decent standard of living	Participation or exclusion
HDI	Life expectancy at birth	1. Adult literacy rate 2. Combined enrolment ratio	GDP per capita (PPP US$)	—
HPI-1	Probability at birth of not surviving to age 40	Adult illiteracy rate	Deprivation in economic provisioning, measured by: 1. Percentage of people without sustainable access to an improved water source 2. Percentage of children under five underweight for age	—
HPI-2	Probability at birth of not surviving to age 60	Percentage of adults lacking functional literacy skills	Percentage of people living below the income poverty line (50% of median adjusted disposable household income)	Long-term unemployment rate (12 months or more)
GDI	Female and male life expectancy at birth	1. Female and male adult literacy rates 2. Female and male combined primary, secondary and tertiary enrolment ratios	Estimated female and male earned income, reflecting women's and men's command over resources	—

Human poverty index

While the HDI measures overall progress in a country in achieving human development, the human poverty index (HPI) reflects the distribution of progress and measures the backlog of deprivations that still exists. The HPI measures deprivation in the same dimensions of basic human development as the HDI.

HPI-1

The HPI-1 measures poverty in developing countries. It focuses on deprivations in three dimensions: longevity, as measured by the probability at birth of not surviving to age 40; knowledge, as measured by the adult illiteracy rate; and overall economic provisioning, public and private, as measured by the percentage of people not using improved water sources and the percentage without sustainable access to an improved water source and the percentage of children under weight for age.

HPI-2

Because human deprivation varies with the social and economic conditions of a community, a separate index, the HPI-2, has been devised to measure human poverty in selected OECD countries, drawing on the greater availability of data. The HPI-2 focuses on deprivation in the same three dimensions as the HPI-1 and one additional one, social exclusion. The indicators are the probability at birth of not surviving to age 60, the adult functional illiteracy rate, the percentage of people living below the income poverty line (with adjusted household disposable income less than 50% of the median) and the long-term unemployment rate (12 months or more).

Gender-related development index

The gender-related development index (GDI) measures achievements in the same dimensions and using the same indicators as the HDI, but captures inequalities in achievement between women and men. It is simply the HDI adjusted downward for gender inequality. The greater is the gender disparity in basic human development, the lower is a country's GDI compared with its HDI.

Gender empowerment measure

The gender empowerment measure (GEM) reveals whether women can take active part in economic and political life. It focuses on participation, measuring gender inequality in key areas of economic and political participation and decision-making. It tracks the percentages of women in parliament, among legislators, senior officials and managers and among professional and technical workers—and the gender disparity in earned income, reflecting economic independence. Differing from the GDI, it exposes inequality in opportunities in selected areas.

Same income, different HDI

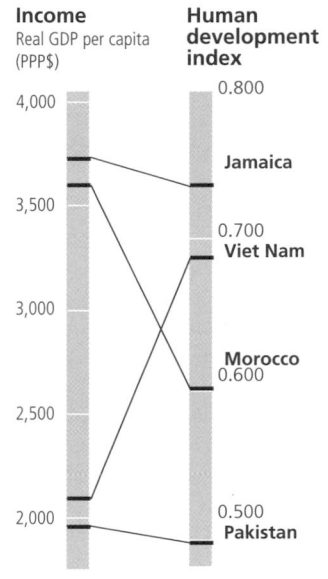

Source: Indicator table 1.

Same HDI, different income

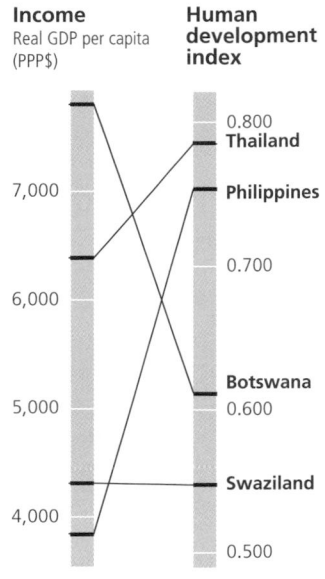

Source: Indicator table 1.

Global disparities in HDI

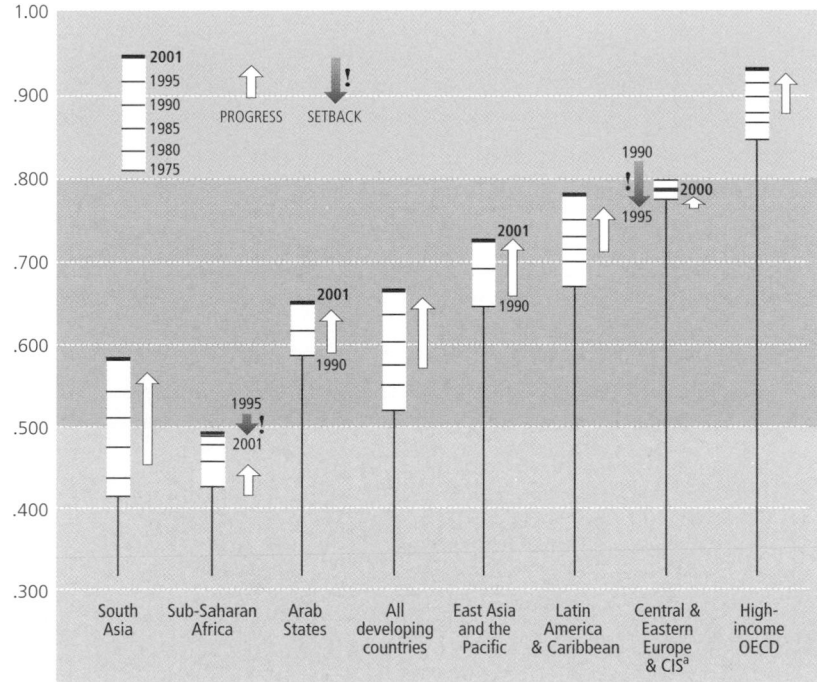

Source: Human Development Report Office calculations based on indicator table 2.

Subnational socio-economic data provide important evidence on inequalities—even for countries that on average have made good progress towards the Millennium Development Goals. Evidence of unbalanced national development helps determine policy priorities. In particular, efforts should go towards eradicating the entrenched human poverty affecting certain areas and groups in countries where human development is otherwise much higher. Some countries provide detailed subnational data for in-depth socio-economic analysis and, where possible, spatial mapping of socio-economic variables. Some of these data are examined below because they provide good examples of growing or lingering gaps—where entire areas or groups (or both) have been left behind in one or more spheres of development.

China: fast progress, driven by the coastland

China is among the few countries performing well overall on the indicators for the Millennium Development Goals. Yet in recent decades China has shown large disparities in economic and social outcomes between coastal and inland regions—a trend that also reflects cleavages between urban and rural areas. Coastal areas have consistently experienced the fastest economic growth: between 1978 and 1998 per capita incomes increased by an astonishing 11% a year. Ignoring inflation, that means that $100 in 1978 would have jumped to $800 just 20 years later.

Moreover, the performance of coastal areas sped up in the 1990s, with annual growth averaging 13%—five times the level in China's slowest-growing north-western regions, which happen to be far from the commercially thriving coast. As a result the bulk of national income is concentrated in metropolitan and coastal regions. Map 1 shows the dispersion in GDP levels across administrative units in 2000. The wealth of coastal areas—with their large ports and harbour cities—owes much to exports.

In 1999 China's three richest metropolises—Shanghai, Beijing and Tianjin—stood at the top of the human development index (HDI) ranking. Those at the bottom were all Western provinces. Moreover, the poorest provinces have the highest inequality. Tibet had the lowest values for education attainment and life expectancy. In income, education and health only some parts of China will achieve the Millennium Development Goals, leaving behind the vast inland areas—and particularly the Western provinces.

Brazil: leaving the North behind?

Brazil has a long legacy of high inequalities. The richest 10% of households have 70 times the income of the poorest 10%. Over the past 10 years illiteracy rates have been widening between the richest and poorest states (table 1). And though poverty started to decline in the early 1990s, it did so unevenly—and is not falling fast enough for Brazil to achieve the first Millennium Development Goal. At current rates of progress, the South is the only region expected to halve poverty by 2015. But the Northeast, the poorest region, has also reduced poverty dramatically, as have the Central and South-eastern regions.

The North is the only region that has seen poverty increase, rising from 36% in 1990 to 44% in 2001. (Data for the North are limited to urban areas.) Why are so many people being left behind when overall growth is good? The culprit is not a shortfall in average resources but persistently high inequality (Mendonça 2003). Not only is the North seeing poverty increase, it is also lagging on the HDI—unlike the wealthy, urban South (São Paulo, Rio de Janeiro and Rio Grande do Sul) and unlike the Northeast, which has seen substantial improvements in its HDI. The policy implications of this are that more resources should be targeted to areas most in need—the North because of the adverse trends and the Northeast because of its still low levels of human development.

MAP 1 **Geographic distribution of income in China, 2000**

Beijing

GDP per capita by county
(10,000 Yuan)

- 0–0.50
- 0.50–1.00
- 1.00–3.03
- No data

Note: Counties with very low population densities (the lowest 20%) were combined to calculate an aggregate GDP per capita for them, because the sparse populations there do not permit high-resolution mapping of per-capita income.
Source: CIESIN 2003.

TABLE 1
Illiteracy rates in Brazil by region, ages 15 and older, 1990 and 2001
Percent

Region	1990	2001	Change
Brazil	18.7	12.4	–6.4
North	12.4	11.2	–1.2
Northeast	36.4	24.3	–12.2
Middle-east	16.9	10.2	–6.7
Southeast	11.4	7.5	–3.9
South	11.7	7.1	–4.6

Source: Mendonça 2003.

Mexico: development excluding the South

Since the early 1990s Mexico's economic, social and political performance has been mixed at best, with its recovery from the debt crisis of the 1980s suffering a blow from the 1994–95 financial crisis. But as a whole, Mexico is on track to achieving most of the Goals. Poverty was lower in 2000 than in 1992, dropping from 15% to 13% (though in 1995 it jumped to 18%). The poorest areas are the South and Southeast. The wealth gap also got worse in the 1990s: by the end of the decade the top 10% of earners had 35 times the income of the bottom 10%, compared with 33 times in 1992. But other development indicators—mainly for health, nutrition and education—improved in the 1990s.

While inequalities divide Mexican society along ethnic and social lines, the most notable gap is that which splits the South from the North, with the South lagging behind in nearly all of the Millennium Development Goals. Southern states are also mainly indigenous and rural, and their economies are largely agricultural and lack infrastructure. Because of poor performance in the South and progress in the North, this historical cleavage has persisted since Mexico's opening to international trade in the 1990s. The North and Northwest have tended to benefit, while distance from the U.S. border has excluded the South from economic integration with Canada and the United States.

In the Southern state of Chiapas more than 30% of the population lives in extreme poverty, and episodes of violence are frequent—as elsewhere in the South. Moreover, large numbers of people in the South are illiterate (map 2). This pattern also reflects gaps between male and female literacy rates, which are much deeper in the most illiterate states of the South.

The Philippines: integrating ethnic minorities

The Philippines is highly fragmented economically and socially. Difficult topography and unfavourable climate make the Southeast more vulnerable to natural disasters than the milder Central and Northwest (metropolitan Manila) states.

Some areas contain large concentrations of minority populations: Moro secessionists in the Autonomous Region of Muslim Mindanao (ARMM) in the Southwest and Central Mindanao in the South and the indigenously dominated Cordillera Administrative Region in the North. Large areas in these regions are lagging behind in many socio-economic indicators relative to the national average. The East Asian financial crisis in 1997, coupled with the El Niño weather phenomenon the following year, contributed to a resurgence in the poverty rate to 28% in 2000. This trend has not been uniform, with poverty increasing in the mountainous central areas of the Northern island of Luzon and the western areas of Mindanao in the South.

Regional disparities in income poverty remain wide, from a low of 12% in the Manila area to 74% in the ARMM. This is reflected in the uneven distribution of the HDI, reflecting closely the ethnic distribution of the population, with ethnic minority areas performing worse (map 3). Similarly heterogeneous performance appears

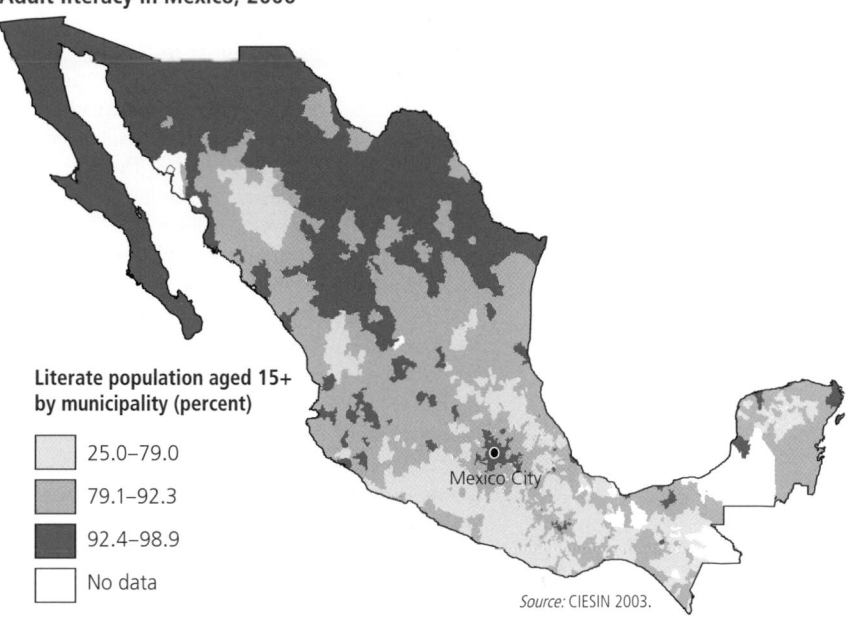

MAP 2
Adult literacy in Mexico, 2000

Literate population aged 15+ by municipality (percent)

- 25.0–79.0
- 79.1–92.3
- 92.4–98.9
- No data

Source: CIESIN 2003.

MAP 3
Human development index in the Philippines, 1994

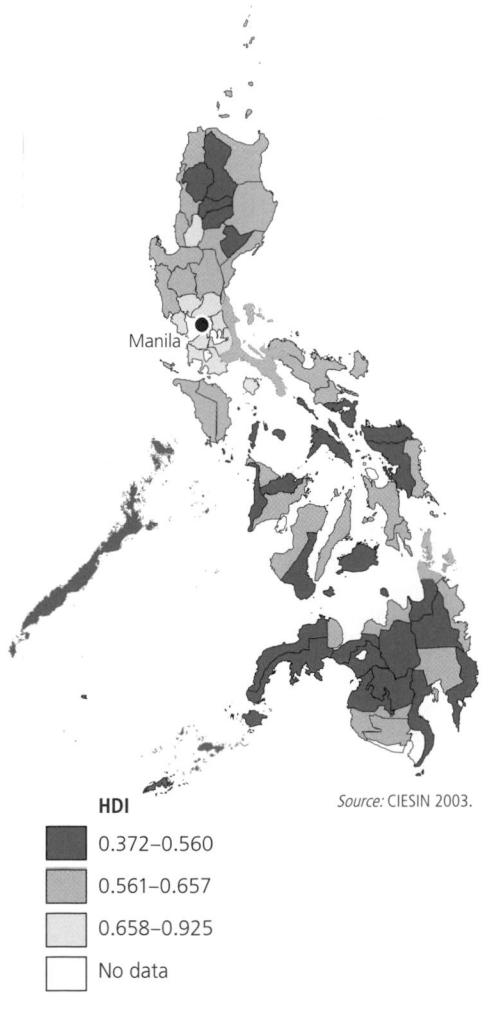

Source: CIESIN 2003.

HDI

- 0.372–0.560
- 0.561–0.657
- 0.658–0.925
- No data

when looking at other indicators, including child mortality rates, with the smallest improvements again recorded in the Mindanao area.

India: general progress, slower for some

India, home to one in six of the world's people, has achieved great progress on most fronts. Poverty has been dramatically reduced and improvements made in education for both males and females. There has been tremendous improvement in gender literacy gaps, particularly in the poor Central states of Madhya Pradesh and, to some extent Rajasthan, Uttar Pradesh and Bihar.

Still, a number of areas appear to have been excluded from these trends, particularly along the Pakistani and Nepalese borders. Furthermore, gaps in literacy between low social classes and the rest of the population remain extremely high, particularly in the poorest states—Rajasthan, Uttar Pradesh, Bihar—and in Karnataka. Shariff and Sudarshan (1996) found that female literacy rates among members of scheduled tribes were as low as 7% in Rajasthan and 9% in Madhya Pradesh.

There are also grave concerns in health. Largely due to widespread undernutrition and poor infrastructure, mortality rates remain high in the poorest, rural, scheduled caste states, particularly among mothers and children (Bajpay 2003). Between 1992/93 and 1997/98 infant mortality fell in all states except Madhya Pradesh and Rajasthan. Moreover, infant mortality rates are substantially higher in rural areas, particularly in Maharasthra and Andhra Pradesh (table 2). High immunization rates are still an almost exclusive characteristic of provinces in the South and Southwest. In numerous areas, particularly in the North and Northeast, less than one-third of children were immunized in 1999.

Guatemala: progress on gender and ethnic gaps

Since 1990 the pace towards the Millennium Development Goals in Guatemala has been slow and uneven. In recent years shocks have included serious drought and lower world prices for coffee, the country's main export staple. In the 1990s, while many groups and areas experienced improvements in human development, outcomes in the North and Northwest were disappointing. These regions, where most indigenous Guatemalans live, had the highest extreme poverty in 2000. There appears to be some overlap between the discrimination facing these ethnic minorities and women. Map 4, for instance, shows that maternal mortality is highest in the North and Northwest, suggesting weak health systems in rural areas with a prevalence of ethnic minorities and women.

Literacy rates illustrate another aspect of the problem. Women in the Northwest were the only group not to see the literacy rate improve. Discrimination by gender and by race occurs in the same areas and probably affects the same people: indigenous women. These trends are compounded by persistent inequalities, especially in land concentration, all of which may impede Guatemala's development. According to a recent study, land concentration increased

TABLE 2

Infant mortality rates in India by state and region, 1990s

| State | Infant mortality rate (per 1,000 live births) | | Rural to urban ratio |
	1992/93	1997/98	1995
Andhra Pradesh	70.4	65.0	1.72
Bihar	89.2	73.0	1.30
Gujarat	73.5	62.2	1.45
Karnataka	65.4	51.5	1.60
Kerala	23.8	16.3	1.23
Madhya Pradesh	85.2	86.1	1.70
Maharashtra	50.5	43.7	1.94
Orissa	112.1	82.0	1.65
Rajasthan	76.3	80.4	1.45
Tamil Nadu	67.7	48.2	1.56
Uttar Pradesh	99.9	86.7	1.35

Source: International Institute of Population Sciences 2000.

between 1979 and 2000, hindering diversification and better distribution of property and risk (Fuentes, Balsells and Arriola 2003).

But while in absolute terms the situation is worrisome, during the 1990s the greatest percentage reduction in extreme poverty occurred among indigenous households, from 32% to 26%. Income poverty also fell fast among female-headed households. While the income progress recorded in many of the indicators relevant to the Millennium Development Goals has been satisfactory, malnutrition (mainly due to droughts) has increased in the Northwest and particularly in the North—overwhelmingly affecting rural indigenous populations and probably suggesting infrastructure deficiencies.

Mali: leaving women behind

Mali has made important progress on many of the indicators for the Millennium Development Goals. Despite some variability, 1992–99 saw overall development

MAP 4

Maternal mortality in Guatemala, 1997

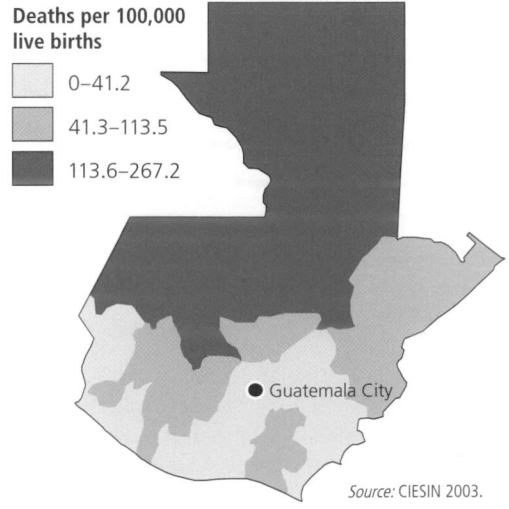

Deaths per 100,000 live births

- 0–41.2
- 41.3–113.5
- 113.6–267.2

Guatemala City

Source: CIESIN 2003.

improve in each region. Still, in many important areas of development, too many women are suffering. In education, 40 of 100 men are literate—and only 33 of 100 women. The Northern rural regions exemplify this national picture, particularly as a consequence of cultural attitudes towards women in rural areas.

Women are also disproportionately hit by HIV/AIDS. In 1992 the infection rate was about 3%. Female sex workers have the highest infection rates (Backiny-Yetna, Raffinot and Coulibaly 2003). The disease has contributed to the high maternal mortality ratio of about 580 deaths per 100,000 live births—unchanged in the past five years.

Burkina Faso: facing drought and disease
One of the world's poorest countries according to the human poverty index (HPI) and GDP per capita, Burkina Faso presents sharp differences in development between its Eastern and Western regions. The East is dry, which complicates agricultural practices. The West is more humid, creating a climate suitable for cotton production. Furthermore, poverty incidence is five times higher in rural areas (50% in rural areas in 1994 and 1998).

Between 1993 and 1999 malnutrition increased in all provinces. Stunting increased from 29% in 1993 to 37% in 1999, with rural areas driving the trend. In the capital city of Ouagadougou an estimated one-fifth of children suffers from malnutrition. In the rest of the country one-third of children do. The rural population has barely improved primary enrolment rates. In 1994 this figure for rural girls was 22%, compared with 69% for urban girls. Four years later the figures had changed to 24% and 99%, indicating extremely slow progress in rural areas.

Russian Federation: development shocks and gender bias
The Russian Federation has undergone a profound transformation since its transition to a market economy. Moreover, two shocks in the 1990s undermined its development indicators. The first was HIV/AIDS, with the number of HIV-positive people reaching 178,000 in 2001 (Zubarevich 2003). The disease has mainly affected people between the ages of 15 and 29 and those in urban areas (Moscow, Saint Petersburg, Sverdlovsk oblast).

The second shock was an increase in poverty and inequality between and within regions. In 2000 Moscow, Tatarstan and oil- and gas-producing Tyumen oblast were the only regions with HDI levels comparable to those of richer countries such as the Czech Republic, Hungary and Slovenia. At the other end of the spectrum were the republics of Siberia and the Far East,

with HDI levels comparable to those of Gabon and Nicaragua (map 5).

Mirroring these differences between regions are gaps within regions. The three richest regions are also experiencing the sharpest polarizations of wealth and poverty. Poverty in Russia has increased in both urban and rural areas, particularly between 1997 and 1999, peaking at 57% in rural areas compared with 47% in urban areas. Poverty has affected different regions in different ways: economic instability in particular (such as the financial shocks in the late 1990s) appears to have exacerbated regional disparities in living standards, with less developed regions getting poorer faster (Zubarevich 2003).

The growth of poverty has hit elderly women and female-headed households particularly hard, illustrating a worrisome "feminization" of poverty in Russia. A driving force behind this trend is job instability and, even more, wage discrimination against women. In early 1999 the female-male wage ratio was 56%. At the end of that year it was down to 52%, and in mid-2000 it reached 50% (Zubarevich 2003). Another study saw this ratio fall from 70% in 1998 to 63% in 2000. Furthermore, women's political representation was very low in the transition period. Gender gaps in education have stayed low, however—close to their levels before the transition.

MAP 5

Human development index in Russian regions, 2000

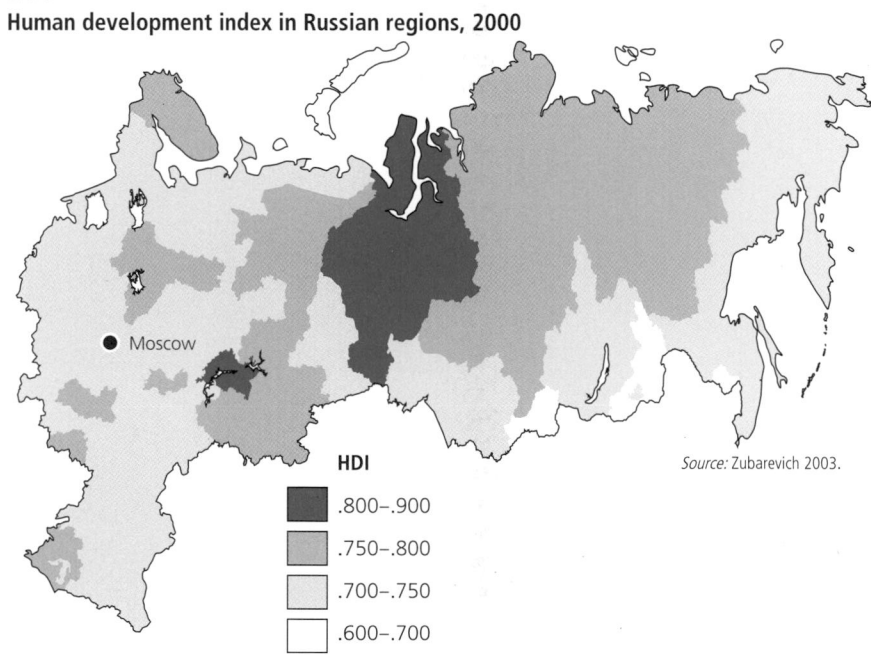

Source: Zubarevich 2003.

HDI

.800–.900
.750–.800
.700–.750
.600–.700

Source: Human Development Report Office based on national human development reports and Mendonça 2003; Bajpay 2003; Baumeister 2002, cited in Fuentes, Balsells and Arriola 2003; Backiny-Yetna, Coulibaly and Raffinot 2003a, b; Zubarevich 2003.

Overcoming structural barriers to growth—to achieve the Goals

The core message of the Millennium Development Compact—and this chapter—is that many of the world's poorest countries and regions face structural impediments that have made it very difficult to achieve sustained economic growth. Thus it is no accident that they are the poorest.

Sustained growth requires that countries first attain basic thresholds on a number of fronts: sound economic governance, basic health care and education, core infrastructure, access to foreign markets. If a country falls short on one or more of these thresholds because of structural conditions—rampant disease, or a location far from world markets, or especially fragile soils and low food production, or high susceptibility to natural disasters—it tends to fall into a poverty trap, making sustained economic growth unlikely. Because these countries face high hurdles and have limited resources, they cannot achieve the thresholds for growth on their own: they require external assistance.

Even in countries otherwise doing well, structural impediments can contribute to pockets of entrenched poverty. China's remote inland regions, for instance, face much longer distances to ports, much poorer infrastructure and much tougher biophysical conditions than the country's coastal regions, which are enjoying the fastest sustained economic growth in human history. Reducing poverty in such highly populated countries as China, Brazil and India requires focusing on how to allocate resources to reduce poverty and inequalities. But this challenge is very different from the one facing the top and high priority countries, which are typically stuck in poverty traps and have insufficient resources to meet the needs of average citizens—let alone the poorest. Resources are insufficient largely due to a lack of economic growth (box 3.1).

Economic growth is necessary to meet the Millennium Development Goals for two reasons.

First, economic growth directly reduces income poverty for many households, increasing their savings and freeing resources for investments in human development. Without economic growth countries cannot expect to halve the proportion of people living in income poverty, the first target of the Goals. Second, economic growth tends to increase government revenue. Because most investments in human development—health, nutrition, education, infrastructure—come from the public sector, greater fiscal resources are critical to meeting the Goals.

But while economic growth is necessary for increased public spending on human development, it is hardly sufficient. Some governments neglect such investments or discriminate in their provision among population groups, weakening the potential benefits that overall economic growth can provide for meeting the Goals. Past *Human Development Report*s have used the term "ruthless growth" to describe growth that does not reach poor people, either because richer households receive most of the increase in income or because governments do not use the additional revenue to invest in the human development

---

BOX 3.1

Growth needed to halve income poverty

Economic growth is important for achieving all the Millennium Development Goals, but it relates most directly to the first target, which calls for halving the proportion of people in poverty between 1990 and 2015. Many studies have calculated an "elasticity of poverty to average income"—the percentage decline in the headcount poverty ratio for each 1% increase in per capita income. A typical estimate in the vast econometric literature, holding constant the distribution of income, is that the poverty rate declines by 2% for each 1% increase in average per capita income, for an elasticity of 2 (Bruno, Ravallion and Squire 1998; see also Adams 2002).

This elasticity estimate suggests that cutting headcount poverty in half requires a 41% increase in per capita income. If the 41% is spread over 25 years (1990 to 2015), annual growth of 1.4% is needed. If a country must accomplish the entire 41% increase between 2003 and 2015, a much higher annual rate (2.9%) is needed. Yet even the higher rate is well within the realm of possibility for a low-income country—if preconditions and policies for growth are in place.

Source: Bruno, Ravallion and Squire 1996; Adams 2002.

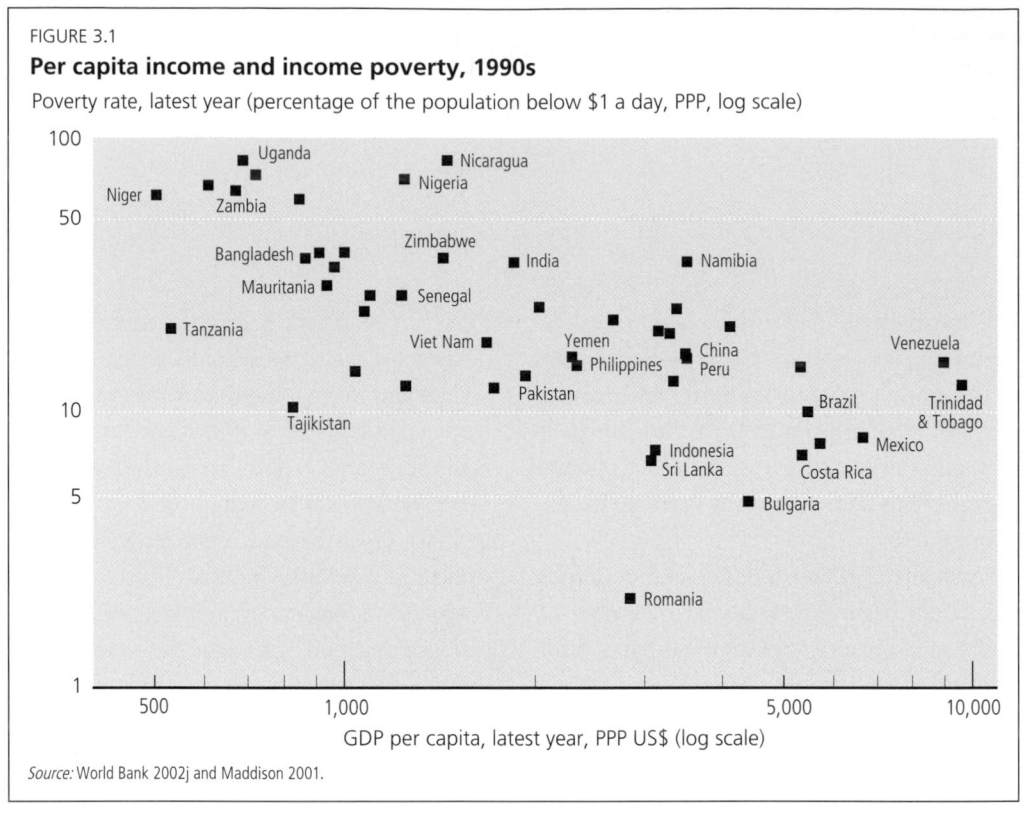

FIGURE 3.1

Per capita income and income poverty, 1990s

Poverty rate, latest year (percentage of the population below $1 a day, PPP, log scale)

Source: World Bank 2002j and Maddison 2001.

needs of poor people. And as *Human Development Report 1996* showed, economic growth cannot be sustained without substantial improvements in education and health.

In countries with higher per capita incomes, a smaller proportion of people fall below the poverty line, suggesting that higher incomes are required to reduce poverty. But while there is an inverse relationship between a country's income poverty and income level, the relationship is far from perfect. Poverty rates can vary considerably across countries with similar per capita incomes: Tanzania and Niger have similar incomes, yet Tanzania has a much lower poverty rate (figure 3.1).

Per capita income is also closely linked to non-income poverty. Still, some countries (such as Viet Nam) have good levels of human development for their income, while other countries (such as Zimbabwe) are performing worse than others with similar levels of economic development (figure 3.2).

Thus the strong links between economic growth and poverty reductions are mediated by policy choices and structural factors. Several countries with economic growth of more than 4% a year since 1990 have not advanced much in some non-income dimensions of poverty (the

Dominican Republic, Mozambique).[1] So while economic growth may provide resources to improve a variety of outcomes, policy-makers need to focus public policies and investments on non-economic outcomes even as they focus on growth. That is why the Millennium Development Compact advocates using public policies to reduce various dimensions of non-income poverty.

FROM HUMAN DEVELOPMENT TO ECONOMIC GROWTH—AND BACK

Good education and health have intrinsic value for people's well-being. And the two are closely linked: education helps improve health, and good health contributes to better education. Moreover, education contributes to economic growth and raises poor people's incomes. Improvements in health also generate significant economic returns.[2]

Consider the average growth in per capita incomes in several dozen developing countries between 1965 and 1995, grouped by their incomes and infant mortality rates in 1965. (Infant mortality is a general proxy for overall disease levels.) In countries starting with per capita incomes below $750 (in constant 1990 dollars adjusted for purchasing power parity) and infant mortality

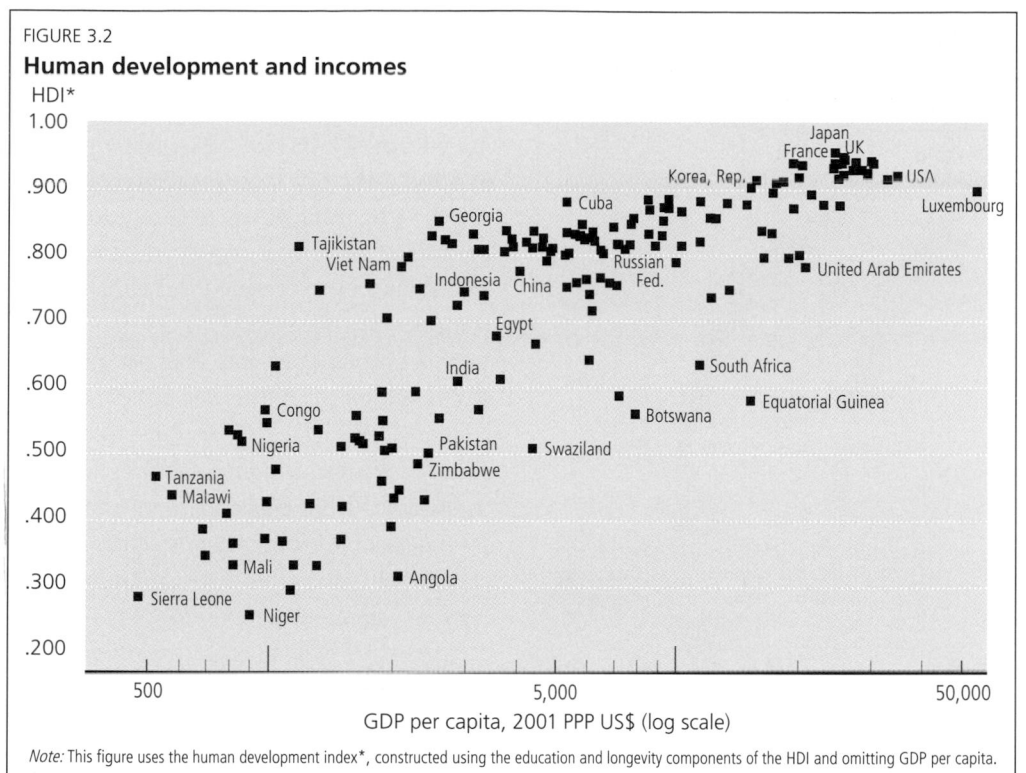

FIGURE 3.2
Human development and incomes

HDI*

Note: This figure uses the human development index*, constructed using the education and longevity components of the HDI and omitting GDP per capita.
Source: Human Development Report Office calculations based on World Bank 2003i.

When poor people have political power protected by civil and political rights, they can be more effective in pressing for policies that create social opportunities

rates above 150 per 1,000 live births, incomes grew by an average of 0.1% a year—while those with rates between 100 and 150 grew by an average of 1.0% a year and those with rates below 100 grew by an average of 3.7% a year.

In countries with initial incomes of $750–1,500, those with infant mortality rates above 150 experienced negative growth averaging –0.7% a year, while those with rates between 100 and 150 averaged 1.1% annual growth and those with rates below 100 averaged 3.4% annual growth.[3] Thus, even after accounting for initial incomes, countries with better health conditions were systematically more successful in achieving higher growth. Moreover, economic growth provides more resources to invest in education and health—and as noted, those investments contribute to higher growth.

This two-way link between human development and economic growth implies virtuous circles—with good human development promoting economic growth, which in turn advances human development (figure 3.3). But it also implies vicious circles—in which poor human development contributes to economic decline, leading to further deterioration in human development. For many countries—particular the top priority ones—achieving the Millennium

Development Goals will require breaking out of vicious circles (or poverty traps, to use a closely related concept) and entering virtuous circles.

The synergies among various aspects of human development are also important: improving health and education requires related interventions in schooling, family planning, health care, nutrition and water and sanitation. For instance, controlling diarrhoea and measles not only improves health, it also reduces malnutrition. Malnutrition severely undermines a person's capacity to learn and grow, and so has important implications for education and the development of a productive workforce. But control of diarrhoea is affected by improved water and sanitation—as well as by hygienic behaviour fostered by education.

Underlying many of these synergies are agency and equity. When poor people have political power protected by civil and political rights, they can be more effective in pressing for policies that create social and economic opportunities.[4] Such power is especially important for women, as well as for ethnic and racial groups that face discrimination. Promoting gender equity and women's capabilities is crucial to advancing economic development and to achieving the Goals (see chapter 4).[5]

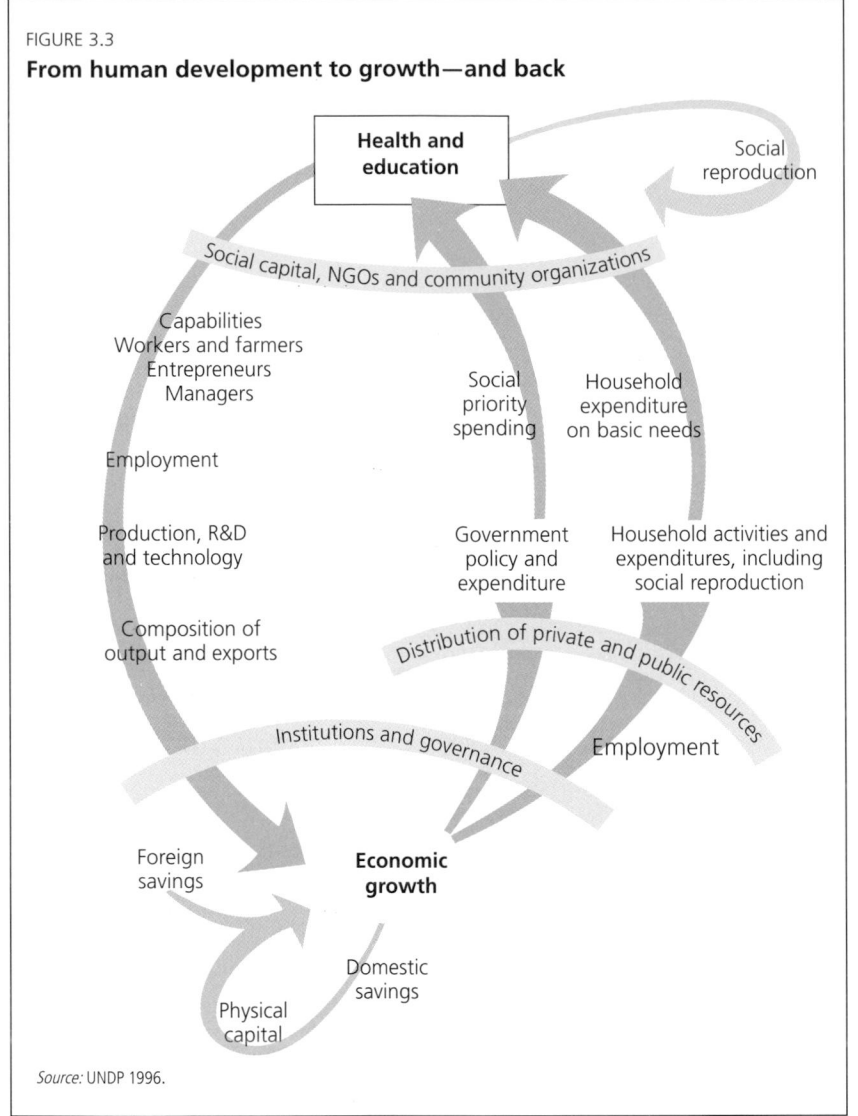

FIGURE 3.3

From human development to growth—and back

Health and education

Social reproduction

Social capital, NGOs and community organizations

Capabilities
Workers and farmers
Entrepreneurs
Managers

Employment

Production, R&D
and technology

Composition of
output and exports

Social priority spending

Household expenditure on basic needs

Government policy and expenditure

Household activities and expenditures, including social reproduction

Distribution of private and public resources

Institutions and governance

Employment

Foreign savings

Economic growth

Physical capital

Domestic savings

Source: UNDP 1996.

To get the most from the complementarities among basic social services, universal primary education should be an early and essential focus, particularly for girls—along with heavy investments in health, family planning and water and sanitation.[6] Most of these investments are not automatic side effects of economic growth: they require major efforts by the public sector.

RECENT PATTERNS—AND PROBLEMS—OF GLOBAL ECONOMIC GROWTH

Of the world's 128 countries with at least 1 million people in 1990 and with sufficient data, 76 saw per capita incomes grow in 1980–98—but 52 saw them shrink (see feature 3.1, table 1). Countries with large populations tended to grow, so when economic trends are measured by num-

bers of people, the outcomes appear much better. More than 4 billion people live in countries that experienced real per capita income growth of more than 1.4% in 1980–98—including China and India, the two most populous countries.[7] This 1.4% figure provides a rough estimate of the per capita growth rate required to achieve the Millennium Development Goal of halving income poverty (see box 3.1).

But economic advance does not guarantee that developing countries will achieve the Millennium Development Goals. Growth could be skewed towards higher-income households, or its fiscal dividends might not be invested in the poorest people. Still, many developing countries are amassing resources to invest in achieving the Goals.

About 1.5 billion people live in developing countries that saw per capita incomes grow by less than 0.7% a year in 1980–98, including many of the poorest countries.[8] If these countries continue to stagnate, they will not have the resources required to achieve the Goals. Finding ways to achieve the Goals, especially in top priority countries that combine widespread poverty with little or no economic growth (see chapter 2), requires understanding why such countries are experiencing little or no growth while so many others are growing rapidly.

Success—or failure—in economic growth is closely linked to how an economy is integrated with global markets. Some forms of globalization help produce economic growth, but some do not. Success or failure is related less to a country's initial income than to the structure of its exports. Excluding transition and fuel-exporting countries, middle-income countries achieved average annual growth of 1.3% in 1980–98, while low-income countries averaged –0.1%.[9] But many low-income countries, including China and India, did extremely well.

Most of the low-income success stories concentrated on manufactured exports (see feature 3.1). Among developing countries with sufficient data on trade and economic growth for 1980–98, 24 exported primarily manufactured goods and 61 exported mainly primary commodities (other than oil) in 1995.[10] Only one of the manufacturing exporters failed to achieve

Bangladesh—large and inland, with access to the coast

Since Bangladesh's birth in 1971, it has evolved into a democracy, achieving major reductions in income and non-income poverty. Income poverty dropped from 48% in 1989 to 34% in 2000. Basic social policies—health, education, reproductive health services, family planning—helped lower population growth and shrink the labour force. Moreover, most of the population is becoming literate. The positive changes unleashed by an export drive reinforced the need for better-educated people.

Growth in manufacturing was a major source of this success. In addition, government agencies have supported the private sector through investments in infrastructure and skills, crucial for launching and sustaining the export drive. The government has also maintained the stability vital for pro-poor growth policies. As a result of these pol-

icy initiatives, Bangladesh's labour-intensive garments exports jumped from $867 million in 1991 to $4.6 billion in 2002 (Bangladesh Garment Manufacturers and Exporters Association 2003).

But though Bangladesh has achieved impressive success in growing out of deep poverty and advancing maternal and children's health over the past 30 years, its experiences may not be universally replicable. The reason: Bangladesh is a large economy, with a population of 133 million people.

Moreover, even with its successes Bangladesh is still far from reaching several of the Millennium Development Goals—including those for hunger and sanitation. So the central recommendation of the Millennium Development Compact still applies: a multipronged approach is required to achieve the Goals across sectors.

Source: World Bank 2003i; Bangladesh Garment Manufacturers and Exporters Association 2003.

economic growth during this period, compared with 32 of the primary commodity exporters.

By recognizing the links between economic growth and economic structure, it is possible to focus on the problems facing the poorest countries. For example, why did China become a manufacturing exporter but not Mali? Was it solely economic policies, or did structural conditions also play a role? And if structural conditions played a role, how can Mali's underlying structures be improved so that it can become a successful manufacturing exporter?

Becoming internationally competitive in products beyond traditional primary commodities is not easy. Returns on manufacturing investments in Mali are not very high, and not just because of economic policies. The country is landlocked and suffers from high levels of malaria, tuberculosis, HIV/AIDS and other diseases. Fragile soils and erratic rainfall over many decades have resulted in low food productivity. Because of few energy resources, fossil fuels must be imported. Finally, Mali's small population means that its domestic market is tiny. Investors consider the country's education and skill levels too low to justify the costs imposed by landlockedness, poor health, low nutrition, a tiny domestic market and related barriers. In short, Mali does not meet the thresholds required to attract many foreign or domestic investors outside traditional sectors.

Thus achieving the Millennium Development Goals in Mali—and many other countries in similar circumstances—will require special investments in a wide range of sectors. Better health, education, water, sanitation, roads, ports and power are needed to reach the thresholds required for private, market-based investments (box 3.2 illustrates the success in Bangladesh). Among other things, Mali could become a successful garment exporter, tourist destination and processor of tropical agricultural products. But such activities will take off only after health, education and other key thresholds are reached. Because the country is much too poor to make these investments on its own, partner countries must provide the financing for economic takeoff.

STRUCTURAL CHALLENGES OF UNFAVOURABLE GEOGRAPHY, SMALL MARKETS AND HIGH TRADING COSTS

To understand why some countries face higher hurdles in reaching thresholds for economic growth, first consider the structural implications of physical geography. For the reason Adam Smith explained more than two centuries ago, a country's ability to sustain the complex division of labour required for internationally competitive manufacturing depends on the extent of the market.

For the reason Adam Smith explained more than two centuries ago, a country's ability to sustain the complex division of labour required for internationally competitive manufacturing depends on the extent of the market

There are two ways for a country to have a large extent of the market. The first is through a large population: countries with small populations tend to have small domestic markets. (Here countries with small populations are defined as those with fewer than 40 million people in 1990.) The second is through low-cost trade with world markets, recognizing that trading costs are strongly influenced by geography. Countries next to major markets (for Mexico, the United States, and for Poland, Germany) or coastal countries with easy access to low-cost ocean shipping have advantages over inland countries far from major markets or ocean ports. (Here inland countries are those where more

than three-quarters of the population lives more than 100 kilometres from a coast.)

In 1980–98 developing countries with large populations, coastal locations or both achieved much higher economic growth than countries with small populations and inland locations. Large coastal countries grew in 3 of 4 cases, at an annual average of 3.2% per capita (see feature 3.1, table 2). Large inland countries grew in 10 of 10 cases, at an average of 2.5%. Small coastal countries grew in 15 of 17 cases, at an average of 1.9% (see feature 3.1). But only 24 of 53 small inland countries grew. Moreover, the group's average per capita growth rate was negative.

Though these data might seem skewed by Sub-Saharan Africa—home to more than 30 small inland countries—the same pattern holds elsewhere: Of the 50 non-African countries in

---

BOX 3.3

Challenges in the Andean region

The Andean countries include Bolivia, Colombia, Ecuador, Peru and Venezuela. Of these, Colombia, Ecuador, Bolivia and Peru share similar structural constraints and policy challenges. These countries have medium human development indicators, yet the region faces persistently high poverty and inequalities. Although average incomes vary greatly across these four countries—measured using purchasing power parity, 2001 per capita income was $2,424 in Bolivia, $3,202 in Ecuador, $4,799 in Peru and $6,248 in Colombia—more than a third of the population is still living on less than $2 a day. Venezuela, despite being the world's sixth largest oil producer, faces equally imposing challenges. Per capita GDP growth has averaged between –0.7% and –1.0% over the past two decades, and nearly a quarter of the population lives on less than 1$ a day.

Several structural features help explain the persistence of economic stagnation and poverty in the Andean countries.
• A first, well-known factor is the persistence of inequalities. Each country has a Gini coefficient above 0.5. These inequalities are particularly pronounced due to ethnic divisions. Any successful development policies for these countries must focus on the public provision of key social services in education, health and water and sanitation to expand opportunities for excluded groups.
• A more commonly overlooked structural factor contributing to these countries' development challenges is that each has a significant amount

of its population living at high inland altitudes. Thus their economies must surmount high transport costs to gain access to global markets. While Bolivia is the only landlocked country, half of Ecuador and Peru's citizens live more than 100 kilometres from the coast. About a quarter of Colombia's population lives inland as well.
• This lack of market access contributes to the countries' dependence on natural resources, and consequent exposure to major fluctuations in commodity prices. In Venezuela oil accounts for more than 80% of exports. More than half of Ecuador's exports are oil (30%) and bananas (21%), while less than a quarter are manufactures (23%). Bolivia is still largely dependent on gas and soy (45% of exports), with manufactures making up a small fraction (14%).
• Another challenge is posed by El Niño, a cyclical climate fluctuation of temperature and rainfall that has major implications for agricultural output. To overcome susceptibility to external fluctuations, these countries require active infrastructure policies, particularly for ports and roads, to provide access to global markets. They also need active industrial policies to help develop a diversified manufacturing base for exports.
• Finally, these countries face a structural constraint that reflects their persistent economic troubles: debt overhang. Bolivia, Ecuador and Peru have each had at least five Paris Club debt reschedulings (with public creditor countries) over the past 20 years. These debt constraints have made it difficult to make domestic invest-

ments that would increase human capabilities and stimulate economic growth.

In Venezuela a lack of export diversification and falling productivity have contributed to economic stagnation. In recent years political unrest, rising inequality and poor economic planning have added to these challenges.

Alongside these structural challenges, the region's social, economic and political instabilities have interacted with the production of coca leaf and cocaine, mainly for US and European markets. The drug industry has led to a proliferation of organized crime, corruption and other ills of public administration, leading to militarization of these societies and persistent threats to social peace and democracy.

Recent estimates based on historical trends indicate that of the five countries only Colombia appears to be on track to meet the poverty Goal, while the other four are expected to see increasing levels of poverty, largely as a consequence of increased inequality, economic slowdown, or both (UNDP, ECLAC and Instituto de Pesquisa Economica Aplicada 2002).

While this combination of challenges is significant, policies can overcome them. Roads and ports can be built. Governments can invest in excluded groups. Markets can be diversified. And debtor relationships can be renegotiated. What is crucial, as outlined in the Millennium Development Compact, is that all these challenges be addressed simultaneously, under a commitment to a compact between each country and its partners.

Source: World Bank 1998b, 2002h, 2002i; UNDP, ECLAC and Instituto de Pesquisa Economica Aplicada 2002.

the sample, 27 of 30 that are large, coastal or both experienced economic growth—while only 11 of 20 that are small and inland did so.

This sample shows that about half the world's people live in large inland countries that have experienced sustained growth, including China and India. Meanwhile, nearly 420 million people live in large coastal countries—with 341 million in robustly growing economies. (The other 77 million live in the Philippines.) Most of the 130 million people in small coastal countries live in growing economies. But almost 420 million people live in small inland economies that are not growing. Some of these countries are in the Andean region (box 3.3).

These numbers do not mean that everyone in growing economies is experiencing greater well-being. Structural constraints can apply within countries as well as between them, and other inequalities might be present. China and India still have large pockets of persistent poverty that require the attention of domestic policies (box 3.4).

Nor do these numbers reflect a high standard of growth, because a country is considered to be growing even if it averaged just 0.1% annual growth in 1980–98. But the numbers highlight the type of countries—small inland economies—facing the greatest challenges in achieving the Goals, requiring the most support from the international community and meriting

---

BOX 3.4

China and India—impressive growth, important differences

China and India, together containing a third of the world's population, have enjoyed tremendous economic growth over the past decade. Their successes in advancing average well-being imply major improvements for a large portion of humanity. But their experiences also point to the importance of looking beyond national averages to understanding differences within countries.

Though both countries have achieved rapid, sustained economic growth, their rates of progress have been quite different. China has enjoyed the fastest sustained economic advance in human history, averaging real per capita growth of 8% a year over the past decade. Its per capita income is now $3,976 in purchasing power parity (PPP) terms. Meanwhile, real per capita income in India grew at a robust though more modest average rate of 4.4%, reaching $2,358 in 2001. Reflecting their successful economic growth, both countries have seen significant reductions in poverty. According to World Bank estimates based on consumption surveys, the proportion of people living on less than $1 a day declined in China from 33% in 1990 to 16% in 2000, and in India from 42% in 1993/94 to 35% in 2001 (World Bank 2003i). While highly contested because of differences in methodology, survey design, and samples, these calculations nonetheless provide a rough indication of poverty trends in these countries.

Market reforms
China's exceptional growth is partly explained by its market-based reforms that started in 1978, well before India's similar reforms began in 1991.

These reforms have enabled China to integrate with the global economy at a phenomenal pace. Today it is the largest recipient of foreign direct investment among developing countries, with annual investment rising from almost zero in 1978 to about $52 billion in 2002 (nearly 5% of GDP). Foreign direct investment in India has also increased significantly, though at much lower levels, growing from $129 million in 1991 to $4 billion in 2002 (less than 1% of GDP).

Robust export growth has contributed to the economic performance of both countries, with a growing dominance of manufactured exports—though again, China has had much more success in this realm. Its exports reached $320 billion in 2001, compared with $35 billion for India. Manufactured exports accounted for 53% of China's total exports in 1981 and for 90% in 2001; in India that share rose from 60% to 77%. China has had particular success in moving from labour-intensive to technology-intensive exports: telecommunications equipment and computers now account for a quarter of its exports.

Social investments
Social investments are required for sustained economic growth. In China public spending on education is 2.3% of GDP while that on health is 2.1% of GDP. The outcomes for human development are clear. Literacy stands at 84%, infant mortality rates at 32 per 1,000 live births and under five mortality rates at 40 per 1,000 live births.

India, in contrast, has traditionally had lower spending levels. Health spending stands at 1.3% of GDP (central and state governments combined).

Spending on education has increased significantly, from 0.8% of GDP in 1950 to 3.2% today, though it still falls short of the government target of 6% of GDP. Human development indicators for India remain much lower than for China. Literacy stands at 65%, infant mortality at 68 per 1,000 live births, and under-five mortality rates at 96 per 1,000 live births.

Regional variations and other challenges
It would be misleading to talk solely in terms of national averages for two countries so large in population and area. As noted in chapter 2, in China the highest economic growth has occurred in the coastal provinces—while the geographically isolated north-western provinces have experienced much lower growth. India also harbours stark regional variations. In 1992–97 per capita economic growth ranged from –0.2% in Bihar to 7.8% in Gujarat. Similar variations appear in other human development indicators, such as those for education and health.

Both countries still face challenges, such as the spread of HIV/AIDS and other sexually transmitted diseases accompanying increased labour migration and international trade. And both face the challenge of fostering a knowledge-based economy to maintain consistently high economic growth as average skill levels increase. Both also need to focus on spreading the gains of growth to regions, communities and ethnic groups that have seen so little benefit from the new prosperity. Inclusive public policies should focus on investments in health, education and infrastructure for future development.

Source: Woo and Bao 2003; World Bank 2003e, 2003f, 2003i and calculations by Shaohua Chen of the World Bank and Angus Deaton of Princeton University; India 2003; China 2003; Bajpay 2003; UNCTAD 2002b.

the greatest attention under the Millennium Development Compact. This is not to say that some large countries with significant coastal regions, such as Pakistan, should be ignored. They too face major challenges in reducing poverty and advancing human development.

Some additional points on geography:
- Geography can be a boon as well as a bane. It is no coincidence that all the East Asian success stories of the late 20th century have access to coasts and major shipping routes—thus access to large markets can help counter the effects of small populations.
- Natural resources—another manifestation of geography—can provide a major boost if their financial dividends are properly managed. The best example is Botswana's diamond discoveries, where revenues invested in education and health helped a fairly tiny, landlocked country quadruple its per capita income in 25 years (though these advances have recently been hindered by a heavy HIV/AIDS burden).
- A country's market size and coastal orientation are not the only geophysical issues requiring urgent attention. Some regions are vulnerable to climatic shocks (such as El Niño) while others are not. Some regions are vulnerable to natural disasters (earthquakes, tropical storms, volcanic eruptions, floods) while others are not. Some regions are prone to environmentally based diseases (malaria) while others are not. Some regions are suffering from extreme water stress while others are not. All these geophysical constraints can weigh heavily on an economy—and require policy attention.

BUT GEOGRAPHY IS NOT DESTINY

While geography can pose challenges, it does not define a country's destiny. The focus on geography here highlights the need for policies tailored to each country's challenges. With proper policies even the difficulties of small markets—or poor soils, or climatic fluctuations—can be overcome. In geographically isolated countries better roads and communications can trounce many of the disadvantages of distance.

In countries with small populations, integration with neighbouring countries can provide the requisite scale for markets. Moreover, rich

countries can open their markets to exports from small developing countries. That is how the small or landlocked countries of Western Europe have succeeded: through the close economic integration of the European Union.

If an economy is burdened by poor soils, soil nutrient supplements are needed (through fertilizers, leguminous trees, better crop rotation and other means). And tropical diseases can be controlled through interventions such as insecticide-impregnated bednets to fight malaria. The problem is not that geophysical obstacles are insurmountable. The problem is that they are too often overlooked—and addressing them costs money.

GOOD POLICIES, ECONOMIC GROWTH AND HUMAN DEVELOPMENT

A first step in economic progress often involves increasing the productivity of poor small farmers. This can happen when market forces yield agricultural advances or governments invest in research and development. Poor farming households often produce food for their own subsistence, with little left over for the market. So, increasing agricultural productivity—say, through improved seed varieties and fertilizers, as during the green revolution of the 1970s—raises household income and nutrition. It also enables poor households to invest more in their children's health and education. Many of these children end up migrating to urban areas, particularly since food needs can now be met by fewer (but more productive) farmers.

In manufacturing, increased productivity comes from a stable macroeconomic environment, sound public institutions and reliable physical infrastructure. Growing urban populations also support larger and more productive manufacturing. In addition, manufacturing productivity is often given a major push by higher-technology imports. In East Asia manufacturing productivity increased when domestic companies became suppliers to multinational corporations, using technologies and products specified by those corporations. Common early-stage manufacturing exports include toys, apparel, footwear, electronics components, automotive components and the like.

The focus on geography here highlights the need for policies tailored to each country's challenges. With proper policies even the difficulties of small markets—or poor soils, or climatic fluctuations—can be overcome

Rising incomes lead households to spend more on health and education. They invest in safer water, or send their children to school or buy drugs when illness hits. They also improve their nutrition. People can afford safer homes—buying screens for windows to keep out disease-bearing mosquitoes or stoves fuelled by propane rather than highly polluting wood. Household investments in health and education are often accompanied by public investments in social services.

As incomes rise, so do national saving rates (the proportion of national income remaining after household and government consumption). At very low incomes, households are too poor to save: they must spend all they have simply to survive. Most spending goes for food, shelter and clothing—and when an emergency hits, health care. As incomes rise above the survival threshold, households can afford to save money for their future well-being and economic security. National savings give another boost to economic growth because it enables investments by private business and government. Such investments lead to rising physical capital and infrastructure stocks per person.

Another vital boost to economic growth comes when fertility rates fall in response to public policies and rising household incomes. Poor households with many children are rarely able to invest enough in each child's health and education. Perhaps only the eldest son has the chance to attend school for more than a few years. But when fertility drops, even poor families can provide a good education for, say, two children instead of six—and can invest more equally in sons and daughters. By this stage an economy is on a robust, self-sustaining growth path. No longer mired in subsistence agriculture, the dynamics for persistent economic growth are under way.

At a later stage another important trend emerges. As education levels rise and domestic companies produce more sophisticated goods and services (often supported by investments, know-how and technology transferred from foreign corporations), domestic scientists and engineers begin developing new products. Private spending on research and development increases, as do government outlays. In addition, local universities make critical contributions to economic growth by training scientists and engineers and by being home to a growing amount of research and development.

WEAK POLICIES, ECONOMIC DECLINE AND HUMAN POVERTY

So what happens—or does not—in countries that fail to achieve this kind of economic take-off? As before, such economies start out poor and primarily rural, with limited urban manufacturing. But unlike in growing economies, agricultural productivity—and so the rural economy—is stagnant or falling because of depleted soils and climatic shocks. As populations have grown, so has deforestation and water scarcity. No new technologies, public or private, have been introduced to boost agriculture. Farmers cannot even get their products to markets because governments cannot afford to build or maintain roads.

In these countries children in farming households work from very young ages—for example, often walking several kilometres a day to fetch water and firewood. Even if schooling is available, children have no time or energy to attend. They also have no access to the primary health care required to prevent or treat malaria, worm parasites and other ailments because their families cannot afford doctors and governments cannot afford doctor salaries or needed medicines. Many children—perhaps 15 of every 100—die before age five. As a result parents have many children.

Making matters worse, productivity is low in urban areas. Moreover, manufacturing activities may be cut off from world markets because a country is landlocked and remote from ports or because its main export is subject to trade barriers around the world. Perhaps the road from the capital to the nearest port passes through another country hostile to the economic interests of its landlocked neighbour. Or maybe the coastal economy is poorly managed, so that even if a landlocked country builds a well-functioning trunk road to the border of the transit country, the coastal economy will not build, maintain and police the road all the way to the port.

As noted, small populations add to the burdens of many poor landlocked economies. As

As education levels rise and domestic companies produce more sophisticated goods and services, domestic scientists and engineers begin developing new products

a result international investors have little interest in establishing local production operations to serve local markets. If they sell anything, they will do so through exports to the country rather than local production.

Under such circumstances, even with the most efficient government policies, local manufacturing is unlikely to trigger self-sustaining growth. Local manufacturers may provide local markets with some basic goods—soap, processed foods, wooden furniture, bricks and other building materials, a few chemicals—but little else. Technology is basic, and firms are not competitive enough to sell to world markets, especially with the high costs of transporting goods to ports (and the prohibitive costs of air transport for basic items). With no engine of growth in manufacturing, such economies are unlikely to start growing.

Even if the public sector is making the most of its resources, such countries face numerous bottlenecks to growth:

- Private saving rates are low—if not negative.
- Governments use most or all of their revenues to pay public employees (army, police, teachers, public administration), leaving little or nothing to invest in health, education and infrastructure.
- Agricultural productivity is low partly because there are few inputs from domestic manufacturing, such as fertilizers. And severe transport problems make importing fertilizers prohibitively expensive for most small farmers.
- Fertility rates remain high, reflecting low education for girls and women, large rural populations, high child mortality rates and lack of family planning and reproductive health services.
- Maternal health suffers because women have little access to education or health care, with negative implications for their children. Most people stay in rural areas because they are needed to grow food for swelling national populations—resulting in high food costs for urban residents.
- With rising rural populations, farmland per agricultural worker falls, reducing output per farmer. That, combined with lack of health care, worsens public health, contributes to the spread of infectious disease (partly prompted by weakened immune system due to malnutrition) and reduces labour productivity.

In short, such countries are trapped in poverty. They have insufficient resources to overcome structural challenges and fall short of critical thresholds—in health, education and infrastructure—to achieve self-sustaining economic growth. Many of the top priority countries identified in chapter 2 fall into this category. Though good economic governance and sound economic policies are needed to escape poverty traps, they are not enough. In most cases enormous structural constraints must also be overcome to reach the thresholds for sustained growth.

Note the distinction between structural constraints to the thresholds for sustained growth and economic governance constraints to those thresholds. Corrupt or incompetent governments wreak havoc on many countries, preventing the investments needed for economic development. This burden can be due to kleptocratic politicians, weak legal institutions, corrupt bureaucrats or political or armed conflicts (box 3.5).

ESCAPING POVERTY TRAPS

So what can be done for countries stuck in poverty traps? This Report's Millennium Development Compact, building on a baseline of sound macroeconomic management, aims to bolster human development by combining six clusters of policies:

- *Investments in the social sectors.* Major progress can be made in health, nutrition, education and water and sanitation in low-income settings when additional donor resources are available, because the needed interventions are well known and long proven, and the main investments can be made by the public sector backed by donor financing. Big gains in health and education are required before per capita incomes can be raised substantially.
- *Investments to raise agricultural productivity.* Agricultural productivity can be raised by introducing better technology (improved seeds, tillage and crop rotation systems, soil nutrient management, pest management) and improving rural infrastructure (irrigation projects, storage and transport facilities, roads connecting villages to larger markets). In addition, security in land holding can protect farmer rights and encourage them to invest in land improvements that raise long-term productivity.

Though good economic governance and sound economic policies are needed to escape poverty traps, they are not enough

BOX 3.5

The Millennium Development Goals and conflict countries

Any serious attempt to launch a successful campaign to achieve the Millennium Development Goals must pay special attention to conflict-affected areas. Nearly 60 countries experienced violent conflict during the 1990s. Beyond its direct cost in human lives, conflict can undermine economies, destabilize governments, damage infrastructure, disrupt social service delivery and provoke mass movements of people. More than 14 million people face hunger due to present or recent conflicts. HIV/AIDS and other infectious disease often spread ferociously in conflict-affected areas. In some militaries of Sub-Saharan Africa more than half the soldiers are HIV-positive. Maternal and infant mortality often increases substantially in war zones, with health services destroyed and childbirths during flight.

Analysis of the 25 countries hit hardest by conflict between 1960 and 1995 reveals substantial variation in the human and economic costs of war. Ethiopia, Liberia and Uganda, for example, had significantly higher infant mortality rates during conflict than in peacetime. Yet, El Salvador, Guatemala and Mozambique experienced rates below their regional average even during war. The findings suggest that policies can be adopted—even during conflicts—to reduce the human and economic costs.

Reducing the human costs of conflict

Broad policy prescriptions are difficult given the heterogeneity and complexity of war-affected economies. War aims may include depriving certain regions of essential services (Sudan). Conflict may also severely weaken governments, leaving them unable to provide services to any group (Afghanistan, Sierra Leone, Somalia). Indeed, the collapse of government without the emergence of substitute structures has led to particularly adverse human and economic war outcomes (Uganda). Countries able to reduce the human and economic costs of war, and in some cases make progress towards development targets, did so only when all households—on both sides of the battle lines—had access to food, basic health care and primary education (Guatemala, Mozambique, Sri Lanka).

Adequate public funding of essential services can often be maintained even with the rising military spending that accompanies war. Mozambique, Nicaragua and Sudan markedly increased per capita social spending during their conflicts. But even if cuts in social spending are necessary, they should not automatically translate into slashing basic social service budgets. Even in peacetime these services account for only a fraction of social spending.

Social spending cutbacks are often compounded by depletions in human resources, as teachers and doctors flee conflict-affected regions. And the cuts are coupled with unpredictable breakdowns in delivery mechanisms. So, flexible approaches to service provision are essential using diverse actors, such as non-governmental organizations (NGOs) and quasi-governmental structures. Mozambique experimented with mobile clinics and classrooms when health and education buildings became war targets. In El Salvador both sides halted fighting on three different occasions to allow for child immunizations.

People in conflict-affected areas are particularly vulnerable to severe malnourishment, as food production declines and conflict disrupts normal relief efforts. Escalating food prices are often a key threat to food security. During their wartime periods many rich countries subsidized and rationed food to prevent price escalation. Nicaragua also used these mechanisms to improve the nutritional status of people in war-affected regions.

In urban areas such efforts are relatively easy to administer. Rural communities, however, may benefit more from agricultural support in the form of supplies, loans and paid work. Food delivery through schools and clinics can also improve access without encouraging movement into camps. Such delivery can help promote school attendance and reduce incentives for children to become soldiers or thieves.

Reducing the economic costs of conflict

The economic costs of conflict affect human well-being in numerous ways, from rising food costs to declining employment opportunities. On average, countries hardest hit by conflict between 1960 and 1995 experienced significant declines in economic growth, reductions in export production, falling consumption levels and dminished government revenue (as a percentage of GDP) compared with non-war countries. Most countries also faced rising budget deficits and spiraling debts, as significant increases in military expenditure were met with substantial declines in government revenue. But some countries were able to defy the average, even showing impressive economic performance during wartime. Sri Lanka, for example, sustained 2% economic growth during the same

decade as it experienced conflict. Countries experiencing ongoing conflicts should focus on (at least) four key policy areas:

- *Maintaining fiscal revenue* in wartime economies is difficult because sharply declining tax revenue often meets escalating military spending. Institutional structures used in revenue collection need to be maintained throughout the war. Tax rates prevailing before the conflict should also be maintained, in addition to levying other taxes such as on luxury items and war-related goods. Governments could also issue compulsory savings bonds as well as sell food aid to tap new revenue sources. Indeed, Nigeria, Sri Lanka and Sudan succeeded in sustaining revenue levels (as a percentage of GDP) during their conflicts.
- *Preventing runaway inflation* is necessary because escalating inflation creates uncertainty and promotes private sector speculation. Such inflation also makes public budgetary and financial control extremely difficult. Price liberalization during conflicts, given low supply elasticities, is a main contributor to escalating inflation. In Mozambique, for example, such liberalization led to huge increases in the price of rationed goods, such as maize, cooking oil and sugar.
- *Securing foreign exchange resources* is essential because declining foreign exchange resources contribute to reductions in output. Some Sub-Saharan countries have experienced devastating famines due to a mix of conflicts, output reductions and droughts. To sustain output, national and international policies should aim to finance productive imports by keeping open and assisting export markets and providing aid and loan support for such imports. National policies should also ensure that available foreign exchange resources are used to purchase essential goods, such as medicines and agricultural inputs. Import controls, such as quotas and tariffs, may be used to ensure this occurs.
- *Maintaining a competitive real exchange rate.* Conflict-affected countries face enormous difficulties in managing their balance of payments under conditions of uncertain export income and aid commitments. Policies must maintain a competitive real exchange rate to avoid disincentives to exports. Countries should also secure control over nominal exchange rates given the inevitable macroeconomic disequilibria of war. In Angola, for example, inflation rose from 160% to 246% between 1991 and 1992, hitting poor Angolans hardest.

Source: Stewart 2003; Fitzgerald 2001.

- *Investments in infrastructure.* Reaching an adequate threshold of roads, power, ports and communications to support economic diversification into non-traditional areas will be relatively easy in some areas, such as coastal port cities. But it will be much harder elsewhere, such as landlocked or mountainous countries suffering from high transport costs.

- *Industrial development policies to bolster private activities.* Successful development of non-traditional activities often requires special industrial policies, including selective, temporary and well designed tax holidays, export processing zones, special economic zones, science parks, investment tax credits, promotion of science and technology, targeted research and development funding and public grants of infrastructure and land.

- *A broad emphasis on equity throughout society.* Political institutions must allow poor people—especially women—to participate in decisions that affect their lives and protect them from arbitrary and unaccountable actions by governments and other forces. Thus strategies for achieving the Millennium Development Goals must ensure women's rights to education, reproductive health services, property ownership, labour force participation and secure land tenure. Strategies must also focus on eliminating all other forms of discrimination, including by race, ethnicity or regional origin.

- *An emphasis on environmental sustainability and urban management.* Many of the world's poorest places are in regions of enormous climatic variability and vulnerability, requiring sound ecological management. These include tropical and subtropical regions vulnerable to El Niño-driven fluctuations in rainfall and temperature—regions also experiencing the pressures of long-term climate change. Another ecological challenge is managing rapid urbanization through careful planning and large public investments.

These policies can trigger a takeoff out of poverty. Countries can start to supply labour-intensive goods (apparel, electronics components) for external markets. Tourism and information-based services (such as data transcription and back-office computer operations) may lead to a comparable boom in service exports. This growth in non-traditional exports can drive the cumulative processes of growth described earlier, including rising saving rates, rising government revenues, rising urbanization, falling fertility and rising agricultural productivity (partly because of more inputs from manufacturing).

To achieve long-term growth, all these policies need to be addressed simultaneously, regardless of a country's stage of economic development. But the poorest countries cannot afford these investments on their own. For them the Millennium Development Compact stresses that donors should help cover the costs—assuming that low-income countries hold up their side of the deal by promoting good economic governance, protecting human rights and pursuing transparent and efficient policies (box 3.6).

The key idea here is that poor countries in stagnation or decline can be pushed above the basic thresholds and establish self-sustaining growth if they receive enough aid to invest in health, education and basic infrastructure. External financing is not needed to fund the entire growth process—merely to support the takeoff. In most cases that takeoff can be achieved within a generation.

GROWTH POLICIES THAT BENEFIT POOR PEOPLE

This chapter has emphasized the need for comprehensive, multisectoral strategies to achieve economic growth, including policies to promote manufacturing exports. Considering the different structural barriers facing countries, it is clear that each needs to pursue policies that make sense for its conditions (see the special contribution by Nobel Laureate Joseph Stiglitz). This section addresses two related issues aimed at ensuring that growth benefits poor people. First, what policies can promote the growth of labour-intensive (rather than capital-intensive) manufacturing exports? Such products can directly expand employment opportunities and increase real wages for poor people. Second, what policies can also ensure higher incomes for poor people not directly employed by manufacturing? Such policies are needed in low-income countries as well as in middle-income countries with persistent pockets of poverty.

What's needed to make the Millennium Development Compact work in Uganda

Uganda has made excellent economic progress over the past decade. But despite average real growth of 3.7% in 1992–97, Uganda still has a per capita income of just $330.

Uganda is small and landlocked, with agriculture employing 80% of the workforce. In 1997 the poverty headcount was 44% of the population, infant mortality was 83 per 1,000 live births (in 2000), maternal mortality was 505 per 100,000 and under-five mortality was 161 per 1,000.

In 1997 Uganda pioneered a poverty-oriented development strategy by designing a Poverty Eradication Action Plan, which in 2000 was revised as the country's Poverty Reduction Strategy Paper in agreement with the World Bank and International Monetary Fund. In the paper Uganda set four goals:

• Reducing absolute poverty to 10% of the population by 2017.
• Raising the educational achievements of Ugandans.
• Improving people's health.
• Giving voice to poor people.

To achieve these goals, the government formulated policies based on four pillars that overlap in many ways with the policy dimensions in the Millennium Development Compact. These pillars include creating a framework for economic growth and transformation through macroeconomic stability; focusing on strategic exports; and promoting the private sector. For this Uganda will have to attract much more foreign direct investment and diversify its economy—both difficult given the country's landlocked status and high transport costs.

The fourth pillar includes promoting good economic governance and security, actions that directly increase poor people's ability to raise their incomes (through a plan to modernize agriculture) and that directly improve their quality of life (through better health, education and safe water and sanitation). But the key question is whether Uganda will be able to make the investments to implement these strategies and achieve these goals.

Budget planning is being aligned with the Poverty Reduction Strategy Paper, and social

spending will draw on funds freed up by debt relief. According to a 2002 estimate by the Economic Policy Research Center, implementing the paper's plans would generate a resource gap of $417 million in 2003, or 6.4% of GDP—and this is based on a fairly low estimate of health care costs. Indeed, if the costs of achieving all the Millennium Development Goals were included—such as providing safe water and sanitation, alleviating hunger and providing infrastructure—this gap would be even wider.

These projections are of great value to the international community because they provide an indication of the increased spending required at the national level. Spending on HIV/AIDS needs to increase by 83%, on education by 109% and on health by 212%. So despite the best commitment and planning at the country level, the Millennium Development Goals will remain unattainable unless supported by much larger financial flows from the international community—which constitute a major part of the role of rich countries in the Millennium Development Compact.

Source: Uganda 2002; IMF 2002a; World Bank 2000b.

POLICIES TO PROMOTE LABOUR-INTENSIVE MANUFACTURING

Over the past 20 years too much development thinking and practice have confused market-based economic growth with laissez faire. Even when economic growth is based on private ownership and market forces, government policies must promote efficient and competitive national industries. Supporting the creation of manufacturing exports, for example, can be half the battle of achieving sustained growth—especially if a country's economic history has involved exporting primary commodities.

Similarly, policies can be central to promoting labour-intensive rather than capital-intensive activities, increasing employment and, in the long run, raising productivity and lifting real wages. Policies have long played a key role in spurring industrial development, as in East Asia's "tiger" economies since the 1960s. But this depended on a number of conditions—particularly disciplined institutional capacity within governments.

Pro-poor industrial development policies should follow a few general guidelines. First, as this chapter has shown, manufacturing

exports are crucial to long-term growth. To that end, macroeconomic and trade policies are key to diversifying economic structures. Overvalued exchange rates that hurt exporters can severely limit possibilities for employment growth. The transition to export orientation is complex (and debated at length elsewhere). But especially for small economies, macroeconomic policies require an export orientation. In China and the Republic of Korea government protection to domestic markets coexisted with export incentives. Korea provided exporters with tax incentives and duty-free imports of inputs, which raised returns to capital invested in desired sectors.

Second, financing incentives are needed to get industries started in capital-scarce economies. A variety of policy instruments have been used: directed and subsidized credit, support to chosen subsectors, export subsidies, technology acquisition institutions and a host of other sector-specific interventions. Several South-East Asian countries have used export credits and fiscal incentives to raise returns to investments in exports. But as relative latecomers, foreign direct investment has typically played a larger role

Poverty, globalization and growth: perspectives on some of the statistical links

Several recent econometric studies have tried to show a systematic relationship between globalization and growth—and between growth and poverty reduction. The message of these studies is clear: open your economy, liberalize and you will grow, and as you grow, poverty will be reduced. This research is supposed to lay to rest the attacks on globalization and, though it shuns the words, breathe new life into long-discredited trickle-down economics, which held that "a rising tide lifts all boats".

Trickle-down economics became discredited for an obvious reason: it was not true. Sometimes growth helps poor people, but sometimes it does not. By some measures poverty increased in Latin America in the 1990s, even in many countries where there was growth. It was not just that well-off people gained disproportionately from growth: some of their gains may even have been at the expense of poor people.

Though there are a number of technical problems with these recent studies, the most telling problem is that they asked the wrong question: globalization and growth are endogenous, the result of particular policies. The debate is not about whether growth is good or bad, but whether certain policies—including policies that may lead to closer global integration—lead to growth; and whether those policies lead to the kind of growth that improves the welfare of poor people. A look at the most successful countries, in growth and poverty reduction, shows how misleading these studies are.

China and other East Asian countries have not followed the Washington consensus. They were slow to remove tariff barriers, and China still has not fully liberalized its capital account. Though the countries of East Asia "globalized", they used industrial and trade policies to promote exports and global technology transfers, against the advice of the international economic institutions. Perhaps most important, unlike the Washington consensus, policies promoting equity were an explicit part of their development strategies. So too for perhaps the most successful country in Latin America, Chile, which during its high-growth days of the early 1990s effectively imposed a tax on short-term capital inflows.

The policy issue is not "to globalize or not to globalize" or "to grow or not to grow". In some cases it is not even "to liberalize or not to liberalize". Instead the issues are: To liberalize short-term capital accounts—and if so, how? At what pace to liberalize trade, and what policies should accompany it? Are there pro-poor growth strategies that do more to reduce poverty as they promote growth? And are there growth strategies that increase poverty as they promote growth—strategies that should be shunned?

For instance, neither theory nor evidence supports the view that opening markets to short-term, speculative capital flows increases economic growth. But there is considerable evidence and theory that it increases economic instability, and that economic instability contributes to insecurity and poverty. So, such forms of capital market liberalization might in some ways increase "globalization". But they do not enhance growth—and even if growth increased slightly, this form of it might increase poverty, especially in countries without adequate social safety nets.

Similarly, trade liberalization is supposed to allow resources to move from low-productivity protected sectors to high-productivity export sectors. But what if export markets in areas of comparative advantage (such as agriculture) are effectively closed, or credit is not available (or available only at exorbitant interest rates) to create the new export-related jobs? Then workers simply move from low-productivity protected sector jobs to unemployment. Growth is not enhanced, and poverty is increased.

Even often-praised measures, such as tariffication, have proven to be double-edged swords, because they have exposed developing countries to additional risks that they are ill prepared to cope with. Again, whether tariffication leads to faster growth is not clear; that the increased variability increases poverty is far more evident.

There are policies that in the long run may enhance growth and reduce poverty, such as enhancing education opportunities for disadvantaged groups, which allows countries to tap into vast reservoirs of underused talent. But the returns to investments in preschool education today will not manifest themselves for two decades or more—not the kind of results that show up in typical econometric studies.

Hidden beneath the surface in these econometric studies of globalization is another subtext: because globalization has proven so good for growth and poverty reduction, critics of globalization must be wrong. But these cross-sectional studies cannot address the most fundamental criticisms of globalization as it has been practiced: that it is unfair and that its benefits have disproportionately gone to rich people. After the last round of trade negotiations, the Uruguay Round, a World Bank study showed that Sub-Saharan Africa was actually worse off. Asymmetric liberalization had global terms of trade effects. The globalization studies suggest that Africa has suffered because it has not globalized. That may be partly true. But it is also true that Africa has suffered from the way that globalization has been managed.

Thus these econometric studies on globalization, growth and poverty have been a misleading distraction, shifting the debate away from where it should be—on the appropriateness of particular policies for particular countries, on how globalization can be shaped (including the rules of the game) and on international economic institutions, to better promote growth and reduce poverty in the developing world. The antiglobalization movement has often been charged with being unthinking in simply asking whether globalization is good or bad. But the econometric studies, for all the seeming sophistication of their statistics, are equally guilty.

Joseph E. Stiglitz

Joseph E. Stiglitz
Nobel Laureate in Economics, 2002

in their export drives—and in China's—than was the case for the East Asian tigers.

Third, a competent, professional, reasonably independent public bureaucracy is needed to support such policies. Undue political interference has been damaging to state institutions, in some cases leading to state failure. The response should not be to abandon the state. No matter how difficult, reviving state institutions may be vital in removing economic governance constraints to growth (see feature 3.1).

Public sector employment policy is important here. The state cannot be an "employer of last resort". In East Asia fairly high public sector salaries, particularly for managers, attract and retain skilled civil servants. These technocratic groups are reasonably insulated from political pressures, which helps ensure clarity in decision-making and builds market confidence. Getting this right has been as important as any policy intervention, because the "right" policies can have perverse effects when there is institutional incoherence.

Fourth, the public sector must support and build the private sector rather than compete with it. Public bodies can support private capacities in several ways. Japan, the Republic of Korea, Malaysia and Thailand established formal deliberation councils to reduce the information and transaction costs of private agents. A new form of deliberation council is being used for technology policy. In Costa Rica and Ireland technology foresight programmes and processes bring together government departments, the private sector, international organizations and non-governmental organizations to lower information and transaction costs—and to reach consensus on how to upgrade national technological capacities. These bodies can be particularly important for the development of export-oriented small and medium-size enterprises. Furthermore, efforts should be made to increase corporate social responsibility and transparency. In addition, international private businesses have an important role in encouraging local capital formation and local private sector development, fostering additional jobs in local labour markets. Finally, pro-poor growth can be achieved through more ambitious public-private partnerships, especially in the construction of basic infrastructure and the provision of services (such as electricity) in developing regions.

POLICIES OUTSIDE MANUFACTURING

The preceding industrial development policies can help develop an economy's engine of growth. But many (if not most) poor people work outside manufacturing—particularly at the early stages of development. Thus policies must address their needs as industrial development policies are pursued.

First, government needs an effective fiscal system to mobilize enough revenue to invest in poor people's basic needs. In the poorest countries this will require not only more domestic revenue, invested wisely, but also more donor assistance. An effective fiscal system does not imply high taxes. A more sensible course is to have rather low direct income tax rates—but to emphasize compliance and end abuse as well as politically motivated exemptions. A major revenue problem in many countries is that rich people simply do not pay direct taxes.

Second, countries with many farmers should invest in increasing agricultural productivity and diversifying cash crops for export markets. (Chapter 4 analyses agricultural productivity in greater detail.) Such efforts could include developing site-specific seeds and soil nutrient strategies to generate high yields under local conditions. Governments can also provide exporters with financial incentives and marketing assistance to diversify crops. They could also guarantee minimum prices for farmers in areas with fragile markets. Thailand did so when it moved from traditional crops to sophisticated crops for exports such as asparagus, which is not eaten domestically.

Third, policies must ensure poor people's access to economic assets. Without assets, poor people cannot participate in markets. They need land, finance and skills—and public action to acquire them. Investing in human development to expand social opportunities for all is one of the six policy clusters discussed in chapter 4. Here the focus is on land and finance.

Access to land. More than 500 million people, or roughly 100 million households in developing countries, lack ownership rights or owner-like rights to the land they farm. Most are tenant farmers, agricultural labourers or former collective farm workers. Also included are agricultural households with insecure tenancy rights, such as squatters or customary or traditional rights holders who do not hold formal rights to the land they occupy.

Lack of formal legal rights to land hinders these people's ability to generate income and earn livelihoods, undermining economic growth. Because land is their primary source of income and provides security and social status, formalizing their ownership rights through agrarian reform would serve several purposes:
• Creating transferable land rights with determinable market value makes land an intergenerational asset.

A major revenue problem in many countries is that rich people simply do not pay direct taxes

This chapter highlights the structural problems holding back economic growth in the top priority and high priority countries for achieving the Millennium Development Goals

- Smaller holdings are often more productive than larger ones, hectare for hectare—especially if they are owned and operated by families.[11]
- Landowners have an incentive and ability to make long-term capital investments that directly increase agricultural productivity.
- Access to land improves household nutrition—and increases non-farm incomes for some farming households.
- Strong legal ownership rights for women, often the food producers in a household, lead to more equitable income and welfare outcomes.
- Secure rights strengthen environmental management and increase community participation.

Even though land reforms have been politically contentious and difficult to implement—as many experiences of the 1970s and 1980s show—their strong link with equity has returned them to the political agenda in many countries such as Brazil and China.

For the benefits of ownership to reach the most people, such rights must be provided on a large scale—especially to the female members of farming households. In addition, reasonable compensation should be provided to private landowners whose land is being redistributed. Similarly, reforms should be set in the context of customary land tenure systems so that traditional landowners do not lose their rights. Potential beneficiaries should be included in the design of such reforms. Finally, accompanying regulations should ensure secure tenure and impose the right incentives so that land transfer is real, and not just in name.

Access to credit. Microfinance—both microcredit and microsavings—provides poor people with a way to procure and build up assets. It encourages borrowers to invest in productive activities, and savers to amass assets and earn interest. Borrowers can also use the funds to smooth income flows and plan economic decisions over longer periods. The number of poor people with access to microcredit schemes rose from 7.6 million in 1997 to 26.8 million in 2001—21 million of them women, enabling them to control assets, make economic decisions and assume control of their lives.[12] According to some estimates, 5% of microfinance programme participants could lift their families out of poverty each year.[13]

From a macroeconomic perspective, microfinance is useful for channelling and generating credit for poor people. It remains an important policy instrument for large-scale poverty reduction. But its success depends on the scheme, the participating community and the support from donors, the local government and the administering agency. Scaling up depends on macroeconomic stability, on the health, coverage and efficacy of the financial sector and (in the long run) on the government's ability to reach poor people through the financial sector on a national scale.

*   *   *

This chapter highlights the structural problems holding back economic growth in the top priority and high priority countries for achieving the Millennium Development Goals. It also offers practical remedies to overcome those problems. These countries must look well beyond market reforms to surmount basic challenges posed by widespread disease, geographic isolation, poor infrastructure, low human capital and limited markets. Major public investments are needed to reach the basic thresholds for health, education and other outcomes. Because these countries are too poor to fund these investments, rich countries must follow through on their commitment to the Millennium Development Goals by helping to finance core public investments that will yield long-term success in economic and human development.

Map 1 divides the world into five categories. First are countries with high economic innovation, as measured by the number of patents per million people, shown in dark blue. These tend to be the high-income countries. Second are developing country exporters of manufactured goods, shown in lighter blue. In 1995 at least half of these countries' exports were in the manufacturing sector. Third are the fuel-exporting economies, shown in blue-grey. Fourth are transition countries, in grey. Fifth are the commodity (non-fuel) exporting developing countries, in black.

MAP 1

Classification of countries by economic structure, 1995

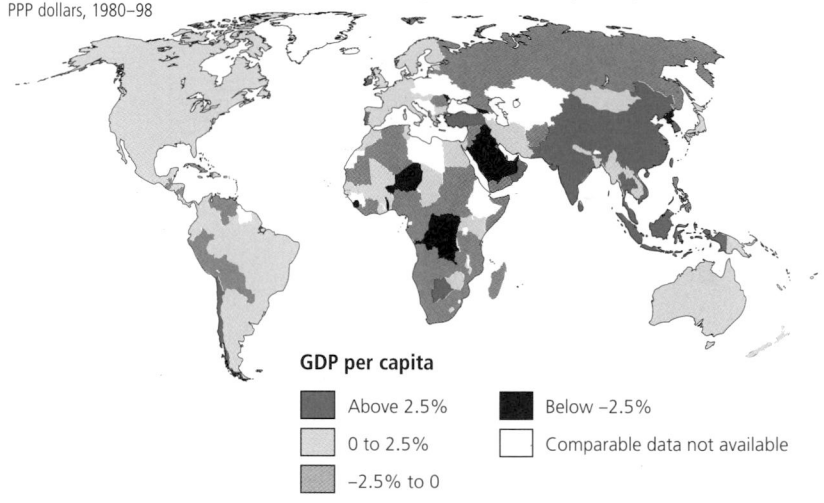

- Technology innovators, high levels of patenting
- Manufacturing exporters
- Fuel exporters
- Transition countries
- Commodity (non-fuel) exporters

Map 2 highlights patterns of economic growth during 1980–98 using constant per capita GDP in purchasing power parity terms. Note the remarkable relationship with the first map. The countries that are either innovators or manufacturing exporters tended to have economic growth, shown in dark blue, while other groups of countries (oil exporters, transition, commodity exporters) tended to experience economic decline. The growing economies include the regions of North America, Western Europe, Oceania, East Asia and South Asia. The declining countries are concentrated in Sub-Saharan Africa, the former Soviet Union, the Middle East, and parts of Latin America, mainly the Andes and Central America. Sub-Saharan Africa is the worst-performing region, with two thirds of its countries and three quarters of its population experiencing economic decline in 1990–98.

MAP 2

Country classification by average annual growth in GDP per capita, 1990
PPP dollars, 1980–98

GDP per capita

- Above 2.5%
- 0 to 2.5%
- −2.5% to 0
- Below −2.5%
- Comparable data not available

Source: Maddison 2001; Gallup, Sachs and Mellinger 1999; World Bank 2003i.

Table 1 breaks down patterns of economic growth by economic structure. Grouping countries in the same five categories as map 1, the table shows that the main problems in economic growth have come in three types of economies: transition countries, oil-exporting economies (which faced a huge loss of purchasing power from their single or dominant export commodity) and commodity (non-fuel) exporting developing countries. Most of the commodity exporting countries are in Sub-Saharan Africa, Latin America and Central Asia. Innovating economies and manufacturing exporters among developing countries by and large experienced economic growth.

TABLE 1

Economic growth rates by country group, 1980–98

Group	Countries that grew in GDP per capita	Average annual growth in GDP per capita (%)
Technology innovators	18 out of 18	1.7
Transition countries	4 out of 12	−1.7
Fuel exporters	2 out of 13	−1.5
Manufacturing exporters	23 out of 24	2.7
Commodity (non-fuel) exporters	29 out of 61	−0.1

Note: GDP per capita is measured in purchasing power parity.
Source: Maddison 2001; World Bank 2002j.

TABLE 2
Economic growth rates by population size and location, 1980–98

Geographic location	Small countries			Large countries		
	Countries that grew in GDP per capita	Average annual growth in GDP per capita (%)	Population living in countries that grew, 2001 (millions)	Countries that grew in GDP per capita	Average annual growth in GDP per capita (%)	Population living in countries that grew, 2001 (millions)
Inland populations	24 of 53	–0.2	379 of 799	10 of 10	2.5	3,087 of 3,087
Coastal populations	15 of 17	1.9	118 of 130	3 of 4	3.2	341 of 418

Note: GDP per capita is measured in purchasing power parity.
Source: Maddison 2001; Gallup, Sachs and Mellinger 1999; World Bank 2003i.

Table 2 highlights patterns of economic growth by looking through a different lens, that of geography. This figure assesses growth rates for all developing, transition and commodity (non-fuel) exporting countries for which data are available. It categorizes countries by their population size and the concentration of population near maritime trade routes. Small countries are those with fewer than 40 million people in 1990. Coastal countries are those with more than three-quarters of their populations living more than 100 kilometres from the coast. The data highlight how groups of countries that are large or coastal experienced systematic average per capita economic growth from 1980–98. Small and inland countries enjoyed much less economic success over the same period. The findings are particularly relevant for Africa, since 33 of the 53 countries counted as small and inland are on that continent.

Source: McArthur and Sachs 2002; World Bank 2002j, 2003i; IMF 2002b; Maddison 2001.

CHAPTER 4

Public policies to improve people's health and education

As the Millennium Development Compact argues, the first cluster of policies required for top and high priority countries to break out of their poverty traps involve investing in health and education. These investments contribute to economic growth, which feeds back into human development (see chapter 3). Education, health, nutrition and water and sanitation complement each other, with investments in any one contributing to better outcomes in the others. A major message of this chapter is that policy-makers need to recognize the synergies among the many aspects of human development as they invest in achieving the Millennium Development Goals.

Education affects all types of human development outcomes. More than just a source of knowledge, education promotes better hygiene and increases the use of health services. Safe water and adequate sanitation also determine health outcomes. By reducing infectious diseases, they improve children's nutritional status and increase their learning abilities. Together such interventions contribute to a health transition—from having communicable diseases account for most of a country's disease burden to having chronic diseases as the main source.

The health transition hastens the demographic transition from high to low birth and death rates. In addition, higher education levels are associated with better family planning. As more children survive, families reduce the number of children they have. Desired family sizes decline, a process helped by the ready availability of contraceptives. So, over time, lower infant and child mortality plays a major role in falling fertility rates.[1] This notion of synergies among social investments is central to reducing hunger, malnutrition, disease and illiteracy—and to advancing human capabilities.

To get the most from the synergies among basic social services, it is crucial to focus on universal primary education early on, particularly

for girls. But doing so requires available, fully functional family planning, water and sanitation services. Thus these services are integral to achieving all the Millennium Development Goals.

This chapter also argues that gender equality is not just a Goal in its own right—it is central to achieving all the other Goals. The lifecycles of educated girls illustrate the synergies among social sector interventions (figure 4.1). Educated girls are likely to marry later—especially if their schooling extends to the junior secondary level and they engage in economic activity outside the home. Educated girls and women also have fewer children, seek medical attention sooner for themselves and their children and provide better care and nutrition for their children.[2] Such behaviour reduces the probability of disease and increases the odds of children surviving past age five.

Over time reduced child mortality leads to smaller families and increased contraceptive use—lowering overall fertility. With smaller households child care improves, and with lower fertility the school-age population shrinks. Thus the benefits of girls' education accrue from generation to generation. But while strengthening women's

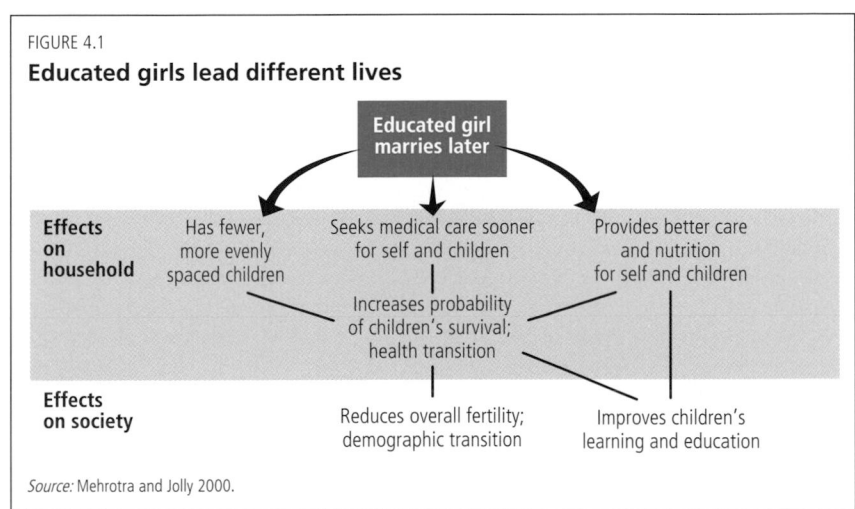

FIGURE 4.1

Educated girls lead different lives

Source: Mehrotra and Jolly 2000.

health and education capabilities in this way is important, action is also needed to reinforce their role in society as agents of change (box 4.1).

Past progress shows what is possible. Over the past 50 years most developing countries achieved advances in health and education that took nearly 200 years in rich countries. But a dozen or so developing countries made especially fast progress, achieving social indicators comparable to those in rich countries. These high performers offer policy lessons for other countries in reaching the Millennium Development Goals (box 4.2).

If there is any doubt that the Goals can be achieved in less than a generation, consider the following gains. Sri Lanka added 12 years to life expectancy at birth in just seven years (1945–52).[3] In nine years (1953–62) China added 13 years.[4] Between 1960 and 1980 Botswana more than doubled its gross primary enrolment ratio, from 40% to 91%.[5] And in Zimbabwe the gross primary enrolment ratio rose from 75% in 1960 to 124% in 1985, five years after independence.[6]

Some high performers combined rapid economic and social progress—and now have high-performing economies (Republic of Korea, Malaysia, Mauritius). They achieved social progress early in their development processes, when national incomes were still low—suggesting a certain sequence for investments. In other high-achieving countries economic growth was slower and less consistent. Still, all of these high

---

BOX 4.1

Women's capabilities and agency—key to achieving the Millennium Development Goals

Unless women's capabilities are improved and gender equality increased, the other Millennium Development Goals will not be achieved. Strengthening women's agency and voice is essential to enhancing their capabilities—and strengthening their capabilities is essential to enhancing their agency and voice. Though education is the only official target ("Eliminate gender disparity in primary and secondary education, preferably by 2005, and in all levels of education by 2015") used to assess progress towards the gender equality Goal, several other indicators have been established to monitor performance:
- The ratio of girls to boys in primary, secondary and tertiary education
- The ratio of literate female to male 15- to 24-year-olds.
- The share of women engaged in wage employment outside agriculture.
- The share of women in national parliaments.

Gender equality in education helps women secure employment outside the home and acquire political power, contributing to their agency in the public sphere. But gender equality must also extend to the private domain.

Today gender inequality undermines women's capabilities in education and health. Still, some progress is being made. For example, between 1990 and 2001 the ratio of literate female to male 15- to 24-year-olds in countries with low human development increased from 70 to 81 women per 100 men, though in countries with medium human development it increased only from 91 to 93. The gender ratio in primary education also made limited progress, rising from 86 to 92 girls per 100 boys in developing countries between 1990 and 1999–2000. At current rates gender equality in education will not be achieved until 2025—20 years after the target set by the Millennium Development Goals.

Among young women (15- to 24-year-olds) in developing countries literacy is 60%, compared with 80% for young men. In addition, more women suffer from HIV/AIDS. Maternal mortality is another dimension of women's additional burdens. And despite biological reasons for women to live longer than men, many developing regions and countries have millions of "missing" women killed by infanticide, gender-based abortions or systematic discrimination over the life cycle (resulting in a lower female population, with 35–37 million fewer million women in South Asia and 38–40 million in China).

Without action to increase women's capabilities in health and education, they will have limited prospects for working outside the home and earning independent incomes. In the 1990s women working outside agriculture accounted for an unchanging 40% of men's employment in developing countries.

Many challenges undermine gender equality in employment and community and political participation. In developing countries most poor female workers outside of agriculture are engaged in informal employment and receive low, irregular pay. And around the world, women account for more than 30% of parliamentarians in just seven countries. More equal political representation often has to be jumpstarted by quotas.

Gender relations are largely determined by social and cultural contexts. Patriarchal values instilled from childhood influence the attitudes and outlooks of both women and men throughout their lives. These values are often enshrined in laws prejudicial to women's rights and claims—especially those related to marriage, divorce, rape, violence and inheritance. Movements for women's rights often focus on reforming such laws.

Although employment and education are considered basic strategies for strengthening women's agency and voice, stronger agency also requires not just:
- Recognizing the importance of education, but also improving its content, provision and returns.
- Creating more jobs for women, but also improving their nature and terms—including sustainable livelihoods.
- Increasing the number of women in parliaments, but also raising women's visibility in positions of authority and decision-making—from the local to the national levels.

Thus empowering women requires policies that address both practical needs (supporting the basic capabilities required to function, such as by improving living conditions and increasing employment, health care and safe water supplies) and strategic needs (strengthening women's voice and agency to renegotiate their roles at home and in society, such as through legal rights to assets and laws ensuring equal wages, reproductive rights and freedom from violence). Moreover, these policies must be backed by laws guaranteeing equal rights—for both women and men in the private and public sectors.

Source: Christiansen, Conway, and Poston 2003; Drèze and Sen 2002; Landuyt 1998.

Policy lessons from high-achieving countries in health and education

There is no global prescription for achieving the Millennium Development Goals, and no set track for being "on track". Diverse national situations require that countries develop different strategies for achieving international targets for health and education. But success stories abound.

• In the 1980s Botswana made strides in education and health much greater than expected based on its income level.

• The state of Kerala, India, has health indicators similar to those of the United States—despite a per capita income 99% lower and annual spending on health of just $28 a person.

• Cuba's per capita income is a small fraction of that in the United States, yet it has the same infant mortality rate and has kept HIV/AIDS under control.

High-performing countries in health and education show the remarkable progress that can be made within a generation, and similarities between success stories provide useful insights into what works:

• Public financing was adequate and equitable. In high-achieving countries political commitment is reflected not just in allocations of public spending to health and education, but also in their equity. Spending has focused on basic rather than tertiary health services, and on primary rather than higher education.

• Education achievements preceded higher health status. From the outset of their development processes, all the high-achieving countries pursued high enrolments for all children, particularly girls. Thus gender inequality in education was lower from the start, and gender differences were narrowed much faster than in lower-achieving countries. As investments in public health infrastructure emerged, high education levels ensured high demand for and effective use of health services.

• Educated women were able to act as agents of change. Children's health and education outcomes are not only the result of adequate food consumption and health services, but also proper child care. In this respect the capabilities and positions of women in the household and in society take on major significance. When women are educated, have ownership rights and are free to work outside the home and earn an independent income, the well-being of the entire household is enhanced (Drèze and Sen 1995). In high-achieving countries women not only had near parity in education, they also had high rates of participation in non-agricultural employment.

Source: Chen and Desai 2000; Mehrotra 2000; Drèze and Sen 1995.

---

performers show that with the right government priorities and policies, high social development is possible even without a thriving economy.

This chapter is about setting the right policy priorities—those of the high-performing countries—to achieve the Millennium Development Goals. The Goals for hunger, education, health and water and sanitation are examined in turn, from the scale of the challenges to the actions required to resolve them. The chapter then proposes an action plan to boost the level, equity and efficiency of public spending—as well as the quantity and quality of official development assistance—for basic services.

ACHIEVING THE HUNGER GOAL

Given past achievements, the Goal of halving the percentage of hungry people by 2015 should be readily achievable. In 1996 the World Food Summit set a similar target: halving to 400 million the number of hungry people in developing countries.[7]

Since the early 1970s food production in developing countries has tripled, more than keeping up with population growth.[8] In addition, the real prices of the main cereal crops have dropped 76%.[9] Between 1980 and 1995 per capita food production increased 27% in Asia and 12% in Latin America. But in Sub-Saharan Africa it fell 8%.[10] Although hunger is most prevalent in South Asia, it is declining—while in Africa about one-third of the population is undernourished, and the number is increasing.[11] If all the food produced worldwide were distributed equally, every person would be able to consume 2,760 calories a day (hunger is defined as consuming fewer than 1,960 calories a day).[12] Addressing hunger means ensuring that people have command over the resources (especially income) needed to acquire food.

Hunger is more than just a lack of available food. It is a problem of deficiencies in food entitlement and deprivations in related essential services (health care, education, safe drinking water, adequate sanitation). Food entitlement differs from food availability in that it indicates what a person can command with income and thus consume, rather than what is available in the market.

SCALE OF THE PROBLEM

Every day 799 million people in developing countries—about 18% of the world's population—go

---

Millennium Development Goals and targets

Goal 1: Eradicate extreme poverty and hunger

Target 1: Halve, between 1990 and 2015, the proportion of people whose income is less than $1 a day

Target 2: Halve, between 1990 and 2015, the proportion of people who suffer from hunger

hungry.[13] In South Asia one person in four goes hungry, and in Sub-Saharan Africa the share is as high as one in three.[14] India is home to the largest number of hungry people, 233 million, while Sub-Saharan Africa has 183 million, China 119 million, the rest of East Asia and the Pacific 74 million, Latin America 55 million and the Arab States 32 million.[15]

Between 1990–92 and 1998–2000 the proportion of hungry people in developing countries fell from 21% to 18%.[16] The largest reductions by far were in China, though substantial declines also occurred in South-East Asia.[17] But with population growth, the number of hungry people is not falling as quickly. Worldwide, the number of hungry people fell by 20 million between 1991 and 1999.[18] Yet that progress came only because 80 million Chinese escaped hunger: in 25 developing countries the number of hungry people increased (figure 4.2).[19]

The hunger Goal also seeks to reduce child malnutrition. In this area, among 33 countries with data, 10 saw reversals or failed to improve in the 1990s.[20] And because data on child malnutrition are more reliable than those on hunger, such trends are worrisome.[21]

More than three-quarters of hungry people are in rural areas of developing countries.[22] About half live in farm households on marginal lands, where environmental degradation threatens agricultural production.[23] Nearly a third live in rural landless and non-farm households, such as those dependent on herding, fishing or forestry.[24] Yet poor fishers are seeing their catches reduced by commercial fishing, and foresters are losing their rights as logging companies move in under government concessions. Moreover, landlessness is rising in most rural regions because of higher farming densities and unequal land distribution. Average land per capita among rural farmers in developing countries declined from 3.6 hectares in 1972 to 0.26 hectares in 1992—and stands to fall further by 2020.[25]

Another worrisome trend is the shift of malnutrition to cities.[26] Urban poor people now account for more than one-fifth of hungry people in developing countries. But this could be rising because urban populations are growing faster than rural.[27]

In any given year 5–10% of hungry people are affected by droughts, plagues, floods, hurricanes, extreme storms or violent conflicts.[28] Among the 21 countries with extreme food emergencies in 2002, in 15 they were sparked by war, civil strife or the lingering effects of past conflicts.[29]

Meeting the Millennium Development Goal for hunger will require improving food distribution and increasing production. Among the top priorities for increasing production:

• *Focusing on technologies that raise agricultural productivity.* Doing so will also raise incomes for people with few assets other than land.

• *Directing more resources to agriculture.* Poor countries have neglected agriculture—a trend that must be reversed.

• *Preventing environmental degradation.* New policies and technologies to raise productivity must also protect critical ecosystems. Poor people suffer the most from environmental degradation, but poverty also leads to environmental degradation. In developing countries low productivity is more often the cause of such degradation—while in Europe and North America high productivity is the cause.

• *Sharing resources more equitably.* Women, who produce most of the food consumed in Sub-Saharan Africa and Asia, must have more secure access to land. The same goes for landless people.

• *Addressing global warming and reducing agricultural tariffs and subsidies in rich countries.* Protection rigs international markets against farmers in developing countries. Meanwhile, global warming can adversely affect weather patterns for farmers dependent on rain.

FOOD BUFFER STOCKS TO IMPROVE DISTRIBUTION AND SMOOTH PRICES

Governments can maintain reserves of essential foods, especially grains, and release them into markets if food prices rise inordinately—enabling poor people to afford them. Such systems may or may not involve public distribution of essential commodities at below-market prices. China and India have long traditions of maintaining buffer stocks (reserves) of food, usually at public expense.

India has maintained food stocks since the 1970s, enabling it to stave off widespread famine.

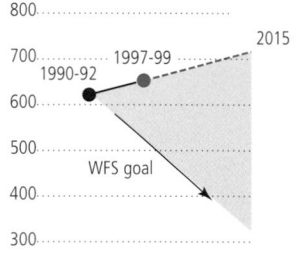

FIGURE 4.2

Food insecurity increases

Number of food-insecure people in all developing countries except China

Note: WFS is World Food Summit.
Source: FAO 2001c.

These efforts have been aided by the increased wheat and rice productivity that resulted from the green revolution, with grains and essential commodities (sugar, cooking oil) provided through a public distribution system. In addition, during droughts food for work programmes ensure subsistence consumption levels.

It is critical that food be kept affordable for poor households, whether through public distribution systems or releases of grains into markets (something the Indian government has failed to do in recent years). One reason for the food security of poor households in Kerala, a high-performing Indian state, is that ration shops distribute grains even in rural areas.[30] Elsewhere in India most public food distribution occurs in urban areas. In China buffer stocks of food are maintained at the community level.

Sri Lanka—another high achiever in social indicators—has maintained food subsidies since independence in 1947. In 1979 universal subsidies for essential commodities (rice, wheat flour, lentils, dried fish, powdered milk) were replaced with a food stamp scheme covering 40% of the population.

In Africa food stocks have not been used as much as might be expected given the continent's low agricultural productivity, fragile soils and frequent famines. One reason for the 2002 famine in Southern Africa was that limited food stocks were run down, partly because fiscal constraints prevented governments from maintaining them.

It is especially important for landlocked countries to hold buffer stocks, because the costs of building and managing warehouses to store them are worth the lives saved, suffering averted and productivity gained. In countries with ports the costs of maintaining stocks must be weighed against the benefits. But even in coastal countries buffer stocks can mitigate the adverse effects of fluctuating food prices.

Policy advice for Africa has tended to push in the opposite direction, arguing that free markets should determine how the continent feeds itself.

Governments facing budget deficits should not provide fertilizer subsidies, crop price supports or cheap loans. A recent report suggests that rural African countries grow cash crops for export—to generate income for poor farmers

and provide foreign exchange for food imports. Though the report acknowledges that bigger food crops would help some farmers, it also suggests that many are so isolated that they should grow only what they need for themselves as cheaply as possible.[31]

INEQUITY—AND WHAT TO DO ABOUT IT

Access to food could be greatly increased by government action to secure the assets and raise the incomes of the most vulnerable groups.

MARGINAL GROUPS

Small farms are more productive than large farms per unit of land. Hence more equitable land distribution increases agricultural efficiency and output. In Piaui, Brazil, farm yields increased 10–40% on non-irrigated and 30–70% on irrigated fields after land was distributed to small farmers.[32] Equitably distributed land also reduces poverty and promotes improves the distribution of income. In El Salvador a 10% increase in land ownership among cultivators raised per capita income by 4%. Similarly, Indian states that implemented land reform saw poverty fall faster between 1958 and 1992.[33]

To make the investments in natural resources needed to raise productivity, poor people need to have secure access to those resources. In Thailand there is a robust relationship between secure title to land and confidence to practice sustainable agriculture.[34]

Poor and hungry people also benefit from common property resources. In recent years Brazil, Cameroon, the Gambia, India, Nepal and Tanzania have set aside public lands for use or comanagement by indigenous communities. Similarly, community forest tenure has been strengthened in Bolivia, Colombia, Indonesia, Mozambique, the Philippines, Uganda and Zambia. And in China and Viet Nam public forest land has been allocated to households. The recognition of indigenous rights and community ownership—and the broader rationalization of public forest tenure—provide opportunities to dramatically improve the livelihoods of millions of forest inhabitants. Poor communities' rights

More equitable land distribution increases agricultural efficiency and output

to water must also be recognized—not just for household needs but also for irrigation, agro-processing and livestock watering.[35]

WOMEN

Women produce most of the food consumed in Sub-Saharan Africa and (to a lesser extent) Asia. But they rarely have secure tenure to the land they work. Fewer than 1 in 10 female farmers in India, Nepal and Thailand own land. Without secure ownership, women lack collateral, access to credit and the means to invest in productivity improvements—hurting the health and nutrition of their families.[36] In some regions women have limited claims to food within households, a particular problem for pregnant and nursing women, who need more calories.

URBAN POOR PEOPLE

Most cities have land available for agriculture—the informal safety net for many poor urban dwellers who grow food in parks, rooftops, wetlands, churchyards, containers, vacant lots, rights of way and plots near railways. They also graze livestock on hillsides, open spaces and rights of way. These residents should not be denied the right to use these lands to feed themselves.

PEOPLE IN FOOD EMERGENCIES

Refugees from wars and natural disasters need emergency help to survive. Response times in food emergencies need to be far shorter so that supplies can get to starving people much faster. Early warning systems for political crises, like those for environmental disasters, would help because political crises have become the main cause of famine.

In addition, a permanent fund should be established so that international agencies can respond to crises immediately, without having to raise funds as they try to respond. A fully capitalized fund would enable the World Food Programme to undertake far more strategic planning for emergency food supplies and post-famine crop and livestock recovery. The UN

Food and Agriculture Organization estimates that it would cost $5.2 billion a year to feed the world's 214 million hungriest people.[37]

To extend the benefits of food security even more, food for such programmes could be purchased from developing countries. International financing for community nutrition and community food bank initiatives could be organized under the World Food Programme as an international bank providing nutrition for all.[38]

RAISING PRODUCTIVITY

Many technologies have been developed to raise agricultural productivity and reduce hunger. Several pro-poor technologies focus on sustainable productivity and suitability for women. Promising management approaches include agroforestry, permaculture, conservation agriculture, biological nitrogen fixation, water use efficiency, gender selection in livestock, integrated pest management, integrated plant nutrient management, integrated intensive farming systems and integrated soil and water management.[39]

For many African farmers the most pressing need is improving soil quality. On many farms fertilizers can double or even quadruple yields of basic food crops.[40] Even farmers who cannot obtain or afford such inputs have many options for raising soil fertility, especially in Africa (box 4.3).

National policies must emphasize rebuilding natural assets. Since 1996 China has rehabilitated 5 million hectares of low- and medium-yield farm land. In some Indian communities better fallows and cover crops have been widely adopted—145 systems have been identified—by farmers on marginal lands forced to reduce fallow periods.[41] Agricultural systems can also be improved by paying farmers, fishers, herders and foresters for their roles in ecosystem management. Such schemes are already in place in many areas: a recent review found 75 that make payments for carbon emission offsets, 72 for biodiversity and 61 for watershed services.[42]

Initiatives can also promote sustainable agriculture in farming communities. A study in 17 African countries found that 730,000 poor households in 45 projects were practicing

Increasing soil fertility in Sub-Saharan Africa

Soil nutrient depletion is traditionally treated through the use of mineral fertilizers. But fertilizers cost two to six times more at the farm gate in Africa than in Europe, North America and Asia. But crops do not care whether the nitrate and phosphorous they absorb come from a bag of fertilizer or a decomposing leaf. Thus the main issue is to replenish plant nutrients in sufficient quantities, and whether this is done with mineral fertilizers or organic inputs is primarily a question of farm economics.

The most advisable approach is to combine the use of both nutrient sources in agronomically sound ways. The Sasakawa Global 2000 network and other organizations have shown on thousands of African farms that mineral fertilizers can double to quadruple yields of basic food crops . But even farmers who cannot obtain or afford purchased inputs can achieve long-term increases in yields through alternative approaches to soil building and replenishment:

• Nitrogen-fixing tree fallows. Leguminous trees are interplanted with young maize crops and allowed to grow as fallows during dry seasons, generating 100–200 kilograms of nitrogen per hectare in 6–24 months in subhumid tropical regions of East and Southern Africa. These fallows are economically and ecologically sound and fit well with farmer customs and work calendars— no surprise, because farmers helped develop the technology.

• Indigenous rock phosphate. Using indigenous rock phosphate deposits provides an alternative to imported superphosphates. The mild acidity of most of these soils (pH 5–6) helps dissolve high-quality rock phosphates at a rate that can supply phosphorus to crops for several years. Over a five-year period their use doubles or triples maize yields 90% as efficiently as superphosphates—at a much lower cost.

• Biomass transfers of leaves of nutrient-accumulating shrubs. Transfers of leaf biomass of the nutrient-accumulating shrub Tithonia diversifolia from roadsides and hedges into cropped fields adds nutrients and routinely doubles maize yields without fertilizer additions.

Tens of thousands of farm families in Kenya, Malawi, Mozambique, Tanzania, Uganda, Zambia and Zimbabwe are using these approaches with good results. Improved fallows are the most widespread practice. Knowledge is being transferred between farmers, villages and community organizations and through national research and extension institutes, universities, non-governmental organizations and development projects.

The challenge now is to accelerate the adoption of such technologies to tens of millions of farm families. The main obstacles are insufficient supplies of high-quality tree germplasm (seeds and seedlings) and rock phosphate and inadequate awareness and knowledge of the technology components. But increased adoption is essential, as these approaches offer major opportunities to drastically and sustainably increase food production—reducing hunger in a way that enhances the natural resource base.

Source: Millennium Project Task Force 2 2003a.

sustainable agriculture—defined to include intensified land use, diversified crops and livestock, increased use of renewable resources and other criteria.[43] In eight Asian countries some 2.9 million poor households using sustainable agriculture have increased food production on 4.9 million hectares.[44] These programmes must be scaled up to involve tens of millions of households.

Farmers in developing countries often lack the roads, warehouses, electricity and communication links required to bring them closer to markets—making them more vulnerable to intermediaries charging high prices for inputs and to monopoly buyers squeezing their incomes. Yet around the world, agriculture is a low priority for governments and donors alike. Most governments have invested much less in marginal lands than in more favoured agricultural areas.[45] In Africa most countries invest less than 5% of their budgets in agricultural development— even though 75% of their citizens depend (directly or indirectly) on farming.[46]

In addition, agricultural research is severely underfunded, with many low-income countries spending only 0.5% of agricultural GDP on it—and nearly all of that focused on higher-quality lands and commercial crops.[47] To benefit poor farmers on marginal lands, agricultural research must support promising initiatives such as multicrop systems, eco-agriculture, early maturing seed varieties and low-cost methods of soil building.

Agricultural services, if available, mainly come from private firms selling inputs and offering advice that is often incorrect and almost always incomplete. Government agricultural extension services have focused on distributing seeds and fertilizers, often promoting varieties and formulations unsuited to local conditions.

When allocating input subsidies or buying grain, most developing countries subsidize or provide privileged access to large producers and processors. Rules for these mechanisms often distort markets, unduly burden small producers, establish official monopoly buyers and set excessive taxes and service charges.[48] Government policies that discriminate against small producers should be immediately reformed, and public financing for subsidies should be redirected to support small farmers (box 4.4).

Farm policies and food security

As the Indian government's interventions in grain markets show, public policies can create different winners—and losers—among different population groups.

Designed to stabilize prices and support grain farmers, the minimum support prices set by the government's Food Corporation of India have instead risen much faster than inflation. This outcome is partly explained by strong farm lobbies (especially for rice and wheat) and government policies that cover farmers' economic costs of production. Economic costs of production are based on input costs, imputed values of land and labour as well as a bonus.

Theoretically, prices in the public food distribution system are based on economic costs (and so minimum support prices). But market prices are lower than the system's prices, increasing food stocks in government warehouses, although India has the largest number of world's hungry, and nearly half of its children are malnourished. Countering the farm lobbies, however, is pressure on political leaders to satisfy voters and so control prices in the public food distribution system.

Source: Kannan, Mahendra Dev and Sharma 2000; India 2002a.

INTERNATIONAL RESPONSIBILITIES

Bilateral official development assistance for agriculture, forestry and fisheries increased between 1971 and 1990, but declined thereafter along with overall official development assistance. Multilateral official development assistance increased from $1.2 billion a year in 1973–74 to $3.6 billion a year 1981–83, but then fell over the next two decades to $1.4 billion a year in 1999–2000 (in 2000 dollars). As a share of total lending of multilateral institutions, assistance to agriculture, forestry and fisheries fell from 15% of total lending in 1997 to 10% in 1999.[49]

But reducing hunger in developing countries requires international action not only on aid, but also on two other issues crucial for increasing food production and farm productivity. First, agricultural subsidies in rich countries—totalling $311 billion in 2002—inhibit agricultural growth in developing countries (see chapter 8).

Second, global warming, caused by emissions of greenhouse gases, is leading to more frequent extreme weather conditions—floods, droughts, mudslides, typhoons, cyclones—increasing the number of people facing food emergencies. Over the next few decades climate change will probably increase precipitation from latitudes 30 degrees North to 30 degrees South—areas that include many of the world's richest countries. But rainfall will likely decrease and become more erratic in many tropical and subtropical regions, causing crop yields to fall in countries already suffering from food insecurity.

Africa's rainfall has been decreasing since 1968. In addition, rainfall fluctuations have widened across the continent, resulting in disastrous floods like the one that devastated Mozambique in March 2000. Sub-Saharan Africa is especially sensitive to climate change because its agriculture is mostly rain-fed—and accounts for 70% of the region's employment and 35% of its GNP. Because of global warming, Africa will become even more dependent on food imports.

Millennium Development Goals and targets

Goal 2: Achieve universal primary education

Target 3: Ensure that, by 2015, children everywhere, boys and girls alike, will be able to complete a full course of primary schooling

Goal 3: Promote gender equality and empower women

Target 4: Eliminate gender disparity in primary and secondary education preferably by 2005 and in all levels of education no later than 2015

ACHIEVING THE EDUCATION GOALS

During the 1990s primary education enrolments increased in every region, and in many a large proportion of children are enrolled. In East Asia and the Pacific, Central and Eastern Europe and the Commonwealth of Independent States (CIS) and Latin America and the Caribbean more than 90% of children are enrolled in primary school. In South Asia 79% are enrolled, and in the Arab States 77%. In Sub-Saharan Africa net primary enrolments increased by 3 percentage points in the 1990s,[50] yet less than 60% of children are enrolled.[51]

SCALE OF THE PROBLEM

Of the 680 million children of primary school age in developing countries, 115 million do not attend school—three-fifths of them girls.[52] In India 40 million children are not in primary school, more than a third of the world's total.[53]

Moreover, enrolment does not mean completion. Just over half the children who start primary school finish it—and in Sub-Saharan Africa, just one in three.[54] Reflecting these shortcomings, one-quarter of adults in the developing world cannot read or write.[55] And of the world's 879 million illiterate adults, two-thirds are women.[56]

Developing countries face three main challenges in expanding primary education:

• *Limited resources.* Relative to rich countries, developing countries spend much less per student and as a proportion of GNP at all levels of education.

• *Inequity.* When spending is low, rich people often capture a much larger share of it—so poor people do not benefit as much.

• *Inefficiency.* Inefficient spending means that a high share of recurrent spending goes for teacher salaries, leaving little for learning materials. In addition, low-quality teaching means that students do not learn as much as they could.

LIMITED RESOURCES—AND WHAT TO DO ABOUT THEM

Governments play a much more important role in the economies of countries where human development is high than in countries where it is medium or low. In 1999 median public spending was 35% of GDP in countries with high human development—while in countries with medium human development it was 25%, and in countries with low human development, 21%.

SMALL EDUCATION BUDGETS

Rich countries rarely spend less than 4.0% of GDP on public education. In countries with high human development median spending on public education is 4.8% of GDP, compared with 4.2% in medium human development countries and 2.8% in low human development countries. Moreover, lower incomes mean that per capita spending is much less in poor countries than in rich ones.

When public spending places high priorities on areas other than education and health, social spending suffers. Debt service is an important non-discretionary component of public spending in many low human development countries (see chapter 8). But military spending—a discretionary expenditure—can also squeeze out education spending (box 4.5).

During 1975–97 developing regions exhibited different patterns of public enrolments and

recurrent spending on primary education.[57] In South Asia, West Asia and Sub-Saharan Africa the number of students enrolled almost doubled, while recurrent spending (in 1995 US dollars) increased modestly.[58] But in East Asia and Latin America and the Caribbean enrolments remained stable, while recurrent spending increased rapidly. Thus some regions invested in quantity (enrolments) and some in quality (higher spending per pupil). If quality is to improve in the first group of regions, more resources are needed.

Some studies argue that public spending levels are not important for education outcomes.[59] They are misguided. True, efficient spending is critical to achieving desired outcomes. But the amount of spending is also important.[60] One basic use of any additional resources would be to hire more teachers. With 26 million primary school teachers in developing countries in 2000, the estimated number of additional teachers required by 2015 ranges from 15–35 million—including more than 3 million in Sub-Saharan Africa, with more than 1 million in Nigeria alone.

THE FUNDING GAP

According to the United Nations Children's Fund, achieving universal primary enrolment (not completion, the aim of the second Millennium Development Goal) in developing and transition countries by 2015 would cost another $9 billion a year.[61] That estimate includes additional capital cost requirements as well as needs to improve schooling quality—and is more than four times what donors now spend, as well as far more than current government spending. Education spending is especially low in heavily indebted poor countries. Another estimate, taking into account a variety of scenarios, is even higher.[62]

WHO WILL FOOT THE BILL?

Economic growth is unlikely to provide enough resources for developing countries to achieve universal primary completion by 2015. In Africa economic growth would have to exceed 8% a year to provide the required resources—an unlikely outcome.[63] Thus much greater donor support is needed.[64]

But donor aid for education is insufficient: in 2000 it totalled $4.1 billion, with just $1.5 billion for primary education. In the 1990s bilateral aid for education fell from $5.0 billion to $3.5 billion, dropping to just 7% of official development assistance—an all-time low.[65] Only France, Germany, Japan, the United Kingdom and the United States devote significant shares of their assistance to education. The gap between donor rhetoric and reality must be reconciled.

In 1996–98 multilateral institutions provided an average of $954 million a year in education-related official development assistance.[66] The amount fell to $799 million in 1999–2001. Commitments for basic education were $402 million a year in 1996–98 and fell sharply to $222 million a year in 1999–2001. The Education for All Fast-Track Initiative, a good example of interagency work, could increase the funding for some countries.

INEQUITY—AND WHAT TO DO ABOUT IT

Who benefits from public spending on primary, secondary and higher education: poor people or non-poor people? In most countries the poorest 20% of the population receives less than 20% of the benefits of public spending on education—

and in some, much less.[67] Meanwhile, the richest 20% generally captures considerably more than 20%. But there are exceptions—including Colombia, Costa Rica and especially Chile—where a larger share of public spending on education goes to the poorest 20%. Not coincidentally, all three countries have made impressive strides towards universal primary enrolments.

Countries performing well on education devote more resources to primary education (averaging 1.7% of GDP) than do countries with average performance (1.4%). High-performing countries also spend more on primary education relative to their per capita incomes. And they allocate less of their education budgets to higher education.

Despite improvements in the 1990s, the countries with the lowest primary enrolments spend more per pupil for higher education than primary education.[68] Indeed, the lower are primary enrolments, the greater is the difference in spending.[69] These countries need to focus on primary education, not spend more on higher education. Still, additional resources are needed for higher education as well if countries are to build capacity to compete in the global economy—but not at the cost of primary education. Entire education budgets need to increase.

IMPROVING POOR PEOPLE'S ACCESS TO PRIMARY SCHOOL

The costs associated with education discriminate against the poorest people by eating up a larger share of limited household budgets.[70] A considerable body of literature argues that school dropouts and child labour can be reduced by lowering the direct and indirect costs of schooling.[71] In Bhutan, Burkina Faso and Uganda high household costs per pupil—ranging from 10–20% of per capita income—discourage primary school attendance, while in Myanmar and Viet Nam lower costs contribute to higher enrolments (figure 4.3).[72]

Uniforms are often the biggest cost for parents. In eight states in India—together containing two-thirds of Indian children out of school—uniforms are one of the largest out-of-pocket education expenses.[73] One policy option is to make uniforms optional, letting school

In Africa economic growth would have to exceed 8% a year to provide the required resources— an unlikely outcome

administrations and parent-teacher associations decide whether to require them.

User fees for education have long been hotly debated, and in the 1980s and early 1990s international financial institutions sent mixed signals about them. But in the early and mid-1990s, after sharp criticism of the consequences for primary schooling, the World Bank came out (albeit late) against fees for primary education.[74] Again, high-achieving countries point the way. To ensure universal primary enrolment and completion early in their development, they largely avoided direct tuition fees—and kept indirect costs low as well.

Thus there is a strong case for reducing the out-of-pocket costs of sending children to school. Sri Lanka eliminated tuition fees in 1945 and began providing free textbooks and free school lunches in the 1950s, and free school uniforms in 1991. Botswana gave enrolments a major boost by halving fees in 1973 and eliminating them in 1980.[75] Malawi also saw enrolments increase sharply after eliminating school fees and uniforms in 1994.

ENDING DISCRIMINATION AGAINST GIRLS

Gender differences in enrolments and dropouts are most severe in South Asia and Sub-Saharan Africa. How, then, can gender disparities in schooling be eliminated by 2005—just two years from now—as called for by the Millennium Development Goals? Countries that have eliminated such differences offer several lessons:[76]

• Getting and keeping girls in school requires that schools be close to their homes. School mapping can identify least-served locations, aiding the establishment of multigrade schools in remote areas.

• Lowering out-of-pocket costs prevents parents from discriminating between boys and girls when deciding whether to send children to school—and in times of declining household income, to keep children from dropping out.

• Scheduling lessons flexibly enables girls to help with household chores and care for siblings.[77]

• Having female teachers provides girls with role models—and gives parents a sense of security about their daughters.[78]

INEFFICIENCY—AND WHAT TO DO ABOUT IT

Efficiency means getting better outcomes from the same amount of resources—and pursuing policies that help rather than hinder learning.

OPERATING INEFFICIENCIES

A major problem in nearly all developing countries is making children repeat class years, a factor in high dropout rates and a significant waste of resources. Countries that have done well in primary education have addressed this inefficiency. Costa Rica cut repetitions in half by introducing automatic promotions to the next class year in the 1960s. Malaysia and Zimbabwe have also adopted automatic promotions.[79] To maintain standards, automatic promotions should be accompanied by a minimum package of inputs, especially classroom materials and teacher training.

Teaching children in the appropriate language also improves education outcomes, as high-performing countries show. In all those countries the mother tongue was used for instruction at the primary level. Students learn to read more quickly when taught in the language most familiar to them and can learn to read a second language more quickly.

This is an important conclusion for, say, francophone Africa, where in most countries French is the language of instruction at all levels.[80] This alienating school experience was hardly conducive to learning.

School feeding programmes are also effective in getting children into school and keeping them

Malawi also saw enrolments increase sharply after eliminating school fees and uniforms in 1994

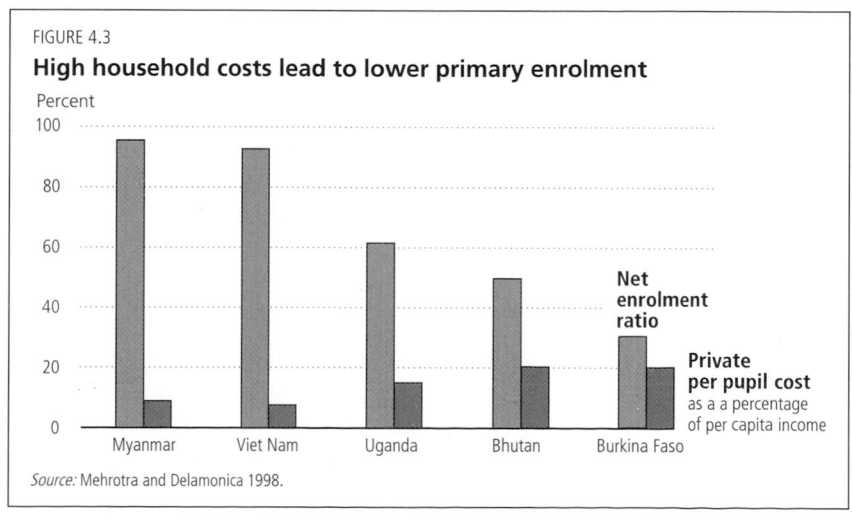

FIGURE 4.3

High household costs lead to lower primary enrolment

Percent

Source: Mehrotra and Delamonica 1998.

there. One of the factors behind increasing enrolments in India in the second half of the 1990s was a mid-day meal programme covering all states.

FINANCIAL INEFFICIENCIES

About 55 developing countries have low primary enrolments and require new buildings and facilities to achieve universal primary education.[81] But such capital investments are often inefficient, and the use of state construction companies and large private contractors often leads to inflated costs.[82]

How can school construction costs be kept low? One way is to use local rather than imported construction materials—an approach that Cameroon and Niger are encouraging to increase efficiency.[83] And since 1994 India has been using not only local materials but also local contractors and construction techniques to contain costs in its District Primary Education Programme.

Managing recurrent costs—to strike a better balance between salary and non-salary spending—is by far the most daunting financial challenge for countries with low enrolments. Wage bills for teachers and administrative staff often account for 90% or more of recurrent spending at the primary level, crowding out non-salary spending and leaving little money for other inputs, such as teaching materials.[84] High performing countries—Botswana, Cuba, Sri Lanka—have recognized this problem and spend reasonable amounts on teaching materials.[85]

Limited budgets also make it difficult for countries to increase the number of teachers, fundamental for universal primary schooling. Increasing salaries can help, but so can changing the salary structure—perhaps even reducing costs. One option is to manage the gap between minimum and maximum teacher salaries. In OECD countries the maximum teacher salary is on average 1.4 times the minimum wage, while in developing countries the range is 1.0 to 2.5 times the minimum.[86] The United Nations Educational, Scientific and Cultural Organization and the International Labour Organization have recommended that it take 10–15 years to reach maximum pay.[87] Another option is to unlink teacher salaries from advanced qualifications, an approach being tested in South Africa.[88]

Better use of teachers' time and better teacher deployment could also do much to help manage teacher costs. Botswana has experimented with paying teachers more to teach double sessions—doubling the number of pupils taught with a small increase in salary cost. Investing in information technology to crack down on "ghost" teachers and incorrect salary payments also generates fairly rapid returns, as shown by the National Education Statistical Information Systems in several Sub-Saharan countries.

Salaries eroded by inflation can also erode teacher morale, forcing them to take second jobs. Teacher absenteeism, a major problem in South Asia and Africa, can be partly addressed by hiring teachers from the neighbourhoods where they are required to teach. In Indonesia and Thailand, which achieved universal primary education early on, teachers have traditionally been hired locally. But teacher salaries are often a reason for absenteeism.

In many middle-income countries teachers have fared well—especially in China, Mauritius, Thailand and Uruguay, where governments have actually managed to increase teacher salaries. But in many low-income countries teacher wages have progressively eroded, including in Cambodia, the Central African Republic, Kyrgyzstan, Madagascar, Moldova, Myanmar, Sierra Leone and Zambia. Such countries will find it difficult to maintain teacher morale without higher salaries. Some of these countries also have to sharply increase the number of teachers to achieve the Millennium Development Goal of universal primary education. For such countries, donor assistance to meet recurrent costs is crucial, at least for a limited period.

A final point on increasing financial efficiency involves official development assistance for education. Such aid tends to emphasize equipment, overseas training and technical assistance. Some 60–80% of education assistance is spent in recipient countries, the rest in donor countries—on education and training for developing country nationals and on consultants and instructors from rich countries.[89] This is not the most efficient use of funds. Technical assistance can undermine local institutions,

In OECD countries the maximum teacher salary is on average 1.4 times the minimum wage, while in developing countries the range is 1.0 to 2.5 times the minimum

particularly if education authorities end up being overwhelmed by an influx of advisors pushing overly elaborate systems. Between 1994 and 1997 Ethiopia conducted 66 studies on its education system, half sponsored by bilateral aid agencies—to little avail.[90]

ACHIEVING THE HEALTH GOALS

A severe shortage of trend data for many developing countries makes it difficult to appraise the likelihood of achieving the Millennium Development Goal of cutting maternal mortality by three-quarters by 2015. Yet many experts believe that already high maternal mortality—a shameful failure of development—is increasing in many countries. The situation is most urgent in Sub-Saharan Africa, which accounts for half of the developing world's maternal deaths—with 1 of every 100 live births resulting in the mother's death.

Lack of data also precludes assessing progress towards the Goal of reversing the spread of HIV/AIDS by 2015. But progress is possible—as in Brazil, Senegal, Thailand (box 4.6), Uganda and Zambia.

Of the measurable health Goals, the world is farther from achieving the one for child mortality—a two-thirds reduction by 2015—than any other. Here the highest-priority countries are in Sub-Saharan Africa and South Asia. South Asia is making progress, with child mortality falling from 12.6% to around 10.0% during the 1990's. But Sub-Saharan Africa trails far behind: there, 17% of children do not reach age five. At current rates the region will not achieve the Goal for child mortality for almost 150 years.[91]

SCALE OF THE PROBLEM

Every day more than 30,000 of the world's children die from preventable causes—dehydration, hunger, disease.[92] In Sierra Leone, an urgent priority country, 18% of children will not see their first birthday.

Every year more than 500,000 women die in pregnancy and childbirth—one every minute of the day. A pregnant woman is 100 times more likely to die in pregnancy and childbirth in Sub Saharan Africa than in a high-income OECD country.[93]

Around the world 42 million people are living with HIV/AIDS. Moreover, the disease has killed the mother or both parents of 13 million children.[94] Tuberculosis is the other leading infectious cause of adult mortality, killing up to 2 million people a year.[95] Malaria kills 1 million people a year, and without effective intervention the number of cases could double in the next 20 years.[96]

Many diseases hurt rural poor people more than city dwellers. For acute respiratory infections, a major child killer, less than half of rural children receive care in most developing regions.[97]

Many of these deaths are readily preventable (box 4.7). Bednets, affordable antibiotics, trained birth attendants and basic hygiene and health education are hardly high-tech solutions. Yet as with education, for broad systemic reasons such solutions remain tragically out of reach for millions of poor people:

- *Limited resources.* Governments do not spend enough on overall health, and they spend even less on basic health.
- *Inequity.* Rural health systems do not have enough staff or enough resources dedicated to women and children.
- *Inefficiency.* Vertical programmes for specific diseases are not integrated with general health systems.

It is here that the links among health, education and income play out most clearly, because it is poor people who lack access to water and sanitation, who cannot afford drugs and who do not receive education about HIV prevention and family planning.

Women are at greater risk than men. Globally, women account for about half of adult HIV/AIDS cases. But among young women the share is far higher and will likely worsen. In many Caribbean countries women account for the majority of new HIV infections. And in many African countries HIV prevalence among 15- to 24-year-olds is up to six times higher for women than for men.[98]

Millennium Development Goals and targets

Goal 4: Reduce child mortality

Target 5: Reduce by two-thirds, between 1990 and 2015, the under-five mortality rate

Goal 5: Improve maternal health

Target 6: Reduce by three-quarters, between 1990 and 2015, the maternal mortality ratio

Goal 6: Combat HIV/AIDS, malaria and other diseases

Target 7: Have halted by 2015 and begun to reverse the spread of HIV/AIDS

Target 8: Have halted by 2015 and begun to reverse the incidence of malaria and other major diseases

---

Thailand's success in preventing HIV/AIDS

Thailand's response to HIV/AIDS is one of the developing world's few successful prevention programmes. Since peaking in the early 1990s, new HIV infections have dropped by more than 80%. How?

Political will
AIDS was first identified in Thailand in 1984, and in 1987 the government established the National AIDS Prevention and Control Program (NAPCP), chaired by the prime minister. Political will has been complemented by financial commitments: between 1987 and 1991 spending by the government and donors jumped from $684,000 to $10 million. By 1997 government spending on AIDS control programmes was $82 million a year.

Multiplayer collaboration
From patients to private practitioners to Buddhist monks, many participants have worked with the national government to plan and implement AIDS programmes. For example, 150 groups of people with HIV/AIDS provide support and advocacy for other patients. The Thai NGO Coalition on AIDS coordinates the AIDS activities of non-governmental organizations. In an

innovative initiative, the government created a programme called Reduce Girls' Vulnerability that provides scholarships to young women for continuing education—aiming to discourage them from becoming prostitutes.

Targeting high-risk groups
In 1989 it was found that 44% of sex workers in Chiang Mai were HIV positive. Instead of denying that prostitution existed, the Thai government focused on reducing male visits to brothels and promoting the use of condoms by sex workers. In 1991 the 100% Condom Use Program was launched, distributing 31 million condoms a year to high-risk groups. Clinics gave away another 600 million condoms a year.

These efforts had dramatic results: between 1988 and 1992 condom use in brothels rose from 14% to 90%. In addition, the average number of men visiting each such establishment dropped from 4.0 to 1.5 a day. As a result HIV prevalence among sex workers fell from 50% in 1991 to less than 10% in 2001.

Education campaigns
A national public information campaign accompanied the 100% Condom Use Program.

AIDS information was made available everywhere—from billboards to cereal boxes to televisions, with one-minute AIDS education spots appeared every hour on television and radio. Thus messages helped dispel the stigma associated with having HIV.

Monitoring and evaluation
Three surveillance systems collect information on HIV and sexually transmitted infections. This information is used to track changes in the distribution of new HIV infections and has been used by policy-makers to guide control efforts.

International support
Thailand has received abundant international financial and technical support for its AIDS programmes. The Joint United Nations Programme on AIDS (UNAIDS), for example, has been active in raising funds, evaluating programmes and helping HIV/AIDS patients. Bilateral cooperation includes partnerships with the US Agency for International Development (USAID), European Union and Australian Agency for International Development (AusAID).

Source: Avert.org 2003; Kongsin and others 1998; Forster-Rothbart and others 2002.

Poor women are especially vulnerable to HIV because of their low nutritional status, limited education and employment opportunities and low social status and consequent inability to negotiate safe sex. And once infected, women are more likely to avoid or postpone seeking care because of gender constraints, such as domestic responsibilities and the costs of travel and treatment. Autonomy is also a problem: in South Asia men often decide whether women should seek medical treatment.[99]

LIMITED RESOURCES—AND WHAT TO DO ABOUT THEM

Every high-income OECD country spends at least 5% of its GDP on public health care. But few developing countries achieve that share—and in most it is less than half that. (Costa Rica—a country with no military that is a high performer in health and education—is a rare exception.) In countries with high human development the

median public spending on health was 5.2% of GDP in 2000—while in medium human development countries it was 2.7% and in low human development countries, 2.1%. In per capita terms public health spending is very low in most developing countries: in 2000 the median was $1,061 in high human development countries, $194 in medium human development countries—and just $38 in low human development countries (in purchasing power parity terms).[100]

The World Health Organization's Commission on Macroeconomics and Health recommends that donor assistance for health systems in low-income countries be substantially increased, along with domestic financial resources in those countries. The commission estimated that an increase in donor assistance for health to $35 billion a year by 2015 (from $5 billion a year in 2001), if properly invested in high-priority areas (infectious diseases, nutritional deficiencies, maternal complications) and if accompanied by greater health spending by

BOX 4.7

Policy priorities and technical interventions

Goal 4: cutting under-five mortality by two-thirds

Achieving Millennium Development Goal 4—reducing under-five mortality by two-thirds between 1990 and 2015—will require addressing the main causes of child mortality. Technical interventions must focus on malnutrition, infectious and parasitic diseases and immunizations, delivered through a strengthened basic health care system.

Malnutrition. Low birth-weight often leads to child malnutrition and is directly related to the mother's health before and during pregnancy. Expanding access to reproductive health care and ensuring adequate nutrition greatly enhance the health of mothers and their children.

Exclusively breastfeeding infants for the first four to six months of their lives greatly benefits their health. But when a mother is HIV-positive, substitutes for breast milk should be explored. As a first step, countries should immediately adopt into law the International Code of Marketing of Breastmilk Substitutes (promulgated by the World Health Organization and United Nations Children's Fund).

Children's health can suffer enormously from micronutrient (vitamin A, iron, zinc and iodine) deficiency, and can be addressed through supplementation (such as iodization of salt). Vitamin A deficiency can be reduced simply by providing two high-dose vitamin A capsules a year. In countries without functioning health systems, vitamin supplements should be delivered through campaigns akin to mass vaccination campaigns. In 1999 such methods enabled the least developed countries to achieve 80% supplementation coverage.

Infectious and parasitic diseases. In the worst-affected areas under-five mortality from HIV/AIDS is expected to more than double by 2010. In many countries combating HIV/AIDS—and explicitly addressing issues specific to women and children—is a top development priority (see box 4.1). Meanwhile, every year malaria kills more than 400,000 children—making it another priority in many countries.

Although under-five deaths from diarrhoea fell in the 1990s, the disease continues to take a high toll on children. Continued reductions will depend on families' ability to treat diarrhoea at home (increased fluids and continued feeding) and to use health services when needed. Increased access to clean water and sanitation, as discussed in this chapter, will also reduce the incidence of the disease.

Finally, acute respiratory infections account for nearly 20% of child deaths in developing countries, yet most are easily preventable. Data from 42 countries show that only half of children with such infections are taken to health care providers. In West Africa that share falls to one-fifth. As discussed in this chapter, a functioning health system that expands the number of health care providers in underserved areas is crucial to attacking this killer.

Immunizations. After increasing for many years, immunizations in South Asia have stagnated at their 1990 level—and in Sub-Saharan Africa they have dropped. But achieving higher levels is possible, as shown by periodic polio campaigns by national governments. Between 1998 and 2000 the campaign cut new polio cases by 99% through mass public education campaigns and better routine immunizations and surveillance.

Goal 5: reducing maternal mortality by three-quarters

Every year about 500,000 women worldwide die from complications arising from pregnancy and childbirth. Thirty times more suffer injuries, infections and other complications related to pregnancy. To achieve Millennium Development Goal 5—reducing maternal mortality ratios by three-quarters between 1990 and 2015—developing countries must expand access to skilled birth attendants, emergency obstetric services and reproductive health care, bringing these services together within a functioning health and referral system. Countries must also address the broader social issues that inhibit women from seeking health care.

Skilled birth attendants. Skilled birth attendants are present for less than half the births in developing countries. Reducing maternal mortality will require substantially increasing the number of skilled attendants, especially in areas underserved by the health system. Skilled attendants help reduce maternal mortality in two ways. First, by using safe and hygienic techniques during routine deliveries, and referring complicated deliveries to clinics and hospitals. Second, by actively managing third-stage labour—potentially reducing post-partum haemorrhages. This requires specific training beyond the distribution of safe birthing kits. Skilled attendants must be able to recognize the onset of complications, perform essential interventions, start treatment, and supervise the referral of mother and baby for emergency care when necessary.

Emergency obstetric services. Even in the best of circumstances, more than 10% of pregnant women experience potentially fatal complications. To reduce maternal mortality, skilled attendants must be able to refer complicated deliveries to emergency obstetric care. Developing countries are grossly lacking in emergency obstetric care, with more than 80% of deliveries occurring in areas without such facilities. Thus countries must commit themselves to the first UN indicator in this area: having such a facility for every 500,000 people.

Reproductive health care. Increasing access to contraception can significantly reduce maternal deaths simply by reducing the number of times that a woman becomes pregnant—and so the risks from related complications. If the unmet need for contraception were filled and women had only the number of pregnancies at the intervals they wanted, maternal mortality would drop 20–35%. In addition, unsafe abortions—those performed by untrained providers, under unhygienic conditions or both—kill an estimated 78,000 women a year, or about 13% of all maternal deaths. Thus achieving Goal 5 will require rapidly expanding access to reproductive health care.

Goal 6: reversing the spread of HIV/AIDS

In 2002, 3.1 million people died of AIDS. Another 42 million people are infected with HIV/AIDS. One of the most crippling plagues in modern history, AIDS has struck every country, devastating many in Sub-Saharan Africa. Though daunting, the first target of Millennium Development Goal 6—reversing the disease's spread by 2015—can draw on more than 20 years of successful prevention and treatment efforts. Moreover, in 2001 the UN General Assembly adopted an unambiguous declaration on the gravity of the epidemic, highlighting the need for decisive action to guide policy.

In tackling HIV/AIDS, strong leadership is essential to thwart institutional inertia and to address social issues that fuel the epidemic, including stigma, discrimination and unequal power relations between men and women. The proportion of women living with HIV/AIDS has risen steadily, from 41% in 1997 to 50% by the end of 2002. In Southern Africa young women are 4 to 6 times more likely to be HIV-positive than men of the same age group. Prevention and treatment programmes must explicitly address the conditions that make some groups more vulnerable to infection and less likely to seek health care. Strong community leadership, such as through discussions of

Continued on next page

BOX 4.7 (continued)

Policy priorities and technical interventions

behaviours and values that increase the spread of HIV/AIDS, can help generate locally acceptable responses.

Strong leadership is also needed to address disorganized, overwhelmed and grievously underfunded health systems, to promote multisectoral responses to the epidemic, to invest in effective prevention technologies (such as condoms and disposable needles) and to increase capacity through better training of health and community workers. Such efforts are being aided by HIV/AIDS control collaboration among developing countries. Thailand is sharing its expertise with Cambodia, as is Brazil with its neighbours.

In addition, prevention efforts must be intensified to curb the spread of the disease. Though control programmes will differ based on local needs, many effective interventions are available (see box 4.6). Effective prevention has enabled many countries to make remarkable progress in reducing infection rates.

Expanded treatment is also widely supported—most notably by the World Health Organization, which has placed antiretroviral drugs on its essential medicines list and issued guidelines for treatment where resources are limited. But significant constraints to scaling up these programs exist, and the timeline for expanding treatment should be ambitious, yet realistic. Involving diverse groups in planning and implementation has contributed to successful treatment programmes in Brazil, Thailand and Uganda.

Weak health systems severely constrain expanding treatment. Ensuring patient compliance with treatment regimens and monitoring drug resistance will require a larger number of well-trained health professionals, new drug distribution and storage systems and more clinics and laboratories in areas with high infection rates.

Goal 6: reversing the incidence of malaria and other major diseases

Malaria and tuberculosis are among the leading infectious causes of adult mortality, particularly in developing countries. To achieve the second target of Millennium Development Goal 6—reversing the spread of malaria and other major diseases by 2015—every developing country will need to identify and tackle the diseases that cause the most damage to its population.

Malaria. Every year malaria infects 500 million people—nearly 10% of the world's population—and kills more than 1 million. Many

researchers fear that the situation could get even worse due to environmental change, civil unrest, population growth, widespread travel and increasing drug and insecticide resistance. But new approaches to malaria control have emerged, and growing international awareness has boosted resources for research and control activities. Still, reversing malaria's spread will require sustained political and financial commitments to scale up successful programmes and to invest in research that could dramatically enhance these efforts.

Because the distribution of malaria cases differs markedly across regions, control programmes must be tailored to local needs. A variety of interventions can be incorporated into local strategies:
• Distributing insecticide-treated nets to people in high-risk areas and ensuring that the nets are retreated each year.
• Training community health workers to diagnose and treat malaria by providing simple diagnostic tools and prepackaged treatment regimens.
• Ensuring that infants and pregnant women receive preventive treatment as part of routine immunizations and antenatal care (though the latter assumes a functional health system).
• Providing antimalarial drugs in combination to decrease the likelihood of resistant parasites.
• Using new techniques to facilitate service delivery by mapping the distribution of populations, health facilities and transport networks. Tools are also available to forecast malaria epidemics—making control efforts in epidemic-prone areas more timely and effective.
• There is also an urgent need to increase research for new drugs and vaccines, because resistance to current treatments undermines their efficacy. Public-private partnerships, such as the Medicines for Malaria Venture, have combined scientists, financial resources and managerial capabilities to accelerate the development of new drugs. Finally, health system capacity must be significantly increased to ensure that existing and emerging treatments are delivered effectively.

Tuberculosis. Fifty years after the introduction of effective chemotherapy, tuberculosis still kills nearly 2 million people a year—making it, along with AIDS, the leading infectious killer of adults worldwide. And its toll is rising. Between 1997 and 1999 the number of new tuberculosis cases rose from 8.0 to 8.4 million. If this trend continues, tuberculosis will still be among the leading causes of adult mortality beyond 2015.

But reversing these trends is possible. The Stop TB partnership, formed in 2000, has made remarkable strides in formulating a plan, complete with financial requirements, to achieve international targets for halting the spread of tuberculosis. This framework calls for expanding, adapting and improving directly observed therapy short-course (DOTS)—a remarkably effective programme in which health workers, while supervising treatment regimens, form close bonds with their patients.

Expanding such therapy requires strengthening tuberculosis control programmes, as well as the overall health system, in four ways:
• Increasing political support to expand DOTS.
• Increasing financial support to expand DOTS.
• Improving health system capacity to expand DOTS.
• Procuring sustainable supplies of quality drugs to expand DOTS.

Adapting DOTS to meet the challenges of drug resistance will involve moving towards "DOTS plus"—the cornerstone of managing multidrug-resistant tuberculosis, which requires strict supervision of therapy regimens. In Russia the incidence of tuberculosis rose by more than 300% between 1990 and 1996, with a substantial proportion of the cases drug resistant. There is an urgent need for clinical, epidemiological and operational research to define the most effective approaches for implementing DOTS plus.

The growing number of tuberculosis cases, combined with HIV/AIDS, places an immense burden on tuberculosis control activities—a burden exacerbated by shortages of trained health personnel, laboratory resources and drug supplies. Establishing joint tuberculosis-HIV/AIDS programmes would address overlaps between the epidemics. But it would also require substantial reconfiguration of and increased outreach between country and community agencies.

Finally, DOTS could be improved by increasing research on:
• New diagnostic tools to detect active tuberculosis cases more quickly, easily and accurately.
• Better drugs to simplify treatment regimens and improve responses to multidrug-resistant tuberculosis and latent infections.
• A better vaccine.

One step towards improving DOTS has been the formation of the Global Alliance for Tuberculosis Drug Development, which will advance such research.

Source: Millennium Project Task Force 5 2003a, p. 2; Millennium Project Task Force 4 2003; Weiss 2002; WHO 2003.998; Forster-Rothbart and others 2002.

the countries themselves, would avert 8 million deaths a year, with economic benefits on the order of $360 billion a year.

Most developing countries implementing economic stabilization or adjustment programmes have no way of expanding health spending without increasing revenues from other sources. Heavily indebted poor countries in particular do not have the fiscal space to increase social spending. Yet basic services account for less than half of public spending on education and health in such countries.[101] (The private sector's role in health care is described in chapter 5.)

What can governments do in the face of severe fiscal constraints? One source of extra funds is official development assistance, and for health such assistance has been rising—with commitments averaging $3.6 billion a year in 1999–2001, up from $3.3 billion a year in 1996–98. Still, official development assistance for health is equal to just $0.01 of every $100 of donor countries' GNP—too little to meet even the basic health needs of developing countries.

In 1996–98 multilateral institutions provided an average of $872 million a year in health-related official development assistance, though in 1999–2001 that fell to $673 million a year.[102] But commitments for basic health were $264 million a year in 1996–98 and stayed at much the same level ($249 million a year) in 1999–2001.

At the end of the 1990s, 37% of health aid from members of the OECD's Development Assistance Committee went to basic health, 23% to general health and the rest to reproductive health (figure 4.4). Thus, unlike for education, official development assistance for health is focused on basic services—good for the Goals. In the 1990s official development assistance for reproductive health rose from $572 million to $897 million a year.[103]

INEQUITY—AND WHAT TO DO ABOUT IT

How should small health budgets be shared among services and users? This is a key issue for equity, because today poor people lose out. A recent survey of developing countries found that in every case the poorest 20% of the population receives less than 20% of the

benefits from public health spending. They also receive less than the richest 20% (which in many countries includes a large portion of the middle class).[104]

But spending on basic health care is shared more equitably than total health spending. In some countries poor people make disproportionate use of primary health facilities. In Kenya the poorest 20% receive 22% of government spending on primary health care, compared with 14% of total health spending. In Chile—a high performer in health—the poorest 20% receive 30% of spending on primary health care. And in Costa Rica, another high performer, the poorest 20% receive 43%.[105] Thus, if poor people are to benefit, more resources must go to primary health care.

More egalitarian spending is strongly reflected in health outcomes. In countries where fewer than 70 of 1,000 children die before age five, the poorest 20% receive more than 25% of public spending on primary health care—while in countries with child mortality rates above 140, the poorest 20% get less than 15%. Moreover, in countries with high child mortality rates, the poorest 20% account for less than 10% of hospital use—the richest 20%, around 40%.[106]

When resources are limited, less developed rural areas bear the brunt of shortages in medical personnel. Moreover, efforts to deploy medical personnel in underserved areas are usually unsuccessful. In Cambodia 85% of people live in rural areas but only 13% of government health staff are located there, while in Angola 65% of the population is rural but just 15% of government health professionals work in those areas.[107] In Nepal only 20% of rural physician posts are filled, compared with 96% in urban areas.[108]

Several measures can be taken to redress imbalances in health care coverage:

• *Increase the number of nurses, paramedics and community health workers.* Nurses, trained birth attendants and community health workers are the limbs of the health system, enabling the outreach that is critical to successful reproductive health services. For example, high-achieving countries—those where life expectancy is high and under-five mortality is low relative to the average for developing countries—tend to have more nurses per doctor. Compare

FIGURE 4.4

A large share of aid for health goes to basic services

Aid for health from Development Assistance Committee members

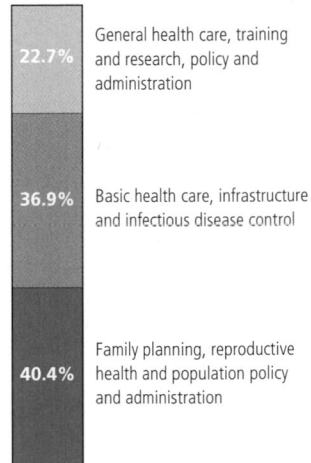

22.7% General health care, training and research, policy and administration

36.9% Basic health care, infrastructure and infectious disease control

40.4% Family planning, reproductive health and population policy and administration

Source: OECD, Development Assistance Committee 2003a.

Zimbabwe (9.5 nurses per doctor in 1990) and Thailand (4 in 1990) with India (1.5 in the late 1980s) and Bangladesh (1 in 1990). More recent data confirm this observation.[109]

• Use service contracts to require medical personnel to spend a certain number of years in public service. Such contracts, common in Latin America, have also been implemented in the Philippines and Tanzania. In the 1970s Malaysia, another high performer, required all holders of medical degrees to work three years for the government health service—enabling the government to post doctors to rural areas they had previously avoided. In addition, policies ensured that the poorest groups received a larger share of public health spending than the middle and upper classes.[110]

• Have donors fund some recurrent costs. The World Health Organization has recommended a package of essential health services for developing countries, including public health and clinical interventions. But this package cannot be provided without more staff, so donors should cover some recurrent staff costs.

INEFFICIENCY—AND WHAT TO DO ABOUT IT

Unless the performance of health systems improves, any extra funds could be wasted.

BOX 4.8

Integrating vertical programmes into working health systems

Where disease specific programmes are integrated into a working health structure, their likelihood of success is high, as India's tuberculosis programme demonstrates. More than 200,000 health workers have been trained. Some 436 million people (more than 40% of the population) have access to services. And 200,000 deaths have been prevented, with indirect savings of more than $400 million—more than eight times the cost of programme implementation.

Using the strategy of directly observed therapy short-course (DOTS), India's programme uses the existing health structure but supplements its activities with additional resources, staff and drugs, with diagnosis and treatment free of charge to patients. Once a decision is made to start a programme in a district, the health administration forms a society, which hires staff for a tuberculosis unit—covering 500,000 people. The state government trains the doctors and hires the lab technicians. Policy direction, drugs and microscopes are provided by the central government, with financial assistance from the World Bank and bilateral donors.

There are several levels of support, monitoring and supervision. Staff from the government and World Health Organization (WHO) make site visits. WHO-hired consultants, with mobile phones and Internet access, provide support to tuberculosis units. The government provides detailed feedback each quarter on the performance of each state and district.

Source: Khatri and Frieden 2002, pp. 1420–25.

FOCUSING ON ESSENTIAL INTERVENTIONS

Cash-strapped governments have traditionally tried to ration health care by limiting overall budgets—not directing resources to specific illnesses or diseases. A different approach would be to ration funds based on essential interventions. Mexico has taken this approach, and Bangladesh, Colombia and Zambia are beginning to.[111]

TAKING AN INTEGRATED APPROACH

The smallpox and malaria eradication campaigns of the 1960s started a trend towards donor-driven, disease-specific vertical programmes imposed on developing country health systems. Since the 1980s—with the launch of myriad structural adjustment programmes and especially since the World Health Organization–United Nations Children's Fund campaign promoting universal immunization of children (1985–90)—donors have tilted the balance even more towards such efforts. And with the increasing prevalence of tuberculosis, malaria and HIV/AIDS, this trend has been further reinforced.

Such programmes have risks. Resources are concentrated in these areas at the expense of the overall health system. Public health care efforts outside of such vertical structures may be gutted. And even vertical programmes, expensive to maintain, may be threatened if donor funds disappear. Vertical programmes may be affordable and prudent only for diseases that offer a reasonable possibility of eradication in a foreseeable period.

Disease-specific programmes should be integrated with overall health structures, as India's successful tuberculosis programme shows (box 4.8). But maternal and child health services are also crying out for integration: in many countries primary health care has focused on family planning to the exclusion of maternal and child health services. To avert more maternal deaths, care during pregnancy and especially during childbirth must be linked to reliable systems that ensure the availability of advanced treatment in cases of obstetrical emergencies.

Ensuring essential medicines for all—success in Bhutan

Bhutan, a small landlocked Asian kingdom, shows how a coherent national drug policy—backed by concerted international assistance—can achieve impressive results in providing essential medicines. Until 1986 public drug supplies in Bhutan were in disarray, with poor availability, erratic quality, irrational prescriptions and high costs. Then the country embarked on an essential drugs programme with extensive technical and financial assistance from the World Health Organization and donor countries. In 1987 a comprehensive national drug policy and enabling legislation were adopted. Key components of the programme include:

• National procurement and distribution facilities.

• Quality assurance through careful supplier selection and product testing.

• More rational prescriptions through the creation of standard treatment guides and better training and supervision of pharmacy technicians.

• Reduced waste and increased efficiency through workshops for storekeepers on proper drug storage and management.

• Free public provision of essential drugs and vaccines.

Since 1993 the programme has been operated by Bhutanese staff, with minimal assistance from international experts. Results include:

• Access to high-quality essential drugs for more than 90% of the population, with 90% of core essential drugs available.

• Reduced errors in medication bookkeeping, from 76% in 1989 to 14% in 1997.

• Reduced waste, with only 0.75% of the drug budget spent on drugs that expire before their use.

• Much lower prices paid by the essential drugs programme (which procures 85–90% of drugs), falling to about half of average international prices.

Source: Stapleton 2000, p. 2.

PROVIDING ESSENTIAL DRUGS IN CLINICS TO ATTRACT PATIENTS

Grossly inadequate drug supplies are one reason public health systems become dysfunctional. When patients do not receive therapeutic drugs, they have little incentive to seek public health care. This kills the demand for medical services, causing medical professionals and paramedics to skip work.

In India public health facilities in four southern states—Andhra Pradesh, Karnataka, Kerala, Tamil Nadu—function better because drugs are distributed through the primary health care network, giving patients a reason to visit the facilities. In other countries providing essential drugs through decentralized facilities could help revive primary health systems. Providing curative services would also expand the coverage of preventive services.

In countries with high human development almost the entire population has access to essential drugs. In countries with medium human development there is a huge range: in China 80–94% of the population has access (depending on the region), in India 0–49%. Most countries with low human development have low access (defined by the World Health Organization as 50–79%). Bhutan is a low human development country but has succeeded in providing essential medicines for 80–94% of its population (box 4.9).

Many low-income countries will require concessional donor financing to provide essential drugs. High-performing countries have provided essential drugs at public health centres—stimulating local demand for other services from these centres. Increasing beneficiary interest in the public health system also improves supervision of public health workers through community monitoring.

ACHIEVING THE WATER AND SANITATION GOALS

Access to safe water and adequate sanitation is crucial for survival. Water is essential for the environment, food security and sustainable development. And adequate sanitation can also make the difference between life and death.

SCALE OF THE PROBLEM

In 2000 at least 1.1 billion of the world's people—about one in five—did not have access to safe water.[112] Twice as many (2.4 billion people) lacked access to improved sanitation.[113] Asia contains

---

Millennium Development Goals and targets

Goal 7: Ensure environmental sustainability

Target 9: Integrate the principles of sustainable development into country policies and programs and reverse the loss of environmental resources

Target 10: Halve by 2015 the proportion of people without sustainable access to safe drinking water

Target 11: Have achieved by 2020 a significant improvement in the lives of at least 100 million slum dwellers

65% of the population without safe water, and Africa 28%. For sanitation Asia contains 80% of the unserved population, and Africa 13%.[114]

There were some positive developments during the 1990s: about 438 million people in developing countries gained access to safe water, and about 542 million in urban areas gained access to proper sanitation.[115] But due to rapid population growth, the number of urban dwellers lacking access to safe water increased by nearly 62 million.[116]

In the major cities of Europe and North America more than 90% of households are connected to piped water and sewers. But in the rest of the world the situation is very different. If adequate sanitation is taken to mean a toilet connected to a sewer, there is a significant lack of adequate sanitation throughout the developing world—even in large cities. And sanitation coverage is much worse than water coverage in every region (figure 4.5).

In the 1990s the number of children killed by diarrhoea—the result of unsafe water and sanitation—exceeded the number of people killed in armed conflicts since the Second World War.[117] Moreover, half the world's hospital beds are occupied by patients with water-borne diseases, meaning that expensive curative services are being used to treat diseases that could easily have been prevented.

In South Asia only 37% of the population has access to adequate sanitation. Some 1.4 million of the region's people still either defecate in open areas or use unsanitary bucket latrines.[118] In Sub-Saharan Africa the more pressing problem is safe water, available to just 57% of the population[119]—an average masking huge gaps between urban and rural areas.[120]

Rural poor people suffer more from a lack of safe water because they generally rely on land and water resources to sustain their livelihoods. Urban poor people suffer more from inadequate sanitation, made worse by overcrowding in cities.

As with the other Millennium Development Goals, increasing access to safe water and sanitation also requires addressing gender inequities. African women and girls spend three hours a day fetching water, expending more than a third of their caloric intake. Such household chores

keep many girls out of school—and if they attend school, the energy they use performing household chores seriously undermines their school performance. Moreover, when other family members become sick, often due to water- or sanitation-related diseases, girls are more likely to be kept home to care for them. And when water is needed in schools, girls are sent to fetch it, reducing their time for study and play.

The policy priorities for achieving the water and sanitation Goals involve:

• *Increasing resources.* Low-cost technologies are available to increase household and community access to safe water and sanitation. But for cash-strapped governments, wastewater treatment infrastructure is extremely expensive to install and maintain.

• *Increasing equity.* Poor people often cannot afford water and sanitation costs because wealthier users are not paying enough. And in poor households girls and women suffer more from difficult access to water and sanitation.

• *Increasing appropriate maintenance.* Too often, water and sanitation delivery systems are poorly maintained by governments and do not respond to local needs.

• *Limiting environmental damage.* Sustainable water supplies require rational water use—especially in agriculture.

APPROPRIATE TECHNOLOGIES FOR EFFICIENT USE

In water supply low-tech, low-cost technologies include household connections, public standpipes, boreholes, rainwater collection and protected springs and wells. These technologies are far better than alternatives such as bottled water, tanker truck provision of water and unprotected springs and wells. Some of these alternatives are unsafe, while others are inappropriate because they cannot be secured in sufficient quantities.

In sanitation there is a pressing need to provide technologies that people want to use, because decisions about sanitation are made at the household level. Households do not need to be convinced about the merits of a well or a standpipe. But they may need to be sold on the merits of onsite sanitation, as well as

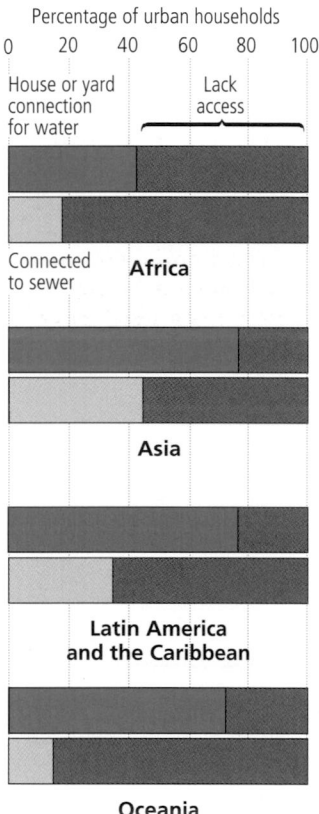

FIGURE 4.5

Many urban households lack water and sanitation

Percentage of urban households

House or yard connection for water — Lack access

Connected to sewer

Africa

Asia

Latin America and the Caribbean

Oceania

Source: WHO, UNICEF and WSSCC 2000.

given adequate hygiene education. The best way to do so is through products that match consumer demand in both price and quality (box 4.10). Appropriate technologies include pour-flush latrines, simple pit latrines, ventilated pit latrines and connections to septic tanks or covered public sewers. In rural areas waste disposal through composting is sometimes appropriate.

Such technologies are affordable to and can be easily maintained by poor communities. In the past governments often took a top-down approach, installing hand pumps, tube wells and even ventilated pit latrines regardless of whether there was demand for them. As a result communities generally neglected maintenance or relied on the government to perform it. But when communities—especially women—are involved in providing and financing facilities and trained to maintain them, ownership and sustainability increase.

Many city governments are reluctant to invest in basic sanitation without addressing the broader challenges of drainage and solid waste disposal. In developing countries very little urban wastewater is treated before being returned to the environment. But treating wastewater is much more expensive than simply providing access to safe water and household sanitation. Thus research is needed on feasible, affordable approaches to the full range of sanitation services.

It may also be necessary to accept an increase in environmental pollution as a first step towards improving sanitation. In Europe and North America, for example, improved household sanitation initially came at the cost of polluting rivers and waterways.

LIMITED RESOURCES—AND WHAT TO DO ABOUT THEM

In developing countries the domestic public sector finances 65–70% of water infrastructure, donors 10–15%, international private companies 10–15% and the domestic private sector 5%.[121] In 90% of developing countries water and sanitation services are provided by the public sector. Funding comes from users who pay bills to local authorities—the usual suppliers of services—but

---

BOX 4.10

Affordable sanitation in India

Much defecation in India still occurs in open spaces. But pioneering work by Sulabh International, a non-governmental organization (NGO), has shown that human waste can be disposed of affordably and in a socially acceptable way. Sulabh's approach is based on partnerships with local governments, backed by community participation, and has substantially improved environmental quality in rural and urban slums inhabited by poor people.

Sulabh's solution is a low-cost, pour-flush water-seal toilet with leach pits for on-site disposal of human waste. The technology is affordable for poor people because designs suit different income levels. Flushing requires only 2 litres of water, compared with the 10 used by other toilets. Moreover, the system is never out of commission because there are two pits—so one can always be used while the other is being cleaned. The latrine can be built with locally available materials and is easy to maintain. It also has high potential for upgrading because it can easily be connected to a sewer system when one is introduced in the area.

Since 1970 more than 1 million of the units have been constructed in houses. In addition, 5,500 have been installed in pay-and-use public toilets, staffed by an attendant around the clock who supplies soap for washing hands. The public toilets include facilities for bathing and doing laundry and offer free services to children and disabled and poor people. As a result more than 10 million people have received improved, low-cost sanitation, and 50,000 jobs have been created.

Sulabh's door-to-door campaigns also provide free health education to millions of people. The organization trains local people to construct more latrines themselves, and has helped set up and maintain fee-based community toilets in slums and other areas.

Source: WSSCC 2002, 2003.

---

cost recovery usually covers only part of the capital and recurrent costs of water infrastructure and services. The financing gap is covered by tax revenue and donor funding. With political commitment and money, access to safe water can be increased—as South Africa showed in the 1990s (box 4.11).

Many developing countries struggle to pay for water and sanitation infrastructure, with funding from the cash flows of water services especially precarious.[122] Inappropriate charges are a big problem. Yet in the absence of core infrastructure, household plumbing and sanitation cannot advance. And without trunk sewerage and treatment plants, wastewater typically flows into open streams and drainage channels—posing health risks and damaging the environment.

International private investment in water services has declined after peaking in 1996–99, apparently because returns are too low.[123] Moreover, water projects require larger initial investments than electricity, telecommunications and natural gas. Currency devaluations—as in the recent economic crisis in Argentina—are another disincentive.

In the 1990s an average of $3 billion a year in official development assistance was allocated

> **BOX 4.11**
>
> ## South Africa and the "right" to water
>
> In 1994, as a new democratic government came to power, more than 15 million South Africans lacked access to 25 litres of clean water a day within 200 meters of their homes. By 2001 that number dropped to 7 million. How?
>
> • Top-level political support has been essential. South Africa's constitution guarantees—as a human right—access to a basic water supply and an environment not harmful to health. As a result a policy ensuring free basic water was recently adopted, providing each household with the first 6,000 litres of water each month free of charge.
>
> • Clear laws and regulations have clarified the roles of water authorities and service providers. In addition, national standards and similar legislation have helped regulate water quality and tariff structures.
>
> • An extensive capital works programme was quickly pursued by the new government to address areas in greatest need. This
>
> programme benefited from substantial government funding and from the support of various actors, including non-governmental organizations, private companies and community groups.
>
> • Devolution of responsibilities to local governments gives local authorities more control over projects, allowing them to be better tailored to local needs.
>
> Despite these achievements, South Africa still faces obstacles to sustaining and expanding access to basic water supplies. Continued political and financial commitments will be necessary to ensure continued success. The viability of the free basic water policy, for example, largely depends on government revenue—as well as the number of wealthy households available to cross-subsidize poorer households. In addition, mixed experiences with private sector participation have left uncertain the extent of its role in future service provision.
>
> *Source:* Millennium Project Task Force 2003; WSP 2002b.

to water and sanitation projects. In 1996–98 such funding was $3.5 billion a year, but in 1999–2001 it fell to $3.1 billion a year. The share of water and sanitation in total official development assistance remained relatively stable in the 1990s, at 6% of bilateral and 4–5% of multilateral aid. Non-concessional lending, mainly by the World Bank, added $1.0–1.5 billion a year. Japan made by far the most significant commitments.[124]

Water supply and sanitation accounted for three-quarters of aid to the water sector in 1997–2001. Most aid to water supply and sanitation goes for large systems.[125] The number of projects drawing on low-cost technologies offering the best prospects of increased coverage for poor people—hand pumps, gravity-fed systems, rainwater collection, latrines—is very small.[126] Thus the composition of aid for water and sanitation has to change. Ten countries accounted for half of the official development assistance for water, and just one donor—Japan—provides one-third of such aid.[127] Worse, only 12% of official development assistance for water went to countries where less than 60% of the population has access to safe water.[128]

To fill part of the financing gap to meet the Goals for water and sanitation, costs must be reduced and revenues from users increased. To reduce costs, local authorities have to improve management—for which there should be more donor support and exchanges among developing countries.

In terms of revenues, local authorities commonly do not include capital costs in their cost recovery policies—and only partly recover recurrent costs. It has been suggested that "for the water and sanitation sector, full cost recovery from users is the ideal long-term aim".[129] Under such a strategy urban users would pay full costs for investments, while peri-urban and rural users would not contribute to capital costs. For operation and maintenance costs urban users would pay full costs, peri-urban users would do so where possible and rural users would pay partial recurrent costs.

But such an approach would be unfair. Since the social benefits of safe water and adequate sanitation far exceed the costs, there is a strong case for a pricing policy that reflects the wider benefits to all from, say, reducing the incidence of diarrhoea. This implies that those with direct household connections should be paying full cost. Today they are the ones paying below cost—and receiving the greatest subsidies. Charging them full cost would generate resources for the sector and make it possible to cross-subsidize those lacking improved water or sanitation or having a lower ability to pay. Such cross-subsidies would also be possible if higher rates were charged to industrial and agricultural users.

Depending on poverty levels in peri-urban and rural areas, there should be only partial cost recovery of recurrent costs. In many areas poor people currently pay exorbitant prices to water vendors. Some form of cost recovery is often desirable, less to generate resources than to ensure efficient use. Communities should be encouraged to provide labour to ensure rapid installation of hand pumps and public toilets.

How difficult is it for poor people to cover the costs of water and sanitation infrastructure? Consider an example from Bolivia and some cost estimates for water and sanitation from a project in El Alto:

- *Average monthly income:* $122 ($0.80 a day per capita).
- *Connection costs:* $229 for traditional water, $276 for sanitation (excluding trunk infrastructure).
- *Connection costs for condominial technology with community participation:* $139 for water, $172 for sanitation.[130]

An important additional cost for poor households is the construction of a bathroom or similar in-house facility, including a toilet. In El Alto these costs averaged $400, plus 16 days of labour. These costs are typically not factored into costing exercises for water and sanitation. Even with microfinance available the costs were too high for most poor people. But with hygiene education, the demand for toilets more than doubled.

Where poor people struggle to cover charges, they should be helped through credit schemes. Bangladesh's Grameen Bank has been extending credit for water and sanitation, on a group basis, for years.

Women face more problems of workload, privacy, safety and hygiene than boys and men—and so are more interested in sanitation improvements. But they often have fewer resources, so it is important to persuade men that sanitation improvements are worth it. The improvements should also be financially affordable for female-headed households, which often have less money and fewer labour resources than households with a man and a woman. Since women are more likely to know what designs and locations are suitable for use by women and children, men and women should share information and decisions.

Women also prove more reliable in maintaining equipment, such as hand pumps—partly because they are commonly responsible for fetching water for the family. Thus they should be encouraged to train as masons and plumbers, because they would feel more comfortable showing another woman where to locate a latrine in a home than showing a man. And with a job in maintenance, they are less likely to move from the community in search of work elsewhere.

Within the social services, particularly health and education, resource allocations have tended to be biased against basic health services and basic education

---

CROSS-CUTTING PRIORITIES

The discussion so far has focused on sectoral policy priorities. Here the focus shifts to policy priorities that cut across the Goals for all groups of countries.

INCREASING THE LEVEL, EFFICIENCY AND EQUITY OF PUBLIC SPENDING ON BASIC SERVICES

In most rich countries the government accounts for more than 40% of GDP—in most developing countries, less than 20%. With development the size of government is expected to rise. The enormous challenges of reducing hunger, preventing deaths and spreading literacy require a big increase in public spending.

But it is difficult to drive through multisectoral action in low-income countries, where tax revenues typically account for less than 15% of GDP. And achieving the Millennium Development Goals will require significant additional resources not likely to be generated by the economic growth of poor countries alone

(see chapter 3). Their fiscal resources are squeezed by debt repayments (see chapters 3 and 8). And the allocation of what is left over is skewed too much towards defence (see box 4.5). Not enough goes for agriculture—less than 5% of budgets in Africa—or for health and education.

Within the social services, particularly health and education, resource allocations have tended to be biased against basic health services and basic education. But the capacity of governments to reallocate spending to basic services to meet the Millennium Development Goals depends partly on shifting spending away from defence and debt servicing, partly on generating more domestic revenues. Things become a lot easier if government revenues are increasing, because discretionary spending on each individual can rise.

The problem facing many developing country governments is that large budget deficits have forced them to undertake macroeconomic stabilization and adjustment. But since the early 1980s adjustment policies have focused on reducing public spending—rather than mobilizing tax and non-tax revenues—to reduce the deficits. In a recent external review of International Monetary Fund (IMF) Extended Structural Adjustment Facility programmes, a group of independent experts concluded that public spending limits have often been set too tight, with detrimental effects on human capital and growth. This was again the case in the policy conditions laid down in the IMF's response to the East Asian economic crisis that started in 1997—conditions relaxed somewhat only after widespread criticism of the IMF on this and other counts.[131]

Another recent study shows that, for all of more than a dozen countries, real per capita public spending on basic social services (basic health, basic education and water and sanitation) declined only when public spending fell as a proportion of GDP.[132] In other words, if public spending is stagnant or falling, it is next to impossible politically for governments to shift funds to social services—particularly to basic social services—without incurring the wrath of those better off.

Much more could be done to strengthen tax collection to prevent tax evasion and tax avoidance. And much more could be done to enhance the tax base, by enlarging the tax net to catch those now escaping it. International financial institutions need to take much more seriously the technical support requirements of most developing countries in tax administration and collection, especially those in Sub-Saharan Africa and Latin America.

The prospects for enhancing the efficiency of spending (by increasing the availability of textbooks in schools, of drugs in public health clinics and so on) and improving the equity of spending on social services would be much brighter if spending was to increase. As noted, health spending—even in countries with stagnating incomes—strongly affects health outcomes. The same goes for education spending: it improves outcomes.[133]

IMPROVING THE QUANTITY AND QUALITY OF AID FOR BASIC SERVICES

Reaching the Goals requires true adherence to the Millennium Development Compact. For the poorest low-income countries a significant proportion of the additional resources needed for social investments will have to come from external sources. For heavily indebted poor countries, from debt cancellation—and much more than so far. And for all low-income countries, from enhanced official development assistance.

How has official development assistance responded? The total share devoted to basic social services (basic health, basic education and water and sanitation) has rarely surpassed 10%, despite an increase in bilateral flows in the new decade. The multilateral contribution has accounted for a third of official development assistance, including UN agencies, the World Bank and regional banks. Official development assistance for small water and sanitation projects in rural areas and for basic education are insufficient.

Official development assistance for basic services must increase. Donors worried about the fungibility of recipient government resources should bear in mind that even if governments shift resources partially to other sectors, they still increase public spending.[134]

IMPROVING SECTORWIDE PROGRAMMES

Moving from project-oriented to sectorwide approaches is an important step forward. A sectorwide approach avoids the weaknesses of the project approach: weak links to other sectors, geographic isolation, lack of ownership and aid conditionality. It is also supposed to build an integrated programme that sets out policy objectives, a comprehensive policy framework, an investment plan, a spending plan and funding commitments for governments and donors.

The idea is that sectorwide programmes should become part of the overall policy environment—rather than bypassing national structures, as project funding does. They could also ensure clear financing commitments from donors, an improvement over unpredictable aid flows to particular projects. Though a complex exercise, because they presuppose homegrown and effective sector policies, at least they involve recipients.

The sectoral approach has had problems, however, and in many cases resource pooling has

If public spending is stagnant or falling, it is next to impossible politically for governments to shift funds to social services—particularly to basic social services—without incurring the wrath of those better off

not yet occurred. First, the approach takes years to develop and finalize. It has been estimated that a sectoral approach planning cycle takes an average of five to seven years.

Second, technical cooperation (with expatriate technical personnel), which tends to dominate the project approach, remains a lingering problem with sectoral programmes. It would be useful to evaluate the opportunity costs of time and funds used for donor-financed training.

Third, donors' differing legislative constraints on spending, rigid and different procedures for resource allocation and reporting needs and weak capacity in recipient countries prevent actions from being fully harmonized. The government cannot be in the driver's seat if donor project implementation units continue to exist over which the line ministry has little control.

In Zambia donors have agreed to release the second tranche of their aid only if the government has spent at least 20% of its budget on education.[135] In addition, all the external agencies involved have linked their financial flows to specific programmes. Indeed, earmarking funds for specific elements of sectorwide approaches is widespread, often depending on donor perceptions of local political leadership and commitment in specific areas.

Donors recognize some of these problems. The February 2003 Rome Declaration on Harmonization calls for donors to commit to "providing budget, sector, or balance of payments support where it is consistent with the mandate of the donor, and when appropriate policy and fiduciary arrangements are in place".[136]

COVERING SOME RECURRENT SPENDING

Most donors have been willing to finance investment costs (building hospitals) but unwilling to finance recurrent costs (doctor salaries). This attitude is changing—but if the Goals are to be met, donors will have to more flexible than in the past in this area. Governments are often unable to absorb multilateral resources for capital costs if, as is often required, they have to show they can match these capital expenditures with funds to meet the running costs of the resulting infrastructure.

In the interim donors will need to cover some recurrent costs, especially for non-salary purposes in areas related to the Goals for heavily indebted poor countries—as long as these countries have raised some revenue from domestic sources. In cases where fiscal constraints are very severe, donors may need to show a willingness to accommodate even the salary costs of school teachers, paramedics or trained birth attendants for a transitional period until the fiscal space can be created for the government to bear those recurrent costs domestically on a sustainable basis.

DEVOTING RESEARCH AND DEVELOPMENT
TO TECHNOLOGIES FOR POOR PEOPLE

For some sectors the lack of research funding is a serious problem. For instance, 90% of global research for pharmaceutical drugs goes to diseases that account for 10% of the disease burden in developing countries. Thus international efforts need to be mobilized to address the need for drugs for tropical diseases. One clear case is the rapid development and testing of a vaccine for HIV/AIDS. The International AIDS Vaccine Initiative is making long strides in this area, trying to develop vaccines specific to the strains of the AIDS virus prevalent in different parts of the developing world. Vaccine trials are expected to begin soon in Uganda on the strain in that part of Africa—and in 2004 in India. But many other areas of research remain neglected.

In many other areas relevant to achieving the Goals, the solution is to diffuse existing technologies. Agricultural output in Sub-Saharan Africa, for instance, has been bedevilled by low productivity, even though high-yielding varieties are available for maize, rice and wheat. Nor have high-yielding varieties been developed for the grains consumed most by poor people, such as sorghum and millet. Part of the problem is the low commercial availability and high prices of inorganic fertilizer. Another is the limited use of organic fertilizer, despite the ease of making it from local resources. Using organic fertilizer would raise

For some sectors the lack of research funding is a serious problem

productivity and promote environmentally sustainable farming in a region where environmental degradation has been reducing already low agricultural yields.

Another example is the lack of diffusion of impregnated (or even ordinary) bednets to control malaria. Similarly, slow deaths from indoor pollution caused by smoke from cooking fires can easily be prevented by going to scale with the commercial production of smokeless ovens. Clearly, what such commercial production requires is appropriate subsidies, reinforced by a communication strategy to reach poor people in remote areas. The Sulabh latrine can promote environmental sanitation in most densely populated urban areas. But to do so, it must be adopted by international agencies as a model for widespread promotion in developing countries.

CHAPTER 5

Private finance and provision of health, education and water

For a number of reasons governments often finance and provide basic social services—basic health care, primary education, water and sanitation. One reason is that because such services are public goods, their market prices alone would not capture their intrinsic value and social benefits. Basic education benefits not only the individual who gains knowledge, it also benefits all members of society by improving health and hygiene behaviour and raising worker productivity.

A second reason for public financing is to ensure that basic social services are available equitably. Poor people usually lack these services, and if they have to pay for them they may not use them—making it difficult to escape poverty.

In addition, the state often plays a dominant role in the provision of these services. Provision by many suppliers (public or private) can result in duplication and higher costs. Moreover, access to basic social services is a fundamental human right—enshrined in the UN Covenant on Economic, Social and Cultural Rights—and governments have an obligation to ensure that these services are provided to their people. Government commitments to the UN Millennium Declaration and Millennium Development Goals reflect this obligation.

But public provision of social services is not always the best solution when institutions are weak and accountability for the use of public resources is low—often the case in developing countries. (Chapter 7 describes how to make governments more accountable in the use of public resources for social services.)

In rich countries private providers dominated health, education and water services in the first half of the 19th century. But these services were limited. In the second half of the century public financing and provision became dominant. Indeed, only when governments intervened did these services become universal in Canada, Western Europe and the United States—in the last quarter of the 19th and first half of the 20th centuries.

In poor countries private health providers and schools coexisted with a growing public sector in the first few decades after the Second World War. But in the 1980s and especially the 1990s, private provision began to increase rapidly. As loss-making state-owned enterprises were privatized in productive sectors—in both industry and services—the same trend was encouraged in social services.

The experiences of rich countries suggest that the sequence for social services should be comprehensive provision by the state early on, followed by more targeted interventions and then public-private partnerships to serve different markets—depending on the nature of services in different sectors.

WHY HAS PRIVATE PROVISION INCREASED IN POOR COUNTRIES?

In developing countries the private sector's growing role in health and education, and the push to privatize water and hospital services, have been driven by three factors: lack of government resources, low-quality public provision and pressure to liberalize the economy.

LACK OF GOVERNMENT RESOURCES

Strapped for cash—whether domestic resources or foreign aid—many governments of poor countries cannot provide social services effectively or fund large investments in infrastructure. Privatization is often pursued with a view towards obtaining revenue, but the biggest returns to government come from eliminating subsidies to loss-making public enterprises.

In some cases, such as domestic water and sanitation (and irrigation water and energy), insufficient government funds have been

Only when governments intervened did health, education and water services become universal in Canada, Western Europe and the United States

compounded by distorted tariff structures. Under state ownership tariffs are often too low to recoup costs, and user failures to pay tariffs are often overlooked. This approach essentially subsidizes rich people—while poor people suffer from lack of access. Moreover, as urban populations increase, fiscally strapped local authorities cannot expand services to cover them. As a result water services decline in quantity and quality in middle-class neighbourhoods—and fail to reach new poor neighbourhoods.

LOW-QUALITY PUBLIC PROVISION

Linked to lack of resources is the weak record of public provision in many countries. Stories abound of governments failing to provide their citizens, especially poor citizens, with basic social services or with services of good quality.

In India and Pakistan poor households cited teacher absenteeism in public schools as their main reason for choosing private ones.[1] Poorly paid public sector doctors often supplement their incomes by selling drugs intended for free distribution.[2] As a result poor (and non-poor) people are forced to use private providers—because such providers are more accessible and often dispense drugs as part of their consultations (unlike government facilities, where drugs may not be available).

To access more and better water, poor people often must pay exorbitant prices for it from private tankers run by small vendors. Most residents of South Asian cities receive water for only a couple hours at a time, and not every day.[3] They get electricity for a few more hours a day, but interruptions increase in the hottest parts of the summer—when temperatures can rise to 48 degrees Celsius.

PRESSURE TO LIBERALIZE THE ECONOMY

The third push for private provision has come from donor policies advocating economic liberalization and free markets to advance growth and development. Social services are frontier issues in this move to expand the private sector's role. In the 1990s many donors supported extending private provision and financing to social services, especially urban water supply. The World Trade Organization's General Agreement on Trade in Services also encourages private entry in social services (box 5.1).

HEALTH

Many developing countries—in Latin America, South Asia and South-East Asia—have substantial, thriving private sectors. In addition, a

---

BOX 5.1

Social services and the General Agreement on Trade in Services

The General Agreement on Trade in Services (GATS) establishes a legal framework for international trade in services through both general trade rules and specific national commitments for accessing domestic markets. Many critics have asked if the GATS goes far enough in protecting countries' ability to decide how best to deliver social services—including determining the extent to which foreign suppliers should engage in their delivery.

On the one hand, the agreement gives governments considerable discretion in deciding how, when and whether to open services to international trade. No country is required to open any specific sector to foreign competition, and countries can set conditions on the nature and pace of such liberalization. Governments can also, with adequate compensation, suspend or modify existing commitments to liberalization. In

addition, the agreement includes a "governmental authority" exclusion, which defines services covered by the GATS as "any service in any sector except services supplied in the exercise of governmental authority". Finally, countries can invoke general exceptions to protect public interests, including national security and public health.

On the other hand, the GATS commits members to "successive rounds of negotiations…with a view to achieving progressively higher levels of liberalization", and countries will come under increased pressure to liberalize new areas of service delivery. More worrisome, undefined terms in the agreement could negate the above safeguards.

The governmental authority exclusion applies only to services provided on neither a commercial nor a competitive basis. Governments, however, rarely deliver social services exclu-

sively, but through an evolving mix of public-private actors that compete for clients. And the precise scope of services fitting the exclusion criteria remains ambiguous. If not covered by the exclusion, legislation used by governments to ensure equitable and efficient delivery of these services could conceivably conflict with the GATS. State aid offered exclusively to non-governmental organizations operating schools and clinics in underserved areas could be challenged if a government liberalized its health and education sectors and these market conditions were not officially registered.

The GATS could be strengthened by eliminating the governmental authority exclusion or by rewording the text to ensure that services provided in the "exercise of governmental authority" is understood relative to function, not means of delivery.

Source: Mehrotra and Delamonica forthcoming; Save the Children 2001; Canadian Centre for Policy Alternatives 2003; UNHCHR 2003; WTO 2003.

large portion of health spending is private in all regions,[4] with more than half of basic health services provided by private providers in low-income countries.[5] In Asia and Latin America a significant share of hospitals and health facilities are privately owned, though preventive measures are largely the responsibility of the public sector.[6]

More than any other developing region, Latin America has experienced a huge shift towards private care since opening the management of its health sector to international companies in the 1990s. Several multinational corporations (Aetna, CIGNA, Prudential, American Insurance Group—all US-based) are providing health insurance and services in the region. And they intend to assume administrative responsibilities for public health institutions and to secure access to social security funds for medical care. These companies invest by:

• Purchasing established companies that sell indemnity insurance or prepaid health plans.
• Associating with other companies in joint ventures.
• Agreeing to manage social security and public health institutions.[7]

About 270 million Latin Americans—60% of the population—receive cash benefits and health care services paid for by (and often delivered by employees of) social security funds. Penetration by multinational corporations in social security funds is most advanced in Argentina and Chile but is growing in Brazil and starting in Ecuador.[8]

IMPACT OF MANAGED CARE

All citizens should have access to basic health services. And private provision can help meet different needs. But is equity ignored in the process?

Latin America has long relied on public social security funds to provide health services. But in the 1990s the management of many funds was offered to foreign health insurance firms. As a result more funding is used to cover higher administrative costs and returns to investors, reducing access for vulnerable groups and spending on clinical services. In Chile in the late 1990s about a quarter of patients under private managed care opted for care from public clinics, citing as their main reason the high co-payments required under managed care.[9]

In Argentina public hospitals that have not converted to managed care face an influx of patients covered by privatized social security funds. These patients have had to resort to public hospitals because they cannot afford their co-payments or because private practitioners have refused to see them (due to non-payment by the social security funds).

Argentina and Brazil's public hospitals now require reimbursements from social security funds and from private insurance, as well as co-payments. To receive free care at public institutions, poor patients must undergo lengthy means testing—with rejection rates averaging 30–40% in some hospitals.[10] And because managed care organizations attract healthier patients, sicker patients are being shifted to the public sector. This two-tier system undercuts the pooling of health risks and undermines cross-subsidies between healthier and more vulnerable groups.

APPROPRIATENESS OF HEALTH CARE AND REGULATION

The supposed benefits of privatizing social services are elusive, with inconclusive evidence on efficiency and quality standards in the private relative to the public sector.[11] Meanwhile, examples of market failures in private provisioning abound.

Clinical services and drugs are essentially private goods, and there is much evidence of failures in markets for them. Limited regulatory capacity compounds the problem. For example, in many developing countries overtreatment is a major problem in private health care. In Brazil caesarean sections are more common among private patients because doctors are paid more for operations than for normal births.[12] In Mumbai, India, private providers engage in unnecessary referrals and tests—with referring providers getting a cut of referred providers' fees.[13] By contrast, even though most Canadian and US and many European physicians are private, strong professional regulation ensures that there is no crisis of overtreatment.

In developing countries unregulated private pharmacists also overtreat illnesses or overprescribe expensive drugs. Such inappropriate

The supposed benefits of privatizing social services are elusive, with inconclusive evidence on efficiency and quality standards in the private relative to the public sector

use of medicines leads to dangerous treatment practices, higher health care costs and growing drug resistance. Drugs account for 30–50% of health care spending in poor countries, compared with 15% in rich.[14] People who cannot afford professional services must go to pharmacies, which often do not follow prescribing regulations—especially in China, South Asia and parts of Africa. In India more than half of out-of-pocket health spending and nearly three-quarters of inpatient spending go to medicines and consultation fees.[15]

COSTS

In many developing countries costs are rising and technology is accumulating in the private health care sector. Thailand's private health sector has as much or more of some high-technology equipment as the private sectors in most European countries, even though Thailand's per capita income is much lower and its disease burden is much different.[16]

In China a shift in focus from preventive to curative services has significantly increased drug sales since economic reforms began. Foreigners have invested in about 1,500 drug manufacturing ventures across the country.[17] With limited access to professional services and aggressive drug production in an unregulated market, the result is irrational drug use—particularly among poor people. In 1993 drugs accounted for 52% of China's health spending, compared with 15–40% in most developing countries.[18] In some rural areas Chinese farmers spend two to five times the average daily per capita income on a typical prescription. Apart from contributing to unnecessarily high medical costs, excessive and inappropriate prescribing of drugs in poor rural areas exposes patients to the risk of ineffective treatment and adverse side effects.[19]

As noted, in Latin America managed care organizations have taken over the administration of public health institutions—diverting funds from clinical services to cover higher administrative costs. To attract patients with private insurance and social security plans, public hospitals in Buenos Aires, Argentina, have hired management firms that receive a fixed percentage of billings, increasing administrative

costs to 20% of health spending.[20] In Chile administrative and promotional costs account for 19% of managed care spending.[21]

BRAIN DRAIN

In developing countries growth in private health care often draws badly needed human resources away from fragile public systems—as in Thailand in the 1980s and 1990s.[22] Public clinics are left to care for the most vulnerable groups—the poor, the elderly, the disabled—with fewer well-trained physicians.

EDUCATION

In most OECD countries about 10% of students attend private primary schools (both independent and government-dependent). That share tends to be higher in developing countries. In Latin America private schools account for more than 14% of primary enrolments, though in high-performing Costa Rica the share is just 7%.[23] Among 22 Sub-Saharan African countries with data the private share in 10 is 10–40%—in the other 12, less than 10%.[24] In India the share of private schools is highest in states with the lowest primary enrolments (Bihar, Uttar Pradesh), indicating that the private sector is the escape route for a poorly performing public sector.[25]

In many (though not most) developing countries private enrolments rise with the level of education.[26] Yet for a large number of countries in all regions, recent data are lacking on private enrolments at all levels—making this an area deserving attention from governments and donors.

Three issues are crucial in the private financing and provision of education. The first affects demand: high household costs compromise universal access to basic education. The other two are related to supply, affecting equity and efficiency. One relates to the comparative performance of public and private schools, the other to public subsidies for private schools.

HIGH FEES, LOWER ENROLMENTS

Requiring poor households to pay for schooling (private or public) is not conducive to achieving

Requiring poor households to pay for schooling is not conducive to achieving universal primary education and so is unlikely to help achieve the Millennium Development Goals

universal primary education and so is unlikely to help achieve the Millennium Development Goals. In Ghana two-thirds of rural families cannot afford to send their children to school consistently, and for three-quarters of street children in Accra (the capital) the inability to pay school fees was their main reason for dropping out.[27] Where school fees have been removed in Africa, children have flooded into schools.

QUALITY ISSUES

Many proponents of private education claim that private schools outperform public ones, are inherently more accountable and help students develop stronger cognitive skills and feel a greater sense of ownership for their education.[28] But little evidence substantiates these claims.[29] Private schools do not systematically outperform public schools with comparable resources. In Peru students in private primary schools outperform their public counterparts—but pay up to 10 times more for their education.[30]

In Brazil achievement scores in maths and language favour private school students to the same degree as in several OECD countries (Greece, Ireland, Spain).[31] But this advantage is linked to the students in each type of school. In every country studied, students in private secondary schools come from wealthier households than do students in public schools.

PUBLIC FINANCING FOR PRIVATE SCHOOLS— POTENTIAL DRAWBACKS AND BENEFITS

The main rationale for government support is that private education meets excess demand for education. But in most cases fee-based private education responds to different demand, not excess demand—particularly in low-income countries, where poor households have limited capacity to pay even public school fees. Thus government support for private education can be inequitable if it is not targeted to poor households. In OECD countries direct support for private primary and secondary schools averages about 10% of government spending on education. By contrast, in India nearly a third of direct education spending supports private

institutions—yet the country is home to more than a third of the world's children of primary school age not in school.[32] In Indonesia most rural private schools are as dependent as public ones on state subsidies.[33]

Many developing country governments also pay the salaries of private school teachers, making them less accountable to parents and principals.[34] Such subsidies place even greater stress on already weak public systems, which must provide services for the most vulnerable groups with fewer human and financial resources.

A study of 16 developing countries found that those with the highest private upper secondary enrolments also have the lowest overall upper secondary enrolments (India, Indonesia, Zimbabwe).[35] But in China, Jamaica, Malaysia and Thailand—which have relatively high enrolments—more than 90% of direct public spending on education reaches public schools.

MAKING PRIVATE PROVISION WORK FOR POOR PEOPLE

Despite its potential drawbacks, public funding of private schools can help in certain circumstances—particularly if governments have trouble paying the full costs (building schools, paying teacher salaries) required to achieve universal primary schooling. In some countries a shortage of public schools has led to expansion in private schools. To ensure that children from poor families unable to pay school fees are able to attend private schools, governments could finance their education through vouchers.

Colombia, for example, introduced a voucher system in response to a shortage of public secondary schools. This approach to public funding of private education can help expand schooling at lower cost for the government, because the only cost the government bears is the voucher. This is slightly different from a voucher system that enables families to enrol their children in the school of their choice, public or private. To avoid giving windfall gains to the middle class that customarily purchase private education, vouchers should be restricted to poor families—as in Bangladesh, Chile, Colombia, Puerto Rico and the United Kingdom.[36]

A study of 16 developing countries found that those with the highest private upper secondary enrolments also have the lowest overall upper secondary enrolments (India, Indonesia, Zimbabwe)

WATER AND SANITATION

Only about 5% of the world's people (about 300 million) receive their water from private companies. Most privatization of water and sanitation services has occurred through public-private partnerships in urban areas, with almost all occurring in the 1990s in highly urbanized countries (table 5.1).

Private companies are unlikely to be interested in providing water services in rural areas in low-income countries—because rural areas are generally considered unprofitable. In sanitation, public-private partnerships sometimes also view poor people as being unprofitable. Reflecting such biases, some private water companies have found ways of excluding poor people from service even in urban areas. In Cartagena, Colombia, a large shantytown did not receive water services because the company considered it outside the city area.[37] Moreover, in some countries the extension of connections has been limited. In Dakar, Senegal, about 80% of the population had access to safe drinking water in 1994. Four years after the service was privatized, only 82% had access.[38]

International private sector involvement in water and sanitation remains limited in the urban areas of low-income countries. Even in middle-income countries, where most people live in urban areas, international private firms may be discouraged by the scale of investments required. Sustained service provision is best achieved through the efforts of local communities and firms (private and public), and building this capacity is an important role for government.

MIXED PERFORMANCE, UNCERTAIN FINANCING

Public-private partnerships in water and sanitation—which have grown from almost none in the early 1990s to more than 2,350 today—have a mixed record of performance. One of the main arguments for privatization is that it provides new capital, enabling public-private partnerships to mobilize additional resources for basic services. But since peaking in 1996, international private financing for water and sanitation has declined. And that decline is expected to continue.[39]

TABLE 5.1
Investments in water and sanitation projects involving private participation, various countries, 1990–94 and 1995–2000
(millions of US dollars)

Country	1990–94	1995–2000
Argentina	4,075	4,173
Brazil	3	2,891
Chile	128	3,720
Czech Republic	16	37
Indonesia	4	883
Malaysia	3,977	1,116
Mali	0	697
Mexico	295	277
Philippines	n.a.	5,820
Romania	n.a.	1,025
South Africa	n.a.	209

Source: World Bank 2002j.

SERVICE CHARGES

The private sector's reluctance to fund less profitable investments in poor rural areas hurts users. But public-private partnerships often do the same, even more directly—through charges that hit poor people disproportionately more. This fact has to be balanced against the even higher prices that poor people previously paid for water from small vendors.

Public-private partnerships are based on the assumption that customers pay for services. Privatization in water and sanitation has led to much higher fees, sometimes overnight—and sometimes with disastrous consequences (box 5.2). But if success requires higher tariffs, state water companies have shown that it is possible to use the additional revenue to improve services and expand coverage.

POSITIVE PRIVATE PROVISION

Not all privatizations of water and sanitation have been failures. In Sub-Saharan Africa, for instance, public-private partnerships have improved water quality.[40] More generally, success in privatizing water services largely depends on government regulation, investor interest and the initial state of the enterprise.[41] Countries with decent services before privatization often continue to do well after.

Where poor people have reaped the benefits of privatized water services, it has been due to political will. In Bolivia water and sanitation concessions in La Paz and El Alto were

User fees in South Africa and Bolivia

Privatization of water services has often led to increased tariffs largely unaffordable to poor households. Under some public systems, households enjoyed low water bills—well below the rate needed to recoup costs—and non-payment of bills was largely overlooked. This approach is undesirable because cash-strapped public companies essentially subsidize both rich and poor people. But an overnight jump from exceptionally low to excessively high water bills also has disastrous consequences for poor households.

South Africa

South Africa has made incredible progress in providing water supplies to its people, though managing fee structures has been a challenge. In August 2000, however, a cholera epidemic broke out in the province of KwaZuluNatal—infecting nearly 14,000 people and claiming more than 250 lives. The epidemic started after local authorities cut water supplies to people living in an informal settlement who were unable to afford new user fees. The minister of water affairs and forestry admitted that the policy of cost recovery

exacerbated the cholera epidemic, forcing households to seek alternative water sources.

In the build-up to privatizing water services, South Africa reversed its policy of keeping tariffs low and overlooking non-payment. But this reversal occurred overnight—and without concurrent measures to ease the financial burden on poor people.

Bolivia

In early 2000 protests broke out in Cochabamba, Bolivia, largely in response to the tripling and quadrupling of household water costs. This price hike came only weeks after Aguas del Tunari, a London-based private company, took over the city's water system. The protests effectively shut down the city for four days. And as protests spread throughout Bolivia, 50 people were detained, dozens injured and 6 died from the violence.

Many analysts agree that the significant increase in water tariffs was driven by the cost of an expensive construction project that households were obliged to pay for up-front. The Misicuni Project, one of the most complex en-

gineering projects in South America, involves building a $130 million dam, a hydroelectric power station and a $70 million, 20-kilometre tunnel used to transport water from the Misicuni River to Cochabamba.

User fees have great potential for impoverishing users and deterring people from using badly needed services. When user fees for basic social services have to be increased, governments must ensure that they are tailored to users. First, governments should be open with citizens about why increases are needed. There should be clear communication between service providers and users in this regard. Second, governments should strategically fix tariffs so that wealthier households can subsidize poorer. Other means of subsidizing poor people should also be sought. For instance, many campaigners in South Africa asked that the government provide 50 litres of water a day free of charge to poor households—the World Health Organization minimum for maintaining health and hygiene. Third, increases in water bills should be instituted progressively, not overnight.

Sources: ICIJ 2003c; Lobina 2000; Sidley 2001, p. 71.

awarded to the bidder that promised to make the most new connections in poor neighbourhoods. The winning bidder was then obliged to connect 72,000 families to piped water and 38,000 to sanitation over a five-year period.

In addition to contractually obliging private providers to expand services, governments have used revenue from privatization towards that end. Financial incentives, such as capital grants, have been offered to providers that service poor neighbourhoods. In addition, the high tariffs that tend to accompany privatization can be offset with subsidies targeting poor people. In Chile government subsidies ensured that no household spent more than 5% of its income on water.[42]

PROMISING APPROACHES

Government programmes have registered many successes in delivering basic social services to all citizens. Thus privatization need not be seen as the only option for reforming poorly run public services.

RELYING ON EFFECTIVE GOVERNMENT SYSTEMS

Many activities in the social sectors produce public goods or have many externalities, requiring state involvement to provide basic services to all. The recent push to privatize basic social services has ignored the past experiences of rich countries—as well as of many developing countries today—which relied on state systems to provide basic social services to most (if not all) of their people when they were developing. Private actors played only a limited role.

Many of today's high-performing developing countries managed to improve health indicators early in their development—providing universal health care paid out of government revenues. In many (Botswana, Costa Rica, Zimbabwe) better-off citizens opted out by taking private health insurance.[43] Or, if private insurance was not available (Sri Lanka and Kerala, India), they paid private providers directly.[44] But for most of these countries' populations, better health was the result of universal and affordable care—financed by government revenues and made effective by allocating resources to the lower levels of the health system.[45]

High-performing developing countries also began pursuing universal primary education early in their development, when their incomes were lower. Countries with literacy rates above those of their neighbours in 1980 also had smaller shares of students in private schools in the 15 years leading to 1980. In South Asia, for example, Sri Lanka's literacy rate in 1980 was 85%—while the regional average was an extraordinarily low 38%.[46] And Sri Lanka's proportion of students in private primary and secondary education was low in the 15 years to 1980.

In water and sanitation there is ample evidence of inefficient, oversized, corrupt state-owned companies. But there are also successful public systems largely ignored by proponents of privatization. Chile, for example, made safe water available to 97% of its urban population by 1990, and sanitation to 80%. And in Bogota, Colombia, municipal water services were threatened with privatization—but, completely reformed, they have expanded coverage (box 5.3).

In Debrecen, Hungary, the state-run water company required considerable investment in the mid-1990s. Attempts were made to contract the service to one transnational water company, then another—but both attempts failed. In 1995 the city council decided that local water managers had the expertise to carry out the work. A new local public company made the needed investments at much lower costs than the bids by the private companies, partly by sourcing supplies locally instead of importing them. As a result prices are 75% lower than predicted by the private companies.

STRENGTHENING THE STATE

Regulatory capacity in developing countries has to be built up so that public and private provision works for all services and users. A key policy recommendation is to retrain government staff. This does not necessarily mean rich countries providing more technical assistance or technical cooperation—it means them paying for transfers of skills and exchanges of experience among poor countries.

In health the need for regulation applies to both privatized companies and existing private services, both to protect consumers and contain costs. Most health ministries in developing countries have extremely weak information systems, undermining their ability (or perhaps indicating their unwillingness) to regulate private

---

BOX 5.3

Successful state-run water systems

Efforts by the Chilean government in water and sanitation show that state-run systems can achieve positive results. By 1990, 97% of Chile's urban population had access to safe water, and 80% had access to sanitation. The cornerstones of the country's success:
• Separating central regulation and regional operation.
• Increasing financial investments in the sector.
• Developing a system for fixing tariffs objectively.
• Introducing incentives for efficiency.

Between 1988 and 1990 Chilean authorities established a new system for fixing tariffs objectively—essential to revitalize the industry. The regulator established a maximum tariff based on a model efficient provider, and any differences of opinion between the company holding the concession and the regulator were to be resolved by a tripartite commission of experts. The reform permitted the gradual adjustment of tariffs to new, higher levels. Objective tariff fixing was a main contributor to the success achieved in the management of water and sanitation services since 1990.

The private sector played a role in Chile's water and sanitation sector, but this role was limited and strictly regulated by the central government. There was a big increase in the contracting out of many activities by all companies, including operation, management and capital investment of entire systems, as well as maintenance of all aspects of the networks, meter reading and billing. Contracting out reduced the number of workers per connection. And in 1995 the average level of unaccounted-for water was 31%, far less than the Latin American norm of 40–60%.

In Colombia's capital, Bogotá, privatization was rejected in the late 1990s. The city refused World Bank money and transformed its public utility into the most successful in Colombia.

Source: ICIJ 2003a; Mehrotra and Delamonica forthcoming.

providers. In South Asia, despite widespread private provision and high private spending, regulation has failed abysmally to ensure quality care for most users of private providers.[47]

Regulation of clinical health services, for instance, requires tackling the proliferation of private providers—often untrained, unlicensed and unregulated. Governments must bring these actors into the public domain, which will require licensing and regular training to improve knowledge and skills. Training has increased provision of antimalaria drugs in Kenya and improved management of acute respiratory infections and diarrhoea in Mexico.[48] In addition, the Rural Medical Association of West Bengal has adopted the World Health Organization's list of 40 essential medicines for recommended use by its members. Getting practitioners to restrict their use of these drugs will improve quality and control. Other measures for regulating providers include developing consumer protection legislation, promoting professional ethics and providing non-financial incentives, such as enhanced prestige.

Accreditation can be used to inform consumers about which private medical providers are registered. A professional body that offers accreditation and training to unregistered providers would benefit both providers and the public. It would build on the desire of providers for social recognition and prestige. And it would help promote the use of essential medicines through public campaigns.

Improving consumer behaviour is also important for health care regulation. This can involve improving consumer knowledge or providing subsidies to make quality services more affordable. Governments can also create institutions that enable consumers to challenge private providers who offer poor care.

Regulation of education and water services is often equally weak. In water privatizations public water authorities often assume the role of regulator. But international private providers rarely adhere to their agreements with host governments (box 5.4).[49] Much more international support is needed to build regulatory capacity in these and other infrastructure areas if the private sector is to do more in achieving the Millennium Development Goals.

BOX 5.4

Metropolitan Manila and Buenos Aires: mixed record of experience with water privatization

Manila

In 1995 the Philippines declared a water crisis. The public water utility had left 3.6 million people unconnected to a water supply. And for those with connections, service was often erratic. In 1997 two private water companies won concessions to take over Manila's water system, dividing the metropolitan area into eastern and western zones. Within five years the companies had connected roughly 2 million more people to the network and service had improved significantly. During this time new service connections tripled from 17,040 a year (before privatization) to 53,921 (after).

Yet six years after privatization the water companies have performed below their targets—and are even asking to withdraw from the concessions. By 2001 one company had supplied water to 85% of its population, slightly below its projection of 87%, while the other company surpassed its target. But much debate surrounds the calculation of these figures, possibly leading to the dampening of reported success rates. Although one private water company saw no decline in the number of leaking pipes and water thefts, the other saw these figures increase. And by January 2003 water tariffs had risen by two to five times 1997 rates in both zones. Indeed, a 2000 survey of residents in 100 districts revealed a mixed perception of privatization, with 33% of respondents noticing better service, 55% noticing no change and 12% noticing deterioration.

Buenos Aires

In 1993 Argentina's government privatized the Buenos Aires water utility, and service quality and expansion subsequently increased. Company figures indicate that it connected roughly 1 million new users to the water system. And in the first year the company reduced water rates by 27%. But this drop simply rolled back significant rate hikes instituted by the public utility prior to privatization. In subsequent years the company repeatedly raised water rates, and in 1996 protests against high water bills occurred in Buenos Aires.

Furthermore, a government review found that by 1997 the company had built only about one-third of the pumping stations and underground mains it had promised to complete by then. And investments in sewerage networks totalled just $9.4 million—one-fifth the level promised. According to recent estimates, the picture is quite different when the country is considered as a whole. In the second half of the 1990s municipalities with privately managed water services have worked better than those publicly managed, particularly in poor areas, contributing to faster reductions in child mortality.

Source: ICIJ 2003b; Galiani, Gertler, and Schargrodsky 2002; ICIJ 2003d.

INVOLVING NON-GOVERNMENTAL ORGANIZATIONS

Social service provision by non-governmental organizations (NGOs) has been viewed as the "middle way" between market and state provision. For some analysts it provides a rationale for increasing the role of civil society organizations in providing these services. NGOs are often quite successful at filling gaps left by the public system (as with the primary schools set up by the Bangladesh Rural Advancement Committee). They are also useful in articulating community concerns, especially for poor people, to make institutions perform better. In water and sanitation, rural areas have been best served through user committees supported by NGOs.

But NGOs should be a complement to, not substitute for, state activities.

NGOs have also joined partnerships among governments, businesses and civil society organizations. When private firms win long-term concessions for urban water and sanitation services, the contracts usually require significantly increasing coverage. Doing so may require skills and resources beyond the scope of private firms, especially foreign ones. NGO partners can improve a firm's understanding of its poor customers (expanding the customer base, improving project design), reducing capital and operation and maintenance costs, as with the water concessions in La Paz and El Alto, Bolivia.

NGOs can also lend credibility and outreach to education and awareness campaigns. Vivendi, the French water company, initiated a partnership with an NGO in its Kwazulu-Natal project to better understand the needs of poor communities in South Africa.[50]

Through the politics of pressure and engagement, NGOs are creating new agendas for businesses. A continuum of protests and partnerships between businesses and NGOs is creating a new form of regulation for global business—civil regulation.[51]

IDENTIFYING BETTER WAYS OF FINANCING SERVICES

Aside from increasing government tax revenues, there are ways of improving service tariffs and charges to make them more rational and equitable. In health sudden, steep out-of-pocket costs can drive patients into (or further into) poverty. Surveys from 60 countries show that among poor groups, a larger proportion of households has high levels of health spending.[52] In the absence of public financing, prepayment schemes—which contain high health costs by spreading risks among pools of individuals—can help deal with this problem. Such schemes have not only helped protect poor households from catastrophic health costs, they have also helped organize communities to sustain local public health systems (box 5.5).

In public education there is scope for much greater cost recovery at higher levels in most developing countries. In the 1990s Africa and India increased cost recovery in public universities.[53] Still, it is nowhere near its potential: higher education provides enormous private benefits, and most people who can access it are not poor. Thus there is scope for much greater cost recovery (combined with exemptions for poor people).

In water and sanitation strategic tariff fixing (whether the provider is public or private) that raises user fees in line with higher use—coupled with targeted subsidies—is a good way to provide water services to more people. Targeting that is geographic (to places that poor people reside), rather than based on income, is more likely to succeed.

BOX 5.5

The Bamako Initiative: pooling community resources for health care

The Bamako Initiative is an initiative that pools community resources to finance local health care. The initiative has been implemented to a varying degree in more than 40 low-income countries, with half in Sub-Saharan Africa. It has not only protected households from catastrophic health costs, but has also organized communities to help strengthen and sustain local public health services. These communities contribute financial resources to local health clinics and have a voice in the management of these services.

The initiative's strategy is to revitalize public health systems by decentralizing decision-making from the national to the district level, instituting community financing and co-management of a minimum package of essential services at the level of basic health units. The aim is to improve services by generating sufficient income to cover some local operating costs, such as supplies of essential drugs, salaries of some support staff and incentives for health workers. Funds generated by community financing do not revert to the central treasury but remain in the community and are controlled by it through a locally elected health committee. From mere recipients of health care, consumers become active partners whose voices count.

After 10 years of implementation of the initiative, community action in most rural health centres in Benin and Guinea has enabled nearly half the population to be regular users of the services. It has also raised and sustained immunization levels close to health for all targets for 2000. Charging modest fees to users is seen in some cases as the most affordable option for the poorest people, who otherwise have to use more expensive alternatives—though it is less clear whether mechanisms exist to protect indigent members of the community.

Much of the success has been in ensuring that affordable essential drugs are readily available in health centres, under the scrutiny of committees. Another factor has been the improved attitude of health workers—traditionally one reason for people, especially women, not to use health services.

This experience suggests that in the absence of adequate government financing of health care, pooling of community resources, with some prepayment by the poor, is a fair and efficient mechanism for providing health services to poor people. Health systems that require individuals to pay out of pocket for many of the costs of health services restrict access to those who can afford to pay, and most likely exclude the poorest people. Fairness of financial risk protection thus requires the highest possible separation between contributions and use. There is consensus on the central role of public financing in public health. But for personal health care it is not the public-private dichotomy that is most important in determining health system performance—but the difference between prepayment and out-of-pocket spending.

Source: Mehrotra and Delamonica forthcoming.

International institutions promoting privatization of social services need to provide much more advance support to build regulatory capacity. The World Bank has some initiatives in this area, such as the International Forum for Utility Regulation, created in 1996 as an umbrella structure for learning and networking initiatives for utility regulators. But international agencies should do more than offer advice. They should also enable field visits of developing country regulators to other countries more experienced in private sector regulation. There is also a need to prepare model clauses for public-private partnerships in water. Such clauses would draw on the lessons discussed in this chapter, so that future contracts can avoid the pitfalls of past ones.

In water all revenues come in local currency, so servicing foreign loans involves an exchange risk for both borrowers and investors. This became a problem in Argentina, Indonesia and the Philippines after devaluations, putting pressure on water subsidiaries to raise tariffs to water users to service the loans. Thus central governments should encourage local authorities, which are usually responsible for water services, to borrow domestically—from national development banks.

Too often it is assumed that private sector involvement in water implies the involvement of foreign multinational companies. In many developing country cities small providers cover significant sections of the population: in Delhi, India, 6%; in Dhaka, Bangladesh, 10%; in Ho Chi Minh City, Viet Nam, 19%; and in Jakarta, Indonesia, 44%.[54]

In all sectors regulatory capacity should be built up before privatization. Otherwise, the private sector may merely respond to different demand, not to excess demand, whether in education, clinical health care or water and sanitation. With better information on the private sector and stronger regulatory capacity, the state can ensure that the private sector plays a complementary role in providing and financing these basic social services.

CHAPTER 6

Public policies to ensure environmental sustainability

Ensuring environmental sustainability—the seventh Millennium Development Goal—requires achieving sustainable development patterns and preserving the productive capacity of natural ecosystems for future generations. Both efforts in turn require a variety of policies that reverse environmental damage and improve ecosystem management. The challenge has two dimensions: addressing natural resource scarcity for the world's poor people and reversing environmental damage resulting from high consumption by rich people.

Many environmental problems arise from the production and consumption patterns of non-poor people, particularly in rich countries. Rich countries consume a lot of fossil fuels and deplete many of the world's fisheries, damaging the global environment. They also use a lot of tropical hardwoods and products from endangered species.

To ensure the sustainability of Earth and its resources, including the development prospects of poor countries, these harmful production and consumption patterns must change. Energy systems will have to generate much lower greenhouse gas emissions. Fisheries will have to be managed based on ecological limits rather than heavily subsidized free-for-alls. And international rules of the game will have to mitigate the overconsumption that endangers ecosystems and certain plants and animals. But with smart policies and new technologies, the costs of these changes can be quite low.

At the same time, many environmental problems stem from poverty—often contributing to a downward spiral in which poverty exacerbates environmental degradation and environmental degradation exacerbates poverty. In poor rural areas, for example, there are close links among high infant mortality, high fertility, high population growth and extensive deforestation, as peasants fell tropical forests for firewood and new farmland.

Given this chain of causation, policies that reduce child mortality can help the environment by lowering population growth and reducing demographic pressures on fragile ecosystems. Other examples of poverty contributing to environmental degradation abound.

Thus reducing poverty can play a pivotal role in environmental protection. Worsening environmental conditions—including depletion of natural resources and degradation of ecosystems and their services—hit poor people the hardest. And when poor people degrade the environment, it is often because they have been denied their rights to natural resources by wealthy elites. In many cases, for example, poor people are forced onto marginal lands more prone to degradation.[1]

Around the world, 900 million people live in absolute poverty in rural areas, depending on the consumption and sale of natural products for much of their livelihoods. In Tanzania poor people derive as much as half of their cash incomes from the sale of forest products such as charcoal, honey, firewood and wild fruits.[2] The least developed countries are the most dependent on agriculture and natural resources. Yet relying on primary products—agricultural and forest products, minerals, fish—for export earnings makes developing countries highly vulnerable to resource depletion and worsening terms of trade.

The relationship between poverty and environmental resources also has a strong gender component. Poor women and girls are hurt disproportionately by environmental degradation, often because they are responsible for collecting fuel, fodder and water. In many countries deforestation forces rural women and girls to walk farther and spend more time and energy collecting fuel wood. In Africa they spend up to three hours a day just fetching water, expending more than a third of their daily food intake.[3]

How global climate change threatens developing countries

Global climate change is expected to increase the economic disparities between rich and poor countries, especially as temperatures increase. The estimated damage for poor countries partly reflects their weaker adaptive capacity. Hence climate change is a major development issue.

Climate change could lead to large-scale, possibly irreversible changes in Earth systems, with effects at the global and continental levels. Though the likelihood and scope of these effects are not well known, they will be significant and so must be reflected in policy-making. Potential effects include:
- Reduced crop yields in most tropical and subtropical regions and increased variability in agricultural productivity due to extreme weather conditions (droughts and floods).
- Increased variability of precipitation during Asian summer monsoons, which could reduce food production and increase hunger.
- Reduced water availability in many water-scarce regions, particularly subtropical regions. Increased water availability in some water-scarce regions—such as parts of South-East Asia.
- Increased destruction of coral reefs and coastal ecosystems and changes in ocean-supported weather patterns.
- Rising sea levels. With a 1 metre rise in sea level, partly due to global warming, Egypt could see 12% of its territory—home to 7 million people—disappear. Rising seas threaten to make several small island nations—such as the Maldives and Tuvalu—uninhabitable, and to swamp vast areas of other countries.
- Increased exposure to vector-borne diseases (malaria, dengue fever) and water-borne diseases (cholera).

Source: IPCC 2001a, b; UNDP 1998.

Poor people tend to suffer the most from air and water pollution. They spend more of their household incomes on energy, yet the services they receive are often of low quality—such as biomass fuels burned in inefficient, polluting stoves, or kerosene lamps that cost more per unit of illumination than lamps powered by an electricity grid.

Poor people are also the most vulnerable to environmental shocks and stresses, including floods, prolonged droughts and the emerging effects of global climate change (box 6.1). Moreover, they are the least capable of coping with such shocks and stresses. In dryland India biodiversity-related products (such as wild fruits or honey) usually account for about 20% of the incomes of poor rural people. But during droughts they account for more than 40% because cultivated crops fail.[4]

Ignoring environmental sustainability, even if doing so leads to short-run economic gains, can hurt poor people and undermine long-run poverty reduction.[5] The strong links between poverty and the environment call for a focus on the needs of people whose livelihoods depend on natural resources and environmental services. In policy and practice, environmental management should create income-generating opportunities, strengthening people's property and user rights and fostering their participation in political decision-making.

The links between poverty and the environment also run in the other direction. Poor people are often deprived of the means and rights to invest in the sustainable use of environmental resources through improved water treatment and sanitation, cleaner energy technologies and so on. Poor people also lack the money to invest in substitutes for environmental services.

Ever-expanding consumption hurts the environment through polluting emissions and wastes. Growing depletion and degradation of renewable resources also undermine livelihoods. Over the past 50 years carbon dioxide emissions quadrupled, with much of the increase occurring in rich countries. In 1999 per capita carbon dioxide emissions in high-income OECD countries exceeded 12 metric tonnes—compared with 0.2 tonnes in the least developed countries.

Because of their larger contributions to global environmental degradation and their greater financial and technological resources, rich countries bear much of the responsibility for addressing environmental concerns. Rich countries also need to help poor ones pursue environmentally sustainable development. Achieving the Millennium Development Goals requires policies that stress the complementarity between sustainable development and environmental management and that minimize the trade-offs. Indeed, ensuring environmental sustainability is essential for achieving the other Goals (table 6.1).

Environmental resources

Ecosystems and natural resources, fundamental to so many productive activities, contribute much to the global economy. In the late 1990s agriculture accounted for nearly a quarter of the GDP of low-income countries.[6] Industrial wood products contributed $400 billion to the global economy in the early 1990s, and fisheries accounted for $55 billion in exports in 2000.[7]

Scarce natural resources and ecosystem stresses often force unwanted trade-offs on poor communities. A community can get more food by converting a forest to farmland, but in doing so it may lose environmental services such as timber, biodiversity, clean water, flood regulation and drought control.

Food

Human well-being depends on natural resources and environmental services that help produce food. People rely on soils to grow crops, grasslands to raise livestock and freshwater and oceans to support fisheries. Underlying much of this productivity: genetic resources. Over centuries farmers have generated crucial stocks of knowledge and productivity by breeding livestock and selecting, storing and propagating plant varieties. Diverse genetic resources enable farmers to adapt to environmental change by creating new livestock and plant varieties better suited to new conditions. In periods of scarcity, wild biodiversity is also a source of alternative food products.

Water

Natural resource mismanagement and degradation threaten vital water services—undermining economic growth, human well-being and environmental resilience. About 1.7 billion people, a third of the developing world's population, live in countries facing water stress (defined as countries that consume more than 20% of their renewable water supply each year). If current trends persist, this number could increase to 5.0 billion people by 2025.[8] Limited access to water is weakening the development prospects of many countries, and conflicts over water use and distribution are a common cause of international disputes.

TABLE 6.1

Why reaching the environmental Goal is so important for the other Goals

Goal	Links to the environment
1. Eradicate extreme poverty and hunger	Poor people's livelihoods and food security often depend on ecosystem goods and services. Poor people tend to have insecure rights to environmental resources and inadequate access to markets, decision-making and environmental information—limiting their capability to protect the environment and improve their livelihoods and well-being. Lack of access to energy services also limits productive opportunities, especially in rural areas.
2. Achieve universal primary education	Time spent collecting water and fuel wood reduces time available for schooling. In addition, the lack of energy, water and sanitation services in rural areas discourages qualified teachers from working in poor villages.
3. Promote gender equality and empower women	Women and girls are especially burdened by water and fuel collection, reducing their time and opportunities for education, literacy and income-generating activities. Women often have unequal rights and insecure access to land and other natural resources, limiting their opportunities and ability to access other productive assets.
4. Reduce child mortality	Diseases (such as diarrhoea) tied to unclean water and inadequate sanitation and respiratory infections related to pollution are among the leading killers of children under five. Lack of fuel for boiling water also contributes to preventable waterborne diseases.
5. Improve maternal health	Inhaling polluted indoor air and carrying heavy loads of water and fuel wood hurt women's health and can make them less fit to bear children, with greater risks of complications during pregnancy. And lack of energy for illumination and refrigeration, as well as inadequate sanitation, undermine health care, especially in rural areas.
6. Combat major diseases	Up to 20% of the disease burden in developing countries may be due to environmental risk factors (as with malaria and parasitic infections). Preventive measures to reduce such hazards are as important as treatment—and often more cost-effective. New biodiversity-derived medicines hold promise for fighting major diseases.
8. Develop a global partnership for development	Many global environmental problems—climate change, loss of species diversity, depletion of global fisheries—can be solved only through partnerships between rich and poor countries. In addition, predatory investments in natural resources can greatly increase pressure to overexploit environmental assets in poor countries.

Source: Based on UNDP; DFID; World Bank.

ENERGY

More than 2 billion people lack access to electricity and the services it provides, including lighting, refrigeration, telecommunications and mechanical power.[9] These services are essential to delivering education and health care and to creating productive employment opportunities.

In the poorest countries more than 80% of energy comes from traditional sources such as dung, crop residue and fuel wood.[10] Inefficient stoves and heating technologies often force local people to gather traditional fuels at a rate that exceeds the natural regeneration of these resources, degrading land. Cooking with such fuels can produce extremely high levels of health-damaging air pollutants, both indoors and out. Solutions to such problems involve linking changes in energy consumption patterns in rich countries to the use of low-cost, low-emission technologies in developing countries.

Transportation, the most energy-intensive sector, is a key challenge for achieving sustainable energy use. Governments should provide incentives for consumers and producers to switch to more efficient vehicles and more sustainable resource use. The price of petrol, much of which is determined by taxes, can make a big difference. Among OECD countries Canada and the United States have some of the lowest petrol prices—and, not surprisingly, the highest

per capita consumption. Austria and Japan have among the highest petrol prices—and per capita consumption one-quarter the US level and one-third the Canadian level (figure 6.1). In India petrol costs four times as much (at market exchange rates) as in the United States.

LIVELIHOODS

Natural resources and environmental services are a direct source of livelihood for many people—especially poor people in rural areas, who are the most severely affected when the environment is degraded or access to environmental assets is limited or denied. By maintaining the environment's health and productivity, natural resources and environmental services maintain livelihood options and potential for diversification. Variety is essential because poor people need to be able to diversify their use of natural resources and environmental services as conditions change.[11]

POLICY RESPONSES

Policy interventions to address natural resource scarcity for the world's poor people—and to reverse environmental damage from overconsumption in rich countries—must take into account the diversity of the natural environment, the many and varying causes of environmental degradation and the complex links between poverty and the environment. Interventions should also draw on past efforts to improve environmental management:

• Environmental management cannot be treated separately from other development concerns. To achieve significant, lasting results, it must be integrated with efforts to reduce poverty and achieve sustainable development. Improving environmental management in ways that benefit poor people requires policy and institutional changes that cut across sectors and lie mostly outside the control of environmental institutions—including changes in governance, domestic economic and social policies and international and rich country policies.[12]

• Successful environmental policies must see poor people not as part of the problem but as part of the solution (boxes 6.2 and 6.3).

FIGURE 6.1

Higher petrol consumption is associated with lower prices in OECD countries, 2001

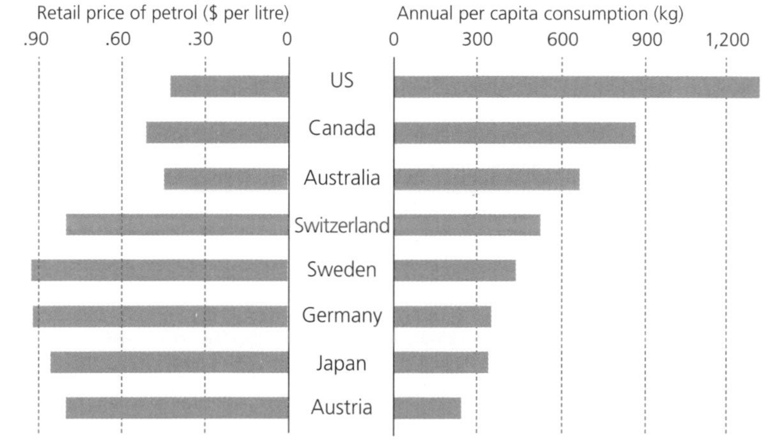

Retail price of petrol ($ per litre)   Annual per capita consumption (kg)

Source: IEA and OECD 2003.

- Environmental problems must be actively managed as part of the growth process. Environmental improvements cannot be deferred until rising incomes make more resources available for environmental protection.

Six policy principles should guide environmental policies:
- Strengthening institutions and governance.
- Making environmental sustainability part of all sector policies.
- Improving markets and removing environmentally damaging subsidies.
- Bolstering international mechanisms for environmental management.
- Investing in science and technology for the environment.
- Increasing efforts to conserve critical ecosystems.

STRENGTHENING INSTITUTIONS AND GOVERNANCE

Many environmental problems are grounded in institutional failures and poor governance. Three institutional failures are especially important for environmental management: inadequate property and user rights, insufficient information and opportunities for local stakeholders to participate in decision-making and weak monitoring and enforcement of environmental standards (box 6.4).

At the international level institutional and governance problems are evident in struggles to develop fair, effective systems to manage global resources such as oceans and the climate. At the national level weak property and user rights are a common cause of environmental problems such as deforestation, overgrazing and overfishing. Managing open access to a common resource is difficult because the decisions of individuals and companies are based on private costs and benefits—and so can reduce environmental and community well-being.

To respond, local people must have the power to manage the environmental systems on which their livelihoods depend. How? Partly by clarifying overall property and user rights to common resources, which may require reforming policies and institutions that control access to land and natural resources. And partly by

strengthening women's property rights, because women tend to be more dependent on environmental resources for their livelihoods.

Decentralization can improve environmental governance (see chapter 7). But it should be accompanied by efforts that build community capacity to manage environmental resources and influence planning and policy-making. Respecting the rights of marginal and indigenous groups, who often rely on natural resources for much of their incomes, is particularly important.

In many developing countries natural resources are plundered by corruption, benefiting powerful elites at the expense of poor people who depend on such resources. Countering corruption requires strengthening governance, with better enforcement, stiffer penalties and increased community involvement. In several countries citizens are assessing how well governments provide access to environmental decision-making and regularly monitoring environmental governance. Both efforts will likely spur further progress.[13]

MAKING ENVIRONMENTAL SUSTAINABILITY PART OF ALL SECTOR POLICIES

Most sector policies affect the environment, but too often environmental considerations do not inform policy-making. More scientific advice can ensure that understanding of the natural world feeds into the political process at all levels. Economic analysis, incorporating valuations of environmental assets, should also inform policy-making in all sectors.

Sector policies with significant effects on the environment should be subject to rigorous environmental impact assessments. In addition, Poverty Reduction Strategy Papers—as well as national development and sector strategies—should explicitly address environmental protection and management. National governments, multilateral organizations and bilateral aid agencies need to systematically incorporate environmental impact assessments into their policies and programmes.

Social policies related to the Millennium Development Goals also affect environmental quality (see chapter 4). Investments in human development, particularly in education for women and girls, offer numerous environmental benefits, including reduced population pressure. So, environmental policies need to address the gender dimensions of the links between poverty and the environment, integrating them into the formulation, implementation and monitoring of Poverty Reduction Strategies and related policy reforms.

National frameworks, such as strategies for sustainable development, should guide policies for natural resource management in light of a country's specific resources and concerns. Many national environmental action plans fail to address their effects on other sectors and on the needs of poor people. To improve environmental policy-making, such plans should explicitly address these concerns—as well as their contributions towards reaching the Goals.

IMPROVING MARKETS AND REMOVING ENVIRONMENTALLY DAMAGING SUBSIDIES

The normal operations of markets drive apart private gains and social costs because productive activities often generate private benefits for economic agents but impose costs on society. Thus regulation or corrective taxation may be required to align private and public incentives with the need for environmental protection.

Especially harmful are government policies, such as direct or hidden subsidies, that send the wrong signals by pricing environmental resources inappropriately. Reducing environmentally damaging subsidies is often far more cost-effective than directly regulating economic activity. Reflecting environmental costs in market prices—through pollution charges and other market-based policies—also promotes environmentally sound practices and sustainable use of natural resources.

Prices for irrigation water are an important example. Even though water is becoming more scarce in many countries, it tends to be provided to users almost free of charge. That approach promotes waste, increases soil waterlogging and salinization and discourages farmers from investing in water conservation. Other environmentally damaging policies include subsidies that promote large-scale commercial fishing and forestry and excessive use of agricultural chemicals such as fertilizers and pesticides (boxes 6.5 and 6.6).

Topping the list of damaging subsidies, however, are those for fossil fuel consumption. Worldwide, their value exceeds all foreign aid from all sources.[14] There is growing consensus that energy subsidies should focus on expanding access to technology, developing and disseminating cleaner fuels and increasing end use efficiency—not promoting consumption. As some European countries show, pricing fossil fuels appropriately can provide a powerful incentive for increasing the use of renewable energy. The lower unit costs of renewable energy technologies benefit both rich countries and developing countries considering their adoption.

Policy interventions should also account for the impact of economic activities on environmental assets. National income accounts (such as GDP) should differentiate between income from sustainable use of natural resources (sustainable agriculture and forestry) and from activities that reduce stocks of natural capital (extracting minerals or oil). These accounts should

also include the effects of economic activities on environmental quality and productivity, such as soil and water degradation.

Such "green" accounts place environmental problems in a framework that economic ministries understand. They also encourage decision-makers in finance, planning and sector ministries to pay more attention to environmental degradation. When the costs of environmental degradation and natural resource

---

depletion are accounted for, Sub-Saharan Africa's net savings rate goes from positive to negative in most years between 1976 and 2000.

BOLSTERING INTERNATIONAL MECHANISMS FOR ENVIRONMENTAL MANAGEMENT

Environmental degradation rarely stops at national borders, yet many environmental policies and institutions do. International watersheds, fisheries, pollution and climate change pose environmental policy challenges that must be addressed by countries working together—because the actions of one country affect the welfare of others. Compounding the problem are the unequally distributed benefits of environmental services and the costs of managing them within and between countries.

Several international environmental agreements have drawn attention to the need to manage the global environment. But implementation of these agreements could be improved. Greater emphasis should be placed on the needs of poor people, particularly in reaching the Goals. And more needs to be done to build developing countries' capacity to implement these agreements and integrate them with national policy-making.

New institutional arrangements may be needed to coordinate national policies in response to regional and global environmental challenges. Stronger cooperation is needed for regional environmental management. The countries along the Rhine river show how costs and benefits can be shared in managing an international watershed.

Intergovernmental processes tend to be difficult to organize and slow to execute, but they are the only realistic way to address cross-border pollution and ecosystem degradation. International agreements should share burdens equitably and ensure that the benefits of better environmental management accrue to the local people who bear the direct costs and lost opportunities of environmental resource protection. The Montreal Protocol—the international agreement to protect the ozone layer—has been a resounding success of global environmental policy. But its implementation was facilitated by cost-effective alternatives to ozone-depleting substances, limiting the need for extensive benefit- and cost-sharing between rich and poor countries.

Although rich countries produce most of the emissions that lead to global warming, the effects are felt all over the world. Meanwhile, progress on curbing these emissions has been mixed (box 6.7).

INVESTING IN SCIENCE AND TECHNOLOGY FOR THE ENVIRONMENT

Available technologies can go a long way towards addressing complex environmental challenges cost-effectively. Needed are ways to provide these technologies to people who need them most. In poor countries this will often require significantly strengthening institutional capacities for technological cooperation.

BOX 6.7

Policy responses to climate change

Scientific evidence strongly supports immediate action to curb the greenhouse gas emissions that cause global warming. The 1997 Kyoto Protocol places most of this burden on rich countries—because while they contain only 16% of the world's population, they generate 51% of such emissions.

The protocol calls on rich countries to reduce carbon dioxide emissions by at least 5% of 1990 levels by 2008–12. Supporters of the protocol see this as an important step towards mitigating climate change. Opponents castigate it for unnecessarily high implementation costs—due to restrictions on emissions trading—and for a lack of emission limits for poor countries. Another criticism is that, even if fully implemented, the protocol would reduce the average global temperature by less than 0.15 degrees Celsius by 2100.

The United States, which produces 25% of global greenhouse gas emissions, has refused to ratify the protocol. Without US participation, no international agreement on climate change is likely to significantly reduce the threat of global warming. But international cooperation is required to provide incentives for the private sector, consumers and governments to reduce greenhouse gas emissions.

To increase acceptance of the protocol, more attention should be paid to minimizing the costs of combating climate change. It will also be important to build on the Clean Development Mechanism, which permits reductions in carbon emissions through innovative international trading systems.

In addition, there is scope for long-term reductions in greenhouse gas emissions in rich and poor countries beyond the terms of the Kyoto Protocol:

• Developing clean energy technologies—solar or wind energy, fuel cells, hydropower, geothermal energy—that release little or no carbon dioxide. Making these technologies cost-competitive with fossil fuels will require increasing public investment in research and development and removing fossil fuel subsidies.

• Developing safe, economical carbon sequestration technologies that prevent the release of carbon dioxide into the atmosphere. Promising examples include natural carbon sinks such as forests, sequestration in deep seas and mines and chemical fixation of carbon dioxide as thermodynamically stable metal carbonates.

• Increasing energy efficiency through more efficient vehicles, appliances, lighting and industrial motors, and through reduced electricity transmission losses.

Source: UN 1997; Nordhaus and Boyer 1999, pp. 93–130; World Bank 2003i; Baumert and others 2002.

Improving technologies for environmental problems will require dramatically reorienting research and development policies. In rich countries public investment in energy research and development—including for renewable energy—has dropped precipitously over the past two decades.[15] Given the need to address climate change, increased investment is essential to expand markets for renewable energy technologies and lower unit costs, benefiting rich countries and enabling poor countries to adopt the same solutions.

Scientific understanding of the natural world is substantial, but a remarkable amount remains unknown. No mechanism exists to track major ecosystems and their continued ability to produce needed goods and services. A Life Observatory should be established to systematically monitor major ecosystems such as coastal habitats, major watersheds and wetlands. Such an observatory would complement current efforts, including the Global Terrestrial Observing System, the Global Climate Observing System and the Global Ocean Observing System.

The Life Observatory should build on the Millennium Ecosystem Assessment, a four-year effort involving 1,500 scientists compiling the best available knowledge on the world's ecosystems and the services they provide. The Life Observatory would ensure that these analyses are continuously updated to map the long-term effects of human activities on specific ecosystems.

To devise responses, policy-makers require reliable scientific forecasts of human-induced environmental change. Environmental indicators that accurately track the environment should be developed and integrated with national policy-making. Long-term planning should factor in projected changes in climate and changes to specific ecosystems to assess how these trends will affect development progress and needs.

INCREASING EFFORTS TO CONSERVE CRITICAL ECOSYSTEMS

Creating protected areas is often the best way to conserve species diversity and critical ecosystems. More than 60% of terrestrial species are found in 25 ecoregions on just over 1% of Earth's land surface. These biodiversity hotspots face extreme threats that have already caused a 70% loss of their original vegetation.[16]

The best hope for conserving biodiversity and critical ecosystems is for the world's governments, scientists and other key stakeholders to set priorities and cooperate on common goals. Conservation efforts are most effective when constructed by experts from a wide array of disciplines, in consultation with local residents.

Well-managed protected areas can generate significant revenues through tourism and innovative financial mechanisms, such as payments for ecosystem services. Local people, particularly poor people, should be seen as part of the solution—not part of the problem. People whose livelihoods depend on protected areas must benefit from them and have a stake in their continued success. Otherwise such efforts will not be sustainable.

Available technologies can go a long way towards addressing complex environmental challenges cost-effectively

CHAPTER 7

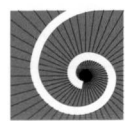 **Mobilizing grass-roots support for the Goals**

Men and women have the right to live their lives and raise their children in dignity, free from hunger and from the fear of violence, oppression or injustice. Democratic and participatory governance based on the will of the people best assures these rights.
— UN Millennium Declaration, p. 2

Implementing the policies and interventions required to meet the Millennium Development Goals requires the commitment of political leaders. But it also requires sustained political pressure, broad popular support and mechanisms for delivering services effectively. An open democratic state that guarantees civil and political freedoms is essential for such popular mobilization and participatory civic engagement, so that poor people can pressure their leaders to deliver on their commitments to the Goals.

Upon his inauguration as president, Brazil's Luiz Inacio "Lula" da Silva vowed to eradicate hunger by 2005 through his Fome Zero (Zero Hunger) programme.[1] This kind of political momentum, support and mobilization is critical for the Goals, and the Brazilian initiative will go a long way beyond halving the country's proportion of hungry people (Goal 1). Such mobilization around the Goals should be encouraged and sustained. Political leaders must be able to use the Goals to structure their political platforms and campaign manifestos, and electorates must be able to judge leaders' performance based on progress towards the Goals.

Such efforts are already under way in many countries:

- In Cambodia and Niger political leaders have articulated political platforms and policy agendas integrating several Goal-related concerns.
- Chile is promoting public debate on the Goals and making them a major part of parliamentary discussions.

- Paraguay has a tradition of community involvement in setting development priorities, including training community leaders.
- Albania has a strategy to follow up its report on the Goals, including a regional advocacy tour and a plan to establish a forum for civil society organizations.
- Poland has a project to integrate poverty reduction and environmental protection efforts with its national strategy for achieving the Goals.
- Kenya is promoting partnerships with civil society organizations on the Goals. The Goals will also be part of a national meeting of stakeholders in Kenya's Poverty Reduction Strategy Paper (PRSP) process.
- Zambia's 2002 national human development report focuses on poverty and hunger, bringing these concerns into public and policy debates.[2]

The risk is that the Millennium Development Goals will be undermined by entrenched groups that resist policies reallocating resources to the poorest, most marginal members of society. It is more the rule than the exception that more schools and health clinics are built in urban areas than in poor rural villages, and that poor communities often pay more for water than rich ones (see chapter 4).

It is also often the case that pro-poor priorities—such as basic health and education—receive little political attention. The more unequal a society, the less likely it is to generate sustained political support for the Goals, because political power is usually concentrated and overlaps with economic wealth and social dominance. In unequal societies, elite-dominated progress towards the Goals is also less likely to benefit the poorest people. Moreover, overall national progress may still mean that large sections of the population are being left behind, as in Brazil, China, India and elsewhere (see chapter 2).

The risk is that the Millennium Development Goals will be undermined by entrenched groups that resist policies reallocating resources to the poorest, most marginal members of society

Whether the Goals succeed partly depends on the local political environment—on whether there are avenues for citizens to participate in decision-making through formal democratic structures or through direct collective mobilization and action

Reversing such inequities requires political pressure, with people making demands on decision-makers. But even if resources are reallocated and political pressure succeeds, a further risk is that mechanisms for effective implementation will not be created. Basic public services closest to the needs of the poorest people—health clinics, schools, hand pumps, standpipes or wells—are usually managed by bureaucrats and government employees who report to their superiors within the vertical hierarchy of line ministries. Such bureaucrats and government employees rarely feel a strong sense of accountability or belonging to the communities or neighbourhoods they administer. If they were instead held accountable to locally elected municipal bodies, services would likely be delivered more effectively. Effective, accountable responses are encouraged by local incentives—and censure.

The Millennium Development Goals are national political commitments with the potential to provide ordinary people with a powerful tool for holding their leaders accountable for results. The Goals are exciting because they articulate the dreams of ordinary people: to have a school nearby with teachers who show up for work and with books and pens for students. To have at least a hand pump that provides safe water and that women and children can walk to easily. To have a local health clinic supplied with drugs and staffed by a doctor and nurse.

But realizing the potential of the Goals requires that poor people organize and take collective action. This is not simple. Poor people tend to be less organized, less capable of articulating their concern politically, less able to gain access to public services and legal protection, less connected to influential people and most vulnerable to economic shocks.

Whether the Goals succeed partly depends on the local political environment—on whether there are avenues for citizens to participate in decision-making through formal democratic structures or through direct collective mobilization and action (box 7.1). The political processes that matter most to poor people are at the local level, because that is where they have the best chance of holding governments accountable.

The major political reforms of recent decades have made such outcomes more feasible. The 1980s and 1990s saw a huge increase in the global spread of democracy. Some 81 countries—29 in Sub-Saharan Africa, 23 in Europe, 14 in Latin America, 10 in Asia and 5 in the Arab States—took steps towards democratization.[3] As part of these political changes there have been moves towards decentralization and an emergence of new social movements, giving citizens new ways to take collective action. This chapter examines these two political developments to draw lessons for political reforms and social actions that can provide the political momentum needed to achieve the Millennium Development Goals.

DECENTRALIZATION—ITS RISE, ITS ROLE, ITS REQUIREMENTS

In recent years a wide variety of countries—transition and developing, solvent and insolvent, authoritarian and democratic, with governments of the left, right and centre—have pursued decentralization. Since the early 1980s such reforms have been introduced in regimes ranging from monarchies to military juntas to single-party systems to multiparty democracies.

Decentralization involves a central government transferring to local entities some of its political authority and, crucially, some of its resources and administrative responsibilities. These local entities then provide some basic public services and functions. Multipurpose local councils have been created for this purpose in more than 60 countries.[4] And in Latin America, except in a few small countries, nearly all legislative and executive authorities are now elected in 13,000 units of local government.[5]

It is widely believed that decentralization increases popular participation in decision-making because it brings government closer to people—making it more accessible and more knowledgeable about local conditions and so more responsive to people's demands. But does evidence support this idea? More important, does decentralizing authority and resources help advance the pro-poor agenda?

THE CASE FOR DECENTRALIZATION

Where decentralization has worked (and this is no mean feat)—as in parts of Botswana, Brazil,

Madhya Pradesh and Rajasthan—education policies that deliver results

Madhya Pradesh and Rajasthan—two of India's poorest states, with the country's worst social indicators—have transformed schooling for poor people. How?

In 1994 Madhya Pradesh became the first state in India to implement the newly resurrected local governance system—*panchayati raj* institutions. The panchayat leadership, along with the state government, made universal primary education a priority. Between 1991 and 2001 Madhya Pradesh increased its literacy rate by 20 percentage points, from 44% to 64%. Similarly, literacy rates in Rajasthan rose by 22 percentage points, from 39% to 61%. Clearly, both governments were doing some things right.

Rajasthan's success in increasing literacy was driven by the 1987 Shiksha Karmi project and 1992 Lok Jumbish project. These projects initiated state-wide processes that created village education councils representing every part of each village, including women and most castes. The councils made decisions about setting up local schools, monitoring teacher and student performance and raising funds for them.

In Madhya Pradesh participatory surveys under the Lok Sampark Abhiyan (Public Interaction Campaign) at the village and panchayat levels found that dropout rates were not especially high, contrary to what teachers had reported. Instead, initial enrolments were low. Low enrolments were caused by several factors—not least the problem of access to schools.

The policy response was to introduce an Education Guarantee Scheme for primary schooling in all hamlets—not just all villages. Under this scheme, if the parents of 40 children in a locality (25 in a tribal area) seek a school for their children, the state government must provide, within 90 days, a lower-paid teacher's salary for that purpose. The village panchayat can appoint the teacher from within the community. It must also make arrangements for spaces where teachers can hold classes.

In the 50 years since independence, 80,000 schools had opened in Madhya Pradesh as part of the regular government primary school system—while within three years of the scheme's announcement in January 1997, 30,000 new schools were created. Of particular importance is that the scheme dramatically increased enrolments of tribal children—who had among the lowest enrolment rates among vulnerable groups. The scheme also led to a larger than proportionate increase in girls' enrolment.

The Education Guarantee Scheme offers lessons for similar situations around the world. Community demand for schools triggered government action. And while state governments pay and train the teachers, communities recommend them from among local people and provide the teaching spaces. The scheme's success shows that even with severe resource constraints, policy changes and innovative participatory and accountable processes can deliver pro-poor outcomes.

The scheme was so successful that it inspired a national campaign for universal primary education. But the national plan overlooked one crucial factor: the 90-day deadline for providing teacher salaries. This change in project design removed the imperative for the government to deliver within a specified period—and predictably, the national plan has stalled. Replicating project design therefore requires the successful integration of all elements of its success.

Source: Mehrotra and Delamonica forthcoming, Institute of Development Studies 2003.

Colombia, Jordan, South Africa and many states in India (Karnataka, Kerala, Madhya Pradesh, Rajasthan, West Bengal)—impressive achievements have been made, including:

• *Faster responses to local needs.* Local authorities tend to act more in line with local preferences and conditions, and no longer have to wait for permission from higher levels before acting. Decentralization also provides opportunities for women to participate at the local level, enabling a more gender-sensitive approach to policy formulation and implementation. Moreover, government health programmes become more widely used because local councillors are better able than bureaucrats to explain the rationale for them in terms that local people can understand—contributing significantly to the success of the health-related Millennium Development Goals.

• *More accountability and transparency, and less corruption.* Because decentralization tends to enhance transparency, the amount of money corruptly diverted from development programmes often declines in countries that pursue it. A recent study of 55 countries found that decentralization of government spending is closely associated with lower corruption among bureaucrats and reduced rent seeking by private parties—leaving more money to spend on basic services for poor people.[6]

• *Improved delivery of basic services.* Decentralization often reduces absenteeism among government employees in local schools and health clinics because elected local officials receive complaints from their constituents and can impose discipline. Thus reduced absenteeism enhances basic services at no extra cost— and is crucial to achieving the Goals for health and education.[7] Increased accountability also encourages local people to monitor programme implementation and to protest when government employees perform badly.

- *Better information flows.* Decentralization provides bureaucrats with early warnings of potential disasters—disease outbreaks, floods, droughts—and allows empowered local authorities to take swift remedial action.

- *More sustainable projects.* Decentralization makes development projects more sustainable because local people are more likely to be involved in their design, execution and monitoring (see chapter 4).[8] In addition, participatory budgeting and accounting enhance efficiency and transparency and make projects more gender-responsive.

- *Stronger means for resolving conflict.* Empowering regions and localities helps promote national unity and resolve conflicts, as in Ethiopia and Rwanda. In Namibia and South Africa decentralization was undertaken to redress inequalities among regions.[9] Reallocating resources ensured a more equitable distribution of national funds to regions previously neglected by dominant groups at the centre. It also enabled debate and renegotiation on the allocation of national resources—a source of long-standing conflicts between regions and ethnic groups.

- *Increased energy and motivation among local stakeholders.* Decentralization encourages local people to find solutions to their everyday problems—yielding innovative ideas and reducing the workload in centralized, hierarchical systems.[10]

- *Expanded opportunities for political representation.* Decentralization provides people with a much stronger voice in public policy decisions that affect their lives. In particular, it has increased representation among women (as in India, where one-third of council seats are reserved for women at the *panchayat*, or local, level[11]) and among previously marginalized ethnic groups (such as the Quechua and Aymara communities in Bolivia, the Kalingas and Gaddangs communities in the Philippines and rural ethnic groups like the Songhai and Dogon in Mali).[12]

Decentralization can make a particularly big difference in the provision of social services. It facilitates community participation in decision-making and can help resolve issues related to sharing the costs of service delivery. For example, in many cases where governments have been unable to provide schools, communities have pooled resources and labour to build them, with teacher salaries usually paid by the state (see chapter 5). Similarly, the Bamako Initiative has ensured the supply of essential drugs to remote rural communities in Mali and helped identify poor community members who cannot cover certain costs.

Decentralized entities are more efficient at delivering services than top-down sectoral ministries because local planning and participation ensure stronger links between interventions in health, education, water and sanitation and other services (see chapter 4). Local crises receive faster responses—especially because of the improved communications that decentralized systems facilitate. For example, in the Dhar district of Madhya Pradesh, India, a rural community intranet project, Gyandoot, started in January 2000, enabling prompt responses to an early e-mail warning and so preventing an outbreak of a cattle epidemic.[13]

Decentralization also improves implementation and monitoring of service delivery—and expedites responses to bad performance. Around the world, increased transparency and improved scrutiny have reduced both the level of corruption and the scale of embezzlement. Political power is no longer concentrated solely in the hands of national elites. As a result state employees— whether local elected representatives, civil servants or service personnel such as nurses, teachers and water engineers—are held accountable not just to the most powerful segments of society but also to the poorest citizens (box 7.2). Such a setup is critical when planning policy interventions for the Goals.

Many experiments with decentralization are under way. And while their full impact is still being assessed, early indications are promising.[14] The creation of locally elected authorities with jurisdiction over social services ensures

Decentralization provides bureaucrats with early warnings of potential disasters—disease outbreaks, floods, droughts—and allows empowered local authorities to take swift remedial action

Mutual pressures for accountability—between local governments and civil society—strengthen governance in Ceará, Brazil

In 1987 the newly elected state government of Ceará, Brazil, facing falling federal transfers and payroll commitments absorbing 87% of state receipts, undertook several innovative measures. It tried to overcome problems in service delivery by forming alliances with local workers and communities. The initiatives put pressure on local municipalities—from above and below—to improve their performance in areas such as public health, agricultural extension, drought relief and infrastructure construction (such as schools).

Having reduced payroll commitments to 45% in 1991, the government initiated programmes for preventive health and for public procurement from informal producers, as well as a large emergency employment generation scheme for workers laid off from government employment. The state recruited grass-roots workers to provide these services, and motivated them by publicizing their work and offering official recognition for their services—reinforcing respect for the workers.

At the same time, the government encouraged the public to have high expectations of the programmes and to hold workers accountable for their performance. It also informed people of what services they should receive, so they could put pressure on local governments to provide them if the services were not forthcoming. This publicity campaign helped mobilize collective action in communities, with technical support where necessary.

Between 1997 and 2001 the state saw impressive improvements in health indicators. Infant mortality fell by more than one-third, from 40 to 26 per 1,000 live births. Immunization coverage increased by more than one-third, with the number of fully immunized children rising from 67% to 91%. The rate of exclusive breastfeeding for the first four months of life increased from 46% to 61%, and the incidence of child malnutrition was halved to 7%.

Source: Fuentes and Niimi 2002, pp. 123–33; Mehrotra and Delamonica forthcoming.

that these authorities are held accountable to local leaders and citizens (box 7.3).

When decentralization initiatives are pursued with appropriate institutions and resources, they mobilize pressures from civil society and engaged citizens. Such reforms can yield significant benefits not just for poor and excluded groups but also for governments. By addressing many of the problems of poverty, such reforms tend to boost the legitimacy and popularity of governments that introduce them.

Decentralization is particularly significant for the Goals because many are contingent on the effective delivery of basic services. For Goals 2–7, for example, outcomes depend on better services and active engagement of the main stakeholders.

PRECONDITIONS FOR EFFECTIVE DECENTRALIZATION

Decentralization tends to be successful when the central government is stable, solvent and committed to transferring both responsibilities and resources, when local authorities are able to assume those responsibilities and when there is effective participation by poor people and by a well-organized civil society. These conditions generally result in responsive policies and services, increasing growth, equity and human development.

Still, the mere existence of a functioning state, capable local authorities and active civil society does not ensure successful decentralization. The relationships between these three levels are crucial: local authorities must feel pressure from both above (for accountability to national governments) and below (for service delivery to local citizens) to ensure effective and appropriate policies. Thus successful decentralization requires more than just certain political reforms—it also requires establishing a three-way dynamic among local governments, civil society and an active central government.[15]

Decentralization efforts are strongly influenced by a country's size, population, history, political climate and geographic and ethnic diversity. These differences call for different arrangements between central and subnational levels, including devolution, delegation and deconcentration.[16] Experiences with decentralization point to the importance of a few core principles, particularly those related to:

- The functions to be decentralized—which must be carefully selected.
- The resources that enable local authorities to deliver services—which must be provided for in decentralization plans.

BOX 7.3

Decentralization helps increase equity in Kerala, India

The Kerala People's Campaign started in 1996, sparked by the state government's decision to devolve 35–40% of state plan funds to village and municipal bodies. In its first two years the campaign led to the construction of 98,494 houses, 240,307 sanitary latrines, 17,489 public taps and 50,162 wells—all far more than in previous years.

The campaign mobilized local volunteers, notably from the Kerala Sastra Sahitya Parishad (People's Science Movement), and retired experts to assist with technical and financial appraisals of the projects, including engineers, doctors, professors and other professionals. The volunteers assessed residents' needs and resources in each locality, compiling information for *panchayats* (local elected councils), urban development reports and earmarked development projects. They also provided training in project planning, implementation and monitoring.

The participatory, consultative local deliberations increased resources by 10% for the projects because of material and labour donations—and delivered a larger percentage of project funds to scheduled caste and scheduled tribe communities (both historically oppressed social groups). More than 30% of project funds were dedicated to providing housing for these groups.

Under its Women Component Plan, 10% of every project budget was committed to projects benefiting women—such as vegetable gardening, sewing cooperatives, mobilization of *anganwadi* (preschool) personnel and the establishment of community centres for women. With new programmes in the public sector for health care and education, there have also been significant increases in literacy and health.

Source: Franke and Chasin 2000; Mehrotra and Delamonica forthcoming.

First, many functions with national scope require standardized, uniform provision by a central authority. Examples include defence, foreign policy, currency regulation and maintenance of national standards for primary education and immunizations and other public health interventions. The central government is best entrusted with tasks involving economies of scale and requiring higher financing and stronger regulation (such as training, oversight, technical assistance and capital-intensive facilities). For instance, Lao People's Democratic Republic experimented with decentralizing currency exchange across regions—leading to varied exchange rates and creating tremendous administrative and financial difficulties.[17]

Second, devolving decision-making to local authorities risks being an empty gesture unless backed by sufficient financial resources, administrative capacity and mechanisms for holding those authorities accountable. Village and town councils can sometimes raise some fiscal resources locally—provided they are given powers to do so, which is seldom the case. But much of the needed funding needs to be devolved from above. This does not necessarily require new spending, but rather transferring control over existing spending. Devolving spending does not risk fiscal irresponsibility, as some argue. Nor does it make councils hopelessly dependent on higher authorities, as others

claim—as long as councils have some power to decide how to use the funds.

Yet most central governments have failed to devolve adequate funds for local service delivery. Sometimes this is because they derive substantial tax revenues from certain sectors, such as forestry or mining, and want to retain control over them rather than turn them over to local councils or communities.[18] But without fiscal decentralization, efforts to decentralize are inevitably stymied.

Patronage systems—whether dominated by political parties or local elites, or reflecting an undemocratic environment—can also hijack decentralization. Inadequate, unreliable financial commitments from national governments, accompanied by political manipulation and favouritism of specific regions and constituencies, have disastrous consequences. Such shortcomings have created serious challenges for decentralization in Bangladesh, Côte d'Ivoire, Ghana, Kenya and Nigeria.

Some myths about preconditions for successful initiatives need to be dispelled. First, some insist that decentralization is doomed without land reform.[19] But experiences in Karnataka, India, and elsewhere show that is not true. Second, some maintain that a market orientation and an entrepreneurial middle class are essential to decentralization.[20] This too is inaccurate: there have been encouraging initiatives in countries such as Mozambique, where the middle class is underdeveloped.[21]

Successful decentralization involves three indispensable elements:

- Effective state capacity.
- Empowered, committed, competent local authorities.
- Engaged, informed, organized citizens and civil societies.

Effective state capacity. For a central government to devolve authority to local authorities effectively, it must have power to start with. Decentralization requires coordination between levels of government and requires more regulation—not less—to guarantee basic transparency, accountability and representation. The state has to oversee, regulate and where necessary sanction local authorities so that poor people really benefit from political reform. The state also has to raise adequate fiscal resources to support decentralization. When a weak state tries to decentralize, problems arise. In Ukraine, for example, it has been a challenge for a weak, unstable central government to keep local governments functioning with vastly shrunken resources and little or no civil society engagement at the local level.[22] Similar problems of weak national and local capacity have plagued other former Soviet countries that have attempted decentralization.

Decentralization is about state potential, not state failure. When a weak state devolves power, more often than not it is simply making accommodations with local elites—creating what has been called decentralized despotism[23]—rather than expanding democratic spaces. Take Sub-Saharan Africa, where centralized regimes have tried to control rural areas by appointing their own people at the local level—the opposite of sharing political power and enhancing local accountability.[24] Such moves have failed to deliver desired development outcomes.

Nor have decentralization efforts in Papua New Guinea given local people a stronger voice. They have been more about staving off a breakup of the country, under pressure from secessionist movements. The absence of a strong national government able to ensure territorial integrity has undermined the country's decentralization efforts. In such circumstances reforms

cannot deliver expected benefits.

Empowered, committed, competent local authorities. Responsibilities for delivering social services need to be devolved to local authorities through legislative or constitutional means that transfer control over both functions and functionaries. But functionaries cannot perform their functions without adequate finance. And whether decentralization serves the interests of poor people depends on whether local authorities promote social justice and are committed to pro-poor mobilization and policies.[25]

In Ceará, Brazil, and Kerala, India, state authorities were strongly committed to reducing poverty and prepared to challenge local elites if they resisted such efforts. For example, in Ceará the Northeast Rural Development Programme was administered by local governments but able to bypass local patronage systems.

Engaged, informed, organized citizens and civil societies. For local authorities to be responsive to people's needs, the two groups must be in constant communication. A well-developed, well-informed civil society, able to collect and articulate the views of the community, is thus indispensable.

In Mozambique committed local authorities working in a decentralized system doubled health staff and focused on outreach—improving vaccination coverage and prenatal consultations by 80%.[26] The government is trying to overcome capacity constraints by engaging partners and commissioning services from a range of providers—public, private, non-governmental organizations (NGOs)—at all levels.

In the state of West Bengal, India, where local authorities (panchayats) were empowered long before the national government required all state governments to create and empower them, poverty declined sharply in the 1980s.[27] Under Operation Barga the panchayats helped improve agricultural technology and reform land tenancy. They also helped register 1.4 million sharecroppers.

Since the late 1980s Mazdoor Kisan Shakti Sangathan (MKSS, or Workers' and Peasants' Strength Organization) in Rajasthan, India, has been campaigning for the right to information. MKSS organizes public hearings to examine official information—detailed accounts derived

For a central government to devolve authority to local authorities effectively, it must have power to start with

from official spending records—and assess its validity. It uses these "social audits" to promote democratic functioning at the most tangible and immediate level: the village.

The Philippines is pursuing decentralization under the 1991 Local Government Code, which allocates new functions to locally elected bodies and provides for wide participation. Civil society has been active in promoting public accountability at the local level.[28] The challenge has been to keep local elites from hijacking the process.

The failures of some decentralization initiatives point to a lack of public awareness and an absence of a culture of participation. Where civil society has demanded accountability and responses from local authorities, decentralization has been more effective.

Ensuring that these three actors—state authorities, local authorities and civil society—interact to improve the lives of poor people is a complex challenge. Indeed, there is nothing automatically pro-poor about decentralization (box 7.4). Dominant groups and narrow interests can hijack it. In Bangladesh, Côte d'Ivoire, Ghana, Kenya, Mexico, Nigeria, Papua New Guinea and Uganda such decentralization led to neither greater participation nor better social and economic outcomes for poor people. Uganda's ambitious but poorly financed and centrally directed decentralization programme has run aground because of its overly centralized technocratic approach and system of local patronage.

SOCIAL MOVEMENTS AND INNOVATIONS IN POPULAR PARTICIPATION

Direct collective action is another way for ordinary people, especially poor people, to influence decision-making and hold authorities accountable. Social movements have brought exclusion and deprivation to the political fore. They are most active where democratic freedoms have been won recently—or remain to be won. More than mere protests in the streets, they demand changes in decision-making processes. Decentralization has created new possibilities for popular engagement at the local level, leading to the proliferation of municipal activism.

MOBILIZING FOR BETTER LIVING CONDITIONS IN BOGOTA, COLOMBIA

For decades, residents of Bogotá, Colombia—particularly those in poor neighbourhoods—have been organizing and mobilizing support to improve the quality of life in the city and reduce violence. These efforts have had some impressive results. Residents were able to elect their mayor for the first time in 1988. In 1994 they elected the first independent mayor, Antanus Mockus, ending the dominance of liberal and conservative parties in the city. The rise of Mockus was largely the result of organization efforts in poor neighbourhoods. His administration put forth a development plan based on "constructing a new city". The following administration, of Enrique Peñalosa—another independent—emphasized the development of public spaces such as parks, plazas, sidewalks and bicycle paths.

Such efforts have tangibly improved living conditions in Bogotá. Deaths from traffic accidents are down, from a peak of 1,387 in 1995 to 745 in 2001. Homicide rates have fallen even more sharply, from a peak of 4,452 in 1993 to 2,000 in 2001. Perhaps most surprising was a voluntary tax campaign that increased city revenues by $500,000 during the same period.[29] A recent study of political, fiscal and administrative indicators by the Colombian National Planning Office gave Bogotá the highest score of all Colombian municipalities.[30]

PROMOTING A DEMOCRATIC CULTURE IN BOLIVIA

Bolivia's Popular Participation system is an example of the recent trend towards administrative and fiscal decentralization in developing countries.[31] The Popular Participation Law, passed in 1992, ensures that decentralization includes participation by local civil society and grass-roots organizations in municipal planning and oversight of development projects.

This approach was driven by the challenges facing local civil society organizations and reflected Bolivia's long tradition of community participation in both indigenous cultures and labour and mining unions. The Popular Participation Law divided the country into 314 municipalities

BOX 7.4

Does decentralization help reduce poverty?

Outcome

Area/country	Participation by or responsiveness to poor people	Impact on social and economic poverty
Bangladesh	Poor: some improvement in participation, but very weak representation of and low responsiveness to poor people	Poor on all criteria, undermined by corruption and political patronage
Brazil	Little evidence, but thought to be poor, as spoilage and patronage systems run by powerful mayors and governors still dominant	Good on equity and human development in exceptional areas where state and federal programmes combined with decentralization; poor on spatial equity
Chile	No evidence	Mixed: growth and equity good as a result of targeting, but human development and spatial equity show negative outcomes
Colombia	Fairly good: ambiguous evidence on participation and representation, but improved responsiveness	Fairly good: little evidence on growth or equity, but good results on human development and spatial equity
Côte d'Ivoire	Poor: low participation and representation, very low responsiveness	Spatial equity probably improved through government allocations to rural areas
Ghana	Mixed: improved participation by poor and community groups—but representation has hardly improved, and responsiveness is quite low	Limited evidence shows that resources were too insignificant to have made much impact; spatial equity may have improved through government allocations
Karnataka, India	Fairly good: improved representation, but poor people's participation is less effective and responsiveness low	Neutral: did little to help pro-poor growth or equity; human development and spatial equity indirectly benefited from funding allocations and development programmes
Kenya	Very poor: deconcentration scheme was politically run	Some impact on spatial equity through politically motivated redistribution
Mexico	No evidence available, but it is assumed that party-dominated patronage system has changed little	Poor despite significant central funding; equity, spatial equity and human development undermined by political patronage
Nigeria	Very poor: low participation and representation, bad record of responsiveness and lack of accountability	Poor: bad record on equity and human development; spatial equity subject to political manipulation and urban bias
Philippines	Mixed: representation and participation improved through people's organizations and nongovernmental organizations (NGOs), but evidence on responsiveness contested—and local elites remain powerful	No evidence
West Bengal, India	Good: improved participation, representation and responsiveness	Good: increased growth, equity and human development; evidence lacking on spatial equity

Source: Adapted from Crook and Sturla Sverrisson 2001, forthcoming.

that receive central funding for projects based on their populations.

While these reallocations have had mixed results in reducing poverty, they have reduced spatial inequality by providing resources to regions—such as remote rural areas—previously neglected. Decentralization has also increased participation by indigenous populations, especially the Quechua and Aymara communities. Among the new system's most important effects has been promoting an inclusive democratic culture.

RAISING AWARENESS OF HIV/AIDS IN THAILAND

Since the early 1990s Thailand's Population and Community Development Association, a nongovernmental organization (NGO) previously focused on family planning, has made enormous strides in raising awareness about HIV/AIDS. It helped promote compulsory informational broadcasts on radio and television for 30 seconds every hour. It also helped establish a national AIDS education programme. And it has conducted "condom nights" and "Miss Anti-AIDS beauty pageants" in the most frequented sex districts of Bangkok, providing an opportunity to educate high-risk groups—prostitutes and their clients—and to distribute condoms.

Such efforts have helped reduce new HIV cases, highlighting the importance of local mobilization. Building awareness, promoting contraceptive use and fostering local participation and support are thus critical for achieving the Millennium Development Goal of reversing the spread of HIV/AIDS, malaria and other infectious diseases.

MAINSTREAMING GENDER INTO BUDGET POLICIES IN SOUTH AFRICA

In 1995 the South African Women's Budget Initiative was established by the Gender and Economic Policy Group of the Parliamentary Committee on Finance and by two policy-oriented NGOs focused on research and advocacy. By linking researchers and parliamentarians, the research was assured of being advanced into advocacy—while the parliamentarians were given

a solid basis for their advocacy. Not restricted to economics, the exercise promoted a multidisciplinary approach, integrating issues that conventional economic analysis does not address. Such oversights had often resulted in gender-blind policies. The initiative documented this gender blindness as well as the emerging problem of HIV/AIDS.

This work was extended when the Gender Advocacy Programme, a women's NGO, performed research in Western Cape Province on budget allocations in 2000 related to the Domestic Violence Act of 1998. Supported by the provincial government, the research examined the budget provisions made in the departments (justice, safety and security, welfare) responsible for implementing the act. Though such initiatives are still too recent to have affected policy outcomes, they are a step towards increasing participation and inputs for policy-making.[32]

Such policy formulation and budget measures have great significance for the Goals, especially those for hunger, education, women's empowerment, child mortality, maternal health and HIV/AIDS and other diseases. Providing basic services for targeted people and groups improves their outcomes, as do specialized services for vulnerable groups.

PARTICIPATORY BUDGETING IN PORTO ALEGRE, BRAZIL

In Porto Alegre, in Rio Grande do Sul, Brazil, the Workers' Party initiated participatory budgeting in 1988, thereafter strengthened with its electoral wins in 1992 and 1996.[33] Clientelistic budgeting was transformed into a fully accountable, bottom-up deliberative system, driven by the needs of city residents.

The scheme has had several good results.[34] Citizen participation in preparing and ranking public policies has increased impressively. The share of the city population with access to water rose from 49% in 1989 to 98% in 1996.[35] The number of children enrolled in elementary or secondary schools doubled in the same period.

All this was made possible by a 48% increase in local revenue collection that accompanied the interventions. Municipal funding has been redistributed to fund works in poor

In Bolivia decentralization has also increased participation by indigenous populations, especially the Quechua and Aymara communities

areas of the city. Transportation has expanded to outlying zones. The quality and reach of public works and services—such as road paving, housing and urban development projects—have increased. Many slums have been urbanized. Half the street pavement deficit has been eliminated. And corruption has been reduced.

The high level of civil society engagement and the change in attitude of the political authorities has been an enormous advantage for deliberation and consensus building. Representatives of the city's 16 administrative regions meet twice a year at plenary assemblies to settle budget issues. The events are coordinated jointly by the municipal government and community delegates, and attendees include city executives, administrators, representatives of neighbourhood associations and youth and health clubs and any other interested residents.

An annual assembly of the 16 regions in March assesses the previous year's budget and elects representatives to participate in weekly meetings for the next three months to work out the region's spending priorities for the coming year. The three months spent preparing for the second regional assembly involve local and neighbourhood consultations on issues such as transportation, sewerage, land regulation, day care centres and health care, and these findings are reported at the second assembly. Also at the second assembly, two delegates and their substitutes are elected to represent the region in the citywide Participatory Budgeting Council, to work for five months on formulating the city budget, incorporating the regional agendas.

The council is made up of the regional delegates, elected thematic representatives and delegates representing the municipal workers union, the neighbourhood associations union and central municipal agencies. This body meets weekly from July until September to formulate a municipal budget to be presented to the mayor. On 30 September every year, the annual municipal budget is presented, which the mayor can accept or remand to the council by his veto. The council can then respond by amending the budget or by overriding the mayoral veto with a two-thirds vote.

This participatory budgeting exercise has become popular, with more than 100,000 people (8% of the adult population) participating in the 1996 round of regional assemblies and the various intermediate meetings.[36] The work of several civil society organizations sustains the popular momentum by providing support to various meetings and raising awareness, advocating and researching for common community objectives.

The Porto Alegre experiment has been so successful that it has spread to many other Brazilian cities, including São Paulo, Santos, Belo Horizonte, Campinas and Vitoria, as well as other Latin American countries. These experiences offer important lessons for formulating strategies to address the Millennium Development Goals, especially those aimed at improving the lives of slum dwellers and ensuring sustainable access to safe drinking water and improved sanitation.

*   *   *

The examples of decentralization and local mobilization provided here focus on the redistribution of public spending, especially for social services. But they do not address other key issues of access to economic opportunities and productive assets. They are less likely to be effective in exerting political pressure for public policies that contribute to growth and that raise the incomes of poor households, such as tax reform, asset redistribution and promotion of investments in employment-generating industries.

That does not mean that the scope and ambition of such efforts are modest. There are other constitutional and legal commitments for which governments are accountable where social mobilization can also play a role: the elimination of poverty, the provision of employment, the reduction of inequality and the progressive realization and guarantee of human rights. The Millennium Development Goals put a spotlight on these objectives, which are properly the focus of human development. The path for reaching those Goals also matters and, as stated in the Millennium Declaration, democratic and participatory forms are best equipped for this.

The Porto Alegre experiment has been so successful that it has spread to many other Brazilian cities, including São Paulo, Santos, Belo Horizonte, Campinas and Vitoria, as well as other Latin American countries

CHAPTER 8

Policy, not charity: what rich countries can do to help achieve the Goals

This chapter analyses the role of rich countries in the international compact to achieve the Millennium Development Goals, a compact that leverages the global commitments to reducing poverty by building on mutual responsibilities between poor and rich countries. Poor countries must improve governance to mobilize and manage resources more effectively and equitably. Rich countries must increase aid, debt relief, market access and technology transfers.

The UN Millennium Declaration and the Monterrey Consensus (the result of the March 2002 International Conference on Financing for Development in Monterrey, Mexico) make it clear that poor countries are primarily responsible for achieving Goals 1–7. But these frameworks also reflect a new approach, with rich countries basing their support for poor countries more on performance—and seeing it less as an entitlement. Thus rich countries will increase assistance for poor countries that demonstrate good-faith efforts to mobilize domestic resources, undertake policy reforms, strengthen institutions and tackle corruption and other aspects of weak governance.

The commitments made by rich countries in the Millennium Declaration are spelled out in Goal 8 (box 8.1). These commitments have since been reaffirmed in various forums:

• The Monterrey Consensus recognized the need for a substantial increase in aid, urging donor countries to make concrete efforts to reach the aid target of 0.7% of gross national income set in 1970—and to vigorously pursue debt relief for countries that take steps to strengthen governance.

• The Doha ministerial declaration, issued at the 2001 meeting of the World Trade Organization (WTO) in Doha, Qatar, affirmed poverty reduction goals and committed to making the interests of poor countries central to the future work of the trade ministers. The declaration also committed to the objective of duty-free, quota-free market access for products from the least developed countries.

• The September 2002 World Summit on Sustainable Development in Johannesburg, South Africa, reaffirmed the need to increase aid, urging donors to work towards the 0.7% target and to reduce unsustainable debt for countries that demonstrate efforts to strengthen governance. It also called on WTO members to fulfil their commitments on market access.

If Goal 8 is ignored, it is hard to imagine the poorest countries achieving Goals 1–7. This Report shows what is needed to accelerate progress towards the Goals: Allocating sufficient funds to social spending. Restoring crumbling health infrastructure. Hiring more female teachers to encourage more girls to go to school. Removing inequities in public spending on water supply. Securing women's rights to land. Investing in agricultural research. Seeking new export markets. Taking a multitude of other practical steps to change policies, improve institutions and increase investments.

Governments of poor countries must lead the way in taking these steps, but they cannot take them on their own. Indeed, as the Millennium Development Compact argues, countries that have the steepest slopes to climb—the top priority and high priority countries—will need large injections of donor financing to invest much more heavily in health, education, agriculture, water, sanitation and key infrastructure. They cannot wait until economic growth generates enough domestic savings and raises household incomes. Indeed, these core investments lay the foundation for economic growth.

In addition, poor countries face constraints that can only be eased through policy changes in rich countries. They often face barriers to

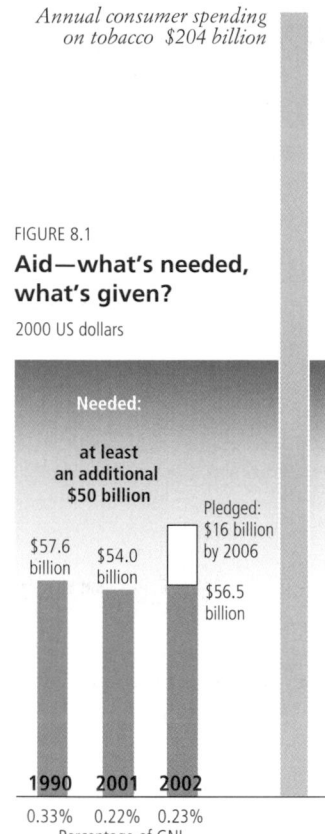

Annual consumer spending on tobacco $204 billion

FIGURE 8.1

Aid—what's needed, what's given?

2000 US dollars

Needed:

at least an additional $50 billion

$57.6 billion | $54.0 billion | Pledged: $16 billion by 2006

$56.5 billion

1990 2001 2002

0.33% 0.22% 0.23%
Percentage of GNI
in donor countries

Source: Total needed: World Bank and IMF 2001; total given: OECD, Development Assistance Committee 2003c; *Economist* 2001.

FIGURE 8.2

Official development assistance (ODA) in decline

Index, 1990=100
1990–2001

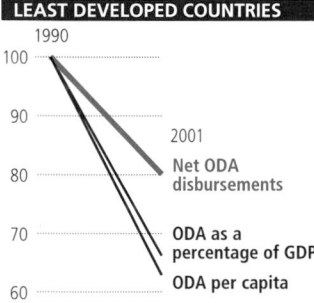

LEAST DEVELOPED COUNTRIES

1990

2001

Net ODA disbursements

ODA as a percentage of GDP

ODA per capita

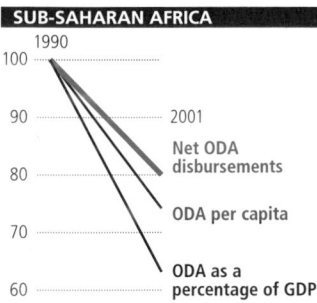

SUB-SAHARAN AFRICA

1990

2001

Net ODA disbursements

ODA per capita

ODA as a percentage of GDP

Source: OECD, Development Assistance Committee 2003a.

international trade. They are also hobbled by insurmountable external debts inherited from past administrations. And their lack of technological prowess demands global resources and know-how to solve problems of health, communication and energy.

AID—MORE AND MORE EFFECTIVE

Estimating the additional external funding needed to reach the Goals is difficult because it requires information on costs that vary enormously by country. Moreover, prospects for domestic resource mobilization depend on future growth and reforms. Various studies have estimated that external aid will need to increase by $40–100 billion a year. One frequently cited, conservative estimate by the UN Zedillo Commission calls for an additional $50 billion a year[1]—consistent with the World Bank's estimate.[2] This would require nearly doubling official development assistance from the 23 members of the OECD's Development Assistance Committee, bringing the total to about 0.43% of these countries' gross national income—still less than the 0.7% benchmark used since 1970 (box 8.2; figure 8.1).

These figures may seem huge, but they are not far from the situation before the 1990s. Between 1990 and 2001 official development assistance fell from 0.33% to 0.22% of donor countries' gross national income. But that drop mainly occurred in the early and mid-1990s, and by the end of the decade aid had increased considerably. The latest data show this trend continuing, with official development assistance increasing by 5% between 2001 and 2002. Still, such resources fall far short of what is needed—particularly to achieve the Goals.

Declining aid has hit hardest the regions and countries in greatest need. For example, Sub-Saharan Africa and South Asia saw dramatic drops in per capita aid in the 1990s (table 8.1; figures 8.2 and 8.3). These downward trends have continued to reverse since the UN Millennium Declaration was adopted in 2000, with announced increases in aid of about $16 billion a year—to 0.26% of donors' gross national income by 2006.[3] Though a good start, this is not enough to meet the needs. To increase financing, innovative ways of raising funds from capital markets have been proposed (box 8.3).

Though the Millennium Development Goals target aid to the least developed countries, these countries have not been fully protected from aid cuts. Of the 49 least developed countries, 31 receive less aid today (8.5% of their average GDP) than in 1990 (12.9%).[4]

Since the early 1990s human development advocates have campaigned to increase social spending to at least 20% of national and aid budgets. But aid for basic social services—critical for achieving the health, education, hunger and water and sanitation Goals—remains less

BOX 8.2

Official development assistance: the 0.7% target

The idea that rich countries should give 0.7% of their GNP for global development was first proposed in 1969 in the Report on International Development, led by former Canadian Prime Minister Lester Pearson. This figure has been widely accepted as a reference target for official development assistance. Endorsed by the UN General Assembly in 1970, it was part of the international development strategy for that decade. More recently:

• The Millennium Declaration calls on rich countries to give "more generous development assistance".

• The Monterrey Consensus calls on "developed countries that have not done so to make concrete efforts towards the target of 0.7% of GNP as ODA [official development assistance] to developing

countries and 0.15% to 0.20%...to the least developed countries".

• The World Summit on Sustainable Development also urged "developed countries that have not done so, to make concrete efforts towards the target of 0.7% of GNP as ODA to developing countries, and to effectively implement their commitments on such assistance to the least developed countries".

If members of the OECD's Development Assistance Committee (the world's 23 largest donors) actually delivered official development assistance equal to 0.7% of their GNP, aid would be $165 billion a year—three times the current level and well above current estimates of what is needed to achieve the Millennium Development Goals.

Source: UN 2002e.

TABLE 8.1
Net receipts of official development assistance by region, 1990 and 2001
(2000 US dollars)

Region	Per capita of recipient 1990	Per capita of recipient 2001	Percentage of GDP 1990	Percentage of GDP 2001
All developing countries	15	10	1.61	0.81
Least developed countries	33	20	12.92	8.45
Arab States	59	18	2.85	1.00
East Asia and the Pacific	5	4	0.77	0.32
Latin America and the Caribbean	13	12	0.48	0.32
South Asia	6	4	1.18	0.84
Sub-Saharan Africa	34	21	6.13	4.55
World	14	10	1.28	0.77

Source: OECD, Development Assistance Committee 2003a.

FIGURE 8.3
Official development assistance, net disbursements

2000 US$ billions

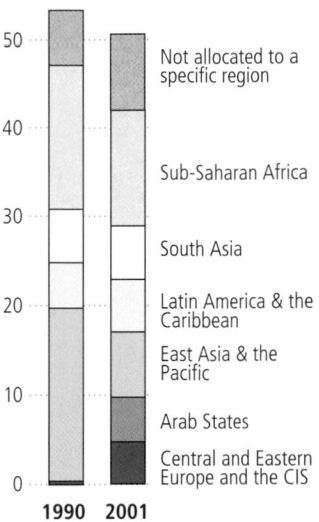

Not allocated to a specific region

Sub-Saharan Africa

South Asia

Latin America & the Caribbean

East Asia & the Pacific

Arab States

Central and Eastern Europe and the CIS

Source: OECD, Development Assistance Committee 2003a.

than 15% of bilateral donor allocations. It is rising, however, and Austria, Ireland, Luxembourg, the Netherlands, the United Kingdom and the United States have hit the 20% target.

MAKING AID MORE EFFECTIVE

Increasing aid will not be enough. As a recent World Bank study finds, at different times and in different places aid has been "highly effective, totally ineffective, and everything in between".[5] Aid contributed to many of the spectacular development successes of recent decades—Indonesia and the Republic of Korea in the 1970s, Bolivia and Ghana in the 1980s, Uganda and Viet Nam in the 1990s. International programmes drove the green revolution, efforts to control river blindness and expanded immunizations against childhood diseases. But too much aid has gone to countries with rampant corruption and misguided policies—conditions where aid can only be squandered.

What should be done to ensure that aid is more effective, especially in accelerating progress towards the Goals? Three issues that have dominated recent analyses—stronger governance, increased ownership and better aid practices—are central to the principles of stronger partnership that emerged from the Monterrey and Johannesburg conferences.

BOX 8.3

New financing for the Goals

Pledges since Monterrey
At the 2002 International Conference on Financing for Development in Monterrey, Mexico, the international community agreed to a coherent, principled approach to development—and to the first increase in aid in 20 years, with an additional $16 billion a year by 2006 (including pledges made since the conference).

The United States will nearly double official development assistance—to $15 billion a year—by 2006. The European Union will increase aid to 0.39% of GNP by 2006—about $11 billion more a year. Among individual members:

- Austria pledged to reach 0.33% of gross national income (GNI) by 2006.
- Belgium pledged to reach 0.7% of GNI by 2010.
- Finland pledged to reach 0.4% of GNI by 2007.
- France pledged to reach 0.5% of GNI by 2007.

- Germany pledged to reach 0.33% of GNI by 2006.
- Greece pledged to reach 0.33% of GNI by 2006.
- Ireland pledged to reach 0.7% of GNI by 2007.
- Italy pledged to reach 0.33% of GNI by 2006.
- Luxembourg pledged to reach 1.0% of GNI by 2005.
- The Netherlands pledged to reach 1.0% of GNI by 2005.
- Portugal pledged to reach 0.33% of GNI by 2006.
- Spain pledged to reach 0.33% of GNI by 2006.
- Sweden promised to aim for 1.0% of GNI by 2006.
- The United Kingdom agreed to reach 0.4% of GNI by 2005–06.

Other donors have also made important pledges. Canada agreed to increase aid by 8% a year, or by about $1.7 billion—by 2010 that would reach 0.28% of its GNI. Norway agreed to raise aid from 0.92% of GNI to 1.0% by 2005, equivalent to an annual increase of $250 million. Switzerland agreed to increase aid to 0.37% of GNI by 2010. And Australia agreed to a 3% real increase in 2002–03.

A proposal for a new financing mechanism
The United Kingdom has proposed creating a new mechanism—an international finance facility—to provide predictable, stable aid for the investments required to achieve the Goals by 2015. This temporary facility would raise funds until 2015. Donors would make long-term pledges for annual payments to the facility, which would then raise funds by issuing bonds in international capital markets—making resources available now, when they are needed.

Source: UN 2002a; United Kingdom, Her Majesty's Treasury 2003; OECD, Development Assistance Committee 2003d.

Governance—the policies and institutions that regulate interactions among individuals and groups in society—is seen as part of the foundation for sustained growth and human development. Thus many donors have predicated their support on efforts to strengthen governance—and provided support to strengthen it, primarily through technical cooperation. Fighting corruption, adopting sound macroeconomic policies and implementing efficient, accountable systems for the use of public resources are key to ensuring that external resources are not wasted. The rule of law, sound contract enforcement and strong public regulatory institutions are important for making a market economy function. These are important elements of good economic governance.

But other dimensions of governance are also important. As *Human Development Report 2002* argues, human development demands democratic governance that responds to the needs of poor people. Democratic governance requires more than policies and institutions that ensure efficient public services. It requires fair institutions and rules, as well as decision-making processes that give people a say and allow them to hold authorities accountable. So, political institutions that enhance the voice of people and the accountability of government are important for accelerating progress towards the Goals—though a pro-poor agenda might run counter to the vested interests of elites (see chapter 7).

Many countries have implemented programmes to strengthen democratic governance. Africa has launched a major regional initiative, the New Partnership for Africa's Development, that places a major emphasis on governance. And many donors have made support for governance a priority.

The second issue, ownership, is about countries being in charge. A lesson of the 1990s is that policy reforms are not implemented if they are not deeply embedded in a national commitment involving all of a country's stakeholders. This reinforces the findings of governance studies that participation matters. How decisions are made—the process—matters. But ownership is difficult to achieve when capacity and power are uneven. Most poor countries lack not only financial resources but also the institutional and human capacity to manage and drive development. Aid agencies often complain of institutional weaknesses in recipient countries that "force" them to take charge of designing aid interventions. But this asymmetry has undesirable consequences for ownership. Finding aid delivery mechanisms that minimize the burden on recipient countries is an important challenge in making aid more effective.

The final issue has long been part of the debate about making aid more effective: tied aid and donor coordination. Tied aid is costly for recipient countries because it limits choices in making the most economical use of resources. A recent World Bank study estimates that tied aid is 25% less effective than untied aid.[6] Members of the OECD's Development Assistance Committee have agreed to reduce (and report on) tied aid, and it has declined to about one-fifth of their overall assistance. But it remains high for a few countries—accounting for more than half of non–technical cooperation aid for Canada, Greece and Italy, while four countries (Austria, New Zealand, Luxembourg, the United States) do not report on it.

Lack of donor coordination can undermine recipient priorities. It has put a costly burden on recipient countries where public services are already overstretched. Ministers receive dozens of donor missions, and their staff spend enormous amounts of time preparing documents at various stages of the aid project process—from preparation to negotiation to implementation. Civil servants who should be designing policies and implementing programmes are instead spending their time receiving donor missions and preparing donor reports. In February 2003 the heads of bilateral donor agencies and multilateral institutions met at a high-level forum to review these issues. The Rome Declaration on Harmonization adopted at the meeting reflects strong commitment to action.[7]

WHAT SHOULD BE DONE?

Achieving the Goals will require much more ambitious aid programmes that tackle resource, policy and institutional constraints. As emphasized in the Millennium Development Compact, aid must focus on the poorest countries. But massive injections of resources—financial and technical—can create distortions, overwhelm weak national programmes and create resource dependency.

To avoid such outcomes, external resources must be embedded in nationally owned programmes and processes. That requires integrating the Goals and their targets with national budgeting, programming and planning processes—at the local, sectoral and national levels—that identify external financing resources. To be assessed is the gap between current external resources and domestic policies and the external resources and policy reforms required to achieve the Goals.

Most top priority and high priority countries are already using Poverty Reduction Strategy Papers as frameworks for agreements with external partners. As proposed in the Compact, these papers should assess what is needed to reach the Goals. As things stand, the papers set targets based on what can realistically be achieved given available resources and prevailing institutions and policies. Instead, gaps between the funds required to reach the Goals and the funds now available must be identified, as well as the capacity and governance weaknesses that need to be overcome through policy and institutional reforms. Determining how to fill these gaps, and integrating the results with the framework of the Poverty Reduction Strategy Papers, will need to be negotiated country by country.

Local coordination and dialogue can also strengthen consensus on priorities between donors and developing country governments. Tanzania shows how local aid can be coordinated based on a Poverty Reduction Strategy Paper (box 8.4).

Resources for the Goals could also be channelled through underfunded multilateral programmes such as the Global Fund to Fight HIV/AIDS, Tuberculosis and Malaria, the Consultative Group on International Agricultural Research and the Integrated Framework for Capacity Development in Trade.

Address aid selectivity: country performance relative to need. To make aid more effective, donors are moving towards greater policy selectivity. The donors that made pledges at the 2002 conference in Monterrey sent a clear

Gaps between the funds required to reach the Goals and the funds now available must be identified, as well as the capacity and governance weaknesses that need to be overcome through policy and institutional reforms

---

BOX 8.4

Making government-led partnerships work in Tanzania

The Tanzanian government and its development partners are pursuing two complementary approaches to improve aid coordination. The country's Poverty Reduction Strategy sets out a coherent, strategic national development programme. It is supported by the Tanzania Assistance Strategy, which maps out the role of partners.

The result is a widely endorsed, government-led process for coordinating external assistance. Achieving this was not easy, however. When Tanzania, a major aid recipient, stalled on its economic and structural reforms in 1995, partners had serious concerns about governance and accountability. As a result partners assessed their relationship with Tanzania and, perhaps for the first time, considered their own practices and began to engage more constructively with government—eschewing conditionality in favour of promoting national ownership and undertaking concerted attempts to develop capacity. A 2002 independent assessment of the development partnership found relations much improved, providing for a more solid foundation for sustainable poverty reduction.

The Tanzania Assistance Strategy sets out government priorities for building capacity using national, rather than parallel, aid management systems.

It also encourages development partners to provide more predictable funding. Doing so would strengthen planning, increase the impact of aid (through better coordination), promote sustainability, and increase oversight and accountability.

Government leadership in the process—complemented by reforms in financial management, local governments and the civil service—means that the Poverty Reduction Strategy has emerged as the country's overarching policy framework. Sector and thematic programmes are nested in the strategy, and government-partner dialogue is structured around its implementation. Strong government commitment to poverty reduction has ensured that the strategy informs the national budget and all sector programmes. In addition, an innovative, comprehensive Poverty Monitoring System ensures constant feedback between resource allocations (domestic and external) and poverty-related outcomes while Tanzania's Development Assistance Committee is an important element for building consensus among all partners. When combined with a strong policy framework, demonstrated national ownership and concerted efforts to develop domestic capacity, the country's positive experiences highlight much that could be replicated elsewhere.

Source: Hendra and Courtnadge 2003.

---

message: they will channel more resources to countries that demonstrate a commitment to reducing poverty by adopting pro-poor policies, taking steps to improve governance and achieving some results in the right direction—rather than just stating intentions and expectations. Without sound economic governance, large financial injections are likely to be wasted. And without democratic governance that gives voice to people, development efforts will not empower poor people.

Aid given in the absence of such preconditions, motivated by interests other than eradicating poverty and promoting sustainable development, has little impact. But if selectivity means no help, the Millennium Development Goals cannot be achieved. Aid allocations based on policy selectivity will help countries with good policies and strong institutions. But they will leave behind countries with poor policies and weak institutions. These countries need not only financial resources but also support—technical cooperation—to strengthen policy and institutional capacity. That does not require large amounts of financing, but is an important element of external assistance that also needs to be done right, as discussed below.

Strengthen policy and institutional capacity. For many countries, strengthening policies and institutions—reforming governance—is where they need the most outside help. Building such capacity should be a focus of development aid, though not a dominant portion of the financial resources allocated. It requires not finance, but technical cooperation for capacity development.

But technical cooperation has a mixed record. It has been much more effective at "getting the job done" than at developing national capacity. Many evaluations have found that once external support ends, project activities end as well—and whatever capacity was developed dissipates. For more than a decade, donors and recipients have debated the underlying constraints to capacity development and sought more effective approaches. For example, the conventional approach of sending foreign advisers to train national staff members can undermine the self-confidence of national staff. And sending national staff abroad

for degree-oriented training can simply increase the brain drain.

In the early 1990s the OECD's Development Assistance Committee adopted new principles for technical cooperation.[8] Though those principles remain valid, they have not been fully applied. Recent work by UNDP calls for a new paradigm and new principles for capacity development that recognize that capacity matters as much for development as do economic policies, that capacity is not just individual but institutional and societal, and that knowledge cannot be transferred but must be learned. The new approach also calls for new practices to make capacity development work (box 8.5).

Provide aid to countries in or recovering from conflict. Violent political conflict is a major obstacle to the Millennium Development Goals. Some 60 countries are in or recently recovering from such conflict—many of them among the top and high priority countries. It is critical for donors to support these countries through their crises, going beyond humanitarian relief to development aid. Some donors refuse to support such countries because resources could be diverted to fund war efforts. But evidence shows that denying aid to such countries results in greater human suffering and does not hasten the end of conflict.[9] Of course, donors should be aware of the potential misuses of aid, as when relief supplies are stolen or aid is used for political gain or further terror.

Supporting the state's authority is also critical—because when the state collapses, the economy also collapses, undermining human well-being. Many countries have shown remarkable success in sustaining the provision of essential services during conflict—or even improving them, achieving significant human development gains, as in Guatemala, Nicaragua and Sri Lanka (see chapter 3). Often this has been thanks to the work of non-governmental organizations (NGOs), local communities and foreign humanitarian organizations still able to reach people in need.

Improve aid practices. Key principles that should govern the aid practices of donors and recipients—to ensure aid reaches poor people—were recently summarized by former Bolivian President Jorge Quiroga under the acronyms of Mr. DUCCA and Mr. LIPPO.

Aid allocations based on policy selectivity will help countries with good policies and strong institutions. But they will leave behind countries with poor policies and weak institutions

Refocusing technical cooperation on capacity development

The importance of country ownership and national capacity has long been recognized, but technical cooperation often focuses on getting the job done rather than on developing capacity. Ten principles offer starting propositions for national stakeholders and external partners in search of promising approaches to building capacity:

• *Think and act in terms of sustainable capacity outcomes.* Capacity development is at the core of development. Every action should be analysed to see whether it serves this end.

• *Don't rush.* Capacity development is a long-term process, not amenable to delivery pressures, quick fixes and short-term results. Engagement for capacity development needs to have a reliable, long-term time horizon.

• *Scan globally, reinvent locally.* There are no blueprints: capacity development means learning. Learning is a voluntary process that requires genuine commitment and interest. Knowledge cannot be transferred; it must be acquired.

• *Use existing capacities rather than create new ones.* This implies using primarily national expertise, strengthening national institutions and protecting social and cultural capital.

• *Integrate external inputs with national priorities, processes and systems.* External inputs need to correspond to national demand and respond to national needs and possibilities. Where national systems are not strong enough, they need to be reformed and strengthened, not bypassed.

• *Establish incentives for capacity development.* Distortions in public employment are major obstacles to capacity development. Ulterior motives and perverse incentives need to be aligned with the objective of capacity development.

• *Challenge mindsets and power differentials.* Capacity development is not power neutral, and challenging vested interests is difficult.

Establishing frank dialogue and moving to a collective culture of transparency is essential to overcoming these challenges.

• *Stay engaged in difficult circumstances.* The weaker is the capacity, the greater is the need. Weak capacity is not an argument for withdrawal or for pushing external agendas. People should not be hostage to irresponsible governance.

• *Be accountable to ultimate beneficiaries.* Even if governments are not responsive to the needs of their people, external partners need to be accountable to their ultimate beneficiaries and help make national authorities responsible. Approaches need to be discussed and negotiated with national stakeholders.

• *Respect values and foster self-esteem.* The imposition of alien values can undermine confidence. Self-esteem is at the root of ownership and empowerment.

Source: Lopes and Thieson 2003.

For donor countries, Mr. DUCCA:

• *Decentralized decision-making.* A lot of donor decision-making is still centralized in donor capitals, where decisions are based on second guessing about local constraints and priorities—about matters such as water, schools and sanitation that are at the centre of achieving the Goals. Decentralizing donor decision-making to national levels enhances the role of recipients and increases their ownership.

• *Untied aid.* With tied aid so financially costly to recipients, untying it would give them more options and be more concessional and less prone to corruption.

• *Concessional aid.* Aid for most of the top and high priority countries—especially those that are heavily indebted or least developed—should be grants, because further loans would only add to already unsustainable debt burdens.

• *Coordination of donor projects and programmes.* Better coordination among donors would relieve administrative burdens on poor country governments and help governments align donor inputs with national priorities. Recent experiences have shown the value of sector-wide programmes for health systems (see chapter 4). Donors must also finance recurrent costs—often a critical bottleneck.

• *Accountability to the public based on programme results.* All aid delivery mechanisms should be underpinned by accountability. But accountability in aid relationships is often one-sided, emphasizing the legal accountability of recipients to donors and donors to taxpayers. Another aspect of accountability is even more important—to the beneficiaries, framed not in money spent but in results.

For recipient countries, Mr. LIPPO:

• *Local government and decentralization.* Local governments, closer and more responsive to the people, can be the main drivers for expanding health, education and other key services—if the right conditions are in place (see chapter 7).

• *Institutional reform to combat corruption and promote democratic governance.* Fighting corruption requires strong institutions. Democratic institutions give people a say and hold decision-makers accountable to the public.

• *Popular participation in development activities.* More widespread participation generally produces better development outcomes, particularly for poor people.

• *Progressive, more equitable assignment of resources.* More often than not, resources are allocated inequitably—and so require adjustment.

• *Oversight by civil society, individuals and NGOs.* An alert citizenry is essential for ensuring the accountability of public institutions and decision-makers.

DEBT RELIEF—FASTER AND DEEPER

Many of the top and high priority countries are extremely indebted, with two-thirds (31 of 59) eligible for debt relief under the Heavily Indebted Poor Countries (HIPC) initiative. (Only 11 of the 42 HIPCs are not among the top or high priority countries.) Important in reaching the Goals, debt relief will help put these countries on a course of sustainable development and release resources that could finance additional social spending and other priority investments identified in the Millennium Development Compact.

FOLLOWING THROUGH ON COMMITMENTS TO RELIEVING DEBT

Since the mid-1990s donor countries have committed themselves to addressing the debt crisis in poor countries and ensuring that none faces a debt burden it cannot manage (figure 8.4). In 1996 donors introduced the HIPC initiative to reduce debt and release funds to support poverty reduction (box 8.6). Spurring this unprecedented initiative was pressure from Jubilee 2000, a global

campaign for action on debt relief. Campaigners convincingly argued that debts owed by developing countries to well-funded institutions such as the International Monetary Fund (IMF) and the World Bank and to rich country governments were an unjust burden on poor people, who were paying for debts often incurred by since-displaced corrupt leaders. They argued that these debts were taking scarce resources from government budgets, leaving little for health care, schools and clean water.

Donor countries had another reason to cancel some of the debt. They were locked into "defensive lending"—endless rounds of debt rescheduling and new grants and loans to help poor countries pay back old loans, hardly a good use of new aid money.[10]

By early 2003 the HIPC initiative had benefited 26 countries.[11] Eight countries have reached their completion points, meaning that some of their debt has been forgiven. Another 18 countries have reached their decision points, meaning that they will begin to benefit from debt service relief. For these countries debt service declined from $3.7 billion in 1998 to $2.2 billion in 2001, or from 17.5% of exports to 9.8%. Annual debt service payments will be one-third (about $1.2 billion) lower in 2001–05 than in 1998–99.

Governments in these 26 countries are using their debt savings to increase spending on education and health, with about 40% directed

---

FIGURE 8.4

For the poorest: caught between falling aid and level debt

Percentage of GDP in least developed countries, 1990–2001

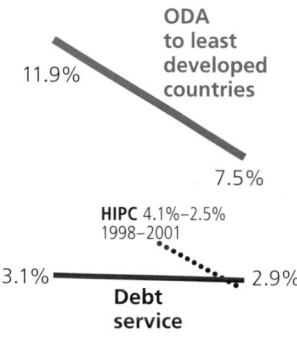

ODA to least developed countries

11.9%

7.5%

HIPC 4.1%–2.5%
1998–2001

3.1% — Debt service — 2.9%

Source: Human Development Report Office calculations based on data from OECD, Development Assistance Committee 2003c and debt service data from World Bank 2003i.

BOX 8.6

What is the Heavily Indebted Poor Countries initiative?

The Heavily Indebted Poor Countries (HIPC) initiative, launched in 1996 by the International Monetary Fund (IMF) and the World Bank and endorsed by 180 governments, has two main objectives. The first is to relieve certain low-income countries of their unsustainable debt to donors. The second is to promote reform and sound policies for growth, human development and poverty reduction.

The enhanced HIPC framework, approved in 1999, introduces broader eligibility criteria and increases debt relief. To be eligible, countries must be eligible for highly concessional assistance such as from the World Bank's International Development Association and the IMF's Poverty Reduction and Growth Facility. In addition, countries must face unsustainable debt even

after the full application of traditional debt relief mechanisms. They must also have a proven track record in implementing strategies focused on reducing poverty and building the foundations for sustainable economic growth.

Debt relief occurs in two steps:
• At the decision point the country gets debt *service* relief after having demonstrated adherence to an IMF programme and progress in developing a national poverty strategy.
• At the completion point the country gets debt *stock* relief upon approval by the World Bank and the IMF of its Poverty Reduction Strategy Paper. The country is entitled to at least 90% debt relief from bilateral and multilateral creditors to make debt levels sustainable.

Of the 42 countries participating in the initiative, 34 are in Sub-Saharan Africa. None had a per capita income above $1,500 (in purchasing power parity terms) in 2001, and all rank low on the human development index. Between 1990 and 2001 HIPCs grew by an average of just 0.5% a year.

HIPCs have been overindebted for at least 20 years: by poor country standards their ratios of debt to exports were already high in the 1980s. At the same time, HIPCs have received considerable official development assistance. Net transfers of such aid averaged about 10% of their GNP in the 1990s, compared with about 2% for all poor countries. To date 16 HIPCs have reached the decision point and 8 have reached the completion point (Benin, Bolivia, Burkina Faso, Mali, Mauritania, Mozambique, Tanzania, Uganda).

Source: World Bank 2003c; IMF and IDA 2003; Birdsall, Williamson and Deese 2002.

---

to education and 25% to health. Uganda has achieved almost universal primary enrolment. Mali, Mozambique and Senegal plan to use their freed debt to increase spending on HIV/AIDS prevention.[12] Another review of 10 African countries that have reached their decision points shows clear increases in social spending (figure 8.5).[13]

Yet the pace of relief is neither fast nor deep enough—and not enough countries have benefited. According to the original schedule of the HIPC initiative, 19 countries should have reached their completion points by now, not 8. Achieving the Goals will require additional resources—at least $50 billion a year in addition to domestically mobilized resources. More debt relief can help fill this gap.

There is also concern that the HIPC initiative will not be adequate for countries to escape their debt traps. Of the eight countries that have reached their completion points, two have returned to a ratio of net present value of debt to exports above 150%—the threshold considered sustainable under the initiative. Initial IMF and World Bank projections of debt sustainability were calculated during a global economic boom. This analysis relied on three assumptions that have since proven overly optimistic:

• *Exports would increase.* In the coming decade exports would have to grow at almost twice the rate of the 1990s if HIPC countries are to be able to service their debts. This would require the terms of trade for these countries to improve by 0.5% a year—even though they deteriorated by 0.7% a year in the 1990s.

• *Borrowing would decline.* New annual borrowing is projected to decline from 9.5% to 5.5% of GNP, and grants are projected to double. But already a few HIPC countries are borrowing at higher than expected interest rates.

• *Shocks would not matter much.* But most HIPCs are vulnerable to droughts, floods, civil conflicts and plunging commodity prices.[14]

WHAT SHOULD BE DONE?

The HIPC initiative did not provide enough debt sustainability for enough countries and needs further enhancement, especially given the larger financing needs of the Millennium Development Goals. Debt relief is more efficient

than aid as a way for donors to help poor countries reach the Goals because debt relief provides more flexible funding. It targets countries in need. And being untied, it provides budget support that can be applied to national priorities defined under poverty reduction strategies.

Strengthen links with the Goals. As recommended in the Millennium Development Compact, the financing requirements of the Goals should be assessed explicitly in Poverty Reduction Strategy Papers. Assessments of debt sustainability by the World Bank and IMF should be extended beyond the mere capacity to service debt to freeing up enough resources to reach the Goals.

More relief. Debt servicing capacity should be assessed relative to the country's needs for achieving the Goals. For many countries this will require full debt cancellation. The HIPC debt-export measure of debt sustainability has little to do with the needs of poor people. If debtor countries and donors want to prevent the diversion of resources from basic social investments to debt payments, one proposed measure of debt sustainability should be the ratio of debt service to GNP. Rich countries could extend debt relief until debt service falls under 2% of GDP. (Most HIPCs collect about 20% of GNP in tax revenue, and 10% of tax revenue would be a reasonable amount to pay for debt service.)[15]

Provide better insurance against shocks. HIPCs are particularly prone to natural disasters and price collapses for their commodity exports. An innovative proposal calls for a contingency facility. Under this proposal, when a shock results in debt service of more than 2% of GNP, external finance would finance debt service beyond this threshold.[16]

Other ideas outside current HIPC arrangements also merit consideration. Jubilee Research, the successor to Jubilee 2000, has proposed a debt restructuring programme for the Millennium Development Goals that would be a case-by-case process, overseen by an independent panel or court that would rule on the sovereign debtor's petition for protection from creditors. This approach has the appeal of placing the onus on the creditor as much on the debtor (box 8.7). But there may be unintended consequences—diverting resources away from the creditor's aid

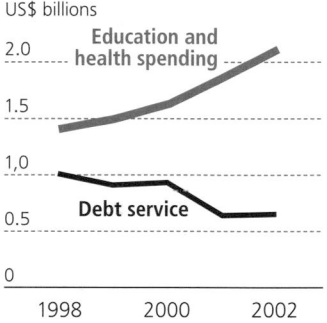

FIGURE 8.5

Spending shifts from debt service to human development in 10 countries benefitting from HIPC debt relief

US$ billions

Source: OECD, Development Assistance Committee 2003a.

BOX 8.7

A proposal for restructuring debt to reach the Goals

Since 1995 the Jubilee 2000 movement has campaigned to resolve international debt crises. Jubilee Research, the movement's successor, has proposed a radical new approach that would follow three principles.

Apply justice and reason to the resolution of debt crises

No one party to a debt crisis would be able to act as plaintiff, judge and jury in the court of sovereign debt.

Recognize the responsibilities of both debtors and creditors for the crisis

Under current procedures liabilities fall more heavily on debtors. Any assessment of how losses should be distributed would take into account the interests of creditors, but also the need to protect the human rights and dignity of the people of the debtor nation.

Ensure an open, accountable, transparent process

These are public, not private, assets and liabilities. Recognizing that there are three parties to any debt crisis—the debtor, the creditors and the taxpayers—all three should participate in the resolution of the crisis.

Source: Pettifor and Greenhill 2003.

As with Chapter 9 of the US legal code, affected citizens would have a legal right to have their voices heard in the resolution of a crisis. Such transparency and accountability help prevent future crises.

The debtor government would initiate the process by applying to the United Nations for an independent, transparent, accountable framework for arbitration. The grounds for the framework would be that debt service payments were crowding out spending on basic human rights, preventing the country from meeting the Goals.

During the next stage an independent arbitration panel would be appointed, with members appointed in equal numbers by the debtor and its creditors. These members would select a neutral judge or chairperson. In considering how much debt should be cancelled, the panel would require a full assessment of the resources required by the country to meet the Goals.

The United Nations would be responsible for ensuring that the process is conducted transparently, independently and fairly—for both the debtor and the creditors—and for ensuring that funds released by the process are used to achieve the Goals.

TABLE 8.2

Trade: exploiting the opportunities—or not

	Exports of goods, services and income (1995 US$ billions)	
	1990	2001
High human development	3,959	7,602
Medium human development	780	1,599
Low human development	41	61

Source: Human Development Report Office calculations based on data on exports and GDP deflator from World Bank 2003i.

petitive in the products they export and diversify into others. Yet countries with low human development have been slow to increase or diversify their exports (table 8.2).

Today's highly competitive global markets make export diversification difficult for countries with low human development. With open markets, capital, technological and human resource requirements have increased. International buyers of commodities demand high reliability and quality from suppliers in developing countries. These trends place a greater premium on knowledge, skills and flexibility. They also put more pressure on the poorest countries—which have the least skills, savings and capacity to adapt to changing environments.[18]

Faster progress in reaching the Millennium Development Goals—particularly in education and health—will help countries strengthen their exports. Healthy, well-educated people make a workforce more adaptable and an economy more productive. That changes patterns of trade—from exporting primary commodities to more processed goods, from low-skill manufactured goods to more skill-intensive goods.[19]

WHAT SHOULD BE DONE?

There is enormous scope for rich countries to expand market access and promote imports from poor countries by reducing tariffs and subsidies. Despite some significant recent initiatives, trade policies in rich countries remain highly discriminatory against the products produced in the poorest countries—especially in agriculture and textiles. The most important expectation of poor countries in the Uruguay Round of international trade negotiations (1986–94) was that rich coun-

---

programmes. Unlike the HIPC initiative, the programme also lacks a mechanism to ensure that resources released are used for poverty reduction.

TRADE—OPENING MARKETS, REDUCING SUBSIDIES

One reason for the debt problem is that like other poor countries, most HIPCs rely heavily on exports of primary commodities—which have suffered from declining prices. Countries dependent on such exports are being left behind by global economic growth (see chapter 3).[17] Although aid and debt relief will be essential to getting many developing countries on the right track, they are not sustainable solutions.

CHANGING TRADE PATTERNS

To compete and prosper in the world economy, developing countries need to drive their own development. They need to become com-

TABLE 8.3

Post–Uruguay Round tariffs and reductions in selected countries and groups
(percent)

Product category	European Union		United States		Poor countries		Rich countries	
	Tariff	Reduction	Tariff	Reduction	Tariff	Reduction	Tariff	Reduction
Agriculture[a]	15.7	–5.9	10.8	–1.5	17.4	–43.0	26.9	–26.9
Textiles	8.7	–2.0	14.8	–2.0	21.2	–8.5	8.4	–2.6
Metals	1.0	–3.3	1.1	–3.8	10.8	–9.5	0.9	–3.4
Chemicals	3.8	–3.3	2.5	–4.9	12.4	–9.7	2.2	–3.7

a. Data exclude fish and include the tariff equivalents of non-tariff barriers.
Source: Finger and Harrison 1996.

tries would open their markets in these two sectors. But the results have been largely disappointing. Protection in most rich countries remains extremely high, through a variety of instruments:[20]

Tariffs. Most rich countries apply higher tariffs to agricultural goods and simple manufactures—the very goods that developing countries produce and can export. In agriculture, the tariffs of OECD countries are heavily biased against low-priced farm products produced by developing countries (table 8.3). Tariffs against developing country manufactures also remain high. In the 1990s the average OECD tariff on manufactured goods from the developing world was 3.4%, more than four times the average of 0.8% on OECD manufactures. Bangladesh exports about $2.4 billion to the United States each year and pays 14% in tariffs—while France exports more than $30 billion and pays 1% in tariffs.[21] Moreover, the Uruguay Round did not change peak tariffs (those above 15%) on many developing country exports—60% of the imports from developing countries by Canada, the European Union, Japan and the United States were subject to peak tariffs.[22]

The poorest countries often also face tariff escalation—higher tariffs if they try to process their exports rather than simply export primary products. In New Zealand this "development tax" imposes a 5% tariff on coffee beans and a 15% tariff on ground coffee[23]—and in Japan a 0.1% tariff on unprocessed textiles and an 8.6% tariff on fully processed textiles.[24]

Quotas. Import quotas are a more extreme version of the same policy. Rather than just making developing country products less competitive, quotas do not allow those products past a certain volume to compete at all. OECD countries subject imports to a wide variety of quotas, particularly for clothing and footwear—labour-intensive products in which developing countries would have a comparative advantage. Quotas on clothing and textiles are to be phased out by 2005. But in 2002 quotas still governed most of the same clothing products covering quotas in the late 1980s. This lack of progress raises doubts about the seriousness of OECD countries to meet their 2005 commitments.

Export subsidies. Another way rich countries tilt the playing field for trade seems, on its face, to have little to do with trade. Rich countries, to varying degrees, pay large subsidies to their domestic food producers. These subsidies are so large—totalling $311 billion a year—that they affect world market prices of agricultural goods, causing direct harm to poor countries (box 8.8). EU-subsidized exports have contributed to the decline of the dairy industries in Brazil and Jamaica and the sugar industry in South Africa.[25] West African cotton producers have increased the efficiency of their cotton sector, achieving competitive production costs. But they cannot compete against subsidized farmers in rich countries (box 8.9). Indeed, OECD per capita subsidies for cows and cotton bolls are considerably higher than OECD per capita aid for Sub-Saharan Africa (figure 8.6). Annual agricultural subsidies in rich countries considerably exceed the national income of all of Sub-Saharan Africa (figure 8.7).

At the 2001 World Trade Organization (WTO) conference in Doha, Qatar, countries agreed to the eventual elimination of agricultural export subsidies—though no timeframe was set. A timeframe is obviously essential if the Doha declaration is to have any meaning.[26]

In the long term the real solution for commodity-dependent countries is to diversify into other export sectors, especially labour-intensive

FIGURE 8.6

Cows and cotton receive more aid than people, 2000

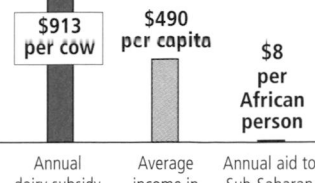

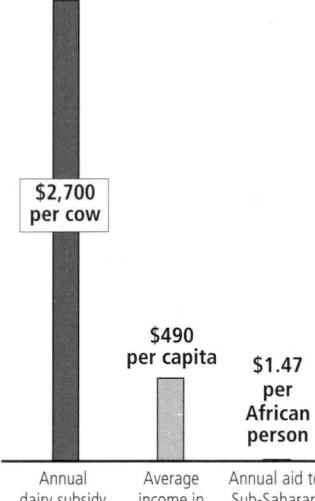

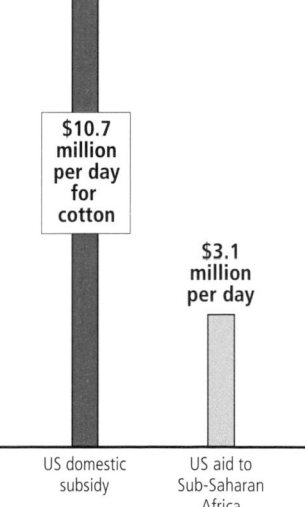

Source: Birdsall and Clemens 2003b.

FIGURE 8.7

OECD agricultural subsidies dwarf aid, 2001

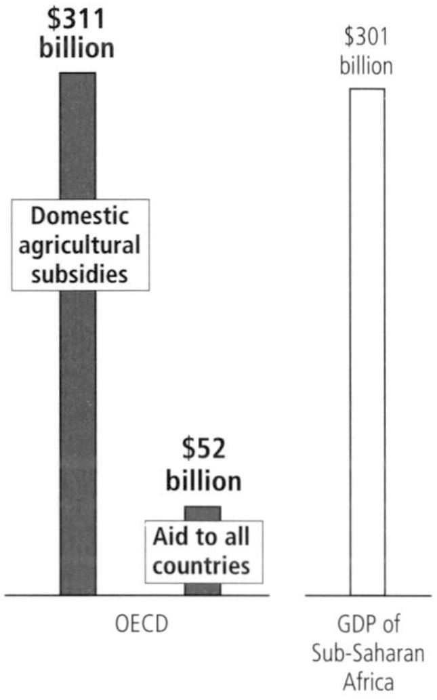

$311 billion

$301 billion

Domestic agricultural subsidies

$52 billion

Aid to all countries

OECD

GDP of Sub-Saharan Africa

Source: OECD, Development Assistance Committee 2003a; indicator tables 12 and 15.

BOX 8.8

The long international reach of domestic subsidies

Rich countries' subsidies to their farmers make their farms more profitable, encouraging greater production and lowering the prices of their output. The result: cheap, abundant agricultural products.

Who are the winners and losers? Domestic producers clearly gain, with higher profits. But domestic consumers unambiguously lose. They pay less for food, but they pay more in taxes to cover the subsidies—and the negative effect outweighs the positive. In addition, subsidies are heavily biased towards large producers. The European Commission estimates that, excluding Greece, half of all subsidies go to just 5% of farms.

But the effects go beyond national frontiers. Producers in poor countries must compete with subsidized producers in rich countries. They often cannot export their products to rich countries because their unsubsidized prices cannot compete with the below-market prices offered by farmers in rich countries. (Such is the case with sugar in the United States.) And they may not even be able to sell their products at home, because the subsidy-inspired surge in rich countries' agricultural production can create surpluses that are exported to poor countries at prices no domestic producer can match. (Such is the case with European milk.)

What about consumers in poor countries? Other things being equal, rich country subsidies should drive down the prices they pay for traded food, so they should benefit. But in many poor countries a large share of consumers are also agricultural producers. Such people are affected in two ways by rich country subsidies: the food they buy is cheaper, but their incomes are lower because of lower prices for the food they produce.

So, whether the subsidies increase or decrease poverty in poor countries depends on how many poor people in those countries earn their livings by selling food. A recent study found that removing subsidies hurts poor people in the short term when less than half of them live in rural areas. But in the average developing country about three-quarters of poor people are rural—and in the poorest African and Asian countries, more than 90%. Net food-importing countries benefit from cheaper world prices. But in the long run low prices dampen incentives to invest, which leads to stagnation of an important sector of the economy on which many poor people depend. That leaves rich country farmers as the sole true beneficiaries of subsidies, with a multitude of losers across the globe.

Source: Cline 2002.

---

manufactures. But in the short term, the international community could address the extreme volatility of commodity prices. Approaches at stabilization through international commodity agreements—tried in the 1970s and 1980s, then abandoned—are unlikely to attract much support given their poor record. A contingency facility could build insurance into the HIPC debt relief agreement, with additional relief provided after exogenous shocks, such as a sudden decline in the world price of a country's exports.[27] In addition, the WTO Agreement on Agriculture should be amended to ensure that no constraints are placed on developing country funding of projects to diversify commodity exports or insure prices for poor farmers.

Though estimates vary of the benefits to poor countries from trade liberalization in rich countries, most show huge gains. Just the static effects—those taking the present economic structure of poor countries—would be about the same as current levels of foreign aid. That does not mean that trade liberalization could or should be substituted for aid. For the top and high priority countries, aid is critical for immediately tackling the

structural constraints to achieving the Millennium Development Goals. For them the gains from trade will take more time to realize as they develop the capacity to respond to new opportunities.

The middle human development countries that export corn, wheat, rice, sugar and other agricultural commodities also have the capacity to export clothing, footwear and other manufactured goods. Thus many of the gains from trade liberalization in rich countries would accrue to them. But low human development countries would also benefit, especially exporters of commodities such as coffee and cotton.

Rich countries could make trade work for human development in many other areas. They could implement provisions friendly to public health under the WTO agreement on Trade-Related Aspects of Intellectual Property Rights (TRIPS; see below). They could exempt basic social services from the progressive liberalization principle under the General Agreement on Services (GATS; see chapter 5). They could address many other developing country concerns about trade, the

The Doha gamble for Africa's cotton exporters

Cotton is crucial to the economic development of several West African countries (Benin, Burkina Faso, Chad, Mali, Togo). Since the 1980s cotton production has quadrupled—and now ranges from 5–10% of GDP and accounts for 30% of exports. Much of the cotton is produced by small farmers, many below the poverty line. For most, cotton is the only product that they can export competitively. Cotton revenues also finance a large part of economic and social infrastructure in rural areas. Thus cotton prices and revenues are central to any poverty reduction strategy in these countries—and to achieving the Goals.

In recent years these countries undertook a number of reforms that significantly improved their productivity and cut their production costs to among the world's lowest levels (considerably below those in the European Union and the United States). Largely as a result, the region accounts for 15% of global cotton exports, second only to the United States.

But a number of exporters—including China, the European Union and the United States—heavily subsidize their cotton producers. In 2002 direct financial assistance was estimated to equal 73% of world production, considerably higher than the 50% recorded five years before. In 2001 these programmes cost $4.9 billion, with about half provided by the United States and most of the rest by the European Union and China. Some of these countries also provide assistance for cotton exports.

These distortions have artificially inflated the supply of cotton in global markets, lowering its price. The greatest price drops occurred in 2001–02. Poor exporting countries like those in West and Central Africa have suffered the most. Their non-subsidized producers must sell cotton at close to production costs, causing steadily declining real returns. The International Cotton Consultative Committee and International Monetary Fund believe that cutting domestic and export subsidies for cotton would return international prices to competitive levels—raising the incomes of poor cotton exporters and setting these countries on a course of sustainable growth. The question is, will the World Trade Organization's Doha Round of trade negotiations respond to and honour the competitive advantage of West African cotton producers?

Source: ICCC 2002.

environment, investment and the movement of persons. And they could increase the effective participation of developing countries in decision-making in WTO negotiations.

The November 2001 Doha Declaration committed all countries to make the needs of development, especially for the least developed countries, a central objective of future trade negotiations.[28] Unlike the other Millennium Development Goals, Goal 8 does not have a time-bound target. But this Report proposes that rich countries also respect a time limit for eliminating tariffs and quotas on exports of manufactures and for removing domestic subsidies on agriculture—a time limit before 2015, when poor countries are to achieve Goals 1–7.

GLOBAL TECHNOLOGY—SHARING THE FRUITS OF GLOBAL KNOWLEDGE

Recent decades have seen unprecedented technological progress, with dramatic advances in medicine, agriculture, energy, genomics and information and communications technology—offering huge opportunities to put the power of technology to work for development. Already

known technological innovations can do much to raise productivity and tackle problems of disease, water supply, sanitation, hygiene and hunger (see chapters 3 and 4). But many more frontiers remain to be crossed: low-cost energy for poor communities, cures for sleeping sickness, vaccines for HIV/AIDS and responses to ever-emerging new challenges. Technological innovations could accelerate progress towards Goals 1–7.

LINKING TECHNOLOGY AND HUMAN DEVELOPMENT—AND HARNESSING GLOBAL KNOWLEDGE

Technological innovations advance human development in two ways—by increasing productivity that raises household incomes (Goal 1) and by providing solutions to problems of disease, transport, energy, water supply, sanitation and information and communications technology for education, all important for achieving Goals 2–7.

Investments in technological innovations deserve high priority because they can overcome the constraints of low incomes and weak institutions. Though the 1980s saw limited

FIGURE 8.8

Oral rehydration therapy (ORT) reduces child mortality despite income stagnation

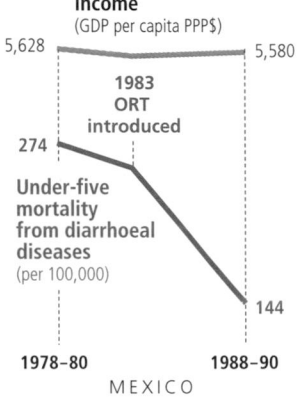

Income
(GDP per capita PPP$)

5,628 — 5,580

1983
ORT
introduced

274

Under-five
mortality
from diarrhoeal
diseases
(per 100,000)

144

1978–80   1988–90
MEXICO

Source: Gutierrez and others 1996.

poverty reduction and stagnant economic growth in most of the developing world, child deaths were cut due to technological interventions: immunizations and oral rehydration therapy (figure 8.8). In agriculture, too, investments in research and development have shown exceptionally high returns. Sharing the fruits of scientific and technological progress is one of the most important ways that rich countries can help poor countries fight poverty.

UNDERINVESTMENT IN TECHNOLOGY FOR POVERTY REDUCTION

Despite enormous potential and recent advances in biotechnology, relatively little investment goes into technology to solve the problems of poverty. In medicine, for example, the World Health Organization's Commission on Macroeconomics and Health has found "gross underinvestment" in the diseases that most afflict poor people.[29] These include tropical diseases such as kala-azar, Chagas disease and sleeping sickness as well as the main infectious killers (HIV/AIDS, tuberculosis, malaria). Together tropical diseases and tuberculosis accounted for 11% of the global disease burden in 1999. Yet of 1,393 new drugs approved between 1975 and 1999, only 16—just over 1%—were specifically developed for these ailments.[30]

In 1990 the World Health Organization's Commission on Health Research and Development found that only 10% of spending on health research and development is directed at the health problems of 90% of the world's people. This has not changed. The imbalance between scientific effort and social need can be measured by assessing the share of total spending on a disease relative to the global disease burden—about 1:20 for malaria, a disease that kills more than 1 million people a year and debilitates the productivity of millions more. Malaria is almost entirely concentrated in poor countries (99% of cases), and remains the primary cause of death in many.

Such outcomes are not surprising when one considers the incentives. Pharmaceutical companies and rich countries account for 93% of global spending on health research and development.[31] Poor countries and poor people's diseases mean little in market terms because

developing countries account for less than 2% of the market for major pharmaceutical products.[32] As a result poor countries benefit from global investments in research only when they suffer from diseases also prevailing in rich countries—as with HIV/AIDS. Even then, poor countries are unable to share in the fruits of such research due to high prices—maintained with the help of patents, as with those for retroviral drugs for HIV/AIDS.

Public funding for technology development—from both national and global sources—continues to be low. That is why public policy needs to step in, to increase investment and to improve access. In health the Tropical Disease Research Programme, jointly managed by the World Health Organization, UNDP and the World Bank, has about $30 million a year for a programme that covers eight tropical diseases. In agriculture research and development continues to be underfunded despite consistently high economic returns. Such investments have increased in Brazil and Mexico but declined in Africa. The premier global research programme for food crops, the Consultative Group on International Agricultural Research, had difficulty raising $377 million. (Meanwhile, the private corporation Monsanto spent $600 million on research and development.)

TECHNOLOGY ACCESS AND INTELLECTUAL PROPERTY RIGHTS

Rich countries, despite their commitment in the TRIPS agreement, have taken no real steps to share their technology in the interests of reducing poverty. The TRIPS agreement includes provisions for technology transfers, but with few details and no discussion on implementation The TRIPS agreement does not provide intellectual property protection for indigenous knowledge such as those used in traditional medicine. Intense public pressure has led to special price deals and donations from corporations in one visible area—medicines for HIV/AIDS—but little else.

The TRIPS agreement introduces a global minimum standard for promoting invention. Intellectual property regimes are intended to balance the two social goals of promoting inventions and promoting the use of inventions. Thus the TRIPS agreement incorporates provisions in the interests of users, such as compulsory licensing or parallel imports that give governments flexibility to allow local manufacturing or imports of goods under patents. But the wording of these provisions is so vague that they are difficult to apply—so clarifying them would be a first step.

The 2001 Doha declaration on TRIPS and public health was a milestone that recognized that intellectual property rights were subservient to public health concerns. It clearly stated that the TRIPS agreement does not and should not prevent members from taking measures to protect public health. It specifically recognizes the flexibility that countries have to use compulsory licensing for local production. The declaration also set a timetable of December 2002 to find a solution for countries that did not have adequate manufacturing capacity. But negotiations ran aground—reopening them is urgent.

The high prices restricting access to lifesaving drugs has become a huge ethical issue that pharmaceutical companies no longer ignore. Differential pricing—voluntary price cuts by pharmaceutical companies—has become an important mechanism for expanding access, especially to HIV/AIDS retroviral drugs. But experience shows that price cuts are no panacea, as the November 2002 report of UK Working Group on Increasing Access to Essential Medicines in the Developing World concluded. Experience also shows that in the absence of generic competition and lobbying, the cuts have limited response. After three years of operation, the most prominent voluntary tiered-pricing scheme, the UN-sponsored Accelerating Access Initiative, has delivered drugs to only around 30,000 patients—and at prices four or more times those of commercially available generic equivalents.

Standing in stark contrast is Brazil's HIV/AIDS treatment scheme, which used generic drugs to deliver cost-effective treatment to more than 115,000 patients in 2001 alone. Brazil's programme has cut the number of AIDS deaths by half and reduced common opportunistic infections among HIV/AIDS patients by 60–80%. Lower hospitalization and medical care costs generated savings of $422 million in 1997–99—almost entirely offsetting the cost of providing the antiretrovirals, and not including the economic benefits of rehabilitating patients to be economically and socially active. Countries with less capacity than Brazil, not able to follow in its footsteps, could benefit from importing products from Brazil—if agreement is reached on the TRIPS agreement.

Developing countries need to develop their own capacity to manufacture pharmaceuticals and other technology products for public health and development. But not all developing countries should do so—among them the poorest, smallest and lowest in human development.

WHAT SHOULD BE DONE?

Investments in global technology for reducing poverty and reaching the Goals need to be expanded to match the needs. Research and development to tackle the enduring problems of poverty need to be far more ambitious, such as in:

- High-yielding, drought- and pest-resistant varieties of food crops such as sorghum, cassava and lentils.
- Clean energy for rural people who now use wood and dung.
- Low-cost, battery-operated, wireless computers that open communications for rural areas with no electricity and telecommunications infrastructure.
- Vaccines and treatment for neglected diseases such as sleeping sickness.

These investments are critical to achieving Goals 1–7 but do not constitute market demand; people surviving on less than $1 a day have little to spend on medicines. Because these investments will not attract private investment, the public sector must take the lead. But partnerships with the private sector, while not only desirable, may be essential in some areas—because it has the know-how and technology.

Technology is a motor for human development. Rich countries, by opening access to technologies, can make a vital contribution to reaching the Goals. Yet the opening has, if anything, slowed—especially in the industrial sector. In the long term this harms everyone. Many economists now argue that the free flow of knowledge can facilitate growth for all, rather than generating high returns at the expense of

Rich countries, by opening access to technologies, can make a vital contribution to reaching the Goals

TABLE 8.4
Rich country responsibilities

	Aid			Debt relief			Trade			
	Net official development assistance (ODA) disbursed		Tied aid (% of total aid disbursements)[a] 2001	Bilateral pledges to the HIPC Trust Fund (US$ millions) As of November 2002	Cancellation of bilateral debt (US$ millions) 1990–2002	Average tariff and non-tariff barriers[b] (tariff-equivalents, %) 2000	Goods imports			
							From developing countries		From least developed countries	
	Total (US$ millions) 2001	As % of GNP 2001					Total (US$ millions) 2001	Share of total imports (%) 2001	Total (US$ millions) 2001	Share of total imports (%) 2001
Australia	873	0.25	41	14	72	13.4	2,274	37.5	11	0.2
Austria	533	0.29	..	44	202	21.8	616	9.4	16	0.3
Belgium	867	0.37	10	45	544	22.1	2,275	12.7	254	1.4
Canada	1,533	0.22	68	114	1,207	12.7	3,558	16.1	35	0.2
Denmark	1,634	1.03	7	60	359	21.6	447	10.0	12	0.3
Finland	389	0.32	13	38	156	21.3	338	10.2	16	0.5
France	4,198	0.32	33	181	13,043	21.4	5,112	17.4	236	0.8
Germany	4,990	0.27	15	226	4,996	21.4	7,488	15.2	218	0.4
Greece	202	0.17	83	11	..	22.5	670	23.8	18	0.6
Ireland	287	0.33	..	24	..	22.9	700	13.6	17	0.3
Italy	1,627	0.15	92	153	1,156	20.1	4,323	18.3	98	0.4
Japan	9,847	0.23	19	200	3,908	34.8	20,582	58.9	110	0.3
Luxembourg	141	0.82	..	318	..	..	28	2.6	1	0.1
Netherlands	3,172	0.82	9	199	1,575	19.9	3,860	23.5	73	0.4
New Zealand	112	0.25	..	29	..	12.0	383	28.8	2	0.1
Norway	1,346	0.83	1	300	237	61.1	405	12.3	12	0.4
Portugal	268	0.25	42	27	460	20.5	556[c]	13.9[c]	29[c]	0.7[c]
Spain	1,737	0.30	31	44	980	21.3	3,373	21.8	136	0.9
Sweden	1,666	0.81	14	189	121	20.5	580	9.8	10	0.2
Switzerland	908	0.34	4	127	311	37.1	694	8.3	9	0.1
United Kingdom	4,579	0.32	6	77	1,886	20.9	6,535	18.9	132	0.4
United States	11,429	0.11	..	40	8,062	9.7	54,798	46.4	982	0.8

Note: This table presents data for members of the OECD Development Assistance Committee.
a. Refers to tied and partially tied aid as a percentage of total aid, excluding technical cooperation. b. This is an aggregate measure of trade barriers towards developing countries. It measures not only monetary barriers (tariffs) but also non-monetary ones, such as import quotas and the effect of domestic subsidies. c. Data refer to 2000.
Source: Columns 1 and 2: OECD, Development Assistance Committee 2003c. Column 3: Human Development Report Office calculations based on data on tied and partially tied aid from OECD, Development Assistance Committee 2003c. Column 4: Geithner and Nankani 2002. Column 5: Human Development Report Office calculations based on data on debt cancellation from OECD, Development Assistance Committee 2003c. Column 6: Birdsall and Roodman 2003. Columns 7–10: UN 2003a.

access. That is why it is vital to reopen negotiations on the TRIPS agreement, operationalizing its provisions for technology transfer.

Rich countries can do much more to expand access to technology by tackling the key obstacles:
- Lack of financing for investments in research and development.
- Ambiguous intellectual property laws.
- Limits of differential pricing.
- National technology capacity, including local production capacity.

LIVING UP TO THE COMMITMENTS OF THE MILLENNIUM DECLARATION: POLICY, NOT CHARITY

More action on aid has been seen in the two years since the Millennium Declaration than in the past decade—with pledges for $16 billion more aid by 2006, debt relief to 26 countries and an agreement that intellectual property rights should not stand in the way of access to technology for protecting public health. Though significant, these achievements fall far short of promises made. Even $16 billion in additional official development assistance would only reach 0.26% of the gross national income of Development Assistance Committee members by 2006—not the target of 0.7%. There has been little concrete action in opening markets, transferring technology and relieving debt, leaving too many countries without benefits. With commitments falling short of the need, poor countries will continue to face stagnant growth, accumulating (and unsustainable) debt and falling export prices.

Rich countries should be encouraged to prepare reports—contributing to a world poverty reduction strategy—that set out their priorities for action.[33] They could pinpoint where they need to do more to live up to their commitments. For example, countries generous

BOX 8.10

The commitment to development index

The commitment to development index (CDI) is a pioneering attempt to monitor how well rich countries live up to their commitments to global partnership. Created by the Center for Global Development and *Foreign Policy* magazine, the index goes beyond looking at the traditional measures of aid—dollar amounts. Instead, it examines a broader set of dimensions and policies, looking at both the quality and quantity of aid, trade barriers, the environment, investment, migration and peacekeeping.

Constructing an index that takes into account the full range of policies affecting poor countries is as difficult as it is important. While the CDI is a significant first step towards holding rich countries accountable to their commitments, a number of questions remain:

• *Valuation of "good" policy.* The CDI is designed to measure a specific set of policies, that, it is assumed, enhance development outcomes. These assumptions inevitably entail value judgements. For example, higher scores are given for aid to countries with good governance than to those where the need may be greater. Another example is foreign direct investment (FDI), a component of the index, where lack of data has led the CDI to assume that it is good in all circumstances.

• *Weighting.* Perhaps the biggest problem in any composite index is what importance to assign each indicator. The CDI uses a variety of methods in each policy area. But the overall index gives equal weight to each of the six components. While this is the simplest approach, it downplays aid and trade—arguably far more important than, say, peacekeeping contributions.

• *Measurement weaknesses.* While all the six components of rich country policies presented here are important for global development, some

are difficult to measure. Migration policies that contribute to development are difficult to measure because there is no clear consensus on what constitutes good migration policy, and data are sparse. The environment is also a complex area that suffers from lack of adequate data.

• *Complexity.* The CDI was designed to target policies very specifically, resulting in a multitude of indicators and a wide range of statistical methods. The cost of this complexity is that to all but dedicated researcher with knowledge of the field, the index will be a black box: the results are clear, but understanding what lies behind them requires specialized knowledge. So for the voter, the non-governmental organization, the journalist or the policy-maker—all key audiences—the take-home message of what needs to change may not be clear.

• *Bias against large economies.* Because key aspects of the index (aid, peacekeeping and FDI contributions) are measured as a proportion of gross national income, large economies—which often give the most in absolute terms—end up with lower scores. Indeed, the top five countries all have populations of less than 20 million.

Some of the results of the index are surprising, sometimes due to the problems discussed above. The Netherlands leads the rankings, leaving in second place Denmark—by far the most generous donor of official development assistance as a share of gross national income of the countries in the index. This result is mainly driven by the Netherlands' extremely high scores in FDI, where Denmark scores very low. This highlights the problems of using FDI as a scorecard for policy: FDI is an outcome, arguably more affected by the structure of the private sector than by government policy. Portugal, another surprise at third place,

is also helped by a perfect score in FDI. It is followed by New Zealand and Switzerland in fourth and fifth place—countries that, like Portugal, are not big donors of official development assistance. Switzerland's high ranking illustrates well the problems of giving equal weight to all the components of the index: it scores low in the important categories of trade and aid, but high in investment and migration—areas that are difficult to measure, and whose impact is more controversial.

Finland, Canada, Australia, the United States and Japan have the lowest scores. The two largest donors of foreign aid in dollar amounts—the United States and Japan—rank at the very bottom. Both countries' scores suffer because their aid and FDI, while huge in absolute terms, are small relative to the size of their economies. Japan receives particularly low scores in peacekeeping, because constitutional barriers and commitments prevent it from contributing troops to peacekeeping. This again illustrates the problem of weighting: in important sectors such as trade and the environment, Japan performs relatively better. The US score is also helped by strong performance in trade—helped by its more open agricultural market, which is not as heavily subsidized as those in Europe.

The most important result of the index, however, lies not in the relative rankings, but in the fact that even the top country is barely halfway to a perfect score. All countries have a long way to go to achieve policies that help poor countries develop.

Intended to be published annually, the first edition of the CDI should sharpen the debate on rich country development policies and stimulate discussions on measuring those policies and improving data.

Source: Birdsall and Roodman 2003.

with aid are not always as open to developing country imports. Consider Norway, which does much to meet the aid commitments but could do more on market access (table 8.4).[34] The current OECD Development Assistance Committee process of peer reviews on aid could also be expanded to include trade and debt relief so that these policies could be reviewed in a coherent framework. Japan imports more from developing countries than any other rich country (59% of total imports), but has low official development assistance as a percentage of gross national income.

A recent research project developed a composite index, the commitment to development index, that encapsulates rich country performance in implementing policies that contribute to development (box 8.10). Like other composite indices, this one helps policy-makers—in this case, rich country policy-makers—assess their situation and pinpoint areas for improvement. It shows how they perform relative to other countries not only in aid, but also in whether they protect their markets from developing country goods, in investments, in opening doors to migrants, in contributing to peacekeeping and in contributing to global environmental stewardship. A product of innovative research, the index intends not to "name and shame" but to diagnose shortcomings and spur action to do more.

As noted, Goal 8 does not have time-bound and quantitative targets. But rich countries can set their own deadlines for targets requiring their action. Proposed here are some indicators of progress, with specificity and deadlines in critical areas:

• Increase official development assistance to fill financing gaps—by a low estimate of $50 billion.

• Increase official development assistance to the least developed countries.

• Develop concrete measures for implementing the Rome Declaration on Harmonization.

• Remove tariffs and quotas on agricultural products, textiles and clothing exported by developing countries.

• Remove agricultural export subsidies.

• Agree and finance, for the HIPCs, a compensatory financing facility against external shocks—including commodity price collapses.

• Finance deeper debt reduction for HIPCs having reached their completion points, to ensure sustainability.

• Introduce protection and remuneration of traditional knowledge in the TRIPS agreement.

• Agree on what countries without sufficient manufacturing capacity can do to protect public health under the TRIPS agreement.

The commitments already made by rich countries show that the world has changed. Global market integration and technological advances have increased—as have exposure to disease, costs of environmental losses and risks of global financial contagion. Actions within national borders are not enough to tackle these problems. Partnership is needed for mutual self-interest. But rich countries also need to act—because eliminating human suffering is an ethical imperative. For rich countries to deliver on their commitments is a matter not just of charity but of policy—policy that is part of the international community's coherent approach to eradicating global poverty.

At the turn of the century the prospect of eradicating poverty seemed possible. The cold war was over and the prospect of all societies converging towards common goals seemed within reach. Yet as this Report goes to press, global challenges—from Iraq to the spread of new deadly diseases—loom large. The global economic slowdown also threatens to undermine rich country action for development as their own economies come under pressure to reduce budget deficits and press home their own trading advantages. That is why it is all the more urgent for all nations to keep their promises. Monitoring progress towards Goal 8, enumerating rich countries' side of the partnership for development, is as important as monitoring Goals 1–7.

Notes

Chapter 1

1. UN 2000a.
2. UN 2000a.
3. UN 2001b.
4. See for example Khor 2000.
5. UN 2002d.
6. Jolly 2003; Foster 2002; Bissio 2003; White and Black 2002.
7. World Bank 2003i.
8. UNICEF 2003b.
9. World Bank 2003i.
10. UNICEF 2003b.
11. WFUNA and North-South Institute 2002.

Chapter 2

1. Except for income, reversals do not include countries with low levels of human poverty in the relevant indicator. For definitions of the human poverty levels, see technical note 2.
2. Measured using the $2 a day poverty line, considered a more appropriate extreme poverty line for Central and Eastern Europe and the CIS (UNDP 2003c).
3. Human Development Report Office calculations based on indicator table 27.
4. Human Development Report Office calculations based on Alvarez and others 2002.
5. World Bank 2003i.
6. Birdsall and Clemens 2003b.
7. World Bank 2002f.
8. World Bank 2002f.
9. Covers different periods between 1990 and the mid- to late 1990s for countries with data on national poverty trends.
10. Data are from World Bank 2000a and 2003i, ECLAC 2002, UNCTAD 2002a and Milanovic 1998.
11. Measured using the $2 a day poverty line, considered a more appropriate extreme poverty line for Central and Eastern Europe and the CIS (UNDP 2003c).
12. UNAIDS 2000.
13. FAO 2001b.
14. UNAIDS 2000.
15. UN 2002g.
16. UNAIDS 2002b.
17. Eberstadt 2002.
18. See technical note 2 for more details on the categorization of top priority and high priority countries.
19. Refers to a score of 4 or greater from Marshall 2000.
20. UNAIDS 2002b.
21. Gwatkin 2002.
22. Vandemoortele 2001.
23. Filmer and Pritchett 1999; Watkins 2000.
24. Data are from demographic and social surveys. Data on wealth are based on household characteristics and possessions. The "wealthy" class is the top fifth of the distribution, determined after ranking households by wealth (Minujin and

Delamonica 2003).
25. Minujin and Delamonica 2003.
26. Watkins 2000.
27. Watkins 2000.
28. Sahn and Stifel 2003.
29. Minujin and Delamonica 2003.
30. Watkins 2000.
31. Klasen and Wink 2002.
32. UNDP 2003c.
33. Minujin and Delamonica 2003.
34. UNAIDS 2002b.
35. Chapter 5 provides a more conceptual and systematic discussion of gender discrimination.

Chapter 3

1. The Dominican Republic is a top-priority country in hunger and sanitation. Mozambique is a top-priority country in primary education and gender equality. See feature 2.1 for further information.
2. Commission on Macroeconomics and Health 2001.
3. Commission on Macroeconomics and Health 2001.
4. Sen 1999.
5. Mehrotra and Jolly 2000.
6. UNICEF 2000.
7. Based on Human Development Report Office calculations using Maddison 2001 and World Bank 2003i.
8. Based on Human Development Report Office calculations using Maddison 2001 and World Bank 2003i.
9. Excludes transition countries and fuel exporters and includes only countries with a population of at least 1 million and for which data on the export structure are available.
10. Prosterman and Hansted 2000.
11. The distribution of social and cultural power adds an important caveat to this ability. Many microfinance schemes have failed to prevent the funds from eventually reaching and being controlled by male heads of household.
12. Daley-Harris 2003.
13. World Bank 1998b.

Chapter 4

1 Caldwell 1979.
2. Carnoy 1992.
3. Caldwell 1986.
4. Caldwell 1986.
5. Mehrotra 2000c; UNESCO 1999.
6. UNICEF 2001b.
7. UN 2002b.
8. Millennium Project Task Force 2 2003b.
9. Millennium Project Task Force 2 2003b.
10. Pinstrup-Andersen, Pandya-Lorch and Rosegrant 1999; Millennium Project Task Force 2 2003b.
11. Millennium Project Task Force 2 2003b.

12. UN 2002b.

13. Panos Institute 2001.

14. MDG indicator table 1.

15. FAO 2002b.

16. MDG indicator table 1.

17. MDG indicator table 1.

18. Millennium Project Task Force 2 2003b.

19. FAO 2002b; MDG indicator table 1.

20. World Bank 2003i.

21. Seventeen countries, including some of the most populous, have achieved reductions of 25% or more over the decade.

22. Millennium Project Task Force 2 2003b.

23. Millennium Project Task Force 2 2003b.

24. Human Development Report Office calculations based on Millennium Project Task Force 2 2003a.

25. Millennium Project Task Force 2 2003b.

26. Millennium Project Task Force 2 2003b.

27. Millennium Project Task Force 2 2003b.

28. Millennium Project Task Force 2 2003b.

29. Millennium Project Task Force 2 2003b.

30. Drèze and Sen 1995.

31. World Bank 2002d.

32. Panos Institute 2001.

33. Panos Institute 2001.

34. Panos Institute 2001.

35. IFAD 2001.

36. Agarwal 1994.

37. FAO 2002a.

38. Swaminathan 2001.

39. Millennium Project Task Force 2 2003b.

40. Millennium Project Task Force 2 2003b.

41. Millennium Project Task Force 2 2003a.

42. Millennium Project Task Force 2 2003a.

43. Millennium Project Task Force 2 2003a.

44. Pretty and Hine 2000; Millennium Project Task Force 2 2003a.

45. Millennium Project Task Force 2 2003a.

46. Millennium Project Task Force 2 2003a.

47. Millennium Project Task Force 2 2003a.

48. Scherr, White and Kaimowitz 2002.

49. OECD, Development Assistance Committee 2003c.

50. MDG indicator table 1.

51. MDG indicator table 1.

52. MDG indicator table 1.

53. India, Planning Commission 2002.

54. Human Development Report Office calculations.

55. Indicator table 10.

56. UNESCO 2002a.

57. UNESCO 2002a.

58. Includes Afghanistan, Bangladesh, Bhutan, India, the Islamic Republic of Iran, Maldives, Nepal, Pakistan and Sri Lanka.

59. Flug, Spilimbergo and Wachtenheim 1998; World Bank forthcoming.

60. See for example Gupta, Verhoeven and Tiongson 2002 and Mehrotra and Delamonica forthcoming.

61. Delamonica, Mehrotra and VandeMoortele 2001.

62. Millennium Project Task Force 3 2003.

63. Hanmer and Naschold 2001.

64. Millennium Project Task Force 3 2003.

65. UNESCO 2002a.

66. Multilateral here refers to the African Development Bank, Asian Development Bank, Inter-American Development Bank (Special Fund), European Development Fund of the European Community, International Development Association (of the World Bank Group), United Nations Development Programme and United Nations Children's Fund (OECD, Development Assistance Committee 2003c).

67. Mehrotra and Delamonica forthcoming.

68. Mehrotra 1999.

69. Mehrotra and Jolly 2000.

70. Mehrotra 1998.

71. Mehrotra and Biggeri 2002.

72. Mehrotra and Delamonica 1998.

73. Mehrotra and others forthcoming.

74. Tilak 1997.

75. Mehrotra 1998.

76. Mehrotra 1998.

77. UNICEF 1999.

78. In many African countries at the junior secondary level and beyond, the phenomenon of teachers becoming "sugar daddies" is seen as a disincentive for sending postpuberty girls to school.

79. Heng and Hoey 2000; Loewenson and Chisvo 2000.

80. Alidou and Jung 2002.

81. Delamonica, Mehrotra and VandeMoortele 2001.

82. World Bank 1996.

83. Mehrotra 1998.

84. At the secondary level in developing countries the share of teacher costs is about 80%, while at the higher level it is about 60% (Mehrotra and Buckland 1998).

85. Mehrotra 1998.

86. UNESCO Institute for Statistics and OECD 2002.

87. UNESCO and ILO 1966.

88. UNESCO and ILO 1966.

89. Buckland, Hofmeyr and Meyer 1993.

90. Watkins 2000.

91. Human Development Report Office calculations based on feature 2.1 in chapter 2.

92. UNICEF 2001b.

93. Millennium Project Task Force 4 2003.

94. UN 2003g; UNDP 2002e.

95. Millennium Project Task Force 5 2003b.

96. Millennium Project Task Force 5 2003d.

97. UNICEF 2001b.

98. Carlsson and Valdivieso 2003.

99. International Institute of Population Sciences 2000.

100. According to estimates by the World Health Organization's Commission on Macroeconomics and Health, the minimum financing needed to cover essential interventions, including those for fighting the AIDS pandemic, is about $30-40 a person per year. Actual health spending in the least developed countries is around $13 a person per year, of which $7 is from budgetary outlays. Other low-income countries spend around $24 a person per year, of which $13 is from budgetary outlays (Commission on Macroeconomics and Health 2001). Clearly, health spending needs to be substantially increased.

101. Mehrotra and Delamonica forthcoming.

102. Multilateral here refers to the African Development Bank, Asian Development Bank, Inter-American Development Bank (Special Fund), European Development Fund of the European Community, International Development Association (of the World Bank Group), United Nations Development Programme and United Nations Children's Fund.

103. OECD, Development Assistance Committee 2003c.

104. Mehrotra and Delamonica forthcoming.

105. Mehrotra and Delamonica forthcoming.

106. Mehrotra and Delamonica forthcoming.

107. Mehrotra and Delamonica forthcoming.

108. WHO 2000.

109. Mehrotra and Delamonica forthcoming.

110. World Bank 1993.

111. WHO 2000.

112. Millennium Project Task Force 7 2003.

113. Millennium Project Task Force 7 2003; UN 2002c.

114. WHO, UNICEF and WSSCC 2000.

115. WHO, UNICEF and WSSCC 2000.

116. UN 2000b.

117. WSSCC 2002.

118. World Bank 2003i; UN 2002c.

119. Indicator table 6.

120. UN 2002c.

121. World Panel on Financing Water Infrastructure 2003.

122. According to the World Bank Operations Evaluation Department.

123. World Panel on Financing Water Infrastructure 2003.

124. OECD 2003b.

125. This includes aid for water resources development, water resources protection, water supply and use, water legislation and management, sanitation (including solid waste management), education and training in water supply and sanitation and water resources policy, planning and programmes. It excludes aid for dams and reservoirs primarily for irrigation and hydropower and activities related to water transport.

126. OECD 2003b.

127. OECD 2003b.

128. OECD 2003b.

129. World Panel on Financing Water Infrastructure 2003.

130. WSP 2002a.

131. Stiglitz 2002a.

132. Mehrotra and Delamonica forthcoming.

133. Reddy 2003; Mehrotra and Delamonica forthcoming.

134. Mehrotra and Delamonica 1998.

135. Mehrotra and Delamonica forthcoming.

136. World Bank 2003g.

Chapter 5

1. For Pakistan, Watkins 2000 and Mehrotra and Delamonica forthcoming; for India, De and Drèze 1999.

2. Van Lerberghe and others 2002.

3. Leipziger and Foster 2003.

4. For evidence, see World Bank 1993.

5. World Bank 2002b.

6. Berman and Rose 1996.

7. Iriart, Merhy and Waitzkin 2001.

8. Iriart, Merhy and Waitzkin 2001.

9. Stocker, Waitzkin and Iriart 1999.

10. Iriart, Merhy and Waitzkin 2001.

11. Mills 1997.

12. Barros, Vaughan and Victora 1986.

13. Yesudian 1994.

14. Velasquez, Madrid and Quick 1998.

15. Iyer and Sen 2000.

16. Yang 1993; Nittayaramphong and Tangcharaoensathien 1994.

17. Saywell 1999.

18. Tomlinson 1997.

19. Shaokang, Shenglan and Youde 1997.

20. Iriart, Waitzkin and Trotta 2002.

21. Iriart, Merhy and Waitzkin 2001.

22. Van Lerberghe and others 2002; Sitthi-Amorn, Janjaroen and Somrongthong 2001.

23. Watkins 2000.

24. UNESCO and OECD 2000.

25. De and Drèze 1999; Mehrotra and others forthcoming.

26. UNESCO Institute of Statistics and OECD 2002.

27. Results USA 2003.

28. Cox and Jimenez 1991; Mehrotra and Delamonica forthcoming; Watkins 2000.

29. Mehrotra and Delamonica forthcoming; Watkins 2000.

30. Watkins 2000.

31. UNESCO Institute for Statistics and OECD 2002.

32. UNESCO Institute for Statistics and OECD 2002.

33. Watkins 2000.

34. Mehrotra and Delamonica forthcoming.

35. UNESCO and OECD 2000.

36. West 1997; Kremer 2003.

37. Hall 2002.

38. Bayliss 2002b.

39. World Panel on Financing Water Infrastructure 2003.

40. Bayliss 2002b.

41. Bayliss 2002b.

42. Leipziger and Foster 2003.

43. Garnier and others 2000; Duncan, Jefferis and Molutsi 2000; Loewenson and Chisvo 2000.

44. Alailama and Sanderante 2000; Krishnan 2000.

45. Mehrotra and Jarrett 2002.

46. UNESCO 1996.

47. Rohde and Vishwanathan 1995.

48. Mills 1997.

49. See detailed accounts at http://www.icij.org such as ICIJ 2003b, 2003d and 2003e.

50. Business Partners for Development 2002.

51. Murphy and Bendell 1999.

52. Mehrotra and Delamonica forthcoming.

53. Kawabata, Xu and Carrin 2002.

54. World Panel on Financing Water Infrastructure 2003.

Chapter 6

1. UNDP, DFID and World Bank 2002.

2. IMF 2000.

3. WEHAB Working Group 2002b.

4. UNDP 2002d; UNDP, DFID and World Bank 2002.

5. UNDP, DFID and World Bank 2002.

6. Khemani 2001.

7. Khemani 2001.

8. IPCC 2001a.

9. UNDP, WEC and UNDESA 2000.

10. UNDP, WEC and UNDESA 2000.

11. Koziell and McNeill 2002.

12. UNDP, DFID and World Bank 2002.

13. Petkova and others 2003.

14. UNDP, WEC and UNDESA 2000.

15. IEA 1999.

16. Myers and others 2000.

Chapter 7

1. Osava 2003. Lula's first high-profile decision was to delay for a year the tender for a $760 million purchase of 12 fighter planes that were to replace the air force's fleet of combat jets, now nearly 30 years old and due to be phased out by 2005. The funds will instead go towards the "Zero Hunger" programme. All ministries will have to cut costs as part of a united effort to allow greater social spending, especially on the Zero Hunger programme.

2. UNDP 2002f.

3. UNDP 2002e.

4. Manor 2003.

5. Mehrotra and Delamonica forthcoming.

6. Fisman and Gatti 2002. The authors discuss decentralization of government expenditure and conclude, based on a study of 55 country cases, that it has a strong and significant association with lower corruption and bureaucratic rents.

7. Manor 2003.

8. Manor 2003.

9. Watson 2002.

10. Turner and Hulme 1997.

11. In India the local administrations at the village, block and district levels are called panchayati raj institutions. In 1992 national legislation under the 73rd and 74th constitutional amendments required that a third of all seats in panchayats be reserved for women.

12. Blair 2000.

13. UNDP 2003d.

14. Much of the evidence on these decentralization initiatives is derived from extensive case studies. The reason is that quantifying many important effects of political reform poses both

an empirical and a conceptual challenge. Some are exceedingly difficult—and in some cases impossible—to measure. For further discussion of this issue, see Manor 2003.

15. Tendler 1997.

16. Decentralization initiatives involve different types of arrangements between central and local authorities. These may take the form of deconcentration, where local offices implement policies decided at the national level; delegation, where local governments have limited decision-making power over funding and policy and act as agents ultimately responsible to the central government; and devolution, where the central government transfers resources, responsibility and decision-making to the local level. Decentralization commonly involves a mix of all three.

17. UNDP 2001b.

18. Manor 2003.

19. For a discussion, see Manor 1999, Evers 1996 and Hessling and Ba 1994.

20. For a discussion, see Manor 1999 and Fuhr 2003.

21. Manor 1999.

22. Blair 2000.

23. Mamdani 1996.

24. Turner and Hulme 1997.

25. Interventions hailed for furthering effective decentralization have been spearheaded by political parties such as the African National Congress in South Africa, the Workers Party in Porto Alegre, Brazil, and the Communist Party of India in Kerala. All these parties have tried to address the dominance of economically and socially entrenched groups through policies and such political measures as decentralization and agrarian reform. For further discussion, see Heller 2001.

26. Foster and Mackintosh-Walker 2001.

27. Crook and Sturla Sverrisson 2001.

28. Blair 2000.

29. Calderón and Pinc 2003.

30. Calderón and Pinc 2003.

31. Rojas 2002.

32. Budlender and others 2002.

33. Calderón and Pinc 2003.

34. Calderón and Pinc 2003.

35. Fung and Wright 2002.

36. Fung and Wright 2002, p. 14.

Chapter 8

1. UN 2001a.

2. Devarajan, Miller and Swanson 2002.

3. OECD, Development Assistance Committee 2003d.

4. Human Development Report Office calculations based on MDG indicator table 7.

5. World Bank 1998a.

6. Birdsall and Clemens 2003b.

7. World Bank 2003g.

8. OECD, Development Assistance Committee 1991.

9. Stewart 2003.

10. Birdsall, Williamson and Deese 2002.

11. IMF and International Development Association 2003.

12. Birdsall and Deese 2002.

13. Pettifor and Greenhill 2003.

14. Birdsall, Williamson and Deese 2002.

15. Birdsall and Deese 2003.

16. Birdsall and Deese 2003.

17. UNCTAD 2002a.

18. UNCTAD 2002a.

19. Wood 1995.

20. Millennium Project Task Force 9 2003.

21. Birdsall and Clemens 2003b.

22. Millennium Project Task Force 9 2003.

23. New Zealand 2003.

24. WTO 2000.

25. CAFOD 2002.

26. UNDP and others 2003.

27. Birdsall, Williamson and Deese 2002.

28. WTO 2001.

29. Commission on Macroeconomics and Health 2001.

30 Trouiller and others 2002.

31 Michaud and Murray 1996.

32. van den Haak, Vounatsos and McAuslane 2001.

33. Birdsall and Clemens 2003a.

34. Birdsall and Roodman 2003.

Bibliographic note

Chapter 1 draws on Barro 1996; Bissio 2003; Booth and Lucas 2002; Chivian 2002; Chwialkowska 2002; Colclough 2002; Foster 2002; IMF and others 2000; Jolly 2001, 2003; Khor 2000; Kraul 2002; Marks 2003; Millennium Project Task Force 1 2003; OECD 1996, 2003b; UN 1966, 1979, 1980, 1989, 2000a, 2000c, 2001b, 2002d; UNDP 1996, 2002g, 2003b; UNESCO Institute for Statistics 2002; UNHCHR 2002a, 2002b; UNICEF 2003a; WFUNA and North-South Institute 2002; White and Black 2002; World Bank 2002j.

Chapter 2 draws on Alvarez and others 2002; Backiny-Yetna, Coulibaly and Raffinot 2003a, 2003b; Bajpay 2003; Bhalla 2002; Birdsall and Clemens 2003b; Birdsall and Londono 1997; Bourguignon 2001; Caldwell 1986; Carson, Laliberie and Khawaja 2001; CNN 1998; Cornia and Kiiski 2001; David 2003; De Vries 2003; Deaton 2003; Deininger and Olinto 2000; Deininger and Squire 1998; Dollar and Kraay 2002; Eberstadt 2002; ECLAC 2002; Fajnzylber, Lederman and Loayza 1998; FAO 2001b, 2002b; Filmer and Pritchett 1999; Fuentes, Balsells and Arriola 2003; Fuentes and Montes 2003; Gwatkin 2002; Henninger and Snel 2002; IFPRI 2002; IFRC 2001; Johnston 2002, 2003; Kanbur and Lustig 1999; Klasen and Wink 2002; Korzeniewicz and Moran 1997; Lee 1997; Macro International 2003; Marshall 2000; McEwin 2003; Mendonça 2003; Milanovic 1998, 2002, 2003; Millennium Project Task Force 5 2003a; Minujin and Delamonica 2003; Monsod and Monsod 2003; OECD, Development Assistance Committee 2003c; Oster, Lake and Oksman 1978; Pettifor and Greenhill 2003; Ravallion 2000, 2002; Reddy and Pogge 2002; Sala-i-Martin 2002; Sarmiento Gómez and others 2003; Schultz 1998; Simonpietri 2003; SIPRI 2002b; Snow and others 2003; Sprout and Weaver 1992; Stewart 2003; Székely and Hilgert 1999; UN 2002g, 2003c, 2003h; UNAIDS 1996, 2000, 2002b; UNCTAD 2002a; UNDP 1996, 2002a, 2002c, 2002e, 2003a, 2003c, 2003e; UNDP, ECLAC and Instituto de Pesquisa Economica Aplicada 2002; UNESCO 2002a; UNHCR 2000; UNICEF 1996, 2003b; UNIFEM 2000; VandeMoortele 2001, 2002; Ward 2003; Watkins 2000; Woo and Bao 2003; World Bank 2000a, 2002a, 2002f, 2002j, 2003d, 2003h; World Bank and IMF 2001; WSP 2002b; Zubarevich 2003.

Chapter 3 draws on Adams 2002; Bajpay 2003; Bruno, Ravallion and Squire 1996; China 2003; Commission on Macroeconomics and Health 2001; Daley-Harris 2003; Fitzgerald 2001; Gallup, Sachs and Mellinger 2003; IMF 2002a, 2002b; India 2003; Khandker 1998; Maddison 2001; McArthur and Sachs 2002; Mehrotra and Jolly 2000; Prosterman and Hansted 2000; Sen 1999; Stewart 2003; Uganda 2002; UNCTAD 2002b; UNDP 1996; UNICEF 2000; Woo and Bao 2003; World Bank 1998b, 2000b, 2002h, 2002i, 2003a, 2003e, 2003f, 2003i.

Chapter 4 draws on Agarwal 1994; Ainsworth, Nyamete and Beegle 1996; Alailama and Sanderante 2000; Alidou and Jung 2002; Avert.org 2003; Barro and Lee 1993; Barros, Vaughan and Victora 1986; Behrman and others 1999; Bennel and Furlong 1997; Bicego and Boerma 1991; Buckland, Hofmeyr and Meyer 1993; Caldwell 1979, 1986; Carlsson and Valdivieso 2003; Carnoy 1992; Chen and Desai 2000; Christiansen, Conway and Poston 2003; Commission on Macroeconomics and Health 2001; Delamonica, Mehrotra and VandeMoortele 2001; de los Angeles 2002; de Moor and Calamai 2003; DFID 2002c; Drèze and Sen 1995; Duncan, Jef-

feris and Molutsi 2000; Economic and Political Weekly 2000; Fan and Hazell 2001; Fan, Hazell and Thorat 1998; FAO 2001c, 2002a, 2002b; Filmer and Pritchett 1997, 1999; Filmer, Hammer and Pritchett 1998; Flug, Spilimbergo and Wachtenheim 1998; Forster-Rothbart and others 2002; Gupta, Verhoeven and Tiongson 2002; Haddad 1999; Haggblade and Tembo 2002; Hall 2003a; Hanmer and Naschold 2001; Heng and Hoey 2000; IFAD 2001; ILO 1991a, 1991b; India, Ministry of Finance 2002; India, Planning Commission 2002; International Institute of Population Sciences 2000; Jha 2002; Jimenez 1987; Kadzamira and Rose 2001; Kannan, Dev and Sharam 2000; Khatri and Frieden 2002; Kongsin and others 1998; Landell-Mills, Bishop and Porras 2002; Landuyt 1998; Lewin and Caillods 2001; Loewenson and Chisvo 2000; Lucas 1988; Maddison 2001; Mehrotra 1998, 1999, 2000a, 2000b, 2000c; Mehrotra and Biggeri 2002; Mehrotra and Buckland 1998; Mehrotra and Delamonica 1998, forthcoming; Mehrotra and Jolly 2000; Mehrotra and others forthcoming; Millennium Project Task Force 2 2003a, 2003b; Millennium Project Task Force 3 2003; Millennium Project Task Force 4 2003; Millennium Project Task Force 5 2003a, 2003b, 2003c, 2003d; Millennium Project Task Force 7 2003; Murthy 1999; OECD 2001, 2003b; OECD, Development Assistance Committee 2003b, 2003c; Paarlberg 2002; Panos Institute 2001; Pinstrup-Andersen, Pandya-Lorch and Rosegrant 1999; Pretty and Hine 2000; Reddy 2003; Saith 1995; Scherr, White and Kaimowitz 2002; Schultz 2001; Siniscalco 2002; SIPRI 2002a, 2002b, 2003; Stapleton 2000; Stiglitz 2002a; Swaminathan 2001; Thomas and Strauss 1998; Tilak 1997; UN 1985, 2000b, 2002b, 2002c, 2003g; UNAIDS 2002a; UNDP 2001d, 2002e; UNESCO 1999, 2002a, 2002b, 2003; UNESCO and ILO 1966; UNESCO and OECD 2000; UNESCO Institute for Statistics and OECD 2002; UNICEF 1991, 1999, 2000, 2001a, 2001b, 2002; Watkins 2000; WEHAB Working Group 2002b; Weiss 2002; White and Martin 2002; WHO 2000, 2003a, 2003b, 2003c; WHO, UNICEF and WSSCC 2000; World Bank 1993, 1996, 2002d, 2002g, 2003b, 2003i, forthcoming; World Bank and UN-Habitat 2003; World Panel on Financing Water Infrastructure 2003; WSP 2002a, 2002b; WSSCC 2002, 2003; WWC 2000.

Chapter 5 draws on Alailama and Sanderante 2000; Barros, Vaughan and Victora 1986; Bayliss 2002b; Bennett 1997; Berman and Rose 1996; Boubakri and Cosset 1998; Business Partners for Development 2002; Canadian Centre for Policy Alternatives 2003; Commission on Macroeconomics and Health 2001; Cornia and Stewart 1995; Cox and Jimenez 1991; De and Drèze 1999; Duncan, Jefferis and Molutsi 2000; Franceys 2001; Garnier and others 2000; GAVI 2003; Hall 2002, 2003b; Hall and Lobina 2001; Hao, Suhua and Lucas 1997; ICIJ 2003a, 2003b, 2003c, 2003d, 2003e; IFC 2002a, 2002b; International Council for Science 2002; Iriart, Merhy and Waitzkin 2001; Iyer and Sen 2000; Kawabata, Xu and Carrin 2002; Kremer 2003; Krishnan 2000; Leipziger and Foster 2003; Lobina 2000, 2001; Lobina and Hall 1999; Loewenson and Chisvo 2000; Mason and others 1980; Mehrotra and Delamonica forthcoming; Mehrotra and Jarrett 2002; Mehrotra and Jolly 2000; Mehrotra and others forthcoming; Mills 1997; Mills and others 2002; Murphy and Bendell 1999; Myers and Kent 1998; Nittayaramphong and Tangcharaoensathien 1994; Polanyi 1994; PSIRU 2000; Results USA 2003; Rohde and Vishwanathan 1995;

Save the Children 2001; Saywell 1999; Schulpen and Gibbon 2001; Shaokang, Shenglan and Youde 1997; Sidley 2001; Sinclair and Grieshaber-Otto 2002; Sitthi-Amorn, Janjaroen and Somrongthong 2001; Social Watch 2003; Stiglitz 2002a; Stocker, Waitzkin and Iriart 1999; Tomlinson 1997; Tornquist and others 2000; UNDP 2001a; UNESCO 1996, 2002a; UNESCO Institute for Statistics and OECD 2002; UNHCHR 2003; Van Lerberghe and others 2002; Velasquez, Madrid and Quick 1998; Watkins 2000; Webster and Sansom 1999; West 1997; Whitehead, Evans and Dahlgren 2001; WHO 2002; World Bank 1990, 1993, 1999, 2000c, 2002b, 2002j; World Panel on Financing Water Infrastructure 2003; WTO 2003; Yang 1993; Yesudian 1994.

Chapter 6 draws on AfDB and others 2003; Annan 2002; Baumert and others 2002; Bryant and others 1998; Campbell 1997; Cavendish 1999; Chivian 2002; Common Dreams Press Wire 1998; DFID 2002b; UNDP, DFID and World Bank 2002; Ezzati and Kammen 2001; FAO 1998, 2001a; Finlayson and others 1999; Fuggle 2001; Gardiner 2002; Goldman and Tran 2002; Graumann 1977; Hardoy, Mitlin and Satterthwaite 2001; Harrison and Stassny 1999; IEA 1999, 2003; IEA and OECD 2003; IFPRI 2002; IMF 2000; Institute for European Environmental Policy 2002; IPCC 2001a, 2001b; IUCN 2002; Janzen 2000; Khemani 2001; Koziell and McNeill 2002; Lvovsky 2001; May and others 2002; Milazzo 1998; Millennium Project Task Force 8 2003; Myers and Kent 1998; Myers and others 2000; Naeem 1998; Nigel and others 1998; Nordhaus and Boyer 1999; OECD 1999; Oldeman, Hakkeling and Sombroek 1990; Petkova and others 2003; Pinstrup-Andersen and Pandya-Lorch 2001; Rainforest Foundation 1998; Repetto and Gillis 1998; Satterthwaite 2002; Sizer 2000; Smith 2000; Toledo 1997; UN 1997, 2002h, 2002i, 2003e, 2003f; UNCHS 1996; UNDP 1998, 2001a, 2002d; UNDP, WEC and UNDESA 2000; UNDP and others 1998, 2000; UNEP 2003; UN-HABITAT 2002; UN World Summit on Sustainable Development 2002; WEHAB Working Group 2002a, 2002b; WHO 1997; World Bank 2002k, 2003i; WRI 2000a, 2000b; WWF 2002.

Chapter 7 draws on Ablo and Reinikka 1998; Adamolekun 1999; Agrodev Canada 2000; Alm and Bahl 2001; Alston and Crawford 2000; Angell, Lowdon and Thorp 2001; Appleton 2001; Asian Development Bank 2002; Augustin-Jean 2002; Baiocchi 2001, 2002; Banerjee 2002; Banner 2002; Bardhan and Mookherjee 2000; Barraclough 1999; Bayliss 2002a; Besley and Burgess 2000, 2002; Blair 2000; Bourguignon and Ferreira 2000; Brinkerhoff and Goldsmith 2003; Brown and others 2000; Bruno, Ravallion and Squire 1996; Budlender and others 2002; Calderón 2002; Calderón and Pinc 2003; Calderón and Szmukler 2002; Cameron 2002; Carrión 2003; Chandler 2001; Choguill 2001; Council of Europe 1998; Crook 2001; Crook and Manor 1998; Crook and Sturla Sverrisson 2001, forthcoming; Cross and Kutengule 2001; Cuéllar-Marchelli 2001; Deshpande 2002; Devarajan, Miller and Swanson 2002; DFID 2000, 2002a; Dillinger and Fay 1999; Drake and others 2003; Drèze and Sen 2002; Evans 2002; Evers 1996; Fabre 2001; Faguet 2001; Ferro, Rosenblatt and Stern 2002; Finan, Sadoulet and de Janvry 2002; Fisman and Gatti 2002; Foster and Mackintosh-Walker 2001; Francis and James 2003; Franke and Chasin 2000; Fuentes and Niimi 2002; Fuhr2003; Fung and Wright 2002;

Furtado 2001; Gargarella 2002; Gaventa and Valderrama 1999; Gloppen, Rakner and Tostensen 2002; Goetz and Jenkins 2001; Goldfrank 2002; Mutebi, Stone and Thin 2003; Gopalakrishnan and Sharma 1999; Grant and others 2001; Greenhill and Blackmore 2002; Harrison 2001; Harriss 2000; Heller 2000, 2001; Herring 2000, forthcoming; Hessling and Ba 1994; Hirschman 1970; Hope 2000; Hossain and Moore 2001; Houtzager 1999; Huizer 1999; ILO 2001; Institute of Development Studies 2003; Iriart, Waitzkin and Trotta 2002; Jenkins and Goetz 1999; Jhabvala and Kanbur 2002; Johnson 2001, 2003; Johnson and Start 2001; Kabeer 2000; Kanbur and Squire 1999; Kawabata, Xu and Carrin 2002; Khemani 2001; Kohl 2002; Kosack 2003; Krishnan 2000; Kudva 2003; Leftwich 1994; Lipton and Ravallion 1994; Lopes 2002; Lopez 2003; MacDonald 2002; Mamdani 1976, 1995, 1996; Manor 1999, 2000, 2003; McIntyre 2002; Mehrotra 2002; Mehrotra and Delamonica forthcoming; Michaud and Murray 1996; Migdal, Kohli and Shue 1994; Millennium Project Task Force 6 2003; Milliken and Krause 2002; Moore and Putzel 1999a, 1999b; Mozambique 2002; Naidu 2002; Narasimahan 2002; Narayan and Patesch 2000; Noman 1997; Ogus 2002; Osava 2003; Øyen 2002; Pande 2003; Paul 2002; Phillips 1995; Rahman and Westley 2001; Reno 2002; Ribot 2001; Roberts 2003; Rojas 2002; Ruggeri 2001; Sahn and Stifel 2003; Schusterman and others 2002; Shah 1998; Shankar and Shah 2001; Shatkin 2000; Social Watch 2003; Steinich 2000; Stiglitz 1996, 2002b, 2003; Tendler 1997; Tinker 2002; Turner and Hulme 1997; UN 2003d; UNDP 2001b, 2002b, 2002e, 2002f, 2003d; Valderrama 1998; Veltmeyer 1997; Walker 2002; Watson 2002; Work 2002; Working Group on Contemporary Forms of Slavery 1997, 1999; Yoder 2003.

Chapter 8 draws on Abrego and Ross 2001; Birdsall and Clemens 2003a, 2003b; Birdsall and Deese 2002, 2003; Birdsall and Roodman 2002, 2003; Birdsall, Williamson and Deese 2002; Business Week 2000; CAFOD 2002; CGIAR 2003; Cline 2002, forthcoming; Commission on Macroeconomics and Health 2001; Damon, Danté and Naudet 1999; Devarajan, Miller and Swanson 2002; Economist 2001; European Commission 2002a, 2002b; Finger and Harrison 1996; Fortucci 2002; Fukuda-Parr, Lopes and Malik 2002; Geithner and Nankani 2002; Gore 2002; Goreaux 2003; Gutierrez and others 1996; Hanlon 1998; Hendra and Courtnadge 2003; Herfkens 2002; Hertel and Martin 1999; IMF and International Development Association 2003; International Cotton Consultative Committee 2002; Khor 2002a, 2002b; Lopes and Thieson 2003; Michaud and Murray 1996; Millennium Project Task Force 9 2003; Millennium Project Task Force 10 2003; Narayan and Patesch 2000; New Zealand 2003; OECD 2003a; OECD, Development Assistance Committee 1991, 2001, 2003a, 2003d; Oxfam 2002; Pettifor and Greenhill 2003; PIPA 2002; Quiroga 2002; Rahman 2003; Randel and German 1998; Ranis and Stewart 2000; Stewart 2003; Trouiller and others 2002; UN 2001a, 2002a, 2002d, 2002e, 2002f , 2003a, 2003b; UNCTAD 2000, 2002a; UNDP 1993, 2000, 2001c; UNDP and others 2003; UNICEF 2003b; United Kingdom 2003; van den Haak, Vounatsos and McAuslane 2001; Van de Walle and Johnston 1996; ; Wood 1995; World Bank 1998a, 2001, 2002c, 2002e, 2002f, 2003c, 2003g, 2003i; WTO 2000, 2001.

Bibliography

Background papers

Birdsall, Nancy, and Michael Clemens. 2003b. "What Rich Countries Can Do: The Global Social Contract."

Calderón, Fernando, and Christopher Pinc. 2003. "Political Reforms and Policies Enabling People's Empowerment and Advancing Human Development: The Challenges for Latin American Countries."

David, Isidoro P. 2003. "The International Statistical System and Statistical Capacity Building: Then and Now."

Deaton, Angus. 2003. "Data for Monitoring the Poverty MDG."

Jolly, Richard. 2003. "Global Goals: The UN Experience."

Manor, James. 2003. "Democratisation with Inclusion: Political Reforms and People's Empowerment at the Grassroots."

Pettifor, Ann, and Romilly Greenhill. 2003. "Debt Relief and the Millennium Development Goals."

Reddy, Sanjay. 2003. "Stagnation! Growth Failures, Coping Strategies and Human Development: Cross-Country Evidence and Policy Implications."

Stewart, Frances. 2003. "Conflict and the MDGs."

Background notes

CIESIN (Center for International Earth Science Information Network). 2003. "Mapping Human Development."

De Vries, Willem. 2003. "Measuring Statistical Capacity."

Johnston, Robert. 2003. "Notes on Statistical Capacity Building Issues."

UNDP (United Nations Development Programme). 2003a. "Conflict Mapping." Bureau for Crisis Prevention and Recovery.

Ward, Michael. 2003. "An Integrated Overview of Poverty and Inequality."

World Bank. 2003d. "Managing the Increasing Demand for Statistics."

———. 2003h. "Successful Statistical Capacity Building."

Country studies

Akder, Halis. 2003. "Human Development Progress towards the Millennium Development Goals: Turkey."

Backiny-Yetna, Prosper, Siaka Coulibaly and Marc Raffinot. 2003a. "Country Case Study on Human Development Progress towards the MDGs at the Sub-National Level: Burkina Faso."

———. 2003b. "Country Case Study on Human Development Progress towards the MDGs at the Sub-National Level: Mali."

Bajpay, Nirupam. 2003. "India: Towards the Millennium Development Goals."

Fuentes, Juan Alberto, Edgar Balsells and Gustavo Arriola. 2003. "Guatemala: Human Development Progress towards the MDGs at the Sub-National Level."

Fuentes, Ricardo, and Andres Montes. 2003. "Millennium Development Goals for Mexico."

Mendonça, Rosane. 2003. "Country Case Study on Human Development Progress towards the MDGs at the Sub-National Level: Brazil."

Monsod, Solita, and Toby T. Monsod. 2003. "Philippines Case Study on Human Development Progress towards the MDGs at the Sub-National Level."

Sarmiento Gómez, Alfredo, Lucía Mina Rosero, Carlos Alonso Malaver and Sandra Álvarez Toro. 2003. "Human Development Progress towards the Millennium Development Goals in Colombia."

Snow, Thomas, Michael Faye, John McArthur and Jeffrey Sachs. 2003. "Country Case Studies on the Challenges Facing Landlocked Developing Countries."

Topinska, Irena. 2003. "Human Development Progress towards the MDGs at the Subnational Level. Poland."

Woo, Wing, and Shuming Bao. 2003. "China Case Study on Human Development Progress towards the Millennium Developmental Goals at the Sub-National Level."

Zubarevich, Natalia. 2003. "Russian Case Study on Human Development Progress towards the MDGs at the Sub-National Level."

Millennium Project task force papers

Millennium Project Task Force 1. 2003. "A Millennium Development Strategy for Achieving Poverty Alleviation and Economic Growth."

Millennium Project Task Force 2. 2003a. "Halving Global Hunger."

———. 2003b. "Halving Global Hunger." Second draft.

Millennium Project Task Force 3. 2003. "Achieving Universal Primary Education by 2015."

Millennium Project Task Force 4. 2003. "Child Health and Maternal Health."

Millennium Project Task Force 5. 2003a. "Combating HIV/AIDS in the Developing World."

———. 2003b. "Combating Tuberculosis."

———. 2003c. "Expanding Access to Essential Medicines in the Developing World."

———. 2003d. "Reducing the Burden of Malaria in the Developing World."

Millennium Project Task Force 6. 2003. "Environmental Sustainability."

Millennium Project Task Force 7. 2003. "Achieving the Millennium Development Goals in Water and Sanitation."

Millennium Project Task Force 8. 2003. "Improving the Lives of Slum Dwellers."

Millennium Project Task Force 9. 2003. "Trade and Finance and the Millennium Development Goals."

Millennium Project Task Force 10. 2003. "Science, Technology and Innovation: Challenges and Opportunities for Implementing the Millennium Development Goals."

References

Ablo, Emmanuel, and Ritva Reinikka. 1998. "Do Budgets Really Matter? Evidence from Public Spending on Education and Health in Uganda." Policy Research Working Paper 1926. World Bank, Washington, DC.

Abrego, Lisandro, and Doris C. Ross. 2001. "Debt Relief under the HIPC Initiative: Context and Outlook for Debt

Sustainability and Resource Flows." IMF Working Paper 01/144. International Monetary Fund, Washington, DC.

Adamolekun, Ladipo. 1999. *Public Administration in Africa*. Boulder, Colo.: Westview Press.

Adams, Richard. 2002. "Economic Growth, Inequality, and Poverty: Findings from a New Data Set." Policy Research Working Paper 2972. World Bank, Washington, DC.

AfDB (African Development Bank), ADB (Asian Development Bank), DFID (UK Department for International Development), DGIS (Netherlands Directorate-General for International Cooperation), EC (European Commission), BMZ (German Federal Ministry for Economic Cooperation and Development), OECD (Organisation for Economic Co-operation and Development), UNDP (United Nations Development Programme), UNEP (United Nations Environment Programme) and World Bank. 2003. "Poverty and Climate Change: Reducing the Vulnerability of the Poor." 23 October. World Bank, Washington, DC. [http://lnweb18.worldbank.org/ESSD/essdext.nsf/46DocByUnid/6449D122940C7A9485256C4F005349D7/$FILE/PovertyAndClimateChange2002.pdf]. March 2003.

Agarwal, Bina. 1994. *A Field of One's Own: Gender and Land Rights in South Asia*. Cambridge: Cambridge University Press.

Agrodev Canada. 2000. "Final Report: Sindh Rural Development Project." Report prepared for the government of Sindh and the Asian Development Bank. Ottawa.

Ainsworth, Martha, Andrew Nyamete and Kathleen Beegle. 1996. "The Impact of Women's Schooling on Fertility and Contraceptive Use: A Study of Fourteen Sub-Saharan African Countries." *World Bank Economic Review* 10 (1): 85–122. [http://www.worldbank.org/research/journals/wber/revjan96/impact.htm]. March 2003.

Alailama, Patricia, and Nimal Sanderante. 2000. "Social Policy in a Slowly Growing Economy: Sri Lanka." In Santosh Mehrotra and Richard Jolly, eds., *Development with a Human Face: Experiences in Social Achievement and Economic Growth*. Oxford: Clarendon Press.

Alidou, Hassana, and Ingrid Jung. 2002. "Education Language Policies in Francophone Africa: What Have We Learned from Field Experiences?" In Steven J. Baker, ed., *Language Policy: Lessons from Global Models*. Monterey, Calif.: Monterey Institute of International Studies. [http://www.miis.edu/docs/langpolicy/ch04.pdf]. March 2003.

Alm, James, and Roy Bahl. 2001. "Can Indonesia Decentralise Successfully? Plans, Problems and Prospects." *Bulletin of Indonesian Economic Studies* 37 (1): 83–102. [http://rspas.anu.edu.au/economics/bies/biesabsv37no1.pdf]. March 2003.

Alston, Philip, and James Crawford, eds. 2000. *The Future of UN Human Rights Treaty Monitoring*. New York: Cambridge University Press.

Alvarez, Michael, Jose Antonio Cheibub, Jennifer Gandhi, Fernando Limongi, Adam Przeworski and Sebastian Saiegh. 2002. "D&D2000." Data set provided in correspondence. March. New York University, Department of Politics, New York.

Angell, Alan, Pamela Lowdon and Rosemary Thorp. 2001. *Decentralizing Development: The Political Economy of Institutional Reform in Colombia and Chile*. New York: Oxford University Press.

Annan, Kofi. 2002. "Towards a Sustainable Future." American Museum of Natural History's Annual Environmental Lecture, delivered by Nane Annan, 14 May, New York. [http://sustsci.harvard.edu/keydocs/fulltext/annan_amnh_020514.pdf]. March 2003.

Appleton, Simon. 2001. "Poverty Reduction during Growth: The Case of Uganda,1992–2000." University of Nottingham, School of Economics. [http://www.uppap.or.ug/docs/simonpaper.pdf]. March 2003.

Asian Development Bank. 2002. "Poverty in Pakistan: Issues, Causes and Institutional Responses." Islamabad. [http://www.adb.org/Documents/Reports/Poverty_PAK/default.asp]. March 2003.

Augustin-Jean, Louis. 2002. "Rural Enterprises and Regional Development in the People's Republic of China: Part One—Institutional Context and Economic Reforms." *Géographie, Économie, Société* 4 (3): 323–36.

Avert.org. 2003. "AIDS in Thailand." [http://www.avert.org/aidsthai.htm]. March 2003.

Baiocchi, Gianpaolo. 2001. "Participation, Activism, and Politics: The Porto Alegre Experiment and Deliberative Democratic Theory." *Politics and Society* 29 (1): 43–72.

———. 2002. "Synergizing Civil Society: State-Civil Society Regimes in Porto Alegre, Brazil." *Political Power and Social Theory* 15. [http://www.pitt.edu/~baiocchi/BaiocchiPPST15.pdf]. March 2003.

Banerjee, Abhijit. 2002. "Who Is Getting the Public Goods in India? Some Evidence and Some Speculation." Massachusetts Institute of Technology, Department of Economics, Cambridge, Mass. [http://www.arts.cornell.edu/econ/indiaconf/Banerjee%20paper.pdf]. March 2003.

Banner, Gerhard. 2002. "Community Governance and the New Central-Local Relationship." *International Social Science Journal* 54 (172): 217–31.

Bardhan, Pranab, and Dilip Mookherjee. 2000. "Capture and Governance at Local and National Levels." *American Economic Review* 90 (2): 135–39.

Barraclough, Salon. 1999. "Land Reform in Developing Countries: The Role of the State and Other Actors." United Nations Research Institute for Social Development, Geneva. [http://www.ifad.org/popularcoalition/pdf/mon2.pdf]. March 2003.

Barro, Robert. 1996. "Democracy and Growth." *Journal of Economic Growth* 1 (1): 1–27.

Barro, Robert, and Jong-Wha Lee. 1993. *Losers and Winners in Economic Growth*. NBER Working Paper 4341. Cambridge, Mass.: National Bureau of Economic Research.

Barros, Fernando, J. Patrick Vaughan and Cesar Victora. 1986. "Why So Many Caesarean Sections? The Need for Further Policy Change in Brazil." *Health, Policy and Planning* 1 (1): 19–29.

Baumert, Kevin A., Odile Blanchard, Silvi Llosa and James Perkaus, eds. 2002. *Building on the Kyoto Protocol: Options for Protecting the Climate*. Washington, DC: World Resources Institute. [http://climate.wri.org/pubs_pdf.cfm?PubID=3762]. March 2003.

Bayliss, Kate. 2002a. "Privatisation and Poverty: The Distributional Impact of Utility Privatisation." *Annals of Public and Co-operative Economics* 73 (4): 603–25.

———. 2002b. "Water Privatization in SSA: Progress, Problems and Policy Implications." Public Services International Research Unit, London. [http://www.psiru.org/]. March 2003.

Behrman, Jere R., Andrew Foster, Mark Rosenzweig and Prem Vashishtha. 1999. "Women's Schooling, Home Teaching, and Economic Growth." *Journal of Political Economy* 107 (4): 682–714.

Bennel, Paul, and Dominic Furlong. 1997. "Has Jomtien Made Any Difference? Trends in Donor Funding for Education and Basic Education since the Late 1980s." IDS Working Paper 51. University of Sussex, Institute of Development Studies, Brighton, England. [http://www.ids.ac.uk/ids/bookshop/wp/wp51.pdf]. March 2003.

Bennett, Sara. 1997. "Private Health Care and Public Policy Objectives." In Christopher Colclough, ed., *Marketizing Education and Health in Developing Countries: Miracle or Mirage?* Oxford: Clarendon Press.

Berman, Peter, and Laura Rose. 1996. "The Role of Private Providers in Maternal and Child Health and Family Planning Services in Developing Countries." *Health Policy and Planning* 11 (2): 142–55. [http://www.hsph.harvard.edu/ihsg/publications/pdf/No-18.PDF]. March 2003.

Besley, Timothy, and Robin Burgess. 2000. "Land Reform, Poverty Reduction, and Growth: Evidence from India." *Quarterly Journal of Economics* 115 (2): 389–430.

———. 2002. "The Political Economy of Government Responsiveness: Theory and Evidence from India." *Quarterly Journal of Economics* 117 (4): 1415–52.

Bhalla, Surjit. 2002. *Imagine There's No Country: Poverty, Inequality and Growth in the Era of Globalization.* Washington, DC: Institute for International Economics. [http://www.cis.org.au/Policy/summer02-03/polsumm0203-9.htm]. March 2003.

Bicego, George, and J. Ties Boerma. 1991. "Maternal Education and Child Survival: A Comparative Analysis of DHS Data." Paper presented at the Demographic and Health Surveys World Conference, 5 August, Washington, DC.

Birdsall, Nancy, and Michael Clemens. 2003a. "From Promise to Performance: How Rich Countries Can Help Poor Countries Help Themselves." CGD Brief 1 (2). Center for Global Development, Washington, DC.

Birdsall, Nancy, and Brian Deese. 2002. "Delivering on Debt Relief." CGD Brief 1. Center for Global Development, Washington, DC.

———. 2003. "Beyond HIPC: Secure Sustainable Debt Relief for Poor Countries." Paper presented at the 2002 Commonwealth HIPC Ministerial Forum, 12 September 2002. Center for Global Development, Washington, DC.

Birdsall, Nancy, and Juan Luis Londono. 1997. "Asset Inequality Does Matter: Lessons from Latin America." Office of the Chief Economist Working Paper 344. Inter-American Development Bank, Washington, DC. [http://bjcu.uca.edu.ni/biblioteca/debates/Birdsall&Londono.pdf]. March 2003.

Birdsall, Nancy, and David Roodman. 2002. "Gold for Debt: From Debt Relief to a New Development Architecture." International Institute of Economics, Washington, DC.

———. 2003. "The Commitment to Development Index: A Scorecard of Rich-Country Policies." Center for Global Development, Washington, DC.

Birdsall, Nancy, John Williamson and Brian Deese. 2002. *Delivering on Debt Relief: From IMF Gold to a New Aid Architecture.* Washington, DC: International Institute for Economics.

Bissio, Roberto. 2003. "Civil Society and the MDGs." Instituto del Tercer Mundo, Montevideo, Uruguay.

Blair, Harry. 2000. "Participation and Accountability at the Periphery: Democratic Local Governance in Six Countries." *World Development* 28 (1): 21–39. [http://www.worldbank.org/participation/participationaccountability.pdf]. March 2003.

Booth, David, and Henry Lucas. 2002. "Monitoring Progress towards the Millennium Development Goals at Country Levels." In Howard White and Richard Black, eds., *Targeting Development: Critical Perspectives on the Millennium Development Goals and International Development Targets.* London: Routledge.

Boubakri, Narjess, and Jean-Claude Cosset. 1998. "Privatization in Developing Countries: An Analysis of the Performance of Newly Privatized Firms." Public Policy for the Private Sector Note 156. World Bank, Private Sector and Infrastructure Network, Washington, DC. [http://www1.worldbank.org/viewpoint/HTMLNotes/156/156cosse.pdf]. March 2003.

Bourguignon, François. 2001. "Crime as a Social Cost of Poverty and Inequality: A Review Focusing on Developing Countries." In Shahid Yusuf, Simon Evenett and Weiping Wu, eds., *Facets of Globalization: International and Local Dimensions of Development.* Washington, DC: World Bank.

Bourguignon, François, and Francisco Ferreira. 2000. "Understanding Inequality in Brazil: A Conceptual Overview." Discussion Paper 434. Catholic University of Rio de Janeiro, Department of Economics. [http://www.econ.puc-rio.br/pdf/td434.pdf]. March 2003.

Brinkerhoff, Derick, and Arthur Goldsmith. 2003. "How Citizens Participate in Macroeconomic Policy: International Experience and Implications for Poverty Reduction." World Development 31 (4): 685–701.

Brown, Adrienne, Mick Foster, Andy Norton and Felix Naschold. 2000. "The Status of Sector-Wide Approaches." Overseas Development Institute, London. [http://www.odi.org.uk/publications/wp142.pdf]. March 2003.

Bruno, Michael, Martin Ravallion and Lyn Squire. 1996. "Equity and Growth in Developing Countries: Old and New Perspectives on the Policy Issues." Policy Research Working Paper 1563. World Bank, Washington, DC. [http://www.worldbank.org/html/dec/Publications/Workpapers/wps1563-abstract.html]. March 2003.

Bryant, Dirk, Lauretta Burke, John McManus and Mark Spalding. 1998. "Reefs at Risk Analysis: A Map-Based Indicator of Threats to the World's Coral Reefs." World Resources Institute, Washington, DC.

Buckland, Peter, Jane Hofmeyr and Susan Meyer. 1993. *Teacher Salaries in South Africa: A Policy Perspective.* Johannesburg: Urban Foundation.

Budlender, Debbie, Diane Elson, Guy Hewitt and Tanni Mukhopadhyay. 2002. *Gender Budgets Make Cents.* London: Commonwealth Secretariat.

Business Partners for Development. 2002. "Putting Partnering to Work: Results and Recommendations for Business." London. [http://www.bpdweb.org/docs/biz4of5.pdf]. March 2003.

Business Week. 2000. "Global Resistance to GM Imperils Monsanto's Future." 12 June.

CAFOD (Catholic Agency for Overseas Development). 2002. "The Rough Guide to the CAP." London.

Calderón, Fernando. 2002. *La Reforma de la Política: Deliberación y Desarrollo.* Caracas and La Paz: Ildis/FES Bolivia/Nueva Sociedad.

Calderón, Fernando, and Alicia Szmukler. 2002. "Political Culture and Development." In Vijayendra Rao and Michael Walton, eds., *Culture and Public Action.* Washington, DC: World Bank. [http://www.worldbank.org/research/conferences/culture/papers/Calderon-English.pdf]. March 2003.

Caldwell, John. 1979. "Education as a Factor in Mortality Decline: An Examination of Nigerian Data." *Population Studies* 33 (3): 395–413.

———. 1986. "Routes to Low Mortality in Poor Countries." *Population Development Review* 12 (2): 171–220.

Cameron, Robert. 2002. "Central-Local Financial Relations in South Africa." *Local Government Studies* 28 (special issue 3): 113–34.

Campbell, H. 1997. "Indoor Air Pollution and Acute Lower Respiratory Infections in Young Gambian Children." *Health Bulletin* 55: 20–31.

Canadian Centre for Policy Alternatives. 2003. "A GATS Primer." [http://www.canadians.org/campaigns/campaigns-tradepub-gats_primer.html]. March 2003.

Carlsson, Helene, and Cecilia Valdivieso. 2003. "Gender Equality and the Millennium Development Goals." World Bank, Gender and Development Group, Washington, DC.

Carnoy, Martin. 1992. *The Case for Investing in Basic Education.* New York: United Nations Children's Fund.

Carrión, Diego. 2003. "Democracy and Social Participation in Latin American Cities." *Development in Practice* 11 (2/3): 208–17.

Carson, Carol, Lucie Laliberie and Sarmad Khawaja. 2001. "Some Challenges of Statistical Capacity Building." Paper presented at the 53rd Session of the International Statistical Institute, 22–29 August, Seoul.

Cavendish, William. 1999. "Empirical Regularities in the Poverty-Environment Relationship of African Rural Households." Working Paper 99-21. Centre for the Study of African Economies, London. [http://www.econ.ox.ac.uk/CSAEadmin/workingpapers/pdfs/9921text.pdf]. March 2003.

CGIAR (Consultative Group on International Agricultural Research). 2003. "Funding." Washington, DC. [http://www.cgiar.org/who/wwa_funding.html]. March 2003.

Chandler, David. 2001. "Active Citizens and the Therapeutic State: The Role of Democratic Participation in Local Government Reform." *Policy & Politics* 29 (1): 3–14.

Chen, Lincoln, and Meghnad Desai. 2000. "Paths to Social Development: Lessons from Case Studies." In Santosh Mehrotra and Richard Jolly, eds., *Development with a Human Face: Experiences in Social Achievement and Economic Growth.* Oxford: Clarendon Press.

China, Ministry of Foreign Trade and Economic Cooperation. 2003. "Statistical Data on Foreign Direct Investment." Beijing. [http://www1.moftec.gov.cn/moftec_en/tjsj/wazi_01_en.html]. March 2003.

Chivian, Eric. 2002. "Biodiversity: Its Importance to Human Health." Harvard Medical School, Boston.

Choguill, Charles. 2001. "Urban Policy as Poverty Alleviation: The Experience of the Philippines." *Habitat International* 25 (1): 1–13.

Christiansen, Karin, Tim Conway and Mark Poston. 2003. "The Millennium Development Goals and the IDC: Driving and Framing the Committee's Work." Overseas Development Institute, London. [http://www.odi.org.uk/pppg/publications/papers_reports/other/IDC/]. March 2003.

Chwialkowska, Luiza. 2002. "U.S. Pledges Aid to Poor Nations That Respect Law." *National Post,* 23 March.

Cline, William. 2002. "An Index of Industrial Country Trade Policy toward Developing Countries." Working Paper 14. Center for Global Development, Washington, DC.

———. Forthcoming. *Trade Policy and Global Poverty.* Washington, DC: Institute for International Economics and Center for Global Development

CNN. 1998. "Researchers Trace First HIV Case to 1959 in the Belgian Congo." 3 February. [http://www.cnn.com/HEALTH/9802/03/earliest.aids/]. March 2003.

Colclough, Christopher. 2002. "Can the Millennium Development Goals for Education Be Achieved?" In Howard White and Richard Black, eds., *Targeting Development: Critical Perspectives on the Millennium Development Goals and International Development Targets.* London: Routledge.

Commission on Macroeconomics and Health. 2001. *Macroeconomics and Health: Investing in Health for Economic Development.* Geneva: World Health Organization. [http://www.un.org/esa/coordination/ecosoc/docs/RT.K.MacroeconomicsHealth.pdf]. March 2003.

Common Dreams Press Wire. 1998. "Massive Government Subsidies Bloat Fishing Industry and Violate World Trade Rules; WWF Calls for New International Fisheries Rules and Mechanisms." 26 March. [http://www.commondreams.org/pressreleases/Sept98/090998h.htm]. March 2003.

Cornia, Giovanni Andrea, and Sampsa Kiiski. 2001. "Trends in Income Distribution in the Post–World War II Period: Evidence and Interpretation." UNU/WIDER Discussion Paper 2001/89. United Nations University, World Institute for Development Economics Research, Helsinki. [http://www.wider.unu.edu/publications/dps/dp2001-89.pdf]. March 2003.

Cornia, Giovanni Andrea, and Frances Stewart. 1995. "Two Errors of Targeting." In Dominique van de Walle and Kimberly Nead, eds., *Public Spending and the Poor: Theory and Evidence.* Baltimore, Md., and London: Johns Hopkins University Press.

Council of Europe. 1998. "Structure and Operation of Local and Regional Democracy: Croatia—Situation in 1998." Report adopted by the Steering Committee on Local and Regional Democracy. Strasbourg, France. [http://www.coe.int/T/E/Legal_Affairs/Local_and_regional_Democracy/Steering_Committee_(CDLR)/Publications/Structure_Series/croatia.pdf]. March 2003.

Cox, Donald, and Emmanuel Jimenez. 1991. "Achieving Social Objectives through Private Transfers: A Review." *World Bank Research Observer* 5 (2): 205–18.

Crook, Richard. 2001. "Strengthening Democratic Governance in Conflict-Torn Societies: Civic Organisations, Democratic Effectiveness and Political Conflict." IDS Working Paper 129. University of Sussex, Institute of Development Studies, Brighton, England. [http://www.ids.ac.uk/ids/bookshop/wp/wp129.pdf]. March 2003.

Crook, Richard, and James Manor. 1998. *Democracy and Decentralisation in South Asia and West Africa: Participation, Accountability and Performance.* Cambridge: Cambridge University Press.

Crook, Richard, and Alan Sturla Sverrisson. 2001. "Decentralisation and Poverty Alleviation in Developing Countries: A Comparative Analysis or, Is West Bengal Unique?" IDS Working Paper 130. University of Sussex, Institute of Development Studies, Brighton, England. [http://www.ids.ac.uk/ids/bookshop/wp/wp130.pdf]. March 2003.

———. Forthcoming. "Does Decentralization Contribute to Poverty Reduction?" In Peter Houtzager and Mick Moore, eds., *Changing Paths: International Development and the New Politics of Inclusion.* Ann Arbor: University of Michigan Press.

Cross, C., and Milton Kutengule. 2001. "Decentralization and Rural Livelihoods in Malawi." LADDER Working Paper 4. Overseas Development Group, Norwich, England.

Cuéllar-Marchelli, Helga. 2001. "Decentralization and Privatization of Education in El Salvador: Assessing the Experience." *International Journal of Educational Development* 23 (2): 145–66.

Daley-Harris, Sam. 2003. "State of the Microcredit Summit Campaign Report 2002." Microcredit Summit Campaign, Washington, DC. [http://www.microcreditsummit.org/pubs/reports/socr/2002/socr02_en.pdf]. March 2003.

Damon, Jacqueline, Indrissa Danté and David Naudet. 1999. "Improving the Effectiveness of Aid Systems: The Case of Mali." United Nations Development Programme, New York.

De, Anuradha, and Jean Drèze. 1999. *Public Report on Basic Education in India.* Delhi: Oxford University Press.

Deininger, Klaus, and Pedro Olinto. 2000. "Asset Distribution, Inequality, and Growth." Policy Research Working Paper 2375. World Bank, Washington, DC. [http://wbln0018.worldbank.org/Research/workpapers.nsf/568b4463f7c6e237852567e500514be6/3d38b10b0587e4f98525690b0054e45e/$FILE/wps2375.pdf]. March 2003.

Deininger, Klaus, and Lyn Squire. 1998. "New Ways of Looking at Old Issues: Inequality and Growth." *Journal of Development Economics* 57 (2): 259–87.

Delamonica, Enrique, Santosh Mehrotra and Jan VandeMoortele. 2001. "Is EFA Affordable? Estimating the Global Minimum Cost of 'Education for All'." Working Paper 87. United Nations Children's Fund, Innocenti Research Centre, Florence, Italy. [http://www.unicef-icdc.org/publications/pdf/iwp87.pdf]. March 2003.

de los Angeles, Ann. 2002. "RUPES: Rewarding Upland Producers for Ecosystem Services." Paper presented at the Forest Trends Katoomba Group Workshop, 14 March, Kew Gardens, England.

de Moor, André, and Peter Calamai. 2003. *Subsidizing Unsustainable Development: Undermining the Earth with Public Funds.* San Jose, Costa Rica: Earth Council. [http://www.ecouncil.ac.cr/econ/sud/subsidizing_unsd.pdf]. March 2003.

Deshpande, Ashwini. 2002. "Assets versus Autonomy? The Changing Face of the Gender-Caste Overlap in India." *Feminist Economics* 8 (2): 19–35.

Devarajan, Shantayanan, Margaret Miller and Eric Swanson. 2002. "Goals for Development: History, Prospects and Costs." Policy Research Working Paper 2819. World Bank, Washington, DC.

DFID (UK Department for International Development). 2000. "Eliminating World Poverty: Making Globalisation Work for the Poor." London. [http://www.globalisation.gov.uk]. March 2003.

———. 2002a. "Better Livelihoods for Poor People: The Role of Land Policy." London. [http://www.dfid.gov.uk/Pubs/files/landpolicy_consult.pdf]. March 2003.

———. 2002b. "Biodiversity: A Crucial Issue for the World's Poorest." London. [http://www.dfid.gov.uk/Pubs/files/biodiversity.pdf]. March 2003.

———. 2002c. "UK Position on EU Themes for World Food Summit Five Years Later." London.

———. 2002d. "Better Livelihoods for Poor People: The Role of Agriculture." London. [http://www.dfid.gov.uk/Pubs/files/agriculture_consult.pdf]. March 2003.

———. 2002e. "A Framework for Increasing Access to Essential Medicines through Voluntary Differential Pricing." London. [http://www.dfid.gov.uk/Pubs/files/access_to_medicines_report28.11.pdf]. March 2003.

Dillinger, William, and Marianne Fay. 1999. "From Centralized to Decentralized Governance." *Finance and Development* 36 (4): 19–21. [http://www.imf.org/external/pubs/ft/fandd/1999/12/dillinge.htm]. March 2003.

Dollar, David, and Aart Kraay. 2002. "Spreading the Wealth." *Foreign Affairs* 81 (1): 120–33. [http://www.foreignaffairs.org/20020101faessay6561/david-dollar-aart-kraay/spreading-the-wealth.html]. March 2003.

Drake, Elizabeth, Ambreen Malik, Ying Xu, Ioanna Kotsioni, Rasha El-Habashy and Vivek Misra. 2003. "Good Governance and the World Bank." Bretton Woods Project, London. [http://www.brettonwoodsproject.org/topic/governance/goodgov/s32goodgovfinal.pdf]. March 2003.

Drèze, Jean, and Amartya Sen. 1995. *India: Economic Development and Social Opportunity*. Oxford: Oxford University Press.

———. 2002. *India: Development and Participation*. Oxford: Oxford University Press.

Duncan, Tyrrell, Keith Jefferis and Patrick Molutsi. 2000. "Botswana: Social Development in a Resource-Rich Economy." In Santosh Mehrotra and Richard Jolly, eds., *Development with a Human Face: Experiences in Social Achievement and Economic Growth*. Oxford: Clarendon Press.

Eberstadt, Nicholas. 2002. "The Future of AIDS." *Foreign Affairs* 81 (6). [http://www.foreignaffairs.org/20021101faessay9990/nicholas-eberstadt/the-future-of-aids.html]. March 2003.

ECLAC (United Nations Economic Commission for Latin America and the Caribbean). 2002. *Social Panorama for Latin America and the Caribbean*. Santiago, Chile. [http://www.eclac.org/cgi-bin/getProd.asp?xml=/publicaciones/xml/5/11245/P11245.xml&xsl=/dds/tpl-i/p9f.xsl&base=\tpl-i\top-bottom.xsl]. March 2003.

Economic and Political Weekly. 2000. "Food Security: On Verge of Collapse." 4–10 March. [http://www.epw.org.in/showArticles.php?root=2000&leaf=03&filename=1047&filetype=html]. March 2003.

Economist. 2001. "Economist Survey: Illegal Drugs—Stumbling in the Dark." 26 July.

European Commission. 2002a. "Analysis of the Nut Sector." Commission Staff Working Paper SEC (2002)797. Brussels. [http://europa.eu.int/comm/agriculture/markets/fruitveg/report/text_en.pdf]. March 2003.

———. 2002b. "Rice: Markets, CMO and Medium-Term Forecasts." Commission Staff Working Paper SEC (2002)788. Brussels. [http://europa.eu.int/comm/agriculture/mtr/ricerep/text_en.pdf]. March 2003.

Evans, Peter. 2002. "Beyond 'Institutional Monocropping': Institutions, Capabilities, and Deliberative Development." University of California, Department of Sociology, Berkeley. [http://sociology.berkeley.edu/faculty/evans/Institutional_Monocropping.pdf]. March 2003.

Evers, Yvette. 1996. "Local Institutions and Natural Resource Management in the West African Sahel: Policy and Practice of 'Gestion de Terroir' in the Republic of Mali." Rural Resources Rural Livelihoods Working Paper 5. University of Manchester, Institute for Development Policy and Management, Manchester, England.

Ezzati, Majid, and Daniel M. Kammen. 2001. "Indoor Air Pollution from Biomass Combustion as a Risk Factor for Acute Respiratory Infections in Kenya: An Exposure-Response Study." *Lancet* 358 (9281): 619–24.

Fabre, Guilhem. 2001. "State, Corruption, and Criminalisation in China." *International Social Science Journal* 53 (169): 459–66.

Faguet, Jean-Paul. 2001. "Does Decentralization Increase Responsiveness to Local Needs? Evidence from Bolivia." Policy Research Working Paper 2516. World Bank, Washington, DC. [http://www1.worldbank.org/publicsector/decentralization/wps2516.pdf]. March 2003.

Fajnzylber, Pablo, David Lederman and Norman Loayza. 1998. "What Causes Violent Crime?" World Bank, Latin America and the Caribbean Region, Office of the Chief Economist, Washington, DC.

Fan, Shenggen, and Peter Hazell. 2001. "Returns to Public Investments in the Less-Favored Areas of India and China." *American Journal of Agricultural Economics* 83 (5): 1217–22.

Fan, Shenggen, Peter Hazell and Sukhadeo Thorat. 1998. "Government Spending, Growth and Poverty: An Analysis of Interlinkages in Rural India." Environment and Production Technology Division Discussion Paper 33. International Food Policy Research Institute, Washington, DC. [http://www.ifpri.org/divs/eptd/dp/papers/eptdp33.pdf]. March 2003.

FAO (Food and Agriculture Organization of the United Nations). 1998. "Time to Save the Aral Sea?" Rome. [http://www.fao.org/WAICENT/FAOINFO/AGRICULT/MAGAZINE/9809/spot2.htm]. March 2003.

———. 2001a. "Global Forest Resources Assessment 2000." Forestry Paper 140. Rome.

———. 2001b. "The Impact of HIV/AIDS on Food Security." Paper presented at the 27th Session of the Committee on World Food Security, 1 May, Rome. [http://www.fao.org/docrep/meeting/003/Y0310E.htm]. March 2003.

———. 2001c. *The State of Food Insecurity in the World 2001*. Rome. [http://www.fao.org/DOCREP/003/Y1500E/Y1500E00.HTM]. March 2003.

———. 2002a. "Anti-Hunger Programme: Reducing Hunger through Sustainable Agricultural and Rural Development and Wider Access to Food." Second draft. Rome. [http://www.fao.org/DOCREP/004/Y7151E/Y7151e00.HTM]. March 2003.

———. 2002b. *The State of Food Insecurity in the World 2002*. Rome. [http://www.fao.org/docrep/005/y7352e/y7352e00.htm]. March 2003.

Ferro, Manuela, David Rosenblatt and Nicholas Stern. 2002. "Policies for Pro-Poor Growth in India." Cornell University, Department of Economics, Ithaca, NY. [http://www.arts.cornell.edu/econ/indiaconf/Stern%20Paper.pdf]. March 2003.

Filmer, Deon, and Lant Pritchett. 1997. "Child Mortality and Public Spending on Health: How Much Does Money Matter?" Policy Research Working Paper 1864. World Bank, Washington, DC.

———. 1999. "The Effect of Household Wealth on Educational Attainment: Evidence from 35 Countries." *Population and Development Review* 26 (1): 85–120.

Filmer, Deon, Jeffrey Hammer and Lant Pritchett. 1998. "Health Policy in Poor Countries: Weak Links in the Chain." Policy Research Working Paper 1874. World Bank, Washington, DC. [http://www.worldbank.org/html/dec/Publications/Workpapers/WPS1800series/wps1874/wps1874.pdf]. March 2003.

Finan, Frederico, Elisabeth Sadoulet and Alain de Janvry. 2002. "Measuring the Poverty Reduction Potential of Land in Rural Mexico." University of California, Department of Agricultural and Resource Economics, Berkeley. [http://are.berkeley.edu/~sadoulet/papers/Landpaper_WP.pdf]. March 2003.

Finger, J. Michael, and Ann Harrison. 1996. "The MFA Paradox: More Protection and More Trade?" In Anne Krueger, ed., *The Political Economy of American Trade Policy*. Chicago: University of Chicago Press.

Finlayson, C. M., N. C. Davidson, A. G. Spiers and N. J. Stevenson. 1999. "Global Wetland Inventory: Current Status and Future Priorities." *Marine and Freshwater Research* 50 (8): 717–28.

Fisman, Raymond, and Roberta Gatti. 2002. "Decentralization and Corruption: Evidence across Countries." *Journal of Public Economics* 83: 325–45.

Fitzgerald, Valpy. 2001. "Paying for the War: Economic Policy in Poor Countries under Conflict Conditions." In Frances Stewart and Valpy Fitzgerald, eds., *War and Underdevelopment*. Vol. 1, *The Economic and Social Consequences of Conflict*. Oxford: Oxford University Press.

Flug, Karnit, Antonio Spilimbergo and Erik Wachtenheim. 1998. "Investment in Education: Do Economic Volatility and Credit Constraints Matter?" Working Paper 301. Inter-American Development Bank, Washington, DC.

Forster-Rothbart, Amy, Shigeaki Kamo, Lee Shigeaki, Moon Sang and Laura Miner-Nordstrom. 2002. "Effective Strategies for Preventing HIV/AIDS in Developing Countries: Lessons from Brazil, Senegal, Thailand, and Uganda." University of Wisconsin, Robert M. La Follette School of Public Affairs, Madison. [http://www.lafollette.wisc.edu/Research/Publications/StudentPapers/2001-2002/Spring/PA869/International/AIDS.pdf]. March 2003.

Fortucci, Paula. 2002. "The Contributions of Cotton to Economies and Food Security in Developing Countries." Food and Agriculture Organization, Rome.

Foster, John. 2002. "The Millennium Declaration: Engaging Civil Society Organisations." World Federation of United Nations Associations, New York.

Foster, Mick, and Sadie Mackintosh-Walker. 2001. "Sector-Wide Programme and Poverty Reduction." ODI Working Paper 157. Overseas Development Institute, London. [http://www.odi.org.uk/pppg/publications/working_papers/157.pdf]. March 2003.

Franceys, Richard. 2001. "Patterns of Public-Private Partnerships." Paper presented at the Water Utility Partnership regional conference on "Reform of the Water Supply and Sanitation Sector in Africa: Enhancing Public-Private Partnership in the Context of the Africa Vision for Water (2025)," 26 February, Kampala. [http://www.wsp.org/english/afr/wup_conf/v2_wup.pdf]. March 2003.

Francis, Paul, and Robert James. 2003. "Balancing Rural Poverty Reduction and Citizen Participation: The Contradictions of Uganda's Decentralization Program." *World Development* 31 (2): 325–37.

Franke, Richard, and Barbara Chasin. 2000. "The Kerala Decentralisation Experiment: Achievements, Origins, and Implications." Paper presented at the International Conference on Democratic Decentralization, Kerala University, 24 May, Thiruvananthapuram, Kerala, India.

Fuentes, Patricio, and Reiki Niimi. 2002. "Motivating Municipal Action for Children: The Municipal Seal of Approval in Ceará, Brazil." *Environment & Urbanization* 14 (2): 123–33.

Fuggle, R. F. 2001. "Lake Victoria: A Case Study of Complex Interrelationship." United Nations Environment Programme, Nairobi.

Fuhr, Harald. 2003. "Decentralized Policies: Expenditure and Revenue Assignment Options—Is There Any Best Practice? What Can We Recommend?" Discussion paper. World Bank, Latin America and the Caribbean Region, Poverty Reduction and Economic Management Unit, Washington, DC.

Fukuda-Parr, Sakiko, Carlos Lopes and Khalid Malik, eds. 2002. *Capacity for Development: New Solutions to Old Problems*. London: Earthscan.

Fung, Archon, and Erik Olin Wright. 2002. "Deepening Democracy: Institutional Innovations Empowered Participatory Governance." *Politics and Society* 29 (1): 5–41. [http://www.archonfung.com/docs/pal218/Deepening020411.pdf]. March 2003.

Furtado, Xavier. 2001. "Decentralization and Capacity Development: Understanding the Links and the Implications for Programming." Capacity Development Occasional Paper 4. Canadian International Development Agency, Ottawa. [http://www.acdi-cida.gc.ca/INET/IMAGES.NSF/vLUImages/CapacityDevelopment/$file/furtado-E.PDF]. March 2003.

Galiani, Sebastian, Paul Gertler and Ernesto Schargrodsky. 2002. "Water for Life: The Impact of the Privatization of Water Services on Child Mortality." Working Paper 154. Stanford University, Stanford Institute for Economic Policy Research, Stanford, Calif. [http://credpr.stanford.edu/pdf/credpr154.pdf]. March 2003.

Gallup, John, Jeffrey Sachs and Andrew Mellinger. 2003. "Geography and Economic Development." *International Regional Science Review* 22 (2): 179–232.

Gardiner, Rosalie. 2002. "Oceans and Seas: Harnessing the Marine Environment for Sustainable Development." Environment Briefing 3, Towards the Earth Summit 2002 Series. Stakeholder Forum for Our Common Future, London. [http://www.earthsummit2002.org/es/issues/oceans/oceans.PDF]. March 2003.

Gargarella, Roberto. 2002. "Too Far Removed from the People: Access to Justice for the Poor—The Case of Latin America." Paper presented at the Chr. Michelsen Institute Workshop, United Nations Development Programme Oslo Governance Centre, 18 November, Oslo. [http://www.cmi.no/announce/UNDP%20conf%202002/Papers/RobertoGargarella.pdf]. March 2003.

Garnier, Leonardo, Rebeca Grynspan, Roberto Hidalgo, Guillermo Monge and Juan Diego Trejos. 2000. "Costa Rica: Social Development and Heterodox Adjustment." In Santosh Mehrotra and Richard Jolly, eds., *Development with a Human Face: Experiences in Social Achievement and Economic Growth*. Oxford: Clarendon Press.

Gaventa, John, and Camilo Valderrama. 1999. "Participation, Citizenship and Local Governance." Background note for the workshop "Strengthening Participation in Local Governance," University of Sussex, Institute of Development Studies, 21 June, Brighton, England.

GAVI (Global Alliance for Vaccines & Immunization). 2003. "GAVI and the Vaccine Fund: Overview." [http://www.vaccinealliance.org/home/General_Information/About_alliance/Background/overview.php]. March 2003.

Geithner, Timothy, and Gobind Nankani. 2002. "The Enhanced HIPC Initiative and the Achievement of Long-Term External Debt Sustainability." International Monetary Fund and International Development Association, Washington, DC.

Gloppen, Siri, Lise Rakner and Arne Tostensen. 2002. "Responsiveness to the Concerns of the Poor and Accountability to the Commitment to Poverty Reduction: An Issues Paper." Paper presented at the Chr. Michelsen Institute Workshop, United Nations Development Programme Oslo Governance Centre, 22 November, Oslo. [http://www.undp.org/governance/docsaccount/concerns-poor-issues-paper.pdf]. March 2003.

Goetz, Anne Marie, and Rob Jenkins. 2001. "Hybrid Forms of Accountability: Citizen Engagement in Institutions of Public Sector Oversight in India." *Public Management Review* 3 (3): 363–83.

Goldfrank, Benjamin. 2002. "The Fragile Flower of Local Democracy: A Case Study of Decentralization/Participation in Montevideo." *Politics & Society* 30 (1): 51–83.

Goldman, L., and N. Tran. 2002. "Toxics and Poverty." World Bank, Washington, DC.

Gopalakrishnan, and Amita Sharma. 1999. "Education Guarantee Scheme." Government of Madhya Pradesh, Bhopal, India.

Gore, Charles. 2002. "Realizing Goal 8: Development Partnership and Poverty Reduction in Low-Income Countries." United

Nations Conference on Trade and Development, Special Programme for Least Developed, Landlocked and Island Developing Countries.

Goreaux, L. 2003. "Préjudices Causés par les Subventions aux Filières Cotonnières de l'AOC." *Agris*, 14 April.

Grant, Ursula, Nick Devas, Philip Amis, Jo Beall, Diana Mitlin, Carole Rakodi and David Satterthwaite. 2001. "Urban Governance, Partnership and Poverty: Lessons from a Study of Ten Cities in the South." University of Birmingham and UK Department for International Development, London.

Graumann, John V. 1977. "Orders of Magnitude of the World's Urban and Rural Population in History." *United Nations Population Bulletin* 8: 16–33.

Greenhill, Romilly, and Sasha Blackmore. 2002. "Relief Works: African Proposals for Debt Cancellation and Why Debt Relief Works." Jubilee Research at the New Economics Foundation, London.

Gupta, Sanjeev, Marijn Verhoeven and Erwin Tiongson. 2002. "The Effectiveness of Government Spending on Education and Health Care in Developing and Transition Economies." *European Journal of Political Economy* 18 (4): 717–37.

Gutierrez, G., H. Tapia-Conyer, H. Guiscafre, H. Reyes, H. Martinez and J. Kumate. 1996. "Impact of Oral Rehydration Therapy and Selected Public Health Interventions on Reduction of Mortality from Childhood Diarrhoeal Diseases in Mexico." *Bulletin of the World Health Organization* 74 (2): 189–97.

Gwatkin, Davidson R. 2002. "Who Would Gain Most from Efforts to Reach the Millennium Development Goals?" Health, Nutrition and Population Discussion Paper. World Bank, Washington, DC. [http://poverty.worldbank.org/files/13920_gwatkin1202.pdf]. March 2003.

Haddad, Lawrence. 1999. "Women's Status: Levels, Consequences, Determinants, Interventions, and Policy." *Asian Development Review* 17 (1–2): 96–131. [http://www.adb.org/Documents/Periodicals/ADR/ADR_Vol_17_1and2.pdf]. March 2003.

Haggblade, Steven, and Gelson Tembo. 2002. "Conservation Farming in Zambia." Paper presented at the International Food Policy Research Institute workshop "Successes in African Agriculture," 10–12 June, Lusaka, Zambia.

Hall, David. 2002. "Water Multinationals: Financial and Other Problems." Public Services International Research Unit, London. [http://www.psiru.org/reports/2002-08-W-MNCs.doc]. March 2003.

———. 2003a. "Financing Water for the World: An Alternative to Guaranteed Profits." Public Services International Research Unit, London. [http://www.psiru.org/reports/2003-03-W-finance.doc]. March 2003.

———. 2003b. "Water Multinationals: No Longer Business as Usual." Public Services International Research Unit, London. [http://www.psiru.org/reports/2003-03-W-MNCs.doc]. March 2003.

Hall, David, and Emanuele Lobina. 2001. "Private to Public: International Lessons of Water Remunicipalisation in Grenoble, France." Public Services International Research Unit, London. [http://www.psiru.org/reports/2001-08-W-Grenoble.doc]. March 2003.

Hanlon, Joseph. 1998. "We've Been Here Before: Debt, Default and Relief in the Past—and How We Are Demanding That the Poor Pay More This Time." Jubilee 2000 Coalition, London.

Hanmer, Lucia, and Felix Naschold. 2001. "Attaining the International Development Targets: Will Growth Be Enough?" Paper presented at the Development Conference on Growth and Poverty, United Nations University, World Institute for Development Economics Research, 25 May, Helsinki. [http://www.wider.unu.edu/conference/conference-2001-1/hamner%20and%20naschold.pdf]. March 2003.

Hao, Yu, Cao Suhua and Henry Lucas. 1997. "Equity in the Utilization of Medical Services: A Survey in Poor Rural China." *Institute of Development Studies Bulletin* 28 (1): 24–31.

Hardoy, Jorge E., Diana Mitlin and David Satterthwaite. 2001. *Environmental Problems in an Urbanizing World*. London: Earthscan.

Harrison, Graham. 2001. "Post-Conditionality Politics and Administrative Reform: Reflections on the Cases of Uganda and Tanzania." *Development and Change* 32 (4): 657–79.

Harrison, Ian J., and Melanie L. J. Stiassny. 1999. "The Quiet Crisis: A Preliminary Listing of the Freshwater Fishes of the World That Are Extinct or Missing in Action." In Ross D. E. MacPhee and Hans-Dieter Sues, eds., *Extinctions in Near Time: Causes, Contexts and Consequences*. New York: Kluwer Academic and Plenum.

Harriss, John. 2000. "The Dialectics of Decentralisation." *Frontline* 17 (13). [http://www.flonnet.com/fl1713/17130700.htm]. March 2003.

Heller, Patrick. 2000. "Degrees of Democracy: Some Comparative Lessons from India." *World Politics* 52 (4): 484–519.

———. 2001. "Moving the State: The Politics of Democratic Decentralization in Kerala, South Africa, and Porto Alegre." *Politics & Society* 29 (1): 131–63.

Hendra, John, and Philip Courtnadge. 2003. "Building Partnerships for Poverty Reduction in Tanzania." United Nations Development Programme, Tanzania.

Heng, Leong Choon, and Tan Siew Hoey. 2000. "Malaysia: Social Development, Poverty Reduction, and Economic Transformation." In Santosh Mehrotra and Richard Jolly, eds., *Development with a Human Face: Experiences in Social Achievement and Economic Growth*. Oxford: Clarendon Press.

Henninger, Norbert, and Mathilde Snel. 2002. *Where Are the Poor? Experiences with the Development and Use of Poverty Maps*. Washington, DC: World Resources Institute. [http://pubs.wri.org/pubs_pdf.cfm?PubID=3758]. March 2003.

Herfkens, Eveline. 2002. "Millennium Development Goals: Building a Global Partnership." United Nations, New York.

Herring, Ronald. 2000. "Political Conditions for Agrarian Reform and Poverty Alleviation." IDS Discussion Paper 375. University of Sussex, Institute of Development Studies, Brighton, England. [http://www.ids.ac.uk/ids/bookshop/dp/dp375.pdf]. March 2003.

———. Forthcoming. "The Political Impossibility Theorem of Agrarian Reform: Path Dependence and Terms of Inclusion." In Peter Houtzager and Mick Moore, eds., *Changing Paths: International Development and the New Politics of Inclusion*. Ann Arbor: University of Michigan Press.

Hertel, Thomas, and Will Martin. 1999. "Would Developing Countries Gain from Inclusion of Manufacturers in the WTO Negotiations?" Paper presented at the conference "WTO and the Millennium Round," 20–21 September, Geneva.

Hessling, G., and B. M. Ba. 1994. "Land Tenure and Resource Management in the Sahel: Regional Synthesis and Summary." Paper presented at the Permanent Inter-State Committee for the Prevention of Drought in the Sahel (CILSS), Organisation for Economic Co-operation and Development and Club du Sahel Regional Conference on Land Tenure and Decentralisation in the Sahel, May, Praia, Cape Verde.

Hirschman, Albert O. 1970. *Exit, Voice and Loyalty: Responses to Decline in Firms, Organizations and States*. Cambridge, Mass.: Harvard University Press.

Hope, Kempe Ronald. 2000. "Decentralisation and Local Governance Theory and the Practice in Botswana." *Development Southern Africa* 17 (4): 519–34.

Hossain, Naomi, and Mick Moore. 2001. "Arguing for the Poor: Elites and Poverty in Developing Countries." IDS Working Paper 148. University of Sussex, Institute of Development Studies, Brighton, England.

Houtzager, Peter. 1999. "Collective Action and Patterns of Political Authority: Rural Workers, Church, and the State in

Brazil." University of Sussex, Institute of Development Studies, Brighton, England. [http://www.ids.ac.uk/ids/govern/pdfs/insho.pdf]. March 2003.

Huizer, Gerrit. 1999. "Peasant Mobilization for Land Reform: Historical Considerations and Theoretical Considerations." Monograph 6. Popular Coalition to Eradicate Hunger and Poverty and United Nations Research Institute for Social Development, Rome and Geneva. [http://www.ifad.org/popularcoalition/pdf/mon6.pdf]. March 2003.

ICCC (International Cotton Consultantive Committee). 2002. "Réduction de la Pauvreté: Initiative Sectorielle en Faveur du Coton." Initiative Conjointe du Benin, du Burkina Faso, du Mali et du Tchad. Négociations agricoles a l'Organisation Mondiale du Commerce. World Trade Organization, Geneva.

ICIJ (International Consortium of Investigative Journalists). 2003a. "A Tale of Two Cities." [http://www.icij.org/dtaweb/water/default.aspx?SECTION=ARTICLE&AID=10]. March 2003.

———. 2003b. "Loaves, Fishes and Dirty Dishes: Manila's Privatized Water Can't Handle the Pressure." [http://www.icij.org/dtaweb/water/default.aspx?SECTION=ARTICLE&AID=]. March 2003.

———. 2003c. "Metered to Death: How a Water Experiment Caused Riots and a Cholera Epidemic." [http://www.icij.org/dtaweb/water/default.aspx?SECTION=CHAPTER&ID=3]. March 2003.

———. 2003d. "The 'Aguas' Tango: Cashing in on Buenos Aires' Privatization." [http://www.icij.org/dtaweb/water/default.aspx?SECTION=ARTICLE&AID=7]. March 2003.

———. 2003e. "Water and Politics in the Fall of Suharto." [http://www.icij.org/dtaweb/water/default.aspx?SECTION=CHAPTER&ID=6]. March 2003.

IEA (International Energy Agency). 1999. *World Energy Outlook*. Paris.

———. 2003. "Renewables in Global Energy Supply." Fact sheet. Paris. [http://www.iea.org/leaflet.pdf]. March 2003.

IEA (International Energy Agency) and OECD (Organisation for Economic Co-operation and Development). 2003. *Energy Statistics of OECD Countries*. Paris.

IFAD (International Fund for Agricultural Development). 2001. *Rural Poverty Report 2001: The Challenge of Ending Rural Poverty*. New York: Oxford University Press.

IFC (International Finance Corporation). 2002a. "IFC Strategic Directions." Washington, DC.

———. 2002b. "Investing in Private Health Care: Strategic Directions for IFC." Washington, DC.

IFPRI (International Food Policy Research Institute). 2002. "Reaching Sustainable Food Security for All by 2020: Priorities and Responsibilites." Washington, DC. [http://www.futureharvest.org/pdf/2020_Vision_02.pdf]. March 2003.

IFRC (International Federation of the Red Cross and Red Crescent Societies). 2001. *World Disasters Report 2001*. Geneva. [http://www.ifrc.org/publicat/wdr2001/]. March 2003.

ILO (International Labour Organization). 1991a. Teachers in Developing Countries: A Survey of Employment Conditions. Geneva.

———. 1991b. *Teachers in Developing Countries: Improving Effectiveness and Managing Costs*. Geneva.

———. 2001. "Bonded Labour and Its Eradication." In *Stopping Forced Labour*. Geneva. [http://www.ilo.org/public/english/standards/decl/publ/reports/fullreport2/part1_ch6-9.pdf]. March 2003.

IMF (International Monetary Fund). 2000. "Poverty Reduction Strategy Paper, Tanzania." [http://www.imf.org/external/NP/prsp/2000/tza/02/100100.pdf]. March 2003.

———. 2002a. "Uganda: A Request for a Three-Year Arrangement under the Poverty Reduction and Growth Facility." Country Report 02/213. Washington, DC.

———. 2002b. *World Economic Outlook*. Washington, DC.

IMF (International Monetary Fund) and International Development Association. 2003. "Heavily Indebted Poor Countries (HIPC) Initiative: Statistical Update." Washington, DC.

IMF (International Monetary Fund), OECD (Organisation for Economic Co-operation and Development), United Nations and World Bank. 2000. *2000: A Better World for All—Progress towards the International Development Goals*. New York. [http://www.paris21.org/betterworld/pdf/bwa_e.pdf]. March 2003.

India, Ministry of Finance. 2002. "Economic Survey 2001–2002: Prices and Food Management." New Delhi. [http://indiabudget.nic.in/es2001-02/prices.htm]. March 2003.

India, Ministry of Finance and Company Affairs. 2003. "Union Budget and Economic Survey 2003." New Delhi. [http://indiabudget.nic.in/ub2003-04/ubmain.htm]. March 2003.

India, Planning Commission. 2002. *India National Human Development Report 2001*. New Delhi. [http://hdr.undp.org/reports/detail_reports.cfm?view=122]. March 2003.

Institute for European Environmental Policy. 2002. "Subsidies to the European Union Fisheries Sector." Paper commissioned by the World Wildlife Fund European Fisheries Campaign. London. [http://www.panda.org/downloads/marine/subsidiesreport.pdf]. March 2003.

Institute of Development Studies. 2003. "Bringing Citizen Voice and Client Focus into Service Delivery: Case Study—Education Guarantee Scheme, Madhya Pradesh, India." Discussion paper. University of Sussex, Brighton, England. [http://www.ids.ac.uk/ids/govern/citizenvoice/pdfs/educationgs-india.pdf]. March 2003.

International Council for Science. 2002. "Resilience and Sustainable Development: Building Adaptive Capacity in a World of Transformations." Paris. [http://www.icsu.org/Library/WSSD-Rep/Vol3.pdf]. March 2003.

International Institute of Population Sciences. 2000. "India: National Family Health Survey, 1998/9." Mumbai.

IPCC (Intergovernmental Panel on Climate Change). 2001a. "Climate Change 2001: Impacts, Adaptation, and Vulnerability." Summary for Policymakers. Geneva. [http://www.grida.no/climate/ipcc_tar/wg2/005.htm]. March 2003.

———. 2001b. "Climate Change 2001: The Scientific Basis." Summary for Policymakers. Geneva. [http://www.grida.no/climate/ipcc_tar/wg1/005.htm]. March 2003.

Iriart, Celia, Emerson Elfas Merhy and Howard Waitzkin. 2001. "Managed Care in Latin America: The New Common Sense in Health Policy Reform." *Social Science & Medicine* 52 (8): 1243–53.

Iriart, Celia, Howard Waitzkin and Carlos Trotta. 2002. "Global Policies, Health Care Systems and Social Movements from Latin America: A Lesson from Argentina." *Global Social Policy* 2 (3): 245–48.

IUCN (International Union for the Conservation of Nature and Natural Resources). 2002. "2002 IUCN Red List of Threatened Species." Cambridge. [http://www.redlist.org]. March 2003.

Iyer, Aditi, and Gita Sen. 2000. "Health Sector Changes and Health Equity in the 1990s in India." In Shobha Raghuram, ed., *Health and Equity-Effecting Change*. Bangalore, India: Humanist Institute for Co-operation with Developing Countries.

Janzen, Daniel. 2000. "Costa Rica's Area de Conservacion Guanacaste: A Long March to Survival through Non-Damaging Biodiversity and Ecosystem Development." Paper presented at the United Nations Conference on the Ecosystem Approach for Sustainable Use of Biological Diversity, 6 September, Trondheim, Norway.

Jenkins, Rob, and Anne Marie Goetz. 1999. "Accounts and Accountability: Theoretical Implications of the Right-to-Information Movement in India." *Third World Quarterly* 20 (3): 603–22.

Jha, Prabhat. 2002. "Improving the Health of the Global Poor." *Science* 295 (5562): 2036–39.

Jhabvala, Renana, and Ravi Kanbur. 2002. "Globalization and Economic Reform as Seen from the Ground: SEWA's Experience in India." Paper presented at the Cornell University Indian Economy Conference, 19 April, Ithaca, NY. [http://www.arts.cornell.edu/poverty/kanbur/Jhabvala-Kanbur MITPress.pdf]. March 2003.

Jimenez, Emmanuel. 1987. *Pricing Policy in the Social Sectors: Cost Recovery for Education and Health in Developing Countries*. Baltimore, Md.: Johns Hopkins University Press.

Johnson, Craig. 2001. "Local Democracy, Democratic Decentralisation and Rural Development: Theories, Challenges and Options for Policy." *Development Policy Review* 19 (4): 521–32.

———. 2003. "Decentralisation in India: Poverty, Politics and Panchayati Raj." Working Paper 199. Overseas Development Institute, London.

Johnson, Craig, and Daniel Start. 2001. "Rights, Claims and Capture: Understanding the Politics of Pro-Poor Policy." Working Paper 145. Overseas Development Institute, London. [http://www.odi.org.uk/publications/wp145.pdf]. March 2003.

Johnston, Robert. 2002. "Discussion Note on the Draft Terms of Reference and Objectives of the Task Team, and Some General Considerations on MDGs Indicators Reporting at the National Level." Paper presented at the United Nations Statistics Division's First Meeting of the PARIS21 Task Team to Improve Statistical Support for Monitoring Development Goals, 15 October, Paris.

Jolly, Richard, ed. 2001. *Jim Grant: UNICEF Visionary*. Florence, Italy: United Nations Children's Fund, Innocenti Research Centre.

Kabeer, Naila. 2000. "Safety Nets and Opportunity Ladders: Addressing Vulnerability and Enhancing Productivity in South Asia." *Development Policy Review* 20 (5): 589–614.

Kadzamira, Esme, and Pauline Rose. 2001. "Educational Policy Choice and Policy Practice in Malawi: Dilemmas and Disjunctures." IDS Working Paper 124. University of Sussex, Institute of Development Studies, Brighton, England. [http://www.ids.ac.uk/ids/bookshop/wp/wp124.pdf]. March 2003.

Kanbur, Ravi, and Nora Lustig. 1999. "Why Is Inequality Back on the Agenda?" Paper presented at the Annual World Bank Conference on Development Economics, 28 April, Washington, DC.

Kanbur, Ravi, and Lyn Squire. 1999. "The Evolution of Thinking about Poverty: Exploring the Interactions." Cornell University, Ithaca, NY. [http://people.cornell.edu/pages/sk145/papers/evolution_of_thinking_about_poverty.pdf]. March 2003.

Kannan, K. P., S. Mahendra Dev and Alakh Narain Sharma. 2000. "Concerns on Food Security." *Economic and Political Weekly*, 4–10 November. [http://www.epw.org.in/showArticles.php?root=2000&leaf=11&filename=1894&filetype=html]. March 2003.

Kawabata, Kei, Ke Xu and Guy Carrin. 2002. "Preventing Impoverishment through Protection against Catastrophic Health Expenditure." *Bulletin of the World Health Organization* 80 (8): 612. [http://www.who.int/bulletin/pdf/2002/bul-8-E-2002/bu0325.pdf]. March 2003.

Khandker, Shahidur. 1998. *Fighting Poverty with Microcredit: Experience in Bangladesh*. New York: Oxford University Press.

Khatri, G. R., and Thomas Frieden. 2002. "Controlling Tuberculosis in India." *New England Journal of Medicine* 347 (18): 1420–25.

Khemani, Stuti. 2001. "Decentralization and Accountability: Are Voters More Vigilant in Local than in National Elections?" Policy Research Working Paper 2557. World Bank, Washington, DC.

Khor, Martin. 2000. "UN Social Conference Ends with Mixed Reaction." Third World Network, Penang, Malaysia. [http://www.twnside.org.sg/title/copen17.htm]. March 2003.

———. 2002a. "Developing a Global Partnership for Development: Critical Issues and Proposals for Trade and Finance." Third World Network, Penang, Malaysia.

———. 2002b. "The WTO, the Post-Doha Agenda and the Future of the Trade System: A Development Perspective." Third World Network, Penang, Malaysia.

Klasen, Stephan, and Claudia Wink. 2002. "A Turning Point in Gender Bias in Mortality? An Update on the Number of Missing Women." *Population and Development Review* 28 (2): 285–312.

Kohl, Benjamin. 2002. "Stabilizing Neoliberalism in Bolivia: Popular Participation and Privatization." *Political Geography* 21 (4): 449–72.

Kongsin, Sukhontha, Charles Cameron, Laksami Suebsaeng and Donald Shepard. 1998. "Levels and Determinants of Expenditure on HIV/AIDS in Thailand." In Fransen Lieve, Mead Over and Martha Ainsworth, eds., *Confronting AIDS: Evidence from the Developing World*. Brussels: European Commission. [http://www.europa.eu.int/comm/development/aids/limelette/html/lim12f.htm]. March 2003.

Korzeniewicz, P., and T. P. Moran. 1997. "World-Economic Trends in the Distribution of Income, 1965–1992." *American Journal of Sociology* 102 (4): 1000–39.

Kosack, Stephen. 2003. "Effective Aid: How Democracy Allows Development Aid to Improve the Quality of Life." *World Development* 31 (1): 1–22.

Koziell, Isabella, and Charles McNeill. 2002. "Building on Hidden Opportunities to Achieve the Millennium Development Goals: Poverty Reduction through Conservation and Sustainable Use of Biodiversity." United Nations Development Programme, Equator Initiative, New York. [http://www.undp.org/equatorinitiative/pdf/poverty_reduction.pdf]. March 2003.

Kraul, Chris. 2002. "U.S., Europe to Tout Pledges of Development Aid at Summit; Mexico: Bush and Other Leaders Say They Want to Boost Grants to Poor Nations by $12 Billion a Year by 2006." *Los Angeles Times*, 21 March.

Kremer, Michael. 2003. "Evidence from a Study of Vouchers for Private Schooling in Colombia." Background paper for the World Bank's *World Development Report 2004: Making Services Work for Poor People*. World Bank, Washington, DC. [http://econ.worldbank.org/files/18764_KremerVouchers.pdf]. March 2003.

Krishnan, T. N. 2000. "The Route to Social Development in Kerala: Social Intermediation and Public Action." In Santosh Mehrotra and Richard Jolly, eds., *Development with a Human Face: Experiences in Social Achievement and Economic Growth*. Oxford: Clarendon Press.

Kudva, Neema. 2003. "Engineering Elections: The Experiences of Women in *Panchayati Raj* in Karnataka, India." *International Journal of Politics: Culture and Society* 16 (3): 445–63.

Landell-Mills, Natasha, Joshua Bishop and Ina Porras. 2002. *Silver Bullet or Fools' Gold? Markets for Forest Environmental Services and the Poor: Emerging Issues*. London: International Institute for Environment and Development.

Landuyt, Katherine. 1998. "Gender Mainstreaming: A How To Manual." International Labour Organization, Geneva. [http://www.ilo.org/public/english/region/asro/mdtmanila/gender/gnanx1.htm]. March 2003.

Lee, Jong-Wha. 1997. "Economic Growth and Human Development in the Republic of Korea, 1945–92." Human Development Report Office Occasional Paper 24. United Nations Development Programme, New York. [http://hdr.undp.org/docs/publications/ocational_papers/oc24aa.htm]. March 2003.

Leftwich, Adrian. 1994. "Governance, the State and Politics of Development." *Development and Change* 25 (2): 363–86.

Leipziger, Danny, and Vivien Foster. 2003. "Is Privatization Good for the Poor?" International Finance Corporation, Washington, DC. [http://www.ifc.org/publications/pubs/impact/issue2/dl-vf/dl-vf.html]. February 2003.

Lewin, Keith, and François Caillods. 2001. *Financing Secondary Education in Developing Countries: Strategies for Sustainable Growth*. Paris: United Nations Educational, Scientific and Cultural Organization, International Institute for Educational Planning. [http://unesdoc.unesco.org/images/0012/001248/124844e.pdf]. March 2003.

Lipton, Michael, and Martin Ravallion. 1994. "Poverty and Policy." In Jere R. Behrman and T. N. Srinivasan, eds., *Handbook of Development Economics*. Vol. 3. Amsterdam: Elsevier.

Lobina, Emanuele. 2000. "Cochabamba: Water War." Public Services International Research Unit, London. [http://www.psiru.org/reports/Cochabamba.doc]. March 2003.

———. 2001. "UK Water Privatisation: A Briefing." Public Services International Research Unit, London. [http://www.psiru.org/reports/2001-02-W-UK-over.doc]. March 2003.

Lobina, Emanuele, and David Hall. 1999. "Public Sector Alternatives to Water Supply and Sewerage Privatisation: Case Studies." Public Services International Research Unit, London. [http://www.psiru.org/reports/9908--W-U-Pubalt.doc]. March 2003.

Loewenson, Rene, and Munhamo Chisvo. 2000. "Rapid Social Transformation despite Economic Adjustment and Slow Growth: The Experience of Zimbabwe." In Santosh Mehrotra and Richard Jolly, eds., *Development with a Human Face: Experiences in Social Achievement and Economic Growth*. Oxford: Clarendon Press.

Lopes, Carlos, and Thomas Thieson. 2003. *Ownership, Leadership and Transformation: Can We Do Better for Capacity Development?* London: Earthscan.

Lopes, Pablo Silva. 2002. "A Comparative Analysis of Government Social Spending Indicators and Their Correlation with Social Outcomes in Sub-Saharan Africa." IMF Working Paper 02/176. International Monetary Fund, Washington, DC.

Lopez, Ramon. 2003. "The Policy Roots of Socioeconomic Stagnation and Environmental Implosion: Latin America 1950–2000." *World Development* 31 (2): 259–80.

Lucas, Robert. 1988. "On the Mechanisms of Economic Development." *Journal of Monetary Economics* 22 (1): 3–42.

Lvovsky, Kseniya. 2001. "Health and Environment." Environment Strategy Paper 1. World Bank, Environment Department, Washington, DC. [http://lnweb18.worldbank.org/ESSD/essdext.nsf/41DocByUnid/7F4D2733EBC5BBAA05256B6E0002918E/$FILE/ESP1Health&Environment2001.pdf]. March 2003.

MacDonald, Laura. 2002. "Globalization and Social Movements: Comparing Women's Movements' Responses to NAFTA in Mexico, the USA and Canada." *International Feminist Journal of Politics* 4 (2): 151–72.

Macro International. 2003. "Demographic and Health Surveys (DHS)." Calverton, Md. [http://www.measuredhs.com]. March 2003.

Maddison, Angus. 2001. *The World Economy: A Millennial Perspective*. Paris: Organisation for Economic Co-operation and Development. [http://www.theworldeconomy.org/about.htm]. March 2003.

Mamdani, Mahmood. 1976. *Politics and Class Formation in Uganda*. Kampala: Fountain Publishers.

———. 1995. *The Politics of Democratic Reform? Critical Reflections on the NRM*. Kampala: Monitor Publications.

———. 1996. *Citizen and Subject: Contemporary Africa and the Legacy of Late Colonialism*. Kampala: Fountain Publishers.

Manor, James. 1999. *The Political Economy of Democratic Decentralization*. Washington, DC: World Bank.

———. 2000. "Local Government in South Africa: Potential Disaster despite Genuine Promise." IDS background paper. University of Sussex, Institute of Development Studies, Brighton, England.

Marks, Stephen. 2003. Correspondence on the benchmarks for the progressive realization of human rights. April. Harvard University, School of Public Health, Boston.

Marshall, Monty G. 2000. "Major Episodes of Political Violence, 1946–1999." University of Maryland, Center for Systematic Peace, College Park. [http://members.aol.com/csp-mgm/warlist.htm]. March 2003.

Mason, Edward, Mah Je Kim, Dwight Perkins, K. S. Kim and David Cole. 1980. *The Economic and Social Modernization of the Republic of Korea*. Cambridge, Mass.: Harvard University Press.

May, Peter, Fernando Veiga Nieto, Valdir Denardin and Wilson Loureiro. 2002. "Using Fiscal Instruments to Encourage Conservation: Municipal Responses to the Ecological Value Added Tax in Parana and Minas Gerais, Brazil." In Stefano Pagiola, Joshua Bishop and Natasha Landell-Mills, eds., *Selling Forest Environment Services*. London: Earthscan.

McArthur, John, and Jeffrey Sachs. 2002. "The Growth Competitiveness Index: Measuring Technological Advancement and the Stages of Development." In Michael Porter and Jeffrey Sachs, eds., *Global Competitiveness Report 2001–2002*. New York: Oxford University Press.

McEwin, Marion. 2003. Correspondence on statistical capacity building issues. March. Belconnen, Australia.

McIntyre, Robert. 2002. "Local-Level Initiatives in the Context of EU Enlargement: Policy and Ownership Alternatives." Paper presented at the Institute for International Economic and Political Studies workshop on Russia and CIS in Recent European Integration Processes, Moscow.

Mehrotra, Santosh. 1998. "Education for All: Lessons from High-Achieving Countries." *International Review of Education* 44 (5/6): 461–84.

———. 1999. "Improving Cost-Effectiveness and Mobilizing Resources for Primary Education in Sub-Saharan Africa." *Prospects* 28 (3).

———. 2000a. "Health and Education Policies in High-Achieving Countries: Some Lessons." In Santosh Mehrotra and Richard Jolly, eds., *Development with a Human Face: Experiences in Social Achievement and Economic Growth*. Oxford: Clarendon Press.

———. 2000b. "Integrating Economic and Social Policy: Good Practices from High-Achieving Countries." Working Paper 80. United Nations Children's Fund, Innocenti Research Centre, Florence, Italy.

———. 2000c. "Social Development in High-Achieving Countries: Common Elements and Diversities." In Santosh Mehrotra and Richard Jolly, eds., *Development with a Human Face: Experiences in Social Achievement and Economic Growth*. Oxford: Clarendon Press.

———. 2002. "Some Methodological Issues in Determining Good Practices in Social Policy: The Case of High-Achieving Countries." In Else Øyen, ed., *Best Practices in Poverty Reduction: An Analytical Framework*. London and New York: Zed Books.

Mehrotra, Santosh, and Mario Biggeri. 2002. "The Subterranean Child Labour Force: A Comparative Analysis of Subcontracted Home-Based Manufacturing in Five Asian Countries." Working Paper 96. United Nations Children's Fund, Innocenti Research Centre, Florence, Italy.

Mehrotra, Santosh, and Peter Buckland. 1998. "Managing Teacher Costs for Access and Quality." UNICEF Staff Working Papers, Evaluation, Policy and Planning Series, no. EPP-EVL-98-004. United Nations Children's Fund, New York.

Mehrotra, Santosh, and Enrique Delamonica. 1998. "Household Cost and Public Expenditure on Primary Education in Five Low-Income Countries: A Comparative Analysis." *International Journal of Educational Development* 18 (1): 41–61.

———. Forthcoming. *Public Spending for the Poor: Basic Services to Enhance Capabilities and Promote Growth*. Oxford: Oxford University Press.

Mehrotra, Santosh, and Stephen W. Jarrett. 2002. "Improving Basic Health Service Delivery in Low-Income Countries:

Voice to the Poor." *Social Science and Medicine* 54 (11): 1685–90.

Mehrotra, Santosh, and Richard Jolly, eds. 2000. *Development with a Human Face: Experiences in Social Achievement and Economic Growth.* Oxford: Clarendon Press.

Mehrotra, Santosh, P. R. Panchamukhi, Ranjava Srivastava and Ravi Srivastava. Forthcoming. *Uncaging the "Tiger" Economy: Financing Elementary Education in India.* Oxford: Oxford University Press.

Michaud, Catherine, and Chris Murray. 1996. "Resources for Health Research and Development 1992: A Global Overview." In World Health Organization, *Investing in Health Research and Development.* Geneva.

Migdal, Joel, Atul Kohli and Vivienne Shue, eds. 1994. *State Power and Social Forces: Domination and Transformation in the Third World.* New York: Cambridge University Press.

Milanovic, Branko. 1998. "Income, Inequality, and Poverty during the Transition from Planned to Market Economy." World Bank, Washington, DC. [http://www-wds.worldbank.org/servlet/WDSContentServer/WDSP/IB/1998/02/01/000009265_3980319100155/Rendered/PDF/multi_page.pdf]. March 2003.

———. 2002. "True World Income Distribution, 1988 and 1993: First Calculation Based on Household Surveys Alone." *Economic Journal* 112 (476): 51–92.

———. 2003. "Worlds Apart: Global and International Inequality, 1950–2000." World Bank, Washington, DC.

Milazzo, Matteo. 1998. *Subsidies in World Fisheries: A Re-Examination.* World Bank Technical Paper 406. Washington, DC.

Milliken, Jennifer, and Keith Krause. 2002. "State Failure, State Collapse, and State Reconstruction: Concepts, Lessons and Strategies." *Development and Change* 33 (5): 753–74.

Mills, Anne. 1997. "Improving the Efficiency of Public Sector Health Services in Developing Countries: Bureaucratic versus Market Approaches." In Christopher Colclough, ed., *Marketizing Education and Health in Developing Countries: Miracle or Mirage?* Oxford: Clarendon Press.

Mills, Anne, Ruairi Brugha, Kara Hanson and Barbara McPake. 2002. "What Can Be Done about the Private Health Sector in Low-Income Countries?" *Bulletin of the World Health Organization* 80 (4): 325–30. [http://www.who.int/bulletin/pdf/2002/bul-4-E-2002/80 (4)325-330.pdf]. March 2003.

Minujin, Alberto, and Enrique Delamonica. 2003. "Equality Matters for a World Fit for Children: Lessons from the '90s." UNICEF Staff Working Papers, Division of Policy and Planning Series, no. 3. United Nations Children's Fund, New York.

Moore, Mick, and James Putzel. 1999a. "Politics and Poverty." Background paper for the World Bank's *World Development Report 2000/2001.* University of Sussex, Institute of Development Studies, Brighton, England.

———. 1999b. "Thinking Strategically about Politics and Poverty." IDS Working Paper 101. University of Sussex, Institute of Development Studies, Brighton, England.

Mozambique, Ministry of State Administration. 2002. "Local Governance for Poverty Reduction in Africa." Speech by the minister of state administration at the Fifth African Governance Forum, 23 May, Maputo, Mozambique.

Murphy, David, and Jem Bendell. 1999. "Partners in Time? Business, NGOs and Sustainable Development." UNRISD Discussion Paper 109. United Nations Research Institute for Social Development, Geneva. [http://www.unrisd.org/unrisd/website/document.nsf/462fc27bd1fce00880256b4a0060d2af/259bb13ad57ac8e980256b61004f9a62/$FILE/dp109.pdf]. March 2003.

Murthy, P. N. 1999. "Meeting the Needs of a Nation: Bhutan Essential Drugs Programme." *UNV Bhutan Newsletter* 1 (June). [http://www.unv.org/Infobase/articles/1999/99_06_01BTN_drugs.htm]. March 2003.

Mutebi, Frederick Golooba, Simon Stone and Neil Thin. 2003. "Rwanda." *Development Policy Review* 21 (2): 253–70.

Myers, Norman, and Jennifer Kent. 1998. *Perverse Subsidies: Tax Dollars Undercutting Our Economies and Environments Alike.* Winnipeg, Canada: International Institute for Sustainable Development.

Myers, Norman, Russel Mittermeier, Cristina Mittermeier, Gustavo Fonseca and Jennifer Kent. 2000. "Biodiversity Hotspots for Conservation Priorities." *Nature* 400: 853–58.

Naidu, Sanusha. 2002. "The New Partnership for Africa's Development (NEPAD) in the Context of Responsiveness and Accountability." Paper presented at the Chr. Michelsen Institute Workshop, United Nations Development Programme Oslo Governance Centre, 18–19 November, Oslo. [http://www.cmi.no/announce/UNDP%20conf%202002/Papers/SanushaNaidu.pdf]. March 2003.

Narasimahan, Sakuntala. 2002. "Gender, Calls, and Caste Schism in Affirmative Action Policies: The Curious Case of India's Women's Reservation Bill." *Feminist Economics* 8 (2): 183–90.

Narayan, Deepa, and Patti Patesch, eds. 2000. *Voices of the Poor: Crying Out for Change.* New York: Oxford University Press.

Naeem, Shahid. 1998. "Species Redundancy and Ecosystem Reliability." *Conservation Biology* 12: 39–45.

New Zealand, Ministry of Foreign Affairs and Trade. 2003. "Tariffs and Tariff Escalation." Wellington. [http://www.mft.govt.nz/foreign/tead/tariff.html]. March 2003.

Nigel, Bruce, Lynnette Neufeld, Erick Boy and Chris West. 1998. "Indoor Biofuel Air Pollution and Respiratory Health: The Role of Confounding Factors among Women in Highland Guatemala." *International Journal of Epidemiology* 27: 454–58.

Nittayaramphong, Sa-nguan, and Viroj Tangcharaoensathien. 1994. "Thailand: Private Health Care Out of Control?" *Health Policy and Planning* 9 (1): 31–40.

Noman, Omar. 1997. *Economic and Social Progress in Asia: Why Pakistan Did Not Become a Tiger.* New York: Oxford University Press.

Nordhaus, William, and Joseph Boyer. 1999. "Tanzania's Poverty Reduction Strategy Paper." *Energy Journal* (special issue on the Costs of the Kyoto Protocol: A Multi-Model Evaluation): 93–130.

OECD (Organisation for Economic Co-operation and Development). 1996. "Shaping the 21st Century: The Contribution of Development Cooperation." Paris.

———. 1999. "Assisting Developing Countries with the Formulation and Implementation of National Strategies for Sustainable Development: The Need to Clarify DAC Targets and Strategies." Paris. [http://www.nssd.net/pdf/IIED11.pdf].

———. 2001. *Policies to Enhance Sustainable Development.* Paris.

———. 2003a. Correspondence on agricultural support estimates. April. Paris.

———. 2003b. *Improving Water Management: Recent OECD Experience.* Paris. [http://www1.oecd.org/publications/e-book/9703021E.PDF]. March 2003.

OECD (Organisation for Economic Co-operation and Development), Development Assistance Committee. 1991. "Principles for New Orientation in Technical Cooperation." Paris.

———. 2001. *Development Cooperation Report 2001.* Paris.

———. 2003a. Correspondence on official development assistance disbursed. April. Paris.

———. 2003b. *CRS Online.* Database. Paris.

———. 2003c. *DAC Online.* Database. Paris.

———. 2003d. "ODA Prospects after Monterrey: Update." Note by the Secretariat. Paris.

Ogus, Anthony. 2002. "Regulatory Institutions and Structures." *Annals of Public and Cooperative Economics* 73 (4): 627–48.

Oldeman, Roell, Ruud Hakkeling and Wim Sombroek. 1990. "World Map of the Status of Human-Induced Soil Degradation."

International Soil Reference and Information Centre, Wageningen, Netherlands.

Osava, Mario. 2003. "Brazil: A New Chance for Old 'Social Revolutionary' Ideas." *Terra Viva Online*. [http://www.ipsnews.net/fsm2003/eng/note4.shtml]. March 2003.

Oster, Sharon, Elizabeth Lake and Conchita Oksman. 1978. *The Definition and Measurement of Poverty*. Boulder, Colo.: Westview Press.

Oxfam. 2002. "Last Chance in Monterrey: Meeting the Challenge of Poverty Reduction." Oxford.

Øyen, Else, ed. 2002. *Best Practices in Poverty Reduction: An Analytical Framework*. London and New York: Zed Books.

Paarlberg, Robert. 2002. "Governance and Food Security in an Age of Globalization." 20/20 Brief 72. International Food Policy Research Institute, Washington, DC. [http://www.ifpri.org/2020/briefs/brief72.pdf]. March 2003.

Pande, Rohini. 2003. "Can Mandated Political Representation Increase Policy Influence for Disadvantaged Minorities? Theory and Evidence from India." Columbia University, Department of Economics, New York. [http://www.columbia.edu/~rp461/aer2rs.pdf]. March 2003.

Panos Institute. 2001. "Food for All: Can Hunger Be Halved?" London.

Paul, Samuel. 2002. "New Mechanisms for Public Accountability: The Indian Experience." Paper presented at the Chr. Michelsen Institute Workshop, United Nations Development Programme Oslo Governance Centre, 18 November, Oslo. [http://www.cmi.no/announce/UNDP%20conf%202002/Papers/SamuelPaul.pdf]. March 2003.

Petkova, Elena, Crescencia Maurer, Norbert Henninger and Fran Irwin. 2003. *Closing the Gap: Information, Participation, and Justice in Decision-Making for the Environment*. Washington, DC: World Resources Institute. [http://pubs.wri.org/pubs_pdf.cfm?PubID=3759]. March 2003.

Phillips, Anne. 1995. *The Politics of Presence*. Oxford: Clarendon Press.

Pinstrup-Andersen, Per, and Rajul Pandya-Lorch, eds. 2001. *The Unfinished Agenda: Perspectives on Overcoming Hunger, Poverty and Environmental Degradation*. Washington, DC: International Food Policy Research Institute.

Pinstrup-Andersen, Per, Rajul Pandya-Lorch and Mark Rosegrant. 1999. "World Food Prospects: Critical Issues for the Early Twenty-First Century." International Food Policy Research Institute, Washington, DC. [http://www.ifpri.org/pubs/fpr/fpr29.pdf]. March 2003.

PIPA (Program on International Policy Attitudes). 2002. "Americans on Foreign Aid and World Hunger: A Study of US Public Attitudes." University of Maryland, College Park.

Polanyi, Karl. 1994. *The Great Transformation: The Political and Economic Origin of Our Time*. New York: Rinehart.

Pretty, Jules N., and Rachel Hine. 2000. "The Promising Spread of Sustainable Agriculture in Asia." *Natural Resources Forum* 24 (2): 107–21.

Prosterman, Roy, and Tim Hansted. 2000. "Land Reform: A Revised Agenda for the 21st Century." RDI Report on Foreign Aid and Development 108. Rural Development Institute, Seattle.

PSIRU (Public Services International Research Unit). 2000. "It Cannot Be Business as Usual: Problems with the Private Models for Water." London. [http://www.psiru.org/reports/2000-03-W-Hmodel.doc]. March 2003.

Quiroga, Jorge. 2002. "The Millennium Challenge Account: A New Model for Increased Aid Effectiveness." Institute of International Economics, Washington, DC.

Rahman, Atiqur, and John Westley. 2001. "The Challenge of Ending Rural Poverty." *Development Policy Review* 19 (4): 553–62.

Rahman, Mustafizur. 2003. "Globalisation, Market Access and Developed Country Policies: Some Insights from the Bangladesh

Experience." Paper presented at the Fourth Annual Conference of the Global Development Network, Global Policy Workshop on the Development Impact of Rich Country Policies, 16 January, Cairo.

Rainforest Foundation. 1998. "Out of Commission: The Environmental and Social Impacts of European Union Development Funding in Tropical Forest Areas." London.

Randel, Judith, and Tony German, eds. 1998. *The Reality of Aid 1998/99*. London: Earthscan.

Ranis, Gustav, and Frances Stewart. 2000. "Economic Growth and Human Development." *World Development* 28 (2): 197–219.

Ravallion, Martin. 2000. "Should Poverty Measures Be Anchored to the National Accounts?" *Economic and Political Weekly* 34 (35/36): 3245–52.

———. 2002. "The Debate on Globalization, Poverty and Inequality: Why Measurement Matters." World Bank, Development Research Group, Washington, DC. [http://poverty.worldbank.org/files/13871_Why_measurement_matters.pdf]. March 2003.

Reddy, Sanjay, and Thomas Pogge. 2002. "How Not to Count the Poor." Columbia University, Department of Economics, New York. [http://www.columbia.edu/~sr793/count.pdf]. March 2003.

Reno, William. 2002. "The Politics of Insurgency in Collapsing States." *Development and Change* 33 (5): 837–58.

Repetto, Robert, and Malcolm Gillis, eds. 1998. *Public Policies and the Misuse of Forest Resources*. Cambridge: Cambridge University Press.

Results USA. 2003. "The World Bank and User Fees." Washington, DC. [http://results.org/website/article.asp?id=274]. March 2003.

Ribot, Jesse. 2001. "Local Actors, Powers and Accountability in African Decentralizations: A Review of Issues." United Nations Research Institute for Social Development, Geneva. [http://www.odi.org.uk/speeches/envgov2002/ribot/Ribot_local_actors.pdf]. March 2003.

Roberts, John. 2003. "Managing Public Expenditure for Development Results and Poverty Reduction." Working Paper 203. Overseas Development Institute, London.

Rohde, John, and Hema Vishwanathan. 1995. *The Rural Private Practitioner*. New Delhi: Oxford University Press.

Rojas, Cristina. 2002. "Forging Civic Culture in Bogota City." Paper presented at the Inter-American Development Bank and Japan International Cooperation Agency workshop "Citizen Participation in the Context of Fiscal Decentralization: Best Practices in Municipal Administration in Latin America and Asia," 2–6 September, Tokyo and Kobe, Japan. [http://www.adb.org/Documents/Events/2002/Citizen_Participation/Colombia.pdf]. March 2003.

Ruggeri, Caterina. 2001. "Participatory Methods in the Analysis of Poverty: A Critical Review." Working Paper 62. University of Oxford, Queen Elizabeth House, Oxford.

Sahn, David, and David Stifel. 2003. "Progress toward the Millennium Development Goals in Africa." *World Development* 31 (1): 23–52.

Saith, Ashwani. 1995. "Reflections on South Asian Prospects in East Asian Perspective." Discussion Paper 7. International Labour Organization, Geneva. [http://www.ilo.org/public/english/employment/strat/publ/iddp7.htm]. March 2003.

Sala-i-Martin, Xavier. 2002. *The Disturbing "Rise" of Global Income Inequality*. NBER Working Paper 8904. Cambridge, Mass.: National Bureau of Economic Research. [http://papers.nber.org/papers/w8904.pdf]. March 2003.

Satterthwaite, David. 2002. "Coping with Rapid Urban Growth." Royal Institution of Chartered Surveyors, London.

Save the Children. 2001. "The Wrong Model: GATS, Trade Liberalisation and Children's Right to Health." London. [http://www.savethechildren.org.uk/development/global_pub/wrongmodel.pdf]. March 2003.

Saywell, T. 1999. "Strong Medicine." *Far Eastern Economic Review* 162 (34): 46.

Scherr, Sara, Andy White and David Kaimowitz. 2002. "Making Markets Work for Forest Communities." Forest Trends, Washington, DC. [http://www.forest-trends.org/resources/pdf/FT_2628_Livelihood%20Final.pdf]. March 2003.

Schulpen, Lau, and Peter Gibbon. 2001. "Private Sector Development: Policies, Practices and Problems." Centre for Development Research, Copenhagen.

Schultz, T. Paul. 1998. "Inequality in the Distribution of Personal Income in the World: How It Is Changing and Why." *Journal of Population Economics* 11 (3): 307–44.

———. 2001. "School Subsidies for the Poor: Evaluating the Mexican Progresa Poverty Program." Economic Growth Center Discussion Paper 834. Yale University, New Haven, Conn.

Schusterman, Ricardo, Florencia Almansi, Ana Hardoy, Cecilia Monti and Gastón Urquiza. 2002. "Poverty Reduction in Action: Participatory Planning in San Fernando, Buenos Aires, Argentina." IIED Working Paper 6. International Institute for Environment and Development, London. [http://www.iied.org/docs/urban/urb_pr7_schusterman.pdf]. March 2003.

Sen, Amartya. 1999. *Development as Freedom.* Oxford: Oxford University Press.

Shah, Anwar. 1998. "Balance, Accountability, and Responsiveness: Lessons about Decentralization." Policy Research Working Paper 2021. World Bank, Washington, DC. [http://www.worldbank.org/html/dec/Publications/Workpapers/wps2000series/wps2021/wps2021-abstract.html]. March 2003.

Shankar, Raja, and Anwar Shah. 2001. "Bridging the Economic Divide within Nations: A Scorecard on the Performance of Regional Development Policies in Reducing Regional Income Disparities." Policy Research Working Paper 2717. World Bank, Washington, DC. [http://econ.worldbank.org/files/2725_wps2717.pdf]. March 2003.

Shaokang, Zahn, Tan Shenglan and Guo Youde. 1997. "Drug Prescribing in Rural Health Facilities in China: Implications for Service Quality and Cost." *IDS Bulletin* 28 (1).

Shatkin, Gavin. 2000. "Obstacles to Empowerment: Local Politics and Civil Society in Metropolitan Manila, the Philippines." *Urban Studies* 12 (37): 2357–75.

Sidley, Pat. 2001. "Cholera Sweeps through South African Province." *British Medical Journal* 322: 71. [http://bmj.com/cgi/reprint/322/7278/71/c.pdf]. March 2003.

Simonpietri, Antoine. 2003. Correspondence on statistical capacity building issues. March. Organisation for Economic Cooperation and Development, Paris.

Sinclair, Scott, and Jim Grieshaber-Otto. 2002. "Facing the Facts: A Guide to the GATS Debate." Canadian Centre for Policy Alternatives, Ottawa. [http://www.policyalternatives.ca/publications/facing-the-facts.pdf]. March 2003.

Siniscalco, Maria Teresa. 2002. *A Statistical Profile of the Teaching Profession.* Geneva: International Labour Organization. [http://www.ilo.org/public/english/dialogue/sector/papers/education/stat_profile02.pdf]. March 2003.

SIPRI (Stockholm International Peace Research Institute). 2002a. "Military and Social Expenditure as a Share of GDP, 1996–2000." Stockholm. [http://projects.sipri.se/milex/mex_share_gdp.html]. March 2003.

———. 2002b. *SIPRI Yearbook 2002.* Oxford: Oxford University Press.

———. 2003. "Arms Transfers to India and Pakistan, 1993–2002." Stockholm. [http://projects.sipri.se/armstrade/atind_pakdata.html]. March 2003.

Sitthi-Amorn, Chitr, Watana Janjaroen and Ratana Somrongthong. 2001. "Some Health Implications of Globalization in Thailand." *Bulletin of the World Health Organization* 79 (9): 889–90.

Sizer, Nigel. 2000. "Perverse Habits: The G8 and Subsidies That Harm Forests and Economies." World Resources Institute, Washington, DC. [http://www.wri.org/forests/g8.html]. March 2003.

Smith, Kirk. 2000. "National Burden of Disease in India from Indoor Air Pollution." *Proceedings of the National Academy of Sciences* 97 (24): 13286–93.

Social Watch. 2003. *Social Watch Report 2003: The Poor and the Market.* Montevideo, Uruguay.

Sprout, Ronald, and James Weaver. 1992. "International Distribution of Income: 1960–1987." *Kyklos* 45: 237–58.

Stapleton, Maire. 2000. "Bhutan Essential Drugs Programme: A Case History." World Health Organization, Department of Essential Drugs and Medicines Policy, Geneva.

Steinich, Markus. 2000. "Monitoring and Evaluating Support to Decentralisation: Challenges and Dilemmas." ECDPM Discussion Paper 19. European Centre for Development Policy Management, Maastricht, Netherlands. [http://www.gtz.de/urbanet/Downloads/imes-eng.pdf]. March 2003.

Stiglitz, Joseph. 1996. "The Role of Government in Economic Development." In Michael Bruno and Boris Pleskovic, eds., *Proceedings of the World Bank's Annual Conference on Development Economics 1996.* Washington, DC: World Bank.

———. 2002a. *Globalization and Its Discontents.* New York: W.W. Norton.

———. 2002b. "Participation and Development: Perspectives from the Comprehensive Development Paradigm." *Review of Development Economics* 6 (2): 163–83.

———. 2003. "Democratizing the International Monetary Fund and the World Bank: Governance and Accountability." *Governance* 17 (1): 111–39.

Stocker, Karen, Howard Waitzkin and Celia Iriart. 1999. "The Exportation of Managed Care to Latin America." *New England Journal of Medicine* 340 (14): 1131–36.

Swaminathan, M. S. 2001. "Nutrition in the Third Millennium: Countries in Transition." Paper presented at the Seventeenth International Congress on Nutrition, 27–31 August, Vienna. [http://www.mssrf.org/talksbymss/Viennalecture.html]. March 2003.

Székely, Miguel, and Marianne Hilgert. 1999. "What's Behind the Inequality We Measure? An Investigation Using Latin American Data." Working Paper 409. Inter-American Development Bank, Washington, DC.

Tendler, Judith. 1997. *Good Governance in the Tropics.* Baltimore, Md.: Johns Hopkins University Press.

Thomas, Duncan, and John Strauss. 1998. "Health, Nutrition and Economic Development." *Journal of Economic Literature* 36 (2): 737–82.

Tilak, Jandhyala. 1997. "Lessons from Cost Recovery in Education." In Christopher Colclough, ed., *Marketizing Education and Health in Developing Countries: Miracle or Mirage?* Oxford: Clarendon Press.

Tinker, Irene. 2002. "Quotas for Women in Elected Legislatures: Does This Really Empower Women?" Paper presented at the Women, Gender and Development Perspectives symposium "Gender and Transnational Networks," 17–19 October, University of Illinois at Urbana-Champaign.

Toledo, Tito. 1997. "Impacto en la Salud del Fenomeno del Niño 1982–83 en el Peru." Paper presented at the World Health Organization's Central American workshop "The Health Impact of the El Niño Phenomenon," 3 November, San Jose, Costa Rica.

Tomlinson, Richard. 1997. "Health Care in China Is Highly Inequitable." *British Medical Journal* 315 (7112): 831–36. [http://bmj.com/cgi/content/full/315/7112/831/i]. March 2003.

Tornquist, C. Sam, Bjorn Wenngren, Nguyen Thi Kim Chuc, Matthias Larsson, Einar Magnusson, Nguyen Thanh Do, Pham Van Ca and Le Dang HaVan Ca. 2000. "Antibiotic Resistance in Vietnam: An Epidemiological Indicator of

Inefficient and Inequitable Use of Health Resources." In P. M. Hung, I. H. Minas, Y. Liu, G. Dalgren and W. C. Hsiao, eds., *Efficient Equity-Oriented Strategies for Health: International Perspectives—Focus on Vietnam.* Melbourne, Australia: University of Melbourne, Centre for International Mental Health.

Trouiller, Patrice, Piero Olliaro, Els Torreele, James Orbinski, Richard Laing and Natahan Ford. 2002. "Drug Development for Neglected Diseases: A Deficient Market and a Public Health Policy Failure." *Lancet* 359: 2188–94.

Turner, Mark, and David Hulme. 1997. *Governance, Administration and Development.* West Hartford, Conn.: Kumarian Press.

Uganda, Ministry of Finance, Planning and Economic Development. 2002. "Uganda Poverty Reduction Strategy Paper Progress Report 2002." Kampala.

UN (United Nations). 1966. *Covenant on Economic, Social and Cultural Rights.* Adopted and opened for signature, ratification and accession by General Assembly Resolution 2200A (XXI), 16 December, New York.

———. 1979. *Convention on Elimination of All Forms of Discrimination Against Women.* Treaty Series, vol. 1249. 18 December. New York.

———. 1980. *International Development Strategy for the Third United Nations Development Decade.* General Assembly Resolution 35/56 and Annex, A/35/592/Add. 1. 11 November. New York.

———. 1985. "Women's Employment and Fertility: A Comparative Analysis of World Fertility Survey Results from 38 Developing Countries." Population Studies, no. 96. Department of Economic and Social Affairs, New York.

———. 1989. *Convention on the Rights of the Child.* Treaty Series, vol. 1577. 15 March. New York.

———. 1997. *Kyoto Protocol to the United Nations Framework Convention on Climate Change.* [http://unfccc.int/resource/docs/convkp/kpeng.pdf]. March 2003.

———. 2000a. *Millennium Declaration.* A/RES/55/2. 18 September. New York. [http://www.un.org/millennium/declaration/ares552e.pdf]. March 2003.

———. 2000b. "Progress Made in Providing Safe Water Supply and Sanitation for All during the 1990s." Report of the Secretary-General. E/CN.17/2000/13s. Commission on Sustainable Development, New York. [http://www.un.org/documents/ecosoc/cn17/2000/ecn172000-13.htm]. March 2003.

———. 2000c. "The Millennium Summit Group Photo: List of Participants." New York. [http://www.un.org/av/photo/ga/caption.htm]. April 2003.

———. 2001a. "Report of the High-Level Panel on Financing for Development." Presented to the General Assembly 28 June, New York.

———. 2001b. "Road Map towards the Implementation of the United Nations Millennium Declaration." Report of the Secretary-General. A/56/326. 6 September. New York.

———. 2002a. "Follow-up Efforts to the International Conference on Financing for Development." Report of the Secretary-General. A/57/319. New York. [http://ods-dds-ny.un.org/doc/UNDOC/GEN/N02/528/72/PDF/N0252872.pdf?OpenElement]. March 2003.

———. 2002b. "Implementing Agenda 21." Report of the Secretary-General. Economic and Security Council Commission on Sustainable Development, New York. [http://www.johannesburgsummit.org/html/documents/no170793sgreport.pdf]. March 2003.

———. 2002c. "Millennium Indicators: India." Statistics Division, New York. [http://unstats.un.org/unsd/mi/mi_results.asp?crID=356&fID=r15]. March 2003.

———. 2002d. "Outcome of the International Conference on Financing for Development, Monterrey Consensus." A/57/344. New York. [http://ods-dds-ny.un.org/doc/UNDOC/GEN/N02/535/43/PDF/N0253543.pdf?OpenElement]. March 2003.

———. 2002e. "Report of the International Conference on Financing for Development." A/CONF.198/11. Monterrey, Mexico. [http://www.tradeobservatory.org/library/uploaded files/Report_of_the_International_Conference_on_Fina.pdf]. March 2003.

———. 2002f. "Report of the World Summit on Sustainable Development." 26 August. Johannesburg.

———. 2002g. "United Nations Millennium Development Goals Data and Trends 2002." Report prepared by Interagency Expert Group on MDG Indicators. New York.

———. 2002h. "Water, Energy, Health, Agriculture and Biodiversity: Synthesis of the Framework Paper of the Working Group on WEHAB." A/CONF.199/L.4. Presented at the World Summit on Sustainable Development, 26 August–4 September, Johannesburg. [http://daccess-ods.un.org/TMP/7654072.html]. March 2003.

———. 2002i. *World Urbanization Prospects: The 2001 Revision—Data Tables and Highlights.* Department of Economic and Social Affairs, Population Division, New York. [http://www.un.org/esa/population/publications/wup2001/wup2001dh.pdf]. March 2003.

———. 2003a. *Comtrade Database.* Statistics Division, New York.

———. 2003b. "Millennium Development Goals." New York. [http://www.un.org/millenniumgoals/]. March 2003.

———. 2003c. *Millennium Indicators.* Database. Statistics Division, New York. [http://unstats.un.org/unsd/mi/mi_goals.asp]. March 2003.

———. 2003d. "Note for the First Meeting of PARIS21 Task Team to Improve Statistical Support for Monitoring Development Goals." 15 October. Statistics Division, New York.

———. 2003e. "Rio Declaration on Environment and Development." A/CONF.151/26 (vol.1). [http://www.un.org/documents/ga/conf151/aconf15126-1annex1.htm]. March 2003.

———. 2003f. *Water for People, Water for Life.* Paris: United Nations Educational, Scientific and Cultural Organization and Berghahn Books.

———. 2003g. "World and Regional Trends: Data for Years around 1990 and 2000." Statistics Division, New York. [http://unstats.un.org/unsd/mi/mi_worldregn.asp]. March 2003.

———. 2003h. *World Population Prospects 1950–2050: The 2002 Revision.* Database. Department of Economic and Social Affairs, Population Division, New York.

UNAIDS (Joint United Nations Programme on HIV/AIDS). 1996. *The Status and Trends of the Global HIV/AIDS Pandemic.* Geneva. [http://www.unaids.org/publications/documents/epidemiology/estimates/statuskme.html]. March 2003.

———. 2000. *Report on the Global HIV/AIDS Epidemic.* Geneva. [http://www.unaids.org/epidemic_update/report/index.html]. March 2003.

———. 2002a. "AIDS Epidemic Update: December 2002." Geneva. [http://www.unaids.org/worldaidsday/2002/press/update/epiupdate2002_en.doc]. March 2003.

———. 2002b. *Report on the Global HIV/AIDS Epidemic.* Geneva. [http://www.unaids.org/epidemic_update/report_july02/index.html]. March 2003.

UNCHS (United Nations Centre for Human Settlements). 1996. *An Urbanizing World: Global Report on Human Settlements.* Oxford: Oxford University Press.

UNCTAD (United Nations Conference on Trade and Development). 2000. "Positive Agenda for Future Trade Negotiations." Geneva.

———. 2002a. *Least Developed Countries Report 2002: Escaping the Poverty Trap.* Geneva.

———. 2002b. *Trade and Development Report: Developing Countries in World Trade.* New York and Geneva.

UNDP (United Nations Development Programme). 1993. "Rethinking Technical Cooperation." New York.

——. 1996. *Human Development Report 1996.* New York: Oxford University Press. [http://hdr.undp.org/reports/global/1996/en/]. March 2003.

——. 1998. *Human Development Report 1998.* New York: Oxford University Press. [http://hdr.undp.org/reports/global/1998/en/]. March 2003.

——. 2000. *Human Development Report 2000.* New York: Oxford University Press. [http://hdr.undp.org/reports/global/2000/en/]. March 2003.

——. 2001a. *Costa Rica: Estado de la Nación en Desarrollo Humano Sostenible 2001.* San Juan.

——. 2001b. "Decentralising Governance for Rural Development." In *National Human Development Report Lao PDR 2001: Advancing Rural Development.* Vientiane.

——. 2001c. *Human Development Report 2001: Making Technology Work for Human Development.* New York: Oxford University Press. [http://hdr.undp.org/reports/global/2001/en/]. March 2003.

——. 2001d. *Malawi National Human Development Report 2001.* Lilongwe.

——. 2002a. "The Data Challenges of the MDGs." New York.

——. 2002b. "A Global Analysis of UNDP Support to Decentralisation and Local Governance Programmes 2001." Bureau for Development Policy, Institutional Development Group, New York. [http://www.undp.org/governance/docsdecentral/global-analysis-of-undp-support.pdf]. March 2003.

——. 2002c. *Aportes para el Desarrollo Humano de la Argentina 2002.* Buenos Aires.

——. 2002d. "Biodiversity and Poverty: Biodiversity under Development, 2002." Bureau for Development Policy, New York.

——. 2002e. *Human Development Report 2002: Deepening Democracy in a Fragmented World.* New York: Oxford University Press. [http://hdr.undp.org/reports/global/2002/en/]. March 2003.

——. 2002f. "Localising the Millennium Development Goals: Some Examples." South and West Asia Sub-Regional Resource Facility, Kathmandu. [http://www.interaction.org/files.cgi/988_Localising_the_MDGs.doc]. March 2003.

——. 2002g. "Millennium Development Goals." Fact sheet. New York. [http://www.undp.org/mdg/]. March 2003.

——. 2003b. Correspondence on MDG success stories. February. Resident Representative Network, New York.

——. 2003c. Correspondence on the use of $2 a day as an extreme poverty line. March. Regional Bureau for Europe and the CIS, New York.

——. 2003d. "Gyandoot: A Community-Owned Self-Sustainable and Low-Cost Rural Intranet Project." Human Development Resource Centre, New Delhi. [http://hdrc.undp.org.in/content/resources/best_practice_docs/]. March 2003.

——. 2003e. "Status of Millennium Development Goal Country Reporting." Paper presented at the 34th Session of the United Nations Statistics Commission, 4–7 March, New York. [http://unstats.un.org/unsd/statcom/doc03/2003-22e.pdf]. March 2003.

UNDP (United Nations Development Programme), DFID (UK Department for International Development) and World Bank. 2002. "Linking Poverty Reduction and Environmental Management: Policy Challenges and Opportunities." Working Paper 24824. New York. [http://www-wds.worldbank.org/servlet/WDSContentServer/WDSP/IB/2002/09/27/000094946_02091704130739/Rendered/PDF/multi0page.pdf]. March 2003.

UNDP (United Nations Development Programme), ECLAC (United Nations Economic Commission for Latin America and the Caribbean) and Instituto de Pesquisa Economica Aplicada. 2002. "Meeting the Millennium Poverty Reduction Targets in Latin America and the Caribbean." United Nations, Santiago, Chile.

UNDP (United Nations Development Programme), WEC (World Energy Council) and UNDESA (United Nations Department of Economic and Social Affairs). 2000. *World Energy Assessment: Energy and the Challenge of Sustainability.* New York. [http://www.undp.org/seed/eap/activities/wea/drafts-frame.html]. March 2003.

UNDP (United Nations Development Programme), UNEP (United Nations Environment Programme), World Bank and WRI (World Resources Institute). 1998. *World Resources: 1998–1999.* New York: Oxford University Press. [http://www.wri.org/wri/wr-98-99/]. March 2003.

——. 2000. *World Resources 2000–2001: People and Ecosystems—The Fraying Web of Life.* Washington, DC: World Resources Institute. [http://www.wri.org/wr2000/]. March 2003.

UNDP (United Nations Development Programme), Heinrich Böll Foundation, Rockefeller Brothers Fund, Rockefeller Foundation and Wallace Global Fund. 2003. *Making Global Trade Work for People.* London: Earthscan.

UNEP (United Nations Environment Programme). 2003. *Global Environment Outlook 3.* London: Earthscan. [http://www.unep.org/geo/]. March 2003.

UNESCO (United Nations Educational, Scientific and Cultural Organization). 1996. *Statistical Yearbook 1996.* Paris.

——. 1999. *Statistical Yearbook 1999.* Paris.

——. 2002a. *EFA Global Monitoring Report 2002: Is the World On Track?* Paris. [http://www.unesco.org/education/efa/monitoring/monitoring_2002.shtml]. March 2003.

——. 2002b. "The Challenge of Achieving Gender Parity in Basic Education: A Statistical Review, 1990–1998." [http://unesdoc.unesco.org/images/0012/001259/125927e.pdf]. March 2003.

——. 2003. Correspondence on teaching staff in primary education. March. Montreal.

UNESCO (United Nations Educational, Scientific and Cultural Organization) and ILO (International Labour Organization). 1966. "Recommendation Concerning the Status of Teachers." Paris. [http://www.ei-ie.org/ressourc/english/erec1966.htm]. March 2003.

UNESCO (United Nations Educational, Scientific and Cultural Organization) and OECD (Organisation for Economic Co-operation and Development). 2000. *World Education Indicators Report.* Paris.

UNESCO Institute for Statistics. 2002. "Statistics Show Slow Progress towards Universal Literacy, and More Literate Women Than Ever Before." Montreal. [http://www.unesco.org/bpi/eng/unescopress/2002/02-59e.shtml]. March 2003.

UNESCO Institute for Statistics and OECD (Organisation for Economic Co-operation and Development). 2002. "Financing Education: Investments and Returns—Analysis of the World Education Indicators." Montreal and Paris.

UN-HABITAT (United Nations Human Settlements Programme). 2002. "Report of the Expert Group Meeting on Urban Indicators." October. Nairobi.

UNHCHR (United Nations High Commissioner on Human Rights). 2002a. "Question of the Realization in All Countries of the Economic, Social and Cultural Rights Contained in the Universal Declaration of Human Rights and in the International Covenant on Economic, Social and Cultural Rights, and Study of Special Problems Which the Developing Countries Face in Their Efforts to Achieve These Human Rights." 2002/24. Geneva. [http://www.unhchr.ch/huridocda/huridoca.nsf/(Symbol)/E.CN.4.RES.2002.24.En?Opendocument]. March 2003.

——. 2002b. "The Right to Development." 2002/69. Geneva. [http://www.unhchr.ch/huridocda/huridoca.nsf/(Symbol)/E.CN.4.RES.2002.69.En?Opendocument]. March 2003.

——. 2003. "Report of the High Commissioner: Liberalization of Trade in Services and Human Rights." E/CN.4/Sub.2/2002/9.

Geneva. [http://www.unhchr.ch/huridocda/huridoca.nsf/
(Symbol)/E.CN.4.Sub.2.2002.9.En?Opendocument]. March
2003.

UNHCR (United Nations High Commissioner for Refugees).
2000. *The State of the World's Refugees: Fifty Years of Humanitarian Action.* Oxford: Oxford University Press.

UNICEF (United Nations Children's Fund). 1991. "Plan of Action for Implementing the World Declaration on the Survival,
Protection and Development of Children in the 1990s." In
The State of the World's Children 1991. New York: Oxford University Press.

———. 1996. "Wars against Children." New York. [http://www.
unicef.org/graca/]. March 2003.

———. 1999. *The State of the World's Children 1999.* New York:
Oxford University Press. [http://www.unicef.org/sowc99/].
March 2003.

———. 2000. *Poverty Reduction Begins with Children.* New York.
[http://www.unicef.org/pubsgen/poverty/povred.pdf]. March
2003.

———. 2001a. "Progress since the World Summit for Children: A Statistical Review." New York. [http://www.unicef.org/pubsgen/
wethechildren-stats/sgreport_adapted_stats_eng.pdf]. March
2003.

———. 2001b. *The State of the World's Children 2001.* New York:
Oxford University Press. [http://www.unicef.org/pubsgen/
sowc01/fullsowc.pdf]. March 2003.

———. 2002. "India: Mortality." New York. [http://www.unicef.org/
statis/Country_1Page79.html]. March 2003.

———. 2003a. "An Initiative for Effective Case Management."
New York. [http://www.childinfo.org/eddb/imci/]. March
2003.

———. 2003b. *The State of the World's Children 2003.* New York:
Oxford University Press. [http://www.unicef.org/sowc03/].
March 2003.

UNIFEM (United Nations Development Fund for Women). 2000.
Progress of the World's Women. New York. [http://www.
unifem.undp.org/progressww/2000/]. March 2003.

United Kingdom, Her Majesty's Treasury. 2003. "International Finance Facility." London. [http://www.hm-treasury.gov.uk/
documents/international_issues/global_new_deal/int_gnd_
iff2003.cfm]. March 2003.

UN (United Nations) World Summit on Sustainable Development.
2002. "WEHAB Framework Papers." Johannesburg.
[http://www.johannesburgsummit.org/html/documents/wehab_
papers.html]. March 2003.

Valderrama, Camilo. 1998. "Promoting Effective Participation: A
Policy-Oriented Study of Community Involvement in Rural
Development Planning." University of Sussex, Institute of De-
velopment Studies, Brighton, England.

Vandemoortele, Jan. 2001. "Absorbing Social Shocks, Protecting
Children and Reducing Poverty: The Role of Basic Social Ser-
vices." UNICEF Staff Working Paper, Evaluation, Policy and
Planning Series, no. 00-001. United Nations Children's Fund,
New York.

———. 2002. "Are the MDGs Feasible?" In Howard White and
Richard Black, eds., *Targeting Development: Critical Perspectives on the Millennium Development Goals and International Development Targets.* London: Routledge.

van den Haak, M. A., F. J. G. Vounatsos and J. McAuslane. 2001.
"International Pharmaceutical R&D Expenditure and Sales
2001: Pharmaceutical Investment and Output Survey 2001,
Data Report 1." Center for Medical Research International,
London.

Van de Walle, Nicholas, and Timothy Johnston. 1996. "Improving Aid to Africa." ODC Policy Essay 21. Overseas Development Council, Washington, DC.

Van Lerberghe, Wim, Claudia Conceicaõ, Wim Van Damme and
Paulo Ferrinho. 2002. "When Staff Is Underpaid: Dealing with
the Individual Coping Strategies of Health Personnel."

Bulletin of the World Health Organization 80 (7): 581–84.
[http://www.who.int/bulletin/pdf/2002/bul-7-E-2002/
80 (7)581-584.pdf]. March 2003.

Velasquez, German, Yvette Madrid and Jonathan Quick. 1998.
"Health Reform and Drug Financing: Selected Topic—
Health Economics and Drugs." DAP Series, no. 6.
WHO/DAP/98.3. World Health Organization, Geneva.
[http://www.who.int/medicines/library/dap/who-dap-98-3/
who-dap-98-3.htm]. March 2003.

Veltmeyer, Henry. 1997. "New Social Movements in Latin America: The Dynamics of Class and Identity." *Journal of Peasant Studies* 25 (1): 139–69.

Walker, Alex. 2002. "Decentralisation." UK Department for International Development, Infrastructure and Urban Development Department, London. [http://www.odi.org.uk/
keysheets/ppip/purple_1_decentralisation.pdf]. March 2003.

Watkins, Kevin. 2000. *The Oxfam Education Report.* Oxford:
Oxfam. [http://www.oxfam.org.uk/educationnow/edreport/
report.htm]. March 2003.

Watson, David. 2002. "Pro-Poor Service Delivery and Decentralization." Issue Paper 3. Fifth African Governance Forum,
23 May, Maputo, Mozambique. [http://www.undp.org/rba/
pubs/agf5/Issue%20paper%20on%20social%20service%20
delivery.pdf]. March 2003.

Webster, Mike, and Kevin Sansom. 1999. "Public-Private Partnership and the Poor: An Initial Review." Loughborough University and London School of Hygiene and Tropical Medicine.

WEHAB Working Group. 2002a. "A Framework for Action on
Biodiversity and Ecosystem Management." Paper presented
at the World Summit on Sustainable Development, 26 August, Johannesburg. [http://www.agora21.org/johannesburg/
wehab_biodiversity.pdf]. March 2003.

———. 2002b. "A Framework for Action on Water and Sanitation."
Paper presented at the World Summit on Sustainable Development, 26 August, Johannesburg. [http://www.agora21.org/
johannesburg/wehab_water_sanitation.pdf]. March 2003.

Weiss, Ursula. 2002. "Malaria." *Nature* 415 (669).

West, Edwin G. 1997. "Education Vouchers in Principle and
Practice: A Survey." *World Bank Research Observer* 12 (1):
83–103. [http://www.worldbank.org/research/journals/wbro/
obsfeb97/pdf/artcle~6.pdf]. March 2003.

WFUNA (World Federation of United Nations Associations) and
North-South Institute. 2002. "The Role of the Civil Society
in the Implementation of the United Nations Millennium Declaration." Ottawa.

White, Andy, and Alejandra Martin. 2002. "Who Owns the World's
Forests? Forest Tenures and Public Forests in Transition." Forest Trends, Washington, DC. [http://www.forest-trends.org/
resources/pdf/tenurereport_whoowns.pdf]. March 2003.

White, Howard, and Richard Black, eds. 2002. *Targeting Development: Critical Perspectives on the Millennium Development Goals and International Development Targets.*
London: Routledge.

Whitehead, Margaret, Timothy Evans and Göran Dahlgren. 2001.
"Equity and Health Sector Reforms: Can Low-Income Countries Escape the Medical Poverty Trap?" *Lancet* 358 (833):
836. [http://www.healthp.org/article.php?sid=64&mode=
thread&order=0&thold=0]. March 2003.

WHO (World Health Organization). 1997. *Health and Environment in Sustainable Development: Five Years after the
Earth Summit.* Geneva.

———. 2000. *World Health Report 2000: Health Systems Improving Performance.* Geneva.

———. 2002. *World Health Report 2002: Reducing Risks, Promoting Healthy Life.* Geneva.

———. 2003a. Correspondence on data regarding doctors per
person. March. Geneva.

———. 2003b. Correspondence on data regarding nurses per person. March. Geneva.

———. 2003c. "Major Causes of Death among Children under Five, Worldwide, 2000." [http://www.who.int/child-adolescent-health/OVERVIEW/CHILD_HEALTH/piechart1.jpg]. March 2003.

WHO (World Health Organization), UNICEF (United Nations Children's Fund) and WSSCC (Water Supply and Sanitation Collaborative Council). 2000. *Global Water Supply and Sanitation Assessment 2000*. Geneva. [http://www.who.int/water_sanitation_health/Globassessment/GlasspdfTOC.htm]. March 2003.

Wood, Adrian. 1995. "Gains from Human Development through Trade." United Nations Development Programme, New York.

Work, Robertson. 2002. "Overview of Decentralisation Worldwide: A Stepping Stone to Improved Governance and Human Development." Paper presented at the Second International Conference on Decentralization, "Federalism: The Future of Decentralizing States?" 25 July, Manila. [http://www.undp.org/governance/docsdecentral/overview-decentralisation-worldwide-paper.pdf]. March 2003.

Working Group on Contemporary Forms of Slavery. 1997. "Report by Shakeel Ahmed Pathan, Co-ordinator, Special Task Force for Sindh, Human Rights Commission of Pakistan (HRCP)." United Nations Economic and Social Council, 1 June, Geneva. [http://www.antislavery.org/archive/submission/submission1997-06Pakistan.htm]. March 2003.

———. 1999. "Bonded Labour in Pakistan." United Nations Economic and Social Council, 24th Session, 23 June, Geneva. [http://www.antislavery.org/archive/submission/submission1999-08Pakistan.htm]. March 2003.

World Bank. 1990. *Financing Health Services in Developing Countries: An Agenda for Reform*. Washington, DC.

———. 1993. *World Development Report 1993: Investing in Health*. New York: Oxford University Press.

———. 1996. *World Development Report 1996: From Plan to Market*. New York: Oxford University Press.

———. 1998a. *Assessing Aid: What Works, What Doesn't, and Why*. New York: Oxford University Press. [http://www.worldbank.org/research/aid/aidtoc.htm]. March 2003.

———. 1998b. "Memorandum of the President of the International Development Association and the International Finance Corporation to the Executive Directors on a Country Assistance Strategy of the World Bank Group for the Republic of Bolivia." Washington, DC.

———. 1999. "The Kyrgyz Republic: Participatory Poverty Assessment." Paper presented at the Global Synthesis Workshop, 22–23 September, Washington, DC.

———. 2000a. *Making Transition Work for Everyone: Poverty and Inequality in Europe and Central Asia*. Washington, DC. [http://wbln0018.worldbank.org/eca/eca.nsf/General/40F8E9D019CE2E5C8525695800636022?OpenDocument].

———. 2000b. "Memorandum of the President of the International Development Association and the International Finance Corporation to the Executive Directors on a Country Assistance Strategy of the World Bank Group for the Republic of Uganda." Washington, DC.

———. 2000c. *World Development Report 2000/2001: Attacking Poverty*. New York: Oxford University Press. [http://www.worldbank.org/poverty/wdrpoverty/report/index.htm]. March 2003.

———. 2001. *Global Development Network Growth Database*. Washington, DC.

———. 2002a. "Building Statistical Capacity to Monitor Development Progress." Washington, DC.

———. 2002b. "Private Sector Development Strategy: Directions for the World Bank Group." Washington, DC. [http://rru.worldbank.org/documents/PSDStrategy-April%209.pdf]. March 2003.

———. 2002c. *Annual Report 2002*. Washington, DC.

———. 2002d. "From Action to Impact: The Africa Region's Rural Strategy." African Region, Rural Development Operations, Washington, DC.

———. 2002e. *Global Development Finance 2002*. Washington, DC.

———. 2002f. *Global Economic Prospects and the Developing Countries 2002*. Washington, DC. [http://www.worldbank.org/prospects/gep2002/]. March 2003.

———. 2002g. "Health, Nutrition, and Population Development Goals: Measuring Progress Using the Poverty Reduction Strategy Framework." Washington, DC. [http://www1.worldbank.org/hnp/MDG/measureprogress.pdf]. March 2003.

———. 2002h. "Memorandum of the President of the International Bank for Reconstruction and Development and the International Finance Corporation to the Executive Directors on a Country Assistance Strategy of the World Bank Group for the Republic of Colombia." Washington, DC.

———. 2002i. "Memorandum of the President of the International Bank for Reconstruction and Development and the International Finance Corporation to the Executive Directors on a Country Assistance Strategy of the World Bank Group for the Republic of Peru." Washington, DC.

———. 2002j. *World Development Indicators 2002*. CD-ROM. Washington, DC.

———. 2002k. *World Development Report 2003: Sustainable Development in a Dynamic Economy*. New York: Oxford University Press. [http://econ.worldbank.org/wdr/wdr2003/text-17926/]. March 2003.

———. 2003a. "Country Assistance Strategy Documents." Washington, DC. [http://www-wds.worldbank.org/servlet/WDS_IBank_Servlet?dt=540613&psz=20&ptype=advSrch&pcont=results]. March 2003.

———. 2003b. *Education and HIV/AIDS: A Window of Hope*. Washington, DC. [http://www1.worldbank.org/education/pdf/Ed%20&%20HIV_AIDS%20cover%20print.pdf]. March 2003.

———. 2003c. "HIPC: Debt Initiative for Heavily Indebted Poor Countries." Washington, DC. [http://www.worldbank.org/hipc/]. March 2003.

———. 2003e. "Memorandum of the President of the International Bank for Reconstruction and Development and the International Finance Corporation to the Executive Directors on a Country Assistance Strategy of the World Bank Group for the People's Republic of China." Washington, DC.

———. 2003f. "Memorandum of the President of the International Bank for Reconstruction and Development and the International Finance Corporation to the Executive Directors on a Country Assistance Strategy Progress Report of the World Bank Group for India." Report 25057-IN. Washington, DC.

———. 2003g. "Rome Declaration on Harmonization." 24 February, Rome. [http://siteresources.worldbank.org/NEWS/Resources/Harm-RomeDeclaration2_25.pdf].

———. 2003i. *World Development Indicators 2003*. CD-ROM. Washington, DC.

———. Forthcoming. *World Development Report 2004: Making Services Work for Poor People*. New York: Oxford University Press.

World Bank and IMF (International Monetary Fund). 2001. "Financing for Development." Washington, DC. [http://www.imf.org/external/np/pdr/2001/ffd.pdf]. March 2003.

World Bank and UN-Habitat (United Nations Human Settlements Programme). 2003. "Cities Alliance for Cities without Slums: Action Plan." Washington, DC. [http://www.citiesalliance.org/citiesalliancehomepage.nsf/Attachments/Cities+Without+Slums+Action+Plan/$File/brln_ap.pdf]. March 2003.

World Panel on Financing Water Infrastructure. 2003. "Financing Water for All." World Water Council and Global Water

Partnership, Marseilles. [http://www.gwpforum.org/gwp/library/FinPanRep.MainRep.pdf]. March 2003.

WRI (World Resources Institute). 2000a. "Global Forest Watch 2000: A First Look at Logging in Gabon." Washington, DC. [http://www.globalforestwatch.org/common/gabon/english/report.pdf]. March 2003.

———. 2000b. "Global Forest Watch 2000: An Overview of Logging in Cameroon." Washington, DC. [http://www.globalforestwatch.org]. March 2003.

WSP (Water and Sanitation Program). 2002a. "Lower Costs with Higher Benefits: Lessons from the El Alto, Bolivia Pilot Project." Field Note. Lima.

———. 2002b. "The National Water and Sanitation Programme in South Africa: Turning the 'Right of Water' into Reality." Field Note 8. Nairobi. [http://www.wsp.org/pdfs/af_bg_sa.pdf]. March 2003.

WSSCC (Water Supply and Sanitation Collaborative Council). 2002. "WASH Facts and Figures." Geneva. [http://www.wsscc.org/load.cfm?edit_id=292]. March 2003.

———. 2003. "A Guide to Investigating One of the Biggest Scandals of the Last 50 Years." Geneva.

WTO (World Trade Organization). 2000. *Trade Policy Review: Japan.* Geneva.

———. 2001. *Ministerial Declaration, Adopted on 14 November, Doha.* WT/MIN (01)DEC/1. Geneva.

———. 2003. "GATS: Fact and Fiction." Geneva. [http://www.wto.org/english/tratop_e/serv_e/gatsfacts1004_e.pdf]. March 2003.

WWC (World Water Council). 2000. *A Water Secure World: Vision for Water, Life, and the Environment in the 21st Century.* World Water Commission Report. Cairo. [http://www.worldwatercouncil.org/Vision/Documents/CommissionReport.pdf]. March 2003.

WWF (World Wildlife Fund). 2002. "Fishing Madness: 101 Reasons Why the CFP Needs Radical Reform." Surrey, England. [http://www.wwf.org.uk/filelibrary/pdf/fishingmadness.pdf]. March 2003.

Yang, B. M. 1993. "Medical Technology and Inequity in Health Care: The Case of Korea." *Health Policy and Planning* 8 (4): 385–93.

Yesudian, C. A. K. 1994. "Behaviour of the Private Sector in the Health Market in Bombay." *Health Policy and Planning* 9 (1): 72–80.

Yoder, Jennifer. 2003. "Decentralisation and Regionalisation after Communism: Administrative and Territorial Reform in Poland and the Czech Republic." *Europe-Asia Studies* 55 (2): 263–86.

Indicator tables

Note on statistics in the Human Development Report

This Report usually presents two types of statistical information: statistics in the human development indicator tables, which provide a global assessment of country achievements in different areas of human development, and statistical evidence in the thematic analysis in the chapters, which may be based on international, national or subnational data. This year's Report, whose theme is the Millennium Development Goals, also includes indicators relating to the Goals in a special set of tables. These tables provide a statistical reference for assessing the progress in each country towards the Millennium Development Goals and their targets.

DATA SOURCES

The Human Development Report Office is a user, not a producer, of statistics. It therefore relies on international data agencies with the resources and expertise to collect and compile international data on specific statistical indicators.

HUMAN DEVELOPMENT INDICATOR TABLES

To allow comparisons across countries and over time, the Human Development Report Office, to the extent possible, uses internationally comparable data produced by relevant international data agencies or other specialized institutions in preparing the human development indicator tables (for information on the major data agencies providing data used in the Report, see box 1). But many gaps still exist in the data even in some very basic areas of human development. While advocating for improvements in human development data, as a principle and for practical reasons, the Human Development Report Office does not collect data directly from countries or make estimates to fill these data gaps in the Report.

The one exception is the human development index (HDI). The Human Development Report Office strives to include as many UN member countries as possible in the HDI. For a country to be included, data ideally should be available from the relevant international data agencies for all four components of the index (the primary sources of data are the United Nations Population Division for life expectancy at birth, the UNESCO Institute for Statistics for the adult literacy rate and combined primary, secondary and tertiary gross enrolment ratio and the World Bank for GDP per capita [PPP US$]). But for a significant number of countries data are missing for one or more of these components. In response to the desire of countries to be included in the HDI, the Human Development Report Office makes every effort in these cases to identify other reasonable estimates, working with international data agencies, the UN Regional Commissions, national statistical offices and UNDP country offices. In a few cases the Human Development Report Office has attempted to make an estimate in consultation with regional and national statistical offices or other experts.

MILLENNIUM DEVELOPMENT GOAL INDICATOR TABLES

The United Nations Statistics Division maintains the global Millennium Indicators Database (http://millenniumindicators.un.org), compiled from international data series provided by the responsible international data agencies. The database forms the statistical basis for the UN Secretary-General's annual report to the UN General Assembly on global and regional progress towards the Millennium Development

BOX 1

Major sources of data used in the *Human Development Report*

By generously sharing data, the following organizations made it possible for the *Human Development Report* to publish the important human development statistics appearing in the indicator tables.

Carbon Dioxide Information Analysis Center (CDIAC) The CDIAC, a data and analysis centre of the US Department of Energy, focuses on the greenhouse effect and global climate change. It is the source of data on carbon dioxide emissions.

Food and Agriculture Organization (FAO) The FAO collects, analyses and disseminates data and information on food and agriculture. It is the source of data on food insecurity indicators.

International Institute for Strategic Studies (IISS) An independent centre for research, information and debate on the problems of conflict, the IISS maintains an extensive military database. The data on armed forces are from its publication *The Military Balance.*

International Labour Organization (ILO) The ILO maintains an extensive statistical publication programme, with the *Yearbook of Labour Statistics* its most comprehensive collection of labour force data. The ILO is the source of data on wages, employment and occupations and information on the ratification status of labour rights conventions.

International Monetary Fund (IMF) The IMF has an extensive programme for developing and compiling statistics on international financial transactions and balance of payments. Much of the financial data provided to the Human Development Report Office by other agencies originates from the IMF.

International Telecommunication Union (ITU) This specialized UN agency maintains an extensive collection of statistics on information and communications. The data on trends in telecommunications come from its database *World Telecommunication Indicators.*

Inter-Parliamentary Union (IPU) This organization provides data on trends in political participation and structures of democracy. The Human Development Report Office relies on the IPU for data relating to elections and information on women's political representation.

Joint United Nations Programme on HIV/AIDS (UNAIDS) This joint UN programme monitors the spread of HIV/AIDS and provides regular updates. Its *Report on the Global HIV/AIDS Epidemic,* is the primary source of data on HIV/AIDS.

Luxembourg Income Study (LIS) A cooperative research project with 25 member countries, the LIS focuses on poverty and policy issues. It is the source of income poverty estimates for many OECD countries.

Organisation for Economic Co-operation and Development (OECD) The OECD publishes data on a variety of social and economic trends in its member countries as well as on flows of aid. This year's Report presents data from the OECD on aid, energy, employment and education.

Stockholm International Peace Research Institute (SIPRI) SIPRI conducts research on international peace and security. The *SIPRI Yearbook: Armaments, Disarmament and International Security* is the

published source of data on military expenditure and arms transfers that the Human Development Report Office receives electronically.

United Nations Children's Fund (UNICEF) UNICEF monitors the well-being of children and provides a wide array of data. Its *State of the World's Children* is an important source of data for the Report.

United Nations Conference on Trade and Development (UNCTAD) UNCTAD provides trade and economic statistics through a number of publications, including the *World Investment Report.* It is the original source of data on investment flows that the Human Development Report Office receives from other agencies.

United Nations Educational, Scientific and Cultural Organization (UNESCO) The Institute for Statistics of this specialized UN agency is the source of data relating to education. The Human Development Report Office relies on data in UNESCO's statistical publications as well as data received directly from its Institute for Statistics.

United Nations High Commissioner for Refugees (UNHCR) This UN organization provides data on refugees through its *Statistical Yearbook.*

United Nations Interregional Crime and Justice Research Institute (UNICRI) This UN institute carries out international comparative research in support of the United Nations Crime Prevention and Criminal Justice Programme. It is the source of data on crime victims.

United Nations Multilateral Treaties Deposited with the Secretary General (UN Treaty Section) The Human Development Report Office compiles information on the status of major international human rights instruments and environmental treaties based on the database maintained by this UN office.

United Nations Population Division (UNPOP) This specialized UN office produces international data on population trends. The Human Development Report Office relies on *World Population Prospects* and *World Urbanization Prospects,* two of the main publications of UNPOP, for demographic estimates and projections.

United Nations Statistics Division (UNSD) The UNSD provides a wide range of statistical outputs and services. Much of the national accounts data provided to the Human Development Report Office by other agencies originates from the UNSD. This year's Report also draws on the global Millennium Indicators Database, maintained by the UNSD, as the source of data for the Millennium Development Goal indicator tables.

World Bank The World Bank produces and compiles data on economic trends as well as a broad array of other indicators. Its *World Development Indicators* is the primary source for many indicators in the Report.

World Health Organization (WHO) This specialized agency maintains a large array of data series on health issues, the source for the health-related indicators in the Report.

World Intellectual Property Organization (WIPO) As a specialized UN agency, WIPO promotes the protection of intellectual property rights throughout the world through different kinds of cooperative efforts. It is the source of data relating to patents.

Goals and their targets. It also feeds into other international reports providing data on the Millennium Development Goal indicators across countries, such as this Report and the World Bank's annual *World Development Indicators.*

At the time this Report was being prepared, the United Nations Statistics Division was updating the Millennium Indicators Database while the World Bank was completing its *World Development Indicators 2003* for publication. By generously sharing data, the World Bank and other international agencies—such as the Inter-Parliamentary Union, the Joint United Nations Programme on HIV/AIDS (UNAIDS), the United Nations Environment Programme and the World Health Organization—enabled the Report to include not only the existing data in the Millennium Indicators Database but also more recent estimates for some of the Millennium Development Goal indicators. These estimates, being prepared for incorporation into the database, may have been further updated after the cutoff date for this Report.

DATA FOR THEMATIC ANALYSIS

The statistical evidence used in the thematic analysis in the Report is often drawn from the indicator tables. But a wide range of other sources are also used, including commissioned papers, government documents, national human development reports, reports of non-governmental organizations and journal articles and other scholarly publications. Official statistics usually receive priority. But because of the cutting-edge nature of the issues discussed, relevant official statistics may not exist, so that non-official sources of information must be used. Nevertheless, the Human Development Report Office is committed to relying on data compiled through scholarly and scientific research and to ensuring impartiality in the sources of information and in its use in the analysis.

Where information from sources other than the Report's indicator tables is used in boxes or tables in the text, the source is shown and the full citation is given in the bibliography. In addition, for each chapter a summary note outlines the major sources for the chapter, and endnotes specify the sources of statistical information not drawn from the indicator tables.

THE NEED FOR BETTER HUMAN DEVELOPMENT STATISTICS

While the indicator tables in this year's Report present the best data currently available for measuring human development, many gaps and problems remain.

DATA GAPS

Gaps throughout the indicator tables, particularly the Millennium Development Goal indicator tables, demonstrate the pressing need for improvements in the availability of relevant, reliable and timely human development statistics. A stark example of data gaps is the large number of countries excluded from the HDI. The intent is to include all UN member countries along with Hong Kong, China (SAR) and the Occupied Palestinian Territories. But because of a lack of reliable data, 18 UN member countries are excluded from the HDI and therefore from the main indicator tables (what key indicators are available for these countries are presented in table 30). Similarly, the human poverty index covers only 94 developing countries and 17 high-income OECD countries, the gender-related development index 144 countries and the gender empowerment measure 70 countries. For a significant number of countries data for the components of these indices are unreliable and out of date and in some cases need to be estimated (for the definition and methodology of the indices, see technical note 1).

DISCREPANCIES BETWEEN NATIONAL AND INTERNATIONAL ESTIMATES

When compiling international data series, international data agencies often need to apply internationally adopted standards and harmonization procedures to improve comparability across countries. Where the international data are based on national statistics, as they usually are, the national data may need to be adjusted. Where data for a country are missing, an international agency may produce an estimate if other relevant information can be used. And because of the difficulties in coordination between national and international data agencies, international data series may not incorporate the most recent national data. All these factors can lead to significant discrepancies between national and international estimates.

This Report has often brought such discrepancies to light. And while the Human Development Report Office advocates for improvements in international data, it also recognizes that it can play an active role in such efforts. When discrepancies in data have arisen, it has helped to link national and international data authorities to address those discrepancies. In many cases this has led to better statistics in the Report.

TOWARDS STRONGER STATISTICAL CAPACITY

A vital part of the solution to the enormous gaps and deficiencies in statistical information is building sound statistical capacity in countries, an effort requiring financial and political commitment at both national and international levels (see box 2.1 in chapter 2). In contrast to old approaches favouring short-term results, new strategies should focus on long-term sustainability of statistical capacity. The momentum generated by the Millennium Development Goal process has mobilized the entire international statistical community, and many initiatives are under way. Among these are efforts by task forces of the Partnership in Statistics for the 21st Century—the PARIS21 consortium—which have been publicizing the need for better statistics, encouraging countries to develop long-term master plans for statistical development and developing new tools to measure statistical capacity.

One important way to build statistical capacity is by conducting and analysing household surveys. But population censuses also should receive adequate priority and resources (box 2). And international statistical agencies should continue to play an active part in statistical development by improving, promoting and implementing internationally agreed standards, methods and frameworks for statistical activities. The UNESCO Institute for Statistics is developing the Literacy Assessment and Monitoring Programme, a much-improved tool for measuring literacy (box 3). The World Health Organization has been developing a measure of healthy life expectancy (box 4). And other institutions have been working on indicators relating to maternal health, trying to identify process indicators that can help inform policy where adequately measuring the outcome indicators (such as maternal mortality) is difficult and costly (box 5).

BOX 2

Building capacity to ensure the continuity of population censuses

A population census is the primary source of information about the number of people in a country and the characteristics of the population. Several features distinguish it from survey-based sources of data. It can achieve complete coverage of the population. It offers possibilities for relating individual characteristics of the population with those of households. It provides details about subnational population groups. And in a postconflict situation, where the national statistical system has often collapsed, a population census provides the foundation for developing democratic institutions and good governance and may also give the people hope for a better future.

From census data, analysts can derive most of the population-based indicators needed for monitoring national and subnational progress towards the Millennium Development Goals. And no other data source allows such comprehensive sex-disaggregated analysis of population-based indicators. Without a recent census, data gaps are inevitable. Even basic information on the size and age composition of a population will be unavailable or unreliable.

Almost all developing countries have had some experience in census taking in the past several decades, although many still lack the financial and human resources to conduct censuses without at least some external financial or technical assistance. Efforts to build census taking capacity are often impeded by weak national statistical systems, long intervals between censuses and rapid turnover of staff.

Census taking is the most costly data collection activity undertaken by a national statistical system. Rising costs, shrinking public sector budgets and declining aid have all contributed to delays and postponements of censuses in the 2000 round, especially in Sub-Saharan Africa. Without timely and adequate resources, census taking will face an uncertain future. For national statistical systems, partnerships with major stakeholders—civil society, the private sector and bilateral and multilateral organizations—are essential for ensuring the continuity of censuses.

Source: UNFPA 2003.

A new tool for assessing and monitoring literacy

The Literacy Assessment and Monitoring Programme, an initiative being designed by the UNESCO Institute for Statistics in cooperation with international agencies and technical experts, will develop and conduct a survey to measure a range of literacy levels in developing countries. Such a survey is clearly needed. Most current data on adult literacy are too unreliable to serve the needs of national and international users of literacy data. One reason for the lack of reliability is that the data are generally based on self-declarations of literacy or on proxy indicators such as education levels.

Measuring literacy is not just a matter of saying who can read and who cannot. Many different levels of literacy skills are needed, from writing one's name to understanding instructions on a medicine bottle to learning from books. With literacy at the top of the development agenda, good data are needed to help design and target appropriate actions, whether at the national or local level.

How the programme will be conducted

The Literacy Assessment and Monitoring Programme will use assessments to measure people's literacy. It will build on recent advances in assessment method-

Source: UNESCO Institute for Statistics 2003e.

ology, developing them so as to ensure that the entire range of literacy levels can be assessed, from the most basic reading and writing to the highest-level skills.

The programme aims to develop a methodology that meets national needs. It will start as a survey of adults in a small number of developing countries. Once the methodology has been refined, the programme will encourage its use as the standard survey for gathering literacy data worldwide. But the programme will face many challenges, such as ensuring that test questions are compatible with local linguistic and sociocultural circumstances, maintaining international comparability and ensuring the transfer of knowledge.

What outcomes are expected

The programme will show how literacy is distributed throughout a population by providing estimates of literacy rates by age group, gender, education level and other variables. It will also provide a methodology for literacy assessment. And it will ensure that expertise is shared and that national representatives are trained so that countries can adapt the survey to their own purposes. For more information on the programme, see http://www.uis.unesco.org/.

METHODOLOGY

This year's Report presents data for most key indicators with only a two-year lag between the reference date for the indicators and the date of the Report's release. The Millennium Development Goal indicator tables include 191 UN member countries along with Hong Kong, China (SAR) and the Occupied Palestinian Territories. The main human development indicator tables include 175 of these 193 countries and areas—all those for which the HDI can be calculated. Owing to a lack of comparable data, 18 UN member countries cannot be included in the HDI or therefore in the main indicator tables. For these countries basic human development indicators are presented in a separate table (table 30).

COUNTRY CLASSIFICATIONS

Countries are classified in four ways: by human development level, by income, in major world aggregates and by region (see the classification

of countries). These designations do not necessarily express a judgement about the development stage of a particular country or area. The term *country* as used in the text and tables refers, as appropriate, to territories or areas.

Human development classifications. All countries included in the HDI are classified into three clusters by achievement in human development: high human development (with an HDI of 0.800 or above), medium human development (0.500–0.799) and low human development (less than 0.500).

Income classifications. All countries are grouped by income using World Bank classifications: high income (gross national income per capita of $9,206 or more in 2001), middle income ($746–9,205) and low income ($745 or less).

Major world classifications. The three global groups are *developing countries, Central and Eastern Europe and the CIS* and *OECD.* These groups are not mutually exclusive. (Replacing the OECD group with the high-income OECD group would produce mutually exclusive groups; see the classification

Measuring healthy life expectancy

The World Health Organization publishes data on healthy life expectancy as well as total life expectancy in its annual *World Health Report*. Healthy life expectancy reflects years lived in full health. It is calculated by adjusting total life expectancy for years lived in less than full health as a result of diseases and injuries (Mathers and others 2001). Estimates of healthy life expectancy are based on an analysis of mortality in 191 countries and disability from 135 causes in 17 world regions and on analyses of 69 health surveys in 60 countries using new methods to improve the comparability of self-reported data. These estimates are more uncertain than those for total life expectancy, mainly because of data limitations and difficulties in producing comparable measures of disability across countries.

Healthy life expectancy at birth ranges from a low of 39 years in Sub-Saharan Africa to 66 years in developed countries, with a global average in 2000 of 56 years (see table). In Eastern Europe and the former Soviet Union it declined from 62 years to 58 between 1990 and 2000, reflecting worsening adult health. In Sub-Saharan Africa it declined from 42 years to 39 in the same period, reflecting the effect of HIV/AIDS. Without HIV/AIDS, healthy life expectancy at birth in Sub-Saharan Africa would have been almost six years longer in 2000. If malaria and tuberculosis had also been eliminated, it would have been almost nine years longer.

Source: WHO 2003f.

While communicable diseases such as HIV/AIDS, malaria and tuberculosis continue to cause substantial loss of health and life in developing countries, particularly in Africa, non-communicable diseases and injuries account for more than half of all lost years of healthy life in both developing and developed countries.

Healthy life expectancy at birth by region, 2000

Region	Years
Africa	41.4
Northern Africa	57.3
Sub-Saharan Africa	38.7
Asia[a]	55.5
Eastern Asia	60.9
South-Central Asia	51.8
South-Eastern Asia	55.8
Western Asia	50.8
Latin America and the Caribbean	58.0
Oceania[b]	49.6
Developing countries	53.6
Developed countries	66.1
World	56.0

a. Excludes Japan.
b. Excludes Australia and New Zealand.
Source: WHO 2002.

of countries.) Unless otherwise specified, the classification *world* represents the universe of 193 countries covered.

Regional classifications. Developing countries are further classified into the following regions: Arab States, East Asia and the Pacific, Latin America and the Caribbean (including Mexico), South Asia, Southern Europe and Sub-Saharan Africa. These regional classifications are consistent with the Regional Bureaux of UNDP. An additional classification is *least developed countries,* as defined by the United Nations (UNCTAD 2001).

AGGREGATES AND GROWTH RATES

Aggregates. Aggregates for the classifications described above are presented at the end of tables where it is analytically meaningful to do so and data are sufficient. Aggregates that are the total for the classification (such as for popula-

tion) are indicated by a T. As a result of rounding, world totals may not always equal the sum of the totals for subgroups. All other aggregates are weighted averages.

In general, an aggregate is shown for a classification only when data are available for half the countries and represent at least two-thirds of the available weight in that classification. The Human Development Report Office does not fill in missing data for the purpose of aggregation. Therefore, unless otherwise specified, aggregates for each classification represent only the countries for which data are available, refer to the year or period specified and refer only to data from the primary sources listed. Aggregates are not shown where appropriate weighting procedures were unavailable.

Aggregates for indices, for growth rates and for indicators covering more than one point in time are based only on countries for which data exist for all necessary points in time. For the

Using process indicators to monitor maternal health

For years the maternal mortality ratio was the main indicator available for measuring maternal health. This indicator, requiring large household surveys in the absence of vital registration systems, is expensive to generate, subject to many types of errors and particularly unsuitable for monitoring recent changes. Even in countries with good vital registration, maternal mortality can be seriously underestimated as a result of misclassification of deaths. Moreover, while this indicator provides a snapshot of the problem, it gives no indication of what to do about it.

In 1991 Columbia University and the United Nations Children's Fund (UNICEF) developed a set of process indicators (later issued in UNICEF, WHO and UNFPA 1997) to address these problems. While the maternal mortality ratio is an impact indicator and reflects the level of deaths, process indicators show changes in the circumstances known to contribute to maternal death, such as non-availability of medical treatment. Process indicators are therefore useful for planning and monitoring projects to avert maternal deaths (for information on projects using these indicators, see http://www.amdd.hs.columbia.edu).

The process indicators make visible the reality that many health facilities in developing countries do not offer the care women need if they develop obstetric complications. Of every 100 pregnant women, according to the World Health Organization (WHO 1994), at least 15 are likely to develop complications—whether they live in Dhaka or New York. But in New York women can get the life-saving medical treatment they need, such as antibiotics, blood transfusions and caesarean sections. These procedures have been common for decades. And yet the lifetime risk of a woman dying in pregnancy or childbirth is 1 in 16 in Africa, 1 in 65 in Asia and 1 in 3,700 in North America.

Using the process indicators, planners can determine the minimum health facilities needed in a population area (the amount of emergency obstetric care available and the geographic distribution of these services), whether the women who need the services are using them (the proportion of all births in emergency obstetric facilities, the met need for emergency obstetric services and caesarean sections as a share of all births) and whether the quality is adequate (the case fatality rate). The answers can then guide investment in upgrading the facilities for emergency obstetric care.

Compared with the maternal mortality ratio, the process indicators are:

- Less expensive—they do not require surveys but instead are based on facility records and available data or estimates of the population and birth rate.
- More valid—data can be cross-checked.
- More likely to promote action—they emphasize functioning facilities and population coverage.
- More useful—they show change relatively quickly, highlighting needs and progress.

Source: Hijab 2003.

world classification, which refers only to the universe of 193 countries (unless otherwise specified), aggregates are not always shown where no aggregate is shown for one or more regions.

Aggregates in this Report will not always conform to those in other publications because of differences in country classifications and methodology. Where indicated, aggregates are calculated by the statistical agency providing the data for the indicator.

Growth rates. Multiyear growth rates are expressed as average annual rates of change. In calculations of rates by the Human Development Report Office, only the beginning and end points are used. Year-to-year growth rates are expressed as annual percentage changes.

PRESENTATION OF THE INDICATORS

In the Millennium Development Goal indicator tables countries and areas are presented by major world group and by region for developing countries and, within each classification, in alphabetical order. In the human development indicator tables countries and areas are ranked in descending order by their HDI value. To locate a country in these tables, refer to the *key to countries* on the back cover flap, which lists countries alphabetically with their HDI rank.

Sources for all data used in the indicator tables are given in short citations at the end of each table. These correspond to full references in the *statistical references.* When an agency provides data it has collected from another source, both sources are credited in the table notes. But when an agency has built on the work of many other contributors, only the ultimate source is given. The source notes also show the original data components used in any calculations by the Human Development Report Office to ensure that all calculations can be easily replicated.

Indicators for which short, meaningful definitions can be given are included in the *definitions of statistical terms*. All other relevant information appears in the notes at the end of each table.

In the absence of the words *annual, annual rate* or *growth rate,* a hyphen between two years, such as in 1995-2000, indicates that the data were collected during one of the years shown. A slash between two years, such as in 1997/99, indicates an average for the years shown. The following signs are used:

.. Data not available.

(.) Less than half the unit shown.

< Less than.

– Not applicable.

T Total.

Unless otherwise indicated, data for China do not include Hong Kong, China (SAR), Macau, China (SAR) or Taiwan (province of China). In most cases data for Eritrea before 1992 are included in the data for Ethiopia. Data for Indonesia include Timor-Leste through 1999.

Data for Jordan refer to the East Bank only. And data for the Republic of Yemen refer to that country from 1990 onward, while data for earlier years refer to aggregated data for the former People's Democratic Republic of Yemen and the former Yemen Arab Republic.

As a result of periodic revisions of data by international agencies, statistics presented in different editions of the Report often are not comparable. For this reason the Human Development Report Office strongly advises against constructing trend analyses based on data from different editions.

HDI values and ranks similarly are not comparable across editions of the Report. For trend analysis based on consistent data and methodology, refer to table 2 (Human development index trends).

The data presented in the Millennium Development Goal indicator tables and the human development indicator tables are those available to the Human Development Report Office as of 16 April 2003.

¹MDG

GOAL 1 Eradicate extreme poverty and hunger • GOAL 2 Achieve universal primary education

	Halve, between 1990 and 2015, the proportion of people whose income is less than $1 a day			Halve, between 1990 and 2015, the proportion of people who suffer from hunger			Ensure that, by 2015, children everywhere, boys and girls alike, will be able to complete a full course of primary schooling					
	Population living below $1 a day (%)[a] 1990-2001[b]	Poverty gap ratio (%) 1990-2001[b]	Share of poorest 20% in national income or consumption (%) 1990-2001[b,c]	Children under weight for age (% under age 5) 1995-2001[b]	Undernourished people (as % of total population) 1990/1992[d]	1998/2000[d]	Net primary enrolment ratio (%) 1990-1991[e,f]	2000-2001[e,f]	Children reaching grade 5 (%) 1990-1991[e]	1999-2000[e]	Youth literacy rate (% age 15-24) 1990	2001
Arab States												
Algeria	<2	<0.5	7.0	6	5	6	93	98	94	97	77.3	89.2
Bahrain	..	..	..	9	..	..	99	96	89	101	95.6	98.5
Djibouti	..	..	..	18	..	..	32	33	87	77 [g]	73.2	84.9
Egypt	3.1	<0.5	8.6	4	5	4	..	93 [h]	..	..	61.3	70.5
Iraq	..	..	..	16	7	27	79 [i]	93 [i]	..	..	41.0	45.0
Jordan	<2	<0.5	7.6	5	4	6	66	94 [h,j]	100	98 [g,h]	96.7	99.3
Kuwait	..	..	..	10	22	4	45 [k]	66 [j]	..	..	87.5	92.7
Lebanon	..	..	..	3	..	3	..	74	..	97	92.1	95.4
Libyan Arab Jamahiriya	..	..	..	5	..	..	97 [i]	..	..	..	91.0	96.7
Morocco	<2	<0.5	6.5	9 [l]	6	7	58	78	75	80	55.3	68.4
Occupied Palestinian Territories	..	..	..	3	..	..	..	97	..	..	..	..
Oman	..	..	..	24	..	..	70	65	96	96	85.6	98.2
Qatar	..	..	..	6	..	..	87	95 [g]	64	..	90.3	95.0
Saudi Arabia	..	..	..	14	4	3	59	58	83	94	85.4	93.1
Somalia	..	..	..	26	67	71	..	..	..	..	..	..
Sudan	..	..	..	17	31	21	..	46 [j]	94	87 [g]	65.0	78.1
Syrian Arab Republic	..	..	..	13	5	3	98	96	94	..	79.9	87.7
Tunisia	<2	<0.5	5.7	4	..	..	94	99 [h]	87	93 [h]	84.1	93.8
United Arab Emirates	..	..	..	14	3	..	94	87	80	98	84.7	91.0
Yemen	15.7	4.5	7.4	46	36	33	..	67	..	..	50.0	66.5
East Asia and the Pacific												
Brunei Darussalam	..	..	..	..	..	..	91 [k]	..	95 [k]	92	97.9	99.4
Cambodia	..	..	6.9	45	43	36	..	95	..	63	73.5	79.7
China	16.1	3.7	5.9	10	16	9	97	93 [h,j]	86	..	95.3	97.9
Hong Kong, China (SAR)	..	..	5.3	..	..	..	..	..	100	..	98.2	99.4
Fiji	..	..	..	8 [l]	..	..	101 [k]	99 [g]	..	..	97.8	99.2
Indonesia	7.2	1.0	8.4	26	9	6	98	92 [h]	84	97 [h]	95.0	97.9
Kiribati	..	..	..	13 [l]	..	..	..	..	98	..	..	..
Korea, Dem. Rep. of	..	..	..	60	18	34	..	..	..	..	..	..
Korea, Rep. of	<2	<0.5	7.9	..	..	..	104	99 [h]	99	..	99.8	99.8
Lao People's Dem. Rep.	26.3	6.3	7.6	40	29	24	..	81	53 [k]	..	70.1	78.6
Malaysia	<2	<0.5	4.4	18	3	..	..	98 [h]	98	..	94.8	97.7
Marshall Islands	..	..	..	..	..	..	..	..	..	..	..	..
Micronesia, Fed. Sts.	..	..	..	..	..	..	..	..	..	..	..	..
Mongolia	13.9	3.1	5.6	13	34	42	..	89	..	..	98.9	99.1
Myanmar	..	..	..	36	10	6	..	83	..	..	88.2	91.2
Nauru	..	..	..	..	..	..	..	81 [g]	..	..	..	..
Palau	..	..	..	..	..	..	..	111	..	..	..	..
Papua New Guinea	..	..	4.5	35 [l]	25	27	..	84 [j]	59	..	68.6	76.3
Philippines	14.6	2.7	5.4	28	26	23	98 [k]	93 [h]	..	..	97.3	98.8
Samoa (Western)	..	..	..	..	..	..	..	97	..	83 [g]	99.0	99.4
Singapore	..	..	5.0	14 [l]	..	..	..	..	..	..	99.0	99.8
Solomon Islands	..	..	..	21 [l]	..	..	..	..	85	..	..	..
Thailand	<2	<0.5	6.1	19 [l]	28	18	..	85 [h]	..	97 [g,h]	98.1	99.0
Timor-Leste	..	..	..	..	..	..	..	..	..	..	..	..
Tonga	..	..	..	..	..	..	..	91	84	..	..	..
Tuvalu	..	..	..	..	..	..	..	104 [g]	..	..	..	..
Vanuatu	..	..	..	20 [l]	..	..	..	96	90 [k]	101 [g]	..	..
Viet Nam	17.7	3.3	8.0	33	27	18	..	95	..	..	94.1	95.4

	Halve, between 1990 and 2015, the proportion of people whose income is less than $1 a day			Halve, between 1990 and 2015, the proportion of people who suffer from hunger			Ensure that, by 2015, children everywhere, boys and girls alike, will be able to complete a full course of primary schooling					
	Population living below $1 a day (%)[a] 1990-2001[b]	Poverty gap ratio (%) 1990-2001[b]	Share of poorest 20% in national income or consumption (%) 1990-2001[b,c]	Children under weight for age (% under age 5) 1995-2001[b]	Undernourished people (as % of total population) 1990/1992[d]	1998/2000[d]	Net primary enrolment ratio (%) 1990-1991[e,f]	2000-2001[e,f]	Children reaching grade 5 (%) 1990-1991[e]	1999-2000[e]	Youth literacy rate (% age 15-24) 1990	2001
Latin America and the Caribbean												
Antigua and Barbuda	..	..	..	10 [l]	..	..	..	..	..	..	..	..
Argentina	..	..	..	5	..	..	..	107 [h]	..	90 [h]	98.2	98.6
Bahamas	..	..	..	..	..	..	96 [k]	83 [j]	..	..	96.5	97.3
Barbados	..	..	..	6 [l]	..	..	78 [k]	105	..	..	99.8	99.8
Belize	..	..	..	6 [l]	..	..	98 [k]	100	67	..	96.0	98.1
Bolivia	14.4	5.4	4.0	10	26	23	91	97	..	83	92.6	96.1
Brazil	9.9	3.2	2.0	6	13	10	86	97 [h]	72 [k]	..	91.8	95.5
Chile	<2	<0.5	3.2	1	8	4	88	89 [h]	..	101 [h]	98.1	98.9
Colombia	14.4	8.1	1.4	7	17	13	..	89	62	..	94.9	97.0
Costa Rica	6.9	3.4	2.6	5	6	5	86	91	82	80	97.4	98.3
Cuba	..	..	..	4	5	13	92	97	92	95	99.3	99.8
Dominica	..	..	..	5 [l]	..	..	..	..	..	86	..	..
Dominican Republic	<2	<0.5	5.1	5	27	26	..	93	..	75 [g]	87.5	91.4
Ecuador	20.2	5.8	3.3	15	8	5	..	99	..	78	95.5	97.3
El Salvador	21.4	7.9	3.3	12	12	14	75 [i]	81 [j]	58 [k]	71 [g]	83.8	88.5
Grenada	..	..	..	..	..	..	..	84	..	..	..	..
Guatemala	16.0	4.6	2.6	24	14	25	..	84	..	..	73.4	79.6
Guyana	<2	<0.5	4.5	12	19	14	93	98 [j]	87	..	99.8	99.8
Haiti	..	..	..	17	64	50	22	..	..	..	54.8	65.3
Honduras	23.8	11.6	2.0	25	23	21	89 [k]	88	..	..	79.7	85.5
Jamaica	<2	<0.5	6.7	4	14	9	96	95 [h]	..	89 [h]	91.2	94.3
Mexico	8.0	2.1	3.4	8	5	5	100	103 [h]	80	88 [h]	95.2	97.2
Nicaragua	82.3	52.2	2.3	12	30	29	72	81	46	48	68.2	72.0
Panama	7.6	2.9	3.6	7	19	18	91	100	..	92	95.3	96.9
Paraguay	19.5	9.8	1.9	5	18	14	93	92 [h]	70	76 [h]	95.6	97.2
Peru	15.5	5.4	4.4	7	40	11	..	104 [h,j]	..	88 [g,h]	94.5	96.9
Saint Kitts and Nevis	..	..	..	..	..	..	..	..	..	..	..	..
Saint Lucia	..	..	5.2	14 [l]	..	..	..	100	95 [k]	..	..	..
St. Vincent & the Grenadines	..	..	..	..	..	..	..	..	..	..	..	..
Suriname	..	..	..	..	12	11	..	92	..	..	..	..
Trinidad and Tobago	12.4	3.5	5.5	7 [l]	13	12	91	92	96	100	99.6	99.8
Uruguay	<2	<0.5	4.5	5	6	3	91 [k]	90 [h]	94	91 [h]	98.7	99.1
Venezuela	15.0	6.9	3.0	5	11	21	88	88	86	91 [g]	96.0	98.1
South Asia												
Afghanistan	..	..	..	48	63	70	..	..	..	..	..	..
Bangladesh	36.0	8.1	9.0	48	35	35	64	89	..	..	42.0	49.1
Bhutan	..	..	..	19	..	..	..	..	..	90	..	..
India	34.7	8.2	8.1	47	25	24	..	..	..	68 [g,h]	64.3	73.3
Iran, Islamic Rep. of	<2	<0.5	5.1	11	4	5	..	74	90	..	86.3	94.2
Maldives	..	..	..	30	..	..	..	99	..	..	98.1	99.1
Nepal	37.7	9.7	7.6	48	19	19	..	72	52 [k]	..	46.6	61.6
Pakistan	13.4	2.4	8.8	38	25	19	..	66	..	..	47.4	57.8
Sri Lanka	6.6	1.0	8.0	29	29	23	..	97 [g,h]	94	..	95.1	96.9
Southern Europe												
Cyprus	..	..	..	..	..	..	87	95	100	99	99.7	99.8
Turkey	<2	<0.5	6.1	8	..	..	89	..	98	..	92.7	96.7

GOAL 1 **Eradicate extreme poverty and hunger** • GOAL 2 **Achieve universal primary education**

	Halve, between 1990 and 2015, the proportion of people whose income is less than $1 a day			Halve, between 1990 and 2015, the proportion of people who suffer from hunger			Ensure that, by 2015, children everywhere, boys and girls alike, will be able to complete a full course of primary schooling					
	Population living below $1 a day (%)[a] 1990-2001[b]	Poverty gap ratio (%) 1990-2001[b]	Share of poorest 20% in national income or consumption (%) 1990-2001[b,c]	Children under weight for age (% under age 5) 1995-2001[b]	Undernourished people (as % of total population) 1990/1992[d]	1998/2000[d]	Net primary enrolment ratio (%) 1990-1991[e,f]	2000-2001[e,f]	Children reaching grade 5 (%) 1990-1991[e]	1999-2000[e]	Youth literacy rate (% age 15-24) 1990	2001
Sub-Saharan Africa												
Angola	..	..	..	..	61	50	..	37	..	..	..	..
Benin	..	..	..	23	19	13	49 [k]	70 [j]	55	84	40.4	54.3
Botswana	23.5	7.7	2.2	13	17	25	93	84	97	87	83.3	88.7
Burkina Faso	61.2	25.5	4.5	34	23	23	27	36	70	69	24.9	35.8
Burundi	58.4	24.9	5.1	45	49	69	52 [i]	54	62	58	51.6	65.1
Cameroon	33.4	11.8	4.6	21	32	25	..	..	..	81 [g]	81.1	90.5
Cape Verde	..	..	..	14 [l]	..	..	..	99 [g]	..	..	81.5	88.6
Central African Republic	66.6	38.1	2.0	24	49	44	53	55	24	..	52.1	68.7
Chad	..	..	..	28	58	32	..	58	53	54	48.0	68.3
Comoros	..	..	..	25	..	..	..	56	46 [k]	77	56.7	58.8
Congo	..	..	..	14 [l]	37	32	..	..	62	..	92.5	97.6
Congo, Dem. Rep. of the	..	..	..	31	32	73	54	33 [g]	55	..	68.9	82.7
Côte d'Ivoire	12.3	2.4	7.1	21	18	15	47	64	73	91	52.6	62.4
Equatorial Guinea	..	..	..	..	..	..	..	72	..	..	92.7	97.2
Eritrea	..	..	..	44	..	58	..	41	..	..	60.9	71.1
Ethiopia	81.9	39.9	2.4	47	59	44	..	47	..	64	43.0	56.2
Gabon	..	..	..	12	11	8	..	88	..	..	..	..
Gambia	59.3	28.8	4.0	17	21	21	51 [k]	69	87 [k]	69 [g]	42.2	58.6
Ghana	44.8	17.3	5.6	25	35	12	..	58	80	66	81.8	91.6
Guinea	..	..	6.4	23	40	32	..	47	59	84	..	..
Guinea-Bissau	..	..	5.2	23	..	..	..	54 [j]	..	38 [g]	44.1	59.5
Kenya	23.0	6.0	5.6	23	47	44	..	69	..	71 [g]	89.8	95.5
Lesotho	43.1	20.3	1.4	16	27	26	73	78	71	75	87.2	90.8
Liberia	..	..	..	20 [l]	33	39	..	83 [j]	..	33 [g]	57.2	69.8
Madagascar	49.1	18.3	6.4	33	35	40	..	68	22	..	72.2	80.8
Malawi	41.7	14.8	4.9	25	49	33	50	101	64	49	63.2	71.8
Mali	72.8	37.4	4.6	43	25	20	21	43 [g]	72	95	27.6	37.1
Mauritania	28.6	9.1	6.4	32	14	12	..	64	75	61	45.8	49.3
Mauritius	..	..	..	16	6	5	95	95	98	..	91.1	94.0
Mozambique	37.9	12.0	6.5	26	69	55	47	54	33	..	48.8	61.7
Namibia	34.9	14.0	1.4	24	15	9	89 [i]	82	63 [k]	92	87.4	91.9
Niger	61.4	33.9	2.6	40	42	36	25	30	62	74	17.0	23.8
Nigeria	70.2	34.9	4.4	27	13	7	..	..	..	..	73.6	87.8
Rwanda	35.7 [m]	7.7 [m]	9.7 [m]	24	34	40	66	97 [j]	60	39	72.7	84.2
São Tomé and Principe	..	..	..	16	..	..	..	..	..	..	..	..
Senegal	26.3	7.0	6.4	18	23	25	48 [k]	63	85	72	40.1	51.8
Seychelles	..	..	..	6 [l]	..	..	..	..	93 [k]	..	..	..
Sierra Leone	57.0 [m]	39.5 [m]	1.1 [m]	27	46	47	..	..	..	..	..	..
South Africa	<2	<0.5	2.0	12	..	..	103 [k]	89	75	65	88.5	91.5
Swaziland	..	..	2.7	10	10	12	88	93	76	84	85.1	90.8
Tanzania, U. Rep. of	19.9	4.8	6.8	29	36	47	51	47	79	82	83.1	91.1
Togo	..	..	..	25	28	23	75	92	50	74	63.5	76.5
Uganda	82.2	40.1	7.1	23	23	21	..	109	..	..	70.1	79.4
Zambia	63.7	32.7	3.3	25	45	50	..	66	..	81	81.2	88.7
Zimbabwe	36.0	9.6	4.6	13	43	38	..	80 [h]	94	..	93.9	97.4
Central & Eastern Europe & CIS												
Albania	..	..	..	14	..	8	..	98	..	..	94.8	98.0
Armenia	12.8	3.3	6.7	3	..	46	..	69	..	..	99.5	99.8
Azerbaijan	3.7	<1	7.4	17	..	23	..	91 [j]	..	..	..	..
Belarus	<2	<0.5	8.4	..	..	2	..	108	..	..	99.8	99.8
Bosnia and Herzegovina	..	..	..	4	..	6	..	..	..	..	..	..

	Halve, between 1990 and 2015, the proportion of people whose income is less than $1 a day			Halve, between 1990 and 2015, the proportion of people who suffer from hunger			Ensure that, by 2015, children everywhere, boys and girls alike, will be able to complete a full course of primary schooling					
	Population living below $1 a day (%)[a] 1990-2001[b]	Poverty gap ratio (%) 1990-2001[b]	Share of poorest 20% in national income or consumption (%) 1990-2001[b,c]	Children under weight for age (% under age 5) 1995-2001[b]	Undernourished people (as % of total population) 1990/1992[d]	1998/2000[d]	Net primary enrolment ratio (%) 1990-1991[e,f]	2000-2001[e,f]	Children reaching grade 5 (%) 1990-1991[e]	1999-2000[e]	Youth literacy rate (% age 15-24) 1990	2001
Bulgaria	4.7	1.4	6.7	..	..	15	86	94	91	..	99.4	99.7
Croatia	<2	<0.5	8.3	1	..	18	79	..	..	..	99.6	99.8
Czech Republic	<2	<0.5	10.3	1 [l]	..	..	..	90 [h]	..	..	..	..
Estonia	<2	<0.5	7.0	..	..	..	..	98	..	99	99.8	99.7
Georgia	<2	<0.5	6.0	3	..	16	..	95	..	..	..	..
Hungary	<2	<0.5	10.0	2 [l]	..	..	91	90 [h]	98	..	99.7	99.8
Kazakhstan	1.5	0.3	8.2	4	..	8	..	89	..	..	99.8	99.8
Kyrgyzstan	2.0	0.2	9.1	11	..	8	..	82	..	..	..	..
Latvia	<2	<0.5	7.6	..	..	5	83 [i]	92	..	..	99.8	99.8
Lithuania	<2	<0.5	7.9	..	..	3	..	95	..	..	99.8	99.8
Macedonia, TFYR	<2	<0.5	8.4	6	..	4	94	92	..	..	..	..
Moldova, Rep. of	22.0	5.8	7.1	3	..	10	..	78	..	..	99.8	99.8
Poland	<2	<0.5	7.8	..	..	..	97	98 [h]	98	99 [h]	99.8	99.8
Romania	2.1	0.6	8.2	6 [l]	..	..	77 [i]	93	..	..	99.3	99.6
Russian Federation	6.1	1.2	4.9	3	..	5	..	..	..	..	99.8	99.8
Serbia and Montenegro	..	..	..	2	..	8	69	..	..	..	..	..
Slovakia	<2	<0.5	8.8	..	..	..	..	89 [h]	..	..	..	..
Slovenia	<2	<0.5	9.1	..	..	..	..	93	..	..	99.8	99.8
Tajikistan	10.3	2.6	8.0	..	..	64	..	103	..	..	99.8	99.8
Turkmenistan	12.1	2.6	6.1	12	..	8	..	..	..	..	..	..
Ukraine	2.9	0.6	8.8	3	..	5	..	72 [g]	59	..	99.8	99.9
Uzbekistan	19.1	8.1	9.2	19	..	19	..	..	..	..	99.6	99.7
High-income OECD [n]												
Australia	..	..	5.9	..	..	..	99	96 [h]	..	..	..	..
Austria	..	..	7.0	..	..	..	90 [i]	91 [h]	..	..	..	..
Belgium	..	..	8.3	..	..	..	97	101 [h]	..	..	..	..
Canada	..	..	7.3	..	..	..	97	99 [h,j]	..	..	..	..
Denmark	..	..	8.3	..	..	..	98	99 [h,j]	94	..	..	..
Finland	..	..	10.1	..	..	..	99 [i]	100 [h]	100	100 [h]	..	..
France	..	..	7.2	..	..	..	101	100 [h]	96	..	..	..
Germany	..	..	5.7	..	..	..	84 [i]	87 [h,j]	..	..	..	..
Greece	..	..	7.1	..	..	..	94	97 [h]	99	..	99.5	99.8
Iceland	..	..	..	..	..	..	..	102 [h]	..	..	..	..
Ireland	..	..	6.7 [m]	..	..	..	91	90 [h,j]	100	98 [h]	..	..
Italy	..	..	6.0	..	..	..	..	100 [h]	100	..	99.8	99.8
Japan	..	..	10.6	..	..	..	100	101 [h]	100	..	..	..
Luxembourg	..	..	8.0	..	..	..	..	97 [h]	..	99 [h]	..	..
Netherlands	..	..	7.3	..	..	..	95	100 [h]	..	..	..	..
New Zealand	..	..	6.4	..	..	..	101	99 [h]	90	..	..	..
Norway	..	..	9.7	..	..	..	100	101 [h]	100	..	..	..
Portugal	<2	<0.5	5.8	..	..	..	102	..	..	..	99.5	99.8
Spain	..	..	7.5	..	..	..	103	102 [h]	100 [k]	..	99.6	99.8
Sweden	..	..	9.1	..	..	..	100	102 [h]	100	..	..	..
Switzerland	..	..	6.9	..	..	..	84	99 [h]	76	101 [h]	..	..
United Kingdom	..	..	6.1	..	..	..	97	99 [h]	..	..	..	..
United States	..	..	5.2	1 [l]	..	..	96	95 [h]	..	..	..	..

GOAL 1 Eradicate extreme poverty and hunger • GOAL 2 Achieve universal primary education

	Halve, between 1990 and 2015, the proportion of people whose income is less than $1 a day			Halve, between 1990 and 2015, the proportion of people who suffer from hunger			Ensure that, by 2015, children everywhere, boys and girls alike, will be able to complete a full course of primary schooling					
	Population living below $1 a day (%)[a]	Poverty gap ratio (%)	Share of poorest 20% in national income or consumption (%)	Children under weight for age (% under age 5)	Undernourished people (as % of total population)		Net primary enrolment ratio (%)		Children reaching grade 5 (%)		Youth literacy rate (% age 15-24)	
	1990-2001[b]	1990-2001[b]	1990-2001[b,c]	1995-2001[b]	1990/1992[d]	1998/2000[d]	1990-1991[e,f]	2000-2001[e,f]	1990-1991[e]	1999-2000[e]	1990	2001
Other UN member countries												
Andorra	..	..	..	..	..	..	..	..	..	..	..	..
Israel	..	..	6.9	..	..	..	..	101	..	..	98.7	99.5
Liechtenstein	..	..	..	..	..	..	..	..	..	..	..	..
Malta	..	..	..	..	..	..	99	99 [j]	100	100 [g]	97.5	98.6
Monaco	..	..	..	..	..	..	..	..	83	..	..	..
San Marino	..	..	..	..	..	..	..	..	..	..	..	..
Developing countries	..	..	..	..	21	18	80	82	..	..	81.1	84.8
Least developed countries	..	..	..	..	37	38	54	60	..	..	56.5	66.3
Arab States	..	..	..	..	13	13	73	77	..	..	66.5	76.7
East Asia and the Pacific	..	..	..	..	..	..	96	93	..	..	95.2	97.4
Latin America and the Caribbean	..	..	..	..	14	12	87	97	..	..	92.7	95.2
South Asia	..	..	..	..	25	24	73	79	..	..	61.7	70.6
Sub-Saharan Africa	..	..	..	..	35	33	56	59	..	..	67.4	77.9
Central & Eastern Europe & CIS	..	..	..	..	..	9	88	91	..	..	99.7	99.8
OECD	..	..	..	..	..	..	97	98	..	..	..	..
High-income OECD	..	..	..	..	..	..	97	97	..	..	..	..
High human development	..	..	..	..	..	..	97	98	..	..	..	..
Medium human development	..	..	..	..	19	15	86	88	..	..	84.5	87.8
Low human development	..	..	..	..	33	31	50	59	..	..	59.8	71.5
High income	..	..	..	..	..	..	97	97	..	..	..	..
Middle income	..	..	..	..	..	10	92	93	..	..	93.1	95.4
Low income	..	..	..	..	27	25	69	74	..	..	68.0	75.9
World	..	..	..	..	..	..	82	84	..	..	..	..

a. Poverty line is equivalent to $1.08 (1993 PPP US$). b. Data refer to the most recent year available during the period specified. c. For information on survey years and whether data refer to income or consumption, see column 1 of table 13. d. Data refer to the average for the years specified. e. Data refer to the 1990/91, 1999/2000 or 2000/01 school year. Data for some countries may refer to national or UNESCO Institute for Statistics estimates. For details, see http://www.uis.unesco.org/. Because data are from different sources, comparisons across countries should be made with caution. f. The net enrolment ratio is the ratio of enrolled children of the official age for the education level indicated to the total population of that age. Net enrolment ratios exceeding 100% reflect discrepancies between these two data sets. g. Data refer to the 1998/99 school year. h. Data are preliminary and subject to further revision. i. Data refer to the 1992/93 school year. j. Data refer to the 1999/2000 school year. k. Data refer to the 1991/92 school year. l. Data refer to a year or period other than that specified, differ from the standard definition or refer to only part of the country. m. Data refer to a year or period other than that specified. n. Excluding the Republic of Korea; see East Asia and the Pacific.
Source: Columns 1-3: World Bank 2003c; *column 4:* UNICEF 2003b, based on data from a joint effort by the United Nations Children's Fund and the World Health Organization; *columns 5 and 6:* UN 2003a, based on data from the Food and Agriculture Organization; *columns 7 and 8:* World Bank 2003c, based on data from the UNESCO Institute for Statistics; aggregates calculated for the Human Development Report Office by the UNESCO Institute for Statistics; *columns 9-12:* World Bank 2003c, based on data from the UNESCO Institute for Statistics.

GOAL 3 **Promote gender equality and empower women**

Eliminate gender disparity in primary and secondary education,
preferably by 2005, and at all levels of education no later than 2015

| | Ratio of girls to boys [a] | | | | Ratio of literate females to males (age 15-24) [b] | | Female share of non-agricultural wage employment (%) | | Seats in parliament held by women (as % of total) [c] | |
| | In primary education | | In secondary education | In tertiary education | | | | | | |
	1990-91	2000-01	2000-01	2000-01	1990	2001	1990	2001	1990	2003
Arab States										
Algeria	0.81	0.88	1.03	..	0.79	0.90	8	12 [d]	2	6
Bahrain	0.95	0.96	1.01	1.50 [e]	0.99	1.00	7	13	..	0
Djibouti	0.71	0.75	1.28 [f]	0.72	0.78	0.90	..	..	..	11
Egypt	0.80	0.89 [g]	0.90 [g]	..	0.72	0.83	21	20	4	2
Iraq	0.80	0.79 [f]	0.59 [f]	0.52 [f]	0.44	0.50	..	..	11	8
Jordan	0.94	0.95 [f,g]	0.98 [f,g]	1.06 [f,g]	0.97	1.00	23	21	..	1
Kuwait	0.92	0.96 [f]	0.98 [f]	2.09 [e]	0.99	1.02	..	23 [h]	..	0
Lebanon	..	0.93	1.07	1.08	0.93	0.96	..	..	..	2
Libyan Arab Jamahiriya	0.91	0.97	1.00	0.93	0.84	0.94	..	..	..	..
Morocco	0.66	0.84	0.78 [f]	0.78	0.62	0.78	37	27	..	11
Occupied Palestinian Territories	..	0.96	1.02	0.90	..	..	16	16	..	..
Oman	0.89	0.93	0.96	1.38	0.79	0.97	19	25	..	..
Qatar	0.91	0.95	1.00	2.74	1.05	1.05	..	15	..	..
Saudi Arabia	0.84	0.92	0.86	1.27 [f]	0.86	0.96	18	14	..	..
Somalia	..	..	..	..	..	..	..	..	4	..
Sudan	0.75	0.82 [f]	1.61 [f]	0.89 [e]	0.71	0.87	22	..	..	10
Syrian Arab Republic	0.87	0.89	0.87	..	0.73	0.83	17 [i]	17	9	10
Tunisia	0.85	0.91 [g]	1.01 [g]	0.93 [g]	0.81	0.92	..	..	4	12
United Arab Emirates	0.93	0.92	0.98	..	1.08	1.08	..	14 [d]	..	0
Yemen	..	0.60	0.35 [e]	0.26 [e]	0.34	0.58	..	7 [j]	4	1
East Asia and the Pacific										
Brunei Darussalam	..	0.90	0.99	1.84	1.01	1.01	..	..	..	..
Cambodia	..	0.86	0.55	0.38	0.81	0.89	..	52	..	7
China	0.86	0.92 [f,g]	0.83 [f,g]	..	0.95	0.98	38	39	21	22
Hong Kong, China (SAR)	..	..	..	..	0.99	1.01	41	46	..	..
Fiji	..	0.93 [e]	..	..	1.00	1.00	30	38	..	6
Indonesia	0.95	0.95 [g]	0.95 [g]	0.75 [g]	0.97	0.99	29	30 [k]	12	8
Kiribati	0.98	0.96 [f]			..	..	..	..	..	5
Korea, Dem. Rep. of	..	..	..	..	..	..	..	..	21	20
Korea, Rep. of	0.94	0.89 [g]	0.92 [g]	0.55 [g]	1.00	1.00	38	41	2	6
Lao People's Dem. Rep.	0.77	0.83	0.69	0.58	0.76	0.84	..	..	6	23
Malaysia	0.95	0.95 [g]	1.05 [g]	1.04 [g]	0.99	1.00	38	36	5	10
Marshall Islands	..	0.93 [e]	1.02 [e]	..	..	..	..	..	..	3
Micronesia, Fed. Sts.	..	1.01	1.00	..	..	..	..	..	..	0
Mongolia	1.00	1.00	1.19	1.72	1.00	1.01	..	48 [h]	25	11
Myanmar	0.94	0.97	0.93	1.74	0.96	0.99	..	..	..	..
Nauru	..	1.02 [e]	1.05 [e]	..	..	..	..	..	6	0
Palau	..	0.91	0.92	1.74	..	..	..	..	..	0
Papua New Guinea	0.80	0.83 [f]	0.67 [f]	0.55 [e]	0.84	0.90	..	..	..	1
Philippines	0.95	0.96 [g]	1.05 [g]	1.06 [g]	1.00	1.00	40	42	9	18
Samoa (Western)	0.98	0.91	0.98	0.90	1.00	1.00	..	..	..	6
Singapore	0.90	..	..	..	1.00	1.00	43	47	5	12
Solomon Islands	0.80	..	..	..	..	..	..	..	..	0
Thailand	0.94	0.94 [g]	0.94 [g]	0.82 [g]	0.99	0.99	45	47	3	9
Timor-Leste	..	..	..	..	..	..	..	..	..	26
Tonga	0.92	0.87	1.00	1.22 [f]	..	..	..	..	..	..
Tuvalu	0.91	0.85 [e]	0.81 [e]	..	..	..	..	..	8	0
Vanuatu	0.89	0.99	0.77	0.63 [e]	..	..	..	..	4	2
Viet Nam	..	0.91	0.89	0.73	0.99	1.01	..	..	18	27

Eliminate gender disparity in primary and secondary education,
preferably by 2005, and at all levels of education no later than 2015

	Ratio of girls to boys[a]			Ratio of literate females to males (age 15-24)[b]		Female share of non-agricultural wage employment (%)		Seats in parliament held by women (as % of total)[c]	
	In primary education	In secondary education	In tertiary education						
	1990-91	2000-01	2000-01	2000-01	1990	2001	1990	2001	1990	2003
Latin America and the Caribbean										
Antigua and Barbuda	..	1.63	2.53	..	..	..	..	..	..	5
Argentina	..	0.96 [g]	1.04 [g]	1.61 [f, g]	1.00	1.00	37	43	6	31
Bahamas	..	0.93 [f]	0.95 [f]	..	1.02	1.02	49	48	4	20
Barbados	..	0.97	0.98	2.40	1.00	1.00	46	47	4	11
Belize	0.94	0.94	1.05	..	1.01	1.01	37	41	..	7
Bolivia	0.90	0.95	0.93	..	0.93	0.96	35	36	9	19
Brazil	..	0.93 [g]	1.07 [g]	1.28 [g]	1.03	1.03	40	46	5	9
Chile	0.95	0.94 [g]	0.72 [g]	0.89 [g]	1.00	1.00	36	37	..	13
Colombia	1.11	0.96	1.06	1.07	1.01	1.01	40	49	5	12
Costa Rica	0.94	0.93	1.03	1.15	1.01	1.01	37	40	11	35
Cuba	0.93	0.91	1.00	1.11	1.00	1.00	37	38	34	36
Dominica	0.96	0.93	1.09	..	..	..	..	..	10	19
Dominican Republic	..	0.94	1.21	..	1.02	1.02	35	34	8	17
Ecuador	..	0.97	0.99	..	0.99	0.99	37	41	5	16
El Salvador	..	0.93	0.97 [e]	1.23	0.97	0.98	32	31	12	10
Grenada	0.82	0.94	0.47	..	..	..	38 [i]	..	..	27
Guatemala	..	0.88	0.88	..	0.82	0.85	37	39 [k]	7	9
Guyana	0.97	0.95 [f]	0.97 [f]	..	1.00	1.00	..	..	37	20
Haiti	0.93	..	..	..	0.96	1.01	40	..	..	4
Honduras	0.99	0.98	..	1.28	1.03	1.04	48	52	10	6
Jamaica	0.99	0.96 [g]	1.02 [g]	1.86 [g]	1.09	1.07	50	46	5	12
Mexico	0.94	0.95 [g]	1.02 [g]	0.96 [g]	0.98	0.99	35	37	12	16
Nicaragua	1.04	0.98	1.15	..	1.01	1.02	..	..	15	21
Panama	0.92	0.93	1.02	1.62 [f]	0.99	0.99	44	42	8	10
Paraguay	0.93	0.94 [g]	1.00 [g]	..	0.99	1.00	41	38	6	3
Peru	..	0.96 [f, g]	0.92 [e, g]	0.34 [e, g]	0.95	0.97	29	35	6	18
Saint Kitts and Nevis	..	0.97	1.08	..	..	..	..	..	7	13
Saint Lucia	0.95	0.90	1.33	0.86 [e]	..	..	..	..	..	11
St. Vincent & the Grenadines	0.97	0.94	1.18	..	..	..	..	..	10	23
Suriname	0.96	0.96	1.13	..	..	..	39	34	8	18
Trinidad and Tobago	0.97	0.95	1.05	1.50	1.00	1.00	36	40	17	19 [d]
Uruguay	0.95	0.94 [g]	1.09 [g]	1.78 [g]	1.01	1.01	42	47	6	12
Venezuela	0.99	0.94	1.15	1.42	1.01	1.01	35	40	10	10
South Asia										
Afghanistan	0.52	..	..	..	..	..	..	..	4	..
Bangladesh	0.81	0.96	0.99	0.51	0.65	0.71	18	23 [d]	10	2
Bhutan	..	0.86	0.81	0.52	..	..	..	..	2	9
India	0.71	0.77 [f, g]	0.66 [f, g]	0.61 [f, g]	0.74	0.82	13	17	5	9
Iran, Islamic Rep. of	0.86	0.91	0.89	0.89	0.88	0.95	..	..	2	4
Maldives	..	0.95	1.05	..	1.00	1.00	..	37 [d]	6	6
Nepal	0.56	0.79	0.69	0.25	0.41	0.57	..	..	6	6
Pakistan	0.48	0.55	0.63	0.38 [e]	0.49	0.60	7	8	10	22
Sri Lanka	0.93	0.94 [e, g]	1.03 [e, g]	..	0.98	1.00	39	47	5	4
Southern Europe										
Cyprus	0.93	0.94	0.97	1.38 [l]	1.00	1.00	37	43	2	11
Turkey	0.89	0.89 [g]	0.69 [g]	0.69 [g]	0.91	0.95	17	19	1	4

Eliminate gender disparity in primary and secondary education, preferably by 2005, and at all levels of education no later than 2015

	Ratio of girls to boys [a]			Ratio of literate females to males (age 15-24) [b]		Female share of non-agricultural wage employment (%)		Seats in parliament held by women (as % of total) [c]	
	In primary education		In secondary education	In tertiary education						
	1990-91	2000-01	2000-01	2000-01	1990	2001	1990	2001	1990	2003
Sub-Saharan Africa										
Angola	0.92	0.88	0.83	0.64 [f]	..	..	43 [m]	..	15	16
Benin	0.50	0.68	0.45 [f]	0.25 [f]	0.44	0.52	..	..	3	6
Botswana	1.07	0.99	1.06	0.89	1.10	1.09	46	45 [d]	5	17
Burkina Faso	0.62	0.70	0.64	..	0.39	0.52	13	..	..	12
Burundi	0.84	0.80	0.78	0.37	0.77	0.96	..	..	..	18
Cameroon	0.85	0.86	0.78 [e]	..	0.88	0.96	..	..	14	9
Cape Verde	..	0.96	..	..	0.87	0.93	..	..	12	11
Central African Republic	0.65	0.69	..	0.19 [f]	0.60	0.79	..	..	4	7
Chad	0.45	0.63	0.28 [f]	0.18 [f]	0.65	0.83	4	..	..	6
Comoros	0.71	0.85	0.80 [f]	0.72 [f]	0.78	0.79	..	..	..	..
Congo	0.90	0.93	0.85	0.14	0.95	0.99	..	..	14	9
Congo, Dem. Rep. of the	0.74	0.90 [e]	0.52 [e]	..	0.72	0.86	..	..	5	..
Côte d'Ivoire	0.71	0.76	0.55	0.36 [e]	0.62	0.75	..	21 [h]	6	9
Equatorial Guinea	..	0.91	0.43 [f]	0.43 [f]	0.92	0.97	..	..	13	5
Eritrea	0.95	0.82	0.67	0.15	0.68	0.76	..	..	..	22
Ethiopia	0.66	0.68	0.66	0.27	0.66	0.81	40 [i]	..	..	8
Gabon	..	0.98	0.94	0.55 [e]	..	..	..	..	13	9
Gambia	0.68	0.91	0.70	..	0.68	0.76	..	..	8	13
Ghana	0.82	0.90	0.81	0.40	0.86	0.95	..	..	..	9
Guinea	0.46	0.70	0.35 [e]	..	..	..	..	..	..	19
Guinea-Bissau	..	0.67 [f]	0.55 [f]	0.18 [f]	0.43	0.62	..	..	20	8
Kenya	0.95	0.98	0.91	0.77	0.93	0.98	21	38	1	7
Lesotho	1.21	1.02	1.18	1.74	1.26	1.19	..	..	..	12
Liberia	..	0.69 [f]	0.71 [f]	0.75 [f]	0.51	0.63	..	..	..	8
Madagascar	0.97	0.96	0.96 [e]	0.83	0.86	0.92	..	..	7	4
Malawi	0.82	0.96	0.75	0.38 [e]	0.68	0.76	11	12	10	9
Mali	0.59	0.71	0.52 [e]	..	0.45	0.54	..	..	..	10
Mauritania	0.73	0.93	0.88	0.20	0.65	0.72	..	..	..	..
Mauritius	0.98	0.97	0.92	1.32	1.00	1.01	37	39	7	6
Mozambique	0.76	0.77	0.65	0.79	0.48	0.63	..	..	16	30
Namibia	1.08	1.00	1.12	1.23 [f]	1.04	1.04	40 [i]	49 [d]	7	26
Niger	0.57	0.65	0.62	0.33	0.37	0.44	11	..	5	1
Nigeria	0.76	..	..	..	0.82	0.95	..	..	..	3
Rwanda	0.99	1.00	0.96 [f]	0.51	0.86	0.96	..	..	17	26
São Tomé and Principe	..	0.92	1.06	0.56	..	..	..	..	12	9
Senegal	0.72	0.87	0.65	..	0.60	0.71	..	..	13	19
Seychelles	..	0.97	1.02	..	..	..	..	..	16	29
Sierra Leone	0.70	0.76	0.83	0.40	..	..	..	..	..	15
South Africa	0.98	0.94	1.10	1.24	1.00	1.00	..	..	3	30
Swaziland	0.99	0.95	1.00 [f]	0.88	1.01	1.02	35	30	4	3
Tanzania, U. Rep. of	0.98	1.00	0.81	0.31	0.87	0.95	..	..	..	22
Togo	0.65	0.79	0.45	0.20 [f]	0.60	0.74	..	..	5	7
Uganda	0.80	..	0.75	0.52	0.76	0.85	..	..	12	25
Zambia	..	0.93	0.80	0.46	0.88	0.95	..	..	7	12
Zimbabwe	0.99	0.97 [g]	0.88 [g]	0.60 [g]	0.95	0.97	15	20	11	10
Central & Eastern Europe & CIS										
Albania	0.93	0.94	0.95	1.59	0.94	0.97	40	41	29	6
Armenia	..	0.95	1.02	1.20	1.00	1.00	..	..	36	3
Azerbaijan	0.94	0.96 [f]	0.96 [f]	0.89 [f]	..	..	35	45	..	11
Belarus	..	0.94	1.00	1.28	1.00	1.00	56	56	..	10
Bosnia and Herzegovina	..	..	..	..	..	..	..	..	..	17

GOAL 3 **Promote gender equality and empower women**

Eliminate gender disparity in primary and secondary education,
preferably by 2005, and at all levels of education no later than 2015

| | Ratio of girls to boys [a] | | | | Ratio of literate females to males (age 15-24) [b] | | Female share of non-agricultural wage employment (%) | | Seats in parliament held by women (as % of total) [c] | |
| | In primary education | | In secondary education | In tertiary education | | | | | | |
	1990-91	2000-01	2000-01	2000-01	1990	2001	1990	2001	1990	2003
Bulgaria	0.93	0.93	0.93	1.29	1.00	1.00	54	50	21	26
Croatia	0.94	0.94	0.99	1.10	1.00	1.00	44	46	..	21
Czech Republic	0.96	0.94 g	0.98 g	1.00 g	..	..	46	47	..	17
Estonia	0.94	0.91	0.98	1.51	1.00	1.00	52	52	..	18
Georgia	0.96	0.95	0.99	0.96	..	..	43	49	..	7
Hungary	0.95	0.94 g	0.97 f, g	1.21 g	1.00	1.00	47	46	21	10
Kazakhstan	..	0.95	0.95	1.19	1.00	1.00	..	50 h	..	10
Kyrgyzstan	0.99	0.95	0.98	1.03	..	..	48	45	..	10
Latvia	0.96	0.94	0.97	1.62	1.00	1.00	52	53	..	21
Lithuania	0.90	0.94	0.95	1.49	1.00	1.00	58	51	..	11
Macedonia, TFYR	0.93	0.94	0.92	1.26	..	..	38	42	..	18
Moldova, Rep. of	0.97	0.96	0.99	1.26	1.00	1.00	54	53	..	13
Poland	0.95	0.94 g	0.93 g	1.38 g	1.00	1.00	49	47 d	14	20
Romania	0.96	0.94	0.97	1.15	1.00	1.00	43	46	34	11
Russian Federation	0.97	0.95 g	1.03 g	1.26 g	1.00	1.00	50	50	..	8
Serbia and Montenegro	0.95	0.95	0.97	1.16	..	..	..	..	..	7 d
Slovakia	..	0.95 g	0.97 g	1.05 g	..	..	48	52	..	19
Slovenia	..	0.94	0.99 f	1.28	1.00	1.00	49	48	..	12
Tajikistan	0.96	0.90	0.81	0.31	1.00	1.00	39	52	..	13
Turkmenistan	..	..	..	..	..	..	..	..	26	26
Ukraine	0.96	0.95 e	0.87 e	1.11 e	1.00	1.00	50	53	..	5
Uzbekistan	0.96	..	..	..	1.00	1.00	47	38	..	7
High-income OECD [n]										
Australia	0.95	0.95 g	0.96 g	1.19 g	..	..	45	48	6	25
Austria	0.95	0.94 g	0.91 g	1.08 g	..	..	40	44	12	34
Belgium	0.97	0.95 g	1.06 g	1.09 f, g	..	..	40	45	9	23
Canada	0.93	0.95 f, g	0.96 f, g	1.27 f, g	..	..	47	49	13	21
Denmark	0.96	0.95 g	1.00 g	1.29 g	..	..	47	49	31	38
Finland	0.95	0.95 g	1.06 g	1.17 g	..	..	51	50	32	37
France	0.94	0.94 g	0.96 g	1.18 g	..	..	44	46	7	12
Germany	..	0.94 g	0.94 g	0.90 e, g	..	..	41	46	..	32
Greece	0.94	0.94 g	0.97 g	1.05 g	1.00	1.00	35	41	7	9
Iceland	..	0.94 g	1.02 g	1.68 g	..	..	53	52	21	35
Ireland	0.95	0.94 g	1.03 g	1.21 g	..	..	42	47	8	13
Italy	0.95	0.94 g	0.93 g	1.27 g	1.00	1.00	37	41	13	12
Japan	0.95	0.95 g	0.96 g	0.81 g	..	..	38	40	1	7
Luxembourg	1.03	0.95 g	1.02 g	1.18 f, g	..	..	35	38	13	17
Netherlands	0.99	0.94 g	0.93 g	1.02 g	..	..	38	44	21	37
New Zealand	0.94	0.94 g	1.01 g	1.43 g	..	..	47	51	14	29
Norway	0.95	0.95 g	0.97 g	1.45 g	..	..	47	48	36	36
Portugal	0.91	0.94 g	1.01 g	1.33 g	1.00	1.00	42	46	8	19
Spain	0.94	0.94 g	1.00 g	1.10 g	1.00	1.00	33	39	15	28
Sweden	0.95	0.97 g	1.19 g	1.44 g	..	..	51	51	38	45
Switzerland	0.96	0.95 g	0.89 g	0.74 g	..	..	43	47 k	14	23
United Kingdom	0.96	0.95 g	1.11 g	1.20 g	..	..	48	50	6	18
United States	0.94	0.95 g	0.96 g	1.27 g	..	..	47	48	7	14

GOAL 3 **Promote gender equality and empower women**

Eliminate gender disparity in primary and secondary education,
preferably by 2005, and at all levels of education no later than 2015

| | Ratio of girls to boys [a] | | | | Ratio of literate females to males (age 15-24) [b] | | Female share of non-agricultural wage employment (%) | | Seats in parliament held by women (as % of total) [c] | |
| | In primary education | | In secondary education | In tertiary education | | | | | | |
	1990-91	2000-01	2000-01	2000-01	1990	2001	1990	2001	1990	2003
Other UN member countries										
Andorra	..	..	..	..	..	..	44	46 [k]	..	14
Israel	0.98	0.95	0.95	1.31	0.99	1.00	43	49	7	15
Liechtenstein	..	..	..	..	..	..	..	..	4	12
Malta	0.92	0.95 [f]	0.95 [f]	1.14 [f]	1.03	1.02	29	31	3	9
Monaco	1.02	0.94 [f]	1.03 [f]	..	..	..	..	..	11	21
San Marino	0.87	0.92 [f]	0.92 [f]	1.37 [f]	..	..	40	42	12	17
Developing countries	..	..	..	..	0.89	0.91	..	..	..	..
Least developed countries	..	..	..	..	0.72	0.81	..	..	..	..
Arab States	..	..	..	..	0.71	0.83	..	..	..	..
East Asia and the Pacific	..	..	..	..	0.96	0.98	..	..	..	..
Latin America and the Caribbean	..	..	..	..	1.00	1.01	..	..	..	..
South Asia	..	..	..	..	0.72	0.80	..	..	..	..
Sub-Saharan Africa	..	..	..	..	0.80	0.89	..	..	..	..
Central & Eastern Europe & CIS	..	..	..	..	1.00	1.00	..	..	..	..
OECD	..	..	..	..	..	..	..	..	..	..
High-income OECD	..	..	..	..	..	..	..	..	..	..
High human development	..	..	..	..	..	..	..	..	..	..
Medium human development	..	..	..	..	0.91	0.94	..	..	..	..
Low human development	..	..	..	..	0.70	0.81	..	..	..	..
High income	..	..	..	..	..	..	..	..	..	..
Middle income	..	..	..	..	0.95	0.98	..	..	..	..
Low income	..	..	..	..	0.79	0.85	..	..	..	..
World	..	..	..	..	..	..	..	..	..	..

a. Calculated as the ratio of girls' enrolments to boys'. Data refer to the 1990/91 or 2000/01 school year. For the 2000/01 school year, data for some countries may refer to national or UNESCO Institute for Statistics estimates. For details, see http://www.uis.unesco.org/. Because data are from different sources, comparisons across countries should be made with caution. Enrolments for years after 1997 are based on the new International Standard Classification of Education, adopted in 1997 (UNESCO 1997), and so may not be strictly comparable with those for earlier years. b. Calculated on the basis of female and male youth literacy rates. c. Data refer to the lower house only and are as of 1 March 2003. For more detailed information on the status of the parliament in particular countries, see table 27. d. Data refer to 2000. e. Data refer to the 1998/99 school year. f. Data refer to the 1999/2000 school year. g. Preliminary UNESCO Institute for Statistics estimate, subject to further revision. h. Data refer to 1998. i. Data refer to 1991. j. Data refer to 1999. k. Data refer to 2002. l. Excludes Turkish students. m. Data refer to 1992. n. Excluding the Republic of Korea; see East Asia and the Pacific.
Source: Columns 1-4: UN 2003a, based on data from the UNESCO Institute for Statistics; *columns 5 and 6:* World Bank 2003c, based on data from the UNESCO Institute for Statistics; *columns 7 and 8:* UN 2003a, based on data from the International Labour Organization; *column 9:* UN 2003a, based on data from the Inter-Parliamentary Union; *column 10:* IPU 2003b.

³MDG

	Under-five mortality rate (per 1,000 live births)[a]		Infant mortality rate (per 1,000 live births)[a]		One-year-olds fully immunized against measles (%)		Maternal mortality ratio (per 100,000 live births)[b]	Births attended by skilled health personnel (%)
	1990	2001	1990	2001	1990	2001	1995	1995-2001[c]
Arab States								
Algeria	69	49	42	39	83	83	150	92
Bahrain	19	16	15	13	87	98	38	98
Djibouti	175	143	119	100	85	49	520	..
Egypt	104	41	76	35	86	97	170	61
Iraq	50	133	40	107	80	90	370	..
Jordan	43	33	35	27	87	99	41	97
Kuwait	16	10	14	9	66	99	25	98
Lebanon	37	32	32	28	61	94	130	88
Libyan Arab Jamahiriya	42	19	34	16	89	93	120	94
Morocco	85	44	66	39	80	96	390	40
Occupied Palestinian Territories	53 [d]	25	42 [d]	21	..	..	120 [e]	..
Oman	30	13	25	12	98	99	120	91
Qatar	25	16	19	11	79	92	41	..
Saudi Arabia	44	28	34	23	88	94	23	91
Somalia	225	225	133	133	30	38	1,600	34
Sudan	123	107	75	65	57	67	1,500	86 [f]
Syrian Arab Republic	44	28	37	23	87	93	200	76 [f]
Tunisia	52	27	37	21	93	92	70	90
United Arab Emirates	14	9	12	8	80	94	30	99
Yemen	142	107	98	79	69	79	850	22
East Asia and the Pacific								
Brunei Darussalam	11	6	10	6	99	99	22	99
Cambodia	115	138	80	97	34	59	590	32
China	49	39	38	31	98	79	60	89
Hong Kong, China (SAR)	..	..	6	3	..	..	..	..
Fiji	31	21	25	18	84	90	20	100
Indonesia	91	45	60	33	58	59	470	56
Kiribati	88	69	65	51	..	76	..	85
Korea, Dem. Rep. of	55	55	26	42	..	..	35	..
Korea, Rep. of	9	5	8	5	93	97	20	100
Lao People's Dem. Rep.	163	100	120	87	32	50	650	21
Malaysia	21	8	16	8	70	92	39	96
Marshall Islands	92	66	63	54	..	87 [g]	..	95
Micronesia, Fed. Sts.	31	24	26	20	..	84	..	93
Mongolia	107	76	77	61	92	95	65	97
Myanmar	130	109	91	77	90	73	170	..
Nauru	..	..	..	..	..	95	..	..
Palau	..	29	..	24	..	..	..	100
Papua New Guinea	101	94	79	70	67	58	390	53
Philippines	66	38	45	29	85	75	240	56
Samoa (Western)	42	25	33	20	..	92	15	100
Singapore	8	4	7	3	84	89	9	100
Solomon Islands	36	24	29	20	..	..	60	85
Thailand	40	28	34	24	80	94	44	85
Timor-Leste	..	124	..	85	..	..	850	26
Tonga	27	20	25	17	..	93	..	92
Tuvalu	..	..	..	..	..	99	..	99
Vanuatu	70	42	52	34	..	94	32	89
Viet Nam	50	38	36	30	85	97	95	70

Reduce by two-thirds, between 1990 and 2015, the under-five mortality rate

Reduce by three-quarters, between 1990 and 2015, the maternal mortality ratio

	Under-five mortality rate (per 1,000 live births)[a]		Infant mortality rate (per 1,000 live births)[a]		One-year-olds fully immunized against measles (%)		Maternal mortality ratio (per 100,000 live births)[b]	Births attended by skilled health personnel (%)
	1990	2001	1990	2001	1990	2001	1995	1995-2001[c]
Latin America and the Caribbean								
Antigua and Barbuda	..	14	..	12	89	97	..	100 [f]
Argentina	28	19	25	16	93	94	85	98
Bahamas	29	16	24	13	86	93	10	99 [f]
Barbados	16	14	14	12	87	92	33	91
Belize	49	40	39	34	86	96	140	77 [f]
Bolivia	122	77	87	60	53	79	550	59
Brazil	60	36	50	31	78	99	260	88
Chile	19	12	16	10	82	97	33	100
Colombia	36	23	29	19	82	75	120	86
Costa Rica	17	11	15	9	90	82	35	98
Cuba	13	9	11	7	94	99	24	100
Dominica	23	15	19	14	91	99	..	100
Dominican Republic	65	47	53	41	96	98	110	96
Ecuador	57	30	43	24	60	99	210	69
El Salvador	60	39	46	33	98	97	180	51
Grenada	37	25	30	20	85	96	..	100 [f]
Guatemala	82	58	60	43	68	90	270	41
Guyana	90	72	65	54	77	92	150	95
Haiti	150	123	102	79	31	53	1,100	24
Honduras	61	38	47	31	90	95	220	54
Jamaica	20	20	17	17	69	85	120	95
Mexico	46	29	37	24	78	97	65	86
Nicaragua	66	43	52	36	82	99	250	65
Panama	34	25	27	19	73	97	100	90
Paraguay	37	30	30	26	69	77	170	58
Peru	75	39	58	30	64	97	240	59
Saint Kitts and Nevis	36	24	30	20	99	94	..	100
Saint Lucia	24	19	19	17	83	89	..	100
St. Vincent & the Grenadines	26	25	21	22	96	98	..	100 [f]
Suriname	44	32	35	26	65	90	230	85
Trinidad and Tobago	24	20	21	17	99	91	65	99
Uruguay	24	16	20	14	97	94	50	99
Venezuela	27	22	23	19	61	49	43	95
South Asia								
Afghanistan	260	257	167	165	20	46	820	..
Bangladesh	144	77	96	51	65	76	600	12
Bhutan	166	95	75 [d]	74	93	78	500	15 [f]
India	123	93	80	67	56	56	440	43
Iran, Islamic Rep. of	72	42	54	35	85	96	130	..
Maldives	115	77	80	58	96	99	390	70
Nepal	145	91	100	66	57	71	830	11
Pakistan	128	109	96	84	50	54	200	20
Sri Lanka	23	19	19	17	80	99	60	97
Southern Europe								
Cyprus	12	6	11	5	..	86 [g]	0	..
Turkey	74	43	61	36	78	90	55	81

GOAL 4 **Reduce child mortality** • GOAL 5 **Improve maternal health**

	Under-five mortality rate (per 1,000 live births)[a]		Infant mortality rate (per 1,000 live births)[a]		One-year-olds fully immunized against measles (%)		Maternal mortality ratio (per 100,000 live births)[b]	Births attended by skilled health personnel (%)
	1990	2001	1990	2001	1990	2001	1995	1995-2001[c]
Sub-Saharan Africa								
Angola	260	260	166	154	38	72	1,300	23
Benin	185	158	111	94	79	65	880	66
Botswana	58	110	45	80	87	83	480	99
Burkina Faso	210	197	118	104	79	46	1,400	31
Burundi	190	190	114	114	74	75	1,900	25
Cameroon	139	155	85	96	56	62	720	56
Cape Verde	60	38	45	29	79	72	190	53
Central African Republic	180	180	115	115	83	29	1,200	44
Chad	203	200	118	117	32	36	1,500	16
Comoros	120	79	88	59	87	70	570	62
Congo	110	108	83	81	75	35	1,100	..
Congo, Dem. Rep. of the	205	205	128	129	38	46	940	61
Côte d'Ivoire	155	175	100	102	56	61	1,200	47
Equatorial Guinea	206	153	122	101	88	19	1,400	..
Eritrea	155	111	92	72	18 [d]	88	1,100	21
Ethiopia	193	172	128	116	38	52	1,800	6
Gabon	90	90	60	60	76	55	620	86
Gambia	154	126	103	91	86	90	1,100	51
Ghana	126	100	74	57	61	81	590	44
Guinea	240	169	145	109	35	52	1,200	35
Guinea-Bissau	253	211	153	130	53	48	910	35
Kenya	97	122	63	78	78	76	1,300	44
Lesotho	148	132	102	91	80	77	530	60
Liberia	235	235	157	157	..	78	1,000	51
Madagascar	168	136	103	84	47	55	580	47
Malawi	241	183	146	114	81	82	580	56
Mali	254	231	152	141	43	37	630	24
Mauritania	183	183	120	120	38	58	870	53
Mauritius	25	19	21	17	76	90	45	..
Mozambique	235	197	143	125	59	92	980	44
Namibia	84	67	65	55	41	58	370	78
Niger	320	265	191	156	25	51	920	16
Nigeria	190	183	114	110	54	40	1,100	42
Rwanda	178	183	107	96	83	78	2,300	31
São Tomé and Principe	90	74	69	57	71	69	..	86 [f]
Senegal	148	138	90	79	51	48	1,200	51
Seychelles	21	17	17	13	86	95	..	..
Sierra Leone	323	316	185	182	..	37	2,100	42
South Africa	60	71	45	56	79	72	340	84
Swaziland	110	149	77	106	85	72	370	70
Tanzania, U. Rep. of	163	165	102	104	80	83	1,100	36
Togo	152	141	88	79	73	58	980	49
Uganda	165	124	100	79	52	61	1,100	39
Zambia	192	202	108	112	90	85	870	47
Zimbabwe	80	123	53	76	87	68	610	73
Central & Eastern Europe & CIS								
Albania	42	25	37	23	88	95	31	99
Armenia	58	35	50	31	93 [d]	93	29	97
Azerbaijan	106	96	84	77	66 [d]	99	37	88
Belarus	21	20	18	17	94 [d]	99	33	..
Bosnia and Herzegovina	22	18	18	15	52 [d]	92	15	100

	Under-five mortality rate (per 1,000 live births)[a]		Infant mortality rate (per 1,000 live births)[a]		One-year-olds fully immunized against measles (%)		Maternal mortality ratio (per 100,000 live births)[b]	Births attended by skilled health personnel (%)
	Reduce by two-thirds, between 1990 and 2015, the under-five mortality rate						*Reduce by three-quarters, between 1990 and 2015, the maternal mortality ratio*	
	1990	2001	1990	2001	1990	2001	1995	1995-2001[c]
Bulgaria	19	16	15	14	98	90	23	..
Croatia	13	8	11	7	90 [d]	94	18	..
Czech Republic	12	5	11	4	..	..	14	..
Estonia	17	12	12	11	..	95	80	..
Georgia	29	29	24	24	99	73	22	96
Hungary	17	9	15	8	99	99	23	..
Kazakhstan	52	99	42	81	95	96	80	99
Kyrgyzstan	81	61	68	52	94 [h]	99	80	98
Latvia	18	21	14	17	95 [d]	98	70	100
Lithuania	14	9	10	8	89 [d]	97	27	..
Macedonia, TFYR	33	26	32	22	..	92	17	..
Moldova, Rep. of	37	32	30	27	94	81	65	99
Poland	22	9	19	8	95	97	12	..
Romania	36	21	27	19	92	98	60	98
Russian Federation	21	21	17	18	83 [d]	98	75	..
Serbia and Montenegro	26	19	23	17	83	90	15	..
Slovakia	14	9	12	8	..	99	14	..
Slovenia	10	5	8	4	90 [d]	98	17	..
Tajikistan	127	116	98	91	84 [d]	86	120	77
Turkmenistan	98	87	80	69	76 [d]	98	65	97
Ukraine	22	20	18	17	90 [d]	99	45	99
Uzbekistan	65	68	53	52	85	99	60	96
High-income OECD [i]								
Australia	10	6	8	6	86	93	6	100
Austria	9	5	8	5	60	79	11	..
Belgium	9	6	8	5	85	83	8	..
Canada	8	7	7	5	89	96	6	98
Denmark	9	4	8	4	84	94	15	..
Finland	7	5	6	4	97	96	6	..
France	10	6	7	4	71	84	20	..
Germany	9	5	7	4	50	89	12	..
Greece	11	5	10	5	76	88	2	..
Iceland	8	4	6	3	99	88	16	..
Ireland	9	6	8	6	78	73	9	..
Italy	10	6	8	4	43	70	11	..
Japan	6	5	5	3	73	96	12	100
Luxembourg	9	5	7	5	80	91	0	..
Netherlands	8	6	7	5	94	96	10	100
New Zealand	11	6	8	6	90	85	15	100
Norway	9	4	7	4	87	93	9	..
Portugal	15	6	11	5	85	87	12	100
Spain	9	6	8	4	97	94	8	..
Sweden	7	3	6	3	95	94	8	..
Switzerland	8	6	7	5	90	81	8	..
United Kingdom	9	7	8	6	87	85	10	99
United States	11	8	9	7	90	91	12	99

GOAL 4 **Reduce child mortality** • GOAL 5 **Improve maternal health**

	Reduce by two-thirds, between 1990 and 2015, the under-five mortality rate						*Reduce by three-quarters, between 1990 and 2015, the maternal mortality ratio*	
	Under-five mortality rate (per 1,000 live births)[a]		**Infant mortality rate** (per 1,000 live births)[a]		**One-year-olds fully immunized against measles** (%)		**Maternal mortality ratio** (per 100,000 live births)[b]	**Births attended by skilled health personnel** (%)
	1990	2001	1990	2001	1990	2001	1995	1995-2001[c]
Other UN member countries								
Andorra	..	7	..	6	..	90	..	..
Israel	12	6	10	6	91	94	8	..
Liechtenstein	..	11	..	10	..	..	..	..
Malta	14	5	9	5	80	65	0	..
Monaco	..	5	..	4	99	99	..	..
San Marino	..	..	..	..	..	..	..	..
Developing countries	104	90	70	62	71	69	463	56
Least developed countries	182	160	116	101	55	63	1,000	31
Arab States	90	72	63	53	77	84	509	67
East Asia and the Pacific	58	43	42	33	88	77	144	80
Latin America and the Caribbean	53	34	42	28	77	91	188	82
South Asia	126	96	84	69	58	60	427	36
Sub-Saharan Africa	180	172	111	107	56	58	1,098	38
Central & Eastern Europe & CIS	37	36	30	30	86	97	55	96
OECD	22	13	18	11	81	91	25	94
High-income OECD	10	7	8	5	81	90	12	99
High human development	17	11	14	9	82	91	25	96
Medium human development	82	61	58	46	76	74	286	64
Low human development	176	164	112	104	54	57	972	31
High income	10	7	8	5	81	89	12	99
Middle income	52	38	40	31	89	86	118	84
Low income	139	121	90	80	58	60	671	40
World	93	81	63	56	72	72	411	60

a. The primary agencies responsible for these two Millennium Development Goal indicators are the United Nations Children's Fund (UNICEF) and the World Health Organization (WHO). The table shows World Bank estimates, however, because the more recent estimates from UNICEF and the WHO were not ready for release. The estimates shown are largely consistent with the UNICEF and WHO estimates. b. Data are estimates based on available national data and adjusted for the well-documented problems of underreporting and misclassification of maternal deaths or, where national data are unavailable, model-based estimates. The estimates shown are not comparable with the reported maternal mortality ratios in table 8. c. Data refer to the most recent year available during the period specified. d. Data refer to 1992. e. Data refer to the Gaza Strip only. f. Data refer to a year or period other than that specified, differ from the standard definition or refer to only part of the country. g. WHO 2003d. h. Data refer to 1991. i. Excluding the Republic of Korea; see East Asia and the Pacific.
Source: *Columns 1-4:* World Bank 2003c; aggregates calculated for the Human Development Report Office by the World Bank; *column 5:* WHO 2003d, based on data from a joint effort by UNICEF and the WHO; aggregates calculated for the Human Development Report Office by the WHO; *column 6:* UNICEF 2003b, based on data from a joint effort by UNICEF and the WHO; aggregates calculated for the Human Development Report Office by the WHO; *column 7:* UN 2003a, based on data from a joint effort by the WHO, UNICEF and the United Nations Population Fund; aggregates calculated for the Human Development Report Office by the WHO; *column 8:* UN 2003a, based on data from a joint effort by UNICEF and the WHO; aggregates calculated for the Human Development Report Office by the WHO.

GOAL 6 Combat HIV/AIDS, malaria and other diseases

	Have halted by 2015 and begun to reverse the spread of HIV/AIDS					Have halted by 2015 and begun to reverse the incidence of malaria and other major diseases								
	HIV prevalence among pregnant women aged 15-24 (%)a		Condom use at last high-risk sex (% age 15-24)b		Orphans' school attendance rate as % of non-orphans'c	Malaria-related mortality rate (per 100,000)		Malaria cases (per 100,000 people)d	Children under 5 With insecti-cide-treated bed nets (%)	With fever treated with anti-malarial drugs (%)	Tuber-culosis-related mortality rate (per 100,000 people)e	Tuberculosis cases	Detected under DOTS (%)g	Cured under DOTS (%)h
	In major urban areas	Outside major urban areas	Female	Male		All ages	Children aged 0-4					Per 100,000 people f		
	1999-2002 i	1999-2002 i	1996-2002 i	1996-2002 i	1995-2001 i	2000	2000	2000	1999-2002 i	1999-2002 i	2001	2001	2001	2000
Arab States														
Algeria	..	..	..	..	..	22	169	2 j	..	..	2	23	114	87
Bahrain	..	..	..	..	..	0	0	..	..	..	6	34	59	73
Djibouti	..	..	..	..	..	119	620	715 j	..	..	62	382	65	62
Egypt	..	..	..	..	..	0	0	(.)	..	..	4	23	39	87
Iraq	..	..	..	..	..	15	71	14	..	..	27	89	26	92
Jordan	..	..	..	..	..	0	0	3	..	..	1	5	47	90
Kuwait	..	..	..	..	..	0	0	..	..	..	3	27	..	..
Lebanon	..	..	..	69 k	..	0	0	..	..	..	2	11	53	92
Libyan Arab Jamahiriya	..	..	..	..	..	0	0	2	..	..	2	11	..	..
Morocco	..	..	..	..	..	8	49	(.)	..	..	10	47	81	89
Occupied Palestinian Territories	..	..	..	..	..	..	..	..	..	..	3	19	..	..
Oman	..	..	..	..	..	0	0	27	..	..	1	5	113	93
Qatar	..	..	..	..	..	0	0	..	..	..	2	13	119	66
Saudi Arabia	..	..	..	..	..	0	0	32	..	..	5	27	40	73
Somalia	..	..	..	..	65	81	373	118	0.3	18.5	100	281	32	83
Sudan	..	..	..	..	96	70	408	13,934	0.4 l	50.2 l	50	142	35	79
Syrian Arab Republic	..	..	..	..	..	0	0	(.)	..	..	8	47	27	79
Tunisia	..	..	..	..	..	0	0	1	..	..	4	18	73	91
United Arab Emirates	..	..	..	..	..	0	0	..	..	..	2	13	29	74
Yemen	..	..	..	..	..	24	93	15,160 j	..	..	13	70	47	75
East Asia and the Pacific														
Brunei Darussalam	..	..	..	..	..	0	0	..	..	..	4	24	116	63
Cambodia	..	..	43	..	71	14	4	476	..	..	95	560	41	91
China	..	..	..	..	..	0	0	1	..	..	21	107	29	95
Hong Kong, China (SAR)	..	..	..	..	..	..	..	..	..	..	8	39	59	76
Fiji	..	..	..	..	..	7	0	..	..	..	6	23	59	85
Indonesia	..	..	..	..	..	1	0	920	0.1	4.4	68	321	21	87
Kiribati	..	..	..	..	..	17	1	..	..	..	6	38	201	91
Korea, Dem. Rep. of	..	..	..	..	..	0	0	454	..	..	32	158	56	91
Korea, Rep. of	..	..	..	..	..	0	0	9	..	..	12	48	..	..
Lao People's Dem. Rep.	..	..	..	..	..	28	4	759	..	..	27	143	40	82
Malaysia	..	..	..	..	..	1	1	57	..	..	18	67	..	..
Marshall Islands	..	..	..	..	..	15	0	..	..	..	12	55	76	91
Micronesia, Fed. Sts.	..	..	..	..	..	10	1	..	..	..	12	64	17	93
Mongolia	..	..	..	..	..	0	0	..	..	..	35	124	73	87
Myanmar	..	..	..	..	..	20	3	224	..	..	34	113	59	82
Nauru	..	..	..	..	..	13	0	..	..	..	4	15	106	25
Palau	..	..	..	..	..	6	0	..	..	..	12	76	..	..
Papua New Guinea	..	..	..	..	..	28	3	1,688	..	..	53	283	9	63
Philippines	..	..	..	..	..	2	3	15	..	..	56	226	58	88
Samoa (Western)	..	..	..	..	..	6	0	..	..	..	5	22	50	92
Singapore	..	..	..	..	..	0	0	..	..	..	5	22	21	85
Solomon Islands	..	..	..	..	..	8	0	15,172	..	..	12	52	67	81
Thailand	..	..	..	..	..	8	9	130	..	..	18	100	75	69
Timor-Leste	..	..	..	..	..	..	..	..	..	..	..	..	..	..
Tonga	..	..	..	..	..	9	0	..	..	..	4	15	53	93
Tuvalu	..	..	..	..	..	14	0	..	..	..	6	30	..	..
Vanuatu	..	..	..	..	..	11	1	3,260	..	..	13	63	60	88
Viet Nam	..	..	..	..	..	9	1	95	15.8	6.5	23	93	85	92

GOAL 6 Combat HIV/AIDS, malaria and other diseases

	Have halted by 2015 and begun to reverse the spread of HIV/AIDS					Have halted by 2015 and begun to reverse the incidence of malaria and other major diseases								
	HIV prevalence among pregnant women aged 15-24 (%)[a]		Condom use at last high-risk sex (% age 15-24)[b]		Orphans' school attendance rate as % of non-orphans'[c]	Malaria-related mortality rate (per 100,000)		Malaria cases	Children under 5		Tuberculosis-related mortality rate	Tuberculosis cases		
	In major urban areas	Outside major urban areas	Female	Male		All ages	Children aged 0-4	(per 100,000 people)[d]	With insecticide-treated bed nets (%)	With fever treated with anti-malarial drugs (%)	(per 100,000 people)[e]	Per 100,000 people[f]	Detected under DOTS (%)[g]	Cured under DOTS (%)[h]
	1999-2002[i]	1999-2002[i]	1996-2002[i]	1996-2002[i]	1995-2001[i]	2000	2000	2000	1999-2002[i]	1999-2002[i]	2001	2001	2001	2000
Latin America and the Caribbean														
Antigua and Barbuda	..	..	..	..	..	0	0	..	..	..	1	3	52	100
Argentina	..	..	..	..	..	0	0	1	..	..	6	30	39	54
Bahamas	..	..	..	..	..	0	0	..	..	..	4	19	..	..
Barbados	..	..	..	..	..	0	0	..	..	..	3	11	30	..
Belize	..	..	..	..	..	0	0	657	..	..	3	18	126	78
Bolivia	..	..	8	22	82	1	2	378	..	..	32	116	81	79
Brazil	..	..	32	59	..	0	2	344	..	..	8	44	8	73
Chile	..	..	18	33	..	0	0	..	..	..	2	10	97	82
Colombia	..	..	29	..	..	0	1	250	0.7	..	6	29	..	..
Costa Rica	..	..	..	..	..	0	0	42	..	..	1	7	89	76
Cuba	..	..	..	..	..	0	0	..	..	..	1	6	85	93
Dominica	..	..	..	..	..	0	0	..	..	..	2	9	..	..
Dominican Republic	..	..	12	48	87	0	0	6	..	..	24	88	7	79
Ecuador	..	..	..	..	..	0	1	728	..	..	28	94	5	..
El Salvador	..	..	..	..	..	0	2	11	..	..	10	36	58	79
Grenada	..	..	..	..	..	0	0	..	..	..	1	3	..	..
Guatemala	..	..	..	..	98	1	1	386	1.2	..	13	48	39	86
Guyana	..	..	..	..	..	4	10	3,074	8.1	2.6	17	65	21	91
Haiti	3.7 [m]	..	19	30	82	1	2	15 [j]	..	11.7	55	190	31	73
Honduras	..	..	..	..	..	1	3	541	..	..	10	46	105	89
Jamaica	..	..	..	..	..	0	0	..	..	..	1	3	84	45
Mexico	..	..	..	57 [k]	..	0	0	8	..	..	5	19	95	76
Nicaragua	..	..	17	..	..	0	1	402	..	..	9	35	94	82
Panama	..	..	..	..	..	0	0	36	..	..	6	28	71	67
Paraguay	..	..	79	..	..	0	0	124	..	..	12	43	5	77
Peru	..	..	19	..	..	1	2	258	..	..	21	94	94	90
Saint Kitts and Nevis	..	..	..	..	..	0	0	..	..	..	2	7	0	..
Saint Lucia	..	..	..	..	..	0	0	..	..	..	2	9	55	100
St. Vincent & the Grenadines	..	..	..	..	..	0	0	..	..	..	..	..	..	..
Suriname	..	..	..	..	89	1	5	2,954	2.7	..	11	44	..	..
Trinidad and Tobago	..	..	..	..	..	0	0	1	..	..	2	9	..	..
Uruguay	..	..	..	..	..	0	0	..	..	..	3	15	78	85
Venezuela	..	..	..	..	..	0	0	94	..	..	5	22	68	76
South Asia														
Afghanistan	..	..	..	..	..	8	14	937	..	..	91	305	15	86
Bangladesh	..	..	..	..	..	1	1	40	..	..	56	211	26	83
Bhutan	..	..	..	..	..	5	8	285	..	..	24	114	26	90
India	..	..	40	51	..	3	6	7	..	..	42	199	23	84
Iran, Islamic Rep. of	..	..	..	..	..	0	0	27	..	..	6	32	33	85
Maldives	..	..	..	..	..	3	4	..	..	..	4	21	88	95
Nepal	..	..	..	52	..	8	11	33	..	..	28	135	60	86
Pakistan	..	..	..	..	..	4	11	58	..	..	45	178	6	74
Sri Lanka	..	..	..	44	..	9	4	1,110	..	..	11	50	74	77
Southern Europe														
Cyprus	..	..	..	..	..	0	0	..	..	..	1	5	..	..
Turkey	..	..	..	..	..	0	1	17	..	..	6	25	..	..

GOAL 6 Combat HIV/AIDS, malaria and other diseases

	Have halted by 2015 and begun to reverse the spread of HIV/AIDS					Have halted by 2015 and begun to reverse the incidence of malaria and other major diseases								
	HIV prevalence among pregnant women aged 15-24 (%)[a]		Condom use at last high-risk sex (% age 15-24)[b]		Orphans' school attendance rate as % of non-orphans'[c]	Malaria-related mortality rate (per 100,000)		Malaria cases (per 100,000 people)[d]	Children under 5		Tuberculosis-related mortality rate (per 100,000 people)[e]	Tuberculosis cases		
	In major urban areas	Outside major urban areas	Female	Male		All ages	Children aged 0-4		With insecticide-treated bed nets (%)	With fever treated with anti-malarial drugs (%)		Per 100,000 people[f]	Detected under DOTS (%)[g]	Cured under DOTS (%)[h]
	1999-2002[i]	1999-2002[i]	1996-2002[i]	1996-2002[i]	1995-2001[i]	2000	2000	2000	1999-2002[i]	1999-2002[i]	2001	2001	2001	2000
Sub-Saharan Africa														
Angola	..	..	..	..	90	354	1,624	8,773	2.3	63.0	47	197	..	..
Benin	..	..	19	34	..	177	960	10,697 [n]	7.4	60.4	10	36	..	..
Botswana	33.3	31.4	75	88	99	15	72	48,704	..	..	31	224	75	77
Burkina Faso	5.4	3.1	41	55	..	292	1,444	619	..	..	38	157	15	60
Burundi	..	..	..	..	70	143	714	48,098	1.3	31.3	40	170	39	80
Cameroon	11.9 [m]	..	16	31	94	108	620	2,900 [o]	1.3	66.1	24	96	..	..
Cape Verde	..	..	..	..	..	22	145	..	..	..	46	188	40	..
Central African Republic	13.9	13.4	..	..	91	137	777	2,207 [p]	1.5	68.8	57	255	8	57
Chad	..	..	3	2	96	207	1,008	197 [j]	0.6	31.9	44	168	..	..
Comoros	..	..	..	..	59	80	402	1,930	9.3	62.7	9	49	..	..
Congo	11.0 [m]	..	12	..	..	78	395	5,880	..	..	19	122	104	69
Congo, Dem. Rep. of the	..	..	13	..	72	224	1,000	2,960 [i]	0.7	45.4	49	184	61	78
Côte d'Ivoire	8.8	3.8	25	56	83	76	438	12,152	1.1	57.5	51	207	10	..
Equatorial Guinea	..	..	..	..	95	152	769	2,744 [q]	0.7	48.6	32	102	..	..
Eritrea	1.3	..	..	..	..	74	391	3,479	..	3.6	46	249	15	76
Ethiopia	15.0	12.7	17	30	60	198	1,006	556 [q]	..	3.0	39	179	42	80
Gabon	..	..	33	48	98	80	470	2,148 [o]	..	..	38	187	..	..
Gambia	..	..	..	..	85	52	305	17,340 [o]	14.7	55.2	68	283	..	..
Ghana	3.0	2.8	20	33	93	70	448	15,344	..	60.7	38	145	44	50
Guinea	..	..	17	32	113	200	1,037	75,386	..	..	38	134	..	..
Guinea-Bissau	..	..	..	..	103	150	749	2,421 [j]	7.4	58.4	34	135	..	..
Kenya	21.8 [m]	..	14	43	74	63	334	545	2.9	64.5	62	289	47	80
Lesotho	22.0	16.1	..	..	87	84	549	0 [j]	..	..	55	277	..	..
Liberia	..	..	..	..	..	201	1,004	26,699 [o]	..	..	47	176	..	..
Madagascar	..	..	13	..	65	184	904	..	0.2	60.7	47	158	60	70
Malawi	..	..	32	38	93	275	1,288	25,948	2.9	27.0	49	242	40	73
Mali	0.9 [m]	..	14	30	72	454	2,046	4,008 [o]	..	..	72	295	..	..
Mauritania	..	..	..	..	..	108	553	11,150 [j]	..	..	51	209	..	..
Mauritius	..	..	..	..	..	0	0	1 [j]	..	..	12	57	24	93
Mozambique	16.1	7.9	..	..	47	232	1,159	18,115	..	..	33	125	68	75
Namibia	17.9 [m]	..	..	..	92	52	300	1,502	..	..	35	221	98	53
Niger	..	..	..	..	107	469	1,998	1,693 [o]	1.0	48.1	39	150	..	..
Nigeria	..	..	21	38	87	141	729	30	..	..	47	196	16	79
Rwanda	..	..	23	55	80	200	1,049	6,510	5.0	12.6	46	188	32	61
São Tomé and Principe	..	..	..	..	123	80	509	..	22.8	61.2	35	143	..	..
Senegal	..	..	..	..	74	72	377	11,925	1.7	36.2	30	103	85	52
Seychelles	..	..	..	..	..	4	40	..	..	..	6	26	77	82
Sierra Leone	..	..	..	..	71	312	1,481	..	1.5	60.7	67	258	39	77
South Africa	24.1 [m]	..	20	..	95	0	0	143	..	..	55	237	72	66
Swaziland	39.4 [m]	..	..	..	91	0	0	2,835	0.1	25.5	130	627	..	..
Tanzania, U. Rep. of	..	15.0	21	31	74	130	676	1,207 [j]	2.1	53.4	47	212	47	78
Togo	..	..	22	41	96	47	256	7,701 [o]	2.0	60.0	29	114	..	..
Uganda	..	..	44	62	95	152	650	46	0.2	..	48	187	52	63
Zambia	11.6 [m]	..	38	38	87	141	721	34,204	1.1	58.0	94	445	..	..
Zimbabwe	32.3 [m]	..	42	69	85	1	0	5,410	..	..	54	291	47	69
Central & Eastern Europe & CIS														
Albania	..	..	..	..	..	0	0	..	..	..	5	21	20	..
Armenia	..	..	..	43	..	0	0	4	..	..	13	47	22	87
Azerbaijan	..	..	..	..	..	0	2	19	1.4	0.8	11	56	(.)	91
Belarus	..	..	..	..	..	0	0	..	..	..	12	57	..	..
Bosnia and Herzegovina	..	..	..	..	..	0	0	..	..	..	9	35	71	94

	Have halted by 2015 and begun to reverse the spread of HIV/AIDS				Have halted by 2015 and begun to reverse the incidence of malaria and other major diseases								
	HIV prevalence among pregnant women aged 15-24 (%) [a]		Condom use at last high-risk sex (% age 15-24) [b]		Orphans' school attendance rate as % of non-orphans' [c]	Malaria-related mortality rate (per 100,000)		Malaria cases (per 100,000 people) [d]	Children under 5 With insecti-cide-treated bed nets (%)	With fever treated with anti-malarial drugs (%)	Tuber-culosis-related mortality rate (per 100,000 people) [e]	Tuberculosis cases		
	In major urban areas	Outside major urban areas	Female	Male		All ages	Children aged 0-4					Per 100,000 people [f]	Detected under DOTS (%) [g]	Cured under DOTS (%) [h]
	1999-2002 [i]	1999-2002 [i]	1996-2002 [i]	1996-2002 [i]	1995-2001 [i]	2000	2000	2000	1999-2002 [i]	1999-2002 [i]	2001	2001	2001	2000
Bulgaria	..	..	..	..	..	0	0	..	..	..	4	20	15	..
Croatia	..	..	..	..	..	0	0	..	..	..	9	40	..	..
Czech Republic	..	..	..	..	..	0	0	..	..	..	2	7	59	70
Estonia	..	..	..	..	..	0	0	..	..	..	8	27	67	70
Georgia	..	..	0	..	..	0	0	5	..	..	15	58	48	63
Hungary	..	..	..	..	..	0	0	..	..	..	5	22	35	64
Kazakhstan	..	..	65	28	..	0	0	(.)	..	..	24	94	69	79
Kyrgyzstan	..	..	..	..	..	0	0	(.)	..	..	21	88	45	82
Latvia	..	..	66	69	..	0	0	..	..	..	11	43	77	72
Lithuania	..	..	..	..	..	0	1	..	..	..	9	48	30	92
Macedonia, TFYR	..	..	..	..	..	0	0	..	..	..	7	26	51	86
Moldova, Rep. of	..	..	..	..	..	0	0	..	..	..	21	104	37	83
Poland	..	..	..	..	..	0	0	..	..	..	5	23	3	72
Romania	..	..	..	..	..	0	0	..	..	..	20	94	11	80
Russian Federation	..	..	..	..	..	0	0	1	..	..	24	93	5	68
Serbia and Montenegro	..	..	..	..	..	0	0	..	..	..	6	27	25	..
Slovakia	..	..	..	..	..	0	0	..	..	..	4	15	38	82
Slovenia	..	..	18	17	..	0	0	..	..	..	3	12	68	84
Tajikistan	..	..	..	..	..	0	0	303	1.9	68.9	22	83	..	..
Turkmenistan	..	..	..	..	..	0	0	1	..	..	12	56	36	69
Ukraine	..	..	..	..	..	0	0	..	..	..	11	57	0	..
Uzbekistan	..	..	..	..	..	0	0	1	..	..	12	63	8	80
High-income OECD [f]														
Australia	..	..	..	..	..	0	0	..	..	..	1	4	14	74
Austria	..	..	..	..	..	0	0	..	..	..	1	6	46	73
Belgium	..	..	..	..	..	0	0	..	..	..	1	6	75	..
Canada	..	..	72	72	..	0	0	..	..	..	1	3	56	80
Denmark	..	..	..	..	..	0	0	..	..	..	1	6	..	..
Finland	..	..	..	..	..	0	0	..	..	..	1	5	..	..
France	..	..	77	66	..	0	0	..	..	..	1	6	..	..
Germany	..	..	..	..	..	0	0	..	..	..	1	5	46	77
Greece	..	..	..	..	..	0	0	..	..	..	3	11	..	..
Iceland	..	..	..	..	..	0	0	..	..	..	(.)	2	69	..
Ireland	..	..	..	..	..	0	0	..	..	..	1	6	..	..
Italy	..	..	..	..	..	0	0	..	..	..	1	4	10	74
Japan	..	..	..	..	..	0	0	..	..	..	4	21	28	70
Luxembourg	..	..	..	..	..	0	0	..	..	..	1	6	40	..
Netherlands	..	..	..	..	..	0	0	..	..	..	1	3	56	76
New Zealand	..	..	..	..	..	0	0	..	..	..	1	5	37	30
Norway	..	..	..	..	..	0	0	..	..	..	1	3	50	70
Portugal	..	..	..	..	..	0	0	..	..	..	4	17	83	79
Spain	..	..	33	49	..	0	0	..	..	..	3	14	..	..
Sweden	..	..	..	..	..	0	0	..	..	..	(.)	2	54	79
Switzerland	..	..	..	..	..	0	0	..	..	..	1	5	..	..
United Kingdom	..	..	..	..	..	0	0	..	..	..	1	5	..	..
United States	..	..	..	65 [k]	..	0	0	..	..	..	(.)	2	90	76

GOAL 6 **Combat HIV/AIDS, malaria and other diseases**

	Have halted by 2015 and begun to reverse the spread of HIV/AIDS					*Have halted by 2015 and begun to reverse the incidence of malaria and other major diseases*								
	HIV prevalence among pregnant women aged 15-24 (%) [a]		Condom use at last high-risk sex (% age 15-24) [b]		Orphans' school attendance rate as % of non-orphans' [c]	Malaria-related mortality rate (per 100,000)		Malaria cases (per 100,000 people) [d]	Children under 5		Tuber-culosis-related mortality rate (per 100,000 people) [e]	Tuberculosis cases		
	In major urban areas	Outside major urban areas	Female	Male		All ages	Children aged 0-4		With insecti-cide-treated bed nets (%)	With fever treated with anti-malarial drugs (%)		Per 100,000 people [f]	Detected under DOTS (%) [g]	Cured under DOTS (%) [h]
	1999-2002 [i]	1999-2002 [i]	1996-2002 [i]	1996-2002 [i]	1995-2001 [i]	2000	2000	2000	1999-2002 [i]	1999-2002 [i]	2001	2001	2001	2000
Other UN member countries														
Andorra	..	..	..	..	..	0	0	..	..	..	2	10	34	50
Israel	..	..	..	..	..	0	0	..	..	..	1	5	63	78
Liechtenstein	..	..	..	..	..	..	..	..	..	..	..	..	..	..
Malta	..	..	..	..	..	0	0	..	..	..	1	3	25	100
Monaco	..	..	..	..	..	0	0	..	..	..	(.)	1	..	..
San Marino	..	..	..	..	..	0	0	..	..	..	1	2	0	0
Developing countries	..	..	..	..	..	..	..	..	..	..	32	144	..	..
Least developed countries	..	..	..	..	..	..	..	..	..	..	49	192	..	..
Arab States	..	..	..	..	..	..	..	..	..	..	15	57	..	..
East Asia and the Pacific	..	..	..	..	..	..	..	..	..	..	28	137	..	..
Latin America and the Caribbean	..	..	..	..	..	..	..	..	..	..	9	41	..	..
South Asia	..	..	..	..	..	..	..	..	..	..	42	188	..	..
Sub-Saharan Africa	..	..	..	..	..	..	..	..	..	..	47	198	..	..
Central & Eastern Europe & CIS	..	..	..	..	..	..	..	..	..	..	16	66	..	..
OECD	..	..	..	..	..	..	..	..	..	..	3	11	..	..
High-income OECD	..	..	..	..	..	..	..	..	..	..	2	9	..	..
High human development	..	..	..	..	..	..	..	..	..	..	3	12	..	..
Medium human development	..	..	..	..	..	..	..	..	..	..	29	137	..	..
Low human development	..	..	..	..	..	..	..	..	..	..	45	188	..	..
High income	..	..	..	..	..	..	..	..	..	..	2	9	..	..
Middle income	..	..	..	..	..	..	..	..	..	..	18	85	..	..
Low income	..	..	..	..	..	..	..	..	..	..	45	197	..	..
World	..	..	..	..	..	..	..	..	..	..	26	119	..	..

a. Data are median estimates based on data collected from surveillance sites, mainly antenatal clinics. b. Because of data limitations, comparisons across countries should be made with caution. Data for another agreed indicator under the HIV/AIDS target, the percentage of young people aged 15-24 who correctly identify two ways of preventing the sexual transmission of HIV and who reject major misconceptions about HIV transmission, are not yet available. Data for two proxy indicators of HIV/AIDS knowledge and misconceptions among 15- to 24-year-olds are available. For details, see http://millenniumindicators.un.org. c. Data refer to children aged 10-14. d. Data refer to malaria cases reported to the World Health Organization (WHO) and may represent only a fraction of the true number in a country because of incomplete reporting systems, incomplete coverage by health services or both. Because of the diversity of case detection and reporting systems, comparisons across countries should be made with caution. e. Excluding HIV-related deaths. f. Data refer to the prevalence of smear-positive cases of tuberculosis. g. Calculated by dividing the new smear-positive cases of tuberculosis detected under the directly observed treatment, short course (DOTS) case detection and treatment strategy by the estimated annual incidence of new smear-positive cases. Values can exceed 100% because of intense case detection in an area with a backlog or chronic cases, overreporting (for example, double counting), overdiagnosis or underestimation of incidence (WHO 2003e). h. Data refer to the percentage of new smear-positive cases registered for treatment under the DOTS case detection and treatment strategy in 2000 that were successfully treated. i. Data refer to the most recent year available during the period specified. j. Data refer to 1999. k. Data refer to both sexes combined. l. Data refer to Northern Sudan only. m. Estimate based on data from all antenatal clinics. n. Data refer to 1997. o. Data refer to 1998. p. Data refer to 1994. q. Data refer to 1995. r. Excluding the Republic of Korea; see East Asia and the Pacific.

Source: Columns 1 and 2: UN 2003a, based on data from a joint effort by the WHO and the Joint United Nations Programme on HIV/AIDS (UNAIDS); *columns 3 and 4:* UN 2003a, based on data from a joint effort by the United Nations Children's Fund (UNICEF), UNAIDS and the WHO; *columns 5, 9 and 10:* UN 2003a, based on data from UNICEF; *columns 6-8 and 11-14:* UN 2003a, based on data from the WHO.

*Integrate the principles of sustainable development into country policies and programmes
and reverse the loss of environmental resources* [a]

	Land area covered by forests (%)		Ratio of protected area to surface area [b]	GDP per unit of energy use (PPP US$ per kg of oil equivalent)		Carbon dioxide emissions per capita (metric tons)		Consumption of ozone-depleting chlorofluorocarbons (ODP metric tons) [c]	
	1990	2000	2003	1990	2000	1990	1999	1990	2001
Arab States									
Algeria	0.8	0.9	0.05	5.4	6.4	3.2	3.0	3,570 [d]	1,022
Bahrain	(.)	(.)	0.01	1.2	1.6	23.3	29.4	107	106
Djibouti	(.)	(.)	(.)	..	..	0.7	0.6	..	..
Egypt	(.)	(.)	0.01	3.9	4.8	1.4	2.0	2,144	1,335
Iraq	1.8	1.8	(.)	..	..	2.7	3.3	..	..
Jordan	1.0	1.0	0.03	2.8	3.6	3.2	3.1	540	321
Kuwait	(.)	(.)	0.01	1.3 [d]	1.8	19.9	24.9	1,757 [d]	354
Lebanon	3.6	3.5	(.)	2.8	3.5	2.5	4.0	432 [d]	533
Libyan Arab Jamahiriya	0.2	0.2	(.)	..	..	8.8	8.3	67	985
Morocco	6.8	6.8	0.01	9.8	9.5	1.0	1.3	604	435
Occupied Palestinian Territories	..	..	..	..	..	..	..	..	..
Oman	(.)	(.)	0.11	3.5	3.0	7.1	8.5	305 [d]	207
Qatar	(.)	0.1	(.)	..	..	28.2	91.5	85 [d]	85
Saudi Arabia	0.7	0.7	0.34	2.8	2.6	11.3	11.7	3,688 [d]	1,594 [e]
Somalia	13.2	12.0	0.01	..	..	(.)	0.0 [f]	..	..
Sudan	30.0	25.9	0.05	2.5	3.8	0.1	0.1	601 [g]	266
Syrian Arab Republic	2.5	2.5	..	2.2	2.9	3.0	3.4	1,272	1,392
Tunisia	3.0	3.1	(.)	5.3	7.4	1.6	1.8	730	570
United Arab Emirates	2.9	3.8	..	2.4	2.0 [f]	33.0	31.3	448	423
Yemen	1.0	0.9	..	2.4	4.0	0.7 [g]	1.1	..	1,023
East Asia and the Pacific									
Brunei Darussalam	85.8	83.9	0.21	3.0	3.0 [f]	22.6	14.2	64 [d]	31
Cambodia	56.1	52.9	0.18	..	..	(.)	0.1	..	..
China	15.6	17.5	0.07	1.7	4.1	2.1	2.3	41,829	33,923
Hong Kong, China (SAR)	..	..	0.42	8.7	10.9	4.6	6.2	..	..
Fiji	45.5	44.6	(.)	..	..	1.1	0.9	38	0
Indonesia	65.2	58.0	0.16	3.5	4.2	0.9	1.2	1,457 [d]	5,003
Kiribati	38.4	38.4	0.39	..	..	0.3	0.3	..	(.) [f]
Korea, Dem. Rep. of	68.2	68.2	0.03	..	..	12.3	9.4	950 [d]	77 [e]
Korea, Rep. of	63.8	63.3	0.07	3.4	3.6	5.6	8.4	24,126 [d]	6,724
Lao People's Dem. Rep.	56.7	54.4	0.10	..	..	0.1	0.1	4 [h]	41
Malaysia	65.9	58.7	0.05	3.7	4.3	3.0	5.4	3,384	1,947
Marshall Islands	..	..	..	..	..	..	..	1	1 [e]
Micronesia, Fed. Sts.	34.8	21.7	..	..	..	..	..	..	..
Mongolia	7.2	6.8	0.12	..	..	4.7	3.2	7 [d]	9
Myanmar	60.2	52.3	(.)	..	..	0.1	0.2	16 [h]	39
Nauru	..	..	..	..	..	..	..	..	..
Palau	76.1	76.1	..	..	..	..	12.9	..	1
Papua New Guinea	70.1	67.6	0.02	..	..	0.6	0.5	28 [g]	15
Philippines	22.4	19.4	0.06	6.8	6.8	0.7	1.0	2,981	2,049
Samoa (Western)	46.1	37.2	0.04	..	..	0.8	0.8	4 [g]	2
Singapore	3.3	3.3	0.05	2.7	3.9	13.8	13.7	3,167	22
Solomon Islands	90.3	88.8	..	..	..	0.5	0.4	2	1
Thailand	31.1	28.9	0.14	4.7	5.1	1.7	3.3	6,660	3,375
Timor-Leste	36.6	34.3	..	..	..	..	..	..	..
Tonga	5.5	5.5	0.05	..	..	0.8	1.2	2 [d]	1
Tuvalu	..	..	..	..	..	..	..	(.) [d]	0
Vanuatu	36.2	36.7	..	..	..	0.4	0.4	..	..
Viet Nam	28.6	30.2	0.03	2.7	4.2	0.3	0.6	303 [g]	243

GOAL 7 Ensure environmental sustainability: land and air

Integrate the principles of sustainable development into country policies and programmes and reverse the loss of environmental resources [a]

	Land area covered by forests (%)		Ratio of protected area to surface area [b]	GDP per unit of energy use (PPP US$ per kg of oil equivalent)		Carbon dioxide emissions per capita (metric tons)		Consumption of ozone-depleting chlorofluorocarbons (ODP metric tons) [c]	
	1990	2000	2003	1990	2000	1990	1999	1990	2001
Latin America and the Caribbean									
Antigua and Barbuda	20.5	20.5	0.15	..	..	4.7	5.2	421	3
Argentina	13.7	12.7	0.07	5.3	7.2	3.4	3.8	2,138	3,293
Bahamas	84.1	84.1	0.11	..	..	7.6	6.0	57 [d]	66 [e]
Barbados	4.7	4.7	0.01	..	..	4.2	7.6	21	12
Belize	74.7	59.1	0.44	..	..	1.6	2.7	20 [d]	28
Bolivia	50.4	48.9	0.12	4.1	3.9	0.8	1.4	14 [g]	77
Brazil	67.0	64.3	0.06	5.9	6.7	1.4	1.8	8,539	6,231
Chile	21.0	20.7	0.19	4.5	5.6	2.7	4.2	662	470
Colombia	49.6	47.8	0.08	7.7	10.3	1.6	1.5	2,026	1,165
Costa Rica	41.6	38.5	0.22	9.1	11.7	1.0	1.6	267 [g]	145
Cuba	18.9	21.4	0.15	..	..	3.0	2.3	778	504
Dominica	66.7	61.3	0.23	..	..	0.8	1.1	..	1 [i]
Dominican Republic	28.4	28.4	..	6.5	7.4	1.3	2.8	256 [d]	486
Ecuador	43.1	38.1	0.11	4.9	4.9	1.6	1.9	604	207
El Salvador	9.3	5.8	(.)	6.8	8.1	0.5	0.9	423 [g]	117
Grenada	14.7	14.7	0.02	..	..	1.3	2.2	4 [d]	4 [f]
Guatemala	31.2	26.3	0.19	6.3	7.1	0.6	0.9	357	265
Guyana	80.8	78.5	(.)	..	..	1.5	2.2	19	20
Haiti	5.7	3.2	(.)	8.7	7.5	0.2	0.2	..	169
Honduras	53.4	48.1	0.06	4.7	6.0	0.5	0.8	..	122
Jamaica	35.0	30.0	0.80	2.7	2.4	3.3	4.0	424	49
Mexico	32.2	28.9	0.10	4.0	5.5	3.7	3.9	12,037	2,224
Nicaragua	36.7	27.0	0.15	3.6	4.6 [f]	0.7	0.8	87	35
Panama	45.6	38.6	0.21	6.0	6.5	1.3	2.9	252	180
Paraguay	61.9	58.8	0.03	6.1	7.2	0.5	0.8	171 [d]	116
Peru	53.0	50.9	0.06	6.7	9.5	1.0	1.2	801	189
Saint Kitts and Nevis	11.1	11.1	(.)	..	..	1.6	2.4	6 [d]	3 [i]
Saint Lucia	23.0	14.8	0.09	..	..	1.2	2.1	8 [d]	3
St. Vincent & the Grenadines	17.9	15.4	0.21	..	..	0.8	1.4	2 [d]	7
Suriname	90.5	90.5	0.04	..	..	4.5	5.2	..	..
Trinidad and Tobago	54.8	50.5	0.06	1.2	1.3	13.9	19.4	138	79
Uruguay	4.5	7.4	(.)	8.1	9.4	1.3	2.0	416 [g]	102
Venezuela	58.6	56.1	0.62	2.1	2.3	5.8	5.3	3,343	2,546
South Asia									
Afghanistan	2.1	2.1	(.)	..	..	0.1	(.)	..	..
Bangladesh	9.0	10.2	0.01	8.1	10.8	0.1	0.2	195	805 [e]
Bhutan	64.2	64.2	0.25	..	..	0.2	0.5	..	..
India	21.4	21.6	0.05	3.8	5.5	0.8	1.1	4,358 [d]	5,614 [e]
Iran, Islamic Rep. of	4.5	4.5	0.05	3.0	3.2	3.9	4.8	1,366	4,205
Maldives	3.3	3.3	..	..	..	0.7	1.7	4	14
Nepal	32.7	27.3	0.09	2.6	3.7	(.)	0.1	20 [g]	94 [e]
Pakistan	3.6	3.1	0.05	3.4	4.0	0.6	0.7	751	1,666
Sri Lanka	35.4	30.0	0.13	5.7	7.8	0.2	0.5	209	190
Southern Europe									
Cyprus	12.9	18.6	0.08	5.4	6.3	6.8	8.0	240	138
Turkey	13.0	13.3	0.02	4.6	5.3	2.6	3.1	3,519	731

Integrate the principles of sustainable development into country policies and programmes
and reverse the loss of environmental resources [a]

	Land area covered by forests (%)		Ratio of protected area to surface area [b]	GDP per unit of energy use (PPP US$ per kg of oil equivalent)		Carbon dioxide emissions per capita (metric tons)		Consumption of ozone-depleting chlorofluorocarbons (ODP metric tons) [c]	
	1990	2000	2003	1990	2000	1990	1999	1990	2001
Sub-Saharan Africa									
Angola	56.9	56.0	0.07	3.4	3.6	0.5	0.8	116 [d]	9
Benin	30.3	24.0	0.11	1.9	2.5	0.1	0.2	58	54
Botswana	24.0	21.9	0.18	..	..	1.7	2.4	6 [d]	2 [e]
Burkina Faso	26.5	25.9	0.10	..	..	0.1	0.1	28	20
Burundi	9.4	3.7	0.05	..	..	(.)	(.)	43	46
Cameroon	56.0	51.3	0.04	3.4	3.8	0.1	0.3	78	364
Cape Verde	8.7	21.1	..	..	..	0.2	0.3	..	..
Central African Republic	37.3	36.8	0.09	..	..	0.1	0.1	43 [g]	4 [e]
Chad	10.7	10.1	0.09	..	..	(.)	(.)	26	32
Comoros	6.5	4.3	..	..	..	0.2	0.1	1 [g]	2
Congo	65.1	64.6	0.05	1.7	3.2	0.9	0.8	53 [g]	2
Congo, Dem. Rep. of the	62.0	59.6	0.05	4.6	2.5	0.1	(.)	..	639
Côte d'Ivoire	30.7	22.4	0.06	3.9	3.6	1.0	0.8	258 [g]	148
Equatorial Guinea	66.2	62.5	..	..	..	0.3	1.5	..	..
Eritrea	13.9	13.5	0.04	..	..	..	0.1	..	..
Ethiopia	4.5	4.2	0.17	1.9	2.6	0.1	0.1	33 [d]	39 [e]
Gabon	85.1	84.7	0.03	3.7	4.7	7.1	3.0	10 [g]	6
Gambia	43.6	48.1	0.02	..	..	0.2	0.2	15	6
Ghana	33.1	27.8	0.05	4.3	5.5	0.2	0.3	107	36
Guinea	29.6	28.2	0.01	..	..	0.2	0.2	28	35
Guinea-Bissau	66.5	60.5	..	..	..	0.8	0.2	..	..
Kenya	31.7	30.0	0.08	1.7	1.9	0.2	0.3	230	169
Lesotho	0.5	0.5	(.)	..	..	..	..	6 [d]	2 [e]
Liberia	38.1	31.3	0.02	..	..	0.2	0.1	..	..
Madagascar	22.2	20.2	0.03	..	..	0.1	0.1	..	14 [e]
Malawi	34.7	27.2	0.11	..	..	0.1	0.1	23 [g]	51 [i]
Mali	11.6	10.8	0.04	..	..	(.)	(.)	..	29 [e]
Mauritania	(.)	(.)	0.02	..	..	1.3	1.2	17 [d]	13 [i]
Mauritius	8.4	7.9	0.08	..	..	1.1	2.1	76 [d]	14
Mozambique	39.8	39.0	0.08	1.2	2.5	0.1	0.1	18 [d]	14 [i]
Namibia	10.7	9.8	0.14	10.6 [g]	12.0	..	0.1	21 [d]	24
Niger	1.5	1.0	0.08	..	..	0.1	0.1	16	29
Nigeria	19.2	14.8	0.03	1.0	1.2	0.9	0.3	934	3,666
Rwanda	18.5	12.4	0.06	..	..	0.1	0.1	..	..
São Tomé and Principe	28.3	28.3	..	..	..	0.6	0.6	..	..
Senegal	34.6	32.2	0.11	3.7	4.5	0.4	0.4	97	98
Seychelles	66.7	66.7	1.11	..	..	1.6	2.7	3	1
Sierra Leone	19.8	14.7	0.02	..	..	0.1	0.1	..	..
South Africa	7.4	7.3	0.05	3.7	4.4	8.3	7.9	6,804	16
Swaziland	27.0	30.3	0.03	..	..	0.6	0.4	10 [d]	1
Tanzania, U. Rep. of	45.0	43.9	0.28	0.9	1.1	0.1	0.1	88 [d]	131
Togo	13.2	9.4	0.08	5.5	4.9	0.2	0.3	41	35
Uganda	25.6	21.0	0.21	..	..	(.)	0.1	14	13
Zambia	53.5	42.0	0.31	1.1	1.2	0.3	0.2	35	23 [e]
Zimbabwe	57.5	49.2	0.12	2.5	3.1	1.6	1.4	476 [d]	259
Central & Eastern Europe & CIS									
Albania	39.0	36.2	0.04	3.2	6.7	2.2	0.5	40 [d]	69
Armenia	11.0	12.4	0.07	1.8 [h]	4.5	1.0 [h]	0.8	..	163
Azerbaijan	11.5	13.1	0.06	..	1.9	6.4 [h]	4.2	481 [d]	52
Belarus	33.0	45.3	0.04	1.6 [h]	3.0	9.3 [h]	5.7	1,230	0
Bosnia and Herzegovina	44.6	44.6	0.01	..	5.2	1.1 [h]	1.2	145 [g]	200

Integrate the principles of sustainable development into country policies and programmes
and reverse the loss of environmental resources [a]

	Land area covered by forests (%)		Ratio of protected area to surface area[b]	GDP per unit of energy use (PPP US$ per kg of oil equivalent)		Carbon dioxide emissions per capita (metric tons)		Consumption of ozone-depleting chlorofluorocarbons (ODP metric tons)[c]	
	1990	2000	2003	1990	2000	1990	1999	1990	2001
Bulgaria	31.5	33.4	0.04	1.9	2.8	8.6	5.1	2,034	0
Croatia	31.5	31.9	0.07	4.0 [h]	4.9	3.5 [h]	4.8	464	114
Czech Republic	34.0	34.1	0.16	2.5 [h]	3.6	13.1 [h]	10.6	5,498 [d]	3
Estonia	45.8	48.7	0.11	1.5 [h]	2.9	16.1 [h]	11.7	190 [d]	(.)
Georgia	43.7	43.7	0.03	2.0 [h]	4.5	2.8 [h]	1.0	766 [d]	19
Hungary	19.1	19.9	0.07	3.3	4.9	5.6	5.6	4,390	0
Kazakhstan	3.7	4.5	0.03	1.1 [h]	2.2	15.3 [h]	7.4	1,214	524 [e]
Kyrgyzstan	4.0	5.2	0.04	2.6 [h]	5.4	2.4 [h]	1.0	118 [g]	53
Latvia	45.1	47.1	0.13	2.3 [h]	4.6	4.8 [h]	2.8	4,736 [d]	35 [e]
Lithuania	31.1	31.9	0.10	2.4 [h]	3.9	5.8 [h]	3.8	4,179	0
Macedonia, TFYR	35.6	35.6	0.07	..	..	5.5 [h]	5.6	1,174 [d]	47
Moldova, Rep. of	9.6	9.9	0.01	2.0 [h]	3.1	4.8 [h]	1.5	..	23
Poland	29.1	29.7	0.10	2.2	4.0	9.1	8.1	4,939	179
Romania	27.4	28.0	0.05	1.9	3.4	6.7	3.6	..	186
Russian Federation	50.3	50.4	0.03	1.4 [h]	1.6	13.3 [h]	9.8	98,752	0
Serbia and Montenegro	28.4	28.3	0.03	..	..	12.4	3.7	1,449	549 [i]
Slovakia	41.5	45.3	0.22	2.3	3.6	8.1 [h]	7.2	1,979 [d]	3
Slovenia	53.9	55.0	0.06	4.2 [h]	5.0	6.1 [h]	7.3	343	3
Tajikistan	2.7	2.8	0.04	1.1 [h]	2.3	3.7 [h]	0.8	91 [g]	28
Turkmenistan	8.0	8.0	0.03	1.8 [h]	1.4	6.9 [h]	6.4	141	19 [i]
Ukraine	16.0	16.5	0.04	1.5 [h]	1.4	11.5 [h]	7.5	4,518	1,077
Uzbekistan	4.6	4.8	(.)	..	1.2	5.3 [h]	4.8	2,454 [d]	53 [i]
High-income OECD[j]									
Australia	20.5	20.1	..	3.2	4.3	15.6	18.2	7,416	6
Austria	46.0	47.0	0.29	5.6	7.5	7.4	7.6	.. [k]	.. [k]
Belgium	22.6 [l]	22.2 [l]	0.03	3.7	4.4	10.1	10.2	.. [k]	.. [k]
Canada	26.5	26.5	..	2.5	3.3	15.4	14.4	13,174	(.)
Denmark	10.5	10.7	0.10	5.7	7.9	9.9	9.3	.. [k]	.. [k]
Finland	71.8	72.0	0.08	2.9	3.8	10.6	11.3	.. [k]	.. [k]
France	26.8	27.9	0.13	4.3	5.4	6.3	6.1	.. [k]	.. [k]
Germany	30.7	30.7	0.31	4.0	6.1	11.1 [g]	9.7	.. [k]	.. [k]
Greece	25.6	27.9	0.04	5.2	6.3	7.1	8.2	.. [k]	.. [k]
Iceland	(.)	(.)	0.10	2.5	2.4	7.9	7.4	133	0
Ireland	7.1	9.6	0.01	4.2	7.9	8.5	10.8	.. [k]	.. [k]
Italy	33.0	34.0	0.08	6.6	8.2	7.0	7.3	.. [k]	.. [k]
Japan	63.9	64.0	0.07	5.3	6.1	8.7	9.1	97,723	6
Luxembourg	.. [m]	.. [m]	0.14	2.3	6.4	25.9	18.6	.. [k]	.. [k]
Netherlands	10.8	11.1	0.10	4.1	5.7	10.0	8.5	.. [k]	.. [k]
New Zealand	28.2	29.7	0.37	3.2	3.7	6.9	8.1	558	0
Norway	27.9	28.9	0.06	3.7	5.1	7.5	8.7	722	48
Portugal	33.8	40.1	0.07	6.5	7.2	4.3	6.0	.. [k]	.. [k]
Spain	27.0	28.8	0.08	5.6	6.4	5.5	6.8	.. [k]	.. [k]
Sweden	65.9	65.9	0.08	3.2	4.4	5.7	5.3	.. [k]	.. [k]
Switzerland	29.2	30.3	0.20	6.4	7.5	6.4	5.7	2,920	6 [e]
United Kingdom	10.9	11.6	0.20	4.4	6.0	9.9	9.2	.. [k]	.. [k]
United States	24.3	24.7	0.17	3.0	4.2	19.3	19.7	198,308	2,805

5

Integrate the principles of sustainable development into country policies and programmes
and reverse the loss of environmental resources [a]

	Land area covered by forests (%)		Ratio of protected area to surface area[b]	GDP per unit of energy use (PPP US$ per kg of oil equivalent)		Carbon dioxide emissions per capita (metric tons)		Consumption of ozone-depleting chlorofluorocarbons (ODP metric tons)[c]	
	1990	2000	2003	1990	2000	1990	1999	1990	2001
Other UN member countries									
Andorra	..	..	..	..	..	..	..	..	..
Israel	4.0	6.4	0.15	5.3	6.5	7.4	10.0	4,560 [d]	0
Liechtenstein	40.0	46.7	0.39	..	..	..	..	3	0 [e]
Malta	(.)	(.)	0.01	3.2	6.7	4.6	8.8	179	63
Monaco	..	..	0.26	..	..	..	..	6 [d]	0
San Marino	..	..	..	..	..	..	..	..	..
Developing countries	..	..	..	3.2	4.6	1.6	1.9	..	..
Least developed countries	..	..	..	..	..	0.1	0.2	..	..
Arab States	..	..	..	3.5	3.8	3.2	3.7	..	..
East Asia and the Pacific	..	..	..	..	..	2.0	2.3	..	..
Latin America and the Caribbean	..	..	..	4.9	6.1	2.2	2.5	..	..
South Asia	..	..	..	3.8	5.2	0.8	1.1	..	..
Sub-Saharan Africa	..	..	..	2.5	2.9	1.0	0.8	..	..
Central & Eastern Europe & CIS	..	..	..	..	2.2	..	7.2	..	..
OECD	..	..	..	3.7	4.9	10.5	10.8	..	..
High-income OECD	..	..	..	3.8	4.9	11.9	12.3	..	..
High human development	..	..	..	3.8	4.9	10.5	10.8	..	..
Medium human development	..	..	..	3.0	4.0	1.7	2.3	..	..
Low human development	..	..	..	..	4.0	0.4	0.4	..	..
High income	..	..	..	3.8	4.9	11.9	12.4	..	..
Middle income	..	..	..	3.1	4.0	2.6	3.2	..	..
Low income	..	..	..	2.2	2.5	0.7	1.0	..	..
World	..	..	..	3.5	4.5	3.4	3.8	..	..

a. The World Health Organization is collecting country data for another indicator under this target, the proportion of the population using solid fuels, to be published in *World Health Report 2003* (WHO forthcoming).
b. Refers to the ratio of area protected to maintain biological diversity to surface area. Surface area is a country's total area, including areas under inland bodies of water and some coastal waterways but excluding sea areas. Data for some countries include overseas territories. c. Data refer to chlorofluorocarbons controlled under the Montreal Protocol on Substances That Deplete the Ozone Layer, measured in metric tons multiplied by a factor of ozone-depleting potential (ODP). d. Data refer to 1989. e. Data refer to 2000. f. Data refer to 1998. g. Data refer to 1991. h. Data refer to 1992. i. Data refer to 1999. j. Excluding the Republic of Korea; see East Asia and the Pacific. k. No data are available for individual member countries of the European Union (EU). The member countries are Austria, Belgium, Denmark, Finland, France, Germany, Greece, Ireland, Italy, Luxembourg, the Netherlands, Portugal, Spain, Sweden and the United Kingdom. Estimates for EU member countries as a group are 170,331.4 ODP metric tons in 1990 and 2,317.1 ODP metric tons in 2001. l. Including Luxembourg. m. Included in data for Belgium.
Source: Columns 1 and 2: UN 2003a, based on data from the Food and Agriculture Organization; *column 3:* UNEP World Conservation Monitoring Centre and IUCN World Commission on Protected Areas 2003; *columns 4 and 5:* World Bank 2003c, based on data from a joint effort by the International Energy Agency and the World Bank; aggregates calculated for the Human Development Report Office by the World Bank; *columns 6 and 7:* World Bank 2003c, based on data from a joint effort by the United Nations Framework Convention on Climate Change and the Carbon Dioxide Information Analysis Center; aggregates calculated for the Human Development Report Office by the World Bank; *columns 8 and 9:* UN 2003a, based on data from the United Nations Environment Programme's Ozone Secretariat.

GOAL 7 **Ensure environmental sustainability: water and sanitation**

	Halve, by 2015, the proportion of people without sustainable access to safe drinking water				Have achieved, by 2020, a significant improvement in the lives of at least 100 million slum dwellers [a]	
	Population with sustainable access to an improved water source				Urban population with access to improved sanitation	
	Rural (%)		Urban (%)		(%)	
	1990	2000	1990	2000	1990	2000
Arab States						
Algeria	..	82	..	94	..	99
Bahrain	..	..	..	..	..	..
Djibouti	..	100	..	100	..	99
Egypt	92	96	97	99	96	100
Iraq	..	48	..	96	..	93
Jordan	92	84	99	100	100	100
Kuwait	..	..	..	..	..	..
Lebanon	..	100	..	100	..	100
Libyan Arab Jamahiriya	68	68	72	72	97	97
Morocco	58	56	94	98	88	86
Occupied Palestinian Territories	..	86	..	97	..	100
Oman	30	30	41	41	98	98
Qatar	..	..	..	..	..	..
Saudi Arabia	..	64	..	100	..	100
Somalia	..	..	..	..	..	..
Sudan	60	69	86	86	87	87
Syrian Arab Republic	..	64	..	94	..	98
Tunisia	54	58	91	92	96	96
United Arab Emirates	..	..	..	..	..	..
Yemen	..	68	..	74	69	89
East Asia and the Pacific						
Brunei Darussalam	..	..	..	..	..	..
Cambodia	..	26	..	54	..	56
China	60	66	99	94	56	69
Hong Kong, China (SAR)	..	..	..	..	..	..
Fiji	..	51	..	43	..	75
Indonesia	62	69	92	90	66	69
Kiribati	..	25	..	82	..	54
Korea, Dem. Rep. of	..	100	..	100	..	99
Korea, Rep. of	..	71	..	97	..	76
Lao People's Dem. Rep.	..	29	..	61	..	67
Malaysia	..	94	..	..	..	..
Marshall Islands	..	..	..	..	..	..
Micronesia, Fed. Sts.	..	..	..	..	..	..
Mongolia	..	30	..	77	..	46
Myanmar	..	66	..	89	..	84
Nauru	..	..	..	..	..	..
Palau	..	20	..	100	..	100
Papua New Guinea	32	32	88	88	92	92
Philippines	82	79	93	91	85	93
Samoa (Western)	..	100	..	95	..	95
Singapore	..	..	100	100	100	100
Solomon Islands	..	65	..	94	..	98
Thailand	78	81	87	95	95	96
Timor-Leste	..	..	..	..	..	..
Tonga	..	100	..	100	..	..
Tuvalu	..	..	..	..	..	..
Vanuatu	..	94	..	63	..	100
Viet Nam	48	72	86	95	52	82

	Halve, by 2015, the proportion of people without sustainable access to safe drinking water				*Have achieved, by 2020, a significant improvement in the lives of at least 100 million slum dwellers* [a]	
	Population with sustainable access to an improved water source				**Urban population with access to improved sanitation**	
	Rural (%)		**Urban** (%)		(%)	
	1990	2000	1990	2000	1990	2000
Latin America and the Caribbean						
Antigua and Barbuda	..	89	..	95	..	98
Argentina	73	..	97	..	87	..
Bahamas	..	86	..	98	..	100
Barbados	..	100	..	100	..	100
Belize	..	82	..	100	..	71
Bolivia	47	64	91	95	73	86
Brazil	54	53	93	95	82	84
Chile	49	58	98	99	98	96
Colombia	84	70	98	99	96	96
Costa Rica	..	92	..	99	..	89
Cuba	..	77	..	95	..	99
Dominica	..	90	..	100	..	86
Dominican Republic	71	78	92	90	70	70
Ecuador	58	75	82	90	88	92
El Salvador	48	64	88	91	87	89
Grenada	..	93	..	97	..	96
Guatemala	69	88	88	98	82	83
Guyana	..	91	..	98	..	97
Haiti	50	45	59	49	33	50
Honduras	78	81	89	95	88	93
Jamaica	87	85	98	98	99	99
Mexico	52	69	90	95	87	88
Nicaragua	44	59	93	91	97	95
Panama	..	79	..	99	..	99
Paraguay	46	59	80	93	96	94
Peru	42	62	88	87	77	79
Saint Kitts and Nevis	..	..	..	..	..	..
Saint Lucia	..	..	..	..	..	..
St. Vincent & the Grenadines	..	..	..	..	..	..
Suriname	..	50	..	93	..	99
Trinidad and Tobago	..	..	..	..	..	..
Uruguay	..	93	..	98	..	95
Venezuela	..	70	..	85	..	71
South Asia						
Afghanistan	..	11	..	19	..	25
Bangladesh	93	97	99	99	81	71
Bhutan	..	60	..	86	..	65
India	61	79	88	95	44	61
Iran, Islamic Rep. of	..	83	..	98	..	86
Maldives	..	100	..	100	..	100
Nepal	64	87	93	94	69	73
Pakistan	77	87	96	95	77	95
Sri Lanka	62	70	91	98	94	97
Southern Europe						
Cyprus	100	100	100	100	100	100
Turkey	72	86	83	81	97	97

	Halve, by 2015, the proportion of people without sustainable access to safe drinking water				Have achieved, by 2020, a significant improvement in the lives of at least 100 million slum dwellers [a]	
	Population with sustainable access to an improved water source				Urban population with access to improved sanitation	
	Rural (%)		Urban (%)		(%)	
	1990	2000	1990	2000	1990	2000
Sub-Saharan Africa						
Angola	..	40	..	34	..	70
Benin	..	55	..	74	46	46
Botswana	88	90	100	100	87	88
Burkina Faso	..	37	..	66	..	39
Burundi	67	77	96	91	65	68
Cameroon	32	39	78	78	97	92
Cape Verde	..	89	..	64	..	95
Central African Republic	35	57	71	89	38	38
Chad	..	26	..	31	70	81
Comoros	84	95	97	98	98	98
Congo	..	17	..	71	..	14
Congo, Dem. Rep. of the	..	26	..	89	..	54
Côte d'Ivoire	69	72	97	92	70	71
Equatorial Guinea	..	42	..	45	..	60
Eritrea	..	42	..	63	..	66
Ethiopia	17	12	80	81	24	33
Gabon	..	47	..	95	..	55
Gambia	..	53	..	80	..	41
Ghana	36	62	85	91	56	74
Guinea	36	36	72	72	94	94
Guinea-Bissau	..	49	..	79	87	95
Kenya	31	42	91	88	91	96
Lesotho	..	74	..	88	..	72
Liberia	..	..	..	..	..	..
Madagascar	31	31	85	85	70	70
Malawi	43	44	90	95	96	96
Mali	52	61	65	74	95	93
Mauritania	40	40	34	34	44	44
Mauritius	100	100	100	100	100	100
Mozambique	..	41	..	81	..	68
Namibia	63	67	98	100	84	96
Niger	51	56	65	70	71	79
Nigeria	37	49	83	78	69	66
Rwanda	..	40	..	60	..	12
São Tomé and Principe	..	..	..	..	..	..
Senegal	60	65	90	92	86	94
Seychelles	..	..	..	..	..	..
Sierra Leone	..	46	..	75	..	88
South Africa	73	73	99	99	93	93
Swaziland	..	..	..	..	..	..
Tanzania, U. Rep. of	28	57	76	90	84	99
Togo	38	38	82	85	71	69
Uganda	40	47	81	80	..	93
Zambia	28	48	88	88	86	99
Zimbabwe	69	73	99	100	70	71
Central & Eastern Europe & CIS						
Albania	..	95	..	99	..	99
Armenia	..	..	..	..	..	..
Azerbaijan	..	58	..	93	..	90
Belarus	..	100	..	100	..	..
Bosnia and Herzegovina	..	..	..	..	..	..

GOAL 7 Ensure environmental sustainability: water and sanitation

6 MDG

	Halve, by 2015, the proportion of people without sustainable access to safe drinking water				*Have achieved, by 2020, a significant improvement in the lives of at least 100 million slum dwellers* [a]	
	Population with sustainable access to an improved water source				**Urban population with access to improved sanitation**	
	Rural (%)		**Urban** (%)		(%)	
	1990	2000	1990	2000	1990	2000
Bulgaria	..	100	..	100	..	100
Croatia	..	..	..	..	..	..
Czech Republic	..	..	..	..	..	..
Estonia	..	..	..	..	..	93
Georgia	..	61	..	90	..	100
Hungary	98	98	100	100	100	100
Kazakhstan	..	82	..	98	..	100
Kyrgyzstan	..	66	..	98	..	100
Latvia	..	..	..	..	..	..
Lithuania	..	..	..	..	..	..
Macedonia, TFYR	..	..	..	..	..	..
Moldova, Rep. of	..	88	..	97	..	100
Poland	..	..	..	..	..	..
Romania	..	16	..	91	..	86
Russian Federation	..	96	..	100	..	..
Serbia and Montenegro	..	97	..	99	..	100
Slovakia	..	100	..	100	..	100
Slovenia	100	100	100	100	100	..
Tajikistan	..	47	..	93	..	97
Turkmenistan	..	..	..	..	..	..
Ukraine	..	94	..	100	..	100
Uzbekistan	..	79	..	94	..	97
High-income OECD [b]						
Australia	100	100	100	100	100	100
Austria	100	100	100	100	100	100
Belgium	..	..	..	..	..	..
Canada	99	99	100	100	100	100
Denmark	..	100	..	100	..	..
Finland	100	100	100	100	100	100
France	..	..	..	..	..	..
Germany	..	..	..	..	..	..
Greece	..	..	..	..	..	..
Iceland	..	..	..	..	..	..
Ireland	..	..	..	..	..	..
Italy	..	..	..	..	..	..
Japan	..	..	..	..	..	..
Luxembourg	..	..	..	..	..	..
Netherlands	100	100	100	100	100	100
New Zealand	..	..	100	100	..	..
Norway	100	100	100	100	100	..
Portugal	..	..	..	..	..	..
Spain	..	..	..	..	..	..
Sweden	100	100	100	100	100	100
Switzerland	100	100	100	100	100	100
United Kingdom	100	100	100	100	100	100
United States	100	100	100	100	100	100

GOAL 7 **Ensure environmental sustainability: water and sanitation**

	Halve, by 2015, the proportion of people without sustainable access to safe drinking water				Have achieved, by 2020, a significant improvement in the lives of at least 100 million slum dwellers [a]	
	Population with sustainable access to an improved water source				**Urban population with access to improved sanitation**	
	Rural (%)		Urban (%)		(%)	
	1990	2000	1990	2000	1990	2000
Other UN member countries						
Andorra	..	100	..	100	..	100
Israel	..	..	..	..	..	..
Liechtenstein	..	..	..	..	..	..
Malta	100	100	100	100	100	100
Monaco	..	100	..	100	..	100
San Marino	..	..	..	..	..	..
Developing countries	..	69	..	92	..	77
Least developed countries	..	55	..	82	..	71
Arab States	..	76	..	94	..	96
East Asia and the Pacific	..	67	..	93	..	73
Latin America and the Caribbean	..	65	..	94	..	86
South Asia	66	81	90	95	52	68
Sub-Saharan Africa	39	44	86	83	75	74
Central & Eastern Europe & CIS	..	82	..	99	..	..
OECD	..	..	..	..	..	..
High-income OECD	..	..	..	..	..	..
High human development	..	..	..	..	..	..
Medium human development	..	73	..	94	..	77
Low human development	47	53	86	83	72	77
High income	..	..	..	..	..	..
Middle income	..	70	..	95	..	82
Low income	..	69	..	90	58	72
World	..	71 [c]	..	95 [c]	..	85 [c]

a. The United Nations Human Settlements Programme (HABITAT) has prepared country estimates of slum dwellers for this target using several indicators: the proportion of the urban population with sustainable access to an improved water source, the proportion of the urban population with access to improved sanitation, an indicator of overcrowding and an indicator of the durability of housing. Estimates for another indicator to be used in this exercise, the proportion of households with access to secure tenure, will become available soon. b. Excluding the Republic of Korea; see East Asia and the Pacific. c. Data refer to the world aggregate according to UNICEF 2003b.
Source: Columns 1-6: UN 2003a, based on data from a joint effort by the United Nations Children's Fund and the World Health Organization.

GOAL 8 **Develop a global partnership for development: development assistance and market access**

Develop further an open, rule-based, predictable, non-discriminatory trading and financial system

| | Net official development assistance (ODA) disbursed | | | | | | | |
| | As % of GNI | | To least developed countries (as % of donor's GNI)[a] | | ODA to basic social services (as % of total)[b] | | Untied bilateral ODA (as % of total) | |
	1990[c]	2001	1990	2001	1996/97	2000/01	1990	2001
Australia	0.34	0.25	0.06	0.05	8	19	33	59
Austria	0.25	0.29	0.07	0.05	5	21	32	..
Belgium	0.46	0.37	0.19	0.12	11	15	..	90
Canada	0.44	0.22	0.13	0.03	6	19	47	32
Denmark	0.94	1.03	0.37	0.33	10	9	0	93
Finland	0.65	0.32	0.24	0.09	6	12	31	87
France	0.60	0.32	0.19	0.08	..	..	64	67
Germany	0.42	0.27	0.12	0.06	10	10	62	85
Greece	..	0.17	..	0.02	17	5	..	17
Ireland	0.16	0.33	0.06	0.17	(.)	21	..	100
Italy	0.31	0.15	0.13	0.04	7	6	22	8
Japan	0.31	0.23	0.06	0.04	3	7	89	81
Luxembourg	0.21	0.82	0.08	0.26	..	21	..	..
Netherlands	0.92	0.82	0.30	0.25	12	22	56	91
New Zealand	0.23	0.25	0.04	0.07	..	8	100	..
Norway	1.17	0.83	0.52	0.28	13	9	61	99
Portugal	0.24	0.25	0.17	0.11	6	3	..	58
Spain	0.20	0.30	0.04	0.03	14	12	..	69
Sweden	0.91	0.81	0.35	0.22	11	14	87	86
Switzerland	0.32	0.34	0.14	0.10	9	11	78	96
United Kingdom	0.27	0.32	0.09	0.11	24	27	..	94
United States	0.21	0.11	0.04	0.02	23	22	..	..
DAC	0.33	0.22	0.09	0.05	9	15	68	79

Note: This table presents data for members of the Development Assistance Committee (DAC) of the Organisation for Economic Co-operation and Development (OECD).
a. Includes imputed multilateral flows that make allowance for contributions through multilateral organizations. These are calculated using the geographic distribution of disbursements for the year specified. b. Data refer to the average for the years specified. c. Data for individual countries (but not the DAC average) include forgiveness of non-ODA claims.
Source: Columns 1-8: UN 2003a, based on data from the OECD; aggregates calculated by the OECD.

| | OECD country support to domestic agriculture (as % of GDP) | |
	1990	2001
Australia	0.8	0.3
Canada	1.7	0.7
Czech Republic	..	1.2
European Union[a]	2.1	1.4
Hungary	..	1.4
Iceland	4.6	1.6
Japan	1.7	1.4
Korea, Rep. of	9.4	4.7
Mexico	2.9	1.3
New Zealand	0.5	0.3
Norway	3.2	1.4
Poland	..	1.0
Slovak Republic	..	0.9
Switzerland	3.1	1.9
Turkey	4.2	4.3
United States	1.2	0.9
OECD	1.9	1.3

| | Imports by developed countries admitted free of duties (%)[a] | | Average tariffs imposed by developed countries on imports from developing countries (%) | | ODA provided to help build trade capacity (%) | |
	1996	2000	1996	2000	1990	2001
From developing countries	49	65	–	–	–	–
From least developed countries	77	66	–	–	–	–
On textiles	–	–	7	6	–	–
On clothing	–	–	11	10	–	–
By all donors	–	–	–	–	..	2

a. Imports are measured by value and exclude arms.
Source: Columns 1-4: UN 2003a, based on data from the World Trade Organization (WTO); *columns 5 and 6:* UN 2003a, based on data from a joint effort by the OECD and the WTO.

a. No data are available for individual member countries of the European Union. The member countries are Austria, Belgium, Denmark, Finland, France, Germany, Greece, Ireland, Italy, Luxembourg, the Netherlands, Portugal, Spain, Sweden and the United Kingdom. Austria, Finland and Sweden joined in 1995 and thus are not included in the data for 1990.
Source: UN 2003a, based on data from the OECD; aggregates calculated by the OECD.

Address the special needs of landlocked countries and small island developing states

	Official development assistance received by landlocked countries (as % of GNI)			Official development assistance or official aid received by small island developing states (as % of GNI)	
	1990	2001		1990	2001
Armenia	..	9.7	Antigua and Barbuda	1.3	1.3
Azerbaijan	..	4.3	Aruba	3.5	..
Bhutan	16.5	10.8	Bahamas	0.1	..
Bolivia	11.8	9.4	Bahrain	3.9	0.2
Botswana	4.0	0.6	Barbados	0.2	0.0
Burkina Faso	12.0	15.7	Belize	7.7	2.9
Burundi	23.6	19.3	Cape Verde	31.7	13.1
Central African Republic	17.1	7.9	Comoros	17.3	12.4
Chad	18.2	11.2	Cook Islands	..	..
Ethiopia	15.0	17.5	Cuba	..	..
Kazakhstan	..	0.7	Cyprus	0.7	0.5
Kyrgyzstan	..	12.9	Dominica	12.2	8.5
Lao People's Dem. Rep.	17.3	14.5	Dominican Republic	1.5	0.5
Lesotho	13.8	5.5	Fiji	3.7	1.5
Macedonia, TFYR	..	7.3	Grenada	6.6	3.1
Malawi	27.4	23.4	Guinea-Bissau	55.1	32.0
Mali	20.0	13.9	Guyana	61.4	16.0
Mongolia	..	20.6	Haiti	5.9	4.4
Nepal	11.5	6.7	Jamaica	6.5	0.7
Niger	16.4	12.8	Kiribati	36.0	17.6
Paraguay	1.1	0.9	Maldives	10.9	4.5
Rwanda	11.3	17.3	Malta	0.1	0.0
Swaziland	5.7	2.3	Marshall Islands	..	63.7
Tajikistan	..	15.5	Mauritius	3.8	0.5
Turkmenistan	..	1.2	Micronesia, Fed. Sts.	..	51.6
Uganda	15.8	14.1	Nauru	..	..
Uzbekistan	..	1.4	Netherlands Antilles	..	..
Zambia	16.0	10.7	Niue	..	..
Zimbabwe	4.0	1.8	Palau	..	25.0
			Papua New Guinea	13.3	7.2
All landlocked countries	**6.0**	**6.4**	Saint Kitts and Nevis	5.3	3.4
			Saint Lucia	3.4	2.6
			St. Vincent & the Grenadines	8.2	2.6
			Samoa (Western)	29.0	17.0
			São Tomé and Principe	104.2	90.5
			Seychelles	10.1	2.4
			Singapore	0.0	0.0
			Solomon Islands	22.1	22.2
			Suriname	19.9	3.4
			Tokelau	..	..
			Tonga	25.4	14.4
			Trinidad and Tobago	0.4	0.0
			Tuvalu	..	..
			Vanuatu	30.6	15.2
			All small island developing states	**2.6**	**0.9**
			Least developed	15.3	8.8
			High income	0.1	0.1
			Middle income	4.8	1.5

Source: Columns 1 and 2: UN 2003a, based on data from the Organisation for Economic Co-operation and Development (OECD); aggregates calculated by the OECD.

Source: Columns 1 and 2: UN 2003a, based on data from the OECD; aggregates calculated by the OECD.

Deal comprehensively with the debt problems of developing countries through national and international measures

	Total debt service (as % of exports of goods and services)		Debt relief committed under HIPC initiative [a]
	1990	2001	
Arab States			
Algeria	63.7	19.5	..
Djibouti	4.4 [b]	5.4 [c]	..
Egypt	25.7	8.8	..
Iraq	..	..	..
Jordan	22.1	14.7	..
Lebanon	3.2	40.5	..
Libyan Arab Jamahiriya	..	..	..
Morocco	27.9	21.9	..
Occupied Palestinian Territories	..	..	..
Oman	12.0	6.8	..
Saudi Arabia	..	..	..
Somalia	14.6	..	.. [d, e]
Sudan	4.8	3.2	.. [d, e]
Syrian Arab Republic	20.3	2.1	..
Tunisia	25.6	13.4	..
Yemen	7.1	6.3	.. [d, e]
East Asia and the Pacific			
Cambodia	3.8 [b]	1.1	..
China	10.6	4.2	..
Fiji	9.0	1.5	..
Indonesia	25.6	13.8	..
Kiribati	..	..	..
Korea, Dem. Rep. of	..	..	..
Lao People's Dem. Rep.	8.5	9.0	.. [d, e]
Malaysia	10.6	3.6	..
Marshall Islands	..	..	..
Micronesia, Fed. Sts.	..	..	..
Mongolia	0.3	7.9	..
Myanmar	8.8	2.8	.. [d, e]
Nauru	..	..	..
Palau	..	..	..
Papua New Guinea	18.4	7.1	..
Philippines	25.6	13.3	..
Samoa (Western)	10.6	7.1 [c]	..
Solomon Islands	11.3	2.7 [c]	..
Thailand	11.4	7.9	..
Timor-Leste	..	..	..
Tonga	3.5	7.9	..
Tuvalu	..	..	..
Vanuatu	1.6	1.1	..
Viet Nam	..	6.5	.. [d, e]
Latin America and the Caribbean			
Antigua and Barbuda	..	..	..
Argentina	34.7	48.6	..
Barbados	14.6	4.3 [c]	..
Belize	7.0	24.5	..
Bolivia	33.5 [f]	16.1 [f]	2,060 [d, g]
Brazil	18.5	28.6	..
Chile	18.1	5.2	..
Colombia	34.5	28.1	..
Costa Rica	22.0	8.2	..
Cuba	..	..	..
Dominica	6.0	11.9	..
Dominican Republic	10.7	6.6	..
Ecuador	31.0	22.0	..
El Salvador	18.2	7.4	..
Grenada	3.1	5.4 [c]	..
Guatemala	11.6	8.5	..
Guyana	20.6 [b]	8.0	1,030 [d, h]
Haiti	7.1 [i]	4.5	..
Honduras	33.0 [f]	5.7 [f]	900 [d, h]
Jamaica	27.0	16.8	..
Mexico	18.3	14.1	..
Nicaragua	2.3 [f]	22.2 [f]	4,500 [d, h]
Panama	4.1	11.2	..
Paraguay	11.5	8.3	..
Peru	7.3	20.8	..
Saint Kitts and Nevis	3.4	13.5	..
Saint Lucia	2.1	6.9	..
St. Vincent & the Grenadines	3.1	6.9	..
Suriname	..	..	..
Trinidad and Tobago	15.6	3.8	..
Uruguay	35.2	30.3	..
Venezuela	19.6	20.9	..
South Asia			
Afghanistan	..	..	..
Bangladesh	37.5	9.0	..
Bhutan	5.3	3.3	..
India	29.2	12.6	..
Iran, Islamic Rep. of	1.3	4.1	..
Maldives	4.0	4.3	..
Nepal	14.7	6.2	..
Pakistan	25.1	21.3	..
Sri Lanka	14.8	9.2	..
Southern Europe			
Turkey	29.9	24.6	..
Sub-Saharan Africa			
Angola	7.1	26.0	.. [d, e]
Benin	9.2 [f]	10.0 [f]	460 [d, g]
Botswana	4.4	1.7	..
Burkina Faso	7.8 [f, j]	11.0 [f, j]	930 [d, g]
Burundi	41.7	36.3	.. [d, e]
Cameroon	14.7 [f]	9.9 [f]	2,000 [d, h]
Cape Verde	8.9	7.0	..
Central African Republic	12.5	11.5	.. [d, e]
Chad	3.8 [f]	10.0 [f]	260 [d, h]
Comoros	2.4	5.6	.. [d, e]
Congo	32.2	3.3	.. [d, e]
Congo, Dem. Rep. of the	12.7	(.)	.. [d, e]
Côte d'Ivoire	19.1	8.1	800 [d, e]
Equatorial Guinea	11.5	0.1	..
Eritrea	0.0 [b]	4.5	..
Ethiopia	33.7 [f]	20.6 [f]	1,930 [d, h]
Gabon	4.8	13.6	..
Gambia	21.8 [f]	13.8 [f]	90 [d, h]

GOAL 8 **Develop a global partnership for development: debt sustainability**

Deal comprehensively with the debt problems of developing countries through national and international measures

	Total debt service (as % of exports of goods and services)		Debt relief committed under HIPC initiative [a]		Total debt service (as % of exports of goods and services)		Debt relief committed under HIPC initiative [a]
	1990	2001			1990	2001	
Ghana	34.9 [f]	8.9 [f]	3,700 [d, h]	Macedonia, TFYR	..	10.3	..
Guinea	19.6 [f]	9.2 [f]	800 [d, h]	Moldova, Rep. of	..	15.3	..
Guinea-Bissau	22.1 [f]	0.7 [f]	790 [d, h]	Poland	4.4	11.5	..
Kenya	28.6	11.4	.. [d, e]	Romania	0.0	13.7	..
Lesotho	4.2	12.4	..	Russian Federation	..	12.0	..
Liberia	..	0.6	.. [d, e]	Serbia and Montenegro	..	2.0	..
Madagascar	44.4 [f]	3.4 [f]	1,500 [d, h]	Slovakia	..	6.2	..
Malawi	28.0 [f]	15.5 [f]	1,000 [d, h]	Tajikistan	0.0 [b]	6.3	..
Mali	14.7 [f]	4.5 [f]	895 [d, g]	Turkmenistan	0.0 [i]	..	..
Mauritania	28.8 [f, j]	16.5 [f, j]	1,100 [d, g]	Ukraine	..	6.5	..
Mauritius	7.3	4.7	..	Uzbekistan	..	20.6	..
Mozambique	17.3 [f]	2.7 [f]	4,300 [d, g]	**Other UN member countries**			
Namibia	..	..	..	Malta	0.4	2.6	..
Niger	6.6 [f]	6.6 [f]	900 [d, h]				
Nigeria	22.3	11.5	..	Developing countries	15.3	11.0	..
Rwanda	10.6 [f]	7.6 [f]	800 [d, h]	Least developed countries	16.1	9.5	..
São Tomé and Principe	28.7	21.3	200 [d, h]	Arab States	13.8	8.6	..
Senegal	18.3 [f]	9.3 [f]	850 [d, h]	East Asia and the Pacific	12.0	6.4	..
Seychelles	7.8	2.1	..	Latin America and the Caribbean	20.4	19.7	..
Sierra Leone	10.1 [f]	74.3 [f]	950 [d, h]	South Asia	17.9	11.0	..
South Africa	0.0	6.8	..	Sub-Saharan Africa	11.3	9.0	..
Swaziland	5.6	2.5	..	Central & Eastern Europe & CIS	13.7	9.5	..
Tanzania, U. Rep. of	31.3 [f, k]	7.3 [f, k]	3,000 [d, g]	OECD	..	..	..
Togo	11.5	5.9	.. [d, e]	High-income OECD	..	..	..
Uganda	56.9 [f]	9.7 [f]	1,950 [d, g]	High human development	..	..	..
Zambia	14.6 [f]	13.4 [f]	3,850 [d, h]	Medium human development	15.3	10.2	..
Zimbabwe	19.4	3.4	..	Low human development	19.7	12.9	..
Central & Eastern Europe & CIS				High income	..	..	..
Albania	0.9	3.1	..	Middle income	15.0	11.1	..
Armenia	..	8.1	..	Low income	23.4	11.4	..
Azerbaijan	..	4.7	..	World	..	..	..
Belarus	..	2.7	..				
Bosnia and Herzegovina	..	18.3	..				
Bulgaria	18.6	15.5	..				
Croatia	..	13.7	..				
Czech Republic	..	4.4	..				
Estonia	(.) [b]	0.9	..				
Georgia	..	8.1	..				
Hungary	33.4	8.5	..				
Kazakhstan	..	4.7	..				
Kyrgyzstan	..	12.0	..				
Latvia	(.) [b]	2.9	..				
Lithuania	..	5.9	..				

Note: The table excludes high-income countries (as defined by the World Bank; see classification of countries) because the debt indicators it presents are not produced for these countries.

a. Data are as of March 2003. The Debt Initiative for Heavily Indebted Poor Countries (HIPCs) is a mechanism for debt relief, jointly overseen by the International Monetary Fund (IMF) and the World Bank. Bilateral and multilateral creditors have provided debt relief through this framework to heavily indebted poor countries since 1996. By March 2003, 26 countries had reached their decision points, and of these, 8 had also reached their completion points (see the definitions of statistical terms). b. Data refer to 1992. c. Data refer to 2000. d. Country included in the HIPC initiative. e. Decision and completion points not yet reached under the HIPC initiative. f. Data are from debt sustainability analyses undertaken as part of the HIPC initiative. Present value estimates for these countries are for public and publicly guaranteed debt only, and export figures exclude workers' remittances. g. Completion point reached under the HIPC initiative. h. Decision point reached under the HIPC initiative. i. Data refer to 1991. j. Estimates reflecting assistance under the enhanced HIPC initiative will be presented in World Bank forthcoming. k. Data refer to mainland Tanzania only.

Source: Columns 1 and 2: World Bank 2003c, based on data from a joint effort by the IMF and the World Bank; aggregates calculated for the Human Development Report Office by the World Bank; *column 3:* World Bank 2003b.

GOAL 8 **Develop a global partnership for development: work opportunities, access to drugs and access to new technologies**

	Develop and implement strategies for decent and productive work for youth						*Provide access to affordable essential drugs in developing countries*	*Make available the benefits of new technologies, especially information and communications*					
	Youth unemployment (% of labour force aged 15-24) [a]						**Population with sustainable access to affordable essential drugs** (%) [b]	**Telephone mainlines and cellular subscribers** (per 100 people)		**Internet users** (per 100 people)		**Personal computers in use** (per 100 people)	
	Total		**Female**		**Male**								
	1990	2001	1990	2001	1990	2001	1999	1990	2001	1990	2001	1990	2001
Arab States													
Algeria	39	..	14	..	46	..	95-100	3.2	6.4	..	0.6	0.1	0.7
Bahrain	..	..	..	..	..	..	95-100	20.2	72.8	..	20.3	..	15.4
Djibouti	..	..	..	..	..	..	80-94	1.1	2.0	..	0.5	0.2	1.1
Egypt	..	20 [c]	..	37 [c]	..	14 [c]	80-94	3.0	14.7	..	0.9	..	1.5
Iraq	..	..	..	..	..	..	80-94	3.9	2.9	..	..	..	..
Jordan	..	..	..	..	..	..	95-100	7.2	29.6	..	4.5	..	3.3
Kuwait	..	..	..	..	..	..	95-100	20.0	59.4	..	8.8	0.5	12.0
Lebanon	..	..	..	..	..	..	80-94	15.5	41.6	..	7.8	..	7.5
Libyan Arab Jamahiriya	..	..	..	..	..	..	95-100	4.8	11.8	..	0.4	..	..
Morocco	31	15 [c]	32	15 [c]	31	16 [c]	50-79	1.6	20.4	..	1.4	..	1.4
Occupied Palestinian Territories	..	..	..	..	..	..	..	4.1 [d]	17.9	..	1.8	..	..
Oman	..	..	..	..	..	..	80-94	6.1	21.3	..	4.6	0.2	3.2
Qatar	..	..	..	..	..	..	95-100	19.8	56.8	..	6.6	..	16.4
Saudi Arabia	..	..	..	..	..	..	95-100	7.8	25.8	..	1.3	2.4	6.3
Somalia	..	..	..	..	..	..	0-49	0.2	0.4 [c]	..	(.)	..	..
Sudan	..	..	..	..	..	..	0-49	0.3	1.8	..	0.2	..	0.4
Syrian Arab Republic	..	..	..	..	..	..	80-94	4.1	11.5	0.0	0.4	..	1.6
Tunisia	..	..	..	..	..	..	50-79	3.8	14.9	..	4.1	0.3	2.6
United Arab Emirates	..	..	..	..	..	..	95-100	22.4	95.6	..	31.5	2.9 [d]	13.5
Yemen	..	..	..	..	..	..	50-79	1.1	3.0	..	0.1	..	0.2
East Asia and the Pacific													
Brunei Darussalam	..	..	..	..	..	..	95-100	14.3	65.9	..	10.2	1.1 [d]	7.3
Cambodia	..	..	..	..	..	..	0-49	(.)	1.9	..	0.1	..	0.1
China	3	3 [e]	1	..	1	..	80-94	0.6	24.8	..	2.6	(.)	1.9
Hong Kong, China (SAR)	3	11	3	9	4	14	..	47.5	143.9	0.1 [f]	38.7	4.7	38.7
Fiji	..	..	..	..	..	..	95-100	5.8	21.1	..	1.8	..	4.6
Indonesia	9 [g]	..	9 [g]	..	9 [g]	..	80-94	0.6	6.6	..	1.9	0.1	1.1
Kiribati	..	..	..	..	..	..	50-79	1.7	4.8	..	2.3	..	1.0
Korea, Dem. Rep. of	..	..	..	..	..	..	..	2.5	2.1	..	0.0	..	..
Korea, Rep. of	7	10	6	8	10	12	95-100	30.8	110.6	(.)	52.1	3.7	48.1
Lao People's Dem. Rep.	..	..	..	..	..	..	50-79	0.2	1.5	..	0.2	..	0.3
Malaysia	..	..	..	..	..	..	50-79	9.4	51.2	(.) [d]	27.3	0.8	12.6
Marshall Islands	..	..	..	..	..	..	80-94	1.1	8.6	0.0	1.6	(.)	4.6
Micronesia, Fed. Sts.	..	..	..	..	..	..	95-100	2.5	8.7	..	4.3	..	..
Mongolia	..	..	..	..	..	..	50-79	3.2	13.3	..	1.7	..	1.5
Myanmar	..	..	..	..	..	..	50-79	0.2	0.6	..	(.)	..	0.1
Nauru	..	..	..	..	..	..	95-100	13.3 [f]	29.0	..	..	..	..
Palau	..	..	..	..	..	..	95-100	..	..	..	..	..	..
Papua New Guinea	..	..	..	..	..	..	80-94	0.8	1.4	..	0.9	..	5.7
Philippines	15	19	19	23	13	17	50-79	1.0	19.2	..	2.6	0.3	2.2
Samoa (Western)	..	..	..	..	..	..	95-100	2.6	7.2	..	1.7	..	0.6
Singapore	4 [g]	5 [e]	4 [g]	6 [e]	4 [g]	4 [e]	95-100	36.3	119.6	0.2 [f]	41.2	6.6	50.8
Solomon Islands	..	..	..	..	..	..	80-94	1.5	1.9	..	0.5	..	3.9
Thailand	4	7 [e]	4	6 [e]	4	7 [e]	95-100	2.5	22.2	0.0	5.8	0.4	2.8
Timor-Leste	..	..	..	..	..	..		..	..	..	..	..	..
Tonga	..	..	..	..	..	..	95-100	4.6	11.2	..	2.8	..	1.4
Tuvalu	..	..	..	..	..	..	80-94	1.3	6.5	..	10.0	..	..
Vanuatu	..	..	..	..	..	..		1.8	3.5	..	2.7	..	0.1
Viet Nam	..	..	..	..	..	..	80-94	0.1	5.3	..	1.2	(.) [d]	0.9

GOAL 8 **Develop a global partnership for development: work opportunities, access to drugs and access to new technologies**

	Develop and implement strategies for decent and productive work for youth						*Provide access to affordable essential drugs in developing countries*	*Make available the benefits of new technologies, especially information and communications*					
	Youth unemployment (% of labour force aged 15-24)[a]						**Population with sustainable access to affordable essential drugs** (%)[b]	**Telephone mainlines and cellular subscribers** (per 100 people)		**Internet users** (per 100 people)		**Personal computers in use** (per 100 people)	
	Total		**Female**		**Male**								
	1990	2001	1990	2001	1990	2001	1999	1990	2001	1990	2001	1990	2001
Latin America and the Caribbean													
Antigua and Barbuda	..	..	..	..	..	..	50-79	17.4 [h]	80.4	..	9.0	..	..
Argentina	13	32	16	33	12	31	50-79	9.3	41.6	(.) [d]	10.1	0.7	8.0
Bahamas	..	16 [c]	..	22 [c]	..	11 [c]	80-94	28.1	59.7	..	5.5	..	..
Barbados	31	22 [c]	41	27 [c]	22	18 [c]	95-100	28.1	67.9	..	5.6	..	9.3
Belize	..	23 [c]	..	35 [c]	..	15 [c]	80-94	9.2	30.2	..	7.3	..	13.4
Bolivia	5	9 [e]	9	10 [e]	3	7 [e]	50-79	2.8	15.8	..	2.2	0.2 [f]	2.1
Brazil	7	18	7	22	7	15	0-49	6.5	38.5	(.) [f]	4.7	0.3	6.3
Chile	13	19	12	22	13	17	80-94	6.7	57.5	(.) [d]	20.1	0.9	10.6
Colombia	27	36 [e]	31	41 [e]	23	32 [e]	80-94	6.9	24.9	..	2.7	0.9 [d]	4.2
Costa Rica	8	13	10	16	8	12	95-100	10.1	30.5	(.) [d]	9.3	..	17.0
Cuba	..	..	..	..	..	..	95-100	3.1	5.2	..	1.1	..	2.0
Dominica	..	..	..	..	..	..	80-94	16.4	39.8	..	11.6	..	7.7
Dominican Republic	..	23 [e]	..	34 [e]	..	16 [e]	50-79	4.8	25.7	..	2.1	..	..
Ecuador	8	20	12	27	6	15	0-49	4.8	17.0	(.) [d]	2.6	0.2 [f]	2.3
El Salvador	15 [f]	13 [c]	14 [f]	10 [c]	15 [f]	14 [c]	80-94	2.4	23.6	..	2.3	..	2.2
Grenada	27 [f]	..	27 [f]	..	28 [f]	..	95-100	17.8	39.2	0.0	5.2	..	13.0
Guatemala	4 [g]	3 [i]	6 [g]	4 [i]	3 [g]	3 [i]	50-79	2.1	16.2	..	1.7	..	1.3
Guyana	27 [d]	..	38 [d]	..	21 [d]	..	0-49	2.0	17.8	..	10.9	..	2.6
Haiti	..	..	..	..	..	..	0-49	0.7	2.1	..	0.4	..	..
Honduras	11 [f]	7	15 [f]	8 [c]	9 [f]	7 [c]	0-49	1.7	8.4	..	1.4	..	1.2
Jamaica	30 [f]	34 [c]	43 [f]	46 [c]	20 [f]	24 [c]	95-100	4.5	44.9	..	3.8	..	5.0
Mexico	5 [f]	4	6 [f]	5	5 [f]	4	80-94	6.6	35.4	(.) [f]	3.6	0.8	6.9
Nicaragua	11	20	17	20	9	20	0-49	1.3	5.9	..	1.4	..	2.5
Panama	31 [f]	29 [e]	41 [f]	37 [e]	26 [f]	25 [e]	80-94	9.3	29.4	..	4.1	..	3.8
Paraguay	16	14	17	17	15	12	0-49	2.7	25.5	..	1.1	..	1.4
Peru	16	15 [i]	20	14	13	13	50-79	2.6	13.7	..	7.7	..	4.8
Saint Kitts and Nevis	..	..	..	..	..	..	50-79	19.7 [g]	53.7	..	7.9	..	17.5
Saint Lucia	..	44 [j]	..	52 [j]	..	38 [j]	50-79	9.7 [g]	33.4	..	8.2	..	14.6
St. Vincent & the Grenadines	36 [f]	..	43 [f]	..	33 [f]	..	80-94	12.4	29.2	..	4.8	..	11.3
Suriname	37	84 [c]	46	58 [c]	29	94 [c]	95-100	9.2	37.4	..	3.3	..	4.5
Trinidad and Tobago	36	25 [c]	43	31 [c]	33	22 [c]	50-79	14.1	43.7	..	9.2	0.4 [f]	6.9
Uruguay	25	34	28	42	23	29	50-79	13.4	43.8	..	11.9	..	11.0
Venezuela	19	23	18	28	20	20	80-94	7.7	37.3	(.) [d]	4.7	1.0	5.3
South Asia													
Afghanistan	..	..	..	..	..	..	50-79	0.2	0.1	..	..	..	..
Bangladesh	3 [g]	11 [e]	2 [g]	10 [e]	3 [g]	11 [e]	50-79	0.2	0.8	..	0.1	..	0.2
Bhutan	..	..	..	..	..	..	80-94	0.4	2.6	..	0.7	..	1.0
India	..	..	..	..	..	..	0-49	0.6	4.4	(.) [d]	0.7	(.)	0.6
Iran, Islamic Rep. of	..	..	..	..	..	..	80-94	4.0	20.1	..	1.6	..	7.0
Maldives	..	..	..	..	..	..	50-79	2.9	16.8	0.0	3.6	..	2.2
Nepal	..	..	..	..	..	..	0-49	0.3	1.4	0.0	0.3	..	0.4
Pakistan	5	13 [e]	1	29 [e]	6	11 [e]	50-79	0.8	2.9	..	0.3	0.1	0.4
Sri Lanka	33	24 [e]	47	31 [e]	23	20 [e]	95-100	0.7	8.0	..	0.8	(.)	0.9
Southern Europe													
Cyprus	..	7	..	10	..	4	95-100	42.4	108.7	0.1 [d]	21.8	0.9	24.7
Turkey	16	20	15	18	17	21	95-100	12.2	58.1	..	6.0	0.5	4.1

GOAL 8 Develop a global partnership for development: work opportunities, access to drugs and access to new technologies

	Develop and implement strategies for decent and productive work for youth	Provide access to affordable essential drugs in developing countries	Make available the benefits of new technologies, especially information and communications

	Youth unemployment (% of labour force aged 15-24) [a]						Population with sustainable access to affordable essential drugs (%) [b]	Telephone mainlines and cellular subscribers (per 100 people)		Internet users (per 100 people)		Personal computers in use (per 100 people)	
	Total		Female		Male								
	1990	2001	1990	2001	1990	2001	1999	1990	2001	1990	2001	1990	2001
Sub-Saharan Africa													
Angola	..	..	..	..	..	..	0-49	0.8	1.2	..	0.1	..	0.1
Benin	..	..	..	..	..	..	50-79	0.3	2.9	..	0.4	..	0.2
Botswana	..	43 [j]	..	47 [j]	..	38 [j]	80-94	2.1	27.3	0.0	3.0	..	3.9
Burkina Faso	..	..	..	..	..	..	50-79	0.2	1.1	..	0.2	(.)	0.1
Burundi	..	..	..	..	..	..	0-49	0.1	0.7	0.0	0.1	..	..
Cameroon	..	..	..	..	..	..	50-79	0.3	2.7	..	0.3	..	0.4
Cape Verde	..	..	..	..	..	..	80-94	2.4	21.5	..	2.7	..	6.9
Central African Republic	..	..	..	..	..	..	50-79	0.2	0.5	..	0.1	..	0.2
Chad	..	..	..	..	..	..	0-49	0.1	0.4	..	0.1	..	0.2
Comoros	..	..	..	..	..	..	80-94	0.8	1.2	..	0.3	(.)	0.6
Congo	..	..	..	..	..	..	50-79	0.7	5.5	..	(.)	..	0.4
Congo, Dem. Rep. of the	..	..	..	..	..	..	..	0.1	0.3	..	(.)	..	..
Côte d'Ivoire	..	..	..	..	..	..	80-94	0.6	6.3	..	0.4	..	0.7
Equatorial Guinea	..	..	..	..	..	..	0-49	0.4	4.7	..	0.2	..	0.5
Eritrea	..	..	..	..	..	..	50-79	0.4 [d]	0.8	..	0.2	..	0.2
Ethiopia	..	..	..	..	..	..	50-79	0.3	0.5	..	(.)	..	0.1
Gabon	..	..	..	..	..	..	0-49	2.2	23.4	..	1.3	..	1.2
Gambia	..	..	..	..	..	..	80-94	0.7	6.7	..	1.3	..	1.3
Ghana	..	..	..	..	..	..	0-49	0.3	2.1	..	0.2	(.)	0.3
Guinea	..	..	..	..	..	..	80-94	0.2	1.1	..	0.2	..	0.4
Guinea-Bissau	..	..	..	..	..	..	0-49	0.6	1.0	..	0.3	..	..
Kenya	..	..	..	..	..	..	0-49	0.8	3.0	..	1.6	(.)	0.6
Lesotho	..	..	..	..	..	..	80-94	0.7	3.7	..	0.2	..	..
Liberia	..	..	..	..	..	..	0-49	0.4	0.3	..	(.)	..	..
Madagascar	..	..	..	..	..	..	50-79	0.3	1.3	..	0.2	..	0.3
Malawi	..	..	..	..	..	..	0-49	0.3	1.1	..	0.2	..	0.1
Mali	..	..	..	..	..	..	50-79	0.1	0.9	..	0.3	..	0.1
Mauritania	..	..	..	..	..	..	50-79	0.3	5.3	..	0.3	..	1.0
Mauritius	..	..	..	..	..	..	95-100	5.5	48.3	..	13.2	0.4	10.8
Mozambique	..	..	..	..	..	..	50-79	0.3	1.4	..	0.2	..	0.4
Namibia	..	..	..	..	..	..	80-94	3.9	11.9	..	2.5	..	5.5
Niger	1	..	(.)	..	1	..	50-79	0.1	0.2	..	0.1	..	0.1
Nigeria	..	..	..	..	..	..	0-49	0.3	0.8	..	0.1	..	0.7
Rwanda	..	..	..	..	..	..	0-49	0.2	1.1	..	0.3	..	..
São Tomé and Principe	..	..	..	..	..	..	0-49	1.9	3.6	..	6.0	..	..
Senegal	..	..	..	..	..	..	50-79	0.6	5.6	..	1.0	0.2	1.9
Seychelles	..	..	..	..	..	..	80-94	12.4	80.0	..	11.0	..	14.7
Sierra Leone	..	..	..	..	..	..	0-49	0.3	1.0	..	0.1	..	..
South Africa	..	56 [e]	..	53 [e]	..	58 [e]	80-94	9.4	35.3	(.) [f]	6.5	0.7	7.0
Swaziland	..	..	..	..	..	..	95-100	1.7	8.5	..	1.4	..	..
Tanzania, U. Rep. of	..	..	..	..	..	..	50-79	0.3	1.7	..	0.3	..	0.4
Togo	..	..	..	..	..	..	50-79	0.3	3.6	0.0	3.2	..	2.6
Uganda	..	..	..	..	..	..	50-79	0.2	1.4	..	0.3	..	0.3
Zambia	..	..	..	..	..	..	50-79	0.8	2.0	..	0.2	..	0.7
Zimbabwe	..	..	..	..	..	..	50-79	1.3	5.1	..	0.9	(.)	1.7
Central & Eastern Europe & CIS													
Albania	..	..	..	..	..	..	50-79	1.2	14.9	..	0.3	..	0.8
Armenia	..	..	..	..	..	..	0-49	15.7	14.6	..	1.8	..	0.9
Azerbaijan	..	..	..	..	..	..	50-79	8.6	21.4	..	0.3	..	..
Belarus	..	..	..	..	..	..	50-79	15.4	30.2	..	4.2	..	..
Bosnia and Herzegovina	..	..	..	..	..	..	80-94	14.0 [d]	17.1	..	1.1	..	..

	Develop and implement strategies for decent and productive work for youth						Provide access to affordable essential drugs in developing countries	Make available the benefits of new technologies, especially information and communications					
	Youth unemployment (% of labour force aged 15-24)[a]						**Population with sustainable access to affordable essential drugs** (%)[b]	**Telephone mainlines and cellular subscribers** (per 100 people)		**Internet users** (per 100 people)		**Personal computers in use** (per 100 people)	
	Total		Female		Male								
	1990	2001	1990	2001	1990	2001	1999	1990	2001	1990	2001	1990	2001
Bulgaria	..	38	..	35	..	42	80-94	24.2	55.1	..	7.5	1.1 [d]	3.2
Croatia	..	37	..	39	..	36	95-100	17.2	76.0	..	11.1	1.5 [f]	13.3
Czech Republic	..	17	..	17	..	16	80-94	15.8	105.7	..	14.7	1.2	14.7
Estonia	2	22	2	26	2	19	95-100	20.4	80.9	0.1 [d]	30.0	..	17.5
Georgia	..	20	..	20	..	20	0-49	9.9	23.5	..	0.9	..	2.9
Hungary	19 [d]	11	15 [d]	10	22 [d]	12	95-100	9.6	87.3	(.) [f]	14.8	1.0	9.5
Kazakhstan	..	..	..	..	..	..	50-79	8.0	15.7	..	0.9	..	..
Kyrgyzstan	..	..	..	..	..	..	50-79	7.2	8.3	..	3.0	..	1.3
Latvia	..	21	..	21	..	20	80-94	23.4	58.6	..	7.2	..	15.3
Lithuania	..	29 [e]	..	26 [e]	..	31 [e]	80-94	21.2	58.9	..	6.8	..	7.1
Macedonia, TFYR	..	..	..	..	..	..	50-79	14.8	37.3	..	3.4	..	..
Moldova, Rep. of	..	..	..	..	..	..	50-79	10.6	19.7	..	1.4	..	1.6
Poland	28 [d]	41	30 [d]	42	26 [d]	40	80-94	8.6	55.4	(.) [f]	9.8	0.8	8.5
Romania	..	18	..	17	..	18	80-94	10.2	35.6	..	4.5	0.2	3.6
Russian Federation	16 [d]	25 [c]	16 [d]	26 [c]	17 [d]	24 [c]	50-79	14.0	29.6	(.) [d]	2.9	0.3	5.0
Serbia and Montenegro	..	..	..	..	..	..	80-94	16.6	41.6	..	5.6	..	2.3
Slovakia	..	39	..	36	..	42	95-100	13.5	68.9	..	12.5	..	14.9
Slovenia	..	16	..	18	..	15	95-100	21.1	113.9	..	30.1	3.2 [f]	27.6
Tajikistan	..	..	..	..	..	..	0-49	4.5	3.6	..	0.1	..	..
Turkmenistan	..	..	..	..	..	..	50-79	6.0	8.2	..	0.2	..	..
Ukraine	..	24 [e]	..	25 [e]	..	23 [e]	50-79	13.6	25.6	..	1.2	0.2	1.8
Uzbekistan	..	..	..	..	..	..	50-79	6.9	6.9	..	0.6	..	..
High-income OECD[k]													
Australia	13	13	12	12	14	13	95-100	46.7	111.5	0.6	37.1	15.0	51.6
Austria	4	6	4	6	4	5	95-100	42.7	128.5	0.1	38.7	6.5	33.5
Belgium	15	15	19	17	10	14	95-100	39.7	124.4	(.)	31.0	8.8	23.3
Canada	12	13	11	11	14	15	95-100	58.7	103.8	0.4	46.7	10.7	47.3
Denmark	12	8	12	9	11	7	95-100	59.6	146.1	0.1	42.9	11.5	54.2
Finland	9	20	8	20	10	20	95-100	58.6	135.1	0.4	43.0	10.0	42.3
France	19	19	24	22	15	16	95-100	50.0	117.9	0.1	26.4	7.1	32.9
Germany	5 [f]	8	6 [f]	8	5 [f]	9	95-100	44.5	131.7	0.1	37.4	9.0	38.2
Greece	23	28	33	36	15	21	95-100	38.9	128.1	(.) [f]	13.2	1.7	8.1
Iceland	1	5	1	4	1	5	95-100	54.9	152.9	0.5 [f]	59.9	3.9	41.8
Ireland	18	6	16	6	19	6	95-100	28.8	125.8	0.1 [f]	23.3	8.6	39.1
Italy	32	27	38	32	26	23	95-100	39.2	135.5	(.)	26.9	3.6	19.5
Japan	4	10	4	9	5	11	95-100	44.8	117.4	(.)	38.4	6.0	35.8
Luxembourg	4	7	5	5	3	8	95-100	48.3	170.0	0.2 [d]	36.0	..	51.7
Netherlands	11	6	12	6	10	6	95-100	46.9	138.8	0.3	49.1	9.4	42.8
New Zealand	14	12	13	12	15	12	95-100	45.0	107.6	0.3 [d]	46.1	9.7 [f]	39.3
Norway	12	11	11	10	12	11	95-100	54.8	154.7	0.7	46.4	14.5 [f]	50.8
Portugal	10	9	13	12	7	7	95-100	24.3	119.9	0.1 [f]	28.1	2.7	11.7
Spain	30	21	40	27	23	16	95-100	31.7	116.7	(.)	18.3	2.8	16.8
Sweden	5	12	4	11	5	13	95-100	73.5	152.9	0.6	51.6	10.5	56.1
Switzerland	3 [f]	6	3 [f]	6	3 [f]	6	95-100	59.2	146.0	0.6	30.7	8.7	53.8
United Kingdom	10	11	9	9	11	12	95-100	46.0	135.8	0.1	33.0	10.8	36.6
United States	11	11	11	10	12	11	95-100	56.9	111.8	0.8	50.1	21.8	62.5

GOAL 8 **Develop a global partnership for development: work opportunities, access to drugs and access to new technologies**

	Develop and implement strategies for decent and productive work for youth						*Provide access to affordable essential drugs in developing countries*	*Make available the benefits of new technologies, especially information and communications*					
	Youth unemployment (% of labour force aged 15-24)[a]						**Population with sustainable access to affordable essential drugs** (%)[b]	**Telephone mainlines and cellular subscribers** (per 100 people)		**Internet users** (per 100 people)		**Personal computers in use** (per 100 people)	
	Total		**Female**		**Male**								
	1990	2001	1990	2001	1990	2001	1999	1990	2001	1990	2001	1990	2001
Other UN member countries													
Andorra	..	..	..	..	..	..	..	41.4	74.0 [e]	..	9.0 [e]	..	..
Israel	22	19	23	18	21	19	95-100	34.6	137.3	0.1	27.7	6.3	24.6
Liechtenstein	..	..	..	..	..	..	..	..	106.2	..	44.7	..	..
Malta	..	..	..	..	..	..	95-100	36.0	114.1	..	25.3	1.4	23.0
Monaco	..	..	..	..	..	..	95-100	81.5	152.9	..	46.6	..	..
San Marino	10	10 [c]	16	16 [c]	5	6 [c]	..	60.6 [d]	134.6	..	51.3	..	75.9
Developing countries	..	..	..	..	..	..	..	2.1	16.3	..	2.6	..	2.5
Least developed countries	..	..	..	..	..	..	..	0.3	1.2	..	0.2	..	0.3
Arab States	..	..	..	..	..	..	..	3.5	13.4	..	1.6	..	2.1
East Asia and the Pacific	..	..	..	..	..	..	..	1.8	23.5	..	4.1	..	3.3
Latin America and the Caribbean	..	..	..	..	..	..	..	6.2	32.3	..	4.9	..	5.9
South Asia	..	..	..	..	..	..	..	0.7	4.5	..	0.6	..	0.8
Sub-Saharan Africa	..	..	..	..	..	..	..	1.1	4.2	..	0.8	..	1.1
Central & Eastern Europe & CIS	..	..	..	..	..	..	..	12.6	34.5	..	4.3	..	5.5
OECD	..	..	..	..	..	..	..	40.2	106.2	0.3	33.2	9.4	36.3
High-income OECD	..	..	..	..	..	..	..	47.8	120.2	0.3	40.0	11.5	43.7
High human development	..	..	..	..	..	..	..	39.2	104.0	0.3	32.8	9.4	35.9
Medium human development	..	..	..	..	..	..	..	2.6	17.5	..	2.2	..	2.0
Low human development	..	..	..	..	..	..	..	0.4	1.8	..	0.3	..	0.4
High income	..	..	..	..	..	..	..	47.4	120.0	0.3	39.7	11.3	43.3
Middle income	..	..	..	..	..	..	..	4.1	28.0	..	3.7	..	3.5
Low income	..	..	..	..	..	..	..	1.0	4.0	..	0.6	..	0.6
World	..	..	..	..	..	..	..	10.0	32.2	..	8.0	..	8.7

Note: The targets covered in this table read in full as follows: In cooperation with developing countries, develop and implement strategies for decent and productive work for youth. In cooperation with pharmaceutical companies, provide access to affordable essential drugs in developing countries. In cooperation with the private sector, make available the benefits of new technologies, especially information and communications.
a. As a result of limitations in the data, comparisons of labour statistics over time and across countries should be made with caution. For detailed notes on the data, see ILO 2002a, 2002b and 2003b. b. The data on access to essential drugs are based on statistical estimates received from World Health Organization (WHO) country and regional offices and regional advisers and through the World Drug Situation Survey carried out in 1998-99. These estimates represent the best information available to the WHO Department of Essential Drugs and Medicines Policy to date and are currently being validated by WHO member states. The department assigns the estimates to four groupings: very low access (0-49%), low access (50-79%), medium access (80-94%) and good access (95-100%). These groupings, used here in presenting the data, are often employed by the WHO in interpreting the data, as the actual estimates may suggest a higher level of accuracy than the data afford. c. Data refer to 1999. d. Data refer to 1992. e. Data refer to 2000. f. Data refer to 1991. g. Data refer to 1989. h. Data refer to 1988. i. Data refer to 2002. j. Data refer to 1998. k. Excluding the Republic of Korea; see East Asia and the Pacific.
Source: Columns 1-6: UN 2003a, based on data from the International Labour Organization; *column 7:* UN 2003a, based on data from the WHO; *columns 8-13:* UN 2003a, based on data from the International Telecommunication Union.

1 Human development index

HDI rank [a]		Life expectancy at birth (years) 2001	Adult literacy rate (% age 15 and above) 2001	Combined primary, secondary and tertiary gross enrolment ratio (%) 2000-01 [b]	GDP per capita (PPP US$) 2001	Life expectancy index	Education index	GDP index	Human development index (HDI) value 2001	GDP per capita (PPP US$) rank minus HDI rank [c]
High human development										
1	Norway	78.7	.. [d]	98 [e]	29,620	0.90	0.99	0.95	0.944	4
2	Iceland	79.6	.. [d]	91 [e]	29,990	0.91	0.96	0.95	0.942	2
3	Sweden	79.9	.. [d]	113 [e, f]	24,180	0.91	0.99	0.92	0.941	15
4	Australia	79.0	.. [d]	114 [e, f]	25,370	0.90	0.99	0.92	0.939	8
5	Netherlands	78.2	.. [d]	99 [e]	27,190	0.89	0.99	0.94	0.938	3
6	Belgium	78.5	.. [d]	107 [e, f, g]	25,520	0.89	0.99	0.92	0.937	5
7	United States	76.9	.. [d]	94 [e]	34,320	0.86	0.97	0.97	0.937	-5
8	Canada	79.2	.. [d]	94 [e, g]	27,130	0.90	0.97	0.94	0.937	1
9	Japan	81.3	.. [d]	83 [e]	25,130	0.94	0.94	0.92	0.932	5
10	Switzerland	79.0	.. [d]	88 [e]	28,100	0.90	0.95	0.94	0.932	-3
11	Denmark	76.4	.. [d]	98 [e]	29,000	0.86	0.99	0.95	0.930	-5
12	Ireland	76.7	.. [d]	91 [e, h]	32,410	0.86	0.96	0.96	0.930	-9
13	United Kingdom	77.9	.. [d]	112 [e, f]	24,160	0.88	0.99	0.92	0.930	6
14	Finland	77.8	.. [d]	103 [e, f, h]	24,430	0.88	0.99	0.92	0.930	3
15	Luxembourg	78.1	.. [d]	73 [e, i]	53,780 [j]	0.88	0.90	1.00	0.930	-14
16	Austria	78.3	.. [d]	92 [e]	26,730	0.89	0.97	0.93	0.929	-6
17	France	78.7	.. [d]	91 [e]	23,990	0.90	0.96	0.91	0.925	3
18	Germany	78.0	.. [d]	89 [e, g]	25,350	0.88	0.96	0.92	0.921	-5
19	Spain	79.1	97.7 [d]	92 [e]	20,150	0.90	0.97	0.89	0.918	5
20	New Zealand	78.1	.. [d]	99 [e]	19,160	0.88	0.99	0.88	0.917	8
21	Italy	78.6	98.5 [d]	82 [e]	24,670	0.89	0.93	0.92	0.916	-5
22	Israel	78.9	95.1	90	19,790	0.90	0.93	0.88	0.905	4
23	Portugal	75.9	92.5 [d]	93 [e]	18,150	0.85	0.97	0.87	0.896	7
24	Greece	78.1	97.3 [d]	81 [e, h]	17,440	0.89	0.93	0.86	0.892	7
25	Cyprus	78.1	97.2	74 [g, k]	21,190 [l]	0.88	0.90	0.89	0.891	-3
26	Hong Kong, China (SAR)	79.7	93.5	63 [h]	24,850	0.91	0.83	0.92	0.889	-11
27	Barbados	76.9	99.7 [d]	89	15,560	0.87	0.96	0.84	0.888	9
28	Singapore	77.8	92.5	75 [h]	22,680	0.88	0.87	0.91	0.884	-7
29	Slovenia	75.9	99.6 [d]	83 [h]	17,130	0.85	0.94	0.86	0.881	3
30	Korea, Rep. of	75.2	97.9 [d]	91 [e]	15,090	0.84	0.96	0.84	0.879	7
31	Brunei Darussalam	76.1	91.6	83	19,210 [g]	0.85	0.89	0.88	0.872	-4
32	Czech Republic	75.1	.. [d]	76 [e]	14,720	0.83	0.91	0.83	0.861	7
33	Malta	78.1	92.3	76 [g]	13,160 [l]	0.88	0.87	0.81	0.856	8
34	Argentina	73.9	96.9	89 [e, g]	11,320	0.81	0.94	0.79	0.849	11
35	Poland	73.6	99.7 [d]	88 [e]	9,450	0.81	0.95	0.76	0.841	17
36	Seychelles	72.7 [m]	91.0 [m]	.. [n]	17,030 [o]	0.80	0.87	0.86	0.840	-3
37	Bahrain	73.7	87.9	81 [g]	16,060	0.81	0.86	0.85	0.839	-2
38	Hungary	71.5	99.3 [d]	82 [e, g]	12,340	0.77	0.93	0.80	0.837	4
39	Slovakia	73.3	100.0 [d, p, q]	73 [e]	11,960	0.80	0.90	0.80	0.836	5
40	Uruguay	75.0	97.6	84 [e]	8,400	0.83	0.93	0.74	0.834	19
41	Estonia	71.2	99.8 [d]	89	10,170	0.77	0.96	0.77	0.833	7
42	Costa Rica	77.9	95.7	66	9,460	0.88	0.86	0.76	0.832	9
43	Chile	75.8	95.9	76 [e]	9,190	0.85	0.89	0.75	0.831	10
44	Qatar	71.8	81.7	81	19,844 [g, r]	0.78	0.82	0.88	0.826	-19
45	Lithuania	72.3	99.6 [d]	85	8,470	0.79	0.94	0.74	0.824	12
46	Kuwait	76.3	82.4	54 [g]	18,700 [l]	0.86	0.73	0.87	0.820	-17
47	Croatia	74.0	98.4	68 [h]	9,170	0.82	0.88	0.75	0.818	7
48	United Arab Emirates	74.4	76.7	67 [g]	20,530 [g, l]	0.82	0.73	0.89	0.816	-25
49	Bahamas	67.2	95.5	74 [h]	16,270 [g]	0.70	0.88	0.85	0.812	-15
50	Latvia	70.5	99.8 [d]	86	7,730	0.76	0.95	0.73	0.811	11

1 Human development index

HDI rank [a]		Life expectancy at birth (years) 2001	Adult literacy rate (% age 15 and above) 2001	Combined primary, secondary and tertiary gross enrolment ratio (%) 2000-01 [b]	GDP per capita (PPP US$) 2001	Life expectancy index	Education index	GDP index	Human development index (HDI) value 2001	GDP per capita (PPP US$) rank minus HDI rank [c]
51	Saint Kitts and Nevis	70.0 [s]	97.8 [s]	70 [s]	11,300	0.75	0.89	0.79	0.808	-5
52	Cuba	76.5	96.8	76	5,259 [g, r]	0.86	0.90	0.66	0.806	38
53	Belarus	69.6	99.7 [d]	86	7,620	0.74	0.95	0.72	0.804	9
54	Trinidad and Tobago	71.5	98.4	67	9,100	0.78	0.88	0.75	0.802	1
55	Mexico	73.1	91.4	74 [e]	8,430 [l]	0.80	0.86	0.74	0.800	3

Medium human development

HDI rank [a]		Life expectancy at birth (years) 2001	Adult literacy rate (% age 15 and above) 2001	Combined primary, secondary and tertiary gross enrolment ratio (%) 2000-01 [b]	GDP per capita (PPP US$) 2001	Life expectancy index	Education index	GDP index	Human development index (HDI) value 2001	GDP per capita (PPP US$) rank minus HDI rank [c]
56	Antigua and Barbuda	73.9 [s]	86.6 [s]	69 [s]	10,170	0.82	0.81	0.77	0.798	-8
57	Bulgaria	70.9	98.5	77	6,890	0.76	0.91	0.71	0.795	12
58	Malaysia	72.8	87.9	72 [e]	8,750 [l]	0.80	0.83	0.75	0.790	-2
59	Panama	74.4	92.1	75 [g]	5,750	0.82	0.86	0.68	0.788	23
60	Macedonia, TFYR	73.3	94.0 [q, t]	70	6,110	0.81	0.86	0.69	0.784	15
61	Libyan Arab Jamahiriya	72.4	80.8	89 [e]	7,570 [g, u]	0.79	0.84	0.72	0.783	2
62	Mauritius	71.6	84.8	69	9,860	0.78	0.80	0.77	0.779	-12
63	Russian Federation	66.6	99.6 [d]	82 [e]	7,100	0.69	0.93	0.71	0.779	3
64	Colombia	71.8	91.9	71	7,040	0.78	0.85	0.71	0.779	3
65	Brazil	67.8	87.3	95 [e]	7,360	0.71	0.90	0.72	0.777	-1
66	Bosnia and Herzegovina	73.8	93.0 [p, q]	64 [v]	5,970	0.81	0.83	0.68	0.777	13
67	Belize	71.7	93.4	76 [e]	5,690	0.78	0.88	0.67	0.776	16
68	Dominica	72.9 [s]	96.4 [s]	65 [s]	5,520	0.80	0.86	0.67	0.776	18
69	Venezuela	73.5	92.8	68	5,670	0.81	0.84	0.67	0.775	15
70	Samoa (Western)	69.5	98.7	71	6,180	0.74	0.89	0.69	0.775	4
71	Saint Lucia	72.2	90.2 [s]	82 [g]	5,260	0.79	0.88	0.66	0.775	17
72	Romania	70.5	98.2	68	5,830	0.76	0.88	0.68	0.773	9
73	Saudi Arabia	71.9	77.1	58 [g]	13,330	0.78	0.71	0.82	0.769	-33
74	Thailand	68.9	95.7	72 [e]	6,400	0.73	0.88	0.69	0.768	-2
75	Ukraine	69.2	99.6 [d]	81 [g]	4,350	0.74	0.93	0.63	0.766	23
76	Kazakhstan	65.8	99.4 [d]	78	6,500	0.68	0.92	0.70	0.765	-5
77	Suriname	70.8	94.0 [p, q]	77 [e]	4,599 [l, o]	0.76	0.88	0.64	0.762	18
78	Jamaica	75.5	87.3	74 [e]	3,720	0.84	0.83	0.60	0.757	27
79	Oman	72.2	73.0	58 [g]	12,040 [g]	0.79	0.68	0.80	0.755	-36
80	St. Vincent & the Grenadines	73.8	88.9 [s]	58 [s]	5,330	0.81	0.79	0.66	0.755	7
81	Fiji	69.3	93.2	76 [e, g]	4,850	0.74	0.88	0.65	0.754	11
82	Peru	69.4	90.2	83 [e, g]	4,570	0.74	0.88	0.64	0.752	14
83	Lebanon	73.3	86.5	76	4,170	0.80	0.83	0.62	0.752	18
84	Paraguay	70.5	93.5	64 [e, h]	5,210	0.76	0.84	0.66	0.751	7
85	Philippines	69.5	95.1	80 [e]	3,840	0.74	0.90	0.61	0.751	19
86	Maldives	66.8	97.0	79	4,798 [l, o]	0.70	0.91	0.65	0.751	7
87	Turkmenistan	66.6	98.0 [q, t]	81 [h]	4,320	0.69	0.92	0.63	0.748	13
88	Georgia	73.4	100.0 [d, p, q]	69	2,560	0.81	0.89	0.54	0.746	33
89	Azerbaijan	71.8	97.0 [p, q]	69 [g]	3,090	0.78	0.88	0.57	0.744	24
90	Jordan	70.6	90.3	77 [e, g]	3,870	0.76	0.86	0.61	0.743	13
91	Tunisia	72.5	72.1	76 [e]	6,390	0.79	0.73	0.69	0.740	-18
92	Guyana	63.3	98.6	84 [e, g]	4,690	0.64	0.94	0.64	0.740	2
93	Grenada	65.3 [s]	94.4 [s]	63	6,740	0.67	0.84	0.70	0.738	-23
94	Dominican Republic	66.7	84.0	74 [e]	7,020	0.70	0.81	0.71	0.737	-26
95	Albania	73.4	85.3	69	3,680	0.81	0.80	0.60	0.735	11
96	Turkey	70.1	85.5	60 [e, g]	5,890	0.75	0.77	0.68	0.734	-16
97	Ecuador	70.5	91.8	72 [e]	3,280	0.76	0.85	0.58	0.731	12
98	Occupied Palestinian Territories	72.1	89.2 [w]	77 [g]	.. [x]	0.79	0.85	0.56	0.731	19
99	Sri Lanka	72.3	91.9	63 [e, g]	3,180	0.79	0.82	0.58	0.730	13
100	Armenia	72.1	98.5	60	2,650	0.78	0.86	0.55	0.729	19

HDI rank [a]		Life expectancy at birth (years) 2001	Adult literacy rate (% age 15 and above) 2001	Combined primary, secondary and tertiary gross enrolment ratio (%) 2000-01 [b]	GDP per capita (PPP US$) 2001	Life expectancy index	Education index	GDP index	Human development index (HDI) value 2001	GDP per capita (PPP US$) rank minus HDI rank [c]
101	Uzbekistan	69.3	99.2 [d]	76 [h]	2,460	0.74	0.91	0.53	0.729	21
102	Kyrgyzstan	68.1	97.0 [p, q]	79	2,750	0.72	0.91	0.55	0.727	16
103	Cape Verde	69.7	74.9	80 [e]	5,570 [l]	0.75	0.77	0.67	0.727	-18
104	China	70.6	85.8	64 [e, g]	4,020	0.76	0.79	0.62	0.721	-2
105	El Salvador	70.4	79.2	64	5,260	0.76	0.74	0.66	0.719	-17
106	Iran, Islamic Rep. of	69.8	77.1	64	6,000	0.75	0.73	0.68	0.719	-29
107	Algeria	69.2	67.8	71 [e]	6,090 [l]	0.74	0.69	0.69	0.704	-31
108	Moldova, Rep. of	68.5	99.0	61	2,150	0.72	0.86	0.51	0.700	21
109	Viet Nam	68.6	92.7	64	2,070	0.73	0.83	0.51	0.688	21
110	Syrian Arab Republic	71.5	75.3	59 [g]	3,280	0.77	0.70	0.58	0.685	-1
111	South Africa	50.9	85.6	78	11,290 [l]	0.43	0.83	0.79	0.684	-64
112	Indonesia	66.2	87.3	64 [e]	2,940	0.69	0.80	0.56	0.682	2
113	Tajikistan	68.3	99.3 [d]	71	1,170	0.72	0.90	0.41	0.677	41
114	Bolivia	63.3	86.0	84 [e]	2,300	0.64	0.85	0.52	0.672	12
115	Honduras	68.8	75.6	62 [e]	2,830	0.73	0.71	0.56	0.667	1
116	Equatorial Guinea	49.0	84.2	58 [g]	15,073 [g, y]	0.40	0.76	0.84	0.664	-78
117	Mongolia	63.3	98.5	64	1,740	0.64	0.87	0.48	0.661	25
118	Gabon	56.6	71.0 [p, q]	83 [e]	5,990	0.53	0.75	0.68	0.653	-40
119	Guatemala	65.3	69.2	57 [e]	4,400	0.67	0.65	0.63	0.652	-22
120	Egypt	68.3	56.1	76 [e, h]	3,520	0.72	0.63	0.59	0.648	-12
121	Nicaragua	69.1	66.8	65 [e, g]	2,450 [g, l]	0.73	0.66	0.53	0.643	2
122	São Tomé and Principe	69.4	83.1 [m]	58 [m]	1,317 [g, r]	0.74	0.75	0.43	0.639	28
123	Solomon Islands	68.7	76.6 [m]	50 [m]	1,910 [l]	0.73	0.68	0.49	0.632	13
124	Namibia	47.4	82.7	74 [g]	7,120 [l]	0.37	0.80	0.71	0.627	-59
125	Botswana	44.7	78.1	80	7,820	0.33	0.79	0.73	0.614	-65
126	Morocco	68.1	49.8	51 [g]	3,600	0.72	0.50	0.60	0.606	-19
127	India	63.3	58.0	56 [e, g]	2,840	0.64	0.57	0.56	0.590	-12
128	Vanuatu	68.3	34.0 [m]	54 [g]	3,190 [l]	0.72	0.41	0.58	0.568	-17
129	Ghana	57.7	72.7	46	2,250 [l]	0.54	0.64	0.52	0.567	-1
130	Cambodia	57.4	68.7	55	1,860	0.54	0.64	0.49	0.556	9
131	Myanmar	57.0	85.0	47	1,027 [g, u]	0.53	0.72	0.39	0.549	28
132	Papua New Guinea	57.0	64.6	41 [g]	2,570 [l]	0.53	0.57	0.54	0.548	-12
133	Swaziland	38.2	80.3	77 [g]	4,330	0.22	0.79	0.63	0.547	-34
134	Comoros	60.2	56.0	40 [g]	1,870 [l]	0.59	0.51	0.49	0.528	4
135	Lao People's Dem. Rep.	53.9	65.6	57	1,620 [l]	0.48	0.63	0.46	0.525	10
136	Bhutan	62.5	47.0 [p, q]	33 [h]	1,833 [o]	0.62	0.42	0.49	0.511	5
137	Lesotho	38.6	83.9	63	2,420 [l]	0.23	0.77	0.53	0.510	-13
138	Sudan	55.4	58.8	34 [g]	1,970	0.51	0.51	0.50	0.503	-4
139	Bangladesh	60.5	40.6	54	1,610	0.59	0.45	0.46	0.502	7
140	Congo	48.5	81.8	57 [e]	970	0.39	0.73	0.38	0.502	22
141	Togo	50.3	58.4	67 [g]	1,650	0.42	0.61	0.47	0.501	3
Low human development										
142	Cameroon	48.0	72.4	48 [e, g]	1,680	0.38	0.64	0.47	0.499	1
143	Nepal	59.1	42.9	64	1,310	0.57	0.50	0.43	0.499	8
144	Pakistan	60.4	44.0	36	1,890	0.59	0.41	0.49	0.499	-7
145	Zimbabwe	35.4	89.3	59 [e]	2,280	0.17	0.79	0.52	0.496	-18
146	Kenya	46.4	83.3	52	980	0.36	0.73	0.38	0.489	14
147	Uganda	44.7	68.0	71	1,490 [l]	0.33	0.69	0.45	0.489	1
148	Yemen	59.4	47.7	52 [g]	790	0.57	0.49	0.34	0.470	21
149	Madagascar	53.0	67.3	41 [g]	830	0.47	0.58	0.35	0.468	17
150	Haiti	49.1	50.8	52 [h]	1,860 [l]	0.40	0.51	0.49	0.467	-11
151	Gambia	53.7	37.8	47 [e]	2,050 [l]	0.48	0.41	0.50	0.463	-20

HDI rank [a]		Life expectancy at birth (years) 2001	Adult literacy rate (% age 15 and above) 2001	Combined primary, secondary and tertiary gross enrolment ratio (%) 2000-01 [b]	GDP per capita (PPP US$) 2001	Life expectancy index	Education index	GDP index	Human development index (HDI) value 2001	GDP per capita (PPP US$) rank minus HDI rank [c]
152	Nigeria	51.8	65.4	45 [h]	850	0.45	0.59	0.36	0.463	13
153	Djibouti	46.1	65.5	21 [g]	2,370	0.35	0.51	0.53	0.462	-28
154	Mauritania	51.9	40.7	43	1,990 [l]	0.45	0.41	0.50	0.454	-21
155	Eritrea	52.5	56.7	33	1,030	0.46	0.49	0.39	0.446	3
156	Senegal	52.3	38.3	38 [e]	1,500	0.46	0.38	0.45	0.430	-9
157	Guinea	48.5	41.0 [p, q]	34 [e]	1,960	0.39	0.39	0.50	0.425	-22
158	Rwanda	38.2	68.0	52 [g]	1,250	0.22	0.63	0.42	0.422	-5
159	Benin	50.9	38.6	49 [e]	980	0.43	0.42	0.38	0.411	1
160	Tanzania, U. Rep. of	44.0	76.0	31	520	0.32	0.61	0.28	0.400	14
161	Côte d'Ivoire	41.7	49.7	39 [g]	1,490	0.28	0.46	0.45	0.396	-13
162	Malawi	38.5	61.0	72 [e]	570	0.22	0.65	0.29	0.387	11
163	Zambia	33.4	79.0	45	780	0.14	0.68	0.34	0.386	7
164	Angola	40.2	42.0 [q, t]	29 [g]	2,040 [l]	0.25	0.38	0.50	0.377	-32
165	Chad	44.6	44.2	33 [g]	1,070 [l]	0.33	0.41	0.40	0.376	-8
166	Guinea-Bissau	45.0	39.6	43 [g]	970	0.33	0.41	0.38	0.373	-4
167	Congo, Dem. Rep. of the	40.6	62.7	27 [g]	680 [l]	0.26	0.51	0.32	0.363	5
168	Central African Republic	40.4	48.2	24 [h]	1,300 [l]	0.26	0.40	0.43	0.363	-16
169	Ethiopia	45.7	40.3	34	810	0.34	0.38	0.35	0.359	-2
170	Mozambique	39.2	45.2	37	1,140 [l]	0.24	0.43	0.41	0.356	-15
171	Burundi	40.4	49.2	31	690 [l]	0.26	0.43	0.32	0.337	0
172	Mali	48.4	26.4	29 [g]	810	0.39	0.27	0.35	0.337	-5
173	Burkina Faso	45.8	24.8	22 [e]	1,120 [l]	0.35	0.24	0.40	0.330	-17
174	Niger	45.6	16.5	17	890 [l]	0.34	0.17	0.36	0.292	-10
175	Sierra Leone	34.5	36.0 [p, q]	51	470	0.16	0.41	0.26	0.275	0
Developing countries		64.4	74.5	60	3,850	0.66	0.70	0.61	0.655	..
Least developed countries		50.4	53.3	43	1,274	0.43	0.50	0.42	0.448	..
Arab States		66.0	60.8	60	5,038	0.70	0.63	0.65	0.662	..
East Asia and the Pacific		69.5	87.1	65	4,233	0.74	0.80	0.63	0.722	..
Latin America and the Caribbean		70.3	89.2	81	7,050	0.75	0.86	0.71	0.777	..
South Asia		62.8	56.3	54	2,730	0.64	0.56	0.55	0.582	..
Sub-Saharan Africa		46.5	62.4	44	1,831	0.36	0.56	0.49	0.468	..
Central & Eastern Europe & CIS		69.3	99.3	79	6,598	0.74	0.92	0.70	0.787	..
OECD		77.0	..	87	23,363	0.87	0.94	0.91	0.905	..
High-income OECD		78.1	..	93	27,169	0.89	0.97	0.94	0.929	..
High human development		77.1	..	89	23,135	0.87	0.95	0.91	0.908	..
Medium human development		67.0	78.1	64	4,053	0.70	0.74	0.62	0.684	..
Low human development		49.4	55.0	41	1,186	0.41	0.50	0.41	0.440	..
High income		78.1	..	92	26,989	0.89	0.96	0.93	0.927	..
Middle income		69.8	86.6	70	5,519	0.75	0.82	0.67	0.744	..
Low income		59.1	63.0	51	2,230	0.57	0.59	0.52	0.561	..
World		66.7	..	64	7,376	0.70	0.75	0.72	0.722	..

Note: As a result of revisions to data and methodology and varying country coverage, human development index values and ranks are not strictly comparable with those in earlier *Human Development Reports*. The index has been calculated for UN member countries with reliable data in each of its components as well as for Hong Kong, China (SAR) and the Occupied Palestinian Territories. For data on the remaining 18 UN member countries, see table 30. Aggregates for columns 5-8 are based on all data in the table.

a. The HDI rank is determined using HDI values to the sixth decimal point. b. Data refer to the 2000/01 school year. Data for some countries may refer to national or UNESCO Institute for Statistics estimates. For details, see http://www.uis.unesco.org/. Because data are from different sources, comparisons across countries should be made with caution. c. A positive figure indicates that the HDI rank is higher than the GDP per capita (PPP US$) rank, a negative the opposite. d. For purposes of calculating the HDI, a value of 99.0% was applied. e. Preliminary UNESCO Institute for Statistics estimate, subject to further revision. f. For purposes of calculating the HDI, a value of 100% was applied. g. Data refer to a year other than that specified. h. Data refer to the 1999/2000 school year. They were provided by the UNESCO Institute for Statistics for *Human Development Report 2001* (see UNESCO Institute for Statistics 2001). i. The ratio is an underestimate, as many secondary and tertiary students pursue their studies in nearby countries. j. For purposes of calculating the HDI, a value of $40,000 (PPP US$) was applied. k. Excludes Turkish students and population. l. Estimate based on regression. m. Data are from national sources. n. Because the combined gross enrolment ratio was unavailable, the Human Development Report Office estimate of 78% was used. o. Preliminary World Bank estimate, subject to further revision. p. UNICEF 2003b. q. Data refer to a year or period other than that specified, differ from the standard definition or refer to only part of the country. r. Aten, Heston and Summers 2002. s. Data are from the Secretariat of the Organization of Eastern Caribbean States, based on national sources. t. UNICEF 2000. u. Aten, Heston and Summers 2001. v. UNDP 2002. w. Birzeit University 2002. x. In the absence of an estimate of GDP per capita (PPP US$), the Human Development Report Office estimate of $2,788, derived using the value of GDP in US dollars and the weighted average ratio of PPP US dollars to US dollars in the Arab States, was used. y. World Bank 2002.

Source: Column 1: unless otherwise noted, calculated on the basis of data on life expectancy from UN 2003d; *column 2:* unless otherwise noted, UNESCO Institute for Statistics 2003a; *column 3:* unless otherwise noted, UNESCO Institute for Statistics 2003b; *column 4:* unless otherwise noted, World Bank 2003c; aggregates calculated for the Human Development Report Office by the World Bank; *column 5:* calculated on the basis of data in column 1; *column 6:* calculated on the basis of data in columns 2 and 3; *column 7:* calculated on the basis of data in column 4; *column 8:* calculated on the basis of data in columns 5-7; see technical note 1 for details; *column 9:* calculated on the basis of data in columns 4 and 8.

2 Human development index trends

HDI rank	1975	1980	1985	1990	1995	2001
High human development						
1 Norway	0.858	0.876	0.887	0.900	0.924	0.944
2 Iceland	0.862	0.884	0.893	0.912	0.918	0.942
3 Sweden	0.862	0.871	0.882	0.893	0.924	0.941
4 Australia	0.843	0.859	0.872	0.886	0.926	0.939
5 Netherlands	0.863	0.876	0.890	0.904	0.925	0.938
6 Belgium	0.840	0.857	0.871	0.892	0.923	0.937
7 United States	0.864	0.883	0.896	0.911	0.923	0.937
8 Canada	0.866	0.881	0.904	0.924	0.929	0.937
9 Japan	0.851	0.875	0.890	0.906	0.920	0.932
10 Switzerland	0.872	0.884	0.891	0.904	0.912	0.932
11 Denmark	0.871	0.879	0.886	0.893	0.910	0.930
12 Ireland	0.819	0.832	0.847	0.871	0.895	0.930
13 United Kingdom	0.840	0.847	0.857	0.877	0.916	0.930
14 Finland	0.835	0.854	0.872	0.894	0.907	0.930
15 Luxembourg	0.835	0.849	0.864	0.886	0.913	0.930
16 Austria	0.839	0.853	0.867	0.890	0.908	0.929
17 France	0.846	0.862	0.874	0.896	0.912	0.925
18 Germany	..	0.859	0.868	0.885	0.908	0.921
19 Spain	0.834	0.851	0.865	0.883	0.901	0.918
20 New Zealand	0.844	0.850	0.861	0.870	0.898	0.917
21 Italy	0.838	0.854	0.862	0.884	0.900	0.916
22 Israel	0.794	0.818	0.838	0.857	0.879	0.905
23 Portugal	0.785	0.799	0.821	0.847	0.876	0.896
24 Greece	0.831	0.847	0.859	0.869	0.875	0.892
25 Cyprus	..	0.800	0.820	0.844	0.864	0.891
26 Hong Kong, China (SAR)	0.755	0.794	0.821	0.857	0.875	0.889
27 Barbados	0.802	0.823	0.835	0.849	0.855	0.888
28 Singapore	0.722	0.755	0.782	0.819	0.858	0.884
29 Slovenia	..	..	..	0.843	0.851	0.881
30 Korea, Rep. of	0.701	0.736	0.774	0.814	0.848	0.879
31 Brunei Darussalam	..	..	..	..	..	0.872
32 Czech Republic	..	..	..	0.835	0.843	0.861
33 Malta	0.716	0.751	0.778	0.812	0.835	0.856
34 Argentina	0.784	0.797	0.804	0.807	0.829	0.849
35 Poland	..	..	..	0.794	0.810	0.841
36 Seychelles	..	..	..	..	..	0.840
37 Bahrain	..	0.742	0.773	0.796	0.823	0.839
38 Hungary	0.775	0.791	0.803	0.803	0.807	0.837
39 Slovakia	..	..	..	..	..	0.836
40 Uruguay	0.756	0.775	0.779	0.799	0.814	0.834
41 Estonia	..	0.811	0.818	0.814	0.793	0.833
42 Costa Rica	0.749	0.774	0.776	0.794	0.815	0.832
43 Chile	0.700	0.735	0.752	0.780	0.811	0.831
44 Qatar	..	..	..	..	..	0.826
45 Lithuania	..	..	..	0.819	0.785	0.824
46 Kuwait	0.760	0.780	0.784	..	0.822	0.820
47 Croatia	..	..	..	0.801	0.794	0.818
48 United Arab Emirates	..	..	..	..	..	0.816
49 Bahamas	..	..	..	..	..	0.812
50 Latvia	..	0.791	0.803	0.803	0.761	0.811

HUMAN DEVELOPMENT INDICATORS

HDI rank	1975	1980	1985	1990	1995	2001
51 Saint Kitts and Nevis	..	..	..	..	..	0.808
52 Cuba	..	..	..	..	..	0.806
53 Belarus	..	..	..	0.806	0.774	0.804
54 Trinidad and Tobago	0.733	0.765	0.784	0.787	0.788	0.802
55 Mexico	0.684	0.729	0.748	0.757	0.771	0.800
Medium human development						
56 Antigua and Barbuda	..	..	..	..	..	0.798
57 Bulgaria	..	0.769	0.790	0.792	0.784	0.795
58 Malaysia	0.615	0.658	0.692	0.721	0.759	0.790
59 Panama	0.710	0.729	0.744	0.745	0.768	0.788
60 Macedonia, TFYR	..	..	..	..	..	0.784
61 Libyan Arab Jamahiriya	..	..	..	..	..	0.783
62 Mauritius	..	0.654	0.684	0.720	0.744	0.779
63 Russian Federation	..	0.796	0.811	0.809	0.766	0.779
64 Colombia	0.667	0.696	0.711	0.731	0.758	0.779
65 Brazil	0.643	0.678	0.691	0.712	0.738	0.777
66 Bosnia and Herzegovina	..	..	..	..	..	0.777
67 Belize	..	0.709	0.717	0.749	0.768	0.776
68 Dominica	..	..	..	..	..	0.776
69 Venezuela	0.715	0.729	0.737	0.755	0.765	0.775
70 Samoa (Western)	..	..	0.714	0.726	0.743	0.775
71 Saint Lucia	..	..	..	..	..	0.775
72 Romania	..	..	0.782	0.768	0.765	0.773
73 Saudi Arabia	0.596	0.656	0.679	0.716	0.746	0.769
74 Thailand	0.612	0.650	0.673	0.705	0.739	0.768
75 Ukraine	..	..	..	0.797	0.748	0.766
76 Kazakhstan	..	..	..	0.781	0.738	0.765
77 Suriname	..	..	..	..	..	0.762
78 Jamaica	0.690	0.693	0.695	0.723	0.736	0.757
79 Oman	..	..	..	..	..	0.755
80 St. Vincent & the Grenadines	..	..	..	..	..	0.755
81 Fiji	0.654	0.677	0.691	0.717	0.739	0.754
82 Peru	0.639	0.668	0.691	0.702	0.729	0.752
83 Lebanon	..	..	..	0.678	0.728	0.752
84 Paraguay	0.674	0.708	0.714	0.726	0.744	0.751
85 Philippines	0.647	0.680	0.684	0.713	0.731	0.751
86 Maldives	..	..	..	..	..	0.751
87 Turkmenistan	..	..	..	..	..	0.748
88 Georgia	..	..	..	..	..	0.746
89 Azerbaijan	..	..	..	..	..	0.744
90 Jordan	..	0.637	0.659	0.675	0.702	0.743
91 Tunisia	0.514	0.572	0.620	0.654	0.693	0.740
92 Guyana	0.686	0.689	0.680	0.687	0.711	0.740
93 Grenada	..	..	..	..	..	0.738
94 Dominican Republic	0.625	0.654	0.675	0.683	0.703	0.737
95 Albania	..	0.668	0.686	0.697	0.698	0.735
96 Turkey	0.589	0.612	0.649	0.681	0.712	0.734
97 Ecuador	0.627	0.672	0.694	0.704	0.720	0.731
98 Occupied Palestinian Territories	..	..	..	..	..	0.731
99 Sri Lanka	0.609	0.644	0.670	0.692	0.715	0.730
100 Armenia	..	..	..	0.756	0.709	0.729

HDI rank	1975	1980	1985	1990	1995	2001
101 Uzbekistan	..	..	..	0.728	0.712	0.729
102 Kyrgyzstan	..	..	..	..	..	0.727
103 Cape Verde	..	..	0.593	0.632	0.683	0.727
104 China	0.521	0.554	0.591	0.624	0.679	0.721
105 El Salvador	0.595	0.595	0.614	0.653	0.692	0.719
106 Iran, Islamic Rep. of	0.562	0.566	0.607	0.646	0.690	0.719
107 Algeria	0.510	0.559	0.609	0.648	0.668	0.704
108 Moldova, Rep. of	..	0.718	0.739	0.756	0.704	0.700
109 Viet Nam	..	..	0.582	0.603	0.646	0.688
110 Syrian Arab Republic	0.536	0.578	0.612	0.632	0.664	0.685
111 South Africa	0.660	0.676	0.702	0.734	0.741	0.684
112 Indonesia	0.464	0.526	0.578	0.619	0.659	0.682
113 Tajikistan	..	..	0.736	0.736	0.665	0.677
114 Bolivia	0.511	0.546	0.573	0.598	0.631	0.672
115 Honduras	0.522	0.571	0.603	0.626	0.648	0.667
116 Equatorial Guinea	..	..	..	..	..	0.664
117 Mongolia	..	..	0.647	0.655	0.634	0.661
118 Gabon	..	..	..	..	..	0.653
119 Guatemala	0.514	0.551	0.563	0.587	0.617	0.652
120 Egypt	0.433	0.480	0.530	0.572	0.605	0.648
121 Nicaragua	..	..	..	..	..	0.643
122 São Tomé and Principe	..	..	..	..	..	0.639
123 Solomon Islands	..	..	..	..	..	0.632
124 Namibia	..	..	..	..	0.677	0.627
125 Botswana	0.509	0.573	0.626	0.674	0.666	0.614
126 Morocco	0.427	0.472	0.506	0.538	0.567	0.606
127 India	0.416	0.443	0.481	0.519	0.553	0.590
128 Vanuatu	..	..	..	..	..	0.568
129 Ghana	0.444	0.474	0.487	0.515	0.537	0.567
130 Cambodia	..	..	..	0.512	0.543	0.556
131 Myanmar	..	..	..	..	..	0.549
132 Papua New Guinea	0.428	0.450	0.470	0.487	0.527	0.548
133 Swaziland	0.510	0.541	0.567	0.611	0.606	0.547
134 Comoros	..	0.485	0.503	0.507	0.515	0.528
135 Lao People's Dem. Rep.	..	..	0.422	0.449	0.485	0.525
136 Bhutan	..	..	..	..	..	0.511
137 Lesotho	0.477	0.517	0.542	0.565	0.558	0.510
138 Sudan	0.351	0.378	0.399	0.431	0.465	0.503
139 Bangladesh	0.336	0.352	0.384	0.414	0.443	0.502
140 Congo	0.462	0.506	0.553	0.538	0.517	0.502
141 Togo	0.402	0.450	0.449	0.480	0.491	0.501
Low human development						
142 Cameroon	0.402	0.445	0.495	0.510	0.498	0.499
143 Nepal	0.287	0.326	0.368	0.413	0.451	0.499
144 Pakistan	0.344	0.370	0.403	0.440	0.472	0.499
145 Zimbabwe	0.544	0.570	0.626	0.614	0.567	0.496
146 Kenya	0.440	0.487	0.510	0.535	0.519	0.489
147 Uganda	..	..	0.402	0.403	0.412	0.489
148 Yemen	..	..	..	0.392	0.429	0.470
149 Madagascar	0.397	0.431	0.424	0.431	0.438	0.468
150 Haiti	..	0.446	0.461	0.457	0.456	0.467
151 Gambia	0.291	..	..	..	0.426	0.463

HDI rank	1975	1980	1985	1990	1995	2001
152 Nigeria	0.324	0.384	0.400	0.426	0.452	0.463
153 Djibouti	..	..	..	0.459	0.457	0.462
154 Mauritania	0.346	0.369	0.387	0.399	0.427	0.454
155 Eritrea	..	..	..	..	0.419	0.446
156 Senegal	0.311	0.328	0.354	0.378	0.394	0.430
157 Guinea	..	..	..	..	..	0.425
158 Rwanda	0.349	0.394	0.405	0.359	0.343	0.422
159 Benin	0.286	0.322	0.348	0.352	0.378	0.411
160 Tanzania, U. Rep. of	..	..	..	0.408	0.401	0.400
161 Côte d'Ivoire	0.380	0.413	0.422	0.420	0.405	0.396
162 Malawi	0.314	0.341	0.355	0.365	0.404	0.387
163 Zambia	0.462	0.470	0.478	0.461	0.414	0.386
164 Angola	..	..	..	..	..	0.377
165 Chad	0.265	0.265	0.305	0.330	0.342	0.376
166 Guinea-Bissau	0.263	0.267	0.297	0.319	0.347	0.373
167 Congo, Dem. Rep. of the	0.419	0.426	0.429	0.417	0.380	0.363
168 Central African Republic	0.339	0.356	0.378	0.379	0.370	0.363
169 Ethiopia	..	..	0.281	0.305	0.322	0.359
170 Mozambique	..	0.309	0.295	0.317	0.325	0.356
171 Burundi	0.287	0.312	0.338	0.343	0.317	0.337
172 Mali	0.231	0.261	0.268	0.287	0.308	0.337
173 Burkina Faso	0.237	0.260	0.286	0.301	0.313	0.330
174 Niger	0.243	0.262	0.254	0.264	0.270	0.292
175 Sierra Leone	..	..	..	..	..	0.275

Note: The human development index values in this table were calculated using a consistent methodology and data series. They are not strictly comparable with those in earlier *Human Development Reports*.
Source: Columns 1-5: calculated on the basis of data on life expectancy from UN 2003d, data on adult literacy rates from UNESCO Institute for Statistics 2003a, data on combined gross enrolment ratios from UNESCO Institute for Statistics 2003b and data on GDP at market prices (constant 1995 US$), population and GDP per capita (PPP US$) from World Bank 2003c; *column 6:* column 8 of table 1.

3 Human and income poverty
Developing countries

HDI rank	Human poverty index (HPI-1) Rank	Value (%)	Probability at birth of not surviving to age 40 [†] (% of cohort) 2000-05 [a]	Adult illiteracy rate [†] (% age 15 and above) 2001	Population without sustainable access to an improved water source [†] (%) 2000	Children under weight for age [†] (% under age 5) 1995-2001 [b]	Population below income poverty line (%) $1 a day [c] 1990-2001 [b]	$2 a day [d] 1990-2001 [b]	National poverty line 1987-2000 [b]	HPI-1 rank minus income poverty rank [e]
High human development										
25 Cyprus	..	..	2.9	2.8	0	..	..	..	..	..
26 Hong Kong, China (SAR)	..	..	1.8	6.5	..	..	..	..	..	..
27 Barbados	1	2.5	2.6	0.3	0	6 [f]	..	..	..	..
28 Singapore	6	6.3	1.9	7.5	0	14 [f]	..	..	..	..
30 Korea, Rep. of	..	..	3.4	2.1	8	..	<2	<2	..	..
31 Brunei Darussalam	..	..	2.8	8.4	..	..	..	..	..	..
34 Argentina	..	..	5.1	3.1	..	5	..	..	..	..
36 Seychelles	..	..	..	..	..	6 [f]	..	..	..	..
37 Bahrain	..	..	4.0	12.1	..	9	..	..	..	..
40 Uruguay	2	3.6	4.4	2.4	2	5	<2	<2	..	0
42 Costa Rica	4	4.4	3.7	4.3	5	5	6.9	14.3	..	-12
43 Chile	3	4.1	4.1	4.1	7	1	<2	8.7	17.0	1
44 Qatar	..	..	5.1	18.3	..	6	..	..	..	..
46 Kuwait	..	..	2.6	17.6	..	10	..	..	..	..
48 United Arab Emirates	..	..	3.4	23.3	..	14	..	..	..	..
49 Bahamas	..	..	16.0	4.5	3	..	..	..	..	..
51 Saint Kitts and Nevis	..	..	..	..	2	..	..	..	..	..
52 Cuba	5	5.0	6.0	0.3	0	4	<2	<2	41.9	..
54 Trinidad and Tobago	8	7.7	9.1	1.6	10	7 [f]	12.4	39.0	..	..
55 Mexico	13	8.8	7.6	8.6	12	8	8.0	24.3	..	..
Medium human development										
56 Antigua and Barbuda	..	..	..	..	9	10 [f]	..	..	..	..
58 Malaysia	..	..	4.2	12.1	..	18	<2	9.3	..	..
59 Panama	9	7.8	6.8	7.9	10	7	7.6	17.9	..	-12
61 Libyan Arab Jamahiriya	29	15.7	4.5	19.2	28	5	..	..	..	..
62 Mauritius	17	11.1	4.6	15.2	0	16	..	..	..	..
64 Colombia	10	8.2	8.4	8.1	9	7	14.4	26.5	17.7	-17
65 Brazil	18	11.4	11.5	12.7	13	6	9.9	23.7	..	-8
67 Belize	12	8.8	11.3	6.6	8	6 [f]	..	..	..	..
68 Dominica	..	..	..	..	3	5 [f]	..	..	..	..
69 Venezuela	11	8.6	5.9	7.2	17	5	15.0	32.0	..	-18
70 Samoa (Western)	..	..	6.6	1.3	1	..	..	..	..	..
71 Saint Lucia	..	..	5.7	..	2	14 [f]	..	..	..	..
73 Saudi Arabia	30	16.3	5.2	22.9	5	14	..	..	..	..
74 Thailand	24	12.9	10.2	4.3	16	19 [f]	<2	32.5	13.1	12
77 Suriname	..	..	6.5	..	18	..	..	..	..	..
78 Jamaica	14	9.3	4.9	12.7	8	4	<2	13.3	18.7	7
79 Oman	50	31.8	5.0	27.0	61	24	..	..	..	..
80 St. Vincent & the Grenadines	..	..	3.9	..	7	..	..	..	..	..
81 Fiji	41	21.3	5.4	6.8	53	8 [f]	..	..	..	..
82 Peru	19	11.4	10.2	9.8	20	7	15.5	41.4	49.0	-15
83 Lebanon	15	9.5	4.3	13.5	0	3	..	..	..	..
84 Paraguay	16	10.3	8.0	6.5	22	5	19.5	49.3	..	-22
85 Philippines	28	14.8	7.4	4.9	14	28	14.6	46.4	36.8	-6
86 Maldives	20	11.4	10.2	3.0	0	30	..	..	..	..
90 Jordan	7	7.5	6.6	9.7	4	5	<2	7.4	11.7	3
91 Tunisia	37	19.9	4.9	27.9	20	4	<2	10.0	7.6	24
92 Guyana	23	12.7	17.6	1.4	6	12	<2	6.1	..	13
93 Grenada	..	..	..	..	5	..	..	..	..	..
94 Dominican Republic	25	13.9	14.6	16.0	14	5	<2	<2	20.6	14
96 Turkey	22	12.4	8.0	14.5	18	8	<2	10.3	..	..

3 Human and income poverty
Developing countries

HDI rank		Human poverty index (HPI-1)		Probability at birth of not surviving to age 40 [†] (% of cohort) 2000-05 [a]	Adult illiteracy rate [†] (% age 15 and above) 2001	Population without sustainable access to an improved water source [†] (%) 2000	Children under weight for age [†] (% under age 5) 1995-2001 [b]	Population below income poverty line (%)			HPI-1 rank minus income poverty rank [e]
		Rank	Value (%)					$1 a day [c] 1990-2001 [b]	$2 a day [d] 1990-2001 [b]	National poverty line 1987-2000 [b]	
97	Ecuador	21	11.9	10.3	8.2	15	15	20.2	52.3	..	-21
98	Occupied Palestinian Territories	..	..	5.2	..	14	3	..	..	..	..
99	Sri Lanka	34	18.3	5.1	8.1	23	29	6.6	45.4	25.0	10
103	Cape Verde	40	20.1	7.6	25.1	26	14 [f]	..	..	..	..
104	China	26	14.2	7.1	14.2	25	10	16.1	47.3	4.6	-13
105	El Salvador	32	17.2	9.9	20.8	23	12	21.4	45.0	..	-14
106	Iran, Islamic Rep. of	31	16.4	7.0	22.9	8	11	<2	7.3	..	18
107	Algeria	42	22.6	9.3	32.2	11	6	<2	15.1	22.6	26
109	Viet Nam	39	19.9	10.7	7.3	23	33	17.7	63.7	..	-4
110	Syrian Arab Republic	35	18.8	5.7	24.7	20	13	..	..	..	..
111	South Africa	49	31.7	44.9	14.4	14	12	<2	14.5	..	31
112	Indonesia	33	17.9	10.8	12.7	22	26	7.2	55.4	27.1	5
114	Bolivia	27	14.6	16.0	14.0	17	10	14.4	34.3	62.7	-5
115	Honduras	38	19.9	13.8	24.4	12	25	23.8	44.4	53.0	-15
116	Equatorial Guinea	..	..	36.4	15.8	56	..	..	..	..	..
117	Mongolia	36	19.1	13.0	1.5	40	13	13.9	50.0	..	2
118	Gabon	..	..	28.1	..	14	12	..	..	..	..
119	Guatemala	43	22.9	14.1	30.8	8	24	16.0	37.4	..	0
120	Egypt	47	30.5	8.6	43.9	3	4	3.1	43.9	16.7	18
121	Nicaragua	44	24.3	10.3	33.2	23	12	82.3	94.5	47.9	-34
122	São Tomé and Principe	..	..	10.0	..	..	16	..	..	..	..
123	Solomon Islands	..	..	6.8	..	29	21 [f]	..	..	..	..
124	Namibia	62	37.8	52.3	17.3	23	24	34.9	55.8	..	-2
125	Botswana	75	43.6	61.9	21.9	5	13	23.5	50.1	..	11
126	Morocco	56	35.2	9.4	50.2	20	9 [f]	<2	14.3	19.0	34
127	India	53	33.1	15.3	42.0	16	47	34.7	79.9	28.6	-9
128	Vanuatu	..	..	7.3	..	12	20 [f]	..	..	..	..
129	Ghana	46	26.4	25.8	27.3	27	25	44.8	78.5	..	-21
130	Cambodia	73	42.8	24.0	31.3	70	45	..	..	36.1	..
131	Myanmar	45	25.7	24.6	15.0	28	36	..	..	..	..
132	Papua New Guinea	61	37.0	19.0	35.4	58	35 [f]	..	..	..	..
133	Swaziland	..	..	70.5	19.7	..	10	..	..	..	..
134	Comoros	48	31.5	18.1	44.0	4	25	..	..	..	..
135	Lao People's Dem. Rep.	66	40.5	27.9	34.4	63	40	26.3	73.2	38.6	4
136	Bhutan	..	..	17.3	..	38	19	..	..	..	..
137	Lesotho	83	47.7	68.1	16.1	22	16	43.1	65.7	..	4
138	Sudan	52	32.2	27.6	41.2	25	17	..	..	..	..
139	Bangladesh	72	42.6	17.3	59.4	3	48	36.0	82.8	33.7	0
140	Congo	51	32.0	39.3	18.2	49	14 [f]	..	..	..	..
141	Togo	64	38.5	37.9	41.6	46	25	..	..	..	..
Low human development											
142	Cameroon	58	35.9	44.2	27.6	42	21	33.4	64.4	..	-5
143	Nepal	70	41.9	19.3	57.1	12	48	37.7	82.5	..	-2
144	Pakistan	65	40.2	17.8	56.0	10	38	13.4	65.6	32.6	· 22
145	Zimbabwe	90	52.0	74.8	10.7	17	13	36.0	64.2	34.9	14
146	Kenya	63	37.8	49.5	16.7	43	23	23.0	58.6	..	5
147	Uganda	60	36.6	41.1	32.0	48	23	82.2	96.4	..	-24
148	Yemen	67	41.0	19.1	52.3	31	46	15.7	45.2	..	17
149	Madagascar	57	35.9	29.0	32.7	53	33	49.1	83.3	71.3	-13
150	Haiti	68	41.6	37.3	49.2	54	17	..	..	..	..
151	Gambia	79	45.8	29.6	62.2	38	17	59.3	82.9	..	-3

3 Human and income poverty
Developing countries

HDI rank		Human poverty index (HPI-1) Rank	Value (%)	Probability at birth of not surviving to age 40 [†] (% of cohort) 2000-05 [a]	Adult illiteracy rate [†] (% age 15 and above) 2001	Population without sustainable access to an improved water source [†] (%) 2000	Children under weight for age [†] (% under age 5) 1995-2001 [b]	Population below income poverty line (%) $1 a day [c] 1990-2001 [b]	$2 a day [d] 1990-2001 [b]	National poverty line 1987-2000 [b]	HPI-1 rank minus income poverty rank [e]
152	Nigeria	54	34.0	34.9	34.6	38	27	70.2	90.8	34.1	-25
153	Djibouti	55	34.3	42.9	34.5	0	18	..	..	..	..
154	Mauritania	86	48.6	30.5	59.3	63	32	28.6	68.7	46.3	16
155	Eritrea	69	41.8	27.5	43.3	54	44	..	..	..	..
156	Senegal	76	44.5	27.7	61.7	22	18	26.3	67.8	..	10
157	Guinea	..	..	35.9	..	52	23	..	..	..	..
158	Rwanda	77	44.5	54.3	32.0	59	24	35.7 [g]	84.6 [g]	..	5
159	Benin	81	46.4	34.6	61.4	37	23	..	..	..	..
160	Tanzania, U. Rep. of	59	36.2	46.4	24.0	32	29	19.9	59.7	41.6	5
161	Côte d'Ivoire	78	45.0	51.7	50.3	19	21	12.3	49.4	..	31
162	Malawi	82	47.0	59.6	39.0	43	25	41.7	76.1	65.3	4
163	Zambia	89	50.3	70.1	21.0	36	25	63.7	87.4	72.9	0
164	Angola	..	..	49.2	..	62	..	..	..	..	..
165	Chad	88	50.3	42.9	55.8	73	28	..	..	..	..
166	Guinea-Bissau	84	47.8	41.3	60.4	44	23	..	..	..	..
167	Congo, Dem. Rep. of the	74	42.9	47.2	37.3	55	31	..	..	..	..
168	Central African Republic	85	47.8	55.3	51.8	30	24	66.6	84.0	..	-3
169	Ethiopia	92	56.0	43.3	59.7	76	47	81.9	98.4	44.2	0
170	Mozambique	87	50.3	56.0	54.8	43	26	37.9	78.4	..	10
171	Burundi	80	46.3	50.5	50.8	22	45	58.4	89.2	..	-1
172	Mali	91	55.1	35.3	73.6	35	43	72.8	90.6	..	0
173	Burkina Faso	93	58.6	43.4	75.2	58	34	61.2	85.8	45.3	7
174	Niger	94	61.8	38.7	83.5	41	40	61.4	85.3	..	7
175	Sierra Leone	..	..	57.5	..	43	27	57.0 [g]	74.5 [g]	..	..

† Denotes indicators used to calculate the human poverty index (HPI-1). For further details, see technical note 1.

a. Data refer to the probability at birth of not surviving to age 40, times 100. They are medium-variant projections for the period specified. b. Data refer to the most recent year available during the period specified. c. Poverty line is equivalent to $1.08 (1993 PPP US$). d. Poverty line is equivalent to $2.15 (1993 PPP US$). e. Income poverty refers to the percentage of the population living on less than $1 a day. All countries with an income poverty rate of less than 2% were given equal rank. The rankings are based on countries for which data are available for both indicators. A positive figure indicates that the country performs better in income poverty than in human poverty, a negative the opposite. f. Data refer to a year or period other than that specified, differ from the standard definition or refer to only part of the country. g. Data refer to a period other than that specified.

Source: *Column 1:* determined on the basis of the HPI-1 values in column 2; *column 2:* calculated on the basis of data in columns 3-6; see technical note 1 for details; *column 3:* UN 2003d; *column 4:* UNESCO 2003a; *column 5:* calculated on the basis of data on population with sustainable access to an improved water source from UN 2003a, based on data from a joint effort by the United Nations Children's Fund (UNICEF) and the World Health Organization (WHO); *column 6:* UNICEF 2003b, based on data from a joint effort by UNICEF and the WHO; *columns 7-9:* World Bank 2003c; *column 10:* calculated on the basis of data in columns 1 and 7.

HPI-1 ranks for 94 developing countries									
1	Barbados	18	Brazil	38	Honduras	58	Cameroon	78	Côte d'Ivoire
2	Uruguay	19	Peru	39	Viet Nam	59	Tanzania, U. Rep. of	79	Gambia
3	Chile	20	Maldives	40	Cape Verde	60	Uganda	80	Burundi
4	Costa Rica	21	Ecuador	41	Fiji	61	Papua New Guinea	81	Benin
5	Cuba	22	Turkey	42	Algeria	62	Namibia	82	Malawi
6	Singapore	23	Guyana	43	Guatemala	63	Kenya	83	Lesotho
7	Jordan	24	Thailand	44	Nicaragua	64	Togo	84	Guinea-Bissau
8	Trinidad and Tobago	25	Dominican Republic	45	Myanmar	65	Pakistan	85	Central African Republic
9	Panama	26	China	46	Ghana	66	Lao People's Dem. Rep.	86	Mauritania
10	Colombia	27	Bolivia	47	Egypt	67	Yemen	87	Mozambique
11	Venezuela	28	Philippines	48	Comoros	68	Haiti	88	Chad
12	Belize	29	Libyan Arab Jamahiriya	49	South Africa	69	Eritrea	89	Zambia
13	Mexico	30	Saudi Arabia	50	Oman	70	Nepal	90	Zimbabwe
14	Jamaica	31	Iran, Islamic Rep.	51	Congo	71	Iraq	91	Mali
15	Lebanon	32	El Salvador	52	Sudan	72	Bangladesh	92	Ethiopia
16	Paraguay	33	Indonesia	53	India	73	Cambodia	93	Burkina Faso
17	Mauritius	34	Sri Lanka	54	Nigeria	74	Congo, Dem. Rep. of the	94	Niger
		35	Syrian Arab Republic	55	Djibouti	75	Botswana		
		36	Mongolia	56	Morocco	76	Senegal		
		37	Tunisia	57	Madagascar	77	Rwanda		

4 Human and income poverty
OECD, Central & Eastern Europe & CIS

HDI rank		Human poverty index (HPI-2) [a] Rank	Value (%)	Probability at birth of not surviving to age 60 [†] (% of cohort) 2000-05 [b]	People lacking functional literacy skills [†] (% age 16-65) 1994-98 [c]	Long-term unemployment [†] (as % of labour force) [d] 2001	Population below income poverty line (%) 50% of median income [e, †] 1990-2000 [f]	$11 a day 1994-95 [f, g]	$4 a day 1996-99 [f, h]	HPI-2 rank minus income poverty rank [i]
High human development										
1	Norway	2	7.2	8.3	8.5	0.2	6.9	4.3	..	-2
2	Iceland	..	..	7.6	..	0.3	..	..	..	..
3	Sweden	1	6.5	7.3	7.5	1.1	6.6	6.3	..	-2
4	Australia	14	12.9	8.8	17.0	1.4	14.3	17.6	..	-2
5	Netherlands	4	8.4	8.7	10.5	1.6 [j]	8.1	7.1	..	-4
6	Belgium	13	12.4	9.4	18.4 [k]	3.2	8.0	..	..	7
7	United States	17	15.8	12.6	20.7	0.3	17.0	13.6	..	0
8	Canada	12	12.2	8.7	16.6	0.7	12.8	7.4	..	-2
9	Japan	10	11.1	7.5	.. [l]	1.4	11.8 [m]	..	..	-1
10	Switzerland	..	..	9.1	..	0.7	9.3	..	..	..
11	Denmark	5	9.1	11.0	9.6	0.9	9.2	..	..	-4
12	Ireland	16	15.3	9.3	22.6	3.2 [j]	12.3	..	..	4
13	United Kingdom	15	14.8	8.9	21.8	1.3	12.5	15.7	..	2
14	Finland	3	8.4	10.2	10.4	2.4	5.4	4.8	..	1
15	Luxembourg	7	10.3	9.7	.. [l]	0.5 [n]	3.9	0.3	..	6
16	Austria	..	..	9.5	..	0.9	10.6	..	..	..
17	France	8	10.8	10.0	.. [l]	3.3	8.0	9.9	..	2
18	Germany	6	10.2	9.2	14.4	4.2 [o]	7.5	7.3	..	1
19	Spain	9	11.0	8.8	.. [l]	4.6	10.1	..	..	-1
20	New Zealand	..	..	9.8	18.4	0.9	..	..	..	..
21	Italy	11	12.2	8.6	.. [l]	6.1	14.2	..	..	-4
22	Israel	..	..	7.4	..	..	13.5	..	..	..
23	Portugal	..	..	11.7	48.0	1.6	..	..	..	..
24	Greece	..	..	9.1	..	5.5	..	..	..	..
29	Slovenia	..	..	11.8	42.2	..	8.2	..	<1	..
32	Czech Republic	..	..	12.2	15.7	4.3	4.9	..	<1	..
33	Malta	..	..	7.7	..	..	..	..	..	..
35	Poland	..	..	15.6	42.6	8.0	8.6	..	10	..
38	Hungary	..	..	19.6	33.8	2.7	6.7	..	<1	..
39	Slovakia	..	..	15.2	..	9.3	2.1	..	8	..
41	Estonia	..	..	20.4	..	..	12.3	..	18	..
45	Lithuania	..	..	19.5	..	..	..	..	17	..
47	Croatia	..	..	14.5	..	..	..	..	..	..
50	Latvia	..	..	21.4	..	..	..	..	28	..
53	Belarus	..	..	22.8	..	..	..	..	..	..
Medium human development										
57	Bulgaria	..	..	18.6	..	..	..	..	22	..
60	Macedonia, TFYR	..	..	13.3	..	..	..	..	..	..
63	Russian Federation	..	..	28.9	..	..	20.1	..	53	..
66	Bosnia and Herzegovina	..	..	13.7	..	..	..	..	..	..
72	Romania	..	..	20.3	..	..	..	..	23	..
75	Ukraine	..	..	23.0	..	..	..	..	25	..
76	Kazakhstan	..	..	27.0	..	..	..	..	62	..
87	Turkmenistan	..	..	24.8	..	..	..	..	..	..
88	Georgia	..	..	16.2	..	..	..	..	..	..
89	Azerbaijan	..	..	18.5	..	..	..	..	..	..

HDI rank	Human poverty index (HPI-2)[a] Rank	Human poverty index (HPI-2)[a] Value (%)	Probability at birth of not surviving to age 60[†] (% of cohort) 2000-05[b]	People lacking functional literacy skills[†] (% age 16-65) 1994-98[c]	Long-term unemployment[†] (as % of labour force)[d] 2001	Population below income poverty line (%) 50% of median income[e,†] 1990-2000[f]	Population below income poverty line (%) $11 a day 1994-95[f,g]	Population below income poverty line (%) $4 a day 1996-99[f,h]	HPI-2 rank minus income poverty rank[i]
95 Albania	..	..	11.3	..	..	..	..	..	..
100 Armenia	..	..	14.9	..	..	..	..	..	..
101 Uzbekistan	..	..	21.8	..	..	..	..	..	..
102 Kyrgyzstan	..	..	23.7	..	..	..	..	88	..
108 Moldova, Rep. of	..	..	22.8	..	..	..	..	82	..
113 Tajikistan	..	..	22.8	..	..	..	..	..	..

† Denotes indicators used to calculate the human poverty index (HPI-2). For further details, see technical note 1.

Note: This table includes Israel and Malta, which are not OECD member countries, but excludes the Republic of Korea, Mexico and Turkey, which are. For the human poverty index and related indicators for these countries, see table 3.

a. The human poverty index (HPI-2) is calculated for selected high-income OECD countries only. b. Data refer to the probability at birth of not surviving to age 60, times 100. They are medium-variant projections for the period specified. c. Based on scoring at level 1 on the prose literacy scale of the International Adult Literacy Survey. Data refer to the most recent year available during the period specified. d. Data refer to unemployment lasting 12 months or longer. e. Poverty line is measured at 50% of the median adjusted household disposable income. f. Data refer to the most recent year available during the period specified. g. Based on the US poverty line, $11 (1994 PPP US$) a day per person for a family of three. h. Poverty line is $4 (1990 PPP US$) a day. i. Income poverty refers to the percentage of the population living on less than 50% of the median adjusted household disposable income. A positive figure indicates that the country performs better in income poverty than in human poverty, a negative the opposite. j. Data refer to 1999. k. Data refer to Flanders. l. For purposes of calculating the HPI-2, an estimate of 15.1%, the unweighted average for countries with available data, was applied. m. Smeeding 1997. n. Data are based on a small sample and should be treated with caution. o. Data refer to 2000.

Source: Column 1: determined on the basis of the HPI-2 values in column 2; *column 2:* calculated on the basis of data in columns 3-6; see technical note 1 for details; *column 3:* calculated on the basis of survival data from UN 2003d; *column 4:* unless otherwise noted, OECD and Statistics Canada 2000; *column 5:* calculated on the basis of data on long-term unemployment and labour force from OECD 2002a; *column 6:* LIS 2003; *column 7:* Smeeding, Rainwater and Burtless 2002; *column 8:* Milanovic 2002; *column 9:* calculated on the basis of data in columns 1 and 6.

HPI-2 ranks for 17 selected OECD countries

1 Sweden	6 Germany	13 Belgium
2 Norway	7 Luxembourg	14 Australia
3 Finland	8 France	15 United Kingdom
4 Netherlands	9 Spain	16 Ireland
5 Denmark	10 Japan	17 United States
	11 Italy	
	12 Canada	

5 Demographic trends

		Total population (millions)			Annual population growth rate		Urban population (as % of total)[a]			Population under age 15 (as % of total)		Population aged 65 and above (as % of total)		Total fertility rate (per woman)	
HDI rank		1975	2001[b]	2015[b]	1975-2001	2001-15[b]	1975	2001[b]	2015[b]	2001[b]	2015[b]	2001[b]	2015[b]	1970-75[c]	2000-05[b]
High human development															
1	Norway	4.0	4.5	4.7	0.4	0.4	68.2	75.0	78.9	19.8	16.6	15.3	18.0	2.2	1.8
2	Iceland	0.2	0.3	0.3	1.0	0.6	86.6	92.6	94.3	23.2	18.7	11.6	13.5	2.8	2.0
3	Sweden	8.2	8.9	9.0	0.3	0.1	82.7	83.3	84.2	18.1	15.7	17.4	21.4	1.9	1.6
4	Australia	13.9	19.4	21.7	1.3	0.8	85.9	91.1	94.8	20.3	17.3	12.4	15.5	2.5	1.7
5	Netherlands	13.7	16.0	16.8	0.6	0.4	88.4	89.6	91.0	18.4	16.4	13.7	17.4	2.1	1.7
6	Belgium	9.8	10.3	10.5	0.2	0.1	94.9	97.4	98.0	17.3	15.5	17.2	19.5	1.9	1.7
7	United States	220.2	288.0	329.7	1.0	1.0	73.7	77.4	81.0	21.7	20.3	12.3	14.2	2.0	2.1
8	Canada	23.1	31.0	34.1	1.1	0.7	75.6	78.9	81.9	18.7	14.8	12.7	16.4	2.0	1.5
9	Japan	111.5	127.3	127.2	0.5	(.)	75.7	78.9	81.5	14.5	13.0	17.7	26.0	2.1	1.3
10	Switzerland	6.3	7.2	7.0	0.5	-0.2	55.7	67.5	69.5	16.5	12.6	16.2	22.0	1.8	1.4
11	Denmark	5.1	5.3	5.4	0.2	0.1	81.8	85.1	85.7	18.4	16.3	15.0	19.2	2.0	1.8
12	Ireland	3.2	3.9	4.4	0.8	0.9	53.6	59.3	64.0	21.2	20.3	11.3	13.4	3.8	1.9
13	United Kingdom	55.4	58.9	61.3	0.2	0.3	88.7	89.5	90.8	18.9	15.9	15.9	17.8	2.0	1.6
14	Finland	4.7	5.2	5.3	0.4	0.1	58.3	59.0	59.0	18.0	15.8	15.1	20.3	1.6	1.7
15	Luxembourg	0.4	0.4	0.5	0.8	1.2	73.7	91.8	95.0	19.0	17.6	13.6	14.4	2.0	1.7
16	Austria	7.6	8.1	8.1	0.3	(.)	67.4	67.4	71.0	16.4	12.4	15.6	19.5	2.0	1.3
17	France	52.7	59.6	62.8	0.5	0.4	73.0	75.5	78.4	18.7	17.8	16.1	18.5	2.3	1.9
18	Germany	78.7	82.3	82.5	0.2	(.)	81.2	87.7	89.9	15.4	13.2	16.7	20.8	1.6	1.4
19	Spain	35.6	40.9	41.2	0.5	0.1	69.6	77.8	81.1	14.4	13.2	16.9	19.2	2.9	1.2
20	New Zealand	3.1	3.8	4.2	0.8	0.6	82.8	85.9	87.5	22.8	19.3	11.8	14.6	2.8	2.0
21	Italy	55.4	57.5	55.5	0.1	-0.3	65.6	67.1	70.6	14.2	12.3	18.4	22.3	2.3	1.2
22	Israel	3.4	6.2	7.8	2.3	1.6	86.6	91.8	93.5	28.1	24.8	9.9	11.4	3.8	2.7
23	Portugal	9.1	10.0	10.0	0.4	(.)	27.7	65.6	77.5	16.6	15.3	15.8	18.0	2.7	1.5
24	Greece	9.0	10.9	10.9	0.7	(.)	55.3	60.4	65.1	14.9	13.2	17.8	20.9	2.3	1.3
25	Cyprus	0.6	0.8	0.9	1.0	0.6	45.2	70.2	74.6	22.5	18.9	11.7	14.9	2.5	1.9
26	Hong Kong, China (SAR)	4.4	6.9	7.9	1.7	0.9	89.7	100.0	100.0	16.2	12.9	10.8	13.6	2.9	1.0
27	Barbados	0.2	0.3	0.3	0.3	0.3	38.6	50.5	58.4	20.5	16.4	10.1	11.1	2.7	1.5
28	Singapore	2.3	4.1	4.7	2.3	1.0	100.0	100.0	100.0	21.5	12.9	7.4	13.1	2.6	1.4
29	Slovenia	1.7	2.0	1.9	0.5	-0.2	42.4	49.2	51.6	15.4	12.1	14.2	18.5	2.2	1.1
30	Korea, Rep. of	35.3	47.1	49.7	1.1	0.4	48.0	82.4	88.2	20.6	15.5	7.4	11.9	4.3	1.4
31	Brunei Darussalam	0.2	0.3	0.5	2.9	2.0	62.0	72.7	78.7	31.0	25.4	2.9	4.4	5.4	2.5
32	Czech Republic	10.0	10.3	10.1	0.1	-0.1	63.7	74.6	76.4	16.0	13.2	13.9	18.6	2.2	1.2
33	Malta	0.3	0.4	0.4	1.0	0.4	80.4	91.2	93.7	19.7	17.0	12.5	18.0	2.1	1.8
34	Argentina	26.0	37.5	43.4	1.4	1.0	80.7	88.3	90.2	27.5	24.4	9.9	11.0	3.1	2.4
35	Poland	34.0	38.7	38.2	0.5	-0.1	55.4	62.6	66.5	18.6	14.6	12.3	14.8	2.3	1.3
36	Seychelles	0.1	0.1	0.1	1.2	0.8	33.3	64.5	72.3	..	..	..	..	..	..
37	Bahrain	0.3	0.7	0.9	3.6	1.9	79.2	92.5	95.0	29.4	23.2	2.3	3.9	5.9	2.7
38	Hungary	10.5	10.0	9.3	-0.2	-0.5	52.8	64.8	69.4	16.7	13.3	14.7	17.4	2.1	1.2
39	Slovakia	4.7	5.4	5.4	0.5	0.1	46.3	57.6	62.0	19.0	15.4	11.4	13.6	2.5	1.3
40	Uruguay	2.8	3.4	3.7	0.7	0.6	83.1	92.1	94.4	24.7	22.5	13.1	13.7	3.0	2.3
41	Estonia	1.4	1.4	1.2	-0.2	-1.1	67.6	69.4	71.3	17.4	14.2	15.4	18.2	2.2	1.2
42	Costa Rica	2.1	4.0	5.0	2.6	1.6	42.5	59.5	66.5	31.1	23.9	5.5	7.4	4.3	2.3
43	Chile	10.3	15.4	18.0	1.5	1.1	78.4	86.0	89.1	28.1	23.6	7.4	9.8	3.6	2.4
44	Qatar	0.2	0.6	0.7	4.8	1.3	82.9	92.9	95.0	26.9	21.7	1.5	4.6	6.8	3.2
45	Lithuania	3.3	3.5	3.2	0.2	-0.6	55.7	68.7	71.6	19.6	16.0	14.3	16.4	2.3	1.3
46	Kuwait	1.0	2.4	3.4	3.3	2.5	83.8	96.1	96.9	26.3	22.6	1.4	3.5	6.9	2.7
47	Croatia	4.3	4.4	4.3	0.2	-0.3	45.1	58.1	64.4	17.0	16.5	15.9	17.8	2.0	1.7
48	United Arab Emirates	0.5	2.9	3.6	6.7	1.6	65.4	87.1	91.6	26.4	20.8	1.2	4.2	6.4	2.8
49	Bahamas	0.2	0.3	0.4	1.9	1.0	73.4	88.8	91.5	29.3	24.5	5.2	8.3	3.4	2.3
50	Latvia	2.5	2.4	2.1	-0.2	-0.9	65.4	60.4	60.4	17.3	13.0	15.4	18.3	2.0	1.1

5 Demographic trends

HDI rank	Total population (millions)			Annual population growth rate 1975-		Urban population (as % of total)[a]			Population under age 15 (as % of total)		Population aged 65 and above (as % of total)		Total fertility rate (per woman)	
	1975	2001[b]	2015[b]	2001	2001-15[b]	1975	2001[b]	2015[b]	2001[b]	2015[b]	2001[b]	2015[b]	1970-75[c]	2000-05[b]
51 Saint Kitts and Nevis	(.)	(.)	(.)	-0.3	-0.3	35.0	34.3	39.3	..	..	..	..	..	..
52 Cuba	9.3	11.2	11.5	0.7	0.2	64.2	75.5	78.5	20.8	16.3	9.9	14.4	3.5	1.6
53 Belarus	9.4	10.0	9.4	0.2	-0.4	50.3	69.6	72.6	17.9	14.1	13.9	14.3	2.3	1.2
54 Trinidad and Tobago	1.0	1.3	1.3	0.9	0.3	63.0	74.5	79.3	24.1	19.7	6.8	10.0	3.5	1.6
55 Mexico	59.1	100.5	119.6	2.0	1.2	62.8	74.6	77.9	33.3	26.4	4.9	6.8	6.5	2.5
Medium human development														
56 Antigua and Barbuda	0.1	0.1	0.1	0.6	0.4	34.2	37.1	43.3	..	..	..	..	..	..
57 Bulgaria	8.7	8.0	7.2	-0.3	-0.8	57.5	67.5	69.3	15.3	12.6	16.3	18.0	2.2	1.1
58 Malaysia	12.3	23.5	29.6	2.5	1.6	37.7	58.1	66.4	33.4	27.2	4.1	6.1	5.2	2.9
59 Panama	1.7	3.0	3.8	2.1	1.7	49.0	56.6	61.7	31.6	27.5	5.6	7.5	4.9	2.7
60 Macedonia, TFYR	1.7	2.0	2.2	0.7	0.4	50.6	59.5	62.0	22.3	20.0	10.2	12.2	3.0	1.9
61 Libyan Arab Jamahiriya	2.4	5.3	6.9	3.0	1.8	60.9	87.9	90.3	32.0	28.7	3.7	5.5	7.6	3.0
62 Mauritius	0.9	1.2	1.3	1.1	0.8	43.4	41.6	48.6	25.5	21.0	6.2	8.2	3.2	1.9
63 Russian Federation	134.2	144.9	133.4	0.3	-0.6	66.4	72.9	74.0	17.2	13.7	12.8	14.3	2.0	1.1
64 Colombia	25.4	42.8	52.2	2.0	1.4	60.0	75.5	81.3	32.4	27.0	4.8	6.5	5.0	2.6
65 Brazil	108.1	174.0	202.0	1.8	1.1	61.8	81.7	87.7	28.8	24.1	5.3	7.5	4.7	2.2
66 Bosnia and Herzegovina	3.7	4.1	4.3	0.3	0.4	31.3	43.4	50.8	18.3	14.1	10.3	13.6	2.6	1.3
67 Belize	0.1	0.2	0.3	2.3	1.8	50.2	48.1	51.7	38.3	31.1	4.1	4.8	6.3	3.2
68 Dominica	0.1	0.1	0.1	0.3	0.2	55.3	71.3	76.0	..	..	..	..	..	..
69 Venezuela	12.7	24.8	31.2	2.6	1.7	75.8	87.2	90.0	33.5	27.6	4.6	6.6	4.9	2.7
70 Samoa (Western)	0.2	0.2	0.2	0.6	1.1	21.1	22.3	27.6	40.7	35.5	4.6	4.4	5.7	4.1
71 Saint Lucia	0.1	0.1	0.2	1.3	0.7	38.6	38.0	43.6	30.6	26.0	5.4	6.2	5.7	2.3
72 Romania	21.2	22.4	21.6	0.2	-0.3	46.2	55.3	59.3	17.7	15.4	13.6	14.8	2.6	1.3
73 Saudi Arabia	7.3	22.8	32.7	4.4	2.6	58.4	86.6	91.0	39.3	34.5	2.6	3.4	7.3	4.5
74 Thailand	41.3	61.6	69.6	1.5	0.9	15.1	20.0	24.2	25.9	22.0	5.6	8.1	5.0	1.9
75 Ukraine	49.0	49.3	44.4	(.)	-0.8	58.3	68.0	70.4	17.2	13.2	14.2	16.1	2.2	1.2
76 Kazakhstan	14.1	15.5	15.3	0.4	-0.1	52.2	55.9	58.2	26.9	21.4	7.1	8.4	3.5	2.0
77 Suriname	0.4	0.4	0.5	0.6	0.7	49.5	74.7	81.3	31.5	27.0	5.4	6.2	5.3	2.5
78 Jamaica	2.0	2.6	3.0	1.0	1.0	44.1	56.6	63.5	31.2	25.8	7.1	7.7	5.0	2.4
79 Oman	0.9	2.7	3.9	4.1	2.7	19.6	76.5	82.6	37.4	36.0	2.0	3.0	7.2	5.0
80 St. Vincent & the Grenadines	0.1	0.1	0.1	0.8	0.5	27.0	55.8	68.0	31.2	26.0	6.8	7.1	5.5	2.2
81 Fiji	0.6	0.8	0.9	1.4	0.8	36.7	50.2	59.9	32.8	27.6	3.5	5.8	4.2	2.9
82 Peru	15.2	26.4	32.0	2.1	1.4	61.5	73.1	77.9	34.1	27.5	4.9	6.5	6.0	2.9
83 Lebanon	2.8	3.5	4.2	0.9	1.2	67.0	90.0	92.6	30.2	24.0	6.1	6.5	4.9	2.2
84 Paraguay	2.7	5.6	7.7	2.9	2.2	39.0	56.6	65.0	39.2	34.2	3.5	4.3	5.7	3.8
85 Philippines	42.0	77.2	96.3	2.3	1.6	35.6	59.3	69.0	37.1	29.9	3.6	4.9	6.0	3.2
86 Maldives	0.1	0.3	0.4	3.0	2.9	18.1	28.0	35.2	43.4	39.6	3.3	3.1	7.0	5.3
87 Turkmenistan	2.5	4.7	5.8	2.4	1.5	47.6	45.0	49.9	35.6	27.4	4.4	4.6	6.2	2.7
88 Georgia	4.9	5.2	4.7	0.2	-0.7	49.5	56.5	61.4	19.9	15.2	13.3	14.9	2.6	1.4
89 Azerbaijan	5.7	8.2	9.5	1.4	1.0	51.5	51.9	53.9	30.9	23.5	5.8	5.9	4.3	2.1
90 Jordan	1.9	5.2	7.0	3.8	2.1	57.8	78.8	81.1	38.5	31.6	2.9	4.0	7.8	3.6
91 Tunisia	5.7	9.6	11.1	2.0	1.0	49.9	66.1	73.5	29.4	22.6	5.8	6.7	6.2	2.0
92 Guyana	0.7	0.8	0.8	0.1	(.)	30.0	36.7	44.0	30.2	25.5	5.0	6.6	4.9	2.3
93 Grenada	0.1	0.1	0.1	-0.5	-0.3	32.6	38.4	47.2	..	..	..	..	..	..
94 Dominican Republic	5.0	8.5	10.1	2.0	1.3	45.3	66.0	73.0	33.0	28.3	4.5	6.4	5.6	2.7
95 Albania	2.4	3.1	3.4	1.0	0.7	32.7	42.9	51.9	29.0	22.9	6.0	8.1	4.7	2.3
96 Turkey	41.0	69.3	82.1	2.0	1.2	41.6	66.2	71.8	31.2	25.0	5.6	6.7	5.2	2.4
97 Ecuador	6.9	12.6	15.2	2.3	1.3	42.4	63.4	69.4	33.6	27.1	4.9	6.6	6.0	2.8
98 Occupied Palestinian Territories	1.3	3.3	5.3	3.7	3.3	59.6	..	71.7	46.3	42.1	3.4	3.0	7.7	5.6
99 Sri Lanka	13.5	18.8	20.6	1.3	0.7	22.0	23.1	29.9	25.5	21.3	6.8	9.3	4.1	2.0
100 Armenia	2.8	3.1	3.0	0.3	-0.3	63.0	67.3	69.8	22.5	14.4	8.8	9.9	3.0	1.2

HDI rank		Total population (millions)			Annual population growth rate 1975-		Urban population (as % of total) [a]			Population under age 15 (as % of total)		Population aged 65 and above (as % of total)		Total fertility rate (per woman)	
		1975	2001 [b]	2015 [b]	2001	2001-15 [b]	1975	2001 [b]	2015 [b]	2001 [b]	2015 [b]	2001 [b]	2015 [b]	1970-75 [c]	2000-05 [b]
101	Uzbekistan	14.0	25.3	30.7	2.3	1.4	39.1	36.7	38.4	35.4	26.2	4.8	5.0	6.3	2.4
102	Kyrgyzstan	3.3	5.0	5.9	1.6	1.2	37.9	34.4	36.0	33.3	26.4	6.1	5.9	4.7	2.6
103	Cape Verde	0.3	0.4	0.6	1.8	1.9	21.4	63.3	73.5	40.9	32.6	4.5	3.5	7.0	3.3
104	China	927.8 [d]	1,285.2 [d]	1,402.3 [d]	1.3 [d]	0.6 [d]	17.4	36.7	49.5	24.3	19.4	7.0	9.4	4.9	1.8
105	El Salvador	4.1	6.3	7.6	1.6	1.3	41.5	61.3	73.2	35.4	29.4	5.2	6.5	6.1	2.9
106	Iran, Islamic Rep. of	33.4	67.2	81.4	2.7	1.4	45.8	64.7	73.2	33.9	26.8	4.5	4.9	6.4	2.3
107	Algeria	16.0	30.7	38.1	2.5	1.5	40.3	57.7	65.2	34.3	27.4	4.2	4.9	7.4	2.8
108	Moldova, Rep. of	3.8	4.3	4.2	0.4	-0.1	35.8	41.7	45.2	22.1	16.5	9.6	10.9	2.6	1.4
109	Viet Nam	48.0	79.2	94.7	1.9	1.3	18.8	24.5	31.6	32.6	25.3	5.4	5.5	6.7	2.3
110	Syrian Arab Republic	7.5	17.0	23.0	3.1	2.2	45.1	51.8	57.9	39.1	32.2	3.0	3.6	7.5	3.3
111	South Africa	25.8	44.4	44.3	2.1	(.)	48.0	57.6	67.2	33.6	29.2	3.8	6.0	5.4	2.6
112	Indonesia	134.4	214.4	250.4	1.8	1.1	19.4	42.0	55.0	30.4	25.3	5.0	6.4	5.2	2.4
113	Tajikistan	3.4	6.1	7.3	2.2	1.2	35.5	27.6	29.6	38.5	28.5	4.7	4.6	6.8	3.1
114	Bolivia	4.8	8.5	10.8	2.2	1.7	41.3	62.9	69.9	39.3	32.8	4.4	5.3	6.5	3.8
115	Honduras	3.0	6.6	8.8	3.0	2.0	32.1	53.6	64.3	41.2	33.5	3.6	4.5	7.1	3.7
116	Equatorial Guinea	0.2	0.5	0.7	2.8	2.5	27.1	49.2	61.4	43.5	43.0	3.8	3.6	5.7	5.9
117	Mongolia	1.4	2.5	3.1	2.1	1.3	48.7	56.7	59.5	34.2	26.6	3.8	4.1	7.3	2.4
118	Gabon	0.6	1.3	1.6	2.9	1.8	40.0	82.1	88.9	41.3	35.0	4.5	4.3	5.3	4.0
119	Guatemala	6.0	11.7	16.2	2.6	2.3	36.7	40.0	46.2	43.3	37.4	3.6	3.9	6.5	4.4
120	Egypt	39.3	69.1	90.0	2.2	1.9	43.5	42.7	45.8	35.7	31.7	4.5	5.4	5.7	3.3
121	Nicaragua	2.5	5.2	7.0	2.8	2.1	48.9	56.5	62.6	42.2	34.9	3.1	3.8	6.8	3.7
122	São Tomé and Principe	0.1	0.2	0.2	2.4	2.3	27.0	47.6	56.4	41.2	36.4	4.6	3.8	5.4	4.0
123	Solomon Islands	0.2	0.5	0.6	3.3	2.6	9.1	20.2	28.6	43.3	36.5	2.7	3.4	7.2	4.4
124	Namibia	0.9	1.9	2.2	2.8	0.9	20.6	31.4	39.4	43.2	37.5	3.7	4.6	6.6	4.6
125	Botswana	0.8	1.7	1.7	2.9	-0.2	12.8	49.4	56.0	40.0	37.4	2.6	4.5	6.7	3.7
126	Morocco	17.3	29.6	36.5	2.1	1.5	37.8	56.1	64.4	32.3	27.9	4.3	5.1	6.9	2.7
127	India	620.7	1,033.4	1,246.4	2.0	1.3	21.3	27.9	32.2	33.7	27.7	5.0	6.3	5.4	3.0
128	Vanuatu	0.1	0.2	0.3	2.7	2.2	15.7	22.1	28.6	41.6	34.9	3.5	4.0	6.1	4.1
129	Ghana	9.9	20.0	26.4	2.7	2.0	30.1	36.4	42.4	40.6	34.9	3.3	4.1	6.9	4.1
130	Cambodia	7.1	13.5	18.4	2.5	2.2	10.3	17.4	26.1	42.5	37.4	2.9	3.6	5.5	4.8
131	Myanmar	30.2	48.2	55.8	1.8	1.0	23.9	28.2	36.7	32.7	26.8	4.6	5.9	5.8	2.9
132	Papua New Guinea	2.9	5.5	7.2	2.5	1.9	11.9	17.6	22.3	41.4	34.0	2.4	2.8	6.1	4.1
133	Swaziland	0.5	1.1	1.1	2.8	0.1	14.0	26.7	32.7	44.0	39.7	3.2	4.6	6.9	4.5
134	Comoros	0.3	0.7	1.0	3.2	2.6	21.2	33.8	42.6	42.7	38.5	2.3	3.0	7.1	4.9
135	Lao People's Dem. Rep.	3.0	5.4	7.3	2.2	2.1	11.1	19.7	27.1	42.4	36.8	3.5	3.7	6.2	4.8
136	Bhutan	1.2	2.1	3.0	2.3	2.6	3.5	7.4	11.6	42.3	37.8	4.3	4.5	5.9	5.0
137	Lesotho	1.1	1.8	1.7	1.8	-0.3	10.8	28.7	38.9	40.2	38.2	4.6	5.4	5.7	3.8
138	Sudan	16.7	32.2	41.4	2.5	1.8	18.9	37.0	48.7	39.9	34.8	3.5	4.4	6.7	4.4
139	Bangladesh	75.2	140.9	181.4	2.4	1.8	9.9	25.5	34.4	38.8	31.9	3.2	3.8	6.2	3.5
140	Congo	1.5	3.5	5.2	3.2	2.8	35.0	66.0	72.6	46.6	46.2	3.0	2.8	6.3	6.3
141	Togo	2.3	4.7	6.4	2.8	2.2	16.3	33.9	42.7	44.1	40.3	3.2	3.5	7.1	5.3
Low human development															
142	Cameroon	7.6	15.4	18.9	2.7	1.4	26.9	49.6	58.9	42.7	37.8	3.6	4.1	6.3	4.6
143	Nepal	13.4	24.1	32.0	2.3	2.0	5.0	12.2	17.9	40.5	35.6	3.7	4.2	5.8	4.3
144	Pakistan	70.3	146.3	204.5	2.8	2.4	26.4	33.4	39.5	41.8	38.1	3.7	4.0	6.3	5.1
145	Zimbabwe	6.1	12.8	13.0	2.8	0.2	19.6	36.0	45.9	43.5	39.6	3.4	4.2	7.6	3.9
146	Kenya	13.6	31.1	36.9	3.2	1.2	12.9	34.3	47.2	42.7	36.5	2.9	3.4	8.1	4.0
147	Uganda	10.8	24.2	39.3	3.1	3.5	8.3	14.5	20.7	50.0	49.7	2.6	2.3	7.1	7.1
148	Yemen	6.9	18.7	30.7	3.8	3.6	16.6	25.0	31.2	48.9	47.2	2.3	2.2	8.4	7.0
149	Madagascar	7.9	16.4	24.0	2.8	2.7	16.3	30.1	39.4	44.7	41.7	3.0	3.1	6.6	5.7
150	Haiti	4.9	8.1	9.7	1.9	1.3	21.7	36.3	45.6	39.8	35.1	3.9	4.5	5.8	4.0
151	Gambia	0.6	1.4	1.9	3.4	2.3	17.0	31.2	40.5	41.1	36.6	3.5	4.4	6.5	4.7

HDI rank		Total population (millions) 1975	2001[b]	2015[b]	Annual population growth rate 1975-2001	2001-15[b]	Urban population (as % of total)[a] 1975	2001[b]	2015[b]	Population under age 15 (as % of total) 2001[b]	2015[b]	Population aged 65 and above (as % of total) 2001[b]	2015[b]	Total fertility rate (per woman) 1970-75[c]	2000-05[b]
152	Nigeria	54.9	117.8	161.7	2.9	2.3	23.4	44.8	55.5	44.8	40.6	3.1	3.4	6.9	5.4
153	Djibouti	0.2	0.7	0.8	4.4	1.5	68.9	84.2	86.9	43.0	40.3	2.9	3.8	7.2	5.7
154	Mauritania	1.4	2.7	4.0	2.5	2.7	20.3	59.0	73.8	43.2	41.7	3.4	3.5	6.5	5.8
155	Eritrea	2.1	3.8	5.9	2.3	3.1	12.7	19.1	26.2	45.7	41.7	2.1	2.4	6.5	5.4
156	Senegal	4.8	9.6	13.2	2.7	2.2	34.2	48.1	57.4	43.8	39.0	2.4	2.7	7.0	5.0
157	Guinea	4.1	8.2	11.2	2.7	2.2	16.3	27.9	35.5	44.1	41.5	2.8	3.1	7.0	5.8
158	Rwanda	4.4	8.1	10.6	2.3	1.9	4.0	6.3	8.9	45.3	43.5	2.5	2.9	8.3	5.7
159	Benin	3.0	6.4	9.1	2.8	2.5	21.9	43.0	53.0	45.9	42.1	2.7	2.8	7.1	5.7
160	Tanzania, U. Rep. of	16.2	35.6	45.9	3.0	1.8	10.1	33.2	46.2	45.6	40.2	2.3	2.7	6.8	5.1
161	Côte d'Ivoire	6.8	16.1	19.8	3.3	1.5	32.1	44.0	50.9	42.3	37.3	3.1	3.9	7.4	4.7
162	Malawi	5.2	11.6	15.2	3.1	1.9	7.7	15.1	21.3	45.9	44.9	3.5	3.6	7.4	6.1
163	Zambia	5.1	10.6	12.7	2.8	1.3	34.8	39.8	45.2	46.4	44.7	3.0	3.2	7.8	5.6
164	Angola	6.2	12.8	19.3	2.8	2.9	17.8	34.8	44.1	47.4	47.9	2.7	2.6	6.6	7.2
165	Chad	4.1	8.1	12.1	2.6	2.9	15.6	24.2	30.9	46.6	46.5	3.1	2.8	6.7	6.7
166	Guinea-Bissau	0.7	1.4	2.1	3.0	2.9	15.9	32.3	43.0	46.9	46.9	3.1	2.8	7.1	7.1
167	Congo, Dem. Rep. of the	23.9	49.8	74.2	2.8	2.8	29.5	..	39.3	46.8	47.2	2.6	2.6	6.5	6.7
168	Central African Republic	2.1	3.8	4.6	2.3	1.4	33.7	41.7	49.7	43.1	40.4	4.0	4.0	5.7	4.9
169	Ethiopia	33.1	67.3	93.8	2.7	2.4	9.5	15.9	22.0	45.8	43.1	2.9	3.2	6.8	6.1
170	Mozambique	10.6	18.2	22.5	2.1	1.5	8.7	33.2	48.2	44.0	41.2	3.2	3.5	6.6	5.6
171	Burundi	3.7	6.4	9.8	2.1	3.1	3.2	9.3	14.5	47.5	45.8	2.9	2.5	6.8	6.8
172	Mali	6.3	12.3	19.0	2.6	3.1	16.2	30.8	40.7	49.2	48.7	2.4	2.1	7.1	7.0
173	Burkina Faso	6.1	12.3	18.6	2.7	3.0	6.3	16.9	23.1	48.9	47.7	2.7	2.4	7.8	6.7
174	Niger	4.8	11.1	18.3	3.2	3.6	10.6	21.0	29.1	49.9	49.7	2.0	1.9	8.1	8.0
175	Sierra Leone	2.9	4.6	6.4	1.7	2.4	21.4	37.3	46.7	44.0	44.1	2.9	3.0	6.5	6.5
	Developing countries	2,961.2 T	4,863.8 T	5,868.2 T	1.9	1.4	26.3	40.8	48.6	32.6	28.2	5.1	6.4	5.4	2.9
	Least developed countries	353.7 T	684.1 T	941.9 T	2.5	2.3	14.7	25.7	34.5	43.1	40.1	3.1	3.3	6.6	5.1
	Arab States	143.4 T	289.9 T	389.7 T	2.7	2.1	41.5	53.9	59.1	37.5	33.5	3.7	4.3	6.7	3.8
	East Asia and the Pacific	1,310.5 T	1,899.7 T	2,124.6 T	1.4	0.8	20.2	38.8	50.3	26.4	21.4	6.4	8.4	5.0	2.0
	Latin America and the Caribbean	317.9 T	522.6 T	622.5 T	1.9	1.3	61.4	75.8	80.5	31.5	26.3	5.5	7.3	5.1	2.5
	South Asia	842.1 T	1,455.1 T	1,805.3 T	2.1	1.6	21.3	29.5	34.9	35.2	29.6	4.6	5.6	5.6	3.3
	Sub-Saharan Africa	305.8 T	626.4 T	843.1 T	2.8	2.1	21.0	34.8	42.8	44.4	41.9	3.0	3.3	6.8	5.4
	Central & Eastern Europe & CIS	366.6 T	409.8 T	398.4 T	0.5	-0.2	57.0	63.0	64.4	20.1	16.3	11.9	13.2	2.5	1.4
	OECD	925.6 T	1,140.8 T	1,227.7 T	0.8	0.5	70.4	77.1	80.4	20.4	17.9	13.1	16.0	2.5	1.8
	High-income OECD	766.2 T	906.8 T	962.9 T	0.7	0.4	73.7	79.1	82.3	18.3	16.5	14.6	18.0	2.2	1.7
	High human development	972.3 T	1,193.9 T	1,282.0 T	0.8	0.5	71.7	78.3	81.5	20.2	17.8	13.2	16.2	2.5	1.8
	Medium human development	2,678.4 T	4,116.2 T	4,759.1 T	1.7	1.0	28.1	41.6	49.4	29.7	24.7	5.9	7.4	4.9	2.4
	Low human development	354.5 T	737.5 T	1,021.6 T	2.8	2.3	19.1	31.6	39.7	44.6	41.8	3.1	3.3	6.8	5.6
	High income	782.0 T	935.9 T	997.7 T	0.7	0.5	73.8	79.4	82.6	18.5	16.6	14.4	17.7	2.2	1.7
	Middle income	1,847.5 T	2,694.8 T	3,027.9 T	1.5	0.8	35.0	51.6	60.7	27.1	22.5	6.8	8.5	4.6	2.1
	Low income	1,437.1 T	2,515.0 T	3,169.0 T	2.2	1.7	22.1	31.5	38.1	36.9	32.5	4.4	5.1	5.7	3.7
	World	4,068.1 T[e]	6,148.1 T[e]	7,197.2 T[e]	1.6	1.1	37.9	47.7	53.7	29.8	26.1	7.0	8.3	4.5	2.7

a. Because data are based on national definitions of what constitutes a city or metropolitan area, comparisons across countries should be made with caution. b. Data refer to medium-variant projections. c. Data refer to estimates for the period specified. d. Population estimates include Taiwan, province of China. e. Data refer to the total world population according to UN 2003d. The total population of the 175 countries included in the main indicator tables was estimated to be 4,063 million in 1975, and projected to be 6,140 million in 2001 and 7,188 million in 2015.

Source: Columns 1-3, 13 and 14: UN 2003d; column 4: calculated on the basis of data in columns 1 and 2; column 5: calculated on the basis of data in columns 2 and 3; columns 6-8: calculated on the basis of data on urban population and total population from UN 2002b; columns 9 and 10: calculated on the basis of data on population under age 15 and total population from UN 2003d; columns 11 and 12: calculated on the basis of data on population aged 65 and above and total population from UN 2003d.

6 Commitment to health: access, services and resources

HDI rank	Population with access to improved sanitation (%) 2000	Population with sustainable access to an improved water source (%) 2000	Population with sustainable access to affordable essential drugs (%)a 1999	One-year-olds fully immunized — Against tuberculosis (%) 2001	One-year-olds fully immunized — Against measles (%) 2001	Oral rehydration therapy use rate (%) 1994-2000b	Contra-ceptive prevalence rate (%)c 1995-2001b	Births attended by skilled health personnel (%) 1995-2001b	Physicians (per 100,000 people) 1990-2002b	Health expenditure — Public (as % of GDP) 2000	Health expenditure — Private (as % of GDP) 2000	Health expenditure — Per capita (PPP US$) 2000
High human development												
1 Norway	..	100	95-100	92	93	..	..	..	413	6.5	1.1	2,769
2 Iceland	..	..	95-100	..	88	..	..	..	326	7.6	1.4	2,642
3 Sweden	100	100	95-100	..	94	..	..	..	311	6.2	1.8	2,108
4 Australia	100	100	95-100	..	93	..	..	100	260	6.0	2.3	2,213
5 Netherlands	100	100	95-100	..	96	..	..	100	251	5.5	2.6	2,216
6 Belgium	..	..	95-100	..	83	..	..	..	395	6.2	2.5	2,306
7 United States	100	100	95-100	..	91	..	76	99	276	5.8	7.3	4,499
8 Canada	100	100	95-100	..	96	..	75	98	186	6.5	2.5	2,534
9 Japan	..	..	95-100	..	96	..	..	100	197	5.9	1.8	2,009
10 Switzerland	100	100	95-100	..	81	..	82	..	336	6.0	4.7	3,161
11 Denmark	..	100	95-100	..	94	..	..	..	339	6.8	1.5	2,434
12 Ireland	..	..	95-100	90 d	73	..	..	..	226	5.1	1.6	1,908
13 United Kingdom	100	100	95-100	..	85	..	..	99	164	5.9	1.4	1,804
14 Finland	100	100	95-100	99	96	..	..	..	306	5.0	1.7	1,698
15 Luxembourg	..	..	95-100	..	91	..	..	..	253	5.3	0.5	2,785
16 Austria	100	100	95-100	..	79	..	51	..	302	5.6	2.4	2,245
17 France	..	..	95-100	84	84	..	..	..	303	7.2	2.3	2,380
18 Germany	..	..	95-100	..	89	..	..	..	354	8.0	2.6	2,768
19 Spain	..	..	95-100	..	94	..	81	..	436	5.4	2.3	1,547
20 New Zealand	..	..	95-100	..	85	..	75	100	226	6.2	1.8	1,646
21 Italy	..	..	95-100	..	70	..	60	..	567	5.9	2.1	2,028
22 Israel	..	..	95-100	..	94	..	..	..	378	8.1	2.6	2,338
23 Portugal	..	..	95-100	82	87	..	..	100	312	5.8	2.4	1,397
24 Greece	..	..	95-100	88	88	..	..	..	392	4.6	3.7	1,349
25 Cyprus	100	100	95-100	..	86 d	..	..	..	269	3.9	4.1	904
26 Hong Kong, China (SAR)	..	..	..	..	..	..	..	..	..	..	..	..
27 Barbados	100	100	95-100	..	92	..	..	91	121	4.2	2.2	909
28 Singapore	100	100	95-100	97	89	..	..	100	135	1.3	2.3	913
29 Slovenia	..	100	95-100	96	98	..	..	..	215	6.8	1.8	1,463
30 Korea, Rep. of	63	92	95-100	89	97	..	81	100	173	2.6	3.3	899
31 Brunei Darussalam	..	..	95-100	99	99	..	..	99	85	2.5	0.6	618
32 Czech Republic	..	..	80-94	98 d	..	..	72	..	308	6.5	0.6	1,031
33 Malta	100	100	95-100	..	65	..	..	..	263	6.1	2.8	803
34 Argentina	..	..	50-79	99	94	..	..	98	294	4.7	3.9	1,091
35 Poland	..	..	80-94	95	97	..	..	..	233	4.2	1.8	575
36 Seychelles	..	..	80-94	99	95	..	..	..	132	3.9	2.0	749
37 Bahrain	..	..	95-100	..	98	..	62	98	169	2.8	1.3	641
38 Hungary	99	99	95-100	99	99	..	..	..	361	5.1	1.6	838
39 Slovakia	100	100	95-100	93	99	..	..	..	322	5.2	0.6	653
40 Uruguay	94	98	50-79	99	94	..	..	99	375	5.1	5.8	1,007
41 Estonia	..	..	95-100	99	95	..	..	..	307	4.5	1.4	540
42 Costa Rica	93	95	95-100	92	82	..	..	98	178	4.7	2.1	474
43 Chile	96	93	80-94	97	97	..	..	100	115	3.1	4.2	697
44 Qatar	..	..	95-100	99	92	..	43	..	220	2.5	0.7	849
45 Lithuania	..	..	80-94	99	97	..	47	..	394	4.4	1.8	430
46 Kuwait	..	..	95-100	.. d	99	..	50	98	160	2.7	0.4	538
47 Croatia	..	..	95-100	97	94	..	..	..	229	7.5	1.6	665
48 United Arab Emirates	..	..	95-100	98	94	..	28	99	177	2.5	0.7	762
49 Bahamas	100	97	80-94	..	93	..	..	99 e	106	4.4	3.4	1,111
50 Latvia	..	..	80-94	99	98	..	48	100	313	3.5	2.3	406

HDI rank		Population with access to improved sanitation (%) 2000	Population with sustainable access to an improved water source (%) 2000	Population with sustainable access to affordable essential drugs (%)a 1999	One-year-olds fully immunized Against tuberculosis (%) 2001	One-year-olds fully immunized Against measles (%) 2001	Oral rehydration therapy use rate (%) 1994-2000b	Contra-ceptive prevalence rate (%)c 1995-2001b	Births attended by skilled health personnel (%) 1995-2001b	Physicians (per 100,000 people) 1990-2002b	Health expenditure Public (as % of GDP) 2000	Health expenditure Private (as % of GDP) 2000	Health expenditure Per capita (PPP US$) 2000
51	Saint Kitts and Nevis	96	98	50-79	97	94	..	..	100	117	3.1	2.1	658
52	Cuba	98	91	95-100	99	99	..	..	100	590	6.1	1.0	193
53	Belarus	..	100	50-79	99	99	..	50	..	457	4.9	0.1	389
54	Trinidad and Tobago	99	90	50-79	..	91	17 e	..	99	79	2.3	2.2	468
55	Mexico	74	88	80-94	99	97	..	67	86	130	2.5	2.8	477
Medium human development													
56	Antigua and Barbuda	95	91	50-79	..	97	..	..	100 e	17	3.3	2.2	629
57	Bulgaria	100	100	80-94	98	90	..	42	..	344	2.9	0.8	225
58	Malaysia	..	..	50-79	99	92	..	..	96	68	1.8	1.6	310
59	Panama	92	90	80-94	99	97	7	..	90	117	4.8	2.1	464
60	Macedonia, TFYR	..	..	50-79	97	92	..	..	..	300	5.1	0.9	301
61	Libyan Arab Jamahiriya	97	72	95-100	99	93	..	40	94	120	1.5	1.4	370
62	Mauritius	99	100	95-100	89	90	..	..	..	85	2.1	1.2	315
63	Russian Federation	..	99	50-79	97	98	..	73 f	..	423	3.7	1.4	405
64	Colombia	86	91	80-94	86	75	..	77	86	109	5.3	4.0	612
65	Brazil	76	87	0-49	99	99	18	77	88	158	3.4	4.9	631
66	Bosnia and Herzegovina	..	..	80-94	95	92	11	48	100	140	3.1	4.7	259
67	Belize	50	92	80-94	95	96	..	..	77 e	55	2.1	2.5	273
68	Dominica	83	97	80-94	99	99	..	..	100	49	4.3	1.8	340
69	Venezuela	68	83	80-94	94	49	..	..	95	203	2.7	2.0	280
70	Samoa (Western)	99	99	95-100	98	92	..	..	100	70	5.0	1.7	227
71	Saint Lucia	89	98	50-79	99	89	..	..	100	518	2.6	1.6	272
72	Romania	53	58	80-94	99	98	..	64	98	191	1.9	1.1	190
73	Saudi Arabia	100	95	95-100	94	94	..	32	91	153	3.5	1.0	641
74	Thailand	96	84	95-100	99	94	..	72	85	24	2.1	1.6	237
75	Ukraine	99	98	50-79	98	99	..	68	99	299	2.9	1.2	152
76	Kazakhstan	99	91	50-79	96	96	20	66	99	339	2.8	1.0	211
77	Suriname	93	82	95-100	..	90	24	..	85	45	5.5	4.3	424
78	Jamaica	99	92	95-100	96	85	..	66	95	140	2.6	2.9	208
79	Oman	92	39	80-94	98	99	88	24	91	137	2.0	0.5	388
80	St. Vincent & the Grenadines	96	93	80-94	99	98	..	..	100 e	88	4.1	2.2	374
81	Fiji	43	47	95-100	99	90	..	..	100	36	2.6	1.4	194
82	Peru	71	80	50-79	88	97	29	69	59	117	2.8	2.0	238
83	Lebanon	99	100	80-94	..	94	30	61	88	274	3.7	8.5	719
84	Paraguay	94	78	0-49	51	77	..	57	58	117	3.0	4.9	323
85	Philippines	83	86	50-79	45	75	28	47	56	124	1.5	1.8	167
86	Maldives	56	100	50-79	99	99	..	..	70	40	6.3	1.3	254
87	Turkmenistan	..	..	50-79	99	98	31	62	97	300	4.6	0.8	267
88	Georgia	100	79	0-49	97	73	33	41	96	487	0.7	6.3	197
89	Azerbaijan	81	78	50-79	98	99	27	55	88	357	0.9	1.2	57
90	Jordan	99	96	95-100	..	99	..	53	97	205	4.3	3.8	341
91	Tunisia	84	80	50-79	97	92	..	..	90	70	5.5	1.5	472
92	Guyana	87	94	0-49	95	92	7	..	95	48	4.2	0.9	198
93	Grenada	97	95	95-100	..	96	..	..	100 e	50	3.4	1.4	351
94	Dominican Republic	67	86	50-79	96	98	22	64	96	216	1.8	4.6	357
95	Albania	91	97	50-79	93	95	48	58	99	133	2.1	1.3	129
96	Turkey	90	82	95-100	89	90	15	64	81	127	3.6	1.4	315
97	Ecuador	86	85	0-49	99	99	..	66	69	138	1.2	1.2	78
98	Occupied Palestinian Territories	100	86	..	..	..	43	..	..	..	..	..	..
99	Sri Lanka	94	77	95-100	99	99	..	..	97	41	1.8	1.9	120
100	Armenia	..	..	0-49	97	93	30	61	97	305	3.2	4.4	192

HDI rank		Population with access to improved sanitation (%) 2000	Population with sustainable access to an improved water source (%) 2000	Population with sustainable access to affordable essential drugs (%)a 1999	One-year-olds fully immunized Against tuberculosis (%) 2001	Against measles (%) 2001	Oral rehydration therapy use rate (%) 1994-2000b	Contra-ceptive prevalence rate (%)c 1995-2001b	Births attended by skilled health personnel (%) 1995-2001b	Physicians (per 100,000 people) 1990-2002b	Health expenditure Public (as % of GDP) 2000	Private (as % of GDP) 2000	Per capita (PPP US$) 2000
101	Uzbekistan	89	85	50-79	98	99	19	67	96	300	2.8	0.8	86
102	Kyrgyzstan	100	77	50-79	99	99	13	60	98	288	3.5	2.2	145
103	Cape Verde	71	74	80-94	84	72	..	53	53	17	1.9	0.7	106
104	China	40	75	80-94	77	79	29	84	89	167	2.0	3.4	205
105	El Salvador	82	77	80-94	99	97	..	60	51	121	3.8	5.0	391
106	Iran, Islamic Rep. of	83	92	80-94	93	96	..	73	..	110	2.7	3.3	356
107	Algeria	92	89	95-100	97	83	62	64	92	85	3.0	0.6	142
108	Moldova, Rep. of	99	92	50-79	98	81	19	62	99	325	2.9	0.7	65
109	Viet Nam	47	77	80-94	99	97	20	75	70	52	1.4	3.9	130
110	Syrian Arab Republic	90	80	80-94	99	93	..	..	76 e	142	1.6	0.9	51
111	South Africa	87	86	80-94	87	72	..	56	84	443	3.7	5.1	663
112	Indonesia	55	78	80-94	65	59	18	57	56	16	0.6	2.1	84
113	Tajikistan	90	60	0-49	97	86	20	34	77	207	2.0	0.5	29
114	Bolivia	70	83	50-79	94	79	40	53	59	130	4.3	1.8	145
115	Honduras	75	88	0-49	99	95	..	50	54	83	4.3	2.5	165
116	Equatorial Guinea	53	44	0-49	34	19	..	..	..	25	1.0	2.2	168
117	Mongolia	30	60	50-79	98	95	32	60	97	254	4.7	2.0	120
118	Gabon	53	86	0-49	89	55	..	33	86	..	2.0	0.9	171
119	Guatemala	81	92	50-79	92	90	15	38	41	90	2.3	2.5	192
120	Egypt	98	97	80-94	98	97	..	56	61	218	1.8	2.3	143
121	Nicaragua	85	77	0-49	98	99	18	60	65	61	2.3	2.1	108
122	São Tomé and Principe	..	..	0-49	81	69	25	..	86 e	47	1.6	0.8	23
123	Solomon Islands	34	71	80-94	85	..	..	..	85	13	5.5	0.3	97
124	Namibia	41	77	80-94	69	58	..	..	78	29	4.2	2.9	366
125	Botswana	66	95	80-94	99	83	..	40	99	26	3.7	2.2	358
126	Morocco	68	80	50-79	93	96	..	50	40	49	1.6	3.1	174
127	India	28	84	0-49	73	56	..	48 g	43	48	0.9	4.0	71
128	Vanuatu	100	88	..	90	94	..	..	89	12	2.3	1.5	119
129	Ghana	72	73	0-49	91	81	22	22	44	6	2.2	1.9	51
130	Cambodia	17	30	0-49	64	59	..	24	32	30	1.0	6.1	97
131	Myanmar	64	72	50-79	70	73	24	33	..	30	0.4	1.8	24
132	Papua New Guinea	82	42	80-94	74	58	..	26	53	7	3.8	0.4	145
133	Swaziland	..	..	95-100	95	72	7	..	70	15	2.7	1.2	195
134	Comoros	98	96	80-94	90	70	22	21	62	7	3.1	1.2	35
135	Lao People's Dem. Rep.	30	37	50-79	60	50	20	32	21	61	1.3	2.1	52
136	Bhutan	70	62	80-94	81	78	..	..	15 e	16	3.7	0.4	64
137	Lesotho	49	78	80-94	92	77	..	30	60	7	5.2	1.1	100
138	Sudan	62	75	0-49	51	67	21	..	86 e	16	0.9	2.1	43
139	Bangladesh	48	97	50-79	94	76	..	54	12	20	1.5	2.6	47
140	Congo	..	51	50-79	53	35	13	..	..	25	1.5	0.5	23
141	Togo	34	54	50-79	84	58	23	24	49	8	1.5	1.4	35
Low human development													
142	Cameroon	79	58	50-79	77	62	23	19	56	7	1.0	2.9	55
143	Nepal	28	88	0-49	84	71	11	39	11	4	1.6	3.6	64
144	Pakistan	62	90	50-79	78	54	19	28	20	68	0.9	3.2	76
145	Zimbabwe	62	83	50-79	80	68	50	54	73	14	3.7	3.6	170
146	Kenya	87	57	0-49	91	76	30	39	44	14	2.4	6.4	123
147	Uganda	79	52	50-79	81	61	..	23	39	5	1.6	2.4	38
148	Yemen	38	69	50-79	73	79	..	21	22	22	1.5	3.4	69
149	Madagascar	42	47	50-79	72	55	16	19	47	11	2.6	1.0	33
150	Haiti	28	46	0-49	71	53	..	27	24	25	2.4	2.4	56
151	Gambia	37	62	80-94	99	90	26	10	51	4	3.0	0.6	51

HDI rank		Population with access to improved sanitation (%) 2000	Population with sustainable access to an improved water source (%) 2000	Population with sustainable access to affordable essential drugs (%)a 1999	One-year-olds fully immunized Against tuberculosis (%) 2001	One-year-olds fully immunized Against measles (%) 2001	Oral rehydration therapy use rate (%) 1994-2000b	Contraceptive prevalence rate (%)c 1995-2001b	Births attended by skilled health personnel (%) 1995-2001b	Physicians (per 100,000 people) 1990-2002b	Health expenditure Public (as % of GDP) 2000	Health expenditure Private (as % of GDP) 2000	Health expenditure Per capita (PPP US$) 2000
152	Nigeria	54	62	0-49	54	40	24	15	42	19	0.5	1.2	15
153	Djibouti	91	100	80-94	38	49	..	..	..	13	2.4	2.5	63
154	Mauritania	33	37	50-79	70	58	..	8	53	14	3.4	0.9	52
155	Eritrea	13	46	50-79	98	88	..	5	21	5	2.9	1.5	24
156	Senegal	70	78	50-79	89	48	4	13	51	10	2.6	2.0	56
157	Guinea	58	48	80-94	71	52	21	6	35	13	1.9	1.4	56
158	Rwanda	8	41	0-49	74	78	4	13	31	..	2.6	2.5	40
159	Benin	23	63	50-79	94	65	18	19	66	10	1.8	1.4	28
160	Tanzania, U. Rep. of	90	68	50-79	89	83	21	25	36	4	2.2	2.5	27
161	Côte d'Ivoire	52	81	80-94	72	61	25	15	47	9	1.0	1.8	45
162	Malawi	76	57	0-49	93	82	..	31	56	..	3.6	4.0	38
163	Zambia	78	64	50-79	92	85	8	25	47	7	3.5	2.1	49
164	Angola	44	38	0-49	74	72	..	8	23	5	2.0	1.6	52
165	Chad	29	27	0-49	44	36	36	8	16	3	2.3	0.5	16
166	Guinea-Bissau	56	56	0-49	70	48	13	8	35	17	1.8	0.4	12
167	Congo, Dem. Rep. of the	21	45	..	57	46	..	..	61	7	0.3	2.7	..
168	Central African Republic	25	70	50-79	38	29	34	15	44	4	1.4	1.0	31
169	Ethiopia	12	24	50-79	76	52	..	8	6	3	1.1	2.7	14
170	Mozambique	43	57	50-79	97	92	27	6	44	6	2.8	1.6	30
171	Burundi	88	78	0-49	84	75	10	..	25	1	1.7	1.5	16
172	Mali	69	65	50-79	68	37	22	8	24	5	2.2	2.7	32
173	Burkina Faso	29	42	50-79	72	46	37	12	31	3	3.0	1.2	37
174	Niger	20	59	50-79	49	51	38	14	16	4	1.5	1.8	22
175	Sierra Leone	66	57	0-49	74	37	28	4	42	9	2.0	1.7	24
	Developing countries	51	78	..	78	69	..	..	56	..	..	..	..
	Least developed countries	44	62	..	77	63	..	..	31	..	..	..	..
	Arab States	83	86	..	85	84	..	..	67	..	..	..	..
	East Asia and the Pacific	48	76	..	75	77	..	..	80	..	..	..	..
	Latin America and the Caribbean	77	86	..	95	91	..	..	82	..	..	..	..
	South Asia	37	85	..	77	60	..	..	36	..	..	..	..
	Sub-Saharan Africa	53	57	..	73	58	..	..	38	..	..	..	..
	Central & Eastern Europe & CIS	..	93	..	97	97	..	..	96	..	..	..	..
	OECD	..	..	..	..	91	..	..	94	..	..	..	..
	High-income OECD	..	..	..	..	90	..	..	99	..	..	..	..
	High human development	..	..	..	..	91	..	..	96	..	..	..	..
	Medium human development	51	82	..	80	74	..	..	64	..	..	..	..
	Low human development	51	62	..	73	57	..	..	31	..	..	..	..
	High income	..	..	..	..	89	..	..	99	..	..	..	..
	Middle income	60	82	..	85	86	..	..	84	..	..	..	..
	Low income	44	76	..	75	60	..	..	40	..	..	..	..
	World	61 h	82 h	..	79	72	..	..	60	..	..	..	..

a. The data on access to essential drugs are based on statistical estimates received from World Health Organization (WHO) country and regional offices and regional advisers and through the World Drug Situation Survey carried out in 1998-99. These estimates represent the best information available to the WHO Department of Essential Drugs and Medicines Policy to date and are currently being validated by WHO member states. The department assigns the estimates to four groupings: very low access (0-49%), low access (50-79%), medium access (80-94%) and good access (95-100%). These groupings, used here in presenting the data, are often employed by the WHO in interpreting the data, as the actual estimates may suggest a higher level of accuracy than the data afford. b. Data refer to the most recent year available during the period specified. c. Data usually refer to married women aged 15-49; the actual age range covered may vary across countries. d. WHO 2003d. e. Data refer to a year or period other than that specified, differ from the standard definition or refer to only part of the country. f. Data refer to the cities of Ivanovo, Perm and Yekaterinburg. g. Excluding the state of Tripura. h. Data refer to the world aggregate according to UNICEF 2003b.

Source: Columns 1 and 2: UN 2003a, based on data from a joint effort by the United Nations Children's Fund (UNICEF) and the WHO; column 3: UN 2003a, based on data from the WHO; column 4: UNICEF 2003b, based on data from a joint effort by UNICEF and the WHO; aggregates calculated for the Human Development Report Office by the WHO; columns 5 and 8: UN 2003a, based on data from a joint effort by UNICEF and the WHO; aggregates calculated for the Human Development Report Office by the WHO; column 6: UNICEF 2003b; column 7: UN 2003c; column 9: WHO 2003c; columns 10-12: WHO 2003b.

7 Leading global health crises and challenges

HDI rank		Under-nourished people (as % of total population) 1998/2000[a]	Children under weight for age (% under age 5) 1995-2001[b]	Children under height for age (% under age 5) 1995-2001[b]	Infants with low birth-weight (%) 1995-2000[b]	People living with HIV/AIDS			Malaria cases (per 100,000 people) 2000[d]	Tuber-culosis cases (per 100,000 people) 2001[e]	Cigarette consumption per adult (annual average) 1992-2000[f]
						Adults (% age 15-49) 2001[c]	Women (age 15-49) 2001[c]	Children (age 0-14) 2001[c]			
High human development											
1	Norway	..	..	..	5	0.08	400	<100	..	3	739
2	Iceland	..	..	..	4	0.15	<100	<100	..	2	2,013
3	Sweden	..	..	..	4	0.08	880	<100	..	2	1,085
4	Australia	..	..	..	7	0.07	800	140	..	4	1,708
5	Netherlands	..	..	..	..	0.21	3,300	160	..	3	2,775
6	Belgium	..	..	..	8	0.16	2,900	330	..	6	1,830
7	United States	..	1 [g]	2 [g]	8	0.61	180,000	10,000	..	2	2,092
8	Canada	..	..	..	6	0.31	14,000	<500	..	3	1,820
9	Japan	..	..	..	7 [g]	<0.10	6,600	110	..	21	2,950
10	Switzerland	..	..	..	6	0.50	6,000	300	..	5	2,880
11	Denmark	..	..	..	6	0.15	770	<100	..	6	1,847
12	Ireland	..	..	..	4 [g]	0.11	660	190	..	6	2,316
13	United Kingdom	..	..	..	8	0.10	7,400	550	..	5	1,553
14	Finland	..	..	..	6	<0.10	330	<100	..	5	1,171
15	Luxembourg	..	..	..	4	0.16	..	..	..	6	..
16	Austria	..	..	..	7	0.24	2,200	<100	..	6	1,650
17	France	..	..	..	6	0.33	27,000	1,000	..	6	1,757
18	Germany	..	..	..	7	0.10	8,100	550	..	5	1,814
19	Spain	..	..	..	6	0.50	26,000	1,300	..	14	2,826
20	New Zealand	..	..	..	6	0.06	180	<100	..	5	1,038
21	Italy	..	..	..	6	0.37	33,000	770	..	4	2,041
22	Israel	..	..	..	8	0.10	..	..	..	5	2,118
23	Portugal	..	..	..	7	0.52	5,100	350	..	17	2,036
24	Greece	..	..	..	7	0.17	1,800	<100	..	11	3,230
25	Cyprus	..	..	..	..	0.25	150	..	..	5	..
26	Hong Kong, China (SAR)	..	..	..	..	0.08	660	<100	..	39	..
27	Barbados	..	6 [g]	7 [g]	10	1.20 [h]	..	..	..	11	523
28	Singapore	..	14 [g]	11 [g]	8	0.20	860	<100	..	22	..
29	Slovenia	..	..	..	6	<0.10	<100	<100	..	12	2,742
30	Korea, Rep. of	..	..	..	..	<0.10	960	<100	9	48	2,668
31	Brunei Darussalam	..	..	..	..	..	..	..	..	24	..
32	Czech Republic	..	1 [g]	2 [g]	6	<0.10	<100	<10	..	7	1,476
33	Malta	..	..	..	7	0.13	..	..	..	3	..
34	Argentina	..	5	12	7	0.69	30,000	3,000	1	30	1,456
35	Poland	..	..	..	6	0.10 [h]	..	..	..	23	2,473
36	Seychelles	..	6 [g]	5 [g]	10 [g]	..	..	..	..	26	..
37	Bahrain	..	9	10	10	0.26	150	..	..	34	..
38	Hungary	..	2 [g]	3 [g]	9	0.06	300	<100	..	22	2,697
39	Slovakia	..	..	..	7	<0.10	<100	..	..	15	2,039
40	Uruguay	3	5	8	..	0.30	1,400	100	..	15	1,425
41	Estonia	..	..	..	5	1.00	1,500	..	..	27	2,092
42	Costa Rica	5	5	6	6	0.55	2,800	320	42	7	..
43	Chile	4	1	2	5	0.30	4,300	<500	..	10	1,230
44	Qatar	..	6	8	10	..	..	..	..	13	..
45	Lithuania	..	..	..	4	0.07	260	<100	..	48	1,839
46	Kuwait	4	10	24	7	..	..	..	..	27	1,616
47	Croatia	..	1	1	6	<0.10	<100	<10	..	40	2,218
48	United Arab Emirates	..	14	17	..	..	..	..	..	13	..
49	Bahamas	..	..	..	..	3.50	2,700	<100	..	19	..
50	Latvia	..	..	..	5	0.40	1,000	<100	..	43	..

7 Leading global health crises and challenges

HDI rank		Under-nourished people (as % of total population) 1998/2000[a]	Children under weight for age (% under age 5) 1995-2001[b]	Children under height for age (% under age 5) 1995-2001[b]	Infants with low birth-weight (%) 1995-2000[b]	People living with HIV/AIDS			Malaria cases (per 100,000 people) 2000[d]	Tuber-culosis cases (per 100,000 people) 2001[e]	Cigarette consumption per adult (annual average) 1992-2000[f]
						Adults (% age 15-49) 2001[c]	Women (age 15-49) 2001[c]	Children (age 0-14) 2001[c]			
51	Saint Kitts and Nevis	..	..	..	13[g]	..	..	..	..	7	..
52	Cuba	13	4	5	6	<0.10	830	<100	..	6	..
53	Belarus	..	..	..	5	0.27	3,700	..	..	57	2,285
54	Trinidad and Tobago	12	7[g]	4[g]	..	2.50	5,600	300	1	9	673
55	Mexico	5	8	18	9	0.28	32,000	3,600	8	19	752
Medium human development											
56	Antigua and Barbuda	..	10[g]	7[g]	8	..	..	..	..	3	..
57	Bulgaria	..	..	..	9	<0.10[h]	..	..	..	20	3,322
58	Malaysia	..	18	..	9	0.35	11,000	770	57	67	1,262
59	Panama	18	7	14	10	1.50	8,700	800	36	28	..
60	Macedonia, TFYR	..	6	7	6	<0.10	<100	<100	..	26	2,360
61	Libyan Arab Jamahiriya	..	5	15	7[g]	0.24	1,100	..	2	11	..
62	Mauritius	5	16	10	13	0.10	350	<100	1[h]	57	1,349
63	Russian Federation	..	3	13	7	0.90	180,000	..	1	93	2,691
64	Colombia	13	7	14	7	0.40	20,000	4,000	250	29	614
65	Brazil	10	6	11	9	0.65	220,000	13,000	344	44	869
66	Bosnia and Herzegovina	..	4	10	4	<0.10[h]	..	..	..	35	1,546
67	Belize	..	6[g]	..	4	2.00	1,000	180	657	18	1,127
68	Dominica	..	5[g]	6[g]	8[g]	..	..	..	..	9	..
69	Venezuela	21	5	14	6	0.50[h]	..	..	94	22	1,221
70	Samoa (Western)	..	..	..	..	..	..	..	..	22	..
71	Saint Lucia	..	14[g]	11[g]	8[g]	..	..	..	..	9	..
72	Romania	..	6[g]	8[g]	9	<0.10	..	4,000	..	94	1,563
73	Saudi Arabia	3	14	20	3	..	..	..	32	27	..
74	Thailand	18	19[g]	16[g]	7	1.79	220,000	21,000	130	100	798
75	Ukraine	..	3	15	6	0.99	76,000	..	..	57	1,225
76	Kazakhstan	..	4	10	6	0.07	1,200	<100	(.)	94	1,771
77	Suriname	11	..	..	11	1.20	1,800	190	2,954	44	2,285
78	Jamaica	9	4	3	11	1.22	7,200	800	..	3	592
79	Oman	..	24	23	8	0.11	200	..	27	5	..
80	St. Vincent & the Grenadines	..	..	..	10	..	..	..	..	..	..
81	Fiji	..	8[g]	3[g]	12[g]	0.07	<100	..	..	23	819
82	Peru	11	7	25	10	0.35	13,000	1,500	258	94	166
83	Lebanon	3	3	12	6	..	..	..	..	11	..
84	Paraguay	14	5	11	9	..	..	..	124	43	1,838
85	Philippines	23	28	30	18	<0.10	2,500	<10	15	226	1,563
86	Maldives	..	30	25	12	0.06	..	..	..	21	..
87	Turkmenistan	..	12	22	5	<0.10	<100	..	1	56	..
88	Georgia	..	3	12	6	<0.10	180	..	5	58	..
89	Azerbaijan	..	17	20	10	<0.10	280	..	19	56	774
90	Jordan	6	5	8	10	<0.10	150	..	3	5	1,686
91	Tunisia	..	4	12	5	..	..	..	1	18	1,775
92	Guyana	..	12	10	14	2.70	8,500	800	3,074	65	637
93	Grenada	..	..	..	11[g]	..	..	..	..	3	..
94	Dominican Republic	26	5	6	13	2.50	61,000	4,700	6	88	762
95	Albania	..	14	32	5	..	..	..	..	21	1,027
96	Turkey	..	8	16	15	<0.10[h]	..	..	17	25	2,118
97	Ecuador	5	15	27	16	0.30	5,100	660	728	94	259
98	Occupied Palestinian Territories	..	3	8	9	..	..	..	..	19	..
99	Sri Lanka	23	29	14	17	<0.10	1,400	<100	1,110	50	344
100	Armenia	..	3	13	9	0.15	480	<100	4	47	1,389

HDI rank		Under-nourished people (as % of total population) 1998/2000 [a]	Children under weight for age (% under age 5) 1995-2001 [b]	Children under height for age (% under age 5) 1995-2001 [b]	Infants with low birth-weight (%) 1995-2000 [b]	People living with HIV/AIDS			Malaria cases (per 100,000 people) 2000 [d]	Tuber-culosis cases (per 100,000 people) 2001 [e]	Cigarette consumption per adult (annual average) 1992-2000 [f]
						Adults (% age 15-49) 2001 [c]	Women (age 15-49) 2001 [c]	Children (age 0-14) 2001 [c]			
101	Uzbekistan	..	19	31	6	<0.10	150	<100	1	63	501
102	Kyrgyzstan	..	11	25	6	<0.10	<100	..	(.)	88	..
103	Cape Verde	..	14 [g]	16 [g]	13	..	..	..	..	188	..
104	China	9	10	17	6	0.11	220,000	2,000	1	107	1,780
105	El Salvador	14	12	23	13	0.60	6,300	830	11	36	472
106	Iran, Islamic Rep. of	5	11	15	7	<0.10	5,000	<200	27	32	791
107	Algeria	6	6	18	7	0.10 [h]	..	..	2 [h]	23	907
108	Moldova, Rep. of	..	3	10	7	0.24	1,200	..	..	104	..
109	Viet Nam	18	33	36	9	0.30	35,000	2,500	95	93	1,084
110	Syrian Arab Republic	3	13	21	6	..	..	..	(.)	47	1,223
111	South Africa	..	12	25	..	20.10	2,700,000	250,000	143	237	941
112	Indonesia	6	26	..	9	0.10	27,000	1,300	920	321	1,388
113	Tajikistan	..	..	..	13	<0.10	<100	..	303	83	..
114	Bolivia	23	10	26	8	0.10	1,200	160	378	116	..
115	Honduras	21	25	39	6	1.60	27,000	3,000	541	46	960
116	Equatorial Guinea	..	..	..	..	3.38	3,000	420	2,744 [i]	102	..
117	Mongolia	42	13	25	6	<0.10	..	..	..	124	..
118	Gabon	8	12	21	..	..	..	..	2,148 [i]	187	506
119	Guatemala	25	24	46	12	1.00	27,000	4,800	386	48	553
120	Egypt	4	4	19	10	<0.10	780	..	(.)	23	1,201
121	Nicaragua	29	12	25	13	0.20	1,500	210	402	35	..
122	São Tomé and Principe	..	16	26	7 [g]	..	..	..	..	143	..
123	Solomon Islands	..	21 [g]	27 [g]	..	..	..	..	15,172	52	620
124	Namibia	9	24	24	15 [g]	22.50	110,000	30,000	1,502	221	..
125	Botswana	25	13	23	11	38.80	170,000	28,000	48,704	224	..
126	Morocco	7	9 [g]	23 [g]	9 [g]	0.08	2,000	..	(.)	47	717
127	India	24	47	46	26	0.79	1,500,000	170,000	7	199	112
128	Vanuatu	..	20 [g]	19 [g]	7 [g]	..	..	..	3,260	63	..
129	Ghana	12	25	26	9	3.00	170,000	34,000	15,344	145	164
130	Cambodia	36	45	45	9	2.70	74,000	12,000	476	560	..
131	Myanmar	6	36	37	16	..	..	..	224	113	..
132	Papua New Guinea	27	35 [g]	..	..	0.65	4,100	500	1,688	283	..
133	Swaziland	12	10	30	..	33.44	89,000	14,000	2,835	627	..
134	Comoros	..	25	42	18	..	..	..	1,930	49	..
135	Lao People's Dem. Rep.	24	40	41	..	<0.10	350	<100	759	143	..
136	Bhutan	..	19	40	15	<0.10	..	..	285	114	..
137	Lesotho	26	16	44	..	31.00	180,000	27,000	0 [h]	277	..
138	Sudan	21	17	..	..	2.60	230,000	30,000	13,934	142	..
139	Bangladesh	35	48	45	30	<0.10	3,100	310	40	211	234
140	Congo	32	14 [g]	19 [g]	..	7.15	59,000	15,000	5,880	122	401
141	Togo	23	25	22	13	6.00	76,000	15,000	7,701 [i]	114	..
Low human development											
142	Cameroon	25	21	35	10	11.83	500,000	69,000	2,900 [i]	96	..
143	Nepal	19	48	51	21	0.49	14,000	1,500	33	135	512
144	Pakistan	19	38	..	21 [g]	0.11	16,000	2,200	58	178	635
145	Zimbabwe	38	13	27	10	33.73	1,200,000	240,000	5,410	291	493
146	Kenya	44	23	37	9	15.01	1,400,000	220,000	545	289	316
147	Uganda	21	23	39	13	5.00	280,000	110,000	46	187	157
148	Yemen	33	46	52	26	0.12	1,500	..	15,160 [h]	70	794
149	Madagascar	40	33	49	15	0.29	12,000	1,000	..	158	376
150	Haiti	50	17	23	28 [g]	6.10	120,000	12,000	15 [h]	190	221
151	Gambia	21	17	19	14	1.60	4,400	460	17,340 [i]	283	..

HDI rank	Under-nourished people (as % of total population) 1998/2000 [a]	Children under weight for age (% under age 5) 1995-2001 [b]	Children under height for age (% under age 5) 1995-2001 [b]	Infants with low birth-weight (%) 1995-2000 [b]	People living with HIV/AIDS — Adults (% age 15-49) 2001 [c]	People living with HIV/AIDS — Women (age 15-49) 2001 [c]	People living with HIV/AIDS — Children (age 0-14) 2001 [c]	Malaria cases (per 100,000 people) 2000 [d]	Tuber-culosis cases (per 100,000 people) 2001 [e]	Cigarette consumption per adult (annual average) 1992-2000 [f]
152 Nigeria	7	27	46	9	5.80	1,700,000	270,000	30	196	185
153 Djibouti	..	18	26	..	..	..	..	715 [h]	382	..
154 Mauritania	12	32	35	..	..	..	..	11,150 [h]	209	..
155 Eritrea	58	44	38	14	2.80	30,000	4,000	3,479	249	..
156 Senegal	25	18	19	12	0.50	14,000	2,900	11,925	103	330
157 Guinea	32	23	26	10	..	..	..	75,386	134	..
158 Rwanda	40	24	43	12 [g]	8.88	250,000	65,000	6,510	188	..
159 Benin	13	23	31	15	3.61	67,000	12,000	10,697 [k]	36	..
160 Tanzania, U. Rep. of	47	29	44	11	7.83	750,000	170,000	1,207 [h]	212	194
161 Côte d'Ivoire	15	21	25	17	9.65	400,000	84,000	12,152	207	285
162 Malawi	33	25	49	13 [g]	15.00	440,000	65,000	25,948	242	196
163 Zambia	50	25	59	11	21.52	590,000	150,000	34,204	445	..
164 Angola	50	..	..	..	5.50	190,000	37,000	8,773	197	..
165 Chad	32	28	28	24	3.61	76,000	18,000	197 [h]	168	..
166 Guinea-Bissau	..	23	28	20	2.81	9,300	1,500	2,421 [h]	135	..
167 Congo, Dem. Rep. of the	73	31	38	15	4.90	670,000	170,000	2,960 [h]	184	109
168 Central African Republic	44	24	39	13 [g]	12.90	130,000	25,000	2,207 [l]	255	..
169 Ethiopia	44	47	52	12	6.41	1,100,000	230,000	556 [i]	179	..
170 Mozambique	55	26	36	13	13.00	630,000	80,000	18,115	125	..
171 Burundi	69	45	57	16 [g]	8.30	190,000	55,000	48,098	170	..
172 Mali	20	43	..	16	1.65	54,000	13,000	4,008 [j]	295	..
173 Burkina Faso	23	34	37	18	6.50	220,000	61,000	619	157	199
174 Niger	36	40	40	12	..	..	..	1,693 [j]	150	..
175 Sierra Leone	47	27	34	22	7.00	90,000	16,000	..	258	..
Developing countries	18	..	..	..	1.30	18,000,000 T	2,900,000 T	..	144	..
Least developed countries	38	..	..	..	3.50	6,500,000 T	1,400,000 T	..	192	..
Arab States	13	..	..	..	0.40	260,000 T	40,000 T	..	57	..
East Asia and the Pacific	..	..	..	..	0.20	600,000 T	40,000 T	..	137	..
Latin America and the Caribbean	12	..	..	..	0.60	640,000 T	60,000 T	..	41	..
South Asia	24	..	..	..	0.50	1,500,000 T	170,000 T	..	188	..
Sub-Saharan Africa	33	..	..	..	9.00	15,000,000 T	2,600,000 T	..	198	..
Central & Eastern Europe & CIS	9	..	..	..	0.50	270,000 T	15,000 T	..	66	..
OECD	..	..	..	..	0.30	360,000 T	19,000 T	..	11	..
High-income OECD	..	..	..	..	0.30	330,000 T	16,000 T	..	9	..
High human development	..	..	..	..	0.30	420,000 T	25,000 T	..	12	..
Medium human development	15	..	..	..	0.70	6,700,000 T	680,000 T	..	137	..
Low human development	31	..	..	..	5.90	11,300,000 T	2,200,000 T	..	188	..
High income	..	..	..	..	0.30	330,000 T	16,000 T	..	9	..
Middle income	10	..	..	..	0.60	4,200,000 T	390,000 T	..	85	..
Low income	25	..	..	..	2.10	14,000,000 T	2,500,000 T	..	197	..
World	..	..	..	..	1.20	18,500,000 T	3,000,000 T	..	119	..

a. Data refer to the average for the years specified. b. Data refer to the most recent year available during the period specified. c. Data refer to the end of 2001. Aggregates are rounded estimates; regional totals may not sum to the world total. d. Data refer to malaria cases reported to the World Health Organization (WHO) and may represent only a fraction of the true number in a country because of incomplete reporting systems, incomplete coverage by health services or both. Because of the diversity of case detection and reporting systems, comparisons across countries should be made with caution. e. Data refer to the prevalence of smear-positive cases of tuberculosis. f. Data refer to estimates of apparent consumption based on data on cigarette production, imports and exports. Such estimates may under- or overstate true consumption in countries where tobacco products are illegally imported or exported, where there is significant stockpiling of cigarettes or where there are large transient populations. Estimates of apparent consumption cannot provide insights into smoking patterns in a population. Data refer to the most recent three-year moving average available during the period specified. g. Data refer to a year or period other than that specified, differ from the standard definition or refer to only part of the country. h. Data refer to 1999. i. Data refer to 1995. j. Data refer to 1998. k. Data refer to 1997. l. Data refer to 1994.

Source: Column 1: UN 2003a, based on data from the Food and Agriculture Organization; columns 2-4: UNICEF 2003b, based on data from a joint effort by the United Nations Children's Fund and the WHO; columns 5-7: UNAIDS 2002; aggregates calculated for the Human Development Report Office by the Joint United Nations Programme on HIV/AIDS (UNAIDS); columns 8 and 9: UN 2003a, based on data from the WHO; column 10: WHO 2003a.

8 Survival: progress and setbacks

HDI rank	Life expectancy at birth (years)		Infant mortality rate (per 1,000 live births)		Under-five mortality rate (per 1,000 live births)		Probability at birth of surviving to age 65 [a] Female (% of cohort)	Male (% of cohort)	Maternal mortality ratio reported (per 100,000 live births)
	1970-75 [b]	2000-05 [b]	1970	2001	1970	2001	2000-05 [b]	2000-05 [b]	1985-2001 [c]
High human development									
1 Norway	74.4	78.9	13	4	15	4	90.8	83.5	6
2 Iceland	74.3	79.8	13	3	14	4	90.7	85.9	..
3 Sweden	74.7	80.1	11	3	15	3	91.6	86.1	5
4 Australia	71.7	79.2	17	6	20	6	90.7	83.8	..
5 Netherlands	74.0	78.3	13	5	15	6	89.7	83.5	7
6 Belgium	71.4	78.8	21	5	29	6	90.4	82.5	..
7 United States	71.5	77.1	20	7	26	8	86.4	78.1	8
8 Canada	73.2	79.3	19	5	23	7	90.1	83.9	..
9 Japan	73.3	81.6	14	3	21	5	93.0	85.0	8
10 Switzerland	73.8	79.1	15	5	18	6	91.0	82.9	5
11 Denmark	73.6	76.6	14	4	19	4	86.5	79.8	10
12 Ireland	71.3	77.0	20	6	27	6	89.0	82.0	6
13 United Kingdom	72.0	78.2	18	6	23	7	89.4	83.2	7
14 Finland	70.7	78.0	13	4	16	5	91.1	79.9	6
15 Luxembourg	70.7	78.4	19	5	26	5	89.8	82.7	0
16 Austria	70.6	78.5	26	5	33	5	90.7	81.6	..
17 France	72.4	79.0	18	4	24	6	91.0	80.2	10
18 Germany	71.0	78.3	22	4	26	5	90.2	81.7	8
19 Spain	72.9	79.3	27	4	34	6	92.2	82.3	6
20 New Zealand	71.7	78.3	17	6	20	6	88.3	82.6	15
21 Italy	72.1	78.7	30	4	33	6	91.4	82.4	7
22 Israel	71.6	79.2	24	6	27	6	90.5	86.2	5
23 Portugal	68.0	76.2	53	5	62	6	89.3	77.4	8
24 Greece	72.3	78.3	38	5	54	5	91.5	82.3	1
25 Cyprus	71.4	78.3	29	5	33	6	90.8	83.9	0
26 Hong Kong, China (SAR)	72.0	79.9	..	.. [d]	..	..	92.3	84.4	..
27 Barbados	69.4	77.2	40	12	54	14	89.0	82.2	0
28 Singapore	69.5	78.1	22	3	27	4	90.5	83.3	6
29 Slovenia	69.8	76.3	25	4	29	5	88.7	76.2	11
30 Korea, Rep. of	62.6	75.5	43	5	54	5	89.0	73.9	20
31 Brunei Darussalam	68.3	76.3	58	6	78	6	87.9	84.8	0
32 Czech Republic	70.1	75.4	21	4	24	5	88.3	74.8	9
33 Malta	70.6	78.4	25	5	32	5	90.2	85.5	..
34 Argentina	67.1	74.2	59	16	71	19	85.3	72.3	41
35 Poland	70.5	73.9	32	8	36	9	86.5	68.8	8
36 Seychelles	..	..	..	13	..	17	..	..	..
37 Bahrain	63.3	74.0	55	13	75	16	84.8	78.1	46
38 Hungary	69.3	71.9	36	8	39	9	82.6	62.7	15
39 Slovakia	70.0	73.7	25	8	29	9	86.5	68.9	9
40 Uruguay	68.7	75.3	48	14	57	16	85.8	73.2	26
41 Estonia	70.5	71.7	21	11	26	12	83.7	59.9	52
42 Costa Rica	67.8	78.1	62	9	83	11	88.3	81.1	29
43 Chile	63.4	76.1	78	10	98	12	86.3	76.8	23
44 Qatar	62.1	72.2	45	11	65	16	80.3	72.8	10
45 Lithuania	71.3	72.7	23	8	28	9	84.9	62.8	18
46 Kuwait	67.0	76.6	49	9	59	10	87.2	82.3	5
47 Croatia	69.6	74.2	34	7	42	8	86.3	71.1	6
48 United Arab Emirates	62.2	74.7	61	8	83	9	86.6	80.0	3
49 Bahamas	66.5	67.1	38	13	49	16	69.6	56.8	..
50 Latvia	70.1	71.0	21	17	26	21	82.8	59.2	45

HDI rank		Life expectancy at birth (years)		Infant mortality rate (per 1,000 live births)		Under-five mortality rate (per 1,000 live births)		Probability at birth of surviving to age 65 [a] Female (% of cohort)	Male (% of cohort)	Maternal mortality ratio reported (per 100,000 live births)
		1970-75 [b]	2000-05 [b]	1970	2001	1970	2001	2000-05 [b]	2000-05 [b]	1985-2001 [c]
51	Saint Kitts and Nevis	..	..	..	20	..	24	..	..	130
52	Cuba	70.7	76.7	34	7	43	9	85.1	79.1	33
53	Belarus	71.5	70.1	22	17	27	20	81.6	56.4	20
54	Trinidad and Tobago	65.9	71.3	49	17	57	20	78.8	67.5	70
55	Mexico	62.4	73.4	79	24	110	29	82.1	71.5	55
Medium human development										
56	Antigua and Barbuda	..	..	..	12	..	14	..	..	150
57	Bulgaria	71.0	70.9	28	14	32	16	83.2	64.9	15
58	Malaysia	63.0	73.1	46	8	63	8	83.9	73.3	41
59	Panama	66.2	74.7	46	19	68	25	85.1	76.3	70
60	Macedonia, TFYR	67.5	73.6	85	22	120	26	84.1	75.8	7
61	Libyan Arab Jamahiriya	52.8	72.8	105	16	160	19	81.5	73.4	75
62	Mauritius	62.9	72.0	64	17	86	19	82.4	66.6	21
63	Russian Federation	69.7	66.8	29	18	36	21	78.0	48.4	44
64	Colombia	61.6	72.2	69	19	108	23	80.8	70.9	80
65	Brazil	59.5	68.1	95	31	135	36	76.5	59.7	160
66	Bosnia and Herzegovina	67.5	74.0	60	15	82	18	85.2	74.1	10
67	Belize	67.6	71.4	56	34	77	40	77.9	72.5	140
68	Dominica	..	..	..	14	..	15	..	..	65
69	Venezuela	65.7	73.7	47	19	61	22	83.5	73.2	60
70	Samoa (Western)	56.1	70.0	106	20	160	25	78.2	65.1	..
71	Saint Lucia	65.3	72.5	..	17	..	19	77.4	71.2	30
72	Romania	69.2	70.5	46	19	57	21	81.5	63.7	42
73	Saudi Arabia	53.9	72.3	118	23	185	28	81.1	75.7	..
74	Thailand	61.0	69.3	74	24	102	28	79.9	62.4	44
75	Ukraine	70.1	69.7	22	17	27	20	81.1	56.5	25
76	Kazakhstan	64.4	66.3	..	61 [e]	..	76 [e]	76.7	53.1	65
77	Suriname	64.0	71.1	51	26	68	32	79.6	68.4	110
78	Jamaica	69.0	75.7	49	17	64	20	85.4	78.9	95
79	Oman	52.1	72.4	126	12	200	13	82.4	75.4	14
80	St. Vincent & the Grenadines	61.6	74.1	..	22	..	25	84.2	78.6	43
81	Fiji	60.6	69.8	50	18	61	21	75.1	67.3	38
82	Peru	55.4	69.8	115	30	178	39	77.0	68.0	190
83	Lebanon	65.0	73.5	45	28	54	32	83.6	77.2	100 [f]
84	Paraguay	65.9	70.9	57	26	76	30	79.8	71.4	190
85	Philippines	58.1	70.0	60	29	90	38	78.0	69.9	170
86	Maldives	51.4	67.4	157	58	255	77	69.5	69.5	350
87	Turkmenistan	60.7	67.1	..	76 [e]	..	99 [e]	74.2	60.6	65
88	Georgia	69.2	73.6	36	24	46	29	85.6	69.2	50
89	Azerbaijan	69.0	72.2	..	74 [e]	..	105 [e]	81.3	68.0	80
90	Jordan	56.5	71.0	77	27	107	33	77.3	71.2	41
91	Tunisia	55.6	72.8	135	21	201	27	84.6	75.2	70
92	Guyana	60.0	63.2	81	54	101	72	67.1	54.8	110
93	Grenada	..	..	..	20	..	25	..	..	1
94	Dominican Republic	59.7	66.7	91	41	128	47	72.0	62.3	230 [f]
95	Albania	67.7	73.7	68	26 [e]	82	30 [e]	87.7	80.1	..
96	Turkey	57.9	70.5	150	36	201	43	81.0	71.0	130 [f]
97	Ecuador	58.8	70.8	87	24	140	30	78.6	70.3	160
98	Occupied Palestinian Territories	56.6	72.4	..	21	..	24 [e]	81.6	75.1	..
99	Sri Lanka	65.1	72.6	65	17	100	19	84.6	73.5	90
100	Armenia	72.5	72.4	..	31	..	35	85.4	70.3	35

HDI rank		Life expectancy at birth (years)		Infant mortality rate (per 1,000 live births)		Under-five mortality rate (per 1,000 live births)		Probability at birth of surviving to age 65 [a]		Maternal mortality ratio reported (per 100,000 live births)
		1970-75 [b]	2000-05 [b]	1970	2001	1970	2001	Female (% of cohort) 2000-05 [b]	Male (% of cohort) 2000-05 [b]	1985-2001 [c]
101	Uzbekistan	64.2	69.7	..	52	..	68	76.9	65.7	21
102	Kyrgyzstan	63.1	68.6	111	52	146	61	77.2	61.5	65
103	Cape Verde	57.5	70.2	..	29	..	38	79.5	68.1	35
104	China	63.2	71.0	85	31	120	39	81.3	72.7	55
105	El Salvador	58.2	70.7	111	33	162	39	77.6	67.3	120
106	Iran, Islamic Rep. of	55.3	70.3	122	35	191	42	79.5	71.8	37
107	Algeria	54.5	69.7	143	39	234	49	76.9	72.8	140
108	Moldova, Rep. of	64.8	68.9	46	27	61	32	76.4	60.2	28
109	Viet Nam	50.3	69.2	112	30	157	38	77.2	68.8	95
110	Syrian Arab Republic	57.0	71.9	90	23	129	28	80.0	74.7	110 [f]
111	South Africa	53.7	47.7	80	56	115	71	37.4	24.9	..
112	Indonesia	49.2	66.8	104	33	172	45	72.5	64.2	380
113	Tajikistan	63.4	68.8	78	53 [e]	111	72 [e]	75.4	66.2	65
114	Bolivia	46.7	63.9	144	60	243	77	68.0	60.0	390
115	Honduras	53.8	68.9	116	31	170	38	73.4	65.4	110
116	Equatorial Guinea	40.5	49.1	165	101	281	153	44.2	39.2	..
117	Mongolia	53.8	63.9	..	61	..	76	67.4	57.6	150
118	Gabon	48.7	56.6	..	60	..	90	52.0	48.6	520
119	Guatemala	53.7	65.8	115	43	168	58	70.5	59.0	190
120	Egypt	52.1	68.8	157	35	235	41	78.0	67.9	80
121	Nicaragua	55.1	69.5	113	36	165	43	75.2	66.5	150
122	São Tomé and Principe	56.5	69.9	..	57	..	74	79.1	68.9	..
123	Solomon Islands	55.6	69.2	71	20	99	24	76.0	70.2	553 [f]
124	Namibia	49.9	44.3	104	55	155	67	30.8	24.7	270
125	Botswana	56.1	39.7	99	80	142	110	21.7	17.3	330
126	Morocco	52.9	68.7	119	39	184	44	77.1	69.4	230
127	India	50.3	63.9	127	67	202	93	67.5	61.9	540
128	Vanuatu	54.0	68.8	107	34	160	42	73.1	66.3	..
129	Ghana	49.9	57.9	112	57	190	100	55.8	50.1	210 [f]
130	Cambodia	40.3	57.4	..	97	..	138	56.9	47.6	440
131	Myanmar	49.3	57.3	122	77	179	109	58.9	47.7	230
132	Papua New Guinea	44.7	57.6	106	70	147	94	51.5	45.0	370 [f]
133	Swaziland	47.3	34.4	132	106	196	149	15.2	11.0	230
134	Comoros	48.9	60.8	159	59	215	79	61.8	55.3	..
135	Lao People's Dem. Rep.	40.4	54.5	145	87	218	100	52.9	47.8	650
136	Bhutan	43.2	63.2	156	74	267	95	66.1	61.1	380
137	Lesotho	49.5	35.1	125	91	190	132	19.2	8.5	..
138	Sudan	43.6	55.6	104	65	172	107	54.6	48.3	550
139	Bangladesh	45.2	61.4	145	51	239	77	61.1	57.9	400
140	Congo	55.0	48.2	100	81	160	108	37.5	31.1	..
141	Togo	45.5	49.7	128	79	216	141	42.6	36.9	480
Low human development										
142	Cameroon	45.7	46.2	127	96	215	155	36.8	31.7	430
143	Nepal	43.3	59.9	165	66	250	91	57.6	56.4	540
144	Pakistan	49.0	61.0	117	84	181	109	61.9	60.0	..
145	Zimbabwe	56.0	33.1	86	76	138	123	8.3	9.2	700
146	Kenya	50.9	44.6	96	78	156	122	30.6	26.1	590
147	Uganda	46.3	46.2	110	79	185	124	33.5	30.6	510
148	Yemen	39.8	60.0	194	79	303	107	60.0	54.5	350
149	Madagascar	44.9	53.6	109	84	180	136	51.5	46.7	490
150	Haiti	48.5	49.5	148	79	221	123	36.1	34.5	520
151	Gambia	38.0	54.1	183	91	319	126	51.3	45.8	..

HDI rank	Life expectancy at birth (years)		Infant mortality rate (per 1,000 live births)		Under-five mortality rate (per 1,000 live births)		Probability at birth of surviving to age 65 [a]		Maternal mortality ratio reported (per 100,000 live births)
							Female (% of cohort)	Male (% of cohort)	
	1970-75 [b]	2000-05 [b]	1970	2001	1970	2001	2000-05 [b]	2000-05 [b]	1985-2001 [c]
152 Nigeria	44.0	51.5	120	110	201	183	44.5	42.0	..
153 Djibouti	41.0	45.7	160	100	241	143	37.1	33.2	..
154 Mauritania	43.4	52.5	150	120	250	183	50.5	44.4	750
155 Eritrea	44.3	52.7	..	72	..	111	43.7	35.4	1,000
156 Senegal	41.8	52.9	164	79	279	138	52.5	40.0	560
157 Guinea	37.3	49.1	197	109	345	169	42.8	40.3	530
158 Rwanda	44.6	39.3	124	96	209	183	24.1	22.7	1,100
159 Benin	44.0	50.6	149	94	252	158	47.8	38.8	500
160 Tanzania, U. Rep. of	46.5	43.3	129	104	218	165	29.2	26.1	530
161 Côte d'Ivoire	45.4	41.0	158	102	239	175	25.5	24.8	600
162 Malawi	41.0	37.5	189	114	330	183	21.3	19.7	1,100
163 Zambia	49.7	32.4	109	112	181	202	10.6	11.3	650
164 Angola	38.0	40.1	180	154	300	260	31.1	26.4	..
165 Chad	39.0	44.7	..	117	..	200	36.4	32.4	830
166 Guinea-Bissau	36.5	45.3	..	130	..	211	39.4	33.7	910
167 Congo, Dem. Rep. of the	45.8	41.8	148	129	245	205	31.4	27.9	950
168 Central African Republic	43.0	39.5	149	115	248	180	24.0	21.0	1,100
169 Ethiopia	41.8	45.5	160	116	239	172	35.8	32.3	870
170 Mozambique	41.1	38.1	163	125	278	197	26.3	19.8	1,100
171 Burundi	43.9	40.9	138	114	233	190	26.6	25.1	..
172 Mali	38.2	48.6	221	141	391	231	41.0	37.3	580
173 Burkina Faso	41.2	45.7	163	104	290	197	34.5	32.1	480
174 Niger	38.2	46.2	197	156	330	265	39.9	37.6	590
175 Sierra Leone	35.0	34.2	206	182	363	316	23.5	19.4	1,800
Developing countries	55.8	65.1	109	61 [e]	167	89 [e]	69.2	62.0	..
Least developed countries	43.7	51.4	150	99 [e]	244	156 [e]	44.7	40.7	..
Arab States	..	..	128	49 [e]	197	65 [e]	72.5	65.6	..
East Asia and the Pacific	..	..	87	32 [e]	125	42 [e]	79.0	70.0	..
Latin America and the Caribbean	61.0	70.4	86	28	123	34	78.7	66.5	..
South Asia	49.6	63.5	129	69	206	95 [e]	66.4	61.4	..
Sub-Saharan Africa	43.9	46.9	136	107	223	172	36.1	32.0	..
Central & Eastern Europe & CIS	68.7	..	34	18 [e]	43	22 [e]	80.6	58.8	..
OECD	70.4	..	40	11	53	14 [e]	88.1	78.7	..
High-income OECD	71.5	..	22	5	28	7	89.5	80.9	..
High human development	70.2	..	32	9	42	11	88.3	78.8	..
Medium human development	56.9	67.4	102	45 [e]	155	61	74.4	65.3	..
Low human development	43.5	..	139	104	226	162 [e]	41.7	39.1	..
High income	71.5	..	22	5	28	7	89.5	80.9	..
Middle income	62.3	70.7	86	31	122	38	79.5	68.6	..
Low income	48.7	59.6	127	80	203	119 [e]	59.6	54.2	..
World	58.4	66.6	96	56	147	81	72.9	64.4	..

a. Data refer to the probability at birth of surviving to age 65, times 100. b. Data refer to estimates for the period specified. c. The maternal mortality data are those reported by national authorities. The United Nations Children's Fund (UNICEF) and the World Health Organization (WHO) periodically evaluate these data and make adjustments to account for the well-documented problems of underreporting and misclassification of maternal deaths and to develop estimates for countries with no data (for the most recent estimates for 1995, see MDG indicator table 3). Data refer to the most recent year available during the period specified. d. For the World Bank estimate for 2001, see MDG indicator table 3. e. Estimate differs slightly from a more recent World Bank estimate in MDG indicator table 3. f. Data refer to a year or period other than that specified, differ from the standard definition or refer to only part of the country.

Source: Columns 1, 2, 7 and 8: UN 2003d; columns 3 and 5: UNICEF 2003a; columns 4 and 6: UNICEF 2003b; column 9: UNICEF 2003b, based on data from a joint effort by UNICEF and the WHO.

9 Commitment to education: public spending

		Public expenditure on education [a]			Public expenditure on education by level (as % of all levels) [b]					
		As % of GDP		As % of total government expenditure		Pre-primary and primary		Secondary		Tertiary	
HDI rank		1990 [c]	1998-2000 [d]	1990 [c]	1998-2000 [d]	1990 [c]	1998-2000 [d]	1990 [c]	1998-2000 [d]	1990 [c]	1998-2000 [d]
High human development											
1	Norway [e]	7.1	6.8	14.6	16.2	39.5	..	24.7	..	15.2	..
2	Iceland [e]	5.4	..	..	..	59.5	..	25.6	..	14.9	..
3	Sweden [e]	7.4	7.8	13.8	13.4	47.7	..	19.6	..	13.2	..
4	Australia [e]	5.1	4.7 [f]	14.8	..	2.2	33.1	57.4	39.3	32.0	26.0
5	Netherlands [e]	6.0	4.8	14.8	10.7	21.5	..	37.7	..	32.1	..
6	Belgium [e]	5.0	5.9	..	11.6	23.3	..	42.9	..	16.5	..
7	United States [e]	5.2	4.8	12.3	..	..	..	..	..	..	..
8	Canada [e]	6.5	5.5	14.2	..	..	..	62.2	..	28.6	..
9	Japan [e]	..	3.5	..	9.3	..	..	..	..	..	..
10	Switzerland [e]	5.1	5.5	18.7	15.2	49.9	..	25.1	..	19.7	..
11	Denmark [e]	..	8.2	..	15.3	..	..	..	..	..	..
12	Ireland	5.2	4.4	10.2	13.2	37.8	..	40.1	..	20.4	..
13	United Kingdom [e]	4.9	4.5	..	11.4	29.7	33.2	43.8	46.7	19.6	20.1
14	Finland	5.6	6.1	11.9	12.5	27.9	26.7	39.4	39.5	23.9	33.8
15	Luxembourg [e]	3.0	3.7 [f]	10.4	8.5 [f]	..	..	..	..	..	..
16	Austria [e]	5.4	5.8	7.6	12.4	23.7	27.3	46.6	44.1	19.1	26.2
17	France [e]	5.4	5.8	..	11.5	27.3	..	40.7	..	13.8	..
18	Germany	..	4.6	..	9.7	..	..	..	..	..	..
19	Spain [e]	4.4	4.5	9.4	11.3	29.3	33.9	45.0	46.0	15.4	20.1
20	New Zealand [e]	6.2	6.1	..	..	30.5	..	25.3	..	37.4	..
21	Italy [e]	3.1	4.5	..	9.5	33.0	..	63.2	..	..	..
22	Israel	6.3	7.3	11.3	..	43.0	..	31.3	..	16.2	..
23	Portugal [e]	4.2	5.8	..	13.1	44.6	..	32.5	..	16.3	..
24	Greece	2.5	3.8	..	7.0	34.1	..	45.1	..	19.5	..
25	Cyprus [g]	3.5	5.4	11.3	..	38.5	34.7	50.3	50.6	3.8	14.8
26	Hong Kong, China (SAR)	..	..	..	..	26.6	..	38.8	..	30.8	..
27	Barbados	7.8	7.1	22.2	18.5	37.5	35.9 [f]	37.6	32.8	19.2	29.1
28	Singapore	..	3.7	..	23.6 [f]	29.6	27.1 [f]	36.5	28.1 [f]	29.3	26.0 [f]
29	Slovenia	..	..	..	..	..	..	..	..	..	..
30	Korea, Rep. of [e]	3.5	3.8	22.4	17.4	44.4	..	34.1	..	7.4	..
31	Brunei Darussalam	..	4.8	..	9.1 [f]	24.1	..	26.1	..	9.5	..
32	Czech Republic [e]	..	4.4	..	9.7	..	..	..	..	..	..
33	Malta	4.3	4.9 [f]	8.3	..	25.1	28.9	44.7	42.8	14.6	18.2
34	Argentina [e]	1.1	4.0	10.9	11.8	3.4	42.8	44.9	36.9	46.7	17.1
35	Poland [e]	..	5.0	..	11.4	42.8	..	17.5	..	22.0	..
36	Seychelles	7.8	7.6 [f]	14.8	10.7	28.2	23.1	40.7	40.8	9.5	8.1
37	Bahrain	4.2	3.0	14.6	11.4	..	30.1	45.8	34.5	..	0.0
38	Hungary [e]	5.8	5.0	7.8	14.1	55.4	..	23.9	..	15.2	..
39	Slovakia [e]	5.1	4.2	..	13.8	..	..	..	..	..	..
40	Uruguay [e]	3.0	2.8	15.9	..	37.5	..	30.3	..	22.6	..
41	Estonia	..	7.5	..	..	..	44.5	..	34.1	..	16.8
42	Costa Rica	4.4	4.4	20.8	..	..	51.8	..	28.0	..	19.4
43	Chile [e]	2.5	4.2	10.4	17.5	60.1	50.2	17.3	33.3	20.3	16.5
44	Qatar	3.5	3.6 [h]	..	..	..	..	..	..	..	..
45	Lithuania	4.6	6.4	13.8	..	..	..	..	..	..	..
46	Kuwait	4.8	..	3.4	..	53.4	..	13.6	..	16.0	..
47	Croatia	..	4.2 [f]	..	10.4 [f]	..	..	..	..	..	..
48	United Arab Emirates	1.9	1.9	14.6	..	..	53.3	..	45.1	..	0.0
49	Bahamas	4.0	..	17.8	..	..	..	..	..	..	..
50	Latvia	3.8	5.9	10.8	..	11.2	33.3	56.3	48.7	11.6	16.3

HDI rank	Public expenditure on education [a] As % of GDP		As % of total government expenditure		Public expenditure on education by level (as % of all levels) [b] Pre primary and primary		Secondary		Tertiary	
	1990 [c]	1998-2000 [d]	1990 [c]	1998-2000 [d]	1990 [c]	1998-2000 [d]	1990 [c]	1998-2000 [d]	1990 [c]	1998-2000 [d]
51 Saint Kitts and Nevis	2.7	2.9 [f]	..	16.4 [f]	..	59.8 [f]	..	32.3 [f]	..	..
52 Cuba	..	8.5	12.3	15.1	25.7	44.5 [f]	39.0	36.7 [f]	14.4	18.5 [f]
53 Belarus	4.9	6.0	..	..	57.7	..	16.2	..	14.4	..
54 Trinidad and Tobago	3.6	4.0 [f]	11.6	16.7 [f]	42.5	59.6 [f]	36.8	32.3 [f]	11.9	3.7 [f]
55 Mexico [e]	3.6	4.4	12.8	22.6	32.3	..	29.6	..	16.5	..
Medium human development										
56 Antigua and Barbuda	..	3.2	..	..	..	36.9 [f]	..	37.3 [f]	..	15.1 [f]
57 Bulgaria	5.2	3.4	..	..	70.7	41.7	..	43.9	13.9	14.4
58 Malaysia [e]	5.2	6.2	18.3	26.7	34.3	31.8	34.4	32.9	19.9	31.9
59 Panama	4.7	5.9	20.9	..	37.0	40.8 [f]	23.3	33.9 [f]	21.3	25.3 [f]
60 Macedonia, TFYR	..	..	..	..	..	..	..	..	..	..
61 Libyan Arab Jamahiriya	..	..	..	..	..	..	..	..	..	..
62 Mauritius	3.5	3.5	11.8	12.1	37.7	..	36.4	..	16.6	..
63 Russian Federation	3.5	4.4	..	..	..	..	..	..	..	..
64 Colombia	2.5	..	16.0	..	39.3	..	30.9	..	20.7	..
65 Brazil	..	4.7	..	12.9	..	41.0	..	37.6	..	21.4
66 Bosnia and Herzegovina	..	..	..	..	..	..	..	..	..	..
67 Belize	4.7	6.2	18.5	20.9	61.0	46.7 [f]	20.2	36.5 [f]	8.1	4.9 [f]
68 Dominica	..	5.1 [f]	..	..	..	64.4 [f]	..	30.1 [f]	..	0.0
69 Venezuela	3.0	..	12.0	..	23.5	..	4.5	..	40.7	..
70 Samoa (Western)	3.4	4.2 [f]	10.7	13.3 [f]	52.6	..	25.2	..	0.0	..
71 Saint Lucia	..	5.8	..	16.9	48.2	40.1 [f]	23.3	28.9 [f]	12.8	11.6 [f]
72 Romania	2.8	3.5 [f]	7.3	..	52.1	..	22.1	..	9.6	..
73 Saudi Arabia	6.5	9.5	17.8	..	78.8	..	..	..	21.2	..
74 Thailand [e]	3.5	5.4	20.0	31.0	56.2	36.0	21.6	27.1	14.6	24.1
75 Ukraine	5.2	4.4	19.7	15.7	54.9	14.4	15.0	53.1	15.1	19.9
76 Kazakhstan	3.2	..	17.6	..	..	..	..	..	..	..
77 Suriname	8.1	..	..	..	60.5	..	14.5	..	8.8	..
78 Jamaica [e]	4.7	6.3	12.8	11.1	37.4	40.4	33.2	40.0	21.1	18.8
79 Oman	3.1	3.9	11.1	..	54.1	39.1	37.0	50.7	7.4	1.6
80 St. Vincent & the Grenadines	6.4	9.3	13.8	..	..	56.6 [f]	..	29.5 [f]	..	6.0 [f]
81 Fiji	4.6	5.2 [f]	..	17.0 [f]	..	53.4 [f]	..	43.9 [f]	..	2.5 [f]
82 Peru [e]	2.2	3.3	..	21.1	..	41.3	..	26.6	..	20.4
83 Lebanon	..	3.0	..	11.1	..	..	..	..	..	..
84 Paraguay	1.1	5.0	9.1	11.2 [f]	..	..	22.6	..	25.8	..
85 Philippines [e]	2.9	4.2	10.1	20.6	..	..	..	..	..	..
86 Maldives	4.0	3.9 [f]	10.0	11.2 [f]	..	..	..	..	..	..
87 Turkmenistan	4.3	..	21.0	..	..	..	..	..	..	..
88 Georgia	..	..	..	..	..	..	..	..	..	..
89 Azerbaijan	..	4.2	23.5	24.4	..	..	..	..	..	..
90 Jordan [e]	8.4	5.0	17.1	5.0	..	32.9 [f]	62.4	31.5 [f]	35.1	33.0 [f]
91 Tunisia [e]	6.0	6.8	13.5	17.4	39.8	..	36.4	..	18.5	..
92 Guyana	3.4	4.1 [f]	4.4	..	..	..	..	..	..	..
93 Grenada	5.1	4.2 [f]	13.2	..	64.1	72.3 [f]	31.7	23.8 [f]	0.0	0.0
94 Dominican Republic	..	2.5	..	15.7	..	..	..	..	..	..
95 Albania	5.8	..	..	..	..	..	..	..	..	..
96 Turkey [e]	2.2	3.5	..	..	58.1	52.5	29.4	19.6	..	27.9
97 Ecuador	2.8	1.6	17.2	8.0	34.4	49.4 [f]	34.2	42.7 [f]	18.3	6.9 [f]
98 Occupied Palestinian Territories	..	..	..	..	..	..	..	..	..	..
99 Sri Lanka	2.6	3.1	8.1	..	..	..	84.3	..	13.4	..
100 Armenia	7.0	2.9	20.5	..	..	7.2 [f]	..	78.1	..	11.1

HDI rank	Public expenditure on education [a] As % of GDP 1990 [c]	1998-2000 [d]	As % of total government expenditure 1990 [c]	1998-2000 [d]	Public expenditure on education by level (as % of all levels) [b] Pre-primary and primary 1990 [c]	1998-2000 [d]	Secondary 1990 [c]	1998-2000 [d]	Tertiary 1990 [c]	1998-2000 [d]
101 Uzbekistan	..	..	20.4	..	..	..	..	..	..	..
102 Kyrgyzstan	8.3	5.4	22.5	..	8.5	..	57.9	..	10.0	..
103 Cape Verde	..	4.4 f	..	..	..	..	..	..	..	..
104 China	2.3	2.1	12.8	..	..	37.4	..	32.2	..	15.6
105 El Salvador	1.9	2.3 f	16.6	13.4 f	..	15.9 f	..	75.1 f	..	8.8 f
106 Iran, Islamic Rep. of	4.1	4.4	22.4	20.4	33.2	26.7 f	39.2	34.8	13.6	19.4
107 Algeria	5.3	..	21.1	..	..	..	..	..	..	..
108 Moldova, Rep. of	..	4.0	..	15.0	..	19.5	..	69.0	..	11.6
109 Viet Nam	..	..	7.5	..	..	..	..	..	..	..
110 Syrian Arab Republic	4.1	4.1	17.3	11.1	38.5	..	28.2	..	21.3	..
111 South Africa	6.2	5.5	..	25.8	75.6	47.2	..	31.3	21.5	14.5
112 Indonesia [e]	1.0	..	..	..	..	..	..	..	..	..
113 Tajikistan	9.7	2.1	24.7	11.8	6.9	..	57.0	..	9.1	..
114 Bolivia	2.3	5.5	..	23.1	..	52.3 f	..	22.9 f	..	23.8 f
115 Honduras	..	4.0 f	..	..	..	..	..	..	..	..
116 Equatorial Guinea	..	0.6	..	..	..	39.1 f	..	30.7 f	..	30.1 f
117 Mongolia	12.1	2.3	17.6	2.2	13.9	22.0	48.8	60.1	14.5	18.0
118 Gabon	..	3.9 f	..	..	..	35.6 f	..	38.9 f	..	25.5 f
119 Guatemala	1.4	1.7	11.8	11.4	31.1	67.2 f	12.9	32.8 f	21.2	0.0
120 Egypt	3.7	..	..	..	..	..	..	..	..	..
121 Nicaragua	3.4	5.0	9.7	13.8	..	..	..	..	..	..
122 São Tomé and Principe	..	..	..	..	..	..	..	..	..	..
123 Solomon Islands	..	3.6 f	..	15.4 f	..	..	..	..	..	..
124 Namibia	7.6	8.1	..	..	..	58.5	..	27.3	..	12.0
125 Botswana	6.7	8.6 f	17.0	..	..	53.2	..	23.8	..	18.6
126 Morocco	5.3	5.5 f	26.1	26.1	34.8	48.2 f	48.9	50.5 f	16.2	0.4 f
127 India [e]	3.9	4.1	12.2	12.7	38.9	39.4 f	27.0	40.5 f	14.9	20.1 f
128 Vanuatu	4.6	7.3 f	..	17.4 f	59.8	34.6 f	26.6	57.7 f	3.4	6.8 f
129 Ghana	3.2	4.1 f	24.3	..	29.2	..	34.3	..	11.0	..
130 Cambodia	..	1.9	..	10.1	..	65.2 f	..	23.6 f	..	4.9
131 Myanmar	..	0.5	..	9.0 f	..	35.6	..	19.7	..	34.3
132 Papua New Guinea	..	2.3 f	..	17.5 f	..	71.4 f	..	24.3 f	..	4.3 f
133 Swaziland	5.7	1.5	19.5	..	31.2	33.2	24.5	26.9	26.0	32.1
134 Comoros	..	3.8	..	..	42.4	41.6	28.2	41.2	17.3	3.3
135 Lao People's Dem. Rep.	..	2.3	..	8.8	..	47.3 f	..	20.5 f	..	19.8 f
136 Bhutan	..	5.2	..	12.9	..	26.9 f	..	47.9 f	..	19.6 f
137 Lesotho	6.1	10.1	12.2	18.5	..	48.6	..	27.7	..	16.7
138 Sudan	0.9	..	2.8	..	..	..	..	..	..	..
139 Bangladesh	1.5	2.5	10.3	15.7	45.6	46.7 f	42.2	43.0 f	8.7	10.1
140 Congo	5.0	4.2	14.4	12.6	..	..	..	..	..	..
141 Togo	5.5	4.8	26.4	23.2	30.4	51.0 f	25.8	30.8 f	29.0	18.2 f
Low human development										
142 Cameroon	3.2	3.2	19.6	12.5	70.5	..	..	..	29.5	..
143 Nepal	2.0	3.7	8.5	14.1	48.2	60.0 i	15.7	24.6	23.3	11.9
144 Pakistan	2.6	1.8 f	7.4	7.8 f	..	..	..	..	..	..
145 Zimbabwe [e]	..	10.4 f	..	..	54.1	56.1 f	28.6	29.2 f	12.3	14.8 f
146 Kenya	6.7	6.4	17.0	22.5	50.3	1.4 h	18.8	0.7 h	21.6	11.5 h
147 Uganda	1.5	2.3 f	11.5	..	..	..	..	..	..	..
148 Yemen	..	10.0	..	32.8	..	..	..	..	..	..
149 Madagascar	2.1	3.2	..	10.2	49.1	..	35.6	..	..	..
150 Haiti	1.4	1.1 f	20.0	10.9 f	53.1	38.3 f	19.0	61.0 f	9.1	0.8 f
151 Gambia	3.8	2.7 f	14.6	14.2 f	41.6	..	21.2	..	17.8	..

		Public expenditure on education [a]				Public expenditure on education by level (as % of all levels) [b]					
		As % of GDP		As % of total government expenditure		Pre-primary and primary		Secondary		Tertiary	
HDI rank		1990 [c]	1998-2000 [d]	1990 [c]	1998-2000 [d]	1990 [c]	1998-2000 [d]	1990 [c]	1998-2000 [d]	1990 [c]	1998-2000 [d]
152	Nigeria	0.9	..	..	..	..	..	..	..	..	..
153	Djibouti	..	3.5 [f]	10.5	..	58.0	65.9 [f,i]	21.7	..	11.5	..
154	Mauritania	..	3.0 [f]	..	18.9	33.3	..	37.7	..	24.9	..
155	Eritrea	..	4.8	..	..	..	..	..	..	..	..
156	Senegal	3.9	3.2 [f]	26.9	..	43.9	42.5 [h]	25.7	25.3 [h]	24.0	23.1 [h]
157	Guinea	..	1.9 [f]	..	25.6 [f]	..	..	..	..	..	..
158	Rwanda	..	2.8 [f]	..	..	..	..	..	..	..	..
159	Benin	..	3.2 [f]	..	..	..	55.1 [f]	..	26.9 [f]	..	18.0 [f]
160	Tanzania, U. Rep. of	3.2	2.1 [f]	11.4	..	..	..	..	..	..	..
161	Côte d'Ivoire	..	4.6	..	21.5	..	42.4 [f]	..	32.5 [f]	..	25.1 [f]
162	Malawi	3.3	4.1 [f]	11.1	24.6	44.7	..	13.1	..	20.2	..
163	Zambia	2.4	2.3	8.7	17.6	..	..	..	..	..	..
164	Angola	3.9	2.7	10.7	..	96.3	..	..	..	3.7	..
165	Chad	..	2.0 [f]	..	..	..	57.5 [f]	..	25.9 [f]	..	16.6 [f]
166	Guinea-Bissau	..	2.1	..	4.8	..	..	..	..	..	..
167	Congo, Dem. Rep. of the	..	..	..	..	..	..	..	..	..	..
168	Central African Republic	2.2	1.9	..	..	..	..	..	..	..	..
169	Ethiopia	3.4	4.8	9.4	13.8	53.9	..	28.1	..	12.1	..
170	Mozambique	3.9	2.4 [f]	12.0	12.3 [f]	49.8	..	15.7	..	9.9	..
171	Burundi	3.4	3.4	16.7	..	46.8	38.0	29.1	35.0	22.0	26.9
172	Mali	..	2.8 [f]	..	..	..	45.7 [f]	..	39.7 [f]	..	14.6 [f]
173	Burkina Faso	2.7	..	..	..	..	..	..	..	..	..
174	Niger	3.2	2.7 [f]	18.6	..	..	51.6 [f]	..	28.6 [f]	..	19.9
175	Sierra Leone	..	1.0	..	..	..	39.5	..	23.6	..	28.1

Note: As a result of limitations in the data and methodological changes, comparisons of education expenditure data across countries and over time must be made with caution. For detailed notes on the data, see UNESCO 1999 and http://www.uis.unesco.org/.

a. Data refer to total public expenditure on education, including current and capital expenditure. See the definitions of statistical terms. b. Data refer to current public expenditure on education. Data may not be strictly comparable between 1990 and 1998-2000 as a result of methodological changes. Expenditures by level may not sum to 100% as a result of rounding or the omission of the categories expenditures in postsecondary and expenditures not allocated by level. c. Data may not be comparable between countries as a result of differences in methods of data collection. d. Data refer to the most recent year available during the period specified. e. All 1998-2000 data are preliminary UNESCO Institute for Statistics estimates, subject to further revision. f. Data refer to a UNESCO Institute for Statistics estimate where no national estimate is available. g. Data refer to the Office of Greek Education only. h. Data refer to a national estimate. i. Data refer to primary school expenditure only.
Source: Columns 1-10: UNESCO Institute for Statistics 2003c.

10 Literacy and enrolment

HDI rank	Adult literacy rate (% age 15 and above)		Youth literacy rate (% age 15-24)		Net primary enrolment ratio (%)[a]		Net secondary enrolment ratio (%)[a, b]		Children reaching grade 5 (%)	Tertiary students in science, math and engineering (as % of all tertiary students)
	1990	2001	1990	2001	1990-91	2000-01[c]	1990-91	2000-01[c]	1999-2000[c, d]	1994-97[e]
High human development										
1 Norway	..	..	..	..	100	101[f]	88	95[f]	..	18
2 Iceland	..	..	..	..	..	102[f]	..	83[f]	..	20
3 Sweden	..	..	..	..	100	102[f]	85	96[d, f]	..	31
4 Australia	..	..	..	..	99	96[f]	79	90[f]	..	32
5 Netherlands	..	..	..	..	95	100[f]	84	90[f]	..	20
6 Belgium	..	..	..	..	97	101[f]	88	..	..	..
7 United States	..	..	..	..	96	95[f]	86	88[f]	..	..
8 Canada	..	..	..	..	97	99[d, f]	89	98[d, f]	..	..
9 Japan	..	..	..	..	100	101[f]	97	101[f]	..	23
10 Switzerland	..	..	..	..	84	99[f]	80	88[f]	101[f]	31
11 Denmark	..	..	..	..	98	99[d, f]	87	89[d, f]	..	21
12 Ireland	..	..	..	..	91	90[d, f]	80	..	98[f]	30
13 United Kingdom	..	..	..	..	97	99[f]	79	94[f]	..	29
14 Finland	..	..	..	..	99[g]	100[f]	93	95[f]	100[f]	37
15 Luxembourg	..	..	..	..	..	97[f]	..	78[f]	99[f]	..
16 Austria	..	..	..	..	90[g]	91[f]	..	89[f]	..	28
17 France	..	..	..	..	101	100[f]	..	92[f]	..	25
18 Germany	..	..	..	..	84[g]	87[d, f]	..	88[d, f]	..	31
19 Spain	96.3	97.7	99.6	99.8	103	102[f]	..	94[f]	..	31
20 New Zealand	..	..	..	..	101	99[f]	85	92[f]	..	21
21 Italy	97.7	98.5	99.8	99.8	..	100[f]	..	91[f]	..	28
22 Israel	91.4	95.1	98.7	99.5	..	101	..	88	..	..
23 Portugal	87.2	92.5	99.5	99.8	102	..	..	85[f]	..	31
24 Greece	94.9	97.3	99.5	99.8	94	97[f]	83	87[f]	..	..
25 Cyprus	94.3	97.2	99.7	99.8	87	95	..	88	99	17
26 Hong Kong, China (SAR)	89.7	93.5	98.2	99.4	..	..	..	..	..	..
27 Barbados	99.4	99.7	99.8	99.8	78[h]	105	..	85	..	21
28 Singapore	88.8	92.5	99.0	99.8	..	..	..	..	..	..
29 Slovenia	99.6	99.6	99.8	99.8	..	93	..	..	..	29
30 Korea, Rep. of	95.9	97.9	99.8	99.8	104	99[f]	86	91[f]	..	34
31 Brunei Darussalam	85.5	91.6	97.9	99.4	91[h]	..	..	..	92	6
32 Czech Republic	..	..	..	..	..	90[f]	..	..	..	34
33 Malta	88.4	92.3	97.5	98.6	99	99[d]	80	79[i]	100[i]	13
34 Argentina	95.7	96.9	98.2	98.6	..	107[f]	..	79[f]	90[f]	30
35 Poland	99.6	99.7	99.8	99.8	97	98[f]	76	91[f]	99[f]	..
36 Seychelles	..	..	..	..	..	..	..	..	..	..
37 Bahrain	82.1	87.9	95.6	98.5	99	96	85	92	101	..
38 Hungary	99.1	99.3	99.7	99.8	91	90[f]	75	87[d, f]	..	32
39 Slovakia	..	..	..	..	..	89[f]	..	75[f]	..	43
40 Uruguay	96.5	97.6	98.7	99.1	91[h]	90[f]	..	70[f]	91[f]	24
41 Estonia	99.8	99.8	99.8	99.7	..	98	..	83	99	32
42 Costa Rica	93.9	95.7	97.4	98.3	86	91	36	49	80	18
43 Chile	94.0	95.9	98.1	98.9	88	89[f]	55	75[f]	101[f]	43
44 Qatar	77.0	81.7	90.3	95.0	87	95[i]	67	78[i]	..	..
45 Lithuania	99.3	99.6	99.8	99.8	..	95	..	89	..	38
46 Kuwait	76.7	82.4	87.5	92.7	45[h]	66[d]	..	50[i]	..	23
47 Croatia	96.9	98.4	99.6	99.8	79	..	63	..	..	38
48 United Arab Emirates	71.0	76.7	84.7	91.0	94	87	59	67	98	27
49 Bahamas	94.4	95.5	96.5	97.3	96[h]	83[d]	..	72[d]	..	..
50 Latvia	99.8	99.8	99.8	99.8	83[g]	92	..	74	..	29

HDI rank	Adult literacy rate (% age 15 and above)		Youth literacy rate (% age 15-24)		Net primary enrolment ratio (%)[a]		Net secondary enrolment ratio (%)[a, b]		Children reaching grade 5 (%)	Tertiary students in science, math and engineering (as % of all tertiary students)
	1990	2001	1990	2001	1990-91	2000-01[c]	1990-91	2000-01[c]	1999-2000[c, d]	1994-97[e]
51 Saint Kitts and Nevis	..	..	..	..	..	..	..	..	..	..
52 Cuba	95.1	96.8	99.3	99.8	92	97	69	82	95	21
53 Belarus	99.5	99.7	99.8	99.8	..	108	..	76	..	33
54 Trinidad and Tobago	96.8	98.4	99.6	99.8	91	92	..	71	100	41
55 Mexico	87.3	91.4	95.2	97.2	100	103 [f]	45	60 [f]	88 [f]	31
Medium human development										
56 Antigua and Barbuda	..	..	..	..	..	..	..	..	..	..
57 Bulgaria	97.2	98.5	99.4	99.7	86	94	63	88	..	25
58 Malaysia	80.7	87.9	94.8	97.7	..	98 [f]	..	70 [f]	..	..
59 Panama	89.0	92.1	95.3	96.9	91	100	51	62	92	27
60 Macedonia, TFYR	..	..	..	..	94	92	..	81 [d]	..	38
61 Libyan Arab Jamahiriya	68.1	80.8	91.0	96.7	97 [g]	..	..	..	..	..
62 Mauritius	79.8	84.8	91.1	94.0	95	95	..	64	..	17
63 Russian Federation	99.2	99.6	99.8	99.8	..	..	..	..	..	49
64 Colombia	88.4	91.9	94.9	97.0	..	89	..	57	..	31
65 Brazil	82.0	87.3	91.8	95.5	86	97 [f]	15	71 [f]	..	23
66 Bosnia and Herzegovina	..	..	..	..	..	..	..	..	..	..
67 Belize	89.1	93.4	96.0	98.1	98 [h]	100	29	63	..	..
68 Dominica	..	..	..	..	..	..	..	..	86	..
69 Venezuela	88.9	92.8	96.0	98.1	88	88	19	50	91 [i]	..
70 Samoa (Western)	98.0	98.7	99.0	99.4	..	97	..	68	83 [i]	..
71 Saint Lucia	..	..	..	..	..	100	..	80	..	..
72 Romania	97.1	98.2	99.3	99.6	77 [g]	93	..	80	..	32
73 Saudi Arabia	66.2	77.1	85.4	93.1	59	58	31	51	94	18
74 Thailand	92.4	95.7	98.1	99.0	..	85 [f]	..	..	97 [f, i]	21
75 Ukraine	99.4	99.6	99.8	99.9	..	72 [i]	..	..	..	..
76 Kazakhstan	98.8	99.4	99.8	99.8	..	89	..	83	..	42
77 Suriname	..	..	..	..	..	92	..	43	..	..
78 Jamaica	82.2	87.3	91.2	94.3	96	95 [f]	64	74 [f]	89 [f]	20
79 Oman	54.7	73.0	85.6	98.2	70	65	..	59	96	31
80 St. Vincent & the Grenadines	..	..	..	..	..	..	..	..	..	..
81 Fiji	88.6	93.2	97.8	99.2	101 [h]	99 [i]	..	..	..	..
82 Peru	85.5	90.2	94.5	96.9	..	104 [d, f]	..	61 [f, i]	88 [f, i]	..
83 Lebanon	80.3	86.5	92.1	95.4	..	74	..	70 [i]	97	17
84 Paraguay	90.3	93.5	95.6	97.2	93	92 [f]	26	47 [f]	76 [f]	22
85 Philippines	91.7	95.1	97.3	98.8	98 [h]	93 [f]	..	53 [f]	..	..
86 Maldives	94.8	97.0	98.1	99.1	..	99	..	31 [d]	..	..
87 Turkmenistan	..	..	..	..	..	..	..	..	..	..
88 Georgia	..	..	..	..	..	95	..	73 [i]	..	48
89 Azerbaijan	..	..	..	..	..	91 [d]	..	78 [i]	..	..
90 Jordan	81.5	90.3	96.7	99.3	66	94 [d, f]	..	76 [d, f]	98 [f, i]	27
91 Tunisia	59.1	72.1	84.1	93.8	94	99 [f]	..	70 [f]	93 [f]	27
92 Guyana	97.2	98.6	99.8	99.8	93	98 [d]	71	..	..	25
93 Grenada	..	..	..	..	..	84	..	46	..	..
94 Dominican Republic	79.4	84.0	87.5	91.4	..	93	..	40	75 [i]	25
95 Albania	77.0	85.3	94.8	98.0	..	98	..	74	..	22
96 Turkey	77.9	85.5	92.7	96.7	89	..	41	..	..	22
97 Ecuador	87.6	91.8	95.5	97.3	..	99	..	48	78	..
98 Occupied Palestinian Territories	..	..	..	..	..	97	..	78	..	10
99 Sri Lanka	88.7	91.9	95.1	96.9	..	97 [f, i]	..	..	..	29
100 Armenia	97.5	98.5	99.5	99.8	..	69	..	64	..	33

HDI rank	Adult literacy rate (% age 15 and above)		Youth literacy rate (% age 15-24)		Net primary enrolment ratio (%)[a]		Net secondary enrolment ratio (%)[a,b]		Children reaching grade 5 (%)	Tertiary students in science, math and engineering (as % of all tertiary students)
	1990	2001	1990	2001	1990-91	2000-01 [c]	1990-91	2000-01 [c]	1999-2000 [c,d]	1994-97 [e]
101 Uzbekistan	98.7	99.2	99.6	99.7	..	..	..	..	..	..
102 Kyrgyzstan	..	..	..	..	..	82	..	..	..	..
103 Cape Verde	63.8	74.9	81.5	88.6	..	99 [i]	..	..	..	..
104 China	78.3	85.8	95.3	97.9	97	93 [d,f]	..	..	..	53
105 El Salvador	72.4	79.2	83.8	88.5	75 [g]	81 [d]	..	39 [i]	71 [i]	20
106 Iran, Islamic Rep. of	63.2	77.1	86.3	94.2	..	74	..	..	..	36
107 Algeria	52.9	67.8	77.3	89.2	93	98	54	62	97	50
108 Moldova, Rep. of	97.5	99.0	99.8	99.8	..	78	..	68	..	44
109 Viet Nam	90.4	92.7	94.1	95.4	..	95	..	62	..	..
110 Syrian Arab Republic	64.8	75.3	79.9	87.7	98	96	46	39	..	31
111 South Africa	81.2	85.6	88.5	91.5	103 [h]	89	..	57	65	18
112 Indonesia	79.5	87.3	95.0	97.9	98	92 [f]	38	48 [d,f]	97 [f]	28
113 Tajikistan	98.2	99.3	99.8	99.8	..	103	..	76	..	23
114 Bolivia	78.1	86.0	92.6	96.1	91	97	29	68	83	..
115 Honduras	68.1	75.6	79.7	85.5	89 [h]	88	..	..	..	26
116 Equatorial Guinea	73.3	84.2	92.7	97.2	..	72	..	26 [i]	..	..
117 Mongolia	97.8	98.5	98.9	99.1	..	89	..	58	..	25
118 Gabon	..	..	..	..	..	88	..	..	..	..
119 Guatemala	61.0	69.2	73.4	79.6	..	84	..	26	..	..
120 Egypt	47.1	56.1	61.3	70.5	..	93 [f]	..	79 [f]	..	15
121 Nicaragua	62.7	66.8	68.2	72.0	72	81	..	36	48	31
122 São Tomé and Principe	..	..	..	..	..	..	..	..	..	..
123 Solomon Islands	..	..	..	..	..	..	..	..	..	..
124 Namibia	74.9	82.7	87.4	91.9	89 [g]	82	..	38	92	4
125 Botswana	68.1	78.1	83.3	88.7	93	84	34	70	87	27
126 Morocco	38.7	49.8	55.3	68.4	58	78	..	30 [d]	80	29
127 India	49.3	58.0	64.3	73.3	..	..	..	..	68 [f,i]	25
128 Vanuatu	..	..	..	..	..	96	..	23 [i]	101 [i]	..
129 Ghana	58.5	72.7	81.8	91.6	..	58	..	31	66	..
130 Cambodia	62.0	68.7	73.5	79.7	..	95	..	17	63	23
131 Myanmar	80.7	85.0	88.2	91.2	..	83	..	37	..	37
132 Papua New Guinea	56.6	64.6	68.6	76.3	..	84 [d]	..	21 [d]	..	..
133 Swaziland	71.6	80.3	85.1	90.8	88	93	..	44 [d]	84	22
134 Comoros	53.8	56.0	56.7	58.8	..	56	..	..	77	..
135 Lao People's Dem. Rep.	56.5	65.6	70.1	78.6	..	81	..	30	..	..
136 Bhutan	..	..	..	..	..	..	..	..	90	..
137 Lesotho	78.0	83.9	87.2	90.8	73	78	..	21	75	13
138 Sudan	45.8	58.8	65.0	78.1	..	46 [d]	..	..	87 [i]	..
139 Bangladesh	34.2	40.6	42.0	49.1	64	89	18	43	..	..
140 Congo	67.1	81.8	92.5	97.6	..	..	..	..	..	..
141 Togo	44.2	58.4	63.5	76.5	75	92	18	23 [i]	74	11
Low human development										
142 Cameroon	57.9	72.4	81.1	90.5	..	..	..	..	81 [i]	..
143 Nepal	30.4	42.9	46.6	61.6	..	72	..	..	..	14
144 Pakistan	35.4	44.0	47.4	57.8	..	66	..	..	..	..
145 Zimbabwe	80.7	89.3	93.9	97.4	..	80 [f]	..	40 [f]	..	23
146 Kenya	70.8	83.3	89.8	95.5	..	69	..	23	71 [i]	..
147 Uganda	56.1	68.0	70.1	79.4	..	109	..	12 [d]	..	15
148 Yemen	32.7	47.7	50.0	66.5	..	67	..	37 [i]	..	6
149 Madagascar	58.0	67.3	72.2	80.8	..	68	..	11 [i]	..	20
150 Haiti	39.7	50.8	54.8	65.3	22	..	..	..	..	..
151 Gambia	25.6	37.8	42.2	58.6	51 [h]	69	..	35	69 [i]	..

HDI rank	Adult literacy rate (% age 15 and above)		Youth literacy rate (% age 15-24)		Net primary enrolment ratio (%)[a]		Net secondary enrolment ratio (%)[a, b]		Children reaching grade 5 (%)	Tertiary students in science, math and engineering (as % of all tertiary students)
	1990	2001	1990	2001	1990-91	2000-01 [c]	1990-91	2000-01 [c]	1999-2000 [c, d]	1994-97 [e]
152 Nigeria	48.7	65.4	73.6	87.8	..	..	..	..	..	41
153 Djibouti	53.0	65.5	73.2	84.9	32	33	..	..	77 [i]	..
154 Mauritania	34.8	40.7	45.8	49.3	..	64	..	14	61	..
155 Eritrea	46.4	56.7	60.9	71.1	..	41	..	22	..	..
156 Senegal	28.4	38.3	40.1	51.8	48 [h]	63	..	..	72	..
157 Guinea	..	..	..	..	..	47	..	12 [i]	84	42
158 Rwanda	53.3	68.0	72.7	84.2	66	97 [d]	7	..	39	..
159 Benin	26.4	38.6	40.4	54.3	49 [h]	70 [d]	..	17 [d]	84	18
160 Tanzania, U. Rep. of	62.9	76.0	83.1	91.1	51	47	..	5	82	39
161 Côte d'Ivoire	38.5	49.7	52.6	62.4	47	64	..	..	91	..
162 Malawi	51.8	61.0	63.2	71.8	50	101	..	25	49	..
163 Zambia	68.2	79.0	81.2	88.7	..	66	..	19	81	..
164 Angola	..	..	..	..	..	37	..	..	..	..
165 Chad	27.7	44.2	48.0	68.3	..	58	..	8 [d]	54	14
166 Guinea-Bissau	27.2	39.6	44.1	59.5	..	54 [d]	..	..	38 [i]	..
167 Congo, Dem. Rep. of the	47.5	62.7	68.9	82.7	54	33 [i]	..	12 [i]	..	..
168 Central African Republic	33.2	48.2	52.1	68.7	53	55	..	..	..	..
169 Ethiopia	28.6	40.3	43.0	56.2	..	47	..	13	64	36
170 Mozambique	33.5	45.2	48.8	61.7	47	54	..	9	..	46
171 Burundi	37.0	49.2	51.6	65.1	52 [g]	54	..	..	58	..
172 Mali	18.8	26.4	27.6	37.1	21	43 [i]	5	..	95	..
173 Burkina Faso	16.3	24.8	24.9	35.8	27	36	..	8	69	19
174 Niger	11.4	16.5	17.0	23.8	25	30	6	5	74	..
175 Sierra Leone	..	..	..	..	..	..	..	26	..	..
Developing countries	67.2	74.5	81.1	84.8	80	82	..	..	..	..
Least developed countries	43.7	53.3	56.5	66.3	54	60	..	..	..	..
Arab States	50.0	60.8	66.5	76.7	73	77	..	..	..	..
East Asia and the Pacific	80.2	87.1	95.2	97.4	96	93	..	..	..	..
Latin America and the Caribbean	85.0	89.2	92.7	95.2	87	97	..	..	..	..
South Asia	47.7	56.3	61.7	70.6	73	79	..	..	..	..
Sub-Saharan Africa	50.3	62.4	67.4	77.9	56	59	..	..	..	..
Central & Eastern Europe & CIS	98.8	99.3	99.7	99.8	88	91	..	..	..	..
OECD	..	..	..	..	97	98	..	..	..	..
High-income OECD	..	..	..	..	97	97	..	..	..	..
High human development	..	..	..	..	97	98	..	..	..	..
Medium human development	71.8	78.1	84.5	87.8	86	88	..	..	..	..
Low human development	42.8	55.0	59.8	71.5	50	59	..	..	..	..
High income	..	..	..	..	97	97	..	..	..	..
Middle income	80.9	86.6	93.1	95.4	92	93	..	..	..	..
Low income	54.8	63.0	68.0	75.9	69	74	..	..	..	..
World	..	..	..	..	82	84	..	..	..	..

a. Data refer to the 1990/91 or 2000/01 school year. The net enrolment ratio is the ratio of enrolled children of the official age for the education level indicated to the total population of that age. Net enrolment ratios exceeding 100% reflect discrepancies between these two data sets. b. Enrolment ratios are based on the new International Standard Classification of Education, adopted in 1997 (UNESCO 1997), and so may not be strictly comparable with those for earlier years. c. Data for some countries may refer to national or UNESCO Institute for Statistics estimates. For details, see http://www.uis.unesco.org/. Because data are from different sources, comparisons across countries should be made with caution. d. Data refer to the 1999/2000 school year. e. Data refer to the most recent year available during the period specified. f. Preliminary UNESCO Institute for Statistics estimate, subject to further revision. g. Data refer to the 1992/93 school year. h. Data refer to the 1991/92 school year. i. Data refer to the 1998/99 school year.

Source: Columns 1 and 2: UNESCO Institute for Statistics 2003a; *columns 3 and 4:* UNESCO Institute for Statistics 2003a (for data as presented in World Bank 2003c, see MDG indicator table 1); *columns 5 and 6:* UNESCO Institute for Statistics 2003d (for data as presented in World Bank 2003c, see MDG indicator table 1); aggregates calculated for the Human Development Report Office by the UNESCO Institute for Statistics; *columns 7 and 8:* UNESCO Institute for Statistics 2003d; *column 9:* UNESCO Institute for Statistics 2003d (for data as presented in World Bank 2003c, see MDG indicator table 1); *column 10:* calculated on the basis of data on tertiary students from UNESCO 1999.

11 Technology: diffusion and creation

HDI rank	Telephone mainlines (per 1,000 people)		Cellular subscribers (per 1,000 people)		Internet users (per 1,000 people)		Patents granted to residents (per million people)	Receipts of royalties and licence fees (US$ per person)	Research and development (R&D) expenditures (as % of GDP)	Scientists and engineers in R&D (per million people)
	1990	2001	1990	2001	1990	2001	1999	2001	1996-2000[a]	1996-2000[a]
High human development										
1 Norway	502	732	46	815	7.1	463.8	97	34.3	1.7	4,112
2 Iceland	510	664	39	865	5.0 [b]	599.3	21	0.0 [c]	2.3	5,695
3 Sweden	681	739	54	790	5.8	516.3	285	160.5	3.8	4,511
4 Australia	456	541	11	574	5.9	371.4	65	15.4	1.5	3,353
5 Netherlands	464	621	5	767	3.3	490.5	187	107.5	2.0	2,572
6 Belgium	393	498	4	747	(.)	310.4	103	86.3	2.0	2,953
7 United States	547	667	21	451	8.0	501.5	298	135.5	2.7	4,099
8 Canada	565	676	22	362	3.7	466.6	44	48.2	1.8	2,985
9 Japan	441	586	7	588	0.2	384.2	1,057	82.4	3.0	5,095
10 Switzerland	574	732	18	728	5.8	307.0	203	..	2.6	3,592
11 Denmark	567	722	29	740	1.0	429.5	67	..	2.1	3,476
12 Ireland	281	485	7	774	0.6 [b]	233.1	66	90.1	1.2	2,184
13 United Kingdom	441	587	19	770	0.9	329.6	76	134.5	1.9	2,666
14 Finland	534	548	52	804	4.0	430.3	1	112.5	3.4	5,059
15 Luxembourg	481	780	2	920	1.5 [d]	359.8	158	459.1	..	..
16 Austria	418	468	10	817	1.3	387.0	159	16.9	1.8	2,313
17 France	495	573	5	605	0.5	263.8	195	42.3	2.2	2,718
18 Germany	441	634	4	682	1.4	373.6	229	38.3	2.5	3,161
19 Spain	316	434	1	734	0.1	182.7	45	8.9	0.9	1,921
20 New Zealand	434	477	16	599	2.9 [d]	461.2	86	16.0	1.1	2,197
21 Italy	388	471	5	883	0.2	268.9	113	7.6	1.0	1,128
22 Israel	343	466	3	907	1.1	276.6	71	68.0	3.6	1,563
23 Portugal	243	425	1	774	1.0 [b]	281.5	9	2.5	0.7	1,576
24 Greece	389	529	0	751	0.5 [b]	132.1	1	1.3	0.7	1,400
25 Cyprus	419	631	5	456	0.6 [d]	217.5	0	..	0.2	358
26 Hong Kong, China (SAR)	450	580	24	859	1.3 [b]	386.8	4	16.0 [c]	0.4	93 [e]
27 Barbados	281	481	0	198	..	55.9	0	0.9 [c]	..	..
28 Singapore	346	471	17	724	1.6 [b]	411.5	12	..	1.9	4,140
29 Slovenia	211	402	0	737	..	300.8	98	7.2	1.5	2,181
30 Korea, Rep. of	306	486	2	621	0.2	521.1	931	14.6 [c]	2.7	2,319
31 Brunei Darussalam	136	259	7	401	..	102.3	..	..	..	..
32 Czech Republic	158	378	0	679	..	146.7	22	3.6	1.4	1,349
33 Malta	360	530	0	611	..	252.6	26	1.7	..	96 [e]
34 Argentina	93	224	(.)	193	(.) [d]	100.8	4	0.6	0.4	713
35 Poland	86	295	0	259	0.1 [b]	98.4	26	1.2	0.7	1,429
36 Seychelles	124	261	0	539	..	109.9	..	..	..	..
37 Bahrain	191	267	10	460	..	203.4	..	..	..	..
38 Hungary	96	375	(.)	498	(.) [b]	148.4	30	9.4	0.8	1,445
39 Slovakia	135	289	0	399	..	125.3	14	3.0 [c]	0.7	1,844
40 Uruguay	134	283	0	155	..	119.0	3	(.)	0.3	219
41 Estonia	204	354	0	455	0.6 [d]	300.5	4	1.5	0.8	2,128
42 Costa Rica	101	230	0	76	(.) [d]	93.4	0	0.2	0.2	533
43 Chile	66	233	1	342	0.4 [d]	201.4	1	0.3	0.5	370
44 Qatar	190	275	8	293	..	65.6	..	..	..	591 [e]
45 Lithuania	212	313	0	277	..	67.9	26	0.1	..	2,027
46 Kuwait	188	208	12	386	..	87.9	..	0.0	0.2	212
47 Croatia	172	383	(.)	377	..	111.3	14	24.3	1.0	1,187
48 United Arab Emirates	206	340	17	616	..	314.8	0	..	..	..
49 Bahamas	274	400	8	197	..	54.9	..	..	..	..
50 Latvia	234	307	0	279	..	72.3	41	1.1	0.4	1,078

HDI rank	Telephone mainlines (per 1,000 people)		Cellular subscribers (per 1,000 people)		Internet users (per 1,000 people)		Patents granted to residents (per million people)	Receipts of royalties and licence fees (US$ per person)	Research and development (R&D) expenditures (as % of GDP)	Scientists and engineers in R&D (per million people)
	1990	2001	1990	2001	1990	2001	1999	2001	1996-2000 [a]	1996-2000 [a]
51 Saint Kitts and Nevis	237	491	0	46	..	78.5	..	0.0 [c]	..	..
52 Cuba	31	51	0	1	..	10.7	4	..	0.5	480
53 Belarus	154	288	0	14	..	42.4	39	0.1	..	1,893
54 Trinidad and Tobago	141	240	0	197	..	92.3	0	..	0.1	145
55 Mexico	65	137	1	217	0.1 [b]	36.2	1	0.4	0.4	225
Medium human development										
56 Antigua and Barbuda	253	481	0	323	..	90.4	0	0.0	..	..
57 Bulgaria	242	359	0	191	..	74.6	25	0.3	0.6	1,316
58 Malaysia	89	198	5	314	(.) [d]	273.1	..	0.9	0.4	160
59 Panama	93	130	0	164	..	41.4	..	..	0.3	124
60 Macedonia, TFYR	148	263	0	109	..	34.2	16	1.6	..	387
61 Libyan Arab Jamahiriya	48	109	0	9	..	3.6	..	..	..	361
62 Mauritius	52	256	2	227	..	131.6	..	(.) [c]	0.3	360 [e]
63 Russian Federation	140	243	0	53	(.) [d]	29.3	105	0.4	1.0	3,481
64 Colombia	69	172	0	76	..	27.0	(.)	(.)	0.3	101
65 Brazil	65	218	(.)	167	(.) [b]	46.6	3	0.6	0.8	323
66 Bosnia and Herzegovina	0	111	0	60	..	11.1	0	..	..	..
67 Belize	92	143	0	159	..	73.0	..	..	..	..
68 Dominica	164	299	0	99	..	115.7	0	0.0	..	..
69 Venezuela	76	109	(.)	263	0.1 [d]	46.8	..	0.0 [c]	0.3	194
70 Samoa (Western)	26	54	0	18	..	16.8	..	..	..	..
71 Saint Lucia	129	317	0	17	..	82.4	0	0.0 [c]	..	..
72 Romania	102	184	0	172	..	44.7	41	0.7	0.4	913
73 Saudi Arabia	77	145	1	113	..	13.4	(.)	0.0	..	..
74 Thailand	24	99	1	123	0.0	57.7	..	0.1	0.1	74
75 Ukraine	136	212	0	44	..	11.9	12	0.1	0.9	2,118
76 Kazakhstan	80	121	0	36	..	9.3	79	0.0 [c]	0.3	716
77 Suriname	92	176	0	198	..	33.0	..	..	..	..
78 Jamaica	45	205	0	244	..	38.5	(.)	2.3	..	8 [e]
79 Oman	60	90	2	124	..	45.7	..	..	..	4
80 St. Vincent & the Grenadines	124	227	0	65	..	47.8	..	0.0 [c]	..	..
81 Fiji	58	112	0	99	..	18.3	..	..	..	50 [e]
82 Peru	26	78	(.)	59	..	76.6	(.)	0.0	0.1	229
83 Lebanon	155	187	0	229	..	77.6	..	..	..	..
84 Paraguay	27	51	0	204	..	10.6	..	32.0	..	..
85 Philippines	10	42	0	150	..	25.6	(.)	(.)	..	156 [e]
86 Maldives	29	99	0	69	0.0	36.5	..	12.8	..	..
87 Turkmenistan	60	80	0	2	..	1.7	7	..	..	..
88 Georgia	99	174	0	61	..	9.3	38	..	0.3	2,421
89 Azerbaijan	86	120	0	94	..	3.2	0	..	0.2	2,799
90 Jordan	72	129	(.)	167	..	45.2	..	..	..	1,948
91 Tunisia	38	109	(.)	40	..	41.2	..	1.6	0.5	336
92 Guyana	20	92	0	87	..	109.2	..	..	..	..
93 Grenada	177	328	2	64	0.0	52.0	0	0.0 [c]	..	..
94 Dominican Republic	48	110	(.)	146	..	21.5	..	..	..	..
95 Albania	12	50	0	99	..	2.5	0	..	..	..
96 Turkey	121	285	1	295	..	60.4	(.)	0.0	0.6	306
97 Ecuador	48	104	0	67	0.1 [d]	25.9	(.)	..	0.1	83
98 Occupied Palestinian Territories	0	89	0	91	..	18.2	..	..	..	..
99 Sri Lanka	7	44	(.)	36	..	8.0	0	..	0.2	191
100 Armenia	157	140	0	7	..	18.4	46	..	..	1,313

HDI rank	Telephone mainlines (per 1,000 people)		Cellular subscribers (per 1,000 people)		Internet users (per 1,000 people)		Patents granted to residents (per million people)	Receipts of royalties and licence fees (US$ per person)	Research and development (R&D) expenditures (as % of GDP)	Scientists and engineers in R&D (per million people)
	1990	2001	1990	2001	1990	2001	1999	2001	1996-2000 [a]	1996-2000 [a]
101 Uzbekistan	69	67	0	3	..	6.0	20	..	..	1,754 [e]
102 Kyrgyzstan	72	78	0	5	..	30.2	13	0.2	0.2	581
103 Cape Verde	24	143	0	72	..	27.5	..	..	..	..
104 China	6	137	(.)	110	..	25.7	2	0.1	1.0	545
105 El Salvador	24	102	0	134	..	23.4	..	0.2	..	47
106 Iran, Islamic Rep. of	40	169	0	32	..	15.6	2	0.0 [c]	..	590 [e]
107 Algeria	32	61	(.)	3	..	6.5	0	..	..	..
108 Moldova, Rep. of	106	146	0	51	..	13.7	47	0.3	..	334
109 Viet Nam	1	38	0	15	..	12.4	(.)	..	..	274 [e]
110 Syrian Arab Republic	41	103	0	12	0.0	3.6	..	..	0.2	29
111 South Africa	93	111	(.)	242	0.1 [b]	64.9	0	1.2	..	992 [e]
112 Indonesia	6	35	(.)	31	..	19.1	0	..	..	130 [e]
113 Tajikistan	45	36	0	(.)	..	0.5	3	..	..	660 [e]
114 Bolivia	28	63	0	94	..	21.8	..	0.2	0.3	98
115 Honduras	17	47	0	36	..	13.8	1	0.0 [c]	..	..
116 Equatorial Guinea	4	15	0	32	..	1.9	..	..	..	..
117 Mongolia	32	52	0	81	..	16.7	44	0.0	..	531
118 Gabon	22	30	0	205	..	13.5	..	..	..	..
119 Guatemala	21	65	(.)	97	..	17.1	(.)	..	..	103 [e]
120 Egypt	30	104	(.)	43	..	9.3	1	0.7	0.2	493 [e]
121 Nicaragua	13	29	0	30	..	14.4	0	..	0.1	73
122 São Tomé and Principe	19	36	0	0	..	60.0	..	5.1	..	..
123 Solomon Islands	15	17	0	2	..	4.6	..	..	..	..
124 Namibia	39	64	0	55	..	24.6	..	..	..	..
125 Botswana	21	85	0	188	0.0	29.7	0	..	..	..
126 Morocco	16	41	(.)	164	..	13.7	0	0.8	..	..
127 India	6	38	0	6	(.) [d]	6.8	1	0.1 [c]	1.2	157
128 Vanuatu	18	34	0	2	..	27.4	..	..	..	..
129 Ghana	3	12	0	9	..	1.9	0	..	..	..
130 Cambodia	(.)	2	0	17	..	0.7	..	..	..	..
131 Myanmar	2	6	0	(.)	..	0.2	..	(.)	..	..
132 Papua New Guinea	8	12	0	2	..	9.4	..	..	..	..
133 Swaziland	17	31	0	54	..	13.7	0	0.2	..	..
134 Comoros	8	12	0	0	..	3.4	..	..	..	..
135 Lao People's Dem. Rep.	2	10	0	5	..	1.9	..	..	..	..
136 Bhutan	4	26	0	0	..	7.4	..	..	..	..
137 Lesotho	7	10	0	26	..	2.3	0	5.6	..	..
138 Sudan	3	14	0	3	..	1.8	0	0.0 [c]	..	..
139 Bangladesh	2	4	0	4	..	1.4	..	(.) [c]	..	51 [e]
140 Congo	7	7	0	48	..	0.3	..	..	..	33
141 Togo	3	10	0	26	0.0	32.2	..	..	..	102 [e]
Low human development										
142 Cameroon	3	7	0	20	..	2.9	..	..	..	..
143 Nepal	3	13	0	1	0.0	2.6	..	..	..	..
144 Pakistan	8	23	(.)	6	..	3.4	..	(.)	..	69
145 Zimbabwe	13	22	0	29	..	8.7	0	..	..	..
146 Kenya	8	10	0	19	..	16.0	(.)	0.2	..	..
147 Uganda	2	2	0	12	..	2.5	0	..	0.8	24
148 Yemen	11	22	0	8	..	0.9	..	..	..	..
149 Madagascar	3	4	0	10	..	2.3	(.)	(.)	..	12 [e]
150 Haiti	7	10	0	11	..	3.6	0	..	..	..
151 Gambia	7	26	0	41	..	13.5	0	..	..	..

HDI rank	Telephone mainlines (per 1,000 people)		Cellular subscribers (per 1,000 people)		Internet users (per 1,000 people)		Patents granted to residents (per million people)	Receipts of royalties and licence fees (US$ per person)	Research and development (R&D) expenditures (as % of GDP)	Scientists and engineers in R&D (per million people)
	1990	2001	1990	2001	1990	2001	1999	2001	1996-2000 [a]	1996-2000 [a]
152 Nigeria	3	5	0	3	..	1.0	..	..	..	15 [e]
153 Djibouti	11	15	0	5	..	5.1	..	..	..	..
154 Mauritania	3	10	0	43	..	2.7	..	..	..	..
155 Eritrea	0	8	0	0	..	1.6	..	..	..	..
156 Senegal	6	25	0	31	..	10.3	..	..	(.)	2
157 Guinea	2	3	0	7	..	2.0	..	0.0	..	..
158 Rwanda	2	3	0	8	..	2.5	0	0.0 [c]	..	30 [e]
159 Benin	3	9	0	19	..	3.9	..	..	..	174 [e]
160 Tanzania, U. Rep. of	3	4	0	13	..	3.0	0	(.) [c]	..	..
161 Côte d'Ivoire	6	18	0	45	..	4.3	..	(.)	..	..
162 Malawi	3	5	0	5	..	1.9	0	..	..	..
163 Zambia	8	8	0	11	..	2.4	(.)	..	..	..
164 Angola	8	6	0	6	..	1.5	..	1.2 [c]	..	..
165 Chad	1	1	0	3	..	0.5	..	..	..	..
166 Guinea-Bissau	6	10	0	0	..	3.3	0	..	..	..
167 Congo, Dem. Rep. of the	1	(.)	0	3	..	0.1	..	..	..	..
168 Central African Republic	2	2	0	3	..	0.8	..	..	..	47
169 Ethiopia	3	4	0	(.)	..	0.4	0	..	..	..
170 Mozambique	3	5	0	9	..	1.7	..	..	..	..
171 Burundi	1	3	0	4	0.0	0.9	..	..	..	21 [e]
172 Mali	1	5	0	4	..	2.9	..	..	..	..
173 Burkina Faso	2	5	0	6	..	1.6	..	..	0.2	16
174 Niger	1	2	0	(.)	..	1.1	..	..	..	..
175 Sierra Leone	3	5	0	5	..	1.4	0	..	..	..
Developing countries	21	87	(.)	75	..	26.5	..	0.1	..	..
Least developed countries	3	6	0	6	..	1.8	..	(.)	..	..
Arab States	35	76	(.)	58	..	15.6	..	0.3	..	..
East Asia and the Pacific	17	122	(.)	113	..	41.4	..	0.1	1.5	619
Latin America and the Caribbean	62	162	(.)	160	..	49.0	2	0.7	..	..
South Asia	7	38	(.)	7	..	6.3	..	(.)	..	158 [f]
Sub-Saharan Africa	11	15	(.)	28	..	7.8	..	0.1	..	..
Central & Eastern Europe & CIS	124	224	(.)	120	..	42.8	54	1.0	0.9	2,554
OECD	392	523	10	539	2.8	332.0	284	62.7	2.6	2,324 [g]
High-income OECD	465	597	13	605	3.2	400.1	354	78.4	2.6	3,305 [h]
High human development	382	511	10	529	2.6	328.2	273	60.2	2.6	2,335 [g]
Medium human development	26	102	(.)	73	..	22.0	7	0.2	..	588 [f]
Low human development	4	10	(.)	8	..	2.8	..	(.)	..	..
High income	461	592	13	608	3.2	396.9	346	76.4	2.6	3,281 [h]
Middle income	41	152	(.)	128	..	36.8	10	0.4	..	778
Low income	10	30	(.)	10	..	6.4	..	(.)	..	..
World	98	169	2	153	..	79.6	68	11.9	..	..

a. Data refer to the most recent year available during the period specified. b. Data refer to 1991. c. Data refer to 2000. d. Data refer to 1992. e. Data refer to a year before 1996. f. Data refer to 1996. g. Data refer to 1998. h. Data refer to 1997.

Source: Columns 1-4: ITU 2003a; *columns 5 and 6:* UN 2003a, based on data from the International Telecommunication Union; *column 7:* WIPO 2003; *column 8:* World Bank 2003c, based on data from the International Monetary Fund; aggregates calculated on the basis of World Bank aggregates for receipts of royalties and licence fees and population; *columns 9 and 10:* World Bank 2003c, based on data from the United Nations Educational, Scientific and Cultural Organization; aggregates calculated for the Human Development Report Office by the World Bank.

12 Economic performance

HDI rank	GDP US$ billions 2001	GDP PPP US$ billions 2001	GDP per capita US$ 2001	GDP per capita PPP US$ 2001	GDP per capita annual growth rate (%) 1975-2001	GDP per capita annual growth rate (%) 1990-2001	GDP per capita Highest value during 1975-2001 (PPP US$)	Year of highest value	Average annual change in consumer price index (%) 1990-2001	Average annual change in consumer price index (%) 2000-01
High human development										
1 Norway	166.1	133.7	36,815	29,620	2.6	2.9	29,620	2001	2.2	3.0
2 Iceland	7.7	8.5	27,312	29,990	1.7	2.1	29,990	2001	2.9	6.4
3 Sweden	209.8	215.1	23,591	24,180	1.4	1.7	24,180	2001	1.8	2.4
4 Australia	368.7	491.8	19,019	25,370	1.9	2.7	25,370	2001	2.2	4.4
5 Netherlands	380.1	436.2	23,701	27,190	1.9	2.3	27,190	2001	2.4	4.5
6 Belgium	229.6	262.5	22,323	25,520	2.0	1.9	25,520	2001	1.9	2.5
7 United States	10,065.3	9,792.5 [a]	35,277	34,320 [a]	2.0	2.1	34,592	2000	2.7	2.8
8 Canada	694.5	843.2	22,343	27,130	1.5	2.1	27,130	2001	1.7	2.5
9 Japan	4,141.4	3,193.0	32,601	25,130	2.6	1.0	25,309	2000	0.6	-0.7
10 Switzerland	247.1	203.2	34,171	28,100	1.0	0.3	28,100	2001	1.5	1.0
11 Denmark	161.5	155.4	30,144	29,000	1.6	2.0	29,000	2001	2.1	2.4
12 Ireland	103.3	124.4	26,908	32,410	4.2	6.8	32,410	2001	2.4	4.9
13 United Kingdom	1,424.1	1,420.3	24,219	24,160	2.1	2.5	24,160	2001	2.8	1.8
14 Finland	120.9	126.8	23,295	24,430	2.0	2.6	24,430	2001	1.6	2.6
15 Luxembourg	18.5	23.7	42,041	53,780	4.0	4.2	53,780	2001	2.0	2.7
16 Austria	188.5	217.4	23,186	26,730	2.1	1.8	26,730	2001	2.2	2.7
17 France	1,309.8	1,420.0	22,129	23,990	1.7	1.5	23,990	2001	1.6	1.6
18 Germany	1,846.1	2,086.8	22,422	25,350	1.8	1.2	25,350	2001	2.2	2.5
19 Spain	581.8	828.4	14,150	20,150	2.2	2.2	20,150	2001	3.7	3.6
20 New Zealand	50.4	73.7	13,101	19,160	0.9	2.0	19,160	2001	1.8	2.6
21 Italy	1,088.8	1,429.7	18,788	24,670	2.0	1.4	24,670	2001	3.5	2.8
22 Israel	108.3	125.9	17,024	19,790	2.0	2.0	20,376	2000	8.9	1.1
23 Portugal	109.8	181.9	10,954	18,150	3.0	2.6	18,150	2001	4.3	4.4
24 Greece	117.2	184.7	11,063	17,440	1.0	2.0	17,440	2001	8.3	3.4
25 Cyprus	9.1	16.1 [b]	12,004	21,190 [b]	4.8	3.2	21,190	2001	3.5	2.0
26 Hong Kong, China (SAR)	161.9	167.1	24,074	24,850	4.5	2.1	25,037	2000	4.9	-1.6
27 Barbados	2.8	4.2	10,281	15,560	1.3	2.1	15,560	2001	2.5	2.6
28 Singapore	85.6	93.7	20,733	22,680	5.1	4.4	23,804	2000	1.6	1.0
29 Slovenia	18.8	34.1	9,443	17,130	..	3.0	17,130	2001	22.0 [c]	9.4
30 Korea, Rep. of	422.2	714.2	8,917	15,090	6.2	4.7	15,090	2001	4.9	4.1
31 Brunei Darussalam	..	..	..	..	-2.2 [c]	-0.7 [c]	..	..	..	..
32 Czech Republic	56.8	150.5	5,554	14,720	..	1.3	14,720	2001	7.3 [c]	4.7
33 Malta	3.6	5.2 [b]	9,172	13,160 [b]	4.5	3.8	13,427	2000	3.0	2.9
34 Argentina	268.6	424.4	7,166	11,320	0.4	2.3	12,827	1998	7.4	-1.1
35 Poland	176.3	365.3	4,561	9,450	..	4.4	9,450	2001	23.1	5.5
36 Seychelles	0.6	..	6,912	..	2.5	0.1	..	..	2.1	6.0
37 Bahrain	7.9	10.5	12,189	16,060	1.1 [c]	1.9	16,126	2000	0.8	..
38 Hungary	51.9	125.7	5,097	12,340	0.9	2.1	12,340	2001	19.2	9.1
39 Slovakia	20.5	64.6	3,786	11,960	(.) [c]	1.9	11,960	2001	8.5 [c]	7.3
40 Uruguay	18.7	28.2	5,554	8,400	1.4	2.1	9,256	1998	30.2	4.4
41 Estonia	5.5	13.9	4,051	10,170	-0.5 [c]	1.6	10,501	1989	18.9 [c]	5.7
42 Costa Rica	16.1	36.7	4,159	9,460	1.2	2.8	9,529	2000	15.1	11.2
43 Chile	66.5	141.6	4,314	9,190	4.1	4.7	9,190	2001	8.3	3.6
44 Qatar	16.5 [d]	..	28,132 [d]	..	..	..	..	..	2.7	1.4
45 Lithuania	12.0	29.5	3,444	8,470	..	-1.6	11,031	1990	27.0 [c]	1.2
46 Kuwait	32.8	38.2 [b]	16,048	18,700 [b]	-0.7 [c]	-1.0 [c]	29,396	1979	2.0	1.7
47 Croatia	20.3	40.2	4,625	9,170	..	2.1	9,313	1990	72.1	4.8
48 United Arab Emirates	..	..	..	..	-3.7 [c]	-1.6 [c]	..	..	..	..
49 Bahamas	4.8 [d]	5.0	15,797 [d]	16,270	1.5 [c]	0.1 [c]	..	..	2.0	2.0
50 Latvia	7.5	18.2	3,200	7,730	-0.7	-1.0	10,243	1989	25.0 [c]	2.5

HDI rank		GDP US$ billions 2001	GDP PPP US$ billions 2001	GDP per capita US$ 2001	GDP per capita PPP US$ 2001	GDP per capita annual growth rate (%) 1975-2001	GDP per capita annual growth rate (%) 1990-2001	GDP per capita Highest value during 1975-2001 (PPP US$)	GDP per capita Year of highest value	Average annual change in consumer price index (%) 1990-2001	Average annual change in consumer price index (%) 2000-01
51	Saint Kitts and Nevis	0.3	0.5	7,609	11,300	5.4 [c]	3.9	11,377	2000	3.4 [c]	..
52	Cuba	..	..	..	..	..	3.7 [c]	..	..	..	..
53	Belarus	12.2	76.0	1,226	7,620	..	-0.6	8,078	1990	294.7 [c]	61.1
54	Trinidad and Tobago	8.8	11.9	6,752	9,100	0.7	2.9	9,100	2001	5.7	..
55	Mexico	617.8	838.2 [b]	6,214	8,430 [b]	0.9	1.5	8,581	2000	18.6	6.4
Medium human development											
56	Antigua and Barbuda	0.7	0.7	9,961	10,170	4.4 [c]	2.7	10,223	2000	..	..
57	Bulgaria	13.6	55.3	1,690	6,890	(.) [c]	-0.6	8,012	1988	105.3	7.4
58	Malaysia	88.0	208.3 [b]	3,699	8,750 [b]	4.1	3.9	8,996	1997	3.4	1.4
59	Panama	10.2	16.7	3,511	5,750	0.8	2.1	5,821	2000	1.1	0.3
60	Macedonia, TFYR	3.4	12.5	1,676	6,110	..	-0.9	6,990	1991	8.0 [c]	-0.7
61	Libyan Arab Jamahiriya	34.1 [d]	..	6,453 [d]	..	..	..	..	..	..	..
62	Mauritius	4.5	11.8	3,750	9,860	4.7 [c]	3.9	9,860	2001	6.7	5.4
63	Russian Federation	310.0	1,027.9	2,141	7,100	-1.2	-3.5	10,326	1989	85.9 [c]	21.5
64	Colombia	82.4	302.8	1,915	7,040	1.5	0.8	7,539	1997	19.5	8.7
65	Brazil	502.5	1,268.6	2,915	7,360	0.8	1.4	7,360	2001	161.6	6.9
66	Bosnia and Herzegovina	4.8	24.3	1,175	5,970	..	20.5 [c]	..	..	..	..
67	Belize	0.8	1.4	3,258	5,690	2.8	1.6	5,690	2001	1.8	1.2
68	Dominica	0.3	0.4	3,661	5,520	3.5 [c]	1.7	5,756	2000	1.8	1.9
69	Venezuela	124.9	139.5	5,073	5,670	-0.9	-0.6	7,619	1977	45.9	12.5
70	Samoa (Western)	0.3	1.1	1,465	6,180	0.4 [c]	2.0	6,180	2001	3.6	3.8
71	Saint Lucia	0.7	0.8	4,222	5,260	4.1 [c]	0.7	5,529	1999	2.7	0.1
72	Romania	38.7	130.7	1,728	5,830	-1.3 [c]	-0.1	7,325	1987	92.8	34.5
73	Saudi Arabia	186.5	285.3	8,711	13,330	-2.1	-1.1	23,294	1980	0.8	-0.5
74	Thailand	114.7	391.7	1,874	6,400	5.4	3.0	6,763	1996	4.6	1.7
75	Ukraine	37.6	213.3	766	4,350	-7.5 [c]	-7.4	9,303	1989	200.4 [c]	..
76	Kazakhstan	22.4	96.8	1,503	6,500	..	-1.9	7,948	1989	54.8 [c]	8.4
77	Suriname	0.8	..	1,803	..	(.)	2.6	..	..	88.0 [c]	..
78	Jamaica	7.8	9.6	3,005	3,720	0.2	-0.5	4,174	1975	21.4	7.0
79	Oman	19.8 [d]	29.0	8,226 [d]	12,040	2.3 [c]	0.6 [c]	..	..	(.)	-1.1
80	St. Vincent & the Grenadines	0.4	0.6	3,047	5,330	3.9	2.5	5,402	2000	2.2	0.8
81	Fiji	1.7	4.0	2,061	4,850	1.0	1.7	4,961	1999	3.3	4.3
82	Peru	54.0	120.4	2,051	4,570	-0.7	2.4	5,310	1981	23.8	2.0
83	Lebanon	16.7	18.3	3,811	4,170	4.0 [c]	3.6	4,244	1998	..	..
84	Paraguay	7.2	29.4	1,279	5,210	0.6	-0.6	6,052	1981	12.5	7.3
85	Philippines	71.4	301.1	912	3,840	0.1	1.0	3,946	1982	8.0	6.1
86	Maldives	0.6	..	2,082	..	..	2.5 [c]	..	..	6.3	0.6
87	Turkmenistan	6.0	23.5	1,097	4,320	-6.6 [c]	-6.1	7,626	1988	..	..
88	Georgia	3.1	13.5	594	2,560	-5.5	-5.5	8,404	1985	20.6 [c]	4.6
89	Azerbaijan	5.6	25.1	688	3,090	..	-1.3 [c]	4,036	1992	134.5 [c]	1.5
90	Jordan	8.8	19.5	1,755	3,870	0.3	0.9	4,698	1986	3.3	1.8
91	Tunisia	20.0	61.9	2,066	6,390	2.0	3.1	6,390	2001	4.2	1.9
92	Guyana	0.7	3.6	912	4,690	0.5	4.4	4,749	1999	6.0 [c]	2.6
93	Grenada	0.4	0.7	3,965	6,740	3.8 [c]	2.9	7,173	2000	2.3 [c]	..
94	Dominican Republic	21.2	59.7	2,494	7,020	1.8	4.2	7,020	2001	8.5	8.9
95	Albania	4.1	11.6	1,300	3,680	-0.5 [c]	4.3	3,680	2001	24.2 [c]	3.1
96	Turkey	147.7	390.3	2,230	5,890	2.0	1.7	6,495	1998	77.9	54.4
97	Ecuador	18.0	42.3	1,396	3,280	0.2	-0.3	3,517	1997	38.7	37.7
98	Occupied Palestinian Territories	4.0	..	1,286	..	..	-3.0 [c]	..	..	..	..
99	Sri Lanka	15.9	59.6	849	3,180	3.4	3.6	3,273	2000	9.9	14.2
100	Armenia	2.1	10.1	556	2,650	..	-1.3	3,828	1990	55.8 [c]	3.1

HDI rank	GDP		GDP per capita		GDP per capita annual growth rate (%)		GDP per capita Highest value during 1975-2001	Year of highest	Average annual change in consumer price index (%)	
	US$ billions 2001	PPP US$ billions 2001	US$ 2001	PPP US$ 2001	1975-2001	1990-2001	(PPP US$)	value	1990-2001	2000-01
101 Uzbekistan	11.3	61.6	450	2,460	-1.9 c	-1.5	2,950	1989	..	..
102 Kyrgyzstan	1.5	13.6	308	2,750	-4.1 c	-3.9	4,392	1990	21.2 c	6.9
103 Cape Verde	0.6	2.5 b	1,317	5,570 b	3.0 c	3.5	5,570	2001	5.2	3.7
104 China	1,159.0	5,111.2	911	4,020	8.2	8.8	4,020	2001	7.6	0.3
105 El Salvador	13.7	33.7	2,147	5,260	0.1	2.4	5,850	1978	7.8	3.8
106 Iran, Islamic Rep. of	114.1	387.2	1,767	6,000	-0.6	2.0	7,808	1976	24.7	11.3
107 Algeria	54.7	187.9 b	1,773	6,090 b	-0.2	0.1	6,836	1985	15.5	4.2
108 Moldova, Rep. of	1.5	9.2	346	2,150	-5.6 c	-8.2	5,764	1989	19.3 c	9.8
109 Viet Nam	32.7	164.5	411	2,070	4.9 c	6.0	2,070	2001	3.2 c	-0.4
110 Syrian Arab Republic	19.5	54.4	1,175	3,280	0.9	1.9	3,487	1998	5.9	0.4
111 South Africa	113.3	488.2 b	2,620	11,290 b	-0.7	0.2	13,510	1981	8.3	4.8
112 Indonesia	145.3	615.2	695	2,940	4.3	2.3	3,267	1997	13.9	11.5
113 Tajikistan	1.1	7.3	169	1,170	-9.9 c	-9.9	3,731	1988	..	..
114 Bolivia	8.0	19.6	936	2,300	-0.4	1.4	2,613	1978	8.1	1.6
115 Honduras	6.4	18.6	970	2,830	0.1	0.3	3,002	1979	18.0	9.7
116 Equatorial Guinea	1.8	..	3,935	..	11.1 c	18.8	..	..	..	..
117 Mongolia	1.0	4.2	433	1,740	-0.3 c	(.)	2,067	1989	39.0 c	8.0
118 Gabon	4.3	7.6	3,437	5,990	-1.5	-0.1	11,633	1976	4.6	..
119 Guatemala	20.5	51.4	1,754	4,400	0.1	1.4	4,522	1980	9.7	7.6
120 Egypt	98.5	229.4	1,511	3,520	2.8	2.5	3,520	2001	8.1	2.3
121 Nicaragua	..	..	..	..	-4.0 c	-0.1 c	..	..	35.1 c	..
122 São Tomé and Principe	(.)	..	311	..	-0.8 c	-0.6	..	..	..	..
123 Solomon Islands	0.3	0.8 b	614	1,910 b	2.1	-1.4	2,766	1996	10.8 c	..
124 Namibia	3.1	12.8 b	1,730	7,120 b	-0.1 c	2.2	7,378	1980	9.5	9.5
125 Botswana	5.2	13.3	3,066	7,820	5.3	2.5	7,820	2001	10.0	6.6
126 Morocco	34.2	105.0	1,173	3,600	1.3	0.7	3,600	2001	3.5	0.6
127 India	477.3	2,930.0	462	2,840	3.2	4.0	2,840	2001	8.7	3.7
128 Vanuatu	0.2	0.6 b	1,058	3,190 b	(.) c	-1.1	3,817	1991	2.7	3.7
129 Ghana	5.3	44.3 b	269	2,250 b	0.2	1.9	2,250	2001	28.1	32.9
130 Cambodia	3.4	22.8	278	1,860	2.1 c	2.2	1,860	2001	5.3 c	-0.6
131 Myanmar	..	..	..	..	1.8	5.7	..	..	25.0	21.1
132 Papua New Guinea	3.0	13.5 b	563	2,570 b	0.5	1.0	3,108	1994	9.7	9.3
133 Swaziland	1.3	4.6	1,175	4,330	1.9	0.1	4,367	1999	9.3	5.9
134 Comoros	0.2	1.1 b	386	1,870 b	-1.0 c	-1.4	2,359	1984	..	..
135 Lao People's Dem. Rep.	1.8	8.8 b	326	1,620 b	3.3 c	3.9	1,620	2001	29.8	7.8
136 Bhutan	0.5	..	644	..	4.0 c	3.5	..	..	9.6 c	..
137 Lesotho	0.8	5.0 b	386	2,420 b	3.0	2.1	2,452	1997	8.8 c	-9.6
138 Sudan	12.5	62.3	395	1,970	0.8	3.2	1,970	2001	66.8 c	..
139 Bangladesh	46.7	214.1	350	1,610	2.3	3.1	1,610	2001	5.1	1.1
140 Congo	2.8	3.0	886	970	0.3	-1.6	1,382	1984	8.5 c	0.1
141 Togo	1.3	7.7	270	1,650	-1.2	-0.6	2,387	1980	7.8	3.9
Low human development										
142 Cameroon	8.5	25.6	559	1,680	-0.6	-0.3	2,463	1986	5.9	4.5
143 Nepal	5.6	30.9	236	1,310	2.2	2.4	1,310	2001	8.1	2.8
144 Pakistan	58.7	266.7	415	1,890	2.7	1.2	1,890	2001	9.1	3.1
145 Zimbabwe	9.1	29.3	706	2,280	0.2	-0.2	2,780	1998	31.8	76.7
146 Kenya	11.4	30.1	371	980	0.3	-0.6	1,079	1990	14.5	5.7
147 Uganda	5.7	33.9 b	249	1,490 b	2.6 c	3.6	1,490	2001	9.5	2.0
148 Yemen	9.3	14.3	514	790	..	2.4	790	2001	32.6 c	..
149 Madagascar	4.6	13.3	288	830	-1.6	-0.6	1,195	1975	17.5	6.9
150 Haiti	3.7	15.1 b	460	1,860 b	-2.0	-2.5	3,194	1980	20.8	14.2
151 Gambia	0.4	2.7 b	291	2,050 b	-0.2	0.1	2,105	1984	4.0	..

	GDP		GDP per capita		GDP per capita annual growth rate (%)		GDP per capita		Average annual change in consumer price index (%)	
	US$ billions	PPP US$ billions	US$	PPP US$	1975-2001	1990-2001	Highest value during 1975-2001 (PPP US$)	Year of highest value	1990-2001	2000-01
HDI rank	2001	2001	2001	2001						
152 Nigeria	41.4	110.6	319	850	-0.7	-0.3	1,084	1977	30.0	13.0
153 Djibouti	0.6	1.5	894	2,370	-4.6 c	-3.6	4,436	1987	..	..
154 Mauritania	1.0	5.5 b	366	1,990 b	(.)	1.2	2,010	1976	5.9	4.7
155 Eritrea	0.7	4.3	164	1,030	..	2.5 c	1,149	1998	..	..
156 Senegal	4.6	14.7	476	1,500	-0.1	1.1	1,525	1976	5.0	3.1
157 Guinea	3.0	14.8	394	1,960	1.4 c	1.6	1,960	2001	..	..
158 Rwanda	1.7	10.9	196	1,250	-1.2	-1.3	1,643	1983	14.7 c	3.3
159 Benin	2.4	6.3	368	980	0.5	1.9	980	2001	7.9 c	4.0
160 Tanzania, U. Rep. of	9.3	18.0	271	520	0.3 c	0.4	520	2001	19.3	5.1
161 Côte d'Ivoire	10.4	24.4	634	1,490	-2.0	0.1	2,581	1978	6.7	4.3
162 Malawi	1.7	6.0	166	570	0.2	1.5	593	1999	33.5	27.2
163 Zambia	3.6	8.0	354	780	-2.2	-1.7	1,345	1976	80.8 c	..
164 Angola	9.5	27.5 b	701	2,040 b	-2.3 c	-1.1	2,694	1988	633.2	152.6
165 Chad	1.6	8.5 b	202	1,070 b	0.1	-0.5	1,194	1977	7.9	12.4
166 Guinea-Bissau	0.2	1.2	162	970	0.3	-1.3	1,265	1997	30.6	3.3
167 Congo, Dem. Rep. of the	5.2	35.8 b	99	680 b	-5.2	-7.7	2,804	1975	813.4	357.3
168 Central African Republic	1.0	4.9 b	257	1,300 b	-1.5	-0.3	1,825	1977	4.9	3.8
169 Ethiopia	6.2	53.3	95	810	0.1 c	2.4	811	1983	4.7	-8.1
170 Mozambique	3.6	20.6 b	200	1,140 b	1.8 c	4.3	1,140	2001	28.8	9.1
171 Burundi	0.7	4.8 b	99	690 b	-0.8	-4.3	1,034	1991	15.9	9.2
172 Mali	2.6	9.0	239	810	-0.4	1.6	907	1979	4.8	5.2
173 Burkina Faso	2.5	13.0 b	215	1,120 b	1.3	2.0	1,120	2001	5.2	5.0
174 Niger	2.0	9.9 b	175	890 b	-2.0	-0.9	1,473	1979	5.7	4.0
175 Sierra Leone	0.7	2.4	146	470	-3.3	-6.6	1,070	1982	27.0	2.1
Developing countries	6,110.3 T	18,579.4 T	1,270	3,850	2.3	2.9	..	..	..	..
Least developed countries	194.6 T	859.3 T	280	1,274	0.4 c	1.2	..	..	..	..
Arab States	706.5 T	1,424.5 T	2,341	5,038	0.3	0.7	..	..	..	..
East Asia and the Pacific	2,337.3 T	7,962.5 T	1,267	4,233	5.9	5.5	..	..	..	..
Latin America and the Caribbean	1,905.2 T	3,666.7 T	3,752	7,050	0.7	1.5	..	..	..	..
South Asia	727.8 T	3,937.6 T	508	2,730	2.4	3.2	..	..	..	..
Sub-Saharan Africa	300.9 T	1,159.1 T	475	1,831	-0.9	-0.1	..	..	..	..
Central & Eastern Europe & CIS	864.0 T	2,706.9 T	2,094	6,598	-2.5 c	-1.6	..	..	..	..
OECD	25,124.2 T	26,501.8 T	22,149	23,363	2.0	1.7	..	..	..	..
High-income OECD	24,053.3 T	24,567.1 T	26,601	27,169	2.1	1.8	..	..	..	..
High human development	25,935.7 T	27,530.2 T	22,005	23,135	2.0	1.7	..	..	..	..
Medium human development	4,443.6 T	16,505.9 T	1,102	4,053	1.7	2.1	..	..	..	..
Low human development	233.1 T	878.0 T	315	1,186	0.1	0.3	..	..	..	..
High income	24,583.9 T	25,180.8 T	26,395	26,989	2.1	1.7	..	..	..	..
Middle income	5,155.7 T	14,720.0 T	1,928	5,519	1.6	2.2	..	..	..	..
Low income	1,082.1 T	5,587.4 T	432	2,230	1.6	1.4	..	..	..	..
World	30,720.9 T	44,995.3 T	5,133	7,376	1.2	1.2	..	..	..	..

a. In theory, for the United States the value of GDP in PPP US dollars should be the same as that in US dollars, but practical issues arising in the calculation of the PPP US dollar GDP prevent this. b. Estimate based on regression. c. Data refer to a period shorter than that specified. d. Data refer to 2000.

Source: Columns 1, 2 and 4: World Bank 2003c; aggregates calculated for the Human Development Report Office by the World Bank; *column 3:* calculated on the basis of GDP and population data from World Bank 2003c; *columns 5 and 6:* World Bank 2003a; aggregates calculated for the Human Development Report Office by the World Bank; *columns 7 and 8:* calculated on the basis of data on GDP at market prices (constant 1995 US$), population and GDP per capita (PPP US$) from World Bank 2003c; *columns 9 and 10:* calculated on the basis of data on the consumer price index from World Bank 2003c.

13 Inequality in income or consumption

HDI rank	Survey year	Share of income or consumption (%)				Inequality measures		Gini index[b]
		Poorest 10%	Poorest 20%	Richest 20%	Richest 10%	Richest 10% to poorest 10%[a]	Richest 20% to poorest 20%[a]	
High human development								
1 Norway	1995 [c]	4.1	9.7	35.8	21.8	5.3	3.7	25.8
2 Iceland	..	..	..	..	..	..	..	..
3 Sweden	1995 [c]	3.4	9.1	34.5	20.1	5.9	3.8	25.0
4 Australia	1994 [c]	2.0	5.9	41.3	25.4	12.5	7.0	35.2
5 Netherlands	1994 [c]	2.8	7.3	40.1	25.1	9.0	5.5	32.6
6 Belgium	1996 [c]	2.9	8.3	37.3	22.6	7.8	4.5	25.0
7 United States	1997 [c]	1.8	5.2	46.4	30.5	16.6	9.0	40.8
8 Canada	1997 [c]	2.7	7.3	39.3	23.9	9.0	5.4	31.5
9 Japan	1993 [c]	4.8	10.6	35.7	21.7	4.5	3.4	24.9
10 Switzerland	1992 [c]	2.6	6.9	40.3	25.2	9.9	5.8	33.1
11 Denmark	1997 [c]	2.6	8.3	35.8	21.3	8.1	4.3	24.7
12 Ireland	1987 [c]	2.5	6.7	42.9	27.4	11.0	6.4	35.9
13 United Kingdom	1995 [c]	2.1	6.1	43.2	27.5	13.4	7.1	36.0
14 Finland	1995 [c]	4.1	10.1	35.0	20.9	5.1	3.5	25.6
15 Luxembourg	1998 [c]	3.2	8.0	39.7	24.7	7.7	4.9	30.8
16 Austria	1995 [c]	2.3	7.0	37.9	22.4	9.8	5.5	30.5
17 France	1995 [c]	2.8	7.2	40.2	25.1	9.1	5.6	32.7
18 Germany	1998 [c]	2.0	5.7	44.7	28.0	14.2	7.9	38.2
19 Spain	1990 [c]	2.8	7.5	40.3	25.2	9.0	5.4	32.5
20 New Zealand	1997 [c]	2.2	6.4	43.8	27.8	12.5	6.8	36.2
21 Italy	1998 [c]	1.9	6.0	42.6	27.4	14.5	7.1	36.0
22 Israel	1997 [c]	2.4	6.9	44.3	28.2	11.7	6.4	35.5
23 Portugal	1997 [c]	2.0	5.8	45.9	29.8	15.0	8.0	38.5
24 Greece	1998 [c]	2.9	7.1	43.6	28.5	10.0	6.2	35.4
25 Cyprus	..	..	..	..	..	..	..	..
26 Hong Kong, China (SAR)	1996 [c]	2.0	5.3	50.7	34.9	17.8	9.7	43.4
27 Barbados	..	..	..	..	..	..	..	..
28 Singapore	1998 [c]	1.9	5.0	49.0	32.8	17.7	9.7	42.5
29 Slovenia	1998 [c]	3.9	9.1	37.7	23.0	5.8	4.1	28.4
30 Korea, Rep. of	1998 [c]	2.9	7.9	37.5	22.5	7.8	4.7	31.6
31 Brunei Darussalam	..	..	..	..	..	..	..	..
32 Czech Republic	1996 [c]	4.3	10.3	35.9	22.4	5.2	3.5	25.4
33 Malta	..	..	..	..	..	..	..	..
34 Argentina	..	..	..	..	..	..	..	..
35 Poland	1998 [d]	3.2	7.8	39.7	24.7	7.8	5.1	31.6
36 Seychelles	..	..	..	..	..	..	..	..
37 Bahrain	..	..	..	..	..	..	..	..
38 Hungary	1998 [d]	4.1	10.0	34.4	20.5	5.0	3.5	24.4
39 Slovakia	1996 [c]	3.1	8.8	34.8	20.9	6.7	4.0	25.8
40 Uruguay[e]	1998 [c]	1.6	4.5	50.4	33.8	21.6	11.2	44.8
41 Estonia	1998 [c]	3.0	7.0	45.1	29.8	10.0	6.5	37.6
42 Costa Rica[f]	1997 [c]	1.7	4.5	51.0	34.6	20.7	11.5	45.9
43 Chile	1998 [c]	1.1	3.2	61.3	45.4	43.2	19.3	57.5
44 Qatar	..	..	..	..	..	..	..	..
45 Lithuania	2000 [d]	3.2	7.9	40.0	24.9	7.9	5.1	36.3
46 Kuwait	..	..	..	..	..	..	..	..
47 Croatia	2001 [d]	3.4	8.3	39.6	24.5	7.3	4.8	29.0
48 United Arab Emirates	..	..	..	..	..	..	..	..
49 Bahamas	..	..	..	..	..	..	..	..
50 Latvia	1998 [c]	2.9	7.6	40.3	25.9	8.9	5.3	32.4

HDI rank	Survey year	Share of Income or consumption (%)				Inequality measures		
		Poorest 10%	Poorest 20%	Richest 20%	Richest 10%	Richest 10% to poorest 10% [a]	Richest 20% to poorest 20% [a]	Gini index [b]
51 Saint Kitts and Nevis	..	..	..	..	..	..	..	..
52 Cuba	..	..	..	..	..	..	..	..
53 Belarus	2000 [d]	3.5	8.4	39.1	24.1	6.9	4.6	30.4
54 Trinidad and Tobago	1992 [c]	2.1	5.5	45.9	29.9	14.4	8.3	40.3
55 Mexico	1998 [c]	1.2	3.4	57.6	41.6	34.6	17.0	51.9
Medium human development								
56 Antigua and Barbuda	..	..	..	..	..	..	..	..
57 Bulgaria	2001 [c]	2.4	6.7	38.9	23.7	9.9	5.8	31.9
58 Malaysia	1997 [c]	1.7	4.4	54.3	38.4	22.1	12.4	49.2
59 Panama	1997 [d]	1.2	3.6	52.8	35.7	29.8	14.7	48.5
60 Macedonia, TFYR	1998 [d]	3.3	8.4	36.7	22.1	6.8	4.4	28.2
61 Libyan Arab Jamahiriya	..	..	..	..	..	..	..	..
62 Mauritius	..	..	..	..	..	..	..	..
63 Russian Federation	2000 [d]	1.8	4.9	51.3	36.0	20.3	10.5	45.6
64 Colombia [f]	1996 [c]	1.1	3.0	60.9	46.1	42.7	20.3	57.1
65 Brazil [f]	1998 [c]	0.7	2.2	64.1	48.0	65.8	29.7	60.7
66 Bosnia and Herzegovina	..	..	..	..	..	..	..	..
67 Belize	..	..	..	..	..	..	..	..
68 Dominica	..	..	..	..	..	..	..	..
69 Venezuela [f]	1998 [c]	0.8	3.0	53.2	36.5	44.0	17.7	49.5
70 Samoa (Western)	..	..	..	..	..	..	..	..
71 Saint Lucia	1995 [c]	2.0	5.2	48.3	32.5	16.2	9.2	42.6
72 Romania	2000 [d]	3.3	8.2	38.4	23.6	7.2	4.7	30.3
73 Saudi Arabia	..	..	..	..	..	..	..	..
74 Thailand	2000 [d]	2.5	6.1	50.0	33.8	13.4	8.3	43.2
75 Ukraine	1999 [d]	3.7	8.8	37.8	23.2	6.4	4.3	29.0
76 Kazakhstan	2001 [d]	3.4	8.2	39.6	24.2	7.1	4.8	31.2
77 Suriname	..	..	..	..	..	..	..	..
78 Jamaica	2000 [d]	2.7	6.7	46.0	30.3	11.4	6.9	37.9
79 Oman	..	..	..	..	..	..	..	..
80 St. Vincent & the Grenadines	..	..	..	..	..	..	..	..
81 Fiji	..	..	..	..	..	..	..	..
82 Peru	1996 [c]	1.6	4.4	51.2	35.4	22.3	11.7	46.2
83 Lebanon	..	..	..	..	..	..	..	..
84 Paraguay	1998 [c]	0.5	1.9	60.7	43.8	91.1	31.8	57.7
85 Philippines	2000 [d]	2.2	5.4	52.3	36.3	16.5	9.7	46.1
86 Maldives	..	..	..	..	..	..	..	..
87 Turkmenistan	1998 [d]	2.6	6.1	47.5	31.7	12.3	7.7	40.8
88 Georgia	2000 [d]	2.2	6.0	45.2	29.3	13.4	7.6	38.9
89 Azerbaijan	2001 [d]	3.1	7.4	44.5	29.5	9.7	6.0	36.5
90 Jordan	1997 [d]	3.3	7.6	44.4	29.8	9.1	5.9	36.4
91 Tunisia	1995 [d]	2.3	5.7	47.9	31.8	13.8	8.5	41.7
92 Guyana	1999 [d]	1.3	4.5	49.7	33.8	25.9	11.1	44.6
93 Grenada	..	..	..	..	..	..	..	..
94 Dominican Republic	1998 [c]	2.1	5.1	53.3	37.9	17.7	10.5	47.4
95 Albania	..	..	..	..	..	..	..	..
96 Turkey	2000 [d]	2.3	6.1	46.7	30.7	13.3	7.7	40.0
97 Ecuador [f]	1995 [d]	2.2	5.4	49.7	33.8	15.4	9.2	43.7
98 Occupied Palestinian Territories	..	..	..	..	..	..	..	..
99 Sri Lanka	1995 [d]	3.5	8.0	42.8	28.0	7.9	5.3	34.4
100 Armenia	1998 [d]	2.6	6.7	45.1	29.7	11.5	6.8	37.9

HDI rank		Survey year	Share of income or consumption (%)				Inequality measures		
			Poorest 10%	Poorest 20%	Richest 20%	Richest 10%	Richest 10% to poorest 10% [a]	Richest 20% to poorest 20% [a]	Gini index [b]
101	Uzbekistan	2000 [d]	3.6	9.2	36.3	22.0	6.1	4.0	26.8
102	Kyrgyzstan	2001 [d]	3.9	9.1	38.3	23.3	6.0	4.2	29.0
103	Cape Verde	..	..	..	..	..	..	..	..
104	China	1998 [c]	2.4	5.9	46.6	30.4	12.7	8.0	40.3
105	El Salvador	1998 [c]	1.2	3.3	56.4	39.4	33.6	17.3	50.8
106	Iran, Islamic Rep. of	1998 [d]	2.0	5.1	49.9	33.7	17.2	9.7	43.0
107	Algeria	1995 [d]	2.8	7.0	42.6	26.8	9.6	6.1	35.3
108	Moldova, Rep. of	2001 [d]	2.8	7.1	43.7	28.4	10.2	6.2	36.2
109	Viet Nam	1998 [d]	3.6	8.0	44.5	29.9	8.4	5.6	36.1
110	Syrian Arab Republic	..	..	..	..	..	..	..	..
111	South Africa	1995 [d]	0.7	2.0	66.5	46.9	65.1	33.6	59.3
112	Indonesia	2000 [d]	3.6	8.4	43.3	28.5	7.8	5.2	30.3
113	Tajikistan	1998 [d]	3.2	8.0	40.0	25.2	8.0	5.0	34.7
114	Bolivia	1999 [d]	1.3	4.0	49.1	32.0	24.6	12.3	44.7
115	Honduras	1998 [c]	0.5	2.0	61.0	44.4	91.8	30.3	59.0
116	Equatorial Guinea	..	..	..	..	..	..	..	..
117	Mongolia	1998 [d]	2.1	5.6	51.2	37.0	17.8	9.1	44.0
118	Gabon	..	..	..	..	..	..	..	..
119	Guatemala [f]	1998 [c]	1.6	3.8	60.6	46.0	29.1	15.8	55.8
120	Egypt	1999 [d]	3.7	8.6	43.6	29.5	8.0	5.1	34.4
121	Nicaragua	1998 [d]	0.7	2.3	63.6	48.8	70.7	27.9	60.3
122	São Tomé and Principe	..	..	..	..	..	..	..	..
123	Solomon Islands	..	..	..	..	..	..	..	..
124	Namibia	1993 [c]	0.5	1.4	78.7	64.5	128.8	56.1	70.7
125	Botswana	1993 [d]	0.7	2.2	70.3	56.6	77.6	31.5	63.0
126	Morocco	1998-99 [d]	2.6	6.5	46.6	30.9	11.7	7.2	39.5
127	India	1997 [d]	3.5	8.1	46.1	33.5	9.5	5.7	37.8
128	Vanuatu	..	..	..	..	..	..	..	..
129	Ghana	1999 [d]	2.1	5.6	46.6	30.0	14.1	8.4	39.6
130	Cambodia	1997 [d]	2.9	6.9	47.6	33.8	11.6	6.9	40.4
131	Myanmar	..	..	..	..	..	..	..	..
132	Papua New Guinea	1996 [d]	1.7	4.5	56.5	40.5	23.8	12.6	50.9
133	Swaziland	1994 [c]	1.0	2.7	64.4	50.2	49.7	23.8	60.9
134	Comoros	..	..	..	..	..	..	..	..
135	Lao People's Dem. Rep.	1997 [d]	3.2	7.6	45.0	30.6	9.7	6.0	37.0
136	Bhutan	..	..	..	..	..	..	..	..
137	Lesotho	1995 [d]	0.5	1.4	70.7	53.6	117.8	50.0	56.0
138	Sudan	..	..	..	..	..	..	..	..
139	Bangladesh	2000 [d]	3.9	9.0	41.3	26.7	6.8	4.6	31.8
140	Congo	..	..	..	..	..	..	..	..
141	Togo	..	..	..	..	..	..	..	..
Low human development									
142	Cameroon	1996 [d]	1.8	4.6	53.0	36.5	20.0	11.4	47.7
143	Nepal	1995-96 [d]	3.2	7.6	44.8	29.8	9.3	5.9	36.7
144	Pakistan	1998-99 [d]	3.7	8.8	42.3	28.3	7.6	4.8	33.0
145	Zimbabwe	1995 [d]	1.8	4.6	55.7	40.3	22.0	12.0	56.8
146	Kenya	1997 [d]	2.3	5.6	51.2	36.1	15.6	9.1	44.5
147	Uganda	1996 [d]	3.0	7.1	44.9	29.8	9.9	6.4	37.4
148	Yemen	1998 [d]	3.0	7.4	41.2	25.9	8.6	5.6	33.4
149	Madagascar	1999 [d]	2.5	6.4	44.8	28.6	11.4	7.0	46.0
150	Haiti	..	..	..	..	..	..	..	..
151	Gambia	1998 [d]	1.5	4.0	55.2	38.0	25.4	13.8	47.8

HDI rank		Survey year	Share of income or consumption (%)				Inequality measures		Gini index [b]
			Poorest 10%	Poorest 20%	Richest 20%	Richest 10%	Richest 10% to poorest 10% [a]	Richest 20% to poorest 20% [a]	
152	Nigeria	1996-97 [d]	1.6	4.4	55.7	40.8	24.9	12.8	50.6
153	Djibouti	..	..	..	..	..	..	..	..
154	Mauritania	1995 [d]	2.5	6.4	44.1	28.4	11.2	6.9	37.3
155	Eritrea	..	..	..	..	..	..	..	..
156	Senegal	1995 [d]	2.6	6.4	48.2	33.5	12.8	7.5	41.3
157	Guinea	1994 [d]	2.6	6.4	47.2	32.0	12.3	7.3	40.3
158	Rwanda	1983-85 [d]	4.2	9.7	39.1	24.2	5.8	4.0	28.9
159	Benin	..	..	..	..	..	..	..	..
160	Tanzania, U. Rep. of	1993 [d]	2.8	6.8	45.5	30.1	10.8	6.7	38.2
161	Côte d'Ivoire	1995 [d]	3.1	7.1	44.3	28.8	9.4	6.2	36.7
162	Malawi	1997 [d]	1.9	4.9	56.1	42.2	22.7	11.6	50.3
163	Zambia	1998 [d]	1.1	3.3	56.6	41.0	36.6	17.3	52.6
164	Angola	..	..	..	..	..	..	..	..
165	Chad	..	..	..	..	..	..	..	..
166	Guinea-Bissau	1993 [d]	2.1	5.2	53.4	39.3	19.0	10.3	47.0
167	Congo, Dem. Rep. of the	..	..	..	..	..	..	..	..
168	Central African Republic	1993 [d]	0.7	2.0	65.0	47.7	69.2	32.7	61.3
169	Ethiopia	2000 [c]	0.7	2.4	60.8	43.8	59.7	24.8	57.2
170	Mozambique	1996-97 [d]	2.5	6.5	46.5	31.7	12.5	7.2	39.6
171	Burundi	1998 [d]	1.7	5.1	48.0	32.8	19.3	9.5	33.3
172	Mali	1994 [d]	1.8	4.6	56.2	40.4	23.1	12.2	50.5
173	Burkina Faso	1998 [d]	1.8	4.5	60.7	46.3	26.2	13.6	48.2
174	Niger	1995 [d]	0.8	2.6	53.3	35.4	46.0	20.7	50.5
175	Sierra Leone	1989 [d]	0.5	1.1	63.4	43.6	87.2	57.6	62.9

Note: Because the underlying household surveys differ in method and in the type of data collected, the distribution data are not strictly comparable across countries.

a. Data show the ratio of the income or consumption share of the richest group to that of the poorest. Because of rounding, results may differ from ratios calculated using the income or consumption shares in columns 2-5. b. The Gini index measures inequality over the entire distribution of income or consumption. A value of 0 represents perfect equality, and a value of 100 perfect inequality. c. Survey based on income. d. Survey based on consumption. e. Data refer to urban areas only. f. World Bank 2002.

Source: Columns 1-5 and 8: unless otherwise noted, World Bank 2003c; *columns 6 and 7:* unless otherwise noted, calculated on the basis of income or consumption data from World Bank 2003c.

14 The structure of trade

HDI rank	Imports of goods and services (as % of GDP)		Exports of goods and services (as % of GDP)		Primary exports (as % of merchandise exports)		Manufactured exports (as % of merchandise exports)		High-technology exports (as % of manufactured exports)		Terms of trade (1980 = 100) [a]
	1990	2001	1990	2001	1990	2001	1990	2001	1990	2001	2000
High human development											
1 Norway	34	30 [b]	41	47 [b]	67	75	33	21	8	12	86
2 Iceland	33	41	34	40	91	86	8	13	3	3	..
3 Sweden	29	41	30	46	16	10	83	84	13	18	94
4 Australia	17	23 [b]	17	23 [b]	73	65	24	28	5	10	121
5 Netherlands	51	60	54	65	37	29	59	70	16	32	96
6 Belgium	69	81	71	84	19 [c]	17 [c]	77 [c]	79 [c]	..	10	..
7 United States	11	15 [b]	10	11 [b]	22	14	74	82	32	32	91
8 Canada	26	39	26	44	36	31	59	62	12	15	108
9 Japan	9	10	10	10	3	3	96	93	24	26	53
10 Switzerland	36	41	36	45	6	8	94	92	15	21	..
11 Denmark	31	39	36	46	35	29	60	65	15	21	90
12 Ireland	52	80	57	95	26	8	70	88	41	48	102
13 United Kingdom	27	29	24	27	19	17	79	80	23	31	100
14 Finland	24	32	23	40	17	14	83	86	7	23	91
15 Luxembourg	109	135 [b]	112	156 [b]	.. [d]	.. [d]	.. [d]	.. [d]	..	17	..
16 Austria	38	53	40	52	12	13	88	82	8	14	..
17 France	22	26	21	28	23	16	77	82	16	23	..
18 Germany	25	33	29	35	10	9	89	86	12	18 [b]	96
19 Spain	20	31	16	30	24	21	75	78	7	8 [b]	84
20 New Zealand	27	35 [b]	27	37 [b]	75	67	23	29	3	8	91
21 Italy	20	27	20	28	11	10	88	88	8	10	82
22 Israel	45	47 [b]	35	40 [b]	13	6 [b]	87	94 [b]	11	25 [b]	..
23 Portugal	39	41	33	32	19	14 [b]	80	85 [b]	4	6 [b]	..
24 Greece	28	33 [b]	18	25 [b]	46	47	54	52	2	8	133
25 Cyprus	57	48 [e]	52	45 [e]	45	47	55	53	6	3	78
26 Hong Kong, China (SAR)	126	139	134	144	4	4	95	95	0	20	100
27 Barbados	52	52	49	48	55	47	43	51	0	21	82
28 Singapore	177	152	184	174	27	11	72	85	39	60	76
29 Slovenia	..	63 [b]	..	59 [b]	..	10	..	90	..	5	..
30 Korea, Rep. of	30	41	29	43	6	9	94	91	18	29	86
31 Brunei Darussalam	..	..	..	..	100	..	(.)	..	0	..	115
32 Czech Republic	43	74	45	71	..	10	..	89	..	10	..
33 Malta	99	92	85	88	4	4	96	96	44	62	..
34 Argentina	5	10	10	11	71	66	29	33	0	9	82
35 Poland	22	33	29	29	36	19	59	79	0	3	36
36 Seychelles	67	113	62	85	..	..	(.)	..	0	..	..
37 Bahrain	95	59	116	81	91	87	9	13	0	0 [b]	..
38 Hungary	29	63	31	60	35	12	63	85	0	23	117
39 Slovakia	36	82	27	74	..	16	..	84	..	4	..
40 Uruguay	18	20	24	19	61	58	39	42	0	2	101
41 Estonia	..	94	..	91	..	25	..	75	..	19	..
42 Costa Rica	41	45	35	43	66	38	27	62	0	36	123
43 Chile	31	33	35	35	87	80	11	18	1	1	41
44 Qatar	..	..	..	..	84	93	16	7	0	0	83
45 Lithuania	61	56	52	50	..	41	..	58	..	5	..
46 Kuwait	58	37	45	55	94	80 [e]	6	20 [e]	4	1 [e]	117
47 Croatia	..	53	..	47	..	27	..	73	..	10	..
48 United Arab Emirates	40	..	65	..	54	..	46	..	0	..	59
49 Bahamas	..	..	..	..	..	71	..	29	..	..	..
50 Latvia	49	54	48	46	..	40	..	59	..	3	..

		Imports of goods and services (as % of GDP)		Exports of goods and services (as % of GDP)		Primary exports (as % of merchandise exports)		Manufactured exports (as % of merchandise exports)		High-technology exports (as % of manufactured exports)		Terms of trade (1980 = 100) [a]
HDI rank		1990	2001	1990	2001	1990	2001	1990	2001	1990	2001	2000
51	Saint Kitts and Nevis	83	73	52	44	..	27	..	73	..	1 [b]	..
52	Cuba	..	18 [b]	..	16 [b]	..	..	..	..	..	..	75
53	Belarus	44	71	46	68	..	30	..	69	..	8	..
54	Trinidad and Tobago	29	43	45	55	73	54	27	46	0	1 [b]	84
55	Mexico	20	30	19	28	56	15	43	85	7	22	33
Medium human development												
56	Antigua and Barbuda	87	79	89	69	..	..	..	74 [e]	..	..	..
57	Bulgaria	37	63	33	56	..	37 [b]	..	57 [b]	..	2 [b]	..
58	Malaysia	72	98	75	116	46	19	54	80	36	57	48
59	Panama	34	35	38	33	78	87	21	13	0	1 [b]	86
60	Macedonia, TFYR	36	56	26	40	..	30	..	70	..	1	..
61	Libyan Arab Jamahiriya	31	15 [b]	40	36 [b]	95	..	5	..	0	..	82
62	Mauritius	71	63	64	64	34	25	66	74	1	1	97
63	Russian Federation	18	24	18	37	..	66	..	22	..	8 [b]	..
64	Colombia	15	19	21	19	74	61	25	39	0	7	88
65	Brazil	7	14	8	13	47	44	52	54	6	18	135
66	Bosnia and Herzegovina	..	54	..	27	..	..	..	..	..	..	..
67	Belize	62	74	64	55	..	..	15	11 [b]	0	0 [e]	..
68	Dominica	81	64	55	51	..	..	32	57	0	6	..
69	Venezuela	20	18	39	23	90	89	10	11	2	2	65
70	Samoa (Western)	..	82 [b]	..	33 [b]	..	..	4	..	0	..	..
71	Saint Lucia	84	61	73	48	..	79	28	21	0	5	..
72	Romania	26	42	17	34	26	18	73	81	3	6	..
73	Saudi Arabia	36	24	46	42	93	91	7	9	0	(.) [b]	67
74	Thailand	42	60	34	66	36	22	63	74	21	31	67
75	Ukraine	29	54	28	56	..	..	..	..	..	..	..
76	Kazakhstan	..	49	..	46	..	80 [b]	..	20 [b]	..	4 [b]	..
77	Suriname	27	85	28	68	26	22 [b]	74	78 [b]	0	(.) [b]	64
78	Jamaica	52	56	48	41	31	27 [b]	69	73 [b]	0	(.) [b]	73
79	Oman	31	..	53	..	94	87	5	12	11	3 [b]	120
80	St. Vincent & the Grenadines	77	62	66	46	..	..	..	13 [b]	..	0 [b]	..
81	Fiji	66	63 [b]	64	69 [b]	63	..	36	52 [b]	12	(.) [b]	81
82	Peru	14	17	16	16	82	78	18	22	0	2	40
83	Lebanon	100	42	18	12	..	31	..	69	..	3	81
84	Paraguay	39	38	33	23	..	84	10	16	(.)	4	148
85	Philippines	33	47	28	49	31	9	38	91	0	70	109
86	Maldives	64	76	24	93	..	..	..	42	..	0	..
87	Turkmenistan	..	47	..	47	..	92 [b]	..	7 [b]	..	5 [b]	..
88	Georgia	46	38	40	22	..	..	..	..	..	..	..
89	Azerbaijan	39	38	44	42	..	95	..	4	..	8	..
90	Jordan	93	69	62	44	..	34	51	66	2	7	109
91	Tunisia	51	52	44	48	31	23 [b]	69	77 [b]	2	3 [b]	82
92	Guyana	80	111	63	95	..	..	..	..	..	..	69
93	Grenada	63	70	42	59	..	..	20	51	0	0 [e]	..
94	Dominican Republic	44	32	34	24	..	..	..	..	..	..	57
95	Albania	23	42	15	19	..	16	..	84	..	1	..
96	Turkey	18	31	13	34	32	17	68	82	1	5 [b]	..
97	Ecuador	27	34	33	31	98	88	2	12	(.)	4	47
98	Occupied Palestinian Territories	..	71	..	14	..	..	..	..	..	..	..
99	Sri Lanka	38	44	29	37	42	23	54	77	1	3 [e]	114
100	Armenia	46	46	35	26	..	52 [b]	..	43 [b]	..	4 [b]	..

HDI rank	Imports of goods and services (as % of GDP)		Exports of goods and services (as % of GDP)		Primary exports (as % of merchandise exports)		Manufactured exports (as % of merchandise exports)		High-technology exports (as % of manufactured exports)		Terms of trade (1980 = 100)[a]
	1990	2001	1990	2001	1990	2001	1990	2001	1990	2001	2000
101 Uzbekistan	48	28	29	28	..	..	..	..	..	..	..
102 Kyrgyzstan	50	37	29	37	..	40 [e]	..	20 [e]	..	5 [e]	..
103 Cape Verde	44	57	13	26	..	..	..	96	..	..	100
104 China	14	23	18	26	27	11	72	89	0	20	104
105 El Salvador	31	43	19	29	62	44	38	55	0	7	107
106 Iran, Islamic Rep. of	24	21	22	28	..	90	..	10	..	2 [b]	54
107 Algeria	25	21	23	37	97	98 [b]	3	2 [b]	0	4 [b]	59
108 Moldova, Rep. of	51	74	49	50	..	66	..	34	..	3	..
109 Viet Nam	45	57	36	55	..	..	..	..	..	..	..
110 Syrian Arab Republic	28	31	28	38	64	90 [b]	36	8 [b]	0	1 [b]	77
111 South Africa	19	25	24	28	30 [f]	28	22 [f]	59	0	5	..
112 Indonesia	24	33	25	41	65	44	35	56	1	13	53
113 Tajikistan	35	76	28	64	..	..	..	..	..	..	..
114 Bolivia	24	24	23	18	95	78	5	22	0	10	53
115 Honduras	40	55	36	38	91	72	9	27	0	1 [b]	89
116 Equatorial Guinea	70	..	32	..	..	..	..	..	..	..	..
117 Mongolia	53	80	24	64	..	74 [b]	..	26 [b]	..	..	..
118 Gabon	31	41	46	60	..	98 [b]	..	2 [b]	..	..	33
119 Guatemala	25	28	21	19	76	62	24	38	0	8	75
120 Egypt	33	23	20	18	57	60	42	33	0	1	47
121 Nicaragua	46	..	25	..	92	87	8	13	0	3	61
122 São Tomé and Principe	72	86	14	38	..	..	..	..	..	..	..
123 Solomon Islands	73	..	47	..	..	..	..	..	..	..	..
124 Namibia	57	66	44	54	.. [g]	..	.. [g]	..	..	..	..
125 Botswana	50	35	55	51	.. [g]	..	.. [g]	..	..	..	..
126 Morocco	32	36	26	30	48	36 [b]	52	64 [b]	0	11 [b]	111
127 India	10	15	7	14	28	21 [b]	71	77 [b]	4	6 [e]	140
128 Vanuatu	77	..	46	..	..	86 [b]	13	8 [b]	20	1 [b]	..
129 Ghana	26	70	17	52	..	84	..	16	..	1	49
130 Cambodia	13	61	6	53	..	..	..	..	..	..	..
131 Myanmar	5	..	3	(.) [e]	..	..	..	..	..	..	26
132 Papua New Guinea	49	43 [e]	41	47 [e]	89	98 [b]	10	2 [b]	0	19 [b]	..
133 Swaziland	74	81	75	69	.. [g]	..	.. [g]	..	..	..	106
134 Comoros	35	29	14	16	..	..	..	8 [b]	..	1 [b]	59
135 Lao People's Dem. Rep.	25	..	11	..	..	..	..	..	..	..	..
136 Bhutan	32	60 [b]	28	30 [b]	..	60 [e]	..	40 [e]	..	0 [e]	..
137 Lesotho	121	86	17	34	.. [g]	..	.. [g]	..	..	..	59
138 Sudan	..	16	..	13	..	..	..	..	..	..	107
139 Bangladesh	14	22	6	15	..	..	77	..	1	..	89
140 Congo	46	50	54	84	..	..	..	..	..	..	121
141 Togo	45	50	33	33	89	50	9	50	0	1	87
Low human development											
142 Cameroon	17	29	20	32	91	95	9	5	1	(.)	119
143 Nepal	21	32	11	22	..	23 [e]	83	67 [b]	0	0 [b]	..
144 Pakistan	23	19	16	18	21	15	79	85	(.)	(.)	82
145 Zimbabwe	23	21	23	22	68	72 [b]	31	28 [b]	0	0 [b]	108
146 Kenya	31	35	26	26	71	79 [b]	29	21 [b]	4	4 [b]	97
147 Uganda	19	26	7	12	..	93	..	7	..	22 [b]	25
148 Yemen	20	37	14	38	..	..	..	..	..	..	..
149 Madagascar	28	32	17	29	85	48 [e]	14	50 [e]	8	3 [e]	99
150 Haiti	20	33	18	13	15	..	85	..	14	..	44
151 Gambia	72	71	60	54	..	82 [b]	..	17 [b]	..	3 [b]	55

HDI rank	Imports of goods and services (as % of GDP)		Exports of goods and services (as % of GDP)		Primary exports (as % of merchandise exports)		Manufactured exports (as % of merchandise exports)		High-technology exports (as % of manufactured exports)		Terms of trade (1980 = 100) [a]
	1990	2001	1990	2001	1990	2001	1990	2001	1990	2001	2000
152 Nigeria	29	49	43	48	..	100 [b]	..	(.) [b]	..	1 [b]	55
153 Djibouti	..	63 [b]	..	45 [b]	44	..	8	..	0	..	..
154 Mauritania	61	51	46	38	..	..	..	..	..	..	146
155 Eritrea	..	76	..	21	..	..	..	..	..	..	..
156 Senegal	30	38	25	30	77	71	23	29	0	5	91
157 Guinea	31	29	31	28	..	72	..	28	..	(.)	..
158 Rwanda	14	26	6	9	..	..	..	..	..	..	175
159 Benin	26	28	14	15	..	94	..	6	..	..	101
160 Tanzania, U. Rep. of	37 [h]	24 [h]	13 [h]	16 [h]	..	84 [e]	..	15 [e]	..	6 [e]	44
161 Côte d'Ivoire	27	32	32	39	..	85 [b]	..	14 [b]	..	3 [b]	84
162 Malawi	33	38	24	26	95	..	5	..	(.)	..	61
163 Zambia	37	37	36	27	..	87	..	13	..	1	49
164 Angola	21	62	39	74	100	..	(.)	..	0	..	182
165 Chad	28	53	13	14	..	..	..	..	..	..	68
166 Guinea-Bissau	37	74	10	41	..	..	..	..	..	..	74
167 Congo, Dem. Rep. of the	29	17	30	18	..	..	..	..	..	..	77
168 Central African Republic	28	15	15	12	..	..	..	..	..	..	38
169 Ethiopia	12	31	8	15	..	..	..	10 [b]	..	(.) [b]	..
170 Mozambique	36	44	8	22	..	91	..	8	..	(.)	57
171 Burundi	28	18	8	6	..	..	..	(.) [b]	..	0 [b]	43
172 Mali	34	42	17	31	..	..	2	..	0	..	84
173 Burkina Faso	26	26	13	10	..	..	..	..	..	..	153
174 Niger	22	25	15	17	..	95	..	3	..	8	38
175 Sierra Leone	24	37	22	17	..	..	..	..	..	..	99
Developing countries	25	32	26	34	..	..	60	73	8	27	..
Least developed countries	23	30	14	21	..	..	..	..	..	..	..
Arab States	39	29	40	37	..	..	20	19 [e]	1	2 [b]	..
East Asia and the Pacific	39	49	40	54	..	..	75	86	14	32	..
Latin America and the Caribbean	12	19	14	18	65	40	34	49	4	15	..
South Asia	15	18	11	17	..	..	71	55 [b]	..	4 [e]	..
Sub-Saharan Africa	26	33	27	32	..	..	..	33 [b]	..	4 [b]	..
Central & Eastern Europe & CIS	25	40	25	43	..	..	..	55	..	8 [b]	..
OECD	18	23 [b]	18	23 [b]	20	16	78	81	18	22	..
High-income OECD	18	23 [b]	18	23 [b]	19	16	79	81	18	23	..
High human development	19	25 [b]	20	24 [b]	20	17	78	81	17	23	..
Medium human development	19	27	20	29	..	..	48	58	5	19 [b]	..
Low human development	26	30	22	26	..	..	..	29 [b]	..	1 [b]	..
High income	20	24 [b]	20	24 [b]	19	16	79	82	18	24	..
Middle income	19	28	21	30	..	..	47	61	5	22	..
Low income	21	28	18	28	..	..	..	52 [b]	..	7 [e]	..
World	20	28	20	29	..	..	73	78	16	23	..

a. The ratio of the export price index to the import price index measured relative to the base year 1980. A value of more than 100 means that the price of exports has risen relative to the price of imports. b. Data refer to 2000. c. Includes Luxembourg. d. Included in the data for Belgium. e. Data refer to 1999. f. Data refer to the South African Customs Union, which comprises Botswana, Lesotho, Namibia, South Africa and Swaziland. g. Included in the data for South Africa. h. Data refer to mainland Tanzania only.

Source: Columns 1-4 and 7-10: World Bank 2003c; aggregates calculated for the Human Development Report Office by the World Bank; columns 5 and 6: calculated on the basis of data on merchandise trade and exports of food, agricultural raw materials, fuels and ores and metals from World Bank 2003c; column 11: calculated on the basis of data on terms of trade from World Bank 2003c.

15 Flows of aid from DAC member countries

		Net official development assistance (ODA) disbursed			ODA per capita of donor country (2000 US$)		ODA to least developed countries (as % of total) [b]		Net grants by NGOs (as % of GNI) [c]	
		Total (US$ millions) [a]	As % of GNI							
HDI rank		2001	1990 [d]	2001	1990	2001	1990	2001	1990	2001
1	Norway	1,346	1.17	0.83	285	299	44	33	0.13	0.13
3	Sweden	1,666	0.91	0.81	189	207	39	27	0.06	0.01
4	Australia	873	0.34	0.25	49	49	18	20	0.02	0.06
5	Netherlands	3,172	0.92	0.82	160	195	33	31	0.09	0.06
6	Belgium	867	0.46	0.37	83	85	41	34	0.03	0.06
7	United States	11,429	0.21	0.11	57	39	19	15	0.05	0.04
8	Canada	1,533	0.44	0.22	83	51	30	15	0.05	0.02
9	Japan	9,847	0.31	0.23	100	89	19	18	(.)	0.01
10	Switzerland	908	0.32	0.34	108	123	43	28	0.05	0.07
11	Denmark	1,634	0.94	1.03	218	306	39	33	0.02	0.01
12	Ireland	287	0.16	0.33	16	74	37	50	0.07	0.12
13	United Kingdom	4,579	0.27	0.32	53	80	32	36	0.03	0.02
14	Finland	389	0.65	0.32	121	75	38	29	0.03	0.01
15	Luxembourg	141	0.21	0.82	65	325	39	32	0.00	0.03
16	Austria	533	0.25	0.29	47	66	27	20	0.02	0.03
17	France	4,198	0.60	0.32	113	72	32	26	0.02	0.00
18	Germany	4,990	0.42	0.27	93	62	28	24	0.05	0.04
19	Spain	1,737	0.20	0.30	21	43	20	11	0.01	0.00
20	New Zealand	112	0.23	0.25	25	30	19	26	0.03	0.03
21	Italy	1,627	0.31	0.15	50	28	41	30	0.00	(.)
23	Portugal	268	0.24	0.25	16	26	70	45	(.)	(.)
24	Greece	202	..	0.17	..	19	..	11	..	0.00
DAC		52,336 T	0.33	0.22	75	63	28	23	0.03	0.03

Note: DAC is the Development Assistance Committee of the Organisation for Economic Co-operation and Development (OECD).
a. Some non-DAC countries and areas also provide ODA. According to the OECD's Development Assistance Committee (2003a), net ODA disbursed in 2001 by the Czech Republic, Estonia, Iceland, Israel, the Republic of Korea, Kuwait, Poland, Saudi Arabia, Slovakia, Turkey and the United Arab Emirates totalled $1,176 million. China also provides aid but does not disclose the amount. b. Includes imputed multilateral flows that make allowance for contributions through multilateral organizations. These are calculated using the geographic distribution of disbursements for the year specified. c. Does not include disbursements from non-governmental organizations (NGOs) that originate from official sources and are already included in ODA. d. Data for individual countries (but not the DAC average) include forgiveness of non-ODA claims.
Source: Columns 1-9: OECD, Development Assistance Committee 2003a.

16 Flows of aid, private capital and debt

	Official development assistance (ODA) received (net disbursements) [a]				Net foreign direct investment inflows (as % of GDP) [b]		Other private flows (as % of GDP) [b, c]		Total debt service			
	Total (US$ millions)	Per capita (US$)	As % of GDP						As % of GDP		As % of exports of goods and services	
HDI rank	2001	2001	1990	2001	1990	2001	1990	2001	1990	2001	1990	2001
High human development												
22 Israel	172.4 [d]	27.9 [d]	2.6	0.2 [d]	0.3	3.0	..	..	..	..	..	..
23 Portugal	..	..	..	..	3.7	5.4	..	..	..	..	..	..
24 Greece	..	..	..	..	1.2	1.4	..	..	..	..	..	..
25 Cyprus	49.7 [d]	63.0 [d]	0.7	0.5 [d]	2.3	1.8	..	..	..	..	..	..
26 Hong Kong, China (SAR)	3.6 [d]	0.5 [d]	0.1	(.) [d]	..	14.1	..	..	..	..	..	..
27 Barbados	-1.2	-4.3	0.2	(.)	0.7	0.6	-0.8	5.6	8.2	2.5	14.6	4.3 [e]
28 Singapore	1.0 [d]	0.2 [d]	(.)	(.) [d]	15.2	10.1	..	..	..	..	..	..
29 Slovenia	125.6	63.2	..	0.7	..	2.7	..	..	..	..	..	..
30 Korea, Rep. of	-111.1 [d]	-2.4 [d]	(.)	(.) [d]	0.3	0.8	0.1	1.4	3.3	6.2	6.3	7.1
31 Brunei Darussalam	0.4 [d]	1.0 [d]	0.1	..	..	..	..	..	..	..	..	..
32 Czech Republic	313.9 [d]	30.6 [d]	(.) [d]	0.6 [d]	0.2	8.7	1.9	0.5	3.0	8.4	..	4.4
33 Malta	1.7	4.4	0.2	(.)	2.0	8.1	0.0	2.4	2.0	3.8	0.4	2.6
34 Argentina	151.4	4.0	0.1	0.1	1.3	1.2	-1.4	-2.6	4.4	9.0	34.7	48.6
35 Poland	965.9 [d]	25.0 [d]	2.2 [d]	0.5 [d]	0.2	3.2	(.)	2.2	1.6	8.7	4.4	11.5
36 Seychelles	13.5	169.7	9.8	2.4	5.5	10.4	-1.7	-0.6	5.9	2.4	7.8	2.1
37 Bahrain	17.9	25.8	3.2	0.2	..	..	..	..	..	..	..	..
38 Hungary	417.8 [d]	41.9 [d]	0.2 [d]	0.8 [d]	0.9	4.7	-0.9	2.9	12.8	26.4	33.4	8.5
39 Slovakia	164.3 [d]	30.5 [d]	(.) [d]	0.8 [d]	0.0	7.2	1.8	-5.7	2.1	12.8	..	6.2
40 Uruguay	15.5	4.6	0.6	0.1	0.0	1.7	-2.1	2.6	10.6	8.0	35.2	30.3
41 Estonia	68.5 [d]	50.6 [d]	..	1.2 [d]	..	9.8	..	1.5	..	6.9	(.) [f]	0.9
42 Costa Rica	2.2	0.5	4.0	(.)	2.8	2.8	-2.5	1.1	8.8	4.3	22.0	8.2
43 Chile	57.6	3.7	0.3	0.1	2.2	6.7	5.1	1.9	9.1	10.0	18.1	5.2
44 Qatar	1.0 [d]	1.7 [d]	(.)	..	..	..	..	..	..	..	..	..
45 Lithuania	130.3 [d]	37.4 [d]	..	1.1 [d]	..	3.7	..	0.6	..	16.1	..	5.9
46 Kuwait	3.6 [d]	1.5 [d]	(.)	(.) [d]	..	-0.1	..	..	..	..	..	..
47 Croatia	112.5	25.3	..	0.6	..	7.5	..	3.6	..	14.6	..	13.7
48 United Arab Emirates	3.0 [d]	1.0 [d]	(.)	..	..	..	..	..	..	..	..	..
49 Bahamas	8.5 [d]	27.5 [d]	0.1	..	-0.6	5.2 [e]	..	..	..	..	..	..
50 Latvia	106.2 [d]	45.2 [d]	..	1.4 [d]	..	2.3	..	9.3	..	6.8	(.) [f]	2.9
51 Saint Kitts and Nevis	10.6	253.0	5.1	3.1	30.7	24.2	-0.3	7.9	1.9	6.0	3.4	13.5
52 Cuba	50.7	4.5	..	..	..	..	..	..	..	..	..	..
53 Belarus	39.2 [d]	3.9 [d]	..	0.3 [d]	..	0.8	..	-0.1	..	1.9	..	2.7
54 Trinidad and Tobago	-1.7	-1.3	0.4	(.)	2.2	9.4	-3.5	-0.1	8.9	2.6	15.6	3.8
55 Mexico	74.8	0.7	0.1	(.)	1.0	4.0	2.7	0.5	4.3	7.9	18.3	14.1
Medium human development												
56 Antigua and Barbuda	8.6	118.9	1.2	1.3	..	..	..	..	..	..	..	..
57 Bulgaria	346.0 [d]	43.1 [d]	0.1 [d]	2.6 [d]	(.)	5.1	-0.2	2.6	6.6	10.1	18.6	15.5
58 Malaysia	26.7	1.1	1.1	(.)	5.3	0.6	-3.2	0.3	9.8	7.1	10.6	3.6
59 Panama	28.1	9.3	1.9	0.3	2.6	5.0	-0.1	12.7	6.5	11.6	4.1	11.2
60 Macedonia, TFYR	247.7	121.7	..	7.2	..	12.9	..	0.7	..	5.7	..	10.3
61 Libyan Arab Jamahiriya	10.0 [d]	1.9 [d]	0.1	..	..	..	..	..	..	..	..	..
62 Mauritius	21.7	18.1	3.7	0.5	1.7	-1.1	1.9	-0.6	6.5	4.5	7.3	4.7
63 Russian Federation	1,109.8 [d]	7.7 [d]	(.) [d]	0.4 [d]	0.0	0.8	1.0	-0.3	2.0 [g]	5.6	..	12.0
64 Colombia	379.8	8.9	0.2	0.5	1.2	2.8	-0.4	1.5	9.7	7.6	34.5	28.1
65 Brazil	348.9	2.0	(.)	0.1	0.2	4.5	-0.1	0.1	1.8	10.8	18.5	28.6
66 Bosnia and Herzegovina	639.2	157.2	..	13.4	..	4.7	..	0.1	..	6.3	..	18.3
67 Belize	21.4	87.1	7.6	2.7	4.3	4.2	1.4	11.3	5.0	12.1	7.0	24.5
68 Dominica	19.9	254.5	11.9	7.6	7.8	4.5	-0.1	4.5	3.5	6.0	6.0	11.9
69 Venezuela	44.7	1.8	0.2	(.)	0.9	2.8	-1.2	-0.6	10.3	6.0	19.6	20.9
70 Samoa (Western)	43.1	246.6	23.7	16.9	0.0	0.5	0.0	0.0	2.7	2.9	10.6	7.1 [e]

HDI rank		Official development assistance (ODA) received (net disbursements) [a]				Net foreign direct investment inflows (as % of GDP) [b]		Other private flows (as % of GDP) [b, c]		Total debt service			
		Total (US$ millions)	Per capita (US$)	As % of GDP						As % of GDP		As % of exports of goods and services	
		2001	2001	1990	2001	1990	2001	1990	2001	1990	2001	1990	2001
71	Saint Lucia	16.2	110.5	3.1	2.5	11.3	7.7	-0.2	1.1	1.6	3.7	2.1	6.9
72	Romania	647.7 [d]	28.9 [d]	0.6 [d]	1.7 [d]	0.0	3.0	(.)	3.8	(.)	6.7	0.0	13.7
73	Saudi Arabia	27.1	1.2	(.)	(.)	..	..	..	..	..	..	..	..
74	Thailand	281.1	4.6	0.9	0.2	2.9	3.3	2.3	-6.0	6.2	17.5	11.4	7.9
75	Ukraine	519.2 [d]	10.5 [d]	0.3 [d]	1.4 [d]	..	2.1	..	-1.0	..	6.0	..	6.5
76	Kazakhstan	148.2	9.5	..	0.7	..	12.3	..	9.8	..	14.9	..	4.7
77	Suriname	23.2	54.1	19.4	3.1	..	..	..	..	..	..	..	..
78	Jamaica	54.0	20.7	5.9	0.7	3.0	7.9	-1.0	9.9	14.4	8.3	27.0	16.8
79	Oman	1.6	0.6	0.6	..	1.4	0.4 [e]	-3.8	0.1 [e]	7.0	4.4 [e]	12.0	6.8
80	St. Vincent & the Grenadines	8.6	73.0	7.8	2.4	3.9	10.1	0.0	-0.1	2.2	3.9	3.1	6.9
81	Fiji	26.0	31.6	3.7	1.5	6.7	-0.2	-1.1	-0.4	7.7	1.5	9.0	1.5
82	Peru	451.2	17.1	1.5	0.8	0.2	2.0	0.1	0.6	1.8	4.1	7.3	20.8
83	Lebanon	240.8	68.1	9.1	1.4	0.2	1.5	0.2	15.0	3.5	8.7	3.2	40.5
84	Paraguay	61.4	11.0	1.1	0.9	1.5	1.1	-0.2	-1.3	6.2	5.0	11.5	8.3
85	Philippines	576.9	7.5	2.9	0.8	1.2	2.5	0.6	0.4	8.1	10.9	25.6	13.3
86	Maldives	25.0	83.2	9.8	4.3	2.6	2.0	0.5	0.1	4.1	3.7	4.0	4.3
87	Turkmenistan	71.8	15.2	..	1.2	..	2.5	..	-4.7	..	..	0.0 [h]	..
88	Georgia	289.7	55.5	..	9.2	..	5.1	..	0.4	..	2.5	..	8.1
89	Azerbaijan	226.2	27.5	..	4.1	..	4.1	..	-0.2	..	2.4	..	4.7
90	Jordan	431.5	83.3	22.1	4.9	0.9	1.1	5.3	-2.4	15.6	7.6	22.1	14.7
91	Tunisia	377.7	39.2	3.2	1.9	0.6	2.3	-1.6	3.3	11.6	6.8	25.6	13.4
92	Guyana	101.8	133.6	42.6	14.6	2.0	8.0	-4.1	-0.1	74.5	6.3	20.6 [f]	8.0
93	Grenada	11.5	142.6	6.3	2.9	5.8	8.6	0.1	-1.0	1.5	4.1	3.1	5.4 [e]
94	Dominican Republic	105.4	12.4	1.4	0.5	1.9	5.6	(.)	2.5	3.3	2.9	10.7	6.6
95	Albania	268.9	86.1	0.5	6.5	0.0	5.0	1.5	-0.1	0.1	0.9	0.9	3.1
96	Turkey	166.9	2.4	0.8	0.1	0.5	2.2	0.8	-1.6	4.9	15.2	29.9	24.6
97	Ecuador	171.0	13.6	1.5	1.0	1.2	7.4	0.5	0.6	10.1	8.6	31.0	22.0
98	Occupied Palestinian Territories	865.1	261.3	..	21.8	..	..	..	..	..	..	..	..
99	Sri Lanka	330.2	17.6	9.1	2.1	0.5	1.1	0.1	0.4	4.8	4.5	14.8	9.2
100	Armenia	212.2	68.7	..	10.0	..	3.3	..	0.2	..	2.6	..	8.1
101	Uzbekistan	153.2	6.1	..	1.4	..	0.6	..	-0.2	..	7.4	..	20.6
102	Kyrgyzstan	188.1	37.7	..	12.3	..	0.3	..	-5.1	..	11.6	..	12.0
103	Cape Verde	76.5	171.9	31.8	13.0	0.1	0.1	(.)	1.2	1.7	2.4	8.9	7.0
104	China	1,459.9	1.1	0.6	0.1	1.0	3.8	1.3	-0.1	2.0	2.1	10.6	4.2
105	El Salvador	234.5	37.1	7.2	1.7	(.)	1.9	0.1	3.0	4.3	2.8	18.2	7.4
106	Iran, Islamic Rep. of	114.8	1.7	0.1	0.1	-0.3	(.)	(.)	0.9	0.5	1.1	1.3	4.1
107	Algeria	182.0	5.9	0.4	0.3	(.)	2.2	-0.7	-1.7	14.2	8.0	63.7	19.5
108	Moldova, Rep. of	119.2	27.9	..	8.1	..	6.3	..	-1.6	..	12.8	..	15.3
109	Viet Nam	1,434.5	18.1	2.9	4.4	0.2	4.0	0.0	-1.8	2.7	3.7	..	6.5
110	Syrian Arab Republic	152.9	9.0	5.6	0.8	0.6	1.1	-0.1	(.)	9.7	1.4	20.3	2.1
111	South Africa	428.5	9.6	..	0.4	..	6.3	..	-0.5	..	3.8	0.0	6.8
112	Indonesia	1,500.9	7.0	1.5	1.0	1.0	-2.3	2.0	-2.8	8.7	10.7	25.6	13.8
113	Tajikistan	159.2	25.9	..	15.1	..	2.1	..	1.6	..	7.6	0.0 [f]	6.3
114	Bolivia	728.5	85.9	11.2	9.1	0.6	8.3	-0.5	-0.3	7.9	6.8	33.5 [i]	16.1 [i]
115	Honduras	677.7	102.4	14.7	10.6	1.4	3.1	1.0	-1.1	12.8	5.3	33.0 [i]	5.7 [i]
116	Equatorial Guinea	13.3	28.3	46.0	0.7	8.4	4.8	0.0	0.0	3.9	0.2	11.5	0.1
117	Mongolia	212.1	83.9	..	20.2	..	6.0	..	-0.1	..	4.3	0.3	7.9
118	Gabon	8.6	6.7	2.2	0.2	1.2	4.6	0.5	-0.7	3.0	10.5	4.8	13.6
119	Guatemala	225.2	19.2	2.6	1.1	0.6	2.2	-0.1	-0.3	2.8	2.2	11.6	8.5
120	Egypt	1,255.2	18.2	12.6	1.3	1.7	0.5	-0.2	1.6	7.1	2.0	25.7	8.8

		Official development assistance (ODA) received (net disbursements) [a]				Net foreign direct investment inflows (as % of GDP) [b]		Other private flows (as % of GDP) [b, c]		Total debt service			
		Total (US$ millions)	Per capita (US$)	As % of GDP						As % of GDP		As % of exports of goods and services	
HDI rank		2001	2001	1990	2001	1990	2001	1990	2001	1990	2001	1990	2001
121	Nicaragua	928.3	178.4	32.9	..	0.0	..	2.0	..	1.6	..	2.3 [i]	22.2 [i]
122	São Tomé and Principe	37.9	248.2	95.0	80.8	0.0	11.7	-0.2	0.0	4.9	8.5	28.7	21.3
123	Solomon Islands	58.8	130.7	21.7	22.2	4.9	-1.9	-1.5	-1.3	5.5	..	11.3	2.7 [e]
124	Namibia	109.1	56.5	4.4	3.5	..	..	..	..	..	..	..	..
125	Botswana	29.1	16.6	3.9	0.6	2.5	1.1	-0.5	(.)	2.8	1.0	4.4	1.7
126	Morocco	516.5	17.5	4.1	1.5	0.6	7.8	0.7	-0.1	6.9	7.7	27.9	21.9
127	India	1,705.4	1.7	0.4	0.4	0.1	0.7	0.5	(.)	2.6	1.9	29.2	12.6
128	Vanuatu	31.6	156.5	32.6	14.8	8.6	8.5	-0.1	0.0	1.6	0.8	1.6	1.1
129	Ghana	651.8	32.5	9.6	12.3	0.3	1.7	-0.3	2.9	6.3	6.0	34.9 [i]	8.9 [i]
130	Cambodia	408.7	30.3	3.7	12.0	0.0	3.3	0.0	0.0	2.7	0.6	3.8 [f]	1.1
131	Myanmar	126.8	2.6	..	..	..	..	..	..	..	..	8.8	2.8
132	Papua New Guinea	203.1	37.2	12.8	6.9	4.8	2.1	1.5	-2.1	17.2	9.1	18.4	7.1
133	Swaziland	29.3	27.6	6.1	2.3	3.4	1.7	-0.2	1.1	5.3	2.2	5.6	2.5
134	Comoros	27.7	38.1	17.3	12.5	0.2	0.7	0.0	0.0	0.4	1.0	2.4	5.6
135	Lao People's Dem. Rep.	243.3	45.0	17.3	13.8	0.7	1.4	0.0	0.0	1.1	2.5	8.5	9.0
136	Bhutan	59.2	27.9	16.5	11.1	0.6	0.0	-0.9	0.0	1.8	1.2	5.3	3.3
137	Lesotho	54.0	30.1	22.8	6.8	2.7	14.7	(.)	-0.5	3.7	8.6	4.2	12.4
138	Sudan	171.8	5.3	6.2	1.4	0.0	4.6	0.0	0.0	0.4	0.4	4.8	3.2
139	Bangladesh	1,023.9	7.3	7.0	2.2	(.)	0.2	0.2	0.5	2.5	1.4	37.5	9.0
140	Congo	74.8	21.1	7.8	2.7	0.2	2.1	-3.6	0.0	19.0	3.4	32.2	3.3
141	Togo	46.6	9.9	16.0	3.7	1.1	5.3	(.)	0.0	5.3	2.6	11.5	5.9
Low human development													
142	Cameroon	397.7	25.8	4.0	4.7	-1.0	0.9	-0.1	-1.1	4.7	4.0	14.7 [i]	9.9 [i]
143	Nepal	388.1	16.1	11.7	7.0	0.2	0.3	-0.4	(.)	1.9	1.6	14.7	6.2
144	Pakistan	1,938.2	13.2	2.8	3.3	0.6	0.7	-0.2	-1.2	4.8	5.0	25.1	21.3
145	Zimbabwe	159.0	12.5	3.9	1.8	-0.1	0.1	1.1	-0.4	5.4	1.5	19.4	3.4
146	Kenya	452.6	14.6	13.9	4.0	0.7	(.)	0.8	-0.4	9.3	4.1	28.6	11.4
147	Uganda	782.6	32.3	15.5	13.8	0.0	2.5	0.4	(.)	3.4	0.9	56.9 [i]	9.7 [i]
148	Yemen	425.9	22.8	8.4	4.6	-2.7	-2.2	3.3	-0.1	3.5	3.1	7.1	6.3
149	Madagascar	353.9	21.5	12.9	7.7	0.7	0.2	-0.5	(.)	7.2	1.5	44.4 [i]	3.4 [i]
150	Haiti	165.8	20.4	5.9	4.4	0.0	0.1	0.0	0.0	1.2	0.7	7.1 [h]	4.5
151	Gambia	50.9	37.7	31.3	13.0	0.0	9.1	-2.4	0.0	11.9	2.7	21.8 [i]	13.8 [i]
152	Nigeria	184.8	1.6	0.9	0.4	2.1	2.7	-0.4	-0.4	11.7	6.2	22.3	11.5
153	Djibouti	55.1	80.9	46.4	9.6	(.)	0.6	-0.1	0.0	3.6	1.8	4.4 [f]	5.4 [e]
154	Mauritania	261.8	96.1	23.3	26.0	0.7	3.0	-0.1	-0.3	14.3	8.9	28.8 [i, j]	16.5 [i, j]
155	Eritrea	280.1	72.8	..	40.7	..	5.0	..	0.0	..	1.0	0.0 [f]	4.5
156	Senegal	418.9	43.5	14.4	9.0	1.0	2.7	-0.3	0.9	5.7	4.6	18.3 [i]	9.3 [i]
157	Guinea	272.3	33.0	10.4	9.1	0.6	0.1	-0.7	(.)	6.0	3.5	19.6 [i]	9.2 [i]
158	Rwanda	290.5	36.0	11.3	17.1	0.3	0.3	-0.1	0.0	0.8	1.1	10.6 [i]	7.6 [i]
159	Benin	273.2	42.8	14.5	11.5	3.4	5.5	(.)	0.0	2.1	2.1	9.2 [i]	10.0 [i]
160	Tanzania, U. Rep. of	1,233.4	34.7	27.5	13.2	0.0	2.4	0.1	-0.3	4.2 [k]	1.6 [k]	31.3 [i, k]	7.3 [i, k]
161	Côte d'Ivoire	187.0	11.6	6.4	1.8	0.4	2.4	0.1	-1.0	11.7	5.9	19.1	8.1
162	Malawi	401.5	34.5	26.8	23.0	1.2	3.3	0.1	0.0	7.1	2.2	28.0 [i]	15.5 [i]
163	Zambia	373.5	35.3	14.6	10.3	6.2	2.0	-0.3	1.5	6.2	3.6	14.6 [i]	13.4 [i]
164	Angola	268.4	21.0	2.6	2.8	-3.3	11.8	5.6	-2.3	3.2	19.7	7.1	26.0
165	Chad	179.0	22.1	18.0	11.2	0.5	5.0	(.)	(.)	0.7	1.5	3.8 [i]	10.0 [i]
166	Guinea-Bissau	58.6	41.7	52.7	29.4	0.8	15.1	(.)	0.0	3.4	11.7	22.1 [i]	0.7 [i]

16 Flows of aid, private capital and debt

HDI rank	Official development assistance (ODA) received (net disbursements) [a] Total (US$ millions) 2001	Per capita (US$) 2001	As % of GDP 1990	As % of GDP 2001	Net foreign direct investment inflows (as % of GDP) [b] 1990	2001	Other private flows (as % of GDP) [b,c] 1990	2001	Total debt service As % of GDP 1990	2001	As % of exports of goods and services 1990	2001
167 Congo, Dem. Rep. of the	250.9	5.0	9.6	4.8	-0.2	0.6	-0.1	0.0	3.7	0.3	12.7	(.)
168 Central African Republic	76.0	20.2	16.8	7.9	(.)	0.8	(.)	0.0	2.0	1.4	12.5	11.5
169 Ethiopia	1,079.8	16.1	14.8	17.3	0.2	0.3	-0.8	-0.2	3.4	2.9	33.7 [i]	20.6 [i]
170 Mozambique	934.8	51.3	40.7	25.9	0.4	13.3	1.0	-0.8	3.2	2.4	17.3 [i]	2.7 [i]
171 Burundi	130.8	20.4	23.3	19.0	0.1	0.0	-0.5	(.)	3.7	3.3	41.7	36.3
172 Mali	349.9	28.6	19.9	13.2	0.2	3.9	(.)	0.0	2.8	3.0	14.7 [i]	4.5 [i]
173 Burkina Faso	389.0	31.7	12.0	15.6	0.0	1.0	(.)	0.0	1.2	1.5	7.8 [i,j]	11.0 [i,j]
174 Niger	248.6	22.3	16.0	12.7	1.6	0.7	0.4	-0.3	4.0	1.3	6.6 [i]	6.6 [i]
175 Sierra Leone	333.7	73.0	9.4	44.5	5.0	0.5	0.6	0.0	3.3	12.8	10.1 [i]	74.3 [i]
Developing countries	43,811.3 T	9.7	1.6	0.6	0.9	3.0	0.5	(.)	4.3	6.1	15.3	11.0
Least developed countries	13,383.9 T	19.8	11.9	7.5	0.1	2.2	0.5	(.)	3.1	2.9	16.1	9.5
Arab States	5,049.9 T	17.9	3.6	0.8	0.8	1.2	..	..	..	..	13.8	8.6
East Asia and the Pacific	7,332.0 T	3.9	..	0.4	1.7	3.6	0.9	-0.3	..	..	12.0	6.4
Latin America and the Caribbean	5,934.1 T	11.4	0.4	0.2	0.7	3.7	0.5	0.1	4.0	8.4	20.4	19.7
South Asia	6,032.1 T	4.2	1.1	0.8	(.)	0.6	0.3	0.1	2.3	2.1	17.9	11.0
Sub-Saharan Africa	13,018.7 T	20.6	..	..	..	4.1	..	..	..	..	11.3	9.0
Central & Eastern Europe & CIS	4,626.5 T	11.3	..	..	0.1	3.2	..	..	..	..	13.7	9.5
OECD	..	..	..	..	1.0 [l]	2.3 [l]	..	..	..	..	..	..
High-income OECD	..	..	..	..	1.0 [l]	2.2 [l]	..	..	..	..	..	..
High human development	630.9 T	1.9	..	..	1.0 [l]	2.4 [l]	..	..	..	..	..	..
Medium human development	23,263.1 T	5.7	1.3	0.5	0.6	2.6	0.5	-0.1	3.7	5.6	15.3	10.2
Low human development	13,646.1 T	18.4	8.3	5.7	0.4	1.9	0.3	-0.6	6.0	4.7	19.7	12.9
High income	143.5 T	1.9	..	..	1.0 [l]	2.4 [l]	..	..	..	..	..	..
Middle income	15,181.2 T	5.7	1.0	0.3	0.7	3.3	0.6	0.1	3.8	6.9	15.0	11.1
Low income	24,823.2 T	9.9	3.5	2.2	0.4	0.8	0.7	-0.6	4.7	4.0	23.4	11.4
World	51,439.5 T	9.8	..	..	1.0 [l]	2.5 [l]	..	..	..	..	..	..

Note: This table presents data for countries included in parts I and II of the Development Assistance Committee's (DAC) list of aid recipients (OECD, Development Assistance Committee 2003b). The denominator conventionally used when comparing official development assistance and total debt service to the size of the economy is gross national income (GNI), not GDP (see the definitions of statistical terms). GDP is used here, however, to allow comparability throughout the table. With few exceptions the denominators produce similar results.

a. ODA receipts are total net ODA flows from DAC countries, other OECD countries, multilateral organizations and Arab countries as well as Estonia and Israel. A negative value indicates that the repayment of ODA loans exceeds the amount of ODA received. Aggregates do not include net official aid. See the definitions of statistical terms. b. A negative value indicates that the capital flowing out of the country exceeds that flowing in. c. Other private flows combine non-debt-creating portfolio equity investment flows, portfolio debt flows and bank and trade-related lending. See the definitions of statistical terms. d. Data refer to net official aid. See the definitions of statistical terms. e. Data refer to 2000. f. Data refer to 1992. g. Data refer to the debt of the former Soviet Union on the assumption that 100% of all outstanding external debt as of December 1991 has become a liability of the Russian Federation. h. Data refer to 1991. i. Data are from debt sustainability analyses undertaken as part of the Debt Initiative for Heavily Indebted Poor Countries (HIPCs). Present value estimates for these countries are for public and publicly guaranteed debt only, and export figures exclude workers' remittances. j. Estimates reflecting assistance under the enhanced HIPC initiative will be presented in World Bank forthcoming. k. Data refer to mainland Tanzania only. l. Data used to calculate the aggregate include countries not shown in the table.

Source: Column 1: OECD, Development Assistance Committee 2003b; aggregates calculated for the Human Development Report Office by the Organisation for Economic Co-operation and Development (OECD); *column 2:* calculated on the basis of data on ODA from OECD, Development Assistance Committee 2003b and data on population from UN 2003d; aggregates calculated for the Human Development Report Office by the OECD; *columns 3 and 4:* calculated on the basis of data on ODA from OECD, Development Assistance Committee 2003b and data on GDP from World Bank 2003c; *columns 5 and 6:* World Bank 2003c; aggregates calculated for the Human Development Report Office by the World Bank; *columns 7 and 8:* calculated on the basis of data on portfolio investment (bonds and equity), bank and trade-related lending and GDP from World Bank 2003c; *columns 9 and 10:* calculated on the basis of data on total debt service and GDP from World Bank 2003c; *columns 11 and 12:* World Bank 2003c, based on data from a joint effort by the International Monetary Fund and the World Bank; aggregates calculated for the Human Development Office by the World Bank.

17 Priorities in public spending

HDI rank	Public expenditure on education (as % of GDP)[a]		Public expenditure on health (as % of GDP)[b]		Military expenditure (as % of GDP)[c]		Total debt service (as % of GDP)[d]	
	1990[e]	1998-2000[f]	1990	2000	1990	2001	1990	2001
High human development								
1 Norway	7.1	6.8 [g]	6.4	6.6	2.9	1.8	..	..
2 Iceland	5.4	..	6.8	7.5	0.0	0.0	..	..
3 Sweden	7.4	7.8 [g]	7.6	6.5	2.7	2.0	..	..
4 Australia	5.1	4.7 [g, h]	5.3	6.0	2.2	1.7	..	..
5 Netherlands	6.0	4.8 [g]	5.7	5.5	2.5	1.6	..	..
6 Belgium	5.0	5.9 [g]	6.6	6.2	2.4	1.3	..	..
7 United States	5.2	4.8 [g]	4.7	5.8	5.3	3.1	..	..
8 Canada	6.5	5.5 [g]	6.8	6.6	2.0	1.2	..	..
9 Japan	..	3.5 [g]	4.6	6.0	0.9	1.0	..	..
10 Switzerland	5.1	5.5 [g]	5.7	5.9	1.8	1.1	..	..
11 Denmark	..	8.2 [g]	7.0	6.8	2.0	1.6	..	..
12 Ireland	5.2	4.4	4.8	5.1	1.2	0.7	..	..
13 United Kingdom	4.9	4.5 [g]	5.1	5.9	3.9	2.5	..	..
14 Finland	5.6	6.1	6.4	5.0	1.6	1.2	..	..
15 Luxembourg	3.0	3.7 [g, h]	5.7	5.3	0.9	0.8	..	..
16 Austria	5.4	5.8 [g]	5.2	5.6	1.0	0.8	..	..
17 France	5.4	5.8 [g]	6.7	7.2	3.5	2.5	..	..
18 Germany	..	4.6	5.9	8.0	2.8 [i]	1.5	..	..
19 Spain	4.4	4.5 [g]	5.2	5.4	1.8	1.2	..	..
20 New Zealand	6.2	6.1 [g]	5.8	6.2	1.9	1.2	..	..
21 Italy	3.1	4.5 [g]	6.3	6.0	(.)	2.0	..	..
22 Israel	6.3	7.3	3.8	8.3	12.2	7.7	..	..
23 Portugal	4.2	5.8 [g]	4.1	5.8	2.7	2.1	..	..
24 Greece	2.5	3.8	4.7	4.6	4.7	4.6	..	..
25 Cyprus	3.5 [j]	5.4 [j]	..	4.3	5.0	3.1	..	..
26 Hong Kong, China (SAR)	..	..	1.6	..	..	..	..	..
27 Barbados	7.8	7.1	5.0	4.1	..	..	8.2	2.5
28 Singapore	..	3.7	1.0	1.2	4.8	5.0	..	..
29 Slovenia	..	..	..	6.8	..	1.4	..	..
30 Korea, Rep. of	3.5	3.8 [g]	1.8	2.6	3.7	2.8	3.3	6.2
31 Brunei Darussalam	..	4.8	1.6	2.5	6.7 [k]	6.1 [l]	..	..
32 Czech Republic	..	4.4 [g]	4.8	6.6	..	2.1	3.0	8.4
33 Malta	4.3	4.9 [h]	..	6.0	0.9	0.8	2.0	3.8
34 Argentina	1.1	4.0 [g]	4.2	4.7	1.3	1.4	4.4	9.0
35 Poland	..	5.0 [g]	4.8	4.2	2.7	1.9	1.6	8.7
36 Seychelles	7.8	7.6 [h]	3.6	4.1	4.0	1.8	5.9	2.4
37 Bahrain	4.2	3.0	..	2.8	5.1	4.1	..	..
38 Hungary	5.8	5.0 [g]	..	5.1	2.8	1.8	12.8	26.4
39 Slovakia	5.1	4.2 [g]	5.0	5.3	..	1.9	2.1	12.8
40 Uruguay	3.0	2.8 [g]	2.0	5.1	2.1	1.3	10.6	8.0
41 Estonia	..	7.5	1.9	4.7	..	1.7	..	6.9
42 Costa Rica	4.4	4.4	6.7	4.4	0.0	0.0	8.8	4.3
43 Chile	2.5	4.2 [g]	2.2	3.1	3.7	2.9	9.1	10.0
44 Qatar	3.5	3.6 [m]	..	2.5	..	..	..	..
45 Lithuania	4.6	6.4	3.0	4.3	..	1.8	..	16.1
46 Kuwait	4.8	..	4.0	2.6	48.5	11.3	..	..
47 Croatia	..	4.2 [h]	9.5	8.0	..	2.6	..	14.6
48 United Arab Emirates	1.9	1.9	0.8	2.5	4.7	2.5	..	..
49 Bahamas	4.0	..	2.8	4.4	..	..	..	..
50 Latvia	3.8	5.9	2.7	3.5	..	1.2	..	6.8

HDI rank	Public expenditure on education (as % of GDP)[a]		Public expenditure on health (as % of GDP)[b]		Military expenditure (as % of GDP)[c]		Total debt service (as % of GDP)[d]	
	1990[e]	1998-2000[f]	1990	2000	1990	2001	1990	2001
51 Saint Kitts and Nevis	2.7	2.9 [h]	2.7	3.1	..	..	1.9	6.0
52 Cuba	..	8.5	4.9	6.1	..	..	..	..
53 Belarus	4.9	6.0	2.5	4.7	..	1.4	..	1.9
54 Trinidad and Tobago	3.6	4.0 [h]	2.5	2.6	..	..	8.9	2.6
55 Mexico	3.6	4.4 [g]	1.8	2.5	0.4	0.5	4.3	7.9
Medium human development								
56 Antigua and Barbuda	..	3.2	2.8	3.3	..	..	..	..
57 Bulgaria	5.2	3.4	4.1	3.0	3.5	2.7	6.6	10.1
58 Malaysia	5.2	6.2 [g]	1.5	1.5	2.6	2.2	9.8	7.1
59 Panama	4.7	5.9	4.6	5.3	1.4	1.2 [n]	6.5	11.6
60 Macedonia, TFYR	..	..	9.2	5.1	..	7.0	..	5.7
61 Libyan Arab Jamahiriya	..	..	..	1.6	..	..	..	..
62 Mauritius	3.5	3.5	..	1.9	0.3	0.2	6.5	4.5
63 Russian Federation	3.5	4.4	2.5	3.8	12.3 [o]	3.8	2.0 [p]	5.6
64 Colombia	2.5	..	1.2	5.4	2.2	3.8	9.7	7.6
65 Brazil	..	4.7	3.0	3.4	1.9	1.5	1.8	10.8
66 Bosnia and Herzegovina	..	..	..	3.1	..	9.5	..	6.3
67 Belize	4.7	6.2	2.2	2.1	1.2	..	5.0	12.1
68 Dominica	..	5.1 [h]	3.9	4.3	..	..	3.5	6.0
69 Venezuela	3.0	..	2.5	2.7	1.8 [k]	1.5	10.3	6.0
70 Samoa (Western)	3.4	4.2 [h]	2.8	3.9	..	..	2.7	2.9
71 Saint Lucia	..	5.8	2.1	2.7	..	..	1.6	3.7
72 Romania	2.8	3.5 [h]	2.8	1.9	4.6	2.5	(.)	6.7
73 Saudi Arabia	6.5	9.5	..	4.2	12.8	11.3	..	..
74 Thailand	3.5	5.4 [g]	0.9	2.1	2.3	1.4	6.2	17.5
75 Ukraine	5.2	4.4	3.0	2.9	..	2.7	..	6.0
76 Kazakhstan	3.2	..	3.2	2.7	..	1.0	..	14.9
77 Suriname	8.1	..	3.5	5.5	..	..	..	..
78 Jamaica	4.7	6.3 [g]	2.6	2.6	..	..	14.4	8.3
79 Oman	3.1	3.9	2.0	2.3	18.3	12.2	7.0	4.4 [l]
80 St. Vincent & the Grenadines	6.4	9.3	4.4	4.1	..	..	2.2	3.9
81 Fiji	4.6	5.2 [h]	2.0	2.5	2.3	2.2	7.7	1.5
82 Peru	2.2	3.3 [g]	1.3	2.8	2.4	1.7	1.8	4.1
83 Lebanon	..	3.0	..	..	7.6	5.5	3.5	8.7
84 Paraguay	1.1	5.0	0.7	3.0	1.2	0.9	6.2	5.0
85 Philippines	2.9	4.2 [g]	1.5	1.6	1.4	1.0	8.1	10.9
86 Maldives	4.0	3.9 [h]	3.6	6.3	..	..	4.1	3.7
87 Turkmenistan	4.3	..	4.0	4.6	..	3.8 [l]	..	7.6
88 Georgia	..	..	3.0	0.7	..	0.7	..	2.5
89 Azerbaijan	..	4.2	2.7	0.6	..	2.6	..	2.4
90 Jordan	8.4	5.0 [g]	3.6	4.2	9.9	8.6	15.6	7.6
91 Tunisia	6.0	6.8 [g]	3.0	..	2.0	1.6	11.6	6.8
92 Guyana	3.4	4.1 [h]	2.9	4.2	0.9	..	74.5	6.3
93 Grenada	5.1	4.2 [h]	3.3	3.4	..	..	1.5	4.1
94 Dominican Republic	..	2.5	1.6	1.8	..	..	3.3	2.9
95 Albania	5.8	..	3.3	2.1	5.9	1.2	0.1	0.9
96 Turkey	2.2	3.5 [g]	2.2	3.6	3.5	4.9	4.9	15.2
97 Ecuador	2.8	1.6	1.5	1.2	1.9	2.1 [n]	10.1	8.6
98 Occupied Palestinian Territories	..	..	..	..	..	..	..	..
99 Sri Lanka	2.6	3.1	1.5	1.8	2.1	3.9	4.8	4.5
100 Armenia	7.0	2.9	..	3.2	..	3.1	..	2.6

HDI rank	Public expenditure on education (as % of GDP)[a]		Public expenditure on health (as % of GDP)[b]		Military expenditure (as % of GDP)[c]		Total debt service (as % of GDP)[d]	
	1990[e]	1998-2000[f]	1990	2000	1990	2001	1990	2001
101 Uzbekistan	..	..	4.6	2.6	..	1.1	..	7.4
102 Kyrgyzstan	8.3	5.4	4.7	2.2	..	1.7	..	11.6
103 Cape Verde	..	4.4 [h]	..	1.8	..	0.8	1.7	2.4
104 China	2.3	2.1	2.2	1.9	2.7	2.3	2.0	2.1
105 El Salvador	1.9	2.3 [h]	1.4	3.8	2.7	0.8	4.3	2.8
106 Iran, Islamic Rep. of	4.1	4.4	1.5	2.5	2.7	4.8	0.5	1.1
107 Algeria	5.3	..	3.0	3.0	1.5	3.5 [l]	14.2	8.0
108 Moldova, Rep. of	..	4.0	4.4	2.9	..	0.4	..	12.8
109 Viet Nam	..	..	0.9	1.3	7.9	..	2.7	3.7
110 Syrian Arab Republic	4.1	4.1	0.4	1.6	6.9	6.2	9.7	1.4
111 South Africa	6.2	5.5	3.1	3.7	3.8	1.6	..	3.8
112 Indonesia	1.0	..	0.6	0.6	1.8	1.1	8.7	10.7
113 Tajikistan	9.7	2.1	4.9	0.9	..	1.2	..	7.6
114 Bolivia	2.3	5.5	2.1	4.9	2.4	1.6	7.9	6.8
115 Honduras	..	4.0 [h]	3.3	4.3	..	..	12.8	5.3
116 Equatorial Guinea	..	0.6	1.0	2.3	..	..	3.9	0.2
117 Mongolia	12.1	2.3	6.4	4.6	5.7	2.3	..	4.3
118 Gabon	..	3.9 [h]	2.0	2.1	..	..	3.0	10.5
119 Guatemala	1.4	1.7	1.8	2.3	1.5	1.0	2.8	2.2
120 Egypt	3.7	..	1.8	1.8	3.9	2.6	7.1	2.0
121 Nicaragua	3.4	5.0	7.0	2.3	2.1	1.1	1.6	..
122 São Tomé and Principe	..	..	..	1.6	..	..	4.9	8.5
123 Solomon Islands	..	3.6 [h]	5.0	5.6	..	..	5.5	2.7
124 Namibia	7.6	8.1	3.7	4.2	5.6 [k]	2.8	..	..
125 Botswana	6.7	8.6 [h]	1.7	3.8	4.1	3.5	2.8	1.0
126 Morocco	5.3	5.5 [h]	0.9	1.3	4.1	4.1	6.9	7.7
127 India	3.9	4.1 [g]	0.9	0.9	2.7	2.5	2.6	1.9
128 Vanuatu	4.6	7.3 [h]	2.6	2.4	..	..	1.6	0.8
129 Ghana	3.2	4.1 [h]	1.3	2.2	0.4	0.6	6.3	6.0
130 Cambodia	..	1.9	..	2.0	3.1	3.0	2.7	0.6
131 Myanmar	..	0.5	1.0	0.4	3.4	2.3 [l]	..	..
132 Papua New Guinea	..	2.3 [h]	3.1	3.6	2.1	0.8 [l]	17.2	9.1
133 Swaziland	5.7	1.5	1.9	3.0	1.5	1.5	5.3	2.2
134 Comoros	..	3.8	2.9	3.2	..	..	0.4	1.0
135 Lao People's Dem. Rep.	..	2.3	0.0	1.3	..	2.1	1.1	2.5
136 Bhutan	..	5.2	1.7	3.7	..	..	1.8	1.2
137 Lesotho	6.1	10.1	2.6	5.2	3.9	3.1 [l]	3.7	8.6
138 Sudan	0.9	..	0.7	1.0	3.6	3.0 [l]	0.4	0.4
139 Bangladesh	1.5	2.5	0.7	1.4	1.0	1.3	2.5	1.4
140 Congo	5.0	4.2	1.5	1.5	..	..	19.0	3.4
141 Togo	5.5	4.8	1.4	1.5	3.2	..	5.3	2.6
Low human development								
142 Cameroon	3.2	3.2	0.9	1.1	1.5	1.4	4.7	4.0
143 Nepal	2.0	3.7	0.8	0.9	0.9	1.1	1.9	1.6
144 Pakistan	2.6	1.8 [h]	1.1	0.9	5.8	4.5	4.8	5.0
145 Zimbabwe	..	10.4 [g, h]	3.2	3.1	4.5	3.2	5.4	1.5
146 Kenya	6.7	6.4	2.4	1.8	2.9	1.8	9.3	4.1
147 Uganda	1.5	2.3 [h]	..	1.5	3.0	2.1	3.4	0.9
148 Yemen	..	10.0	1.1	..	8.5	6.1	3.5	3.1
149 Madagascar	2.1	3.2	..	2.5	1.2	1.2 [l]	7.2	1.5
150 Haiti	1.4	1.1 [h]	1.2	2.4	..	..	1.2	0.7
151 Gambia	3.8	2.7 [h]	2.2	3.4	1.1	1.0	11.9	2.7

HDI rank	Public expenditure on education (as % of GDP) [a]		Public expenditure on health (as % of GDP) [b]		Military expenditure (as % of GDP) [c]		Total debt service (as % of GDP) [d]	
	1990 [e]	1998-2000 [f]	1990	2000	1990	2001	1990	2001
152 Nigeria	0.9	..	1.0	0.5	0.9	1.1	11.7	6.2
153 Djibouti	..	3.5 [h]	..	..	6.3	..	3.6	1.8
154 Mauritania	..	3.0 [h]	..	3.4	3.8	2.1 [n]	14.3	8.9
155 Eritrea	..	4.8	..	2.8	..	27.5 [n]	..	1.0
156 Senegal	3.9	3.2 [h]	0.7	2.6	2.0	1.5	5.7	4.6
157 Guinea	..	1.9 [h]	2.0	1.9	2.4 [k]	1.7	6.0	3.5
158 Rwanda	..	2.8 [h]	1.7	2.7	3.7	3.9	0.8	1.1
159 Benin	..	3.2 [h]	1.6	1.6	1.8	..	2.1	2.1
160 Tanzania, U. Rep. of	3.2	2.1 [h]	1.6	2.8	2.0 [k]	1.3 [n]	4.2 [q]	1.6 [q]
161 Côte d'Ivoire	..	4.6	1.5	1.0	1.5	..	11.7	5.9
162 Malawi	3.3	4.1 [h]	..	3.6	1.3	0.8	7.1	2.2
163 Zambia	2.4	2.3	2.6	3.5	3.7	0.6 [l]	6.2	3.6
164 Angola	3.9	2.7	1.4	2.0	5.8	3.1	3.2	19.7
165 Chad	..	2.0 [h]	..	2.5	..	1.5	0.7	1.5
166 Guinea-Bissau	..	2.1	1.1	2.6	..	3.1	3.4	11.7
167 Congo, Dem. Rep. of the	..	..	..	1.1	..	..	3.7	0.3
168 Central African Republic	2.2	1.9	..	1.4	1.6 [k]	..	2.0	1.4
169 Ethiopia	3.4	4.8	0.9	1.8	8.5	6.2	3.4	2.9
170 Mozambique	3.9	2.4 [h]	3.6	2.7	10.1	2.3	3.2	2.4
171 Burundi	3.4	3.4	1.1	1.6	3.4	8.1	3.7	3.3
172 Mali	..	2.8 [h]	1.6	2.2	2.1	2.0	2.8	3.0
173 Burkina Faso	2.7	..	1.0	3.0	3.0	1.6	1.2	1.5
174 Niger	3.2	2.7 [h]	..	1.8	..	1.1 [l]	4.0	1.3
175 Sierra Leone	..	1.0	..	2.6	0.9	3.6 [l]	3.3	12.8

a. Data refer to total public expenditure on education, including current and capital expenditure. See the definitions of statistical terms. b. Data for some countries may differ slightly from the data in table 6 (from WHO 2003b). c. As a result of limitations in the data, comparisons of military expenditure data over time and across countries should be made with caution. For detailed notes on the data, see SIPRI 2001. d. For aggregates, see table 16. e. Data may not be comparable between countries as a result of differences in methods of data collection. f. Data refer to the most recent year available during the period specified. g. Preliminary UNESCO Institute for Statistics estimate, subject to further revision. h. Data refer to a UNESCO Institute for Statistics estimate where no national estimate is available. i. Data refer to the Federal Republic of Germany before reunification. j. Data refer to the Office of Greek Education only. k. Data refer to 1991. l. Data refer to 2000. m. Data refer to a national estimate. n. Data refer to 1999. o. Data refer to the former Soviet Union. p. Data refer to the debt of the former Soviet Union on the assumption that 100% of all outstanding external debt as of December 1991 has become a liability of the Russian Federation. q. Data refer to mainland Tanzania only.
Source: Column 1: calculated on the basis of GDP and public expenditure data from UNESCO Institute for Statistics 2003c; column 2: UNESCO 2003c; columns 3 and 4: World Bank 2003c; columns 5 and 6: SIPRI 2003a; columns 7 and 8: calculated on the basis of data on total debt service and GDP from World Bank 2003c.

18 Unemployment in OECD countries

		Unemployment			Youth unemployment		Long-term unemployment [a] (as % of total unemployment)	
HDI rank	Unemployed people (thousands) 2001	Rate (% of labour force) 2001	Average annual rate (% of labour force) 1991-2001	Female rate as % of male rate 2001	Rate (% of labour force aged 15-24) [b] 2001	Female rate as % of male rate 2001	Female 2001	Male 2001
High human development								
1 Norway	83.8	3.5	3.9	96	10.5	97	3.9	6.8
2 Iceland	3.7	2.3	2.8	118	4.8	80	13.8	11.2
3 Sweden	175.7	4.0	4.0	86	11.8	85	20.0	24.2
4 Australia	664.5	6.7	6.3	91	12.7	90	17.9	24.1
5 Netherlands	145.9	2.0	2.7	154	5.8	111	40.4 [c]	47.7 [c]
6 Belgium	296.4	6.6	6.9	123	15.3	116	50.8	52.5
7 United States	6,779.3	4.8	5.8	96	10.6	85	5.7	6.3
8 Canada	1,172.6	7.2	7.6	90	12.8	76	8.2	10.5
9 Japan	3,396.2	5.0	5.5	95	9.7	82	18.3	32.1
10 Switzerland	67.2	1.9	2.7	198	5.6	95	35.5	20.6
11 Denmark	121.9	4.3	4.3	132	8.3	127	18.8	26.2
12 Ireland	70.8	3.9	4.4	92	6.2	91	47.5 [c]	59.5 [c]
13 United Kingdom	1,512.0	5.1	5.2	79	10.5	73	19.5	33.0
14 Finland	237.7	9.2	9.3	112	19.9	103	22.6	30.0
15 Luxembourg	4.9	2.6	3.0	137	6.7	70	23.1 [d]	31.6 [d]
16 Austria	206.5	4.9	5.6	105	6.0	93	23.0	23.8
17 France	2,321.4	8.7	9.0	151	18.7	135	37.6	37.6
18 Germany	3,074.0	7.3	7.8	104	8.4	82	53.1 [e]	50.1 [e]
19 Spain	1,869.1	10.5	11.2	204	20.8	168	48.6	37.9
20 New Zealand	102.5	5.3	5.1	98	11.8	95	13.4	19.6
21 Italy	2,267.0	9.6	9.2	177	27.0	139	63.1	63.7
23 Portugal	211.8	4.1	4.7	158	9.2	165	39.9	35.7
24 Greece	456.1	10.4	10.1	228	28.0	170	56.6	47.0
30 Korea, Rep. of	819.2	3.7	2.9	73	9.7	67	1.2	2.8
32 Czech Republic	421.0	8.2	7.4 [f]	146	16.6	108	53.4	52.0
35 Poland	3,169.8	18.2	19.7 [f]	117	41.0	105	46.2	39.9
38 Hungary	233.3	5.8	5.5 [g]	79	10.8	85	44.1	48.4
39 Slovakia	508.0	19.3	19.0 [h]	95	39.1	85	47.8	48.4
55 Mexico	496.2	2.5	2.8	117	4.1	138	1.0	1.1
Medium human development								
96 Turkey	1,902.0	8.5	8.5	90	19.9	88	32.3	20.1
OECD [i]	32,790.3 T	6.4	6.6 [j]	111	12.4	97	31.4	28.7

a. Data refer to unemployment lasting 12 months or longer. b. The age range for the labour force may be 16-24 for some countries. c. Data refer to 1999. d. Data are based on a small sample and must be treated with caution. e. Data refer to 2000. f. Data refer to the average annual rate in 1993-2001. g. Data refer to the average annual rate in 1992-2001. h. Data refer to the average annual rate in 1994-2001. i. Aggregates are from OECD 2002a and 2002b. j. OECD average does not include the Czech Republic, Hungary, Poland and Slovakia.
Source: Columns 1 and 2: OECD 2002a; column 3: calculated on the basis of data on unemployment rates from OECD 2002a; columns 4 and 6: calculated on the basis of data on male and female unemployment rates from OECD 2002b; columns 5, 7 and 8: OECD 2002b.

19 Energy and the environment

		Traditional fuel consumption (as % of total energy use)	Electricity consumption per capita (kilowatt-hours)		GDP per unit of energy use (PPP US$ per kg of oil equivalent)		Carbon dioxide emissions Per capita (metric tons)		Share of world total (%)	Ratification of environmental treaties [a] Cartagena Protocol on Biosafety	Framework Convention on Climate Change	Kyoto Protocol to the Framework Convention on Climate Change [b]	Convention on Biological Diversity
HDI rank		1997	1980	2000	1980	2000	1980	1999	1999				
High human development													
1	Norway	1.1	18,289	24,422	2.3	5.1	9.5	8.7	0.2	●	●	●	●
2	Iceland	..	12,553	24,779	1.8	2.4	8.2	7.4	(.)	○	●	●	●
3	Sweden	17.9	10,216	14,471	2.0	4.4	8.6	5.3	0.2	●	●	●	●
4	Australia	4.4	5,393	9,006	2.0	4.3	13.8	18.2	1.5		●	○	●
5	Netherlands	1.1	4,057	6,152	2.3	5.7	10.8	8.5	0.6		●	●	●
6	Belgium	1.6	4,402	7,564	2.2	4.4	13.3	10.2	0.4	○	●	●	●
7	United States	3.8	8,914	12,331	1.6	4.2	20.4	19.7	23.2		●	○	○
8	Canada	4.7	12,329	15,620	1.4	3.3	17.1	14.4	1.9	○	●	●	●
9	Japan	1.6	4,395	7,628	3.1	6.1	7.9	9.1	4.9		●	●	●
10	Switzerland	6.0	5,579	7,294	4.4	7.5	6.5	5.7	0.2	●	●	○	●
11	Denmark	5.9	4,222	6,079	3.0	7.9	12.3	9.3	0.2	●	●	●	●
12	Ireland	0.2	2,528	5,324	2.3	7.9	7.4	10.8	0.2	○	●	●	●
13	United Kingdom	3.3	4,160	5,601	2.5	6.0	10.3	9.2	2.3	○	●	●	●
14	Finland	6.5	7,779	14,588	1.7	3.8	11.9	11.3	0.2	○	●	●	●
15	Luxembourg	..	9,803	13,050	1.1	6.4	28.9	18.6	(.)	●	●	●	●
16	Austria	4.7	4,371	6,457	3.4	7.5	6.9	7.6	0.3	●	●	●	●
17	France	5.7	3,881	6,539	2.8	5.4	9.0	6.1	1.5	○	●	●	●
18	Germany	1.3	5,005	5,963	2.2	6.1	..	9.7	3.3	○	●	●	●
19	Spain	1.3	2,401	4,653	3.8	6.4	5.3	6.8	1.2	●	●	●	●
20	New Zealand	0.8	6,269	8,813	2.7	3.7	5.6	8.1	0.1	○	●	●	●
21	Italy	1.0	2,831	4,732	3.9	8.2	6.6	7.3	1.8	○	●	●	●
22	Israel	0.0	2,826	6,188	3.7	6.5	5.4	10.0	0.3		●	○	●
23	Portugal	0.9	1,469	3,834	5.5	7.2	2.8	6.0	0.3	○	●	●	●
24	Greece	4.5	2,064	4,086	4.7	6.3	5.4	8.2	0.4	○	●	●	●
25	Cyprus	..	1,494	3,958	3.3	6.3	5.2	8.0	(.)		●	●	●
26	Hong Kong, China (SAR)	0.7	2,167	5,447	6.2	10.9	3.2	6.2	0.2	–	–	–	–
27	Barbados	..	..	..	..	..	2.7	7.6	(.)	●	●	●	●
28	Singapore	0.0	2,280	6,948	2.2	3.9	12.5	13.7	0.2		●		●
29	Slovenia	1.5	..	5,290	..	5.0	..	7.3	0.1	●	●	●	●
30	Korea, Rep. of	2.4	859	5,607	2.3	3.6	3.3	8.4	1.7	○	●	●	●
31	Brunei Darussalam	..	1,523	7,263	..	3.0 c	35.5	14.2	(.)				
32	Czech Republic	1.6	3,701	4,807	..	3.6	..	10.6	0.5	●	●	●	●
33	Malta	..	1,363	4,018	2.9	6.7	2.7	8.8	(.)		●	●	●
34	Argentina	4.0	1,170	2,038	4.4	7.2	3.8	3.8	0.6	○	●	●	●
35	Poland	0.8	2,390	2,511	..	4.0	12.8	8.1	1.3	○	●	●	●
36	Seychelles	..	..	..	..	..	1.5	2.7	(.)	○	●	●	●
37	Bahrain	..	4,970	8,507	0.9	1.6	23.4	29.4	0.1		●	●	●
38	Hungary	1.6	2,389	2,909	2.0	4.9	7.7	5.6	0.2	○	●	●	●
39	Slovakia	0.5	3,817	4,075	..	3.6	..	7.2	0.2	○	●	●	●
40	Uruguay	21.0	948	1,924	4.8	9.4	2.0	2.0	(.)	○	●	●	●
41	Estonia	13.8	..	3,628	..	2.9	..	11.7	0.1	○	●	●	●
42	Costa Rica	54.2	860	1,630	6.6	11.7	1.1	1.6	(.)	○	●	●	●
43	Chile	11.3	876	2,406	3.0	5.6	2.5	4.2	0.3	○	●	●	●
44	Qatar	..	9,489	14,994	..	..	56.3	91.5	0.2		●		●
45	Lithuania	6.3	..	1,768	..	3.9	..	3.8	0.1	○	●	●	●
46	Kuwait	0.0	5,793	13,995	1.4	1.8	18.0	24.9	0.2		●		●
47	Croatia	3.2	..	2,695	..	4.9	..	4.8	0.1	●	●	○	●
48	United Arab Emirates	..	5,320	10,725	4.9	2.0 c	34.8	31.3	0.4		●		●
49	Bahamas	..	..	..	..	..	38.0	6.0	(.)	○	●	●	●
50	Latvia	26.2	..	1,887	19.8	4.6	..	2.8	(.)		●	●	●

19 Energy and the environment

HDI rank		Traditional fuel consumption (as % of total energy use) 1997	Electricity consumption per capita (kilowatt-hours) 1980	2000	GDP per unit of energy use (PPP US$ per kg of oil equivalent) 1980	2000	Carbon dioxide emissions Per capita (metric tons) 1980	1999	Share of world total (%) 1999	Cartagena Protocol on Biosafety	Framework Convention on Climate Change	Kyoto Protocol to the Framework Convention on Climate Change [b]	Convention on Biological Diversity
51	Saint Kitts and Nevis	..	..	..	..	..	..	2.4	(.)	●	●		●
52	Cuba	30.2	823	1,049	..	..	3.2	2.3	0.1	●	●	●	●
53	Belarus	0.8	..	2,678	..	3.0	..	5.7	0.2	●	●		●
54	Trinidad and Tobago	0.8	1,584	3,692	1.2	1.3	15.4	19.4	0.1	●	●	●	●
55	Mexico	4.5	846	1,655	2.9	5.5	3.7	3.9	1.6	●	●	●	●
Medium human development													
56	Antigua and Barbuda	..	..	..	..	..	2.3	5.2	(.)	○	●	●	●
57	Bulgaria	1.3	3,349	2,962	1.0	2.8	8.5	5.1	0.2	●	●	●	●
58	Malaysia	5.5	631	2,628	2.6	4.3	2.0	5.4	0.5	○	●	●	●
59	Panama	14.4	820	1,331	4.1	6.5	1.8	2.9	(.)	●	●	●	●
60	Macedonia, TFYR	6.1	..	..	..	..	..	5.6	(.)	○	●		
61	Libyan Arab Jamahiriya	0.9	1,588	3,921	..	..	8.8	8.3	0.2		●		●
62	Mauritius	36.1	..	..	..	..	0.6	2.1	(.)	●	●	●	●
63	Russian Federation	0.8	..	4,181	..	1.6	..	9.8	6.1	●	●	○	●
64	Colombia	17.7	561	788	4.7	10.3	1.4	1.5	0.3	○	●	●	●
65	Brazil	28.7	975	1,878	4.2	6.7	1.5	1.8	1.3	●	●	●	●
66	Bosnia and Herzegovina	10.1	..	1,473	..	5.2	..	1.2	(.)		●		●
67	Belize	..	..	..	..	..	1.3	2.7	(.)		●		●
68	Dominica	..	..	..	..	..	0.5	1.1	(.)		●		●
69	Venezuela	0.7	1,823	2,533	1.6	2.3	6.0	5.3	0.5	●	●		●
70	Samoa (Western)	..	..	..	..	..	0.6	0.8	(.)	●	●	●	●
71	Saint Lucia	..	..	..	..	..	1.0	2.1	(.)		●	○	●
72	Romania	5.7	2,434	1,513	..	3.4	8.6	3.6	0.3	○	●	●	●
73	Saudi Arabia	0.0	1,356	4,912	4.0	2.6	14.0	11.7	1.0		●		●
74	Thailand	24.6	279	1,448	2.9	5.1	0.9	3.3	0.8		●	●	○
75	Ukraine	0.5	..	2,293	..	1.4	..	7.5	1.6	●	●	○	●
76	Kazakhstan	0.2	..	2,622	..	2.2	..	7.4	0.5	●	●	○	●
77	Suriname	..	..	..	..	..	6.7	5.2	(.)		●		●
78	Jamaica	6.0	482	2,328	1.8	2.4	4.0	4.0	(.)	○	●	●	●
79	Oman	..	614	2,952	4.5	3.0	5.3	8.5	0.1		●		●
80	St. Vincent & the Grenadines	..	..	..	..	..	0.4	1.4	(.)		●	○	●
81	Fiji	..	..	..	..	..	1.2	0.9	(.)	●	●	●	●
82	Peru	24.6	502	668	4.4	9.5	1.4	1.2	0.1	○	●	●	●
83	Lebanon	2.5	789	1,814	..	3.5	2.1	4.0	0.1		●	●	●
84	Paraguay	49.6	245	838	4.8	7.2	0.5	0.8	(.)	○	●	●	●
85	Philippines	26.9	355	477	5.3	6.8	0.8	1.0	0.3	○	●	○	●
86	Maldives	..	..	..	..	..	0.3	1.7	(.)	●	●	●	●
87	Turkmenistan	..	..	1,071	..	1.4	..	6.4	0.1		●	●	●
88	Georgia	1.0	..	1,212	4.6	4.5	..	1.0	(.)		●	●	●
89	Azerbaijan	0.0	..	1,852	..	1.9	..	4.2	0.1		●	●	●
90	Jordan	0.0	387	1,236	3.1	3.6	2.2	3.1	0.1	○	●	●	●
91	Tunisia	12.4	379	939	3.8	7.4	1.5	1.8	0.1	●	●	●	●
92	Guyana	..	..	..	..	..	2.3	2.2	(.)		●		●
93	Grenada	..	..	..	..	..	0.5	2.2	(.)	○	●	●	●
94	Dominican Republic	14.3	433	788	4.1	7.4	1.1	2.8	0.1		●	●	●
95	Albania	7.3	1,083	1,073	..	6.7	1.8	0.5	(.)		●		●
96	Turkey	3.1	439	1,468	3.2	5.3	1.7	3.1	0.8	○			●
97	Ecuador	17.5	361	624	2.8	4.9	1.7	1.9	0.1	●	●	●	●
98	Occupied Palestinian Territories	..	..	..	..	..	..	..	..				
99	Sri Lanka	46.5	96	293	3.1	7.8	0.2	0.5	(.)	○	●	●	●
100	Armenia	0.0	..	944	..	4.5	..	0.8	(.)		●		●

19 Energy and the environment

HDI rank		Traditional fuel consumption (as % of total energy use) 1997	Electricity consumption per capita (kilowatt-hours) 1980	Electricity consumption per capita (kilowatt-hours) 2000	GDP per unit of energy use (PPP US$ per kg of oil equivalent) 1980	GDP per unit of energy use (PPP US$ per kg of oil equivalent) 2000	Carbon dioxide emissions Per capita (metric tons) 1980	Carbon dioxide emissions Per capita (metric tons) 1999	Carbon dioxide emissions Share of world total (%) 1999	Ratification of environmental treaties[a] Cartagena Protocol on Biosafety	Framework Convention on Climate Change	Kyoto Protocol to the Framework Convention on Climate Change[b]	Convention on Biological Diversity
101	Uzbekistan	0.0	..	1,612	..	1.2	..	4.8	0.5		●	●	●
102	Kyrgyzstan	0.0	..	1,606	..	5.4	..	1.0	(.)		●		●
103	Cape Verde	..	..	..	..	..	0.4	0.3	(.)		●		●
104	China	5.7	253	827	0.7	4.1	1.5	2.3	11.9	○	●		●
105	El Salvador	34.5	274	587	5.0	8.1	0.5	0.9	(.)	○	●		●
106	Iran, Islamic Rep. of	0.7	495	1,474	2.7	3.2	3.0	4.8	1.3	○	●		●
107	Algeria	1.5	265	612	5.5	6.4	3.5	3.0	0.4	○	●		●
108	Moldova, Rep. of	0.5	..	720	..	3.1	..	1.5	(.)	○	●		●
109	Viet Nam	37.8	50	286	..	4.2	0.3	0.6	0.2		●	●	●
110	Syrian Arab Republic	0.0	354	900	2.6	2.9	2.2	3.4	0.2		●		●
111	South Africa	43.4	3,213	3,745	3.1	4.4	7.7	7.9	1.4		●	●	●
112	Indonesia	29.3	44	384	2.0	4.2	0.6	1.2	1.0	○	●	○	●
113	Tajikistan	..	..	2,137	..	2.3	..	0.8	(.)		●		●
114	Bolivia	14.0	226	387	3.0	3.9	0.8	1.4	(.)	●	●	●	●
115	Honduras	54.8	215	499	3.2	6.0	0.6	0.8	(.)	○	●	●	●
116	Equatorial Guinea	..	..	..	..	..	0.3	1.5	(.)		●		●
117	Mongolia	4.3	..	..	..	..	4.1	3.2	(.)		●		●
118	Gabon	32.9	617	697	1.8	4.7	8.9	3.0	(.)		●	●	●
119	Guatemala	62.0	240	335	4.6	7.1	0.7	0.9	(.)		●	●	●
120	Egypt	3.2	380	976	3.3	4.8	1.1	2.0	0.5	○	●	○	●
121	Nicaragua	42.2	303	267	4.0	4.6 c	0.7	0.8	(.)	●	●	●	●
122	São Tomé and Principe	..	..	..	..	..	0.5	0.6	(.)		●		●
123	Solomon Islands	..	..	..	..	..	0.4	0.4	(.)		●	○	●
124	Namibia	..	..	..	..	12.0	..	0.1	(.)	○	●		●
125	Botswana	..	..	..	..	..	1.1	2.4	(.)	●	●		●
126	Morocco	4.0	223	447	6.4	9.5	0.8	1.3	0.2	○	●	●	●
127	India	20.7	130	355	2.2	5.5	0.5	1.1	4.6	●	●	●	●
128	Vanuatu	..	..	..	..	..	0.5	0.4	(.)		●		●
129	Ghana	78.1	424	288	3.1	5.5	0.2	0.3	(.)		●		●
130	Cambodia	89.3	..	..	..	..	(.)	0.1	(.)		●		●
131	Myanmar	60.5	31	69	..	..	0.1	0.2	(.)	○	●		●
132	Papua New Guinea	62.5	..	..	..	..	0.6	0.5	(.)		●	●	●
133	Swaziland	..	..	..	..	..	0.8	0.4	(.)		●		●
134	Comoros	..	..	..	..	..	0.1	0.1	(.)		●		●
135	Lao People's Dem. Rep.	88.7	..	..	..	..	0.1	0.1	(.)		●		●
136	Bhutan	..	..	..	..	..	(.)	0.5	(.)	●	●	●	●
137	Lesotho	..	..	..	..	..	..	..	..	●	●		●
138	Sudan	75.1	34	66	1.6	3.8	0.2	0.1	(.)		●		●
139	Bangladesh	46.0	16	96	5.4	10.8	0.1	0.2	0.1	○	●	●	●
140	Congo	53.0	83	86	0.8	3.2	0.2	0.8	(.)	○	●		●
141	Togo	71.9	..	..	4.9	4.9	0.2	0.3	(.)	○	●		●
Low human development													
142	Cameroon	69.2	154	183	2.7	3.8	0.4	0.3	(.)	○	●		●
143	Nepal	89.6	11	56	1.5	3.7	(.)	0.1	(.)	○	●		●
144	Pakistan	29.5	125	352	2.1	4.0	0.4	0.7	0.4	○	●		●
145	Zimbabwe	25.2	973	845	1.5	3.1	1.3	1.4	0.1	○	●		●
146	Kenya	80.3	92	106	1.0	1.9	0.4	0.3	(.)	●	●		●
147	Uganda	89.7	..	..	..	..	0.1	0.1	(.)	●	●	●	●
148	Yemen	1.4	59	107	..	4.0	..	1.1	0.1		●		●
149	Madagascar	84.3	..	..	..	..	0.2	0.1	(.)	○	●		●
150	Haiti	74.7	41	37	4.7	7.5	0.1	0.2	(.)	○	●		●
151	Gambia	78.6	..	..	..	..	0.2	0.2	(.)	○	●	●	●

19 Energy and the environment

HDI rank	Traditional fuel consumption (as % of total energy use) 1997	Electricity consumption per capita (kilowatt-hours) 1980	2000	GDP per unit of energy use (PPP US$ per kg of oil equivalent) 1980	2000	Carbon dioxide emissions Per capita (metric tons) 1980	1999	Share of world total (%) 1999	Ratification of environmental treaties [a] Cartagena Protocol on Biosafety	Framework Convention on Climate Change	Kyoto Protocol to the Framework Convention on Climate Change [b]	Convention on Biological Diversity
152 Nigeria	67.8	68	81	0.8	1.2	1.0	0.3	0.2	○	●		●
153 Djibouti	..	..	..	..	..	1.0	0.6	(.)	●	●	●	●
154 Mauritania	0.0	..	..	..	..	0.4	1.2	(.)		●		●
155 Eritrea	96.0	..	..	..	..	..	0.1	(.)		●		●
156 Senegal	56.2	96	121	2.2	4.5	0.5	0.4	(.)	○	●	●	●
157 Guinea	74.2	..	..	..	..	0.2	0.2	(.)	○	●	●	●
158 Rwanda	88.3	..	..	..	..	0.1	0.1	(.)	○	●		●
159 Benin	89.2	30	64	1.2	2.5	0.1	0.2	(.)	○	●	●	●
160 Tanzania, U. Rep. of	91.4	37	56	..	1.1	0.1	0.1	(.)		●	●	●
161 Côte d'Ivoire	91.5	..	..	2.7	3.6	0.6	0.8	0.1		●		●
162 Malawi	88.6	..	..	..	..	0.1	0.1	(.)	○	●	●	●
163 Zambia	72.7	1,016	556	0.8	1.2	0.6	0.2	(.)		●	○	●
164 Angola	69.7	67	88	..	3.6	0.8	0.8	(.)		●		●
165 Chad	97.6	..	..	..	..	(.)	(.)	(.)	○	●		●
166 Guinea-Bissau	57.1	..	..	..	..	0.7	0.2	(.)		●		●
167 Congo, Dem. Rep. of the	91.7	148	40	3.8	2.5	0.1	(.)	..		●		●
168 Central African Republic	87.5	..	..	..	..	(.)	0.1	(.)	○	●		●
169 Ethiopia	95.9	16	22	..	2.6	(.)	0.1	(.)	○	●		●
170 Mozambique	91.4	34	53	0.7	2.5	0.3	0.1	(.)	●	●		●
171 Burundi	94.2	..	..	..	..	(.)	(.)	(.)		●	●	●
172 Mali	88.9	..	..	..	..	0.1	(.)	(.)	●	●		●
173 Burkina Faso	87.1	..	..	..	..	0.1	0.1	(.)	○	●		●
174 Niger	80.6	..	..	..	..	0.1	0.1	(.)	○	●	○	●
175 Sierra Leone	86.1	..	..	..	..	0.2	0.1	(.)		●		●
Developing countries	16.7	318	810	2.1	4.6	1.3	1.9	36.6	–	–	–	–
Least developed countries	75.1	59	77	..	..	0.1	0.2	0.5	–	–	–	–
Arab States	5.6	518	1,406	3.6	3.8	3.0	3.7	4.0	–	–	–	–
East Asia and the Pacific	9.4	253	918	..	..	1.4	2.3	17.9	–	–	–	–
Latin America and the Caribbean	15.7	845	1,528	3.6	6.1	2.4	2.5	5.4	–	–	–	–
South Asia	20.3	132	376	2.3	5.2	0.5	1.1	6.4	–	–	–	–
Sub-Saharan Africa	62.9	463	457	..	2.9	1.0	0.8	2.0	–	–	–	–
Central & Eastern Europe & CIS	1.2	..	2,977	..	2.2	..	7.2	12.5	–	–	–	–
OECD	3.3	4,916	7,336	2.2	4.9	11.0	10.8	51.0	–	–	–	–
High-income OECD	3.4	5,687	8,688	2.1	4.9	12.2	12.3	46.4	–	–	–	–
High human development	3.3	4,871	7,245	2.2	4.9	10.9	10.8	53.5	–	–	–	–
Medium human development	10.8	322	939	2.1	4.0	1.3	2.3	38.3	–	–	–	–
Low human development	63.3	116	162	..	4.0	0.4	0.4	1.0	–	–	–	–
High income	3.4	5,637	8,651	2.2	4.9	12.2	12.4	48.2	–	–	–	–
Middle income	7.3	578	1,391	2.0	4.0	2.3	3.2	35.9	–	–	–	–
Low income	29.8	106	352	..	2.5	0.5	1.0	10.3	–	–	–	–
World	8.2	1,442	2,156	2.1	4.5	3.4	3.8	100.0 [d]	–	–	–	–

● Ratification, acceptance, approval, accession or succession. ○ Signature.

a. Information is as of 10 February 2003. The Cartagena Protocol on Biosafety was signed in Cartagena in 2000, the United Nations Framework Convention on Climate Change in New York in 1992, the Kyoto Protocol to the United Nations Framework Convention on Climate Change in Kyoto in 1997 and the Convention on Biological Diversity in Rio de Janeiro in 1992. b. Has not yet entered into force. c. Data refer to 1998. d. Aggregate from CDIAC 2003. Data refer to total carbon dioxide emissions, including those of countries not shown in the main indicator tables as well as emissions not included in national totals, such as those from bunker fuels and oxidation of non-fuel hydrocarbon products.

Source: Column 1: World Bank 2003c; columns 2 and 3: World Bank 2003c; aggregates calculated for the Human Development Report Office by the World Bank; columns 4 and 5: World Bank 2003c, based on data from a joint effort by the International Energy Agency and the World Bank; aggregates calculated for the Human Development Report Office by the World Bank; columns 6 and 7: World Bank 2003c, based on data from the Carbon Dioxide Information Analysis Center; aggregates calculated for the Human Development Report Office by the World Bank; column 8: calculated on the basis of data on carbon dioxide emissions from CDIAC 2003; columns 9-12: UN 2003b.

20 Refugees and armaments

HDI rank	Internally displaced people (thousands) 2001 [a, c]	Refugees [a] By country of asylum (thousands) 2001	Refugees [a] By country of origin (thousands) [d] 2001	Conventional arms transfers (1990 prices) [b] Imports (US$ millions) 1992	Conventional arms transfers (1990 prices) [b] Imports (US$ millions) 2002	Conventional arms transfers (1990 prices) [b] Exports US$ millions 2002	Conventional arms transfers (1990 prices) [b] Exports Share (%) [e] 1998-2002	Total armed forces Thousands 2001	Total armed forces Index (1985 = 100) 2001
High human development									
1 Norway	–	50	..	317	82	203	0.4	27	72
2 Iceland	–	(.)	..	(.)	..	..	..	..	..
3 Sweden	–	146	..	47	45	120	1.2	34	52
4 Australia	–	55	..	250	614	30	0.4	51	72
5 Netherlands	–	152	..	143	236	260	1.6	50	47
6 Belgium	–	12	..	64	29	14	0.1	39	43
7 United States	–	516	..	198	346	3,941	40.8	1,414	66
8 Canada	–	129	..	344	359	318	0.8	52	63
9 Japan	–	3	..	1,523	154	..	(.)	240	99
10 Switzerland	–	58	..	170	36	11	0.2	4	18
11 Denmark	–	73	..	42	7	9	(.)	23	77
12 Ireland	–	4	..	(.)	20	(.)	(.)	10	76
13 United Kingdom	–	149	..	1,166	575	719	5.2	210	63
14 Finland	–	13	..	441	24	12	0.1	32	87
15 Luxembourg	–	1	..	..	..	..	..	1	129
16 Austria	–	14	..	2	79	124	0.2	35	63
17 France	–	132	..	387	22	1,617	9.0	260	56
18 Germany	–	903	..	969	..	..	5.4	296	62
19 Spain	–	7	..	187	132	65	0.3	178	56
20 New Zealand	–	5	..	61	17	..	(.)	9	70
21 Italy	–	9	..	42	308	490	1.9	217	56
22 Israel	–	4	..	1,330	226	178	1.0	162	114
23 Portugal	–	(.)	..	6	103	..	..	44	60
24 Greece	–	7	..	1,994	567	(.)	(.)	178	88
25 Cyprus	–	(.)	..	36	(.)	..	..	10	100
26 Hong Kong, China (SAR)	–	1	..	..	..	..	..	..	..
27 Barbados	–	..	..	..	..	..	..	1	61
28 Singapore	–	(.)	..	100	227	2	(.)	61	110
29 Slovenia	–	2	1	(.)	(.)	..	..	9	..
30 Korea, Rep. of	–	(.)	..	497	229	22	0.3	686	115
31 Brunei Darussalam	–	..	..	(.)	(.)	..	..	7	171
32 Czech Republic	–	1	1	(.)	53	85	0.4	49	24
33 Malta	–	(.)	..	..	(.)	..	..	2	268
34 Argentina	–	2	..	16	210	(.)	(.)	70	65
35 Poland	–	1	3	20	258	43	0.3	163	51
36 Seychelles	–	..	..	..	..	..	..	(.)	38
37 Bahrain	–	(.)	..	35	51	(.)	(.)	11	382
38 Hungary	–	5	1	(.)	(.)	..	(.)	33	32
39 Slovakia	–	(.)	..	(.)	27	40	0.4	26	..
40 Uruguay	–	(.)	..	37	2	..	(.)	24	75
41 Estonia	–	(.)	..	1	1	..	..	6	..
42 Costa Rica	–	8	..	..	..	..	..	..	..
43 Chile	–	(.)	1	182	56	1	(.)	81	80
44 Qatar	–	(.)	..	73	8	..	(.)	12	207
45 Lithuania	–	(.)	..	74	7	3	(.)	14	..
46 Kuwait	–	1	..	897	27	..	0.1	16	129
47 Croatia	23	22	289	24	2	..	(.)	51	..
48 United Arab Emirates	–	1	..	204	452	..	(.)	42	97
49 Bahamas	–	(.)	..	(.)	..	..	..	1	172
50 Latvia	–	(.)	..	..	3	..	..	6	..

HDI rank	Internally displaced people (thousands) 2001 [a,c]	Refugees [a] By country of asylum (thousands) 2001	Refugees [a] By country of origin (thousands) [d] 2001	Conventional arms transfers (1990 prices) [b] Imports (US$ millions) 1992	Imports (US$ millions) 2002	Exports US$ millions 2002	Exports Share (%) [e] 1998-2002	Total armed forces Thousands 2001	Total armed forces Index (1985 = 100) 2001
51 Saint Kitts and Nevis	–	..	..	..	..	..	..	..	..
52 Cuba	–	1	19	(.)	..	..	..	46	28
53 Belarus	–	1	..	(.)	..	(.)	1.2	80	..
54 Trinidad and Tobago	–	..	..	..	(.)	..	..	3	129
55 Mexico	–	15	..	12	19	..	..	193	149
Medium human development									
56 Antigua and Barbuda	–	..	..	..	..	..	..	(.)	170
57 Bulgaria	–	3	..	44	..	20	0.3	68	46
58 Malaysia	–	50	..	16	213	..	(.)	100	91
59 Panama	–	1	..	2	..	..	..	..	..
60 Macedonia, TFYR	16	4	12	(.)	(.)	..	..	12	..
61 Libyan Arab Jamahiriya	–	12	..	(.)	(.)	11	(.)	76	104
62 Mauritius	–	(.)	..	..	..	..	..	..	..
63 Russian Federation	443	18	45	86	170	5,941	22.4	988	19
64 Colombia	720	(.)	18	32	119	..	..	158	239
65 Brazil	–	3	..	66	154	18	(.)	288	104
66 Bosnia and Herzegovina	438	33	450	(.)	..	..	..	20 [f]	..
67 Belize	–	1	..	..	..	..	..	1	175
68 Dominica	–	..	..	..	..	..	..	..	..
69 Venezuela	–	(.)	..	48	50	..	..	82	168
70 Samoa (Western)	–	..	..	..	..	..	..	..	..
71 Saint Lucia	–	0	..	..	..	..	..	..	..
72 Romania	–	2	6	160	186	..	(.)	99	52
73 Saudi Arabia	–	245	..	1,198	478	..	..	125	199
74 Thailand	–	111	..	395	150	..	..	306	130
75 Ukraine	–	3	27	..	..	270	2.9	302	..
76 Kazakhstan	–	20	3	(.)	69	(.)	0.2	60	..
77 Suriname	–	0	..	..	..	..	..	2	92
78 Jamaica	–	0	..	..	..	..	..	3	135
79 Oman	–	..	..	20	48	..	..	42	143
80 St. Vincent & the Grenadines	–	..	..	..	..	..	..	..	..
81 Fiji	–	0	..	..	..	..	..	4	130
82 Peru	–	1	7	132	4	5	(.)	110	86
83 Lebanon	–	3	9	38	..	(.)	(.)	72	413
84 Paraguay	–	(.)	..	1	(.)	..	..	19	129
85 Philippines	–	(.)	45	59	17	..	..	106	92
86 Maldives	–	..	..	..	..	..	..	..	..
87 Turkmenistan	–	14	..	..	..	..	..	18	..
88 Georgia	264	8	18	(.)	(.)	..	0.2	18	..
89 Azerbaijan	573	(.)	269	64	..	..	..	72	..
90 Jordan	–	1	..	(.)	149	..	(.)	100	143
91 Tunisia	–	(.)	..	32	7	..	..	35	100
92 Guyana	–	0	..	..	(.)	..	..	2	24
93 Grenada	–	..	..	..	..	..	..	..	..
94 Dominican Republic	–	0	..	(.)	..	..	..	25	110
95 Albania	–	(.)	8	(.)	(.)	..	..	27	67
96 Turkey	–	3	47	1,347	721	29	0.1	515	82
97 Ecuador	–	2	..	(.)	1	..	..	60	140
98 Occupied Palestinian Territories	–	..	349	..	..	..	..	29 [g]	..
99 Sri Lanka	683	(.)	122	21	9	..	..	158	731
100 Armenia	–	264	7	(.)	..	..	..	45	..

	HDI rank	Internally displaced people (thousands) 2001 [a, c]	Refugees [a] By country of asylum (thousands) 2001	By country of origin (thousands) [d] 2001	Conventional arms transfers (1990 prices) [b] Imports (US$ millions) 1992	2002	Exports US$ millions 2002	Share (%) [e] 1998-2002	Total armed forces Thousands 2001	Index (1985 = 100) 2001
101	Uzbekistan	–	40	3	..	5	170	0.2	50-55 [h]	..
102	Kyrgyzstan	–	9	1	..	..	..	..	11	..
103	Cape Verde	–	0	..	..	..	..	..	1	16
104	China	–	295	117	1,163	2,307	818	1.7	2,270	58
105	El Salvador	–	(.)	7	3	..	..	..	17	40
106	Iran, Islamic Rep. of	–	1,868	92	386	298	..	(.)	520	85
107	Algeria	–	169	8	16	464	..	..	137	80
108	Moldova, Rep. of	1	(.)	4	..	..	(.)	(.)	7	..
109	Viet Nam	–	16	353	(.)	69	..	..	484	47
110	Syrian Arab Republic	–	3	5	317	162	..	(.)	319	79
111	South Africa	–	19	(.)	140	(.)	34	0.1	60	56
112	Indonesia	–	74	9	47	51	70	0.2	297	107
113	Tajikistan	–	15	56	..	..	..	..	6	..
114	Bolivia	–	(.)	..	24	..	..	..	32	114
115	Honduras	–	(.)	..	(.)	..	..	..	8	50
116	Equatorial Guinea	–	..	..	..	(.)	..	..	1	60
117	Mongolia	–	..	..	(.)	..	..	..	9	28
118	Gabon	–	16	..	(.)	..	..	..	5	196
119	Guatemala	–	1	17	(.)	..	..	..	31	99
120	Egypt	–	7	..	995	638	(.)	(.)	443	100
121	Nicaragua	–	(.)	4	(.)	..	..	..	14	22
122	São Tomé and Principe	–	..	..	..	..	..	..	..	..
123	Solomon Islands	–	0	..	..	..	..	..	..	..
124	Namibia	–	31	..	..	11	..	..	9	..
125	Botswana	–	4	..	3	(.)	..	..	9	225
126	Morocco	–	2	..	30	169	..	..	196	132
127	India	–	170	12	871	1,668	(.)	(.)	1,298	103
128	Vanuatu	–	..	..	..	..	..	..	..	..
129	Ghana	–	12	15	(.)	(.)	..	..	7	46
130	Cambodia	–	(.)	35	(.)	..	..	..	125	357
131	Myanmar	–	..	146	52	208	..	..	44	24
132	Papua New Guinea	–	5	..	10	..	..	..	3	97
133	Swaziland	–	1	..	..	(.)	..	..	..	..
134	Comoros	–	(.)	..	..	..	..	..	..	..
135	Lao People's Dem. Rep.	–	0	13	(.)	(.)	..	..	29	54
136	Bhutan	–	..	111	..	..	..	..	..	..
137	Lesotho	–	(.)	..	..	(.)	..	..	2	100
138	Sudan	–	349	490	5	(.)	..	..	117	207
139	Bangladesh	–	22	6	63	21	..	..	137	150
140	Congo	–	119	24	(.)	..	..	..	10	115
141	Togo	–	12	4	(.)	..	..	..	9	263
Low human development										
142	Cameroon	–	41	..	3	(.)	..	..	23	316
143	Nepal	–	131	..	..	8	..	..	51	204
144	Pakistan	–	2,199	12	261	1,278	8	(.)	620	128
145	Zimbabwe	–	9	..	57	(.)	..	..	36	88
146	Kenya	–	239	3	3	..	..	..	24	178
147	Uganda	–	200	40	(.)	..	..	..	50-60 [h]	275
148	Yemen	–	69	..	(.)	496	..	..	67	104
149	Madagascar	–	(.)	..	(.)	..	..	..	14	64
150	Haiti	–	..	7	..	..	..	..	..	..
151	Gambia	–	8	..	..	..	..	..	1	160

HDI rank	Internally displaced people (thousands) 2001 [a,c]	Refugees [a] By country of asylum (thousands) 2001	Refugees [a] By country of origin (thousands) [d] 2001	Conventional arms transfers (1990 prices) [b] Imports (US$ millions) 1992	Imports (US$ millions) 2002	Exports US$ millions 2002	Exports Share (%) [e] 1998-2002	Total armed forces Thousands 2001	Total armed forces Index (1985 = 100) 2001
152 Nigeria	–	7	6	56	2	..	..	79	84
153 Djibouti	–	23	(.)	18	(.)	..	..	10	328
154 Mauritania	–	(.)	30	(.)	..	..	..	16	185
155 Eritrea	–	2	333	(.)	180	..	..	172	..
156 Senegal	–	21	9	(.)	..	..	..	9	93
157 Guinea	–	178	..	(.)	(.)	..	..	10	98
158 Rwanda	–	35	85	2	..	..	..	60-75 [h]	1,298
159 Benin	–	5	..	..	..	..	..	5	101
160 Tanzania, U. Rep. of	–	647	..	20	..	..	..	27	67
161 Côte d'Ivoire	–	126	..	1	7	..	..	17	129
162 Malawi	–	6	..	(.)	..	..	(.)	5	100
163 Zambia	–	284	..	(.)	..	..	..	22	133
164 Angola	202	12	471	(.)	5	1	(.)	100	202
165 Chad	–	13	46	(.)	(.)	..	..	30	249
166 Guinea-Bissau	–	7	1	(.)	..	..	..	9	108
167 Congo, Dem. Rep. of the	3	362	392	2	14	..	..	81	170
168 Central African Republic	–	49	29	..	..	..	..	3	111
169 Ethiopia	–	153	59	(.)	20	..	..	253	116
170 Mozambique	–	(.)	(.)	(.)	..	..	..	10-11 [h]	66
171 Burundi	20	28	554	..	(.)	..	..	46	875
172 Mali	–	8	(.)	(.)	..	..	..	7	150
173 Burkina Faso	–	(.)	..	(.)	..	..	..	10	255
174 Niger	–	(.)	(.)	(.)	..	..	..	5	241
175 Sierra Leone	–	11	179	1	..	..	..	13-14 [h]	435
Developing countries	..	8,716 T	..	..	..	..	..	13,702 T	88
Least developed countries	..	2,692 T	..	..	..	..	..	1,578 T	135
Arab States	..	1,015 T	..	..	..	..	..	2,236 T	83
East Asia and the Pacific	..	552 T	..	..	..	..	..	5,613 T	75
Latin America and the Caribbean	..	36 T	..	..	..	..	..	1,267 T	94
South Asia	..	4,389 T	..	..	..	..	..	2,784 T	110
Sub-Saharan Africa	..	2,719 T	..	..	..	..	..	1,277 T	151
Central & Eastern Europe & CIS	..	865 T	..	..	..	..	..	2,297 T	35
OECD	..	2,465 T	..	..	..	..	..	5,068 T	70
High-income OECD	..	2,439 T	..	..	..	..	..	4,088 T	70
High human development	..	2,506 T	..	..	..	..	..	5,263 T	72
Medium human development	..	4,061 T	..	..	..	..	..	10,845 T	65
Low human development	..	4,874 T	..	..	..	..	..	1,897 T	150
High income	..	2,449 T	..	..	..	..	..	4,417 T	72
Middle income	..	3,551 T	..	..	..	..	..	9,064 T	57
Low income	..	6,024 T	..	..	..	..	..	6,083 T	114
World	..	12,030 T [i]	..	20,454 T [j]	16,492 T [j]	16,496 T [j]	..	19,564 T	71

a. Data refer to the end of 2001. They do not include Palestinian refugees. b. Data are as of 25 February 2003. Figures are trend indicator values, which are an indicator only of the volume of international arms transfers, not of the actual financial value of such transfers. Published reports of arms transfers provide partial information, as not all transfers are fully reported. The estimates presented are conservative and may understate actual transfers of conventional weapons. Zero values are shown as (.). c. Data refer to persons who are displaced within their country and to whom the United Nations High Commissioner for Refugees (UNHCR) extends protection or assistance, generally pursuant to a special request by a competent organ of the United Nations. d. The country of origin for many refugees is unavailable or unreported. These data may therefore be underestimates. e. Calculated using the 1998-2002 totals for all countries and non-state actors with exports of major conventional weapons as defined in SIPRI 2003b. f. In accordance with the Dayton Peace Accords (signed 14 December 1995), Bosnia and Herzegovina comprises two entities: the Federation of Bosnia and Herzegovina and the Republika Srpska. The two entities are subject to ceilings on arms. The armed forces of the Federation of Bosnia and Herzegovina number some 13,200, and those of the Republika Srpska some 6,600. g. Includes paramilitary forces. h. The mid-point value was used for calculating aggregates. i. Aggregate from UNHCR 2002. j. Aggregate from SIPRI 2003b. It includes all countries and non-state actors with transfers of major conventional weapons as defined in SIPRI 2003b.

Source: Columns 1-3: UNHCR 2002; columns 4-6: SIPRI 2003b; column 7: calculated on the basis of data on weapons transfers from SIPRI 2003b; column 8: IISS 2002; column 9: calculated on the basis of data on armed forces from IISS 2002.

21 Victims of crime

	Year[b]	People victimized by crime (as % of total population)[a]					
		Total crime[c]	Property crime[d]	Robbery	Sexual assault[e]	Assault	Bribery (corruption)[f]
National							
Australia	1999	30.1	13.9	1.2	1.0	2.4	0.3
Austria	1995	18.8	3.1	0.2	1.2	0.8	0.7
Belgium	1999	21.4	7.7	1.0	0.3	1.2	0.3
Canada	1999	23.8	10.4	0.9	0.8	2.3	0.4
Denmark	1999	23.0	7.6	0.7	0.4	1.4	0.3
England and Wales	1999	26.4	12.2	1.2	0.9	2.8	0.1
Finland	1999	19.1	4.4	0.6	1.1	2.1	0.2
France	1999	21.4	8.7	1.1	0.7	1.4	1.3
Italy	1991	24.6	12.7	1.3	0.6	0.2	..
Japan	1999	15.2	3.4	0.1	0.1	0.1	(.)
Malta	1996	23.1	10.9	0.4	0.1	1.1	4.0
Netherlands	1999	25.2	7.4	0.8	0.8	1.0	0.4
New Zealand	1991	29.4	14.8	0.7	1.3	2.4	..
Northern Ireland	1999	15.0	6.2	0.1	0.1	2.1	0.2
Poland	1999	22.7	9.0	1.8	0.2	1.1	5.1
Portugal	1999	15.5	7.5	1.1	0.2	0.4	1.4
Scotland	1999	23.2	7.6	0.7	0.3	3.0	..
Slovenia	2000	21.2	7.7	1.1	0.8	1.1	2.1
Sweden	1999	24.7	8.4	0.9	1.1	1.2	0.1
Switzerland	1999	18.2	4.5	0.7	0.6	1.0	0.2 [g]
United States	1999	21.1	10.0	0.6	0.4	1.2	0.2
Major city							
Asunción (Paraguay)	1995	34.4	16.7	6.3	1.7	0.9	13.3
Baku (Azerbaijan)	1999	8.3	2.4	1.6	0.0	0.4	20.8
Beijing (China)	1991	19.0	2.2	0.5	0.6	0.6	..
Bishkek (Kyrgyzstan)	1995	27.8	11.3	1.6	2.2	2.1	19.3
Bogotá (Colombia)	1996	54.6	27.0	11.5	4.8	2.5	19.5
Bratislava (Slovakia)	1996	36.0	20.8	1.2	0.4	0.5	13.5
Bucharest (Romania)	1999	25.4	10.8	1.8	0.4	0.6	19.2
Budapest (Hungary)	1999	32.1	15.6	1.8	9.0	0.8	9.8
Buenos Aires (Argentina)	1995	61.1	30.8	6.4	6.4	2.3	30.2
Cairo (Egypt)	1991	28.7	12.1	2.2	1.8	1.1	..
Dar es Salaam (Tanzania, U. Rep. of)	1991	..	23.1	8.2	6.1	1.7	..
Gaborone (Botswana)	1996	31.7	19.7	2.0	0.7	3.2	2.8
Jakarta (Indonesia)	1995	20.9	9.4	0.7	1.3	0.5	29.9
Johannesburg (South Africa)	1995	38.0	18.3	4.7	2.7	4.6	6.9
Kampala (Uganda)	1995	40.9	20.6	2.3	5.1	1.7	19.5
Kiev (Ukraine)	1999	29.1	8.9	2.5	1.2	1.5	16.2
La Paz (Bolivia)	1995	39.8	18.1	5.8	1.5	2.0	24.4
Manila (Philippines)	1995	10.6	3.3	1.5	0.1	0.1	4.3
Minsk (Belarus)	1999	23.6	11.1	1.4	1.4	1.3	20.6
Moscow (Russian Federation)	1999	26.3	10.9	2.4	1.2	1.1	16.6
Mumbai (India)	1995	31.8	6.7	1.3	3.5	0.8	22.9
New Delhi (India)	1995	30.5	6.1	1.0	1.7	0.8	21.0
Prague (Czech Republic)	1999	34.1	21.6	0.5	0.9	1.1	5.7
Rïga (Latvia)	1999	26.5	9.4	2.8	0.5	1.9	14.3
Rio de Janeiro (Brazil)	1995	44.0	14.7	12.2	7.5	3.4	17.1

	Year[b]	People victimized by crime (as % of total population)[a]					
		Total crime[c]	Property crime[d]	Robbery	Sexual assault[e]	Assault	Bribery (corruption)[f]
San José (Costa Rica)	1995	40.4	21.7	8.9	3.5	1.7	9.2
Skopje (Macedonia, TFYR)	1995	21.1	9.4	1.1	0.3	0.7	7.4
Sofia (Bulgaria)	1999	27.2	16.1	1.5	0.1	0.6	16.4
Tallinn (Estonia)	1999	41.2	22.5	6.3	3.3	3.7	9.3
Tbilisi (Georgia)	1999	23.6	11.1	1.8	0.4	0.9	16.6
Tirana (Albania)	1999	31.7	11.2	2.9	1.2	0.7	59.1
Tunis (Tunisia)	1991	37.5	20.1	5.4	1.5	0.4	..
Ulaanbaatar (Mongolia)	1999	41.8	20.0	4.5	1.4	2.1	21.3
Vilnius (Lithuania)	1999	31.0	17.8	3.2	2.0	1.4	22.9
Zagreb (Croatia)	1999	14.3	4.4	0.5	0.8	0.5	9.5

a. Data refer to victimization as reported in the International Crime Victims Survey. b. Surveys were conducted in 1992, 1995, 1996-97 and 2000-01. Data refer to the year preceding the survey. c. Data refer to people victimized by one or more of 11 crimes recorded in the survey: robbery, burglary, attempted burglary, car theft, car vandalism, bicycle theft, sexual assault, theft from car, theft of personal property, assault and threats and theft of motorcycle or moped. d. Includes car theft, theft from car, burglary with entry and attempted burglary. e. Data refer to female population only. f. Data refer to people who have been asked or expected to pay a bribe by a government official. g. Data refer to 1995.
Source: Columns 1-7: UNICRI 2002.

... AND ACHIEVING EQUALITY FOR ALL WOMEN AND MEN

HDI rank		Gender-related development index (GDI)		Life expectancy at birth (years) 2001		Adult literacy rate (% age 15 and above) 2001		Combined primary, secondary and tertiary gross enrolment ratio (%) 2000-01 [a]		Estimated earned income (PPP US$) 2001 [b]		HDI rank minus GDI rank [c]
		Rank	Value	Female	Male	Female	Male	Female	Male	Female	Male	
High human development												
1	Norway	1	0.941	81.7	75.8	.. [d]	.. [d]	102 [e,f]	94 [f]	23,317 [g]	36,043 [g]	0
2	Iceland	2	0.940	81.8	77.5	.. [d]	.. [d]	96 [f]	87 [f]	23,130	36,799	0
3	Sweden	3	0.940	82.4	77.4	.. [d]	.. [d]	123 [e,f]	103 [e,f]	19,636 [g]	28,817 [g]	0
4	Australia	4	0.938	81.9	76.3	.. [d]	.. [d]	117 [e,f]	112 [e,f]	20,830	29,945	0
5	Netherlands	7	0.934	80.9	75.5	.. [d]	.. [d]	99 [f]	100 [e,f]	18,846	35,675	-2
6	Belgium	8	0.931	81.7	75.4	.. [d]	.. [d]	111 [e,f,h]	104 [e,f,h]	15,835	35,601	-2
7	United States	5	0.935	79.7	74.0	.. [d]	.. [d]	97 [f]	90 [f]	26,389 [g]	42,540 [g]	2
8	Canada	6	0.934	81.8	76.5	.. [d]	.. [d]	96 [f,h]	91 [f,h]	20,990 [g]	33,391 [g]	2
9	Japan	13	0.926	84.7	77.7	.. [d]	.. [d]	82 [f]	84 [f]	15,617	35,061	-4
10	Switzerland	12	0.927	82.2	75.8	.. [d]	.. [d]	86 [f]	90 [f]	18,782	37,619	-2
11	Denmark	9	0.928	78.9	74.0	.. [d]	.. [d]	102 [e,f]	95 [f]	24,086	34,011	2
12	Ireland	16	0.923	79.4	74.1	.. [d]	.. [d]	93 [i]	89 [i]	18,701 [g]	46,280 [g]	-4
13	United Kingdom	11	0.928	80.4	75.4	.. [d]	.. [d]	119 [e,f]	105 [e,f]	18,180	30,476	2
14	Finland	10	0.928	81.3	74.1	.. [d]	.. [d]	108 [e,i]	99 [i]	20,234	28,831	4
15	Luxembourg	18	0.920	81.2	74.8	.. [d]	.. [d]	74 [f,h,j]	72 [f,h,j]	29,569	78,723 [k]	-3
16	Austria	14	0.924	81.3	75.1	.. [d]	.. [d]	93 [f]	91 [f]	17,940 [g]	35,923 [g]	2
17	France	17	0.923	82.6	74.9	.. [d]	.. [d]	93 [f]	90 [f]	18,607	29,657	0
18	Germany	15	0.924	81.0	74.9	.. [d]	.. [d]	93 [i]	95 [i]	18,474	32,557	3
19	Spain	20	0.912	82.6	75.6	96.9 [d]	98.6 [d]	95 [f]	90 [f]	12,331 [g]	28,275 [g]	-1
20	New Zealand	19	0.914	80.6	75.6	.. [d]	.. [d]	104 [e,f]	94 [f]	15,524	22,900	1
21	Italy	21	0.910	81.8	75.4	98.1 [d]	98.9 [d]	84 [f]	81 [f]	15,452 [g]	34,460 [g]	0
22	Israel	22	0.900	80.8	76.9	93.1	97.1	92	88	13,726 [g]	26,011 [g]	0
23	Portugal	23	0.892	79.4	72.3	90.3 [d]	95.0 [d]	97 [f]	90 [f]	12,782	23,940	0
24	Greece	24	0.886	80.8	75.6	96.1 [d]	98.5 [d]	81 [i]	80 [i]	10,833 [g]	24,235 [g]	0
25	Cyprus	25	0.886	80.4	75.8	95.7	98.8	75 [h]	74 [h]	13,513	28,899	0
26	Hong Kong, China (SAR)	26	0.886	82.6	77.1	89.6	96.9	66 [i]	61 [i]	18,028	31,883	0
27	Barbados	27	0.885	79.3	74.3	99.7 [d]	99.7 [d]	94	84	11,852 [g]	19,496 [g]	0
28	Singapore	28	0.880	80.0	75.7	88.7	96.4	75 [i]	76 [i]	14,992	30,262	0
29	Slovenia	29	0.879	79.5	72.2	99.6 [d]	99.7 [d]	85 [i]	80 [i]	13,152 [g]	21,338 [g]	0
30	Korea, Rep. of	30	0.873	79.0	71.4	96.6 [d]	99.2 [d]	84 [f]	97 [f]	9,529	20,578	0
31	Brunei Darussalam	31	0.867	78.7	74.0	88.1	94.6	84	81	11,716 [g,l]	26,122 [g,l]	0
32	Czech Republic	32	0.857	78.4	71.7	.. [d]	.. [d]	77 [f]	76 [f]	10,555	19,113	0
33	Malta	33	0.844	80.4	75.6	93.0	91.5	76 [h]	75 [h]	6,787	19,647	0
34	Argentina	34	0.839	77.4	70.3	96.9	96.9	94 [f,h]	85 [f,h]	6,064 [g]	16,786 [g]	0
35	Poland	35	0.839	77.8	69.4	99.7 [d]	99.8 [d]	91 [f]	86 [f]	7,253 [g]	11,777 [g]	0
36	Seychelles	..	..	..	..	..	..	..	..	..	..	..
37	Bahrain	40	0.829	75.7	72.1	83.2	91.1	84 [m]	78 [m]	7,578	22,305	-4
38	Hungary	36	0.834	75.7	67.3	99.2 [d]	99.5 [d]	83 [f,h]	80 [f,h]	9,183	15,803	1
39	Slovakia	37	0.834	77.2	69.3	.. [d]	.. [d]	74 [f]	72 [f]	9,468 [g]	14,595 [g]	1
40	Uruguay	39	0.830	78.6	71.3	98.1	97.2	89 [f]	79 [f]	5,774 [g]	11,190 [g]	0
41	Estonia	38	0.831	76.5	65.9	99.8 [d]	99.8 [d]	93	85	7,993 [g]	12,720 [g]	2
42	Costa Rica	41	0.824	80.3	75.6	95.8	95.6	66	65	5,189	13,589	0
43	Chile	43	0.821	78.8	72.8	95.7	96.1	71 [f]	81 [f]	5,055 [g]	13,409 [g]	-1
44	Qatar	..	..	75.0	70.1	83.7	80.8	85	78	..	..	..
45	Lithuania	42	0.823	77.3	67.1	99.5 [d]	99.7 [d]	88	83	6,843	10,326	1
46	Kuwait	45	0.813	78.8	74.7	80.3	84.3	57 [m]	52 [m]	8,605 [g]	25,333 [g]	-1
47	Croatia	44	0.814	77.9	70.0	97.4	99.4 [d]	69 [i]	68 [i]	6,612 [g]	11,929 [g]	1
48	United Arab Emirates	49	0.802	77.1	73.0	79.8	75.2	74 [f]	64 [f]	6,041 [g,l]	28,223 [g,l]	-3
49	Bahamas	46	0.811	70.6	63.8	96.3	94.6	77 [i]	72 [i]	12,783 [g,n]	19,857 [g,n]	1
50	Latvia	47	0.810	75.8	65.0	99.8 [d]	99.8 [d]	91	82	6,470	9,215	1

HDI rank		Gender-related development index (GDI)		Life expectancy at birth (years) 2001		Adult literacy rate (% age 15 and above) 2001		Combined primary, secondary and tertiary gross enrolment ratio (%) 2000-01 [a]		Estimated earned income (PPP US$) 2001 [b]		HDI rank minus GDI rank [c]
		Rank	Value	Female	Male	Female	Male	Female	Male	Female	Male	
51	Saint Kitts and Nevis	..	..	..	..	..	..	..	..	..	..	..
52	Cuba	..	..	78.5	74.6	96.7	96.9	77	75	..	..	..
53	Belarus	48	0.803	75.0	64.3	99.6 [d]	99.8 [d]	87	84	6,084 [g]	9,358 [g]	1
54	Trinidad and Tobago	50	0.796	74.6	68.6	97.8	99.0	68	65	5,645 [g]	12,614 [g]	0
55	Mexico	52	0.790	76.1	70.1	89.5	93.5	74 [f]	74 [f]	4,637	12,358	-1
Medium human development												
56	Antigua and Barbuda	..	..	..	..	..	..	..	..	..	..	..
57	Bulgaria	51	0.794	74.6	67.4	98.0	99.0 [d]	79	76	5,484	8,378	1
58	Malaysia	53	0.784	75.3	70.4	84.0	91.7	74 [f]	71 [f]	5,557 [g]	11,845 [g]	0
59	Panama	54	0.781	77.1	72.0	91.4	92.7	78 [h]	73 [h]	3,399 [g]	8,056 [g]	0
60	Macedonia, TFYR	..	..	75.5	71.2	..	..	70	70	..	..	..
61	Libyan Arab Jamahiriya	..	..	75.0	70.4	69.3	91.3	91 [f]	87 [f]	..	..	..
62	Mauritius	59	0.770	75.5	68.0	81.7	88.0	68	70	5,273 [g]	14,497 [g]	-4
63	Russian Federation	56	0.774	72.9	60.6	99.4 [d]	99.7 [d]	82 [i]	75 [i]	5,609 [g]	8,795 [g]	0
64	Colombia	55	0.774	75.0	68.6	91.9	91.9	72	69	4,534 [g]	9,608 [g]	2
65	Brazil	58	0.770	72.3	63.7	87.2	87.4	97 [f]	93 [f]	4,391	10,410	0
66	Bosnia and Herzegovina	..	..	76.5	71.1	..	..	..	..	..	..	..
67	Belize	64	0.756	73.4	70.2	93.3	93.6	76 [f]	75 [f]	2,188 [g]	9,100 [g]	-5
68	Dominica	..	..	..	..	..	..	..	..	..	..	..
69	Venezuela	60	0.767	76.4	70.6	92.4	93.3	70	65	3,288 [g]	8,021 [g]	0
70	Samoa (Western)	..	..	73.0	66.5	98.4	98.9	72	70	..	..	..
71	Saint Lucia	..	..	73.8	70.5	..	..	81 [m]	83 [m]	..	..	..
72	Romania	57	0.771	74.2	67.0	97.4	99.1 [d]	70	67	4,313 [g]	7,416 [g]	4
73	Saudi Arabia	68	0.743	73.3	70.7	68.2	83.5	57 [h]	60 [h]	4,222 [g]	21,141 [g]	-6
74	Thailand	61	0.766	73.2	64.9	94.1	97.3	69 [f]	75 [f]	4,875	7,975	2
75	Ukraine	63	0.761	74.4	64.1	99.5 [d]	99.8 [d]	79 [m]	83 [m]	3,071	5,826	1
76	Kazakhstan	62	0.763	71.5	60.3	99.2 [d]	99.7 [d]	78	77	5,039	8,077	3
77	Suriname	..	..	73.4	68.2	..	..	79 [f]	75 [f]	..	..	..
78	Jamaica	65	0.750	77.5	73.5	91.0	83.4	71 [f, h]	67 [f, h]	2,969 [g]	4,492 [g]	1
79	Oman	71	0.736	74.1	70.8	63.5	80.9	56 [m]	59 [m]	3,919 [g, n]	17,960 [g, n]	-4
80	St. Vincent & the Grenadines	..	..	75.3	72.4	..	..	..	..	..	..	..
81	Fiji	67	0.743	71.1	67.7	91.2	95.2	75 [f, m]	77 [f, m]	2,507 [g]	7,113 [g]	1
82	Peru	72	0.734	72.0	66.9	85.7	94.8	78 [f, m]	89 [f, m]	1,903	7,206	-3
83	Lebanon	70	0.737	74.8	71.7	81.0	92.4	77	75	1,963 [g]	6,472 [g]	0
84	Paraguay	69	0.739	72.8	68.3	92.5	94.5	64 [i]	64 [i]	2,548	7,832	2
85	Philippines	66	0.748	71.6	67.6	95.0	95.3	81 [f]	79 [f]	2,838	4,829	6
86	Maldives	..	..	66.3	67.4	96.9	97.1	79	78	..	..	..
87	Turkmenistan	..	..	70.0	63.3	..	..	81 [i]	81 [i]	..	..	..
88	Georgia	..	..	77.4	69.2	..	..	70	69	1,507	3,712	..
89	Azerbaijan	..	..	75.2	68.3	..	..	69 [h]	69 [h]	..	..	..
90	Jordan	75	0.729	72.1	69.3	85.1	95.2	78 [f, h]	76 [f, h]	1,771	5,800	-2
91	Tunisia	76	0.727	74.5	70.5	61.9	82.3	76 [f]	76 [f]	3,377 [g]	9,359 [g]	-2
92	Guyana	74	0.730	66.5	60.1	98.2	99.0	84 [f, h]	85 [f, h]	2,658 [g]	6,844 [g]	1
93	Grenada	..	..	..	..	..	..	..	..	..	..	..
94	Dominican Republic	77	0.727	69.3	64.4	84.0	84.0	77 [f]	71 [f]	3,663 [g]	10,278 [g]	-1
95	Albania	73	0.732	76.5	70.6	77.8	92.5	70	67	2,608 [g]	4,705 [g]	4
96	Turkey	81	0.726	72.8	67.6	77.2	93.7	54 [f, h]	65 [f, h]	3,717 [g]	8,028 [g]	-3
97	Ecuador	84	0.716	73.2	68.0	90.3	93.4	71 [f]	73 [f]	1,504 [g]	5,040 [g]	-5
98	Occupied Palestinian Territories	..	..	73.7	70.5	..	..	78 [h]	76 [h]	..	..	..
99	Sri Lanka	80	0.726	75.5	69.6	89.3	94.5	64 [f, m]	63 [f, m]	2,095	4,189	0
100	Armenia	78	0.727	75.3	68.7	97.8	99.3 [d]	63	57	2,175 [g]	3,152 [g]	3

HDI rank	Gender-related development index (GDI)		Life expectancy at birth (years) 2001		Adult literacy rate (% age 15 and above) 2001		Combined primary, secondary and tertiary gross enrolment ratio (%) 2000-01 [a]		Estimated earned income (PPP US$) 2001 [b]		HDI rank minus GDI rank [c]
	Rank	Value	Female	Male	Female	Male	Female	Male	Female	Male	
101 Uzbekistan	79	0.727	72.1	66.4	98.9	99.6 [d]	74 [i]	79 [i]	1,951 [g]	2,976 [g]	3
102 Kyrgyzstan	..	..	71.9	64.2	..	..	80	79	..	..	..
103 Cape Verde	82	0.719	72.4	66.6	67.0	84.9	79 [f]	80 [f]	3,557 [g]	7,781 [g]	1
104 China	83	0.718	72.9	68.6	78.7	92.5	62 [f, h]	65 [f, h]	3,169 [g]	4,825 [g]	1
105 El Salvador	85	0.707	73.3	67.3	76.6	81.9	63 [m]	63 [m]	2,771	7,846	0
106 Iran, Islamic Rep. of	86	0.702	71.3	68.5	70.2	83.8	63	66	2,599 [g]	9,301 [g]	0
107 Algeria	88	0.687	70.7	67.7	58.3	77.1	69 [f]	73 [f]	2,784 [g]	9,329 [g]	-1
108 Moldova, Rep. of	87	0.697	71.8	64.9	98.4	99.6 [d]	63	60	1,714 [g]	2,626 [g]	1
109 Viet Nam	89	0.687	71.0	66.3	90.9	94.5	61	67	1,696 [g]	2,447 [g]	0
110 Syrian Arab Republic	93	0.668	72.7	70.2	61.6	88.8	61 [i]	65 [i]	1,423 [g]	5,109 [g]	-3
111 South Africa	90	0.678	54.4	47.7	85.0	86.3	78	78	7,047 [g]	15,712 [g]	1
112 Indonesia	91	0.677	68.2	64.3	82.6	92.1	63 [f]	65 [f]	1,987 [g]	3,893 [g]	1
113 Tajikistan	92	0.673	71.0	65.6	98.9	99.6 [d]	65	78	891 [g]	1,451 [g]	1
114 Bolivia	94	0.663	65.4	61.3	79.9	92.3	80 [f]	88 [f]	1,427 [g]	3,181 [g]	0
115 Honduras	96	0.656	71.3	66.4	75.7	75.4	61 [f]	64 [f]	1,509 [g]	4,131 [g]	-1
116 Equatorial Guinea	..	..	50.4	47.6	76.0	92.8	49 [h]	68 [h]	..	..	..
117 Mongolia	95	0.659	65.3	61.3	98.3	98.6	69	58	1,398 [g]	2,082 [g]	1
118 Gabon	..	..	57.7	55.6	..	..	81 [f]	85 [f]	..	..	..
119 Guatemala	97	0.638	68.4	62.5	61.8	76.6	54 [f]	61 [f]	2,144 [g]	6,620 [g]	0
120 Egypt	99	0.634	70.4	66.3	44.8	67.2	72 [i]	80 [i]	1,970	5,075	-1
121 Nicaragua	98	0.636	71.5	66.8	67.1	66.5	66 [f, h]	63 [f, h]	1,494 [g, l]	3,415 [g, l]	1
122 São Tomé and Principe	..	..	72.4	66.6			..	..	..	..	..
123 Solomon Islands	..	..	70.1	67.5	..	..	..	..	..	..	..
124 Namibia	100	0.622	49.2	45.5	81.9	83.4	75 [h]	72 [h]	4,833 [g]	9,511 [g]	0
125 Botswana	101	0.611	46.0	43.3	80.6	75.3	81	79	5,888 [g]	9,826 [g]	0
126 Morocco	102	0.590	69.9	66.2	37.2	62.6	46 [h]	56 [h]	2,057 [g]	5,139 [g]	0
127 India	103	0.574	64.0	62.8	46.4	69.0	49 [f, h]	63 [f, h]	1,531 [g]	4,070 [g]	0
128 Vanuatu	..	..	70.1	67.1	..	..	54 [m]	54 [m]	..	..	..
129 Ghana	104	0.564	59.3	56.2	64.5	81.1	42	49	1,924 [g]	2,579 [g]	0
130 Cambodia	105	0.551	59.4	55.2	58.2	80.5	49	60	1,621 [g]	2,113 [g]	0
131 Myanmar	..	..	59.8	54.4	81.0	89.1	48	47	..	..	..
132 Papua New Guinea	106	0.544	58.1	56.2	57.7	71.1	39 [m]	43 [m]	1,865 [g]	3,231 [g]	0
133 Swaziland	107	0.536	39.9	36.5	79.4	81.3	75 [h]	78 [h]	2,395 [g]	6,453 [g]	0
134 Comoros	108	0.521	61.6	58.8	48.8	63.3	36 [h]	44 [h]	1,340 [g]	2,395 [g]	0
135 Lao People's Dem. Rep.	109	0.518	55.2	52.7	54.4	76.8	51	63	1,278 [g]	1,962 [g]	0
136 Bhutan	..	..	63.8	61.3	..	..	..	..	..	..	..
137 Lesotho	110	0.497	41.7	35.4	93.9	73.3	65	61	1,375 [g]	3,620 [g]	0
138 Sudan	116	0.483	56.9	54.0	47.7	70.0	32 [m]	36 [m]	935 [g]	2,992 [g]	-5
139 Bangladesh	112	0.495	60.9	60.1	30.8	49.9	54	54	1,153 [g]	2,044 [g]	0
140 Congo	111	0.496	50.3	46.7	75.9	88.2	53 [f]	61 [f]	695 [g]	1,253 [g]	2
141 Togo	118	0.483	52.0	48.6	44.0	73.4	53 [m]	80 [m]	1,058 [g]	2,254 [g]	-4
Low human development											
142 Cameroon	114	0.488	49.4	46.6	65.1	79.9	43 [f, h]	52 [f, h]	1,032 [g]	2,338 [g]	1
143 Nepal	119	0.479	58.9	59.4	25.2	60.5	57	70	867 [g]	1,734 [g]	-3
144 Pakistan	120	0.469	60.3	60.6	28.8	58.2	27 [f]	45 [f]	909 [g]	2,824 [g]	-3
145 Zimbabwe	113	0.489	35.4	35.5	85.5	93.3	58 [f, h]	62 [f, h]	1,667 [g]	2,905 [g]	5
146 Kenya	115	0.488	47.9	44.9	77.3	89.5	52	53	930	1,031	4
147 Uganda	117	0.483	45.4	43.9	58.0	78.1	66	75	1,185 [g]	1,799 [g]	3
148 Yemen	127	0.424	60.5	58.3	26.9	68.5	34 [m]	70 [m]	365 [g]	1,201 [g]	-6
149 Madagascar	121	0.467	54.2	51.9	60.6	74.2	43 [f]	45 [f]	616 [g]	1,046 [g]	1
150 Haiti	122	0.462	49.8	48.5	48.9	52.9	51 [i]	53 [i]	1,339 [g]	2,396 [g]	1
151 Gambia	123	0.457	55.2	52.2	30.9	45.0	43 [f]	51 [f]	1,530 [g]	2,581 [g]	1

HDI rank		Gender-related development index (GDI)		Life expectancy at birth (years) 2001		Adult literacy rate (% age 15 and above) 2001		Combined primary, secondary and tertiary gross enrolment ratio (%) 2000-01 [a]		Estimated earned income (PPP US$) 2001 [b]		HDI rank minus GDI rank [c]
		Rank	Value	Female	Male	Female	Male	Female	Male	Female	Male	
152	Nigeria	124	0.450	52.3	51.3	57.7	73.3	41 [i]	49 [i]	505 [g]	1,191 [g]	1
153	Djibouti	..	..	47.3	44.9	55.5	76.1	19 [h]	23 [h]	..	..	..
154	Mauritania	125	0.445	53.5	50.3	30.7	51.1	40	45	1,429 [g]	2,566 [g]	1
155	Eritrea	126	0.434	54.1	50.9	45.6	68.2	29	38	703	1,361	1
156	Senegal	128	0.420	54.5	50.2	28.7	48.1	34 [f]	41 [f]	1,065 [g]	1,941 [g]	0
157	Guinea	..	..	48.9	48.1	..	..	26 [f]	41 [f]	..	..	..
158	Rwanda	129	0.416	38.7	37.6	61.9	74.5	51 [f]	52 [f]	965 [g]	1,567 [g]	0
159	Benin	131	0.395	53.2	48.6	24.6	53.5	38 [f]	60 [f]	803 [g]	1,163 [g]	-1
160	Tanzania, U. Rep. of	130	0.396	45.0	43.0	67.9	84.5	31	31	432 [g]	610 [g]	1
161	Côte d'Ivoire	134	0.376	42.1	41.2	38.4	60.3	31 [m]	46 [m]	792 [g]	2,160 [g]	-2
162	Malawi	132	0.378	39.1	37.9	47.6	75.0	70 [f]	74 [f]	464 [g]	679 [g]	1
163	Zambia	133	0.376	33.4	33.3	72.7	85.8	43	47	554 [g]	1,009 [g]	1
164	Angola	..	..	41.6	38.8	..	..	26 [h]	31 [h]	..	..	..
165	Chad	135	0.366	45.7	43.5	35.8	53.0	24 [h]	43 [h]	796 [g]	1,350 [g]	0
166	Guinea-Bissau	137	0.353	46.7	43.5	24.7	55.2	34 [h]	52 [h]	636 [g]	1,313 [g]	-1
167	Congo, Dem. Rep. of the	136	0.353	41.7	39.6	51.8	74.2	24 [f,m]	30 [f,m]	486 [g]	879 [g]	1
168	Central African Republic	138	0.352	41.8	39.1	36.6	60.8	20 [i]	29 [i]	987 [g]	1,632 [g]	0
169	Ethiopia	139	0.347	46.7	44.6	32.4	48.1	27	41	550 [g]	1,074 [g]	0
170	Mozambique	140	0.341	40.9	37.4	30.0	61.2	32	42	916 [g]	1,382 [g]	0
171	Burundi	141	0.331	41.0	39.9	42.0	56.9	28	35	573 [g]	814 [g]	0
172	Mali	142	0.327	48.9	47.8	16.6	36.7	26 [f]	38 [f]	615 [g]	1,009 [g]	0
173	Burkina Faso	143	0.317	46.4	45.0	14.9	34.9	18 [f]	27 [f]	927 [g]	1,323 [g]	0
174	Niger	144	0.279	45.9	45.3	8.9	24.4	14	21	646 [g]	1,129 [g]	0
175	Sierra Leone	..	..	35.8	33.2	..	..	44	57	..	..	..

a. Data refer to the 2000/01 school year. Data for some countries may refer to national or UNESCO Institute for Statistics estimates. For details, see http://www.uis.unesco.org/. Because data are from different sources, comparisons across countries should be made with caution. b. Because of the lack of gender-disaggregated income data, female and male earned income are crudely estimated on the basis of data on the ratio of the female non-agricultural wage to the male non-agricultural wage, the female and male shares of the economically active population, the total female and male population and GDP per capita (PPP US$) (see technical note 1). Unless otherwise specified, estimates are based on data for the most recent year available during 1991-2000. c. The HDI ranks used in this column are those recalculated for the 144 countries with a GDI value. A positive figure indicates that the GDI rank is higher than the HDI rank, a negative the opposite. d. For purposes of calculating the GDI, a value of 99% was applied. e. For purposes of calculating the GDI, a value of 100% was applied. f. Preliminary UNESCO Institute for Statistics estimate, subject to further revision. g. No wage data available. For purposes of calculating the estimated female and male earned income, an estimate of 75% was used for the ratio of the female non-agricultural wage to the male non-agricultural wage. h. Data refer to the 1999/2000 school year. i. Data refer to the 1999/2000 school year. They were provided by the UNESCO Institute for Statistics for *Human Development Report 2001* (see UNESCO Institute for Statistics 2001). j. The ratio is an underestimate, as many secondary and tertiary students pursue their studies in nearby countries. k. For purposes of calculating the GDI, a value of $40,000 (PPP US$) was applied. l. Calculated on the basis of GDP per capita (PPP US$) for 1998. m. Data refer to the 1998/99 school year. n. Calculated on the basis of GDP per capita (PPP US$) for 2000.

Source: Column 1: determined on the basis of the GDI values in column 2; *column 2:* calculated on the basis of data in columns 3-10; see technical note 1 for details; *columns 3 and 4:* UN 2003d; *columns 5 and 6:* UNESCO Institute for Statistics 2003a; *columns 7 and 8:* UNESCO Institute for Statistics 2003b; *columns 9 and 10:* unless otherwise noted, calculated on the basis of data on GDP per capita (PPP US$) from World Bank 2003c, data on wages from ILO 2003b, data on the economically active population from ILO 2002a and data on population from UN 2003d; *column 11:* determined on the basis of the recalculated HDI ranks and the GDI ranks in column 1.

GDI ranks for 144 countries										
		23	Portugal	48	Belarus	73	Albania	98	Nicaragua	123 Gambia
		24	Greece	49	United Arab Emirates	74	Guyana	99	Egypt	124 Nigeria
		25	Cyprus	50	Trinidad and Tobago	75	Jordan	100	Namibia	125 Mauritania
1	Norway	26	Hong Kong, China (SAR)	51	Bulgaria	76	Tunisia	101	Botswana	126 Eritrea
2	Iceland	27	Barbados	52	Mexico	77	Dominican Republic	102	Morocco	127 Yemen
3	Sweden	28	Singapore	53	Malaysia	78	Armenia	103	India	128 Senegal
4	Australia	29	Slovenia	54	Panama	79	Uzbekistan	104	Ghana	129 Rwanda
5	United States	30	Korea, Rep. of	55	Colombia	80	Sri Lanka	105	Cambodia	130 Tanzania, U. Rep. of
6	Canada	31	Brunei Darussalam	56	Russian Federation	81	Turkey	106	Papua New Guinea	131 Benin
7	Netherlands	32	Czech Republic	57	Romania	82	Cape Verde	107	Swaziland	132 Malawi
8	Belgium	33	Malta	58	Brazil	83	China	108	Comoros	133 Zambia
9	Denmark	34	Argentina	59	Mauritius	84	Ecuador	109	Lao People's Dem. Rep.	134 Côte d'Ivoire
10	Finland	35	Poland	60	Venezuela	85	El Salvador	110	Lesotho	135 Chad
11	United Kingdom	36	Hungary	61	Iran, Islamic Rep. of	86	Iran, Islamic Rep. of	111	Congo	136 Congo, Dem. Rep. of the
12	Switzerland	37	Slovakia	62	Kazakhstan	87	Moldova, Rep. of	112	Bangladesh	137 Guinea-Bissau
13	Japan	38	Estonia	63	Ukraine	88	Algeria	113	Zimbabwe	138 Central African Republic
14	Austria	39	Uruguay	64	Belize	89	Viet Nam	114	Cameroon	139 Ethiopia
15	Germany	40	Bahrain	65	Jamaica	90	South Africa	115	Kenya	140 Mozambique
16	Ireland	41	Costa Rica	66	Philippines	91	Indonesia	116	Sudan	141 Burundi
17	France	42	Lithuania	67	Fiji	92	Tajikistan	117	Uganda	142 Mali
18	Luxembourg	43	Chile	68	Saudi Arabia	93	Syrian Arab Republic	118	Togo	143 Burkina Faso
19	New Zealand	44	Croatia	69	Paraguay	94	Bolivia	119	Nepal	144 Niger
20	Spain	45	Kuwait	70	Lebanon	95	Mongolia	120	Pakistan	
21	Italy	46	Bahamas	71	Oman	96	Honduras	121	Madagascar	
22	Israel	47	Latvia	72	Peru	97	Guatemala	122	Haiti	

23 Gender empowerment measure

HDI rank	Gender empowerment measure (GEM)		Seats in parliament held by women (as % of total) [a]	Female legislators, senior officials and managers (as % of total) [b]	Female professional and technical workers (as % of total) [b]	Ratio of estimated female to male earned income [c]
	Rank	Value				
High human development						
1 Norway	2	0.837	36.4	26	48	0.65
2 Iceland	1	0.847	34.9	31	55	0.63
3 Sweden	3	0.831	45.3	30	49	0.68
4 Australia	11	0.754	26.5	25	45	0.70
5 Netherlands	6	0.794	33.3	26	48	0.53
6 Belgium	15	0.695	24.9	19 [d]	50 [d]	0.44
7 United States	10	0.760	14.0	46 [d]	54 [d]	0.62
8 Canada	9	0.771	23.6	35	53	0.63
9 Japan	44	0.515	10.0	9 [d]	45 [d]	0.45
10 Switzerland	13	0.720	22.4	24	43	0.50
11 Denmark	4	0.825	38.0	21	51	0.71
12 Ireland	16	0.683	14.2	28	49	0.40
13 United Kingdom	17	0.675	17.1	30	43	0.60
14 Finland	5	0.801	36.5	28	57	0.70
15 Luxembourg	..	..	16.7	..	..	..
16 Austria	7	0.782	30.6	29	48	0.50
17 France	..	..	11.7	..	..	..
18 Germany	8	0.776	31.4	27	50	0.57
19 Spain	14	0.709	26.6	32	45	0.44
20 New Zealand	12	0.750	29.2	38	53	0.68
21 Italy	32	0.561	10.3	19	44	0.45
22 Israel	23	0.612	15.0	27	54	0.53
23 Portugal	21	0.647	19.1	32	50	0.53
24 Greece	40	0.519	8.7	25	47	0.45
25 Cyprus	34	0.542	10.7	18	43	0.47
26 Hong Kong, China (SAR)	..	..	..	25	38	..
27 Barbados	20	0.659	20.4	40 [d]	55 [d]	0.61
28 Singapore	26	0.594	11.8	24	43	0.50
29 Slovenia	27	0.582	12.2	31	54	0.62
30 Korea, Rep. of	63	0.363	5.9	5	34	0.46
31 Brunei Darussalam	..	..	– [e]	..	..	..
32 Czech Republic	28	0.579	15.7	26	53	0.55
33 Malta	..	..	9.2	..	..	..
34 Argentina	..	..	31.3	..	..	..
35 Poland	25	0.594	20.7	32	60	0.62
36 Seychelles	..	..	29.4	..	..	..
37 Bahrain	..	..	6.3	..	..	..
38 Hungary	41	0.518	9.8	34	61	0.58
39 Slovakia	24	0.598	19.3	31	61	0.65
40 Uruguay	43	0.516	11.5	37	52	0.52
41 Estonia	33	0.560	17.8	35	70	0.63
42 Costa Rica	19	0.670	35.1	53	28	0.38
43 Chile	52	0.467	10.1	24 [d]	50 [d]	0.38
44 Qatar	..	..	– [e]	..	..	..
45 Lithuania	48	0.499	10.6	47	69	0.66
46 Kuwait	..	..	0.0	..	..	..
47 Croatia	36	0.534	16.2	25	50	0.55
48 United Arab Emirates	65	0.315	0.0	8	25	0.21
49 Bahamas	18	0.671	23.2 [f]	31	56	0.64
50 Latvia	30	0.576	21.0	38	68	0.70

HDI rank	Gender empowerment measure (GEM)		Seats in parliament held by women (as % of total) [a]	Female legislators, senior officials and managers (as % of total) [b]	Female professional and technical workers (as % of total) [b]	Ratio of estimated female to male earned income [c]
	Rank	Value				
51 Saint Kitts and Nevis	..	..	13.3	..	..	..
52 Cuba	..	..	36.0	..	..	..
53 Belarus	..	..	18.4	..	..	..
54 Trinidad and Tobago	22	0.642	25.4	40	51	0.45
55 Mexico	42	0.516	15.9	25	40	0.38
Medium human development						
56 Antigua and Barbuda	..	..	8.3	..	..	..
57 Bulgaria	..	..	26.3	..	..	..
58 Malaysia	45	0.503	14.5	20 [d]	45 [d]	0.47
59 Panama	50	0.471	9.9	33 [d]	46 [d]	0.42
60 Macedonia, TFYR	..	..	18.3	..	..	..
61 Libyan Arab Jamahiriya	..	..	..	..	..	..
62 Mauritius	..	..	5.7	..	..	..
63 Russian Federation	57	0.440	6.4	37	64	0.64
64 Colombia	46	0.501	10.8	38 [d]	49 [d]	0.47
65 Brazil	..	..	9.1	..	62 [d]	..
66 Bosnia and Herzegovina	..	..	12.3	..	..	..
67 Belize	47	0.501	13.5 [f]	33	53	0.24
68 Dominica	..	..	18.8	..	..	..
69 Venezuela	56	0.441	9.7	24 [d]	58 [d]	0.41
70 Samoa (Western)	..	..	6.1	..	..	..
71 Saint Lucia	..	..	20.7	..	..	..
72 Romania	53	0.460	9.9	29	57	0.58
73 Saudi Arabia	..	..	– [e]	..	..	..
74 Thailand	55	0.457	9.6	27 [d]	55 [d]	0.61
75 Ukraine	61	0.406	5.3	37	63	0.53
76 Kazakhstan	..	..	8.6	..	..	..
77 Suriname	..	..	17.6	28 [d]	51 [d]	..
78 Jamaica	..	..	13.6	..	..	..
79 Oman	..	..	– [e]	..	..	..
80 St. Vincent & the Grenadines	..	..	22.7	..	..	..
81 Fiji	..	..	5.7 [f]	..	..	..
82 Peru	39	0.521	18.3	27	44	0.26
83 Lebanon	..	..	2.3	..	..	..
84 Paraguay	59	0.412	8.0	23 [d]	54 [d]	0.33
85 Philippines	35	0.539	17.2	58	62	0.59
86 Maldives	..	..	6.0	15	40	..
87 Turkmenistan	..	..	26.0	..	..	..
88 Georgia	62	0.381	7.2	23	60	0.41
89 Azerbaijan	..	..	10.5	..	..	..
90 Jordan	..	..	3.3	..	..	..
91 Tunisia	..	..	11.5	..	..	..
92 Guyana	..	..	20.0	..	..	..
93 Grenada	..	..	17.9	..	..	..
94 Dominican Republic	37	0.529	15.4	31	49	0.36
95 Albania	..	..	5.7	..	..	..
96 Turkey	66	0.290	4.4	8	31	0.46
97 Ecuador	49	0.489	16.0	25	44	0.30
98 Occupied Palestinian Territories	..	..	..	11	32	..
99 Sri Lanka	67	0.272	4.4	4	49	0.50
100 Armenia	..	..	3.1	..	..	..

HDI rank	Gender empowerment measure (GEM)		Seats in parliament held by women (as % of total) [a]	Female legislators, senior officials and managers (as % of total) [b]	Female professional and technical workers (as % of total) [b]	Ratio of estimated female to male earned income [c]
	Rank	Value				
101 Uzbekistan	..	..	7.2	..	..	..
102 Kyrgyzstan	..	..	6.7	..	..	..
103 Cape Verde	..	..	11.1	..	..	..
104 China	..	..	21.8	..	..	..
105 El Salvador	54	0.459	9.5	33	47	0.35
106 Iran, Islamic Rep. of	..	..	4.1	..	..	..
107 Algeria	..	..	6.0	..	..	..
108 Moldova, Rep. of	51	0.468	12.9	37	66	0.65
109 Viet Nam	..	..	27.3	..	..	..
110 Syrian Arab Republic	..	..	10.4	..	..	..
111 South Africa	..	..	30.0 [g]	..	..	..
112 Indonesia	..	..	8.0	..	..	..
113 Tajikistan	..	..	12.4	..	..	..
114 Bolivia	38	0.522	17.8	36	40	0.45
115 Honduras	60	0.408	5.5	36 [d]	51 [d]	0.37
116 Equatorial Guinea	..	..	5.0	..	..	..
117 Mongolia	..	..	10.5	..	..	..
118 Gabon	..	..	11.0 [f]	..	..	..
119 Guatemala	..	..	8.8	..	..	..
120 Egypt	68	0.253	2.4	10	29	0.39
121 Nicaragua	..	..	20.7	..	..	..
122 São Tomé and Principe	..	..	9.1	..	..	..
123 Solomon Islands	..	..	0.0	..	..	..
124 Namibia	29	0.578	21.4	30	55	0.51
125 Botswana	31	0.564	17.0	35	52	0.60
126 Morocco	..	..	6.1	..	..	..
127 India	..	..	9.3	..	..	..
128 Vanuatu	..	..	1.9	..	..	..
129 Ghana	..	..	9.0	..	..	..
130 Cambodia	64	0.347	9.3	14	33	0.77
131 Myanmar	..	..	— [h]	..	..	..
132 Papua New Guinea	..	..	0.9	..	..	..
133 Swaziland	..	..	6.3	..	..	..
134 Comoros	..	..	— [i]	..	..	..
135 Lao People's Dem. Rep.	..	..	22.9	..	..	..
136 Bhutan	..	..	9.3	..	..	..
137 Lesotho	..	..	17.0	..	..	..
138 Sudan	..	..	9.7	..	..	..
139 Bangladesh	69	0.218	2.0	8 [d]	25 [d]	0.56
140 Congo	..	..	11.1	..	..	..
141 Togo	..	..	7.4	..	..	..
Low human development						
142 Cameroon	..	..	8.9	..	..	..
143 Nepal	..	..	7.9 [f]	..	..	..
144 Pakistan	58	0.414	20.6	9 [d]	26 [d]	0.32
145 Zimbabwe	..	..	10.0	..	..	..
146 Kenya	..	..	7.1	..	..	..
147 Uganda	..	..	24.7	..	..	..
148 Yemen	70	0.127	0.7	4	15	0.30
149 Madagascar	..	..	6.4	..	..	..
150 Haiti	..	..	9.1	..	..	..
151 Gambia	..	..	13.2	..	..	..

HDI rank	Gender empowerment measure (GEM)		Seats in parliament held by women (as % of total)[a]	Female legislators, senior officials and managers (as % of total)[b]	Female professional and technical workers (as % of total)[b]	Ratio of estimated female to male earned income[c]
	Rank	Value				
152 Nigeria	..	..	3.3	..	..	..
153 Djibouti	..	..	10.8	..	..	..
154 Mauritania	..	..	3.0 [f]	..	..	..
155 Eritrea	..	..	22.0	..	..	..
156 Senegal	..	..	19.2	..	..	..
157 Guinea	..	..	19.3	..	..	..
158 Rwanda	..	..	25.7	..	..	..
159 Benin	..	..	6.0	..	..	..
160 Tanzania, U. Rep. of	..	..	22.3	..	..	..
161 Côte d'Ivoire	..	..	8.5	..	..	..
162 Malawi	..	..	9.3	..	..	..
163 Zambia	..	..	12.0	..	..	..
164 Angola	..	..	15.5	..	..	..
165 Chad	..	..	5.8	..	..	..
166 Guinea-Bissau	..	..	7.8	..	..	..
167 Congo, Dem. Rep. of the	..	..	– [i]	..	..	..
168 Central African Republic	..	..	7.3	..	..	..
169 Ethiopia	..	..	7.8	..	..	..
170 Mozambique	..	..	30.0	..	..	..
171 Burundi	..	..	18.5	..	..	..
172 Mali	..	..	10.2	..	..	..
173 Burkina Faso	..	..	11.7	..	..	..
174 Niger	..	..	1.2	..	..	..
175 Sierra Leone	..	..	14.5	..	..	..

a. Data are as of 1 March 2003. Where there are lower and upper houses, data refer to the weighted average of women's shares of seats in both houses. b. Data refer to the most recent year available during 1992-2001. Estimates for countries that have implemented the recent International Standard Classification of Occupations (ISCO-88) are not strictly comparable with those for countries using the previous classification (ISCO-68). c. Calculated on the basis of data in columns 9 and 10 in table 22. Estimates are based on data for the most recent year available during 1991-2001. d. Data are based on the International Standard Classification of Occupations (ISCO-68) as defined in ILO 2002c. e. The country has never had a parliament. f. Information for the most recent elections was not available in time for publication; data are based on previous elections. g. Calculated on the basis of the 54 permanent seats (that is, excluding the 36 special rotating delegates appointed on an ad hoc basis). h. The parliament elected in 1990 has never been convened nor authorized to sit, and many of its members were detained or forced into exile. i. The parliament has been dissolved or suspended for an indefinite period.

Source: Column 1: determined on the basis of the GEM values in column 2; column 2: calculated on the basis of data in columns 3-6; see technical note 1 for details; column 3: calculated on the basis of data on parliamentary seats from IPU 2003b; columns 4 and 5: calculated on the basis of occupational data from ILO 2003b; column 6: calculated on the basis of data in columns 9 and 10 in table 22.

GEM ranks for 70 countries

1	Iceland	17	United Kingdom	36	Croatia	55	Thailand
2	Norway	18	Bahamas	37	Dominican Republic	56	Venezuela
3	Sweden	19	Costa Rica	38	Bolivia	57	Russian Federation
4	Denmark	20	Barbados	39	Peru	58	Pakistan
5	Finland	21	Portugal	40	Greece	59	Paraguay
6	Netherlands	22	Trinidad and Tobago	41	Hungary	60	Honduras
7	Austria	23	Israel	42	Uruguay	61	Ukraine
8	Germany	24	Slovakia	43	Mexico	62	Georgia
9	Canada	25	Poland	44	Japan	63	Korea, Rep. of
10	United States	26	Singapore	45	Malaysia	64	Cambodia
11	Australia	27	Slovenia	46	Colombia	65	United Arab Emirates
12	New Zealand	28	Czech Republic	47	Belize	66	Turkey
13	Switzerland	29	Namibia	48	Lithuania	67	Sri Lanka
14	Spain	30	Latvia	49	Ecuador	68	Egypt
15	Belgium	31	Botswana	50	Panama	69	Bangladesh
16	Ireland	32	Italy	51	Chile	70	Yemen
		33	Estonia	52	Moldova, Rep. of		
		34	Cyprus	53	Romania		
		35	Philippines	54	El Salvador		

24 Gender inequality in education

		Adult literacy		Youth literacy		Net primary enrolment [a, b]		Net secondary enrolment [a, b]		Gross tertiary enrolment [b, c]	
HDI rank		Female rate (% age 15 and above) 2001	Female rate as % of male rate 2001	Female rate (% age 15-24) 2001	Female rate as % of male rate 2001	Female ratio (%) 2000-01	Ratio of females to males [d] 2000-01	Female ratio (%) 2000-01	Ratio of females to males [d] 2000-01	Female ratio (%) 2000-01	Ratio of females to males [d] 2000-01
High human development											
1	Norway	..	..	..	..	102 [e]	1.00 [e]	95 [e]	1.01 [e]	85 [e]	1.52 [e]
2	Iceland	..	..	..	..	102 [e]	1.00 [e]	86 [e]	1.05 [e]	62 [e]	1.74 [e]
3	Sweden	..	..	..	..	102 [e]	0.99 [e]	98 [e, f]	1.04 [e, f]	85 [e]	1.52 [e]
4	Australia	..	..	..	..	96 [e]	1.01 [e]	91 [e]	1.03 [e]	70 [e]	1.24 [e]
5	Netherlands	..	..	..	..	99 [e]	0.99 [e]	90 [e]	1.00 [e]	57 [e]	1.07 [e]
6	Belgium	..	..	..	..	100 [e]	1.00 [e]	..	..	61 [e, f]	1.13 [e, f]
7	United States	..	..	..	..	96 [e]	1.01 [e]	89 [e]	1.02 [e]	83 [e]	1.32 [e]
8	Canada	..	..	..	..	99 [e, f]	1.00 [e, f]	98 [e, f]	1.01 [e, f]	69 [e, f]	1.33 [e, f]
9	Japan	..	..	..	..	101 [e]	1.00 [e]	101 [e, f]	1.01 [e, f]	44 [e]	0.85 [e]
10	Switzerland	..	..	..	..	99 [e]	0.99 [e]	85 [e]	0.95 [e]	37 [e]	0.78 [e]
11	Denmark	..	..	..	..	99 [e, f]	1.00 [e, f]	91 [e, f]	1.03 [e, f]	68 [e]	1.35 [e]
12	Ireland	..	..	..	..	90 [e, f]	1.00 [e, f]	..	..	53 [e]	1.27 [e]
13	United Kingdom	..	..	..	..	99 [e]	1.00 [e]	95 [e]	1.02 [e]	67 [e]	1.27 [e]
14	Finland	..	..	..	..	100 [e]	1.00 [e]	95 [e]	1.02 [e]	..	..
15	Luxembourg	..	..	..	..	97 [e]	1.01 [e]	81 [e]	1.08 [e]	10 [e, f, g]	1.24 [e, f, g]
16	Austria	..	..	..	..	92 [e]	1.01 [e]	88 [e]	0.99 [e]	62 [e]	1.14 [e]
17	France	..	..	..	..	100 [e]	1.00 [e]	93 [e]	1.02 [e]	59 [e]	1.23 [e]
18	Germany	..	..	..	..	87 [e, f]	1.02 [e, f]	88 [e, f]	1.01 [e, f]	45 [e, h]	0.96 [e, h]
19	Spain	96.9	98	99.8	100	103 [e]	1.01 [e]	95 [e]	1.03 [e]	64 [e]	1.15 [e]
20	New Zealand	..	..	..	..	99 [e]	1.00 [e]	93 [e]	1.02 [e]	84 [e]	1.52 [e]
21	Italy	98.1	99	99.8	100	100 [e]	1.00 [e]	91 [e]	1.01 [e]	57 [e]	1.32 [e]
22	Israel	93.1	96	99.3	100	101	1.00	89	1.01	62	1.39
23	Portugal	90.3	95	99.8	100	..	..	89 [e]	1.08 [e]	58 [e]	1.37 [e]
24	Greece	96.1	97	99.8	100	97 [e]	1.00 [e]	89 [e]	1.03 [e]	..	..
25	Cyprus	95.7	97	99.8	100	95	1.01	89	1.02	22 [f, i]	1.29 [f, i]
26	Hong Kong, China (SAR)	89.6	92	99.8	101	..	..	..	..	..	..
27	Barbados	99.7	100	99.8	100	105	1.01	84	0.97	55	2.45
28	Singapore	88.7	92	99.8	100	..	..	..	..	..	..
29	Slovenia	99.6	100	99.8	100	93	0.99	..	..	70	1.35
30	Korea, Rep. of	96.6	97	99.8	100	100 [e]	1.01 [e]	91 [e]	1.00 [e]	57 [e]	0.59 [e]
31	Brunei Darussalam	88.1	93	99.8	101	..	..	..	..	19	1.96
32	Czech Republic	..	..	..	..	90 [e]	1.00 [e]	..	..	31 [e]	1.05 [e]
33	Malta	93.0	102	99.8	102	100 [f]	1.02 [f]	77 [h]	0.95 [h]	24 [f]	1.22 [f]
34	Argentina	96.9	100	98.8	100	107 [e]	0.99 [e]	82 [e]	1.06 [e]	60 [e, f]	1.64 [e, f]
35	Poland	99.7	100	99.8	100	98 [e]	1.00 [e]	92 [e]	1.03 [e]	66 [e]	1.44 [e]
36	Seychelles	..	..	..	..	..	..	..	..	..	..
37	Bahrain	83.2	91	98.7	100	97	1.01	95	1.07	31 [h]	1.59 [h]
38	Hungary	99.2	100	99.8	100	90 [e]	0.99 [e]	88 [e, f]	1.01 [e, f]	45 [e]	1.27 [e]
39	Slovakia	..	..	..	..	90 [e]	1.01 [e]	75 [e]	1.01 [e]	32 [e]	1.09 [e]
40	Uruguay	98.1	101	99.4	101	91 [e]	1.01 [e]	74 [e]	1.11 [e]	47 [e]	1.83 [e]
41	Estonia	99.8	100	99.8	100	97	0.98	84	1.03	70	1.55
42	Costa Rica	95.8	100	98.6	101	91	1.00	52	1.11	18	1.21
43	Chile	95.7	100	99.1	100	88 [e]	0.99 [e]	64 [e]	0.76 [e]	36 [e]	0.92 [e]
44	Qatar	83.7	104	97.3	105	96 [h]	1.01 [h]	82 [h]	1.10 [h]	38	2.97
45	Lithuania	99.5	100	99.8	100	94	0.99	89	1.01	63	1.51
46	Kuwait	80.3	95	93.6	102	65 [f]	0.95 [f]	50 [h]	1.02 [h]	30 [h]	2.31 [h]
47	Croatia	97.4	98	99.8	100	..	..	..	..	..	..
48	United Arab Emirates	79.8	106	94.7	108	87	1.02	72	1.13	..	..
49	Bahamas	96.3	102	98.3	102	79 [f]	0.92 [f]	71 [f]	0.99 [f]	..	..
50	Latvia	99.8	100	99.8	100	92	1.00	77	1.08	79	1.65

		Adult literacy		Youth literacy		Net primary enrolment [a, b]		Net secondary enrolment [a, b]		Gross tertiary enrolment [b, c]	
		Female rate (% age 15 and above)	**Female rate** as % of male rate	**Female rate** (% age 15-24)	**Female rate** as % of male rate	**Female ratio** (%)	**Ratio of females to males** [d]	**Female ratio** (%)	**Ratio of females to males** [d]	**Female ratio** (%)	**Ratio of females to males** [d]
HDI rank		2001	2001	2001	2001	2000-01	2000-01	2000-01	2000-01	2000-01	2000-01
51	Saint Kitts and Nevis	..	..	..	..	..	..	..	..	..	..
52	Cuba	96.7	100	99.8	100	97	0.99	84	1.05	26	1.16
53	Belarus	99.6	100	99.8	100	107	0.99	76	1.01	63	1.29
54	Trinidad and Tobago	97.8	99	99.8	100	92	1.00	73	1.07	8	1.53
55	Mexico	89.5	96	96.8	99	104 [e]	1.01 [e]	62 [e]	1.08 [e]	20 [e]	0.96 [e]
Medium human development											
56	Antigua and Barbuda	..	..	..	..	..	..	..	..	..	..
57	Bulgaria	98.0	99	99.6	100	93	0.98	87	0.98	47	1.35
58	Malaysia	84.0	92	97.8	100	99 [e]	1.00 [e]	74 [e]	1.11 [e]	29 [e]	1.08 [e]
59	Panama	91.4	99	96.5	99	100	1.00	65	1.09	44 [f]	1.67 [f]
60	Macedonia, TFYR	..	..	..	..	92	1.00	80 [f]	0.98 [f]	28	1.32
61	Libyan Arab Jamahiriya	69.3	76	93.5	94	..	..	..	..	48	0.96
62	Mauritius	81.7	93	94.5	101	95	1.00	65	1.04	13	1.36
63	Russian Federation	99.4	100	99.8	100	..	..	..	..	..	..
64	Colombia	91.9	100	97.7	101	88	1.00	59	1.10	24	1.09
65	Brazil	87.2	100	96.9	103	94 [e]	0.93 [e]	74 [e]	1.08 [e]	19 [e]	1.29 [e]
66	Bosnia and Herzegovina	..	..	..	..	..	..	..	..	..	..
67	Belize	93.3	100	98.8	101	102	1.04	66	1.07	..	..
68	Dominica	..	..	..	..	..	..	..	..	..	..
69	Venezuela	92.4	99	98.8	101	89	1.02	55	1.20	34	1.46
70	Samoa (Western)	98.4	99	99.5	100	95	0.97	71	1.08	11	1.05
71	Saint Lucia	..	..	..	..	100	1.01	90	1.28	24 [h]	0.87 [h]
72	Romania	97.4	98	99.7	100	93	0.99	81	1.02	30	1.20
73	Saudi Arabia	68.2	82	91.0	96	56	0.92	50	0.95	25 [f]	1.29 [f]
74	Thailand	94.1	97	98.4	99	84 [e]	0.97 [e]	..	..	32 [e]	0.82 [e]
75	Ukraine	99.5	100	99.9	100	71 [h]	0.99 [h]	..	..	46 [h]	1.14 [h]
76	Kazakhstan	99.2	100	99.8	100	88	0.99	82	0.98	34	1.19
77	Suriname	..	..	..	..	90	0.96	46	1.13	..	..
78	Jamaica	91.0	109	97.6	107	95 [e]	1.00 [e]	76 [e]	1.04 [e]	22 [e]	1.89 [e]
79	Oman	63.5	78	96.8	97	64	0.99	60	1.01	10	1.40
80	St. Vincent & the Grenadines	..	..	..	..	..	..	..	..	..	..
81	Fiji	91.2	96	99.1	100	100 [h]	1.00 [h]	..	..	..	..
82	Peru	85.7	90	95.5	97	104 [e, f]	1.00 [e, f]	61 [e, h]	0.98 [e, h]	15 [e, h]	0.34 [e, h]
83	Lebanon	81.0	88	93.3	96	74	1.00	73 [h]	1.09 [h]	44	1.09
84	Paraguay	92.5	98	97.2	100	92 [e]	1.01 [e]	48 [e]	1.06 [e]	..	..
85	Philippines	95.0	100	99.0	100	93 [e]	1.01 [e]	57 [e]	1.18 [e]	33 [e]	1.10 [e]
86	Maldives	96.9	100	99.2	100	99	1.01	33 [f]	1.13 [f]	..	..
87	Turkmenistan	..	..	..	..	..	..	..	..	..	..
88	Georgia	..	..	..	..	95	1.00	73 [h]	1.02 [h]	34	0.99
89	Azerbaijan	..	..	..	..	93 [f]	1.03 [f]	78 [h]	1.01 [h]	21 [f]	0.93 [f]
90	Jordan	85.1	89	99.4	100	94 [e, f]	1.01 [e, f]	78 [e, f]	1.07 [e, f]	31 [e, f]	1.14 [e, f]
91	Tunisia	61.9	75	89.8	92	99 [e]	0.99 [e]	72 [e]	1.05 [e]	21 [e]	0.97 [e]
92	Guyana	98.2	99	99.8	100	97 [f]	0.97 [f]	..	..	..	..
93	Grenada	..	..	..	..	..	..	..	..	..	..
94	Dominican Republic	84.0	100	92.2	102	93	1.02	45	1.28	..	..
95	Albania	77.8	84	96.7	97	97	1.00	75	1.03	19	1.69
96	Turkey	77.2	82	94.4	95	..	..	..	..	12 [e, f]	0.70 [e, f]
97	Ecuador	90.3	97	97.1	99	100	1.01	49	1.04	..	..
98	Occupied Palestinian Territories	..	..	..	..	98	1.02	81	1.08	28	0.96
99	Sri Lanka	89.3	94	96.8	100	97 [e, h]	1.00 [e, h]	..	..	..	..
100	Armenia	97.8	98	99.7	100	70	1.02	65	1.06	22	1.25

HDI rank		Adult literacy		Youth literacy		Net primary enrolment [a, b]		Net secondary enrolment [a, b]		Gross tertiary enrolment [b, c]	
		Female rate (% age 15 and above) 2001	Female rate as % of male rate 2001	Female rate (% age 15-24) 2001	Female rate as % of male rate 2001	Female ratio (%) 2000-01	Ratio of females to males [d] 2000-01	Female ratio (%) 2000-01	Ratio of females to males [d] 2000-01	Female ratio (%) 2000-01	Ratio of females to males [d] 2000-01
101	Uzbekistan	98.9	99	99.6	100	..	..	..	..	..	..
102	Kyrgyzstan	..	..	..	..	81	0.97	..	..	42	1.04
103	Cape Verde	67.0	79	85.5	93	99 [h]	1.01 [h]	..	..	..	..
104	China	78.7	85	96.9	98	95 [e, f]	1.03 [e, f]	..	..	..	..
105	El Salvador	76.6	93	87.7	98	87 [f]	1.17 [f]	39 [h]	0.99 [h]	19	1.24
106	Iran, Islamic Rep. of	70.2	84	91.9	95	73	0.98	..	..	10	0.93
107	Algeria	58.3	76	84.6	90	97	0.97	63	1.05	..	..
108	Moldova, Rep. of	98.4	99	99.8	100	78	1.00	69	1.03	31	1.29
109	Viet Nam	90.9	96	95.6	101	92	0.94	..	..	8	0.74
110	Syrian Arab Republic	61.6	69	79.7	83	94	0.95	37	0.90	..	..
111	South Africa	85.0	98	91.5	100	88	0.98	60	1.12	17	1.23
112	Indonesia	82.6	90	97.3	99	92 [e]	0.99 [e]	46 [e, f]	0.96 [e, f]	13 [e]	0.77 [e]
113	Tajikistan	98.9	99	99.8	100	98	0.92	69	0.84	7	0.32
114	Bolivia	79.9	87	94.0	96	97	1.00	67	0.98	..	..
115	Honduras	75.7	100	87.1	104	88	1.02	..	..	17	1.31
116	Equatorial Guinea	76.0	82	95.7	97	68	0.89	14 [h]	0.36 [h]	2 [f]	0.43 [f]
117	Mongolia	98.3	100	99.4	101	91	1.04	64	1.21	42	1.74
118	Gabon	..	..	..	..	87	0.98	..	..	6 [h]	0.55 [h]
119	Guatemala	61.8	81	73.2	85	82	0.95	25	0.94	..	..
120	Egypt	44.8	67	63.7	83	90 [e]	0.95 [e]	77 [e]	0.96 [e]	..	..
121	Nicaragua	67.1	101	72.6	102	81	1.01	38	1.18	..	..
122	São Tomé and Principe	..	..	..	..	..	..	..	..	..	..
123	Solomon Islands	..	..	..	..	..	..	..	..	..	..
124	Namibia	81.9	98	93.7	104	84	1.07	44	1.38	7 [f]	1.24 [f]
125	Botswana	80.6	107	92.4	109	86	1.04	74	1.14	4	0.89
126	Morocco	37.2	59	59.7	78	74	0.91	27 [f]	0.83 [f]	9	0.80
127	India	46.4	67	65.8	82	..	..	..	..	8 [e, f]	0.66 [e, f]
128	Vanuatu	..	..	..	..	100	1.10	25 [h]	1.20 [h]	(.) [h]	0.62 [h]
129	Ghana	64.5	80	89.4	95	57	0.95	28	0.86	2	0.40
130	Cambodia	58.2	72	75.2	89	90	0.90	12	0.59	2	0.38
131	Myanmar	81.0	91	90.8	99	83	0.99	35	0.95	15	1.75
132	Papua New Guinea	57.7	81	72.1	90	80 [f]	0.91 [f]	18 [f]	0.77 [f]	2 [h]	0.66 [h]
133	Swaziland	79.4	98	91.6	102	94	1.02	47 [f]	1.17 [f]	5	0.87
134	Comoros	48.8	77	52.0	79	52	0.87	..	..	1 [f]	0.73 [f]
135	Lao People's Dem. Rep.	54.4	71	71.8	84	78	0.92	27	0.81	2	0.59
136	Bhutan	..	..	..	..	..	..	..	..	..	..
137	Lesotho	93.9	128	98.6	119	82	1.09	25	1.54	3	1.76
138	Sudan	47.7	68	72.9	87	42 [f]	0.83 [f]	..	..	7 [h]	0.92 [h]
139	Bangladesh	30.8	62	40.4	71	90	1.02	44	1.05	5	0.55
140	Congo	75.9	86	97.0	99	..	..	..	..	1	0.13
141	Togo	44.0	60	65.2	74	83	0.82	14 [h]	0.44 [h]	1 [f]	0.20 [f]
Low human development											
142	Cameroon	65.1	82	88.7	96	..	..	..	..	1 [f]	0.17 [f]
143	Nepal	25.2	42	44.4	57	67	0.87	..	..	2	0.27
144	Pakistan	28.8	49	43.1	60	56	0.74	..	..	..	..
145	Zimbabwe	85.5	92	96.0	97	80 [e]	1.00 [e]	39 [e]	0.92 [e]	3 [e]	0.60 [e]
146	Kenya	77.3	86	94.7	98	69	1.02	23	0.97	3	0.77
147	Uganda	58.0	74	73.0	85	106	0.94	10 [f]	0.72 [f]	2	0.52
148	Yemen	26.9	39	48.5	58	49	0.58	21 [h]	0.40 [h]	5 [h]	0.28 [h]
149	Madagascar	60.6	82	77.4	92	68	1.01	12 [h]	1.03 [h]	2	0.84
150	Haiti	48.9	93	65.5	101	..	..	..	..	..	..
151	Gambia	30.9	69	50.8	76	66	0.93	29	0.70	..	..

		Adult literacy		Youth literacy		Net primary enrolment [a, b]		Net secondary enrolment [a, b]		Gross tertiary enrolment [b, c]	
		Female rate (% age 15 and above) 2001	Female rate as % of male rate 2001	Female rate (% age 15-24) 2001	Female rate as % of male rate 2001	Female ratio (%) 2000-01	Ratio of females to males [d] 2000-01	Female ratio (%) 2000-01	Ratio of females to males [d] 2000-01	Female ratio (%) 2000-01	Ratio of females to males [d] 2000-01
HDI rank											
152	Nigeria	57.7	79	85.4	95	..	..	..	..	..	..
153	Djibouti	55.5	73	80.6	90	28	0.77	..	..	1	0.70
154	Mauritania	30.7	60	41.2	72	62	0.93	13	0.78	1	0.20
155	Eritrea	45.6	67	61.5	76	38	0.86	19	0.74	(.)	0.15
156	Senegal	28.7	60	43.2	71	60	0.90	..	..	..	..
157	Guinea	..	..	..	..	41	0.79	6 [h]	0.38 [h]	..	..
158	Rwanda	61.9	83	82.6	96	97 [f]	1.00 [f]	..	..	1	0.50
159	Benin	24.6	46	37.3	52	57 [f]	0.69 [f]	11 [f]	0.46 [f]	1 [f]	0.24 [f]
160	Tanzania, U. Rep. of	67.9	80	88.6	95	48	1.04	5	0.94	(.)	0.31
161	Côte d'Ivoire	38.4	64	53.6	75	55	0.75	..	..	4 [h]	0.36 [h]
162	Malawi	47.6	63	61.9	76	104	1.07	23	0.85	(.) [h]	0.39 [h]
163	Zambia	72.7	85	86.2	95	65	0.99	18	0.87	2	0.47
164	Angola	..	..	..	..	35	0.91	..	..	1 [f]	0.63 [f]
165	Chad	35.8	67	62.0	83	47	0.67	4 [f]	0.31 [f]	(.) [f]	0.17 [f]
166	Guinea-Bissau	24.7	45	45.5	62	45 [f]	0.71 [f]	..	..	(.) [f]	0.18 [f]
167	Congo, Dem. Rep. of the	51.8	70	76.4	86	32 [h]	0.95 [h]	9 [h]	0.58 [h]	..	..
168	Central African Republic	36.6	60	60.8	79	45	0.70	..	..	1 [f]	0.19 [f]
169	Ethiopia	32.4	67	50.2	81	41	0.77	10	0.68	1	0.27
170	Mozambique	30.0	49	47.7	63	50	0.85	8	0.68	(.)	0.79
171	Burundi	42.0	74	63.6	96	49	0.83	..	..	1	0.36
172	Mali	16.6	45	26.0	54	36 [h]	0.71 [h]	..	..	..	..
173	Burkina Faso	14.9	43	24.5	52	29	0.71	6	0.65	..	..
174	Niger	8.9	36	14.5	44	24	0.67	4	0.67	1	0.34
175	Sierra Leone	..	..	..	..	..	..	24	0.83	1	0.40
Developing countries		67.1	82	80.9	91	79	0.93	..	..	..	..
Least developed countries		43.8	70	59.3	81	57	0.90	..	..	..	..
Arab States		48.8	68	69.6	83	73	0.90	..	..	..	..
East Asia and the Pacific		81.3	88	96.6	98	93	1.01	..	..	..	..
Latin America and the Caribbean		88.2	98	95.4	101	96	0.99	..	..	..	..
South Asia		44.8	67	62.4	80	72	0.84	..	..	..	..
Sub-Saharan Africa		54.5	77	73.2	89	56	0.92	..	..	..	..
Central & Eastern Europe & CIS		99.1	99	99.8	100	91	1.02	..	..	..	..
OECD		..	..	..	..	98	1.00	..	..	..	..
High-income OECD		..	..	..	..	98	1.01	..	..	..	..
High human development		..	..	..	..	98	1.01	..	..	..	..
Medium human development		71.6	85	84.8	94	85	0.95	..	..	..	..
Low human development		44.4	68	63.9	81	54	0.86	..	..	..	..
High income		..	..	..	..	97	1.01	..	..	..	..
Middle income		81.8	90	94.9	98	93	1.00	..	..	..	..
Low income		53.9	75	69.8	85	69	0.87	..	..	..	..
World		..	..	..	..	81	0.94	..	..	..	..

a. The net enrolment ratio is the ratio of enrolled children of the official age for the education level indicated to the total population of that age. Net enrolment ratios exceeding 100% reflect discrepancies between these two data sets. b. Data refer to the 2000/01 school year. Data for some countries may refer to national or UNESCO Institute for Statistics estimates. For details, see http://www.uis.unesco.org/. Because data are from different sources, comparisons across countries should be made with caution. c. Tertiary enrolment is generally calculated as a gross ratio. d. Calculated as the ratio of the female enrolment ratio to the male enrolment ratio. e. Preliminary UNESCO Institute for Statistics estimate, subject to further revision. f. Data refer to the 1998/99 school year. g. The ratio is an underestimate, as many students pursue their studies in nearby countries. h. Data refer to the 1999/2000 school year. i. Excludes Turkish students.

Source: Columns 1 and 3: UNESCO Institute for Statistics 2003a; column 2: calculated on the basis of data on adult literacy rates from UNESCO Institute for Statistics 2003a; column 4: calculated on the basis of data on youth literacy rates from UNESCO Institute for Statistics 2003a (for data as presented in World Bank 2003c, as the ratio of literate females to males, see MDG indicator table 2); columns 5 and 6: UNESCO Institute for Statistics 2003d; aggregates calculated for the Human Development Report Office by the UNESCO Institute for Statistics; columns 7-10: UNESCO Institute for Statistics 2003d.

25 Gender inequality in economic activity

HDI rank	Female economic activity rate (age 15 and above) Rate (%) 2001	Index (1990 = 100) 2001	As % of male rate 2001	Agriculture Female 1995-2001[a]	Agriculture Male 1995-2001[a]	Industry Female 1995-2001[a]	Industry Male 1995-2001[a]	Services Female 1995-2001[a]	Services Male 1995-2001[a]	Contributing family workers Female (as % of total) 1995-2000[a]	Male (as % of total) 1995-2000[a]
High human development											
1 Norway	59.5	109	85	2	6	9	33	88	61	63	38
2 Iceland	66.7	101	83	5	12	15	34	80	53	67	33
3 Sweden	62.6	102	89	1	4	12	38	87	59	54	46
4 Australia	56.1	107	77	3	6	10	31	86	63	59	41
5 Netherlands	45.6	106	67	2	4	9	31	84	63	78	22
6 Belgium	39.9	106	66	2	3	13	37	86	60	85	15
7 United States	59.1	106	82	1	4	12	32	86	64	62	38
8 Canada	60.3	104	82	2	5	11	32	87	63	69	31
9 Japan	50.9	103	67	6	5	22	38	73	57	82	18
10 Switzerland	50.8	104	66	4	5	13	36	83	59	..	..
11 Denmark	61.7	100	84	2	5	15	37	83	58	..	..
12 Ireland	37.5	117	53	2	12	15	38	83	50	59	41
13 United Kingdom	53.0	105	74	1	2	12	36	87	61	66	34
14 Finland	56.9	98	87	4	8	14	40	82	52	47	53
15 Luxembourg	38.1	104	58	..	..	..	..	..	..	..	..
16 Austria	44.0	102	65	7	6	14	43	79	52	67	33
17 France	48.8	107	77	..	2	13	35	86	63	..	..
18 Germany	47.9	100	70	2	3	19	46	79	50	75	25
19 Spain	37.8	112	57	5	8	14	41	81	51	64	36
20 New Zealand	57.6	109	80	6	11	12	32	81	56	68	32
21 Italy	38.6	107	59	5	6	21	39	74	55	55	45
22 Israel	48.8	114	68	1	3	13	35	86	61	77	23
23 Portugal	51.4	105	72	14	11	24	44	62	45	66	34
24 Greece	38.2	108	59	20	16	12	29	67	54	69	31
25 Cyprus	49.1	103	62	10	11	18	30	71	58	87	13
26 Hong Kong, China (SAR)	50.9	105	65	..	..	12	28	88	71	..	..
27 Barbados	62.0	107	79	3	5	11	31	85	64	..	..
28 Singapore	50.1	99	64	..	..	23	33	77	67	70	30
29 Slovenia	54.5	98	81	11	11	28	46	61	42	63	37
30 Korea, Rep. of	53.6	111	70	13	10	19	34	68	56	88	12
31 Brunei Darussalam	50.4	112	63	..	..	..	..	..	..	..	..
32 Czech Republic	61.2	100	83	4	6	28	49	69	48	78	22
33 Malta	26.1	112	37	..	..	..	..	..	..	..	..
34 Argentina	36.2	124	47	..	1	10	34	89	65	64	36
35 Poland	57.1	100	80	19	19	21	41	60	39	60	40
36 Seychelles	..	..	..	..	..	..	..	..	..	..	..
37 Bahrain	33.8	119	39	..	..	..	..	..	..	..	..
38 Hungary	48.5	102	71	4	9	25	42	71	48	67	33
39 Slovakia	62.7	99	84	5	10	26	49	69	42	68	32
40 Uruguay	48.3	109	67	1	6	14	34	85	61	68	32
41 Estonia	60.7	95	82	7	11	23	40	70	49	59	41
42 Costa Rica	37.4	113	46	4	22	17	27	79	51	41	59
43 Chile	38.1	119	49	5	19	14	31	82	49	..	..
44 Qatar	41.6	126	46	..	..	..	..	..	..	..	..
45 Lithuania	57.6	97	80	16	24	40	33	63	43	61	39
46 Kuwait	36.5	96	48	..	..	..	..	..	..	..	..
47 Croatia	48.8	102	73	17	16	22	38	61	46	76	24
48 United Arab Emirates	31.8	109	37	..	..	..	..	..	..	..	..
49 Bahamas	66.8	104	84	1	6	5	24	93	69	..	..
50 Latvia	59.6	95	80	14	17	18	35	69	49	52	48

		Female economic activity rate (age 15 and above)			Employment by economic activity (%)						Contributing family workers	
					Agriculture		Industry		Services		Female (as % of total)	Male (as % of total)
		Rate (%)	Index (1990 = 100)	As % of male rate	Female	Male	Female	Male	Female	Male		
HDI rank		2001	2001	2001	1995-2001 [a]	1995-2001 [a]	1995-2001 [a]	1995-2001 [a]	1995-2001 [a]	1995-2001 [a]	1995-2000 [a]	1995-2000 [a]
51	Saint Kitts and Nevis	..	..	..	..	..	..	..	..	..	..	..
52	Cuba	50.2	119	65	..	..	..	..	..	..	..	..
53	Belarus	59.2	98	82	..	..	..	..	..	..	..	..
54	Trinidad and Tobago	44.5	114	59	3	11	13	37	83	52	70	30
55	Mexico	39.8	117	48	7	23	22	29	71	47	49	51
Medium human development												
56	Antigua and Barbuda	..	..	..	..	..	..	..	..	..	..	..
57	Bulgaria	56.4	94	86	..	..	..	..	..	..	..	..
58	Malaysia	48.7	109	61	13	21	29	33	58	46	..	..
59	Panama	43.7	113	55	2	25	10	22	88	52	27	73
60	Macedonia, TFYR	49.8	103	72	..	..	..	..	..	..	..	..
61	Libyan Arab Jamahiriya	25.3	123	34	..	..	..	..	..	..	..	..
62	Mauritius	38.2	110	48	13	15	43	39	45	46	..	..
63	Russian Federation	59.7	98	82	8	15	23	36	69	49	42	58
64	Colombia	48.5	114	61	..	2	20	30	80	68	69	31
65	Brazil	43.8	98	52	19	26	10	27	71	47	..	..
66	Bosnia and Herzegovina	43.1	99	60	..	..	..	..	..	..	..	..
67	Belize	27.3	114	32	6	37	12	19	81	44	30	70
68	Dominica	..	..	..	14	31	10	24	72	40	..	..
69	Venezuela	43.5	115	54	2	16	13	29	85	55	..	..
70	Samoa (Western)	..	..	..	..	..	..	..	..	..	..	..
71	Saint Lucia	..	..	..	16	27	14	24	71	49	..	..
72	Romania	50.6	97	76	45	39	22	33	33	29	71	29
73	Saudi Arabia	21.6	145	28	..	..	..	..	..	..	..	..
74	Thailand	73.1	98	85	47	50	17	20	36	31	66	34
75	Ukraine	55.5	98	80	..	..	..	..	..	..	64	36
76	Kazakhstan	61.1	101	82	..	..	..	..	..	..	..	..
77	Suriname	36.6	123	49	3	7	10	32	86	56	..	..
78	Jamaica	67.2	101	86	10	30	9	26	81	45	66	34
79	Oman	19.6	154	26	..	..	..	..	..	..	..	..
80	St. Vincent & the Grenadines	..	..	..	..	..	..	..	..	..	..	..
81	Fiji	37.9	143	46	..	..	..	..	..	..	..	..
82	Peru	34.9	119	44	3	8	11	25	86	67	62	38
83	Lebanon	29.9	123	39	..	..	..	..	..	..	..	..
84	Paraguay	37.1	110	43	3	7	10	31	87	62	..	..
85	Philippines	49.7	106	61	27	47	13	18	61	36	..	..
86	Maldives	65.4	100	80	..	..	..	..	..	..	57	43
87	Turkmenistan	62.3	105	81	..	..	..	..	..	..	..	..
88	Georgia	55.7	100	78	..	..	..	..	..	..	60	40
89	Azerbaijan	54.8	106	75	..	..	..	..	..	..	..	..
90	Jordan	27.1	160	35	..	..	..	..	..	..	..	..
91	Tunisia	37.2	113	48	..	..	..	..	..	..	..	..
92	Guyana	41.1	115	50	..	..	..	..	..	..	..	..
93	Grenada	..	..	..	10	17	12	32	77	46	..	..
94	Dominican Republic	40.4	118	48	3	24	20	27	77	49	23	77
95	Albania	59.9	103	73	..	..	..	..	..	..	..	..
96	Turkey	50.3	115	62	72	34	10	25	18	41	65	35
97	Ecuador	33.0	119	39	2	11	14	26	84	63	66	34
98	Occupied Palestinian Territories	9.3	148	13	..	..	..	..	..	..	54	46
99	Sri Lanka	43.1	107	55	49	38	22	23	27	37	56	44
100	Armenia	62.4	100	88	..	..	..	..	..	..	..	..

HDI rank	Female economic activity rate (age 15 and above)			Employment by economic activity (%)						Contributing family workers	
	Rate (%) 2001	Index (1990 = 100) 2001	As % of male rate 2001	Agriculture		Industry		Services		Female (as % of total) 1995-2000[a]	Male (as % of total) 1995-2000[a]
				Female 1995-2001[a]	Male 1995-2001[a]	Female 1995-2001[a]	Male 1995-2001[a]	Female 1995-2001[a]	Male 1995-2001[a]		
101 Uzbekistan	62.5	106	85	..	..	..	..	..	..	..	..
102 Kyrgyzstan	61.0	104	84	53	52	8	14	38	34	..	..
103 Cape Verde	46.4	109	53	..	..	..	..	..	..	..	..
104 China	72.6	98	86	..	..	..	..	..	..	..	..
105 El Salvador	46.5	125	55	6	37	25	24	69	38	42	58
106 Iran, Islamic Rep. of	29.5	137	38	..	..	..	..	..	..	..	..
107 Algeria	30.2	158	40	..	..	..	..	..	..	..	..
108 Moldova, Rep. of	60.3	98	84	..	..	..	..	..	..	62	38
109 Viet Nam	73.7	96	91	..	..	..	..	..	..	..	..
110 Syrian Arab Republic	28.9	122	37	..	..	..	..	..	..	..	..
111 South Africa	47.2	102	59	..	..	..	..	..	..	..	..
112 Indonesia	55.6	110	68	42	41	16	21	42	39	..	..
113 Tajikistan	58.1	112	80	..	..	..	..	..	..	..	..
114 Bolivia	48.2	106	58	2	2	16	40	82	58	63	37
115 Honduras	40.8	120	48	9	50	25	21	67	30	40	60
116 Equatorial Guinea	45.7	101	52	..	..	..	..	..	..	..	..
117 Mongolia	73.6	103	88	..	..	..	..	..	..	..	..
118 Gabon	63.2	101	76	..	..	..	..	..	..	..	..
119 Guatemala	36.6	131	42	14	37	19	26	68	38	..	..
120 Egypt	35.4	117	45	35	29	9	25	56	46	43	57
121 Nicaragua	47.7	118	56	..	..	..	..	..	..	..	..
122 São Tomé and Principe	..	..	..	..	..	..	..	..	..	..	..
123 Solomon Islands	81.1	97	92	..	..	..	..	..	..	..	..
124 Namibia	53.7	101	67	39	38	8	19	52	43	..	..
125 Botswana	62.8	96	77	..	..	..	..	..	..	45	55
126 Morocco	41.6	107	52	6	6	40	32	54	63	22	78
127 India	42.2	105	50	..	..	..	..	..	..	..	..
128 Vanuatu	..	..	..	..	..	..	..	..	..	..	..
129 Ghana	80.0	98	98	..	..	..	..	..	..	..	..
130 Cambodia	80.3	98	97	..	..	..	..	..	..	71	29
131 Myanmar	65.8	100	75	..	..	..	..	..	..	..	..
132 Papua New Guinea	67.6	100	79	..	..	..	..	..	..	..	..
133 Swaziland	41.7	106	52	..	..	..	..	..	..	..	..
134 Comoros	62.4	99	73	..	..	..	..	..	..	..	..
135 Lao People's Dem. Rep.	74.5	101	85	..	..	..	..	..	..	..	..
136 Bhutan	57.1	100	65	..	..	..	..	..	..	..	..
137 Lesotho	47.5	102	56	..	..	..	..	..	..	..	..
138 Sudan	35.1	114	41	..	..	..	..	..	..	..	..
139 Bangladesh	66.4	101	76	78	54	8	11	11	34	81	19
140 Congo	58.4	100	71	..	..	..	..	..	..	..	..
141 Togo	53.5	101	62	..	..	..	..	..	..	..	..
Low human development											
142 Cameroon	49.4	105	58	..	..	..	..	..	..	..	..
143 Nepal	56.8	101	66	..	..	..	..	..	..	..	..
144 Pakistan	35.8	125	43	66	41	11	20	23	39	33	67
145 Zimbabwe	65.1	98	78	..	..	..	..	..	..	..	..
146 Kenya	74.7	100	85	16	20	10	23	75	57	..	..
147 Uganda	79.4	98	88	..	..	..	..	..	..	..	..
148 Yemen	30.6	109	37	..	..	..	..	..	..	26	74
149 Madagascar	69.0	99	78	..	..	..	..	..	..	..	..
150 Haiti	55.9	97	70	..	..	..	..	..	..	..	..
151 Gambia	69.7	101	78	..	..	..	..	..	..	..	..

	Female economic activity rate (age 15 and above)			Employment by economic activity (%)						Contributing family workers	
				Agriculture		Industry		Services		Female (as % of total)	Male (as % of total)
	Rate (%)	Index (1990 = 100)	As % of male rate	Female	Male	Female	Male	Female	Male		
HDI rank	2001	2001	2001	1995-2001[a]	1995-2001[a]	1995-2001[a]	1995-2001[a]	1995-2001[a]	1995-2001[a]	1995-2000[a]	1995-2000[a]
152 Nigeria	47.7	102	56	2	4	11	30	87	67	..	..
153 Djibouti	..	..	..	..	..	..	..	..	..	..	..
154 Mauritania	63.3	98	74	..	..	..	..	..	..	..	..
155 Eritrea	74.6	99	87	..	..	..	..	..	..	..	..
156 Senegal	61.7	101	72	..	..	..	..	..	..	..	..
157 Guinea	77.2	98	89	..	..	..	..	..	..	..	..
158 Rwanda	82.5	99	88	..	..	..	..	..	..	..	..
159 Benin	73.4	96	90	..	..	..	..	..	..	..	..
160 Tanzania, U. Rep. of	81.6	98	93	..	..	..	..	..	..	..	..
161 Côte d'Ivoire	43.9	102	51	..	..	..	..	..	..	..	..
162 Malawi	77.8	98	90	..	..	..	..	..	..	..	..
163 Zambia	64.1	98	75	..	..	..	..	..	..	..	..
164 Angola	72.7	98	82	..	..	..	..	..	..	..	..
165 Chad	67.3	101	77	..	..	..	..	..	..	..	..
166 Guinea-Bissau	57.0	100	63	..	..	..	..	..	..	..	..
167 Congo, Dem. Rep. of the	60.5	97	72	..	..	..	..	..	..	..	..
168 Central African Republic	67.5	96	79	..	..	..	..	..	..	..	..
169 Ethiopia	57.3	98	67	88	89	2	2	11	9	..	..
170 Mozambique	82.7	99	92	..	..	..	..	..	..	..	..
171 Burundi	81.9	99	89	..	..	..	..	..	..	..	..
172 Mali	69.9	97	79	..	..	..	..	..	..	..	..
173 Burkina Faso	74.8	97	85	..	..	..	..	..	..	..	..
174 Niger	69.4	99	75	..	..	..	..	..	..	..	..
175 Sierra Leone	44.8	106	54	..	..	..	..	..	..	..	..
Developing countries	55.7	101	67	..	..	..	..	..	..	..	..
Least developed countries	64.2	99	74	..	..	..	..	..	..	..	..
Arab States	32.7	117	41	..	..	..	..	..	..	..	..
East Asia and the Pacific	68.8	99	82	..	..	..	..	..	..	..	..
Latin America and the Caribbean	42.2	109	52	..	..	..	..	..	..	..	..
South Asia	43.6	106	52	..	..	..	..	..	..	..	..
Sub-Saharan Africa	62.2	99	73	..	..	..	..	..	..	..	..
Central & Eastern Europe & CIS	57.5	99	81	..	..	..	..	..	..	..	..
OECD	51.3	106	71	..	..	..	..	..	..	..	..
High-income OECD	52.0	106	73	..	..	..	..	..	..	..	..
High human development	50.7	106	70	..	..	..	..	..	..	..	..
Medium human development	56.7	100	69	..	..	..	..	..	..	..	..
Low human development	56.7	102	66	..	..	..	..	..	..	..	..
High income	51.9	106	73	..	..	..	..	..	..	..	..
Middle income	59.1	100	73	..	..	..	..	..	..	..	..
Low income	51.9	103	62	..	..	..	..	..	..	..	..
World	55.2	102	68	..	..	..	..	..	..	..	..

Note: As a result of limitations in the data, comparisons of labour statistics over time and across countries should be made with caution. For detailed notes on the data, see ILO 2002a, 2002b and 2003b. The percentage shares of employment by economic activity may not sum to 100 because of rounding or the omission of activities not classified.
a. Data refer to the most recent year available during the period specified.
Source: Columns 1-3: calculated on the basis of data on the economically active population and total population from ILO 2002a; *columns 4-9:* ILO 2002b; *columns 10 and 11:* calculated on the basis of data on contributing family workers from ILO 2003b.

26 Gender, work burden and time allocation

| | | Burden of work | | | Time allocation (%) | | | | | |
| | | Total work time (minutes per day) | | Female work time as % of male | Total work time | | Time spent by females | | Time spent by males | |
	Year	Females	Males		Market activities	Non-market activities	Market activities	Non-market activities	Market activities	Non-market activities
Selected developing countries										
Urban areas										
Colombia	1983	399	356	112	49	51	24	76	77	23
Indonesia	1992	398	366	109	60	40	35	65	86	14
Kenya	1986	590	572	103	46	54	41	59	79	21
Nepal	1978	579	554	105	58	42	25	75	67	33
Venezuela	1983	440	416	106	59	41	30	70	87	13
Average [a]	–	481	453	107	54	46	31	69	79	21
Rural areas										
Bangladesh	1990	545	496	110	52	48	35	65	70	30
Guatemala	1977	678	579	117	59	41	37	63	84	16
Kenya	1988	676	500	135	56	44	42	58	76	24
Nepal	1978	641	547	117	56	44	46	54	67	33
Highlands	1978	692	586	118	59	41	52	48	66	34
Mountains	1978	649	534	122	56	44	48	52	65	35
Rural hills	1978	583	520	112	52	48	37	63	70	30
Philippines	1975-77	546	452	121	73	27	29	71	84	16
Average [a]	–	617	515	120	59	41	38	62	76	24
National [b]										
India	2000	457	391	117	61	39	35	65	92	8
Mongolia	2000	545	501	109	61	39	49	51	75	25
South Africa	2000	332	273	122	51	49	35	65	70	30
Average [a]	–	445	388	116	58	42	40	60	79	21
Selected OECD countries [c]										
Australia	1997	435	418	104	46	54	30	70	62	38
Austria [d]	1992	438	393	111	49	51	31	69	71	29
Canada	1998	420	429	98	53	47	41	59	65	35
Denmark [d]	1987	449	458	98	68	32	58	42	79	21
Finland [d]	1987-88	430	410	105	51	49	39	61	64	36
France	1999	391	363	108	46	54	33	67	60	40
Germany [d]	1991-92	440	441	100	44	56	30	70	61	39
Hungary	1999	432	445	97	51	49	41	59	60	40
Israel [d]	1991-92	375	377	99	51	49	29	71	74	26
Italy [d]	1988-89	470	367	128	45	55	22	78	77	23
Japan	1996	393	363	108	66	34	43	57	93	7
Korea, Rep. of	1999	431	373	116	64	36	45	55	88	12
Latvia	1996	535	481	111	46	54	35	65	58	42
Netherlands	1995	308	315	98	48	52	27	73	69	31
New Zealand	1999	420	417	101	46	54	32	68	60	40
Norway [d]	1990-91	445	412	108	50	50	38	62	64	36
United Kingdom [d]	1985	413	411	100	51	49	37	63	68	32
United States [d]	1985	453	428	106	50	50	37	63	63	37
Average [e]	–	423	403	105	52	48	37	64	69	31

Note: Data are estimates based on time use surveys available in time for publication. Time use data are also being collected in other countries, including Benin, Chad, Cuba, the Dominican Republic, Ecuador, Guatemala, the Lao People's Democratic Republic, Mali, Mexico, Morocco, Nepal, Nicaragua, Nigeria, Oman, the Philippines, Thailand and Viet Nam. Market activities refer to market-oriented production activities as defined by the 1993 revised UN System of National Accounts; surveys before 1993 are not strictly comparable with those for later years.

a. Refers to the unweighted average for the countries or areas shown above. b. Classifications of market and non-market activities are not strictly based on the 1993 revised UN System of National Accounts, so comparisons between countries and areas must be made with caution. c. Israel and Latvia are included here, although they are not OECD countries. d. Harvey 1995. e. Refers to the unweighted average for the OECD countries shown above (that is, excluding Israel and Latvia).

Source: For urban and rural areas in developing countries, Goldsmidt-Clermont and Pagnossin Aligisakis 1995 and Harvey 1995; for national studies in developing countries, UN 2002a; for OECD countries and Latvia, unless otherwise noted, Harvey 2001.

27 Women's political participation

HDI rank		Year women received right [a]		Year first woman elected (E) or appointed (A) to parliament	Women in government at ministerial level (as % of total) [b] 2000	Seats in parliament held by women (as % of total) [c]	
		To vote	To stand for election			Lower or single house	Upper house or senate
High human development							
1	Norway	1907, 1913	1907, 1913	1911 A	42.1	36.4	–
2	Iceland	1915	1915	1922 E	33.3	34.9	–
3	Sweden	1861, 1921	1907, 1921	1921 E	55.0	45.3	–
4	Australia	1902, 1962	1902, 1962	1943 E	19.5	25.3	28.9
5	Netherlands	1919	1917	1918 E	31.0	36.7	26.7
6	Belgium	1919, 1948	1921, 1948	1921 A	18.5	23.3	28.2
7	United States	1920, 1960	1788 [d]	1917 E	31.8	14.3	13.0
8	Canada	1917, 1950	1920, 1960	1921 E	24.3	20.6	32.4
9	Japan	1945, 1947	1945, 1947	1946 E	5.7	7.3	15.4
10	Switzerland	1971	1971	1971 E	28.6	23.0	19.6
11	Denmark	1915	1915	1918 E	45.0	38.0	–
12	Ireland	1918, 1928	1918, 1928	1918 E	18.8	13.3	16.7
13	United Kingdom	1918, 1928	1918, 1928	1918 E	33.3	17.9	16.4
14	Finland	1906	1906	1907 E	44.4	36.5	–
15	Luxembourg	1919	1919	1919 E	28.6	16.7	–
16	Austria	1918	1918	1919 E	31.3	33.9	21.0
17	France	1944	1944	1945 E	37.9	12.2	10.9
18	Germany	1918	1918	1919 E	35.7	32.2	24.6
19	Spain	1931	1931	1931 E	17.6	28.3	24.3
20	New Zealand	1893	1919	1933 E	44.0	29.2	–
21	Italy	1945	1945	1946 E	17.6	11.5	8.1
22	Israel	1948	1948	1949 E	6.1	15.0	–
23	Portugal	1931, 1976	1931, 1976	1934 E	9.7	19.1	–
24	Greece	1927, 1952	1927, 1952	1952 E	7.1	8.7	–
25	Cyprus	1960	1960	1963 E	..	10.7	–
26	Hong Kong, China (SAR)	..	..	..	..	..	..
27	Barbados	1950	1950	1966 A	14.3	10.7	33.3
28	Singapore	1947	1947	1963 E	5.7	11.8	–
29	Slovenia	1945	1945	1992 E [e]	15.0	12.2	–
30	Korea, Rep. of	1948	1948	1948 E	6.5	5.9	–
31	Brunei Darussalam	– [f]	– [f]	– [f]	0.0	– [f]	– [f]
32	Czech Republic	1920	1920	1992 E [e]	..	17.0	12.3
33	Malta	1947	1947	1966 E	5.3	9.2	–
34	Argentina	1947	1947	1951 E	7.3	30.7	33.3
35	Poland	1918	1918	1919 E	18.7	20.2	23.0
36	Seychelles	1948	1948	1976 E + A	23.1	29.4	–
37	Bahrain	1973	1973	–	..	0.0	12.5
38	Hungary	1918	1918	1920 E	35.9	9.8	–
39	Slovakia	1920	1920	1992 E [e]	19.0	19.3	–
40	Uruguay	1932	1932	1942 E	..	12.1	9.7
41	Estonia	1918	1918	1919 E	14.3	17.8	–
42	Costa Rica	1949	1949	1953 E	28.6	35.1	–
43	Chile	1931, 1949	1931, 1949	1951 E	25.6	12.5	4.1
44	Qatar	– [f]	– [f]	– [f]	0.0	– [f]	– [f]
45	Lithuania	1921	1921	1920 A	18.9	10.6	–
46	Kuwait	– [f]	– [f]	– [f]	0.0	0.0	–
47	Croatia	1945	1945	1992 E [e]	16.2	20.5	6.2
48	United Arab Emirates	– [f]	– [f]	– [f]	..	0.0	–
49	Bahamas	1961, 1964	1961, 1964	1977 A	16.7	20.0	..
50	Latvia	1918	1918	..	6.7	21.0	–

HDI rank	Year women received right[a] To vote	To stand for election	Year first woman elected (E) or appointed (A) to parliament	Women in government at ministerial level (as % of total)[b] 2000	Seats in parliament held by women (as % of total)[c] Lower or single house	Upper house or senate
51 Saint Kitts and Nevis	1951	1951	1984 E	0.0	13.3	–
52 Cuba	1934	1934	1940 E	10.7	36.0	–
53 Belarus	1919	1919	1990 E[e]	25.7	10.3	31.1
54 Trinidad and Tobago	1946	1946	1962 E + A	8.7	19.4	32.3
55 Mexico	1947	1953	1952 A	11.1	16.0	15.6
Medium human development						
56 Antigua and Barbuda	1951	1951	1984 A	0.0	5.3	11.8
57 Bulgaria	1937	1944	1945 E	18.8	26.3	–
58 Malaysia	1957	1957	1959 E	..	10.4	26.1
59 Panama	1941, 1946	1941, 1946	1946 E	20.0	9.9	–
60 Macedonia, TFYR	1946	1946	1990 E[e]	10.9	18.3	–
61 Libyan Arab Jamahiriya	1964	1964	..	12.5	..	–
62 Mauritius	1956	1956	1976 E	9.1	5.7	–
63 Russian Federation	1918	1918	1993 E[e]	..	7.6	3.4
64 Colombia	1954	1954	1954 A	47.4	12.0	8.8
65 Brazil	1934	1934	1933 E	0.0	8.6	12.3
66 Bosnia and Herzegovina	..	..	..	..	16.7	0.0
67 Belize	1954	1954	1984 E + A	11.1	6.9	..
68 Dominica	1951	1951	1980 E	0.0	18.8	–
69 Venezuela	1946	1946	1948 E	0.0	9.7	–
70 Samoa (Western)	1990	1990	1976 A	7.7	6.1	–
71 Saint Lucia	1924	1924	1979 A	18.2	11.1	36.4
72 Romania	1929, 1946	1929, 1946	1946 E	20.0	10.7	7.9
73 Saudi Arabia	–[f]	–[f]	–[f]	..	–[f]	–[f]
74 Thailand	1932	1932	1948 A	5.7	9.2	10.5
75 Ukraine	1919	1919	1990 E[e]	..	5.3	–
76 Kazakhstan	1924, 1993	1924, 1993	1990 E[e]	17.5	10.4	5.1
77 Suriname	1948	1948	1975 E	..	17.6	–
78 Jamaica	1944	1944	1944 E	12.5	11.7	19.0
79 Oman	–[f]	–[f]	–[f]	..	–[f]	–[f]
80 St. Vincent & the Grenadines	1951	1951	1979 E	0.0	22.7	–
81 Fiji	1963	1963	1970 A	20.7	5.7	..
82 Peru	1955	1955	1956 E	16.2	18.3	–
83 Lebanon	1952	1952	1991 A	0.0	2.3	–
84 Paraguay	1961	1961	1963 E	..	2.5	17.8
85 Philippines	1937	1937	1941 E	..	17.8	12.5
86 Maldives	1932	1932	1979 E	..	6.0	–
87 Turkmenistan	1927	1927	1990 E[e]	..	26.0	–
88 Georgia	1918, 1921	1918, 1921	1992 E[e]	9.7	7.2	–
89 Azerbaijan	1921	1921	1990 E[e]	2.6	10.5	–
90 Jordan	1974	1974	1989 A	0.0	1.3	7.5
91 Tunisia	1957, 1959	1957, 1959	1959 E	10.0	11.5	–
92 Guyana	1953	1945	1968 E	..	20.0	–
93 Grenada	1951	1951	1976 E + A	25.0	26.7	7.7
94 Dominican Republic	1942	1942	1942 E	..	17.3	6.3
95 Albania	1920	1920	1945 E	15.0	5.7	–
96 Turkey	1930	1934	1935 A	0.0	4.4	–
97 Ecuador	1929, 1967	1929, 1967	1956 E	20.0	16.0	–
98 Occupied Palestinian Territories	..	..	..	..	..	..
99 Sri Lanka	1931	1931	1947 E	..	4.4	–
100 Armenia	1921	1921	1990 E[e]	..	3.1	–

HDI rank	Year women received right [a]		Year first woman elected (E) or appointed (A) to parliament	Women in government at ministerial level (as % of total) [b] 2000	Seats in parliament held by women (as % of total) [c]	
	To vote	To stand for election			Lower or single house	Upper house or senate
101 Uzbekistan	1938	1938	1990 E [e]	4.4	7.2	–
102 Kyrgyzstan	1918	1918	1990 E [e]	..	10.0	2.2
103 Cape Verde	1975	1975	1975 E	35.0	11.1	–
104 China	1949	1949	1954 E	5.1	21.8	–
105 El Salvador	1939	1961	1961 E	15.4	9.5	–
106 Iran, Islamic Rep. of	1963	1963	1963 E + A	9.4	4.1	–
107 Algeria	1962	1962	1962 A	0.0	6.2	5.6
108 Moldova, Rep. of	1978, 1993	1978, 1993	1990 E	..	12.9	–
109 Viet Nam	1946	1946	1976 E	..	27.3	–
110 Syrian Arab Republic	1949, 1953	1953	1973 E	11.1	10.4	–
111 South Africa	1930, 1994	1930, 1994	1933 E	38.1	29.8	31.5 [g]
112 Indonesia	1945	1945	1950 A	5.9	8.0	–
113 Tajikistan	1924	1924	1990 E [e]	..	12.7	11.8
114 Bolivia	1938, 1952	1938, 1952	1966 E	..	18.5	14.8
115 Honduras	1955	1955	1957 [h]	33.3	5.5	–
116 Equatorial Guinea	1963	1963	1968 E	..	5.0	–
117 Mongolia	1924	1924	1951 E	10.0	10.5	–
118 Gabon	1956	1956	1961 E	12.1	9.2	..
119 Guatemala	1946	1946	1956 E	7.1	8.8	–
120 Egypt	1956	1956	1957 E	6.1	2.4	–
121 Nicaragua	1955	1955	1972 E	23.1	20.7	–
122 São Tomé and Principe	1975	1975	1975 E	..	9.1	–
123 Solomon Islands	1974	1974	1993 E	..	0.0	–
124 Namibia	1989	1989	1989 E	16.3	26.4	7.7
125 Botswana	1965	1965	1979 E	26.7	17.0	–
126 Morocco	1963	1963	1993 E	4.9	10.8	0.4
127 India	1950	1950	1952 E	10.1	8.8	10.3
128 Vanuatu	1975, 1980	1975, 1980	1987 E	..	1.9	–
129 Ghana	1954	1954	1960 A [h]	8.6	9.0	–
130 Cambodia	1955	1955	1958 E	7.1	7.4	13.1
131 Myanmar	1935	1946	1947 E	..	– [i]	– [i]
132 Papua New Guinea	1964	1963	1977 E	0.0	0.9	–
133 Swaziland	1968	1968	1972 E + A	12.5	3.1	13.3
134 Comoros	1956	1956	1993 E	..	– [j]	– [i]
135 Lao People's Dem. Rep.	1958	1958	1958 E	10.2	22.9	–
136 Bhutan	1953	1953	1975 E	..	9.3	–
137 Lesotho	1965	1965	1965 A	..	11.7	36.4
138 Sudan	1964	1964	1964 E	5.1	9.7	–
139 Bangladesh	1972	1972	1973 E	9.5	2.0	–
140 Congo	1963	1963	1963 E	..	9.3	15.0
141 Togo	1945	1945	1961 E	7.4	7.4	–
Low human development						
142 Cameroon	1946	1946	1960 E	5.8	8.9	–
143 Nepal	1951	1951	1952 A	14.8	5.9	..
144 Pakistan	1947	1947	1973 E	..	21.6	17.0
145 Zimbabwe	1957	1978	1980 E + A	36.0	10.0	–
146 Kenya	1919, 1963	1919, 1963	1969 E + A	1.4	7.1	–
147 Uganda	1962	1962	1962 A	27.1	24.7	–
148 Yemen	1967 [k]	1967 [k]	1990 E [h]	..	0.7	–
149 Madagascar	1959	1959	1965 E	12.5	3.8	11.1
150 Haiti	1950	1950	1961 E	18.2	3.6	25.9
151 Gambia	1960	1960	1982 E	30.8	13.2	–

| HDI rank | Year women received right[a] | | Year first woman elected (E) or appointed (A) to parliament | Women in government at ministerial level (as % of total)[b] 2000 | Seats in parliament held by women (as % of total)[c] | |
	To vote	To stand for election			Lower or single house	Upper house or senate
152 Nigeria	1958	1958	..	22.6	3.4	2.8
153 Djibouti	1946	1986	2003 E	5.0	10.8	–
154 Mauritania	1961	1961	1975 E	13.6	..	..
155 Eritrea	1955	1955	1994 E	11.8	22.0	–
156 Senegal	1945	1945	1963 E	15.6	19.2	–
157 Guinea	1958	1958	1963 E	11.1	19.3	–
158 Rwanda	1961	1961	1965 [h]	13.0	25.7	–
159 Benin	1956	1956	1979 E	10.5	6.0	..
160 Tanzania, U. Rep. of	1959	1959	..	..	22.3	–
161 Côte d'Ivoire	1952	1952	1965 E	9.1	8.5	–
162 Malawi	1961	1961	1964 E	11.8	9.3	–
163 Zambia	1962	1962	1964 E + A	6.2	12.0	–
164 Angola	1975	1975	1980 E	14.7	15.5	–
165 Chad	1958	1958	1962 E	..	5.8	–
166 Guinea-Bissau	1977	1977	1972 A	8.3	7.8	–
167 Congo, Dem. Rep. of the	1967	1970	1970 E	..	– [j]	– [j]
168 Central African Republic	1986	1986	1987 E	..	7.3	–
169 Ethiopia	1955	1955	1957 E	22.2	7.7	8.3
170 Mozambique	1975	1975	1977 E	..	30.0	–
171 Burundi	1961	1961	1982 E	4.5	18.4	18.9
172 Mali	1956	1956	1964 E	33.3	10.2	–
173 Burkina Faso	1958	1958	1978 E	8.6	11.7	–
174 Niger	1948	1948	1989 E	10.0	1.2	–
175 Sierra Leone	1961	1961	..	8.1	14.5	–

a. Data refer to the year in which the right to vote or stand for election on a universal and equal basis was recognized. Where two years are shown, the first refers to the first partial recognition of the right to vote or stand for election. b. Data were provided by states based on their definition of national executive and may therefore include women serving as ministers and vice ministers and those holding other ministerial positions, including parliamentary secretaries. c. Data are as of 1 March 2003. The percentage was calculated using as a reference the number of total seats currently filled in parliament. d. No information is available on the year all women received the right to stand for election. However, the constitution does not mention gender with regard to this right. e. Refers to the year women were elected to the current parliamentary system. f. Women's right to vote and to stand for election has not been recognized. Brunei Darussalam, Oman, Qatar and Saudi Arabia have never had a parliament. g. The figures on the distribution of seats do not include the 36 special rotating delegates appointed on an ad hoc basis; the percentages given are therefore calculated on the basis of the 54 permanent seats. h. No information or confirmation available. i. The parliament elected in 1990 has never been convened nor authorized to sit, and many of its members were detained or forced into exile. j. The parliament has been dissolved or suspended for an indefinite period. k. Refers to the former People's Democratic Republic of Yemen.
Source: Columns 1, 2 and 3: IPU 1995 and 2003a; column 4: IPU 2001; columns 5 and 6: IPU 2003b.

28 Status of major international human rights instruments

HDI rank	International Convention on the Elimination of All Forms of Racial Discrimination 1965	International Covenant on Civil and Political Rights 1966	International Covenant on Economic, Social and Cultural Rights 1966	Convention on the Elimination of All Forms of Discrimination Against Women 1979	Convention Against Torture and Other Cruel, Inhuman or Degrading Treatment or Punishment 1984	Convention on the Rights of the Child 1989
High human development						
1 Norway	●	●	●	●	●	●
2 Iceland	●	●	●	●	●	●
3 Sweden	●	●	●	●	●	●
4 Australia	●	●	●	●	●	●
5 Netherlands	●	●	●	●	●	●
6 Belgium	●	●	●	●	●	●
7 United States	●	●	○	○	●	○
8 Canada	●	●	●	●	●	●
9 Japan	●	●	●	●	●	●
10 Switzerland	●	●	●	●	●	●
11 Denmark	●	●	●	●	●	●
12 Ireland	●	●	●	●	●	●
13 United Kingdom	●	●	●	●	●	●
14 Finland	●	●	●	●	●	●
15 Luxembourg	●	●	●	●	●	●
16 Austria	●	●	●	●	●	●
17 France	●	●	●	●	●	●
18 Germany	●	●	●	●	●	●
19 Spain	●	●	●	●	●	●
20 New Zealand	●	●	●	●	●	●
21 Italy	●	●	●	●	●	●
22 Israel	●	●	●	●	●	●
23 Portugal	●	●	●	●	●	●
24 Greece	●	●	●	●	●	●
25 Cyprus	●	●	●	●	●	●
27 Barbados	●	●	●	●		●
28 Singapore				●		●
29 Slovenia	●	●	●	●	●	●
30 Korea, Rep. of	●	●	●	●	●	●
31 Brunei Darussalam						
32 Czech Republic	●	●	●	●	●	●
33 Malta	●	●	●	●	●	●
34 Argentina	●	●	●	●	●	●
35 Poland	●	●	●	●	●	●
36 Seychelles	●	●	●	●		●
37 Bahrain	●			●	●	●
38 Hungary	●	●	●	●	●	●
39 Slovakia	●	●	●	●	●	●
40 Uruguay	●	●	●	●	●	●
41 Estonia	●	●	●	●	●	●
42 Costa Rica	●	●	●	●	●	●
43 Chile	●	●	●	●	●	●
44 Qatar	●				●	●
45 Lithuania	●	●	●	●	●	●
46 Kuwait	●	●	●	●	●	●
47 Croatia	●	●	●	●	●	●
48 United Arab Emirates	●					●
49 Bahamas	●			●		●
50 Latvia	●	●	●	●	●	●
51 Saint Kitts and Nevis				●		●

HDI rank	International Convention on the Elimination of All Forms of Racial Discrimination 1965	International Covenant on Civil and Political Rights 1966	International Covenant on Economic, Social and Cultural Rights 1966	Convention on the Elimination of All Forms of Discrimination Against Women 1979	Convention Against Torture and Other Cruel, Inhuman or Degrading Treatment or Punishment 1984	Convention on the Rights of the Child 1989
52 Cuba	●			●	●	●
53 Belarus	●	●	●	●	●	●
54 Trinidad and Tobago	●	●	●	●		●
55 Mexico	●	●	●	●	●	●
Medium human development						
56 Antigua and Barbuda	●			●	●	●
57 Bulgaria	●	●	●	●	●	●
58 Malaysia				●		●
59 Panama	●	●	●	●	●	●
60 Macedonia, TFYR	●	●	●	●	●	●
61 Libyan Arab Jamahiriya	●	●	●	●	●	●
62 Mauritius	●	●	●	●	●	●
63 Russian Federation	●	●	●	●	●	●
64 Colombia	●	●	●	●	●	●
65 Brazil	●	●	●	●	●	●
66 Bosnia and Herzegovina	●	●	●	●	●	●
67 Belize	●	●	○	●	●	●
68 Dominica		●		●		●
69 Venezuela	●	●	●	●	●	●
70 Samoa (Western)				●		●
71 Saint Lucia	●			●		●
72 Romania	●	●	●	●	●	●
73 Saudi Arabia	●			●	●	●
74 Thailand	●	●	●	●		●
75 Ukraine	●	●	●	●	●	●
76 Kazakhstan	●			●	●	●
77 Suriname	●	●	●	●		●
78 Jamaica	●	●	●	●		●
79 Oman	●					●
80 St. Vincent & the Grenadines	●	●	●	●	●	●
81 Fiji	●			●		●
82 Peru	●	●	●	●	●	●
83 Lebanon	●	●	●	●	●	●
84 Paraguay	○	●	●	●	●	●
85 Philippines	●	●	●	●	●	●
86 Maldives	●			●		●
87 Turkmenistan	●	●	●	●	●	●
88 Georgia	●	●	●	●	●	●
89 Azerbaijan	●	●	●	●	●	●
90 Jordan	●	●	●	●	●	●
91 Tunisia	●	●	●	●	●	●
92 Guyana	●	●	●	●	●	●
93 Grenada	○	●	●	●		●
94 Dominican Republic	●	●	●	●	○	●
95 Albania	●	●	●	●	●	●
96 Turkey	●	○	○	●	●	●
97 Ecuador	●	●	●	●	●	●
99 Sri Lanka	●	●	●	●	●	●
100 Armenia	●	●	●	●	●	●
101 Uzbekistan	●	●	●	●	●	●

HDI rank	International Convention on the Elimination of All Forms of Racial Discrimination 1965	International Covenant on Civil and Political Rights 1966	International Covenant on Economic, Social and Cultural Rights 1966	Convention on the Elimination of All Forms of Discrimination Against Women 1979	Convention Against Torture and Other Cruel, Inhuman or Degrading Treatment or Punishment 1984	Convention on the Rights of the Child 1989
102 Kyrgyzstan	●	●	●	●	●	●
103 Cape Verde	●	●	●	●	●	●
104 China	●	○	●	●	●	●
105 El Salvador	●	●	●	●	●	●
106 Iran, Islamic Rep. of	●	●	●			●
107 Algeria	●	●	●	●	●	●
108 Moldova, Rep. of	●	●	●	●	●	●
109 Viet Nam	●	●	●	●		●
110 Syrian Arab Republic	●	●	●			●
111 South Africa	●	●	○	●	●	●
112 Indonesia	●			●	●	●
113 Tajikistan	●	●	●	●	●	●
114 Bolivia	●	●	●	●	●	●
115 Honduras	●	●	●	●	●	●
116 Equatorial Guinea	●	●	●	●	●	●
117 Mongolia	●	●	●	●	●	●
118 Gabon	●	●	●	●	●	●
119 Guatemala	●	●	●	●	●	●
120 Egypt	●	●	●	●	●	●
121 Nicaragua	●	●	●	●	○	●
122 São Tomé and Principe	○	○	○	○	○	●
123 Solomon Islands	●		●	●		●
124 Namibia	●	●	●	●	●	●
125 Botswana	●	●		●	●	●
126 Morocco	●	●	●	●	●	●
127 India	●	●	●	●	○	●
128 Vanuatu				●		●
129 Ghana	●	●	●	●	●	●
130 Cambodia	●	●	●	●	●	●
131 Myanmar				●		●
132 Papua New Guinea	●			●		●
133 Swaziland	●					●
134 Comoros	○			●	○	●
135 Lao People's Dem. Rep.	●	○	○	●		●
136 Bhutan	○			●		●
137 Lesotho	●	●	●	●	●	●
138 Sudan	●	●	●		○	●
139 Bangladesh	●	●	●	●	●	●
140 Congo	●	●	●	●		●
141 Togo	●	●	●	●	●	●
Low human development						
142 Cameroon	●	●	●	●	●	●
143 Nepal	●	●	●	●	●	●
144 Pakistan	●			●		●
145 Zimbabwe	●	●	●	●		●
146 Kenya	●	●	●	●	●	●
147 Uganda	●	●	●	●	●	●
148 Yemen	●	●	●	●	●	●
149 Madagascar	●	●	●	●	○	●
150 Haiti	●	●		●		●
151 Gambia	●	●	●	●	○	●

HDI rank	International Convention on the Elimination of All Forms of Racial Discrimination 1965	International Covenant on Civil and Political Rights 1966	International Covenant on Economic, Social and Cultural Rights 1966	Convention on the Elimination of All Forms of Discrimination Against Women 1979	Convention Against Torture and Other Cruel, Inhuman or Degrading Treatment or Punishment 1984	Convention on the Rights of the Child 1989
152 Nigeria	●	●	●	●	●	●
153 Djibouti		●	●	●	●	●
154 Mauritania	●			●		●
155 Eritrea	●	●	●	●		●
156 Senegal	●	●	●	●	●	●
157 Guinea	●	●	●	●	●	●
158 Rwanda	●	●	●	●		●
159 Benin	●	●	●	●	●	●
160 Tanzania, U. Rep. of	●	●	●	●		●
161 Côte d'Ivoire	●	●	●	●	●	●
162 Malawi	●	●	●	●	●	●
163 Zambia	●	●	●	●	●	●
164 Angola		●	●	●		●
165 Chad	●	●	●	●	●	●
166 Guinea-Bissau	○	○	●	●	○	●
167 Congo, Dem. Rep. of the	●	●	●	●		●
168 Central African Republic	●	●	●	●		●
169 Ethiopia	●	●	●	●	●	●
170 Mozambique	●	●		●	●	●
171 Burundi	●	●	●	●	●	●
172 Mali	●	●	●	●	●	●
173 Burkina Faso	●	●	●	●	●	●
174 Niger	●	●	●	●	●	●
175 Sierra Leone	●	●	●	●	●	●
Others [a]						
Afghanistan	●	●	●	○	●	●
Andorra	○	○		●	○	●
Cook Islands						●
Holy See	●				●	●
Iraq	●	●	●	●		●
Kiribati						●
Korea, Dem. Rep. of		●	●	●		●
Liberia	●	○	○	●		●
Liechtenstein	●	●	●	●	●	●
Marshall Islands						●
Micronesia, Fed. Sts.						●
Monaco	●	●	●		●	●
Nauru	○	○			○	●
Niue						●
Palau						●
San Marino	●	●	●		○	●
Serbia and Montenegro	●	●	●	●	●	●
Somalia	●	●	●		●	○
Tonga	●					●
Tuvalu				●		●
Total states parties [b]	167	149	146	170	132	191
Signatures not yet followed by participation	8	8	7	3	12	2

● Ratification, accession or succession. ○ Signature not yet followed by ratification.
Note: The table includes states that have signed or ratified at least one of the six human rights instruments. Information is as of 12 February 2003.
a. States not included in the human development index. b. States that have ratified, acceded or succeeded to the instrument.
Source: Columns 1-6: UN 2003b.

29 Status of fundamental labour rights conventions

HDI rank	Freedom of association and collective bargaining		Elimination of forced and compulsory labour		Elimination of discrimination in respect of employment and occupation		Abolition of child labour	
	Convention 87 [a]	Convention 98 [b]	Convention 29 [c]	Convention 105 [d]	Convention 100 [e]	Convention 111 [f]	Convention 138 [g]	Convention 182 [h]
High human development								
1 Norway	●	●	●	●	●	●	●	●
2 Iceland	●	●	●	●	●	●	●	●
3 Sweden	●	●	●	●	●	●	●	●
4 Australia	●	●	●	●	●	●		
5 Netherlands	●	●	●	●	●	●	●	●
6 Belgium	●	●	●	●	●	●	●	●
7 United States				●				●
8 Canada	●			●	●	●		●
9 Japan	●	●	●		●		●	●
10 Switzerland	●	●	●	●	●	●	●	●
11 Denmark	●	●	●	●	●	●	●	●
12 Ireland	●	●	●	●	●	●	●	●
13 United Kingdom	●	●	●	●	●	●	●	●
14 Finland	●	●	●	●	●	●	●	●
15 Luxembourg	●	●	●	●	●	●	●	●
16 Austria	●	●	●	●	●	●	●	●
17 France	●	●	●	●	●	●	●	●
18 Germany	●	●	●	●	●	●	●	●
19 Spain	●	●	●	●	●	●	●	●
20 New Zealand			●	●	●	●		●
21 Italy	●	●	●	●	●	●	●	●
22 Israel	●	●	●	●	●	●	●	●
23 Portugal	●	●	●	●	●	●	●	●
24 Greece	●	●	●	●	●	●	●	●
25 Cyprus	●	●	●	●	●	●	●	●
27 Barbados	●	●	●	●	●		●	●
28 Singapore		●	●	○	●			●
29 Slovenia	●	●	●	●	●	●	●	●
30 Korea, Rep. of					●	●	●	●
31 Brunei Darussalam								
32 Czech Republic	●	●	●	●	●	●		●
33 Malta	●	●	●	●	●	●	●	●
34 Argentina	●	●	●	●	●	●	●	●
35 Poland	●	●	●	●	●	●	●	●
36 Seychelles	●	●	●	●	●	●	●	●
37 Bahrain			●	●		●		●
38 Hungary	●	●	●	●	●	●	●	●
39 Slovakia	●	●	●	●	●	●	●	●
40 Uruguay	●	●	●	●	●	●	●	●
41 Estonia	●	●	●	●	●			●
42 Costa Rica	●	●	●	●	●	●	●	●
43 Chile	●	●	●	●	●	●	●	●
44 Qatar			●			●		●
45 Lithuania	●	●	●	●	●	●	●	●
46 Kuwait	●		●	●		●	●	●
47 Croatia	●	●	●	●	●	●	●	●
48 United Arab Emirates			●	●	●	●	●	●
49 Bahamas	●	●	●	●	●	●	●	●
50 Latvia	●	●		●	●	●		
51 Saint Kitts and Nevis	●	●	●	●	●	●		●

		Freedom of association and collective bargaining		Elimination of forced and compulsory labour		Elimination of discrimination in respect of employment and occupation		Abolition of child labour	
HDI rank		Convention 87[a]	Convention 98[b]	Convention 29[c]	Convention 105[d]	Convention 100[e]	Convention 111[f]	Convention 138[g]	Convention 182[h]
52	Cuba	●	●	●	●	●	●	●	
53	Belarus	●	●	●	●	●	●	●	●
54	Trinidad and Tobago	●	●	●	●	●	●		
55	Mexico	●		●	●	●	●		●
Medium human development									
56	Antigua and Barbuda	●	●	●	●		●	●	●
57	Bulgaria	●	●	●	●	●	●	●	●
58	Malaysia		●	●	○	●		●	●
59	Panama	●	●	●	●	●	●	●	●
60	Macedonia, TFYR	●	●	●		●	●	●	●
61	Libyan Arab Jamahiriya	●	●	●	●	●	●	●	●
62	Mauritius		●	●	●	●	●	●	●
63	Russian Federation	●	●	●	●	●	●	●	
64	Colombia	●	●	●	●	●	●	●	
65	Brazil		●	●	●	●	●	●	●
66	Bosnia and Herzegovina	●	●	●	●	●	●	●	●
67	Belize	●	●	●	●	●	●	●	●
68	Dominica	●	●	●	●	●	●	●	●
69	Venezuela	●	●	●	●	●	●	●	
70	Samoa (Western)								
71	Saint Lucia	●	●	●	●	●	●		●
72	Romania	●	●	●	●	●	●	●	●
73	Saudi Arabia			●	●	●	●		●
74	Thailand			●	●	●			
75	Ukraine	●	●	●	●	●	●	●	●
76	Kazakhstan	●	●	●	●	●	●	●	
77	Suriname	●	●	●	●				
78	Jamaica	●	●	●	●	●	●		
79	Oman			●					●
80	St. Vincent & the Grenadines	●	●	●	●	●	●		●
81	Fiji	●	●	●	●	●	●	●	●
82	Peru	●	●	●	●	●	●	●	●
83	Lebanon		●	●	●	●	●		●
84	Paraguay	●	●	●	●	●	●		●
85	Philippines	●	●		●	●	●	●	●
86	Maldives								
87	Turkmenistan	●	●	●	●	●	●		
88	Georgia	●	●	●	●	●	●	●	●
89	Azerbaijan	●	●	●	●	●	●	●	
90	Jordan		●	●	●	●	●	●	●
91	Tunisia	●	●	●	●	●	●	●	●
92	Guyana	●	●	●	●	●	●	●	●
93	Grenada	●	●	●	●	●			
94	Dominican Republic	●	●	●	●	●	●	●	●
95	Albania	●	●	●	●	●	●	●	●
96	Turkey	●	●	●	●	●	●	●	●
97	Ecuador	●	●	●	●	●	●	●	●
99	Sri Lanka	●	●	●	●	●	●	●	●
100	Armenia					●	●		
101	Uzbekistan		●	●	●	●	●		

HDI rank	Freedom of association and collective bargaining		Elimination of forced and compulsory labour		Elimination of discrimination in respect of employment and occupation		Abolition of child labour	
	Convention 87[a]	Convention 98[b]	Convention 29[c]	Convention 105[d]	Convention 100[e]	Convention 111[f]	Convention 138[g]	Convention 182[h]
102 Kyrgyzstan	●	●	●	●	●	●	●	
103 Cape Verde	●	●	●	●	●	●		●
104 China					●		●	●
105 El Salvador			●	●	●	●	●	●
106 Iran, Islamic Rep. of			●	●	●	●		●
107 Algeria	●	●	●	●	●	●	●	●
108 Moldova, Rep. of	●	●	●	●	●	●	●	
109 Viet Nam					●	●		●
110 Syrian Arab Republic	●	●	●	●	●	●	●	
111 South Africa	●	●	●	●	●	●	●	●
112 Indonesia	●	●	●	●	●	●	●	●
113 Tajikistan	●	●	●		●	●	●	
114 Bolivia	●	●			●	●	●	
115 Honduras	●	●	●	●	●	●	●	●
116 Equatorial Guinea	●	●	●	●	●	●	●	●
117 Mongolia	●	●			●	●		●
118 Gabon	●	●	●	●	●			●
119 Guatemala	●	●	●	●	●	●	●	●
120 Egypt	●	●	●	●	●	●	●	●
121 Nicaragua	●	●	●	●	●	●	●	●
122 São Tomé and Principe	●	●			●	●		
123 Solomon Islands			●					
124 Namibia	●	●	●	●	●	●	●	●
125 Botswana	●	●	●	●	●	●	●	●
126 Morocco		●	●	●	●	●	●	●
127 India			●	●	●	●		
128 Vanuatu								
129 Ghana	●	●	●	●	●	●		●
130 Cambodia	●	●	●	●	●	●	●	●
131 Myanmar	●		●					
132 Papua New Guinea	●	●	●	●	●	●	●	●
133 Swaziland	●	●	●	●	●	●	●	●
134 Comoros	●	●	●	●	●			
135 Lao People's Dem. Rep.			●					
136 Bhutan								
137 Lesotho	●	●	●	●	●	●	●	●
138 Sudan		●	●	●	●	●		●
139 Bangladesh	●	●	●	●	●	●		●
140 Congo	●	●	●	●	●	●	●	●
141 Togo	●	●	●	●	●	●	●	●
Low human development								
142 Cameroon	●	●	●	●	●	●	●	●
143 Nepal		●	●	●	●	●	●	●
144 Pakistan	●	●	●	●	●	●	●	●
145 Zimbabwe		●	●	●	●	●	●	●
146 Kenya		●	●	●	●	●	●	●
147 Uganda		●	●	●				●
148 Yemen	●	●	●	●	●	●	●	●
149 Madagascar	●	●	●	●	●	●	●	●
150 Haiti	●	●	●	●	●	●		●
151 Gambia	●	●	●	●	●	●	●	●

HDI rank	Freedom of association and collective bargaining		Elimination of forced and compulsory labour		Elimination of discrimination in respect of employment and occupation		Abolition of child labour	
	Convention 87[a]	Convention 98[b]	Convention 29[c]	Convention 105[d]	Convention 100[e]	Convention 111[f]	Convention 138[g]	Convention 182[h]
152 Nigeria	●	●	●	●	●	●	●	●
153 Djibouti	●	●	●	●	●	●		
154 Mauritania	●	●	●	●	●		●	●
155 Eritrea	●	●	●	●	●	●	●	
156 Senegal	●	●	●	●	●	●	●	●
157 Guinea	●	●	●	●	●	●		
158 Rwanda	●	●	●	●	●	●	●	●
159 Benin	●	●	●	●	●	●	●	●
160 Tanzania, U. Rep. of	●	●	●	●	●	●	●	●
161 Côte d'Ivoire	●	●	●	●	●	●		
162 Malawi	●	●	●	●	●	●	●	●
163 Zambia	●	●	●	●	●	●	●	●
164 Angola	●	●	●	●	●	●	●	●
165 Chad	●	●	●	●	●	●		●
166 Guinea-Bissau		●	●	●	●	●		
167 Congo, Dem. Rep. of the	●	●	●	●	●	●	●	●
168 Central African Republic	●	●	●	●	●	●	●	●
169 Ethiopia	●	●		●	●	●	●	
170 Mozambique	●	●		●	●	●		
171 Burundi	●	●	●	●	●	●	●	●
172 Mali	●	●	●	●	●	●	●	●
173 Burkina Faso	●	●	●	●	●	●	●	●
174 Niger	●	●	●	●	●	●	●	●
175 Sierra Leone	●	●	●	●	●	●		
Others [i]								
Afghanistan				●	●			
Iraq		●	●	●	●	●	●	●
Kiribati	●	●	●	●				
Liberia	●	●	●	●		●		
San Marino	●	●	●	●	●	●	●	●
Serbia and Montenegro	●	●	●		●	●	●	
Somalia			●	●		●		
Total ratifications	141	152	161	157	160	157	121	131

● Convention ratified. ○ Ratification denounced.

Note: The table includes states that have ratified at least one of the eight fundamental labour rights conventions. Information is as of 12 February 2003.

a. Freedom of Association and Protection of the Right to Organize Convention (1948). b. Right to Organize and Collective Bargaining Convention (1949). c. Forced Labour Convention (1930). d. Abolition of Forced Labour Convention (1957). e. Equal Remuneration Convention (1951). f. Discrimination (Employment and Occupation) Convention (1958). g. Minimum Age Convention (1973). h. Worst Forms of Child Labour Convention (1999). i. States not included in the human development index.

Source: Columns 1-8: ILO 2003a.

30 Basic indicators for other UN member countries

Human development index components

	Life expectancy at birth (years) 2000-05 [a]	Adult literacy rate (% age 15 and above) 2001	Combined primary, secondary and tertiary gross enrolment ratio (%) 2000-01 [b]	GDP per capita (PPP US$) 2001	Total population (thousands) 2001	Total fertility rate (per woman) 2000-05 [a]	Infant mortality rate (per 1,000 live births) 2001	Under-five mortality rate (per 1,000 live births) 2001	Adults living with HIV/AIDS (% ages 15-49) 2001 [c]	Under-nourished people (as % of total population) 1998/2000 [d]	Population with sustainable access to an improved water source (%) 2000
Afghanistan	43.1	36.0	30	..	22,083	6.8	165	257	..	70	13
Andorra	..	..	..	..	67	..	6	7	..	..	100
Iraq	60.7	39.7	58	..	23,860	4.8	107	133	<0.10	27	85
Kiribati	..	100.0	..	..	85	..	51	69	..	..	48
Korea, Dem. Rep. of	63.1	100.0	..	..	22,409	2.0	42	55	..	34	100
Liberia	41.4	54.8	16	..	3,099	6.8	157	235	..	39	..
Liechtenstein	..	100.0	..	..	33	..	10	11	..	..	..
Marshall Islands	..	91.0	..	..	52	..	54	66	..	..	..
Micronesia, Fed. Sts.	68.6	81.0	..	..	107	3.8	20	24	..	..	..
Monaco	..	..	..	..	34	..	4	5	..	..	100
Nauru	..	95.0	55	..	12	..	25	30	..	..	..
Palau	..	98.0	..	..	20	..	24	29	..	..	79
San Marino	..	..	..	..	27	..	4	6	..	..	..
Serbia and Montenegro	73.2	98.0	52	..	10,545	1.7	17	19	0.19	..	98
Somalia	47.9	24.0	7	..	9,088	7.3	133	225	1.00	71	..
Timor-Leste	49.5	..	..	..	711	3.8	85	124	..	..	..
Tonga	68.6	99.0	81	..	102	3.7	17	20	..	..	100
Tuvalu	..	98.0	67	..	10	..	38	52	..	..	..

Note: This table presents data for UN member countries not included in the main indicator tables.

a. Data refer to estimates for the period specified. b. Data refer to the 2000/01 school year. c. Data refer to the end of 2001. d. Data refer to the average for the years specified.

Source: Columns 1, 5 and 6: UN 2003d; column 2: UNESCO Institute for Statistics 2003a; column 3: UNESCO Institute for Statistics 2003b; column 4: World Bank 2003c; columns 7 and 8: UNICEF 2003b; column 9: UNAIDS 2002; column 10: UN 2003a, based on data from the Food and Agriculture Organization; column 11: UN 2003a, based on data from a joint effort by the United Nations Children's Fund and the World Health Organization.

CALCULATING THE HUMAN DEVELOPMENT INDICES

The diagrams here offer a clear overview of how the five human development indices
used in the *Human Development Report* are constructed, highlighting both their similarities
and their differences. The text on the following pages provides a detailed explanation.

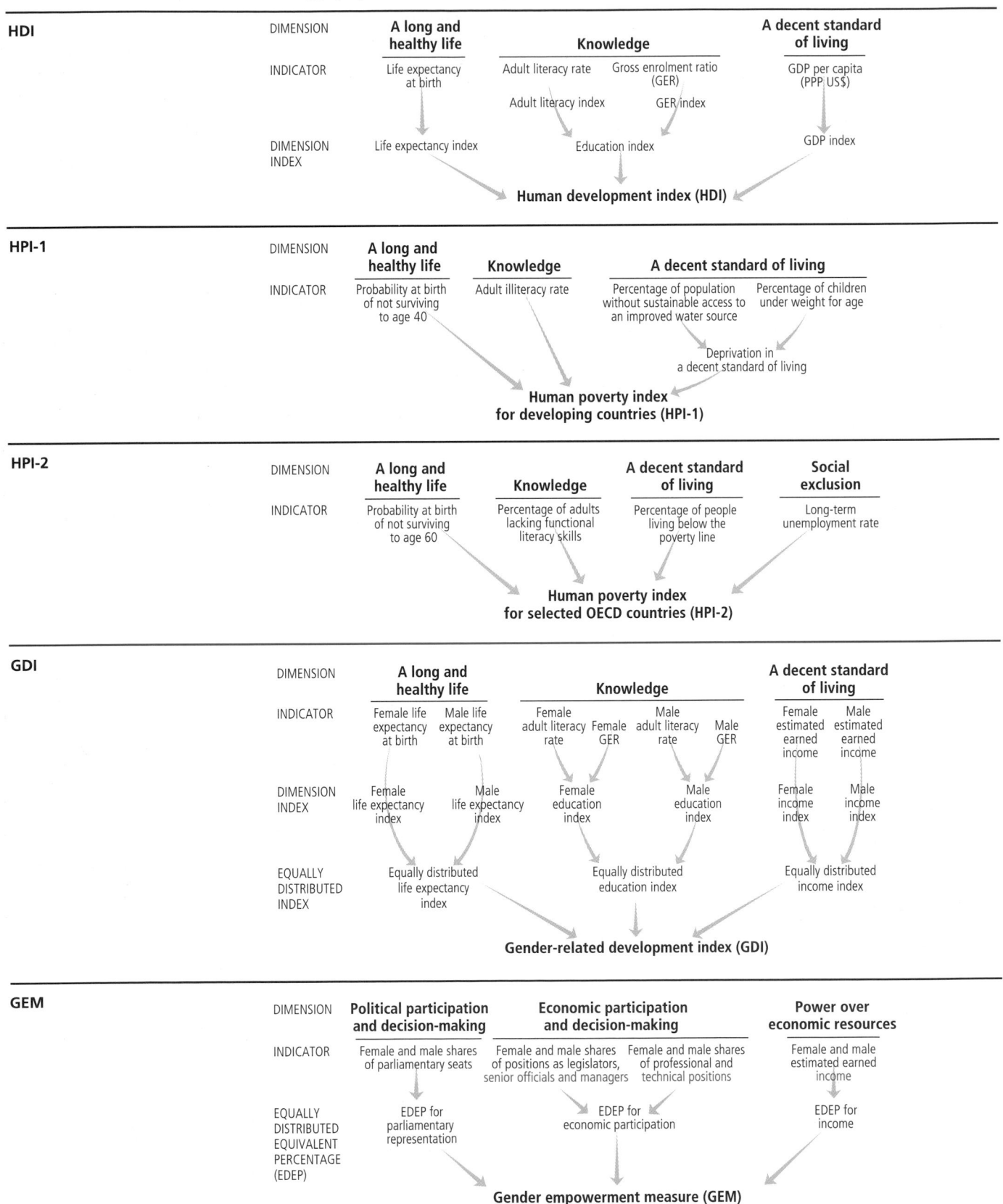

The human development index (HDI)

The HDI is a summary measure of human development. It measures the average achievements in a country in three basic dimensions of human development:

- A long and healthy life, as measured by life expectancy at birth.
- Knowledge, as measured by the adult literacy rate (with two-thirds weight) and the combined primary, secondary and tertiary gross enrolment ratio (with one-third weight).
- A decent standard of living, as measured by GDP per capita (PPP US$).

Before the HDI itself is calculated, an index needs to be created for each of these dimensions. To calculate these dimension indices —the life expectancy, education and GDP indices—minimum and maximum values (goalposts) are chosen for each underlying indicator.

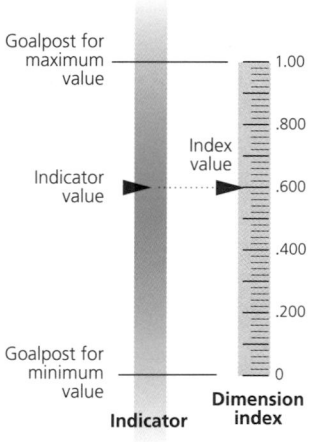

Performance in each dimension is expressed as a value between 0 and 1 by applying the following general formula:

$$\text{Dimension index} = \frac{\text{actual value} - \text{minimum value}}{\text{maximum value} - \text{minimum value}}$$

The HDI is then calculated as a simple average of the dimension indices. The box at right illustrates the calculation of the HDI for a sample country.

Goalposts for calculating the HDI

Indicator	Maximum value	Minimum value
Life expectancy at birth (years)	85	25
Adult literacy rate (%)	100	0
Combined gross enrolment ratio (%)	100	0
GDP per capita (PPP US$)	40,000	100

Calculating the HDI

This illustration of the calculation of the HDI uses data for Albania.

1. Calculating the life expectancy index
The life expectancy index measures the relative achievement of a country in life expectancy at birth. For Albania, with a life expectancy of 73.4 years in 2001, the life expectancy index is 0.807.

$$\text{Life expectancy index} = \frac{73.4 - 25}{85 - 25} = \mathbf{0.807}$$

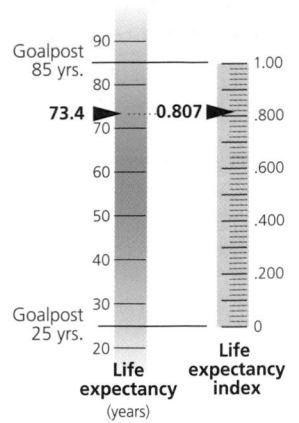

2. Calculating the education index
The education index measures a country's relative achievement in both adult literacy and combined primary, secondary and tertiary gross enrolment. First, an index for adult literacy and one for combined gross enrolment are calculated. Then these two indices are combined to create the education index, with two-thirds weight given to adult literacy and one-third weight to combined gross enrolment. For Albania, with an adult literacy rate of 85.3% in 2001 and a combined gross enrolment ratio of 69% in the school year 2000/01, the education index is 0.798.

$$\text{Adult literacy index} = \frac{85.3 - 0}{100 - 0} = 0.853$$

$$\text{Gross enrolment index} = \frac{69 - 0}{100 - 0} = 0.690$$

Education index = 2/3 (adult literacy index) + 1/3 (gross enrolment index)
= 2/3 (0.853) + 1/3 (0.690) = **0.798**

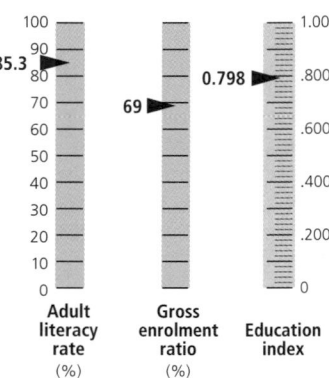

3. Calculating the GDP index
The GDP index is calculated using adjusted GDP per capita (PPP US$). In the HDI income serves as a surrogate for all the dimensions of human development not reflected in a long and healthy life and in knowledge. Income is adjusted because achieving a respectable level of human development does not require unlimited income. Accordingly, the logarithm of income is used. For Albania, with a GDP per capita of $3,680 (PPP US$) in 2001, the GDP index is 0.602.

$$\text{GDP index} = \frac{\log (3,680) - \log (100)}{\log (40,000) - \log (100)} = \mathbf{0.602}$$

4. Calculating the HDI
Once the dimension indices have been calculated, determining the HDI is straightforward. It is a simple average of the three dimension indices.

HDI = 1/3 (life expectancy index) + 1/3 (education index) + 1/3 (GDP index)
= 1/3 (0.807) + 1/3 (0.798) + 1/3 (0.602) = **0.735**

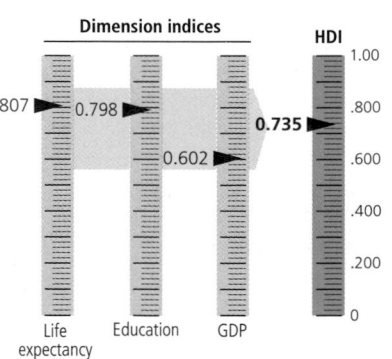

The human poverty index for developing countries (HPI-1)

While the HDI measures average achievement, the HPI-1 measures *deprivations* in the three basic dimensions of human development captured in the HDI:

• A long and healthy life—vulnerability to death at a relatively early age, as measured by the probability at birth of not surviving to age 40.
• Knowledge—exclusion from the world of reading and communications, as measured by the adult illiteracy rate.
• A decent standard of living—lack of access to overall economic provisioning, as measured by the unweighted average of two indicators, the percentage of the population without sustainable access to an improved water source and the percentage of children under weight for age.

Calculating the HPI-1 is more straightforward than calculating the HDI. The indicators used to measure the deprivations are already normalized between 0 and 100 (because they are expressed as percentages), so there is no need to create dimension indices as for the HDI.

Originally, the measure of deprivation in a decent standard of living also included an indicator of access to health services. But because reliable data on access to health services are lacking for recent years, in this year's Report deprivation in a decent standard of living is measured by two rather than three indicators—the percentage of the population without sustainable access to an improved water source and the percentage of children under weight for age.

The human poverty index for selected OECD countries (HPI-2)

The HPI-2 measures deprivations in the same dimensions as the HPI-1 and also captures social exclusion. Thus it reflects deprivations in four dimensions:

• A long and healthy life—vulnerability to death at a relatively early age, as measured by the probability at birth of not surviving to age 60.
• Knowledge—exclusion from the world of reading and communications, as measured by the percentage of adults (aged 16–65) lacking functional literacy skills.
• A decent standard of living—as measured by the percentage of people living below the income poverty line (50% of the median adjusted household disposable income).
• Social exclusion—as measured by the rate of long-term unemployment (12 months or more).

Calculating the HPI-1

1. Measuring deprivation in a decent standard of living
An unweighted average of two indicators is used to measure deprivation in a decent standard of living.

Unweighted average = 1/2 (population without sustainable access to an improved water source) + 1/2 (children under weight for age)

A sample calculation: Central African Republic
Population without sustainable access to an improved water source = 30%
Children under weight for age = 23%

Unweighted average = 1/2 (30) + 1/2 (23) = 26.5%

2. Calculating the HPI-1
The formula for calculating the HPI-1 is as follows:

$$\text{HPI-1} = [1/3\,(P_1^{\alpha} + P_2^{\alpha} + P_3^{\alpha})]^{1/\alpha}$$

Where:
P_1 = Probability at birth of not surviving to age 40 (times 100)
P_2 = Adult illiteracy rate
P_3 = Unweighted average of population without sustainable access to an improved water source and children under weight for age
$\alpha = 3$

A sample calculation: Central African Republic
$P_1 = 55.3\%$
$P_2 = 51.8\%$
$P_3 = 26.5\%$

$$\text{HPI-1} = [1/3\,(55.3^3 + 51.8^3 + 26.5^3)]^{1/3} = \mathbf{47.8}$$

Calculating the HPI-2

The formula for calculating the HPI-2 is as follows:

$$\text{HPI-2} = [1/4\,(P_1^{\alpha} + P_2^{\alpha} + P_3^{\alpha} + P_4^{\alpha})]^{1/\alpha}$$

Where:
P_1 = Probability at birth of not surviving to age 60 (times 100)
P_2 = Adults lacking functional literacy skills
P_3 = Population below income poverty line (50% of median adjusted household disposable income)
P_4 = Rate of long-term unemployment (lasting 12 months or more)
$\alpha = 3$

A sample calculation: United Kingdom
$P_1 = 8.9\%$
$P_2 = 21.8\%$
$P_3 = 12.5\%$
$P_4 = 1.3\%$

$$\text{HPI-2} = [1/4\,(8.9^3 + 21.8^3 + 12.5^3 + 1.3^3)]^{1/3} = \mathbf{14.8}$$

Why $\alpha = 3$ in calculating the HPI-1 and HPI-2

The value of α has an important impact on the value of the HPI. If $\alpha = 1$, the HPI is the average of its dimensions. As α rises, greater weight is given to the dimension in which there is the most deprivation. Thus as α increases towards infinity, the HPI will tend towards the value of the dimension in which deprivation is greatest (for the Central African Republic, the example used for calculating the HPI-1, it would be 55.3%, equal to the probability at birth of not surviving to age 40.

In this Report the value 3 is used to give additional but not overwhelming weight to areas of more acute deprivation. For a detailed analysis of the HPI's mathematical formulation, see Sudhir Anand and Amartya Sen's "Concepts of Human Development and Poverty: A Multidimensional Perspective" and the technical note in *Human Development Report 1997* (see the list of selected readings at the end of this technical note).

The gender-related development index (GDI)

While the HDI measures average achievement, the GDI adjusts the average achievement to reflect the *inequalities* between men and women in the following dimensions:

• A long and healthy life, as measured by life expectancy at birth.
• Knowledge, as measured by the adult literacy rate and the combined primary, secondary and tertiary gross enrolment ratio.
• A decent standard of living, as measured by estimated earned income (PPP US$).

The calculation of the GDI involves three steps. First, female and male indices in each dimension are calculated according to this general formula:

$$\text{Dimension index} = \frac{\text{actual value} - \text{minimum value}}{\text{maximum value} - \text{minimum value}}$$

Second, the female and male indices in each dimension are combined in a way that penalizes differences in achievement between men and women. The resulting index, referred to as the equally distributed index, is calculated according to this general formula:

$$\text{Equally distributed index}$$
$$= \{[\text{female population share (female index}^{1-\epsilon})]$$
$$+ [\text{male population share (male index}^{1-\epsilon})]\}^{1/1-\epsilon}$$

ϵ measures the aversion to inequality. In the GDI $\epsilon = 2$. Thus the general equation becomes:

$$\text{Equally distributed index}$$
$$= \{[\text{female population share (female index}^{-1})]$$
$$+ [\text{male population share (male index}^{-1})]\}^{-1}$$

which gives the harmonic mean of the female and male indices.

Third, the GDI is calculated by combining the three equally distributed indices in an unweighted average.

Goalposts for calculating the GDI

Indicator	Maximum value	Minimum value
Female life expectancy at birth (years)	87.5	27.5
Male life expectancy at birth (years)	82.5	22.5
Adult literacy rate (%)	100	0
Combined gross enrolment ratio (%)	100	0
Estimated earned income (PPP US$)	40,000	100

Note: The maximum and minimum values (goalposts) for life expectancy are five years higher for women to take into account their longer life expectancy.

Calculating the GDI

This illustration of the calculation of the GDI uses data for Thailand.

1. Calculating the equally distributed life expectancy index
The first step is to calculate separate indices for female and male achievements in life expectancy, using the general formula for dimension indices.

FEMALE
Life expectancy: 73.2 years

$$\text{Life expectancy index} = \frac{73.2 - 27.5}{87.5 - 27.5} = 0.762$$

MALE
Life expectancy: 64.9 years

$$\text{Life expectancy index} = \frac{64.9 - 22.5}{82.5 - 22.5} = 0.707$$

Next, the female and male indices are combined to create the equally distributed life expectancy index, using the general formula for equally distributed indices.

FEMALE
Population share: 0.508
Life expectancy index: 0.762

MALE
Population share: 0.492
Life expectancy index: 0.707

$$\text{Equally distributed life expectancy index} = \{[0.508 (0.762^{-1})] + [0.492 (0.707^{-1})]\}^{-1} = \textbf{0.734}$$

2. Calculating the equally distributed education index
First, indices for the adult literacy rate and the combined primary, secondary and tertiary gross enrolment ratio are calculated separately for females and males. Calculating these indices is straightforward, since the indicators used are already normalized between 0 and 100.

FEMALE
Adult literacy rate: 94.1%
Adult literacy index: 0.941
Gross enrolment ratio: 69.3%
Gross enrolment index: 0.693

MALE
Adult literacy rate: 97.3%
Adult literacy index: 0.973
Gross enrolment ratio: 74.6%
Gross enrolment index: 0.746

Second, the education index, which gives two-thirds weight to the adult literacy index and one-third weight to the gross enrolment index, is computed separately for females and males.

$$\text{Education index} = 2/3 \text{ (adult literacy index)} + 1/3 \text{ (gross enrolment index)}$$

$$\text{Female education index} = 2/3 (0.941) + 1/3 (0.693) = 0.858$$

$$\text{Male education index} = 2/3 (0.973) + 1/3 (0.746) = 0.897$$

Finally, the female and male education indices are combined to create the equally distributed education index.

FEMALE
Population share: 0.508
Education index: 0.858

MALE
Population share: 0.492
Education index: 0.897

$$\text{Equally distributed education index} = \{[0.508 (0.858^{-1})] + [0.492 (0.897^{-1})]\}^{-1} = \textbf{0.877}$$

3. Calculating the equally distributed income index
First, female and male earned income (PPP US$) are estimated (for details on this calculation, see the addendum to this technical note). Then the income index is calculated for each gender. As for the HDI, income is adjusted by taking the logarithm of estimated earned income (PPP US$):

$$\text{Income index} = \frac{\log (\text{actual value}) - \log (\text{minimum value})}{\log (\text{maximum value}) - \log (\text{minimum value})}$$

FEMALE
Estimated earned income (PPP US$): 4,875

MALE
Estimated earned income (PPP US$): 7,975

$$\text{Income index} = \frac{\log (4,875) - \log (100)}{\log (40,000) - \log (100)} = 0.649$$

$$\text{Income index} = \frac{\log (7,975) - \log (100)}{\log (40,000) - \log (100)} = 0.731$$

Calculating the GDI continues on next page

Calculating the GDI (continued)

Second, the female and male income indices are combined to create the equally distributed income index:

FEMALE
Population share: 0.508
Income index: 0.649

MALE
Population share: 0.492
Income index: 0.731

Equally distributed income index $= \{[0.508 \, (0.649^{-1})] + [0.492 \, (0.731^{-1})]\}^{-1} = \mathbf{0.687}$

4. Calculating the GDI

Calculating the GDI is straightforward. It is simply the unweighted average of the three component indices—the equally distributed life expectancy index, the equally distributed education index and the equally distributed income index.

GDI = 1/3 (life expectancy index) + 1/3 (education index) + 1/3 (income index)
$= 1/3 \, (0.734) + 1/3 \, (0.877) + 1/3 \, (0.687) = \mathbf{0.766}$

Why $\epsilon = 2$ in calculating the GDI

The value of ϵ is the size of the penalty for gender inequality. The larger the value, the more heavily a society is penalized for having inequalities.

If $\epsilon = 0$, gender inequality is not penalized (in this case the GDI would have the same value as the HDI). As ϵ increases towards infinity, more and more weight is given to the lesser achieving group.

The value 2 is used in calculating the GDI (as well as the GEM). This value places a moderate penalty on gender inequality in achievement.

For a detailed analysis of the GDI's mathematical formulation, see Sudhir Anand and Amartya Sen's "Gender Inequality in Human Development: Theories and Measurement," Kalpana Bardhan and Stephan Klasen's "UNDP's Gender-Related Indices: A Critical Review" and the technical notes in *Human Development Report 1995* and *Human Development Report 1999* (see the list of selected readings at the end of this technical note).

The gender empowerment measure (GEM)

Focusing on women's opportunities rather than their capabilities, the GEM captures gender inequality in three key areas:

- Political participation and decision-making power, as measured by women's and men's percentage shares of parliamentary seats.
- Economic participation and decision-making power, as measured by two indicators—women's and men's percentage shares of positions as legislators, senior officials and managers and women's and men's percentage shares of professional and technical positions.
- Power over economic resources, as measured by women's and men's estimated earned income (PPP US$).

For each of these three dimensions, an equally distributed equivalent percentage (EDEP) is calculated, as a population-weighted average, according to the following general formula:

$$EDEP = \{[\text{female population share (female index}^{1-\epsilon})] + [\text{male population share (male index}^{1-\epsilon})]\}^{1/1-\epsilon}$$

ϵ measures the aversion to inequality. In the GEM (as in the GDI) $\epsilon = 2$, which places a moderate penalty on inequality. The formula is thus:

$$EDEP = \{[\text{female population share (female index}^{-1})] + [\text{male population share (male index}^{-1})]\}^{-1}$$

For political and economic participation and decision-making, the EDEP is then indexed by dividing it by 50. The rationale for this indexation: in an ideal society, with equal empowerment of the sexes, the GEM variables would equal 50%—that is, women's share would equal men's share for each variable.

Finally, the GEM is calculated as a simple average of the three indexed EDEPs.

Calculating the GEM

This illustration of the calculation of the GEM uses data for Venezuela.

1. Calculating the EDEP for parliamentary representation

The EDEP for parliamentary representation measures the relative empowerment of women in terms of their political participation. The EDEP is calculated using the female and male shares of the population and female and male percentage shares of parliamentary seats according to the general formula.

FEMALE
Population share: 0.497
Parliamentary share: 9.7%

MALE
Population share: 0.503
Parliamentary share: 90.3%

$$EDEP\text{ for parliamentary representation} = \{[0.497 (9.7^{-1})] + [0.503 (90.3^{-1})]\}^{-1} = 17.60$$

Then this initial EDEP is indexed to an ideal value of 50%.

$$\text{Indexed EDEP for parliamentary representation} = \frac{17.60}{50} = \textbf{0.352}$$

2. Calculating the EDEP for economic participation

Using the general formula, an EDEP is calculated for women's and men's percentage shares of positions as legislators, senior officials and managers, and another for women's and men's percentage shares of professional and technical positions. The simple average of the two measures gives the EDEP for economic participation.

FEMALE
Population share: 0.497
Percentage share of positions as legislators, senior officials and managers: 24.3%
Percentage share of professional and technical positions: 57.6%

MALE
Population share: 0.503
Percentage share of positions as legislators, senior officials and managers: 75.7%
Percentage share of professional and technical positions: 42.4%

$$EDEP\text{ for positions as legislators, senior officials and managers} = \{[0.497 (24.3^{-1})] + [0.503 (75.7^{-1})]\}^{-1} = 36.90$$

$$\text{Indexed EDEP for positions as legislators, senior officials and managers} = \frac{36.90}{50} = 0.738$$

$$EDEP\text{ for professional and technical positions} = \{[0.497 (57.6^{-1})] + [0.503 (42.4^{-1})]\}^{-1} = 48.80$$

$$\text{Indexed EDEP for professional and technical positions} = \frac{48.80}{50} = 0.976$$

The two indexed EDEPs are averaged to create the EDEP for economic participation:

$$EDEP\text{ for economic participation} = \frac{0.738 + 0.976}{2} = \textbf{0.857}$$

3. Calculating the EDEP for income

Earned income (PPP US$) is estimated for women and men separately and then indexed to goalposts as for the HDI and the GDI. For the GEM, however, the income index is based on unadjusted values, not the logarithm of estimated earned income. (For details on the estimation of earned income for men and women, see the addendum to this technical note.)

FEMALE
Population share: 0.497
Estimated earned income (PPP US$): 3,288

MALE
Population share: 0.503
Estimated earned income (PPP US$): 8,021

$$\text{Income index} = \frac{3,288 - 100}{40,000 - 100} = 0.080$$

$$\text{Income index} = \frac{8,021 - 100}{40,000 - 100} = 0.199$$

The female and male indices are then combined to create the equally distributed index:

$$EDEP\text{ for income} = \{[0.497 (0.080^{-1})] + [0.503 (0.199^{-1})]\}^{-1} = \textbf{0.114}$$

4. Calculating the GEM

Once the EDEP has been calculated for the three dimensions of the GEM, determining the GEM is straightforward. It is a simple average of the three EDEP indices.

$$GEM = \frac{0.352 + 0.857 + 0.114}{3} = \textbf{0.441}$$

Female and male earned income

Despite the importance of having gender-disaggregated data on income, direct measures are unavailable. For this Report crude estimates of female and male earned income have therefore been derived.

Income can be seen in two ways: as a resource for consumption and as earnings by individuals. The use measure is difficult to disaggregate between men and women because they share resources within a family unit. By contrast, earnings are separable because different members of a family tend to have separate earned incomes.

The income measure used in the GDI and the GEM indicates a person's capacity to earn income. It is used in the GDI to capture the disparities between men and women in command over resources and in the GEM to capture women's economic independence. (For conceptual and methodological issues relating to this approach, see Sudhir Anand and Amartya Sen's "Gender Inequality in Human Development" and, in *Human Development Report 1995,* chapter 3 and technical notes 1 and 2; see the list of selected readings at the end of this technical note.)

Female and male earned income (PPP US$) are estimated using the following data:

- Ratio of the female non-agricultural wage to the male non-agricultural wage.
- Male and female shares of the economically active population.
- Total female and male population.
- GDP per capita (PPP US$).

Key

W_f / W_m = ratio of female non-agricultural wage to male non-agricultural wage
EA_f = female share of economically active population
EA_m = male share of economically active population
S_f = female share of wage bill
Y = total GDP (PPP US$)
N_f = total female population
N_m = total male population
Y_f = estimated female earned income (PPP US$)
Y_m = estimated male earned income (PPP US$)

Note

Calculations based on data in the technical note may yield results that differ from those in the indicator tables because of rounding.

Estimating female and male earned income

This illustration of the estimation of female and male earned income uses 2001 data for Ethiopia.

1. Calculating total GDP (PPP US$)
Total GDP (PPP US$) is calculated by multiplying the total population by GDP per capita (PPP US$).

Total population: 67,266 (thousand)
GDP per capita (PPP US$): 810
Total GDP (PPP US$) = 810 (67,266) = 54,485,460 (thousand)

2. Calculating the female share of the wage bill
Because data on wages in rural areas and in the informal sector are rare, the Report has used non-agricultural wages and assumed that the ratio of female wages to male wages in the non-agricultural sector applies to the rest of the economy. The female share of the wage bill is calculated using the ratio of the female non-agricultural wage to the male non-agricultural wage and the female and male percentage shares of the economically active population. Where data on the wage ratio are not available, a value of 75% is used.

Ratio of female to male non-agricultural wage (W_f/W_m) = 0.75
Female percentage share of economically active population (EA_f) = 40.9%
Male percentage share of economically active population (EA_m) = 59.1%

$$\text{Female share of wage bill } (S_f) = \frac{W_f/W_m\,(EA_f)}{[W_f/W_m\,(EA_f)] + EA_m} = \frac{0.75\,(40.9)}{[0.75\,(40.9)] + 59.1} = \mathbf{0.342}$$

3. Calculating female and male earned income (PPP US$)
An assumption has to be made that the female share of the wage bill is equal to the female share of GDP.

Female share of wage bill (S_f) = 0.342
Total GDP (PPP US$) ($Y$) = 54,485,460 (thousand)
Female population (N_f) = 33,892 (thousand)

$$\text{Estimated female earned income (PPP US\$) } (Y_f) = \frac{S_f(Y)}{N_f} = \frac{0.342\,(54,485,460)}{33,892} = \mathbf{550}$$

Male population (N_m) = 33,374 (thousand)

$$\text{Estimated male earned income (PPP US\$) } (Y_m) = \frac{Y - S_f(Y)}{N_m} = \frac{54,485,460 - [0.342\,(54,485,460)]}{33,374} = \mathbf{1,074}$$

Selected readings

Anand, Sudhir, and Amartya Sen. 1994. "Human Development Index: Methodology and Measurement." Occasional Paper 12. United Nations Development Programme, Human Development Report Office, New York. *(HDI)*

———. 1995. "Gender Inequality in Human Development: Theories and Measurement." Occasional Paper 19. United Nations Development Programme, Human Development Report Office, New York. *(GDI, GEM)*

———. 1997. "Concepts of Human Development and Poverty: A Multi-dimensional Perspective." In United Nations Development Programme, *Human Development Report 1997 Papers: Poverty and Human Development.* New York. *(HPI-1, HPI-2)*

Bardhan, Kalpana, and Stephan Klasen. 1999. "UNDP's Gender-Related Indices: A Critical Review." *World Development* 27 (6): 985–1010. *(GDI, GEM)*

United Nations Development Programme. 1995. *Human Development Report 1995.* New York: Oxford University Press. Technical notes 1 and 2 and chapter 3. *(GDI, GEM)*

———. 1997. *Human Development Report 1997.* New York: Oxford University Press. Technical note 1 and chapter 1. *(HPI-1, HPI-2)*

———. 1999. *Human Development Report 1999.* New York: Oxford University Press. Technical note. *(HDI, GDI)*

IDENTIFYING TOP PRIORITY AND HIGH PRIORITY COUNTRIES FOR THE MILLENNIUM DEVELOPMENT GOALS

This year's *Human Development Report* identifies countries that are *top priority* and *high priority* for each Millennium Development Goal for which there are sufficient data, based on human poverty in each Goal and trends in the 1990s. Based on the Goal-by-Goal analysis, the Report then identifies countries that are top priority and high priority overall.

Assessing countries as top priority and high priority for each Goal

For each Millennium Development Goal the assessment of a country is based both on its progress towards the Goal—slow or reversing, moderate, fast—and on its level of human poverty in the Goal—extreme, medium, low (technical note tables 2.1 and 2.2). Progress is measured against the targets and using the indicators defined for the Millennium Development Goals.

Top priority countries for each Goal
A country is designated top priority for a Goal if it has both extreme human poverty in that Goal and slow or reversing progress towards it (technical note figure 2.1).

High priority countries for each Goal
A country is designated high priority for a Goal if:
• It has extreme human poverty in that Goal and moderate progress towards it.

• Or it has medium human poverty in that Goal and slow or reversing progress towards it.

Assessing countries as top priority and high priority across all the Goals

The assessment of whether a country is top priority or high priority for all the Goals is based on the number of Goals for which the country is top priority or high priority. (This overall assessment includes data for the HIV/AIDS target, though it is not assessed separately).

Top priority countries across all the Goals
A country is designated top priority across all the Goals if:
• It is top priority for at least three Goals.
• Or it is top priority for half or more of the Goals for which at least three data points are available for that country.
• Or, where data are available for only two Goals, it is top priority for both.

High priority countries across all the Goals
A country is designated high priority across all the Goals if it does not fall into the top priority category but:
• It is top or high priority for at least three Goals.
• Or it is top priority for two Goals.
• Or it is top or high priority for half or more of the Goals for which at least three data points are available for that country.
• Or, where data are available for only two Goals, it is top or high priority for both.

Technical note table 2.1
Defining progress towards the Millennium Development Goals

Rate of progress	Definition
Slow or reversing	Actual progress towards the Goal is *less than half* the approximate progress required to meet the target if current trends prevail until 2015.
Moderate	Actual progress towards the Goal is *more than half but less than* the approximate progress required to meet the target if current trends prevail until 2015.
Fast	Actual progress towards the Goal is *equal to or greater than* the approximate progress required to meet the target if current trends prevail until 2015.

Note: The year in which the target is to be met is 2015 for all except gender equality in education, for which it is 2005.

Technical note table 2.2
Defining the level of human poverty in the Millennium Development Goals

Target	Indicator	Level of human poverty (x = value of indicator)			Source
		Extreme	Medium	Low	
Halve the proportion of people whose income is less than $1 a day	GDP per capita (PPP US$)[a]	$x < 3,500$	$3,500 \leq x < 7,000$	$x \geq 7,000$	World Bank
Halve the proportion of people who suffer from hunger	Undernourished people (%)	$x > 25$	$10 < x \leq 25$	$x \leq 10$	Food and Agriculture Organization
Ensure that children everywhere will be able to complete a full course of primary schooling	Net primary enrolment ratio (%)	$x < 75$	$75 \leq x < 90$	$x \geq 90$	United Nations Educational, Scientific and Cultural Organization (UNESCO)
Achieve gender equality in education	Ratio of girls to boys in primary and secondary education (%)	$x < 80$	$80 \leq x < 90$	$x \geq 90$	UNESCO
Reduce under-five mortality by two-thirds	Under-five mortality rate (per 1,000 live births)	$x > 100$	$30 < x \leq 100$	$x \leq 30$	World Bank
Halve the proportion of people without sustainable access to safe drinking water	Population with sustainable access to an improved water source (%)	$x < 75$	$75 \leq x < 90$	$x \geq 90$	United Nations Children's Fund (UNICEF) and World Health Organization (WHO)
Halve the proportion of people without access to improved sanitation	Population with sustainable access to improved sanitation (%)	$x < 75$	$75 \leq x < 90$	$x \geq 90$	UNICEF and WHO

a. The average annual GDP per capita growth rate is used as the trend measure.

Technical note figure 2.1
Identifying top priority and high priority countries

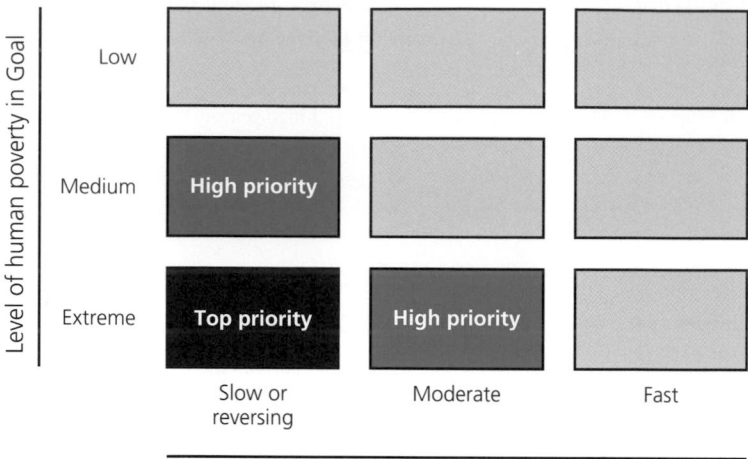

Calculating progress towards each Goal

Progress towards each Goal is assessed by comparing actual annual progress if current trends were to prevail until 2015 with the annual progress needed to meet the target, under the assumption of linear progress.

Assessing actual progress
The actual annual rate of progress is calculated using the general formula:

$$\text{Actual annual rate of progress} = \frac{(x_{t_1} - x_{t_0})\,/\,x_{t_0}}{t_1 - t_0}$$

where t_0 is 1990 or the year closest to 1990 for which data are available; t_1 is the most recent year for which data are available, generally 2001; and x_{t_0} and x_{t_1} are the values of the indicator for those years. For rates of hunger, poverty and under-five mortality, for which the most desirable value is 0, the formula is applied without modification.

For the net primary enrolment ratio, gender equality in education (ratio of girls to boys) and the proportion of the population with access to safe water and sanitation, for which the most desirable value is 100%, progress is expressed as "shortfall reduction" according to the following formula:

$$\text{Actual annual rate of progress} = \frac{(x_{t_1} - x_{t_0})\,/\,(100 - x_{t_0})}{t_1 - t_0}$$

Assessing required progress
The rate of progress required to meet a target by 2015 (by 2005 for gender equality in education) is dictated by the target: α is $-1/2$ for poverty and hunger, $1/2$ for safe water and sanitation, $-2/3$ for under-five mortality and 1 for primary enrolment and gender equality in education. The annual rate of progress required is then calculated by simply dividing α by the number of years between t_{MDG}, the year by which the target is to be met, and t_0, the year closest to 1990 for which data are available:

$$\text{Required annual rate of progress} = \frac{\alpha}{t_{MDG} - t_0}$$

Determining priority status: an example

This illustration of determining priority status uses data on the under-five mortality rate for Chad.

Calculating progress
Data for the under-five mortality rate are available for 1990 and 2001:
$t_0 = 1990$
$t_1 = 2001$

The under-five mortality rate is 203 per 1,000 live births for 1990 and 200 for 2001:
$x_{t_0} = 203$
$x_{t_1} = 200$

The required reduction is two-thirds:
$\alpha = -2/3$

Therefore:

$$\text{Actual annual rate of progress} = \frac{(200 - 203) / 203}{2001 - 1990} = -0.13\%$$

$$\text{Required annual rate of progress} = \frac{-2/3}{2015 - 1990} = -2.67\%$$

The actual progress towards the Goal is less than half the approximate progress required to meet the target.
Therefore, Chad is making slow or reversing progress towards the Goal of reducing under-five mortality.

Determining the level of human poverty
The under-five mortality rate for Chad in 2001 is 200 per 1,000 live births.
Therefore, Chad has an extreme level of human poverty in under-five mortality (see technical note table 2.2).

Determining the priority status for under-five mortality
Chad has an extreme level of human poverty in under-five mortality and slow or reversing progress.
Therefore, Chad is categorized as top priority for the Goal of reducing under-five mortality.

Determining the priority status across all Goals
Of the eight indicators for which Chad has data, it is identified as top priority for five and high priority for another two.
Therefore, Chad is categorized as a top priority country overall.

Note

To measure progress in income poverty, the GDP per capita growth rate in 1990–2001 is used. It is estimated that average annual growth of 1.4% is required in 1990–2015 to meet the income poverty target. Accordingly, the threshold for slow or reversing progress is annual per capita income growth of less than 0.7%; for moderate progress, 0.7% to 1.4%; and for fast progress, 1.4% or more.
Trend data for the prevalence of HIV/AIDS among adults (age 15 and above) in 1990 and 2000 are also used in the overall assessment of countries as top priority and high priority (UNAIDS and WHO 2003). For determining the level of human poverty in HIV/AIDS, a prevalence rate of more than 3% is considered extreme; 3% or less but greater than 1%, medium; and 1% or less, low. Since the target is to halt and begin to reverse the spread of HIV/AIDS, an increase in the prevalence rate of less than 1 percentage point is considered fast progress; an increase of 1 percentage point or more but less than 3, moderate progress; and an increase of 3 percentage points or more, slow or reversing progress.

Definitions of statistical terms

Agriculture, OECD country support to domestic Transfers from taxpayers and consumers arising from policy measures that support agriculture (net of the associated budgetary receipts), regardless of their objectives and impacts on farm production and income or on consumption of farm products.

Armed forces, total Strategic, land, naval, air, command, administrative and support forces. Also included are paramilitary forces such as the gendarmerie, customs service and border guard, if these are trained in military tactics.

Arms transfers, conventional Refers to the voluntary transfer by the supplier (and thus excludes captured weapons and weapons obtained through defectors) of weapons with a military purpose destined for the armed forces, paramilitary forces or intelligence agencies of another country. These include major conventional weapons or systems in six categories: ships, aircraft, missiles, artillery, armoured vehicles and guidance and radar systems (excluded are trucks, services, ammunition, small arms, support items, components and component technology and towed or naval artillery under 100-millimetre calibre).

Births attended by skilled health personnel The percentage of deliveries attended by personnel (including doctors, nurses and midwives) trained to give the necessary care, supervision and advice to women during pregnancy, labour and the postpartum period, to conduct deliveries on their own and to care for newborns.

Birth-weight, infants with low The percentage of infants with a birth-weight of less than 2,500 grams.

Carbon dioxide emissions Anthropogenic (human-originated) carbon dioxide emissions stemming from the burning of fossil fuels, gas flaring and the production of cement. Emissions are calculated from data on the consumption of solid, liquid and gaseous fuels, gas flaring and the production of cement.

Cellular subscribers (also referred to as cellular mobile subscribers) Subscribers to an automatic public mobile telephone service that provides access to the public switched telephone network using cellular technology. Systems can be analogue or digital.

Children reaching grade 5 The percentage of children starting primary school who eventually attain grade 5 (grade 4 if the duration of primary school is four years). The estimates are based on the reconstructed cohort method, which uses data on enrolment and repeaters for two consecutive years.

Chlorofluorocarbons, consumption of ozone depleting The sum of production and imports minus exports of chlorofluorocarbons (CFCs) controlled under the Montreal Protocol on Substances That Deplete the Ozone Layer. CFCs are synthetic compounds formerly used as refrigerants and aerosol propellants and known to be harmful to the ozone layer of the atmosphere. Under the Montreal Protocol, the CFCs to be measured are those found in prepolymers; aerosol products; portable fire extinguishers; vehicle air conditioning units; insulation boards, panels and pipe covers; and domestic and commercial refrigeration, air conditioning and heat pump equipment.

Cigarette consumption per adult The sum of production and imports minus exports of cigarettes divided by the population aged 15 and above.

Computers in use, personal Self-contained computers in use that are designed to be operated by a single user at a time.

Consumer price index Reflects changes in the cost to the average consumer of acquiring a basket of goods and services that may be fixed or may change at specified intervals.

Contraceptive prevalence The percentage of married women (including women in union) aged 15–49 who are using, or whose partners are using, any form of contraception, whether modern or traditional.

Contributing family worker Defined according to the 1993 International Classification by Status in

Employment (ICSE) as a person who works without pay in an economic enterprise operated by a related person living in the same household.

Crime, people victimized by The percentage of the population who perceive that they have been victimized by certain types of crime in the preceding year, based on responses to the International Crime Victims Survey.

Debt relief committed under HIPC initiative Forgiveness of loans as a component of official development assistance under the Debt Initiative for Heavily Indebted Poor Countries (HIPCs). The initiative is the first comprehensive approach to reducing the external debt of the world's poorest, most heavily indebted countries, which total 42 in number.

Debt service, total The sum of principal repayments and interest actually paid in foreign currency, goods or services on long-term debt (having a maturity of more than one year), interest paid on short-term debt and repayments to the International Monetary Fund.

Drugs, affordable essential, population with sustainable access to The estimated percentage of the population for whom a minimum of 20 of the most essential drugs—those that satisfy the health care needs of the majority of the population—are continuously and affordably available at public or private health facilities or drug outlets within one hour's travel from home.

Earned income (PPP US$), estimated (female and male) Roughly derived on the basis of the ratio of the female non-agricultural wage to the male non-agricultural wage, the female and male shares of the economically active population, total female and male population and GDP per capita (PPP US$). For details on this estimation, see technical note 1.

Earned income, ratio of estimated female to male The ratio of estimated female earned income to estimated male earned income. See *earned income (PPP US$), estimated (female and male)*.

Economic activity rate The share of the population aged 15 and above who supply, or are available to supply, labour for the production of goods and services.

Education expenditure, public Includes both capital expenditures (spending on construction, renovation, major repairs and purchase of heavy equipment or vehicles) and current expenditures (spending on goods and services that are consumed within the cur-

rent year and would need to be renewed the following year). It covers such expenditures as staff salaries and benefits, contracted or purchased services, books and teaching materials, welfare services, furniture and equipment, minor repairs, fuel, insurance, rents, telecommunications and travel. See *education levels*.

Education index One of the three indices on which the human development index is built. It is based on the adult literacy rate and the combined primary, secondary and tertiary gross enrolment ratio. For details on how the index is calculated, see technical note 1.

Education levels Categorized as pre-primary, primary, secondary or tertiary in accordance with the International Standard Classification of Education (ISCED). *Pre-primary education* (ISCED level 0) is provided at such schools as kindergartens and nursery and infant schools and is intended for children not old enough to enter school at the primary level. *Primary education* (ISCED level 1) provides the basic elements of education at such establishments as primary and elementary schools. *Secondary education* (ISCED levels 2 and 3) is based on at least four years of previous instruction at the first level and provides general or specialized instruction, or both, at such institutions as middle schools, secondary schools, high schools, teacher training schools at this level and vocational or technical schools. *Tertiary education* (ISCED levels 5–7) refers to education at such institutions as universities, teachers colleges and higher-level professional schools—requiring as a minimum condition of admission the successful completion of education at the second level or evidence of the attainment of an equivalent level of knowledge.

Electricity consumption per capita Refers to gross production, in per capita terms, which includes consumption by station auxiliaries and any losses in the transformers that are considered integral parts of the station. Also included is total electric energy produced by pumping installations without deduction of electric energy absorbed by pumping.

Employment by economic activity Employment in industry, agriculture or services as defined according to the International Standard Industrial Classification (ISIC) system (revisions 2 and 3). *Industry* refers to mining and quarrying, manufacturing, construction and public utilities (gas, water and electricity). *Agriculture* refers to activities in agriculture, hunting, forestry and fishing. *Services* refer to wholesale and retail trade; restaurants and hotels; transport, storage and communications; finance, insurance, real estate and business services; and community, social and personal services.

Energy use, GDP per unit of The ratio of GDP (PPP US$) to commercial energy use, measured in kilograms of oil equivalent. This ratio provides a measure of energy efficiency by showing comparable and consistent estimates of real GDP across countries relative to physical inputs (units of energy use). See *GDP (gross domestic product)* and *PPP (purchasing power parity)*.

Enrolment ratio, gross The number of students enrolled in a level of education, regardless of age, as a percentage of the population of official school age for that level. The gross enrolment ratio can be greater than 100% as a result of grade repetition and entry at ages younger or older than the typical age at that grade level. See *education levels*.

Enrolment ratio, net The number of students enrolled in a level of education who are of official school age for that level, as a percentage of the population of official school age for that level. See *education levels*.

Exports, high technology Exports of products with a high intensity of research and development. They include high-technology products such as in aerospace, computers, pharmaceuticals, scientific instruments and electrical machinery.

Exports, manufactured Defined according to the Standard International Trade Classification to include exports of chemicals, basic manufactures, machinery and transport equipment and other miscellaneous manufactured goods.

Exports of goods and services The value of all goods and other market services provided to the rest of the world. Included is the value of merchandise, freight, insurance, transport, travel, royalties, licence fees and other services, such as communication, construction, financial, information, business, personal and government services. Excluded are labour and property income and transfer payments.

Exports, primary Defined according to the Standard International Trade Classification to include exports of food, agricultural raw materials, fuels and ores and metals.

Fertility rate, total The number of children that would be born to each woman if she were to live to the end of her child-bearing years and bear children at each age in accordance with prevailing age-specific fertility rates.

Foreign direct investment, net inflows of Net inflows of investment to acquire a lasting management interest (10% or more of voting stock) in an enterprise operating in an economy other than that of the investor. It is the sum of equity capital, reinvestment of earnings, other long-term capital and short-term capital.

Fuel consumption, traditional Estimated consumption of fuel wood, charcoal, bagasse (sugar cane waste) and animal and vegetable wastes. Total energy use comprises commercial energy use and traditional fuel use.

GDP (gross domestic product) The sum of value added by all resident producers in the economy plus any product taxes (less subsidies) not included in the valuation of output. It is calculated without making deductions for depreciation of fabricated capital assets or for depletion and degradation of natural resources. Value added is the net output of an industry after adding up all outputs and subtracting intermediate inputs.

GDP (US$) GDP converted to US dollars using the average official exchange rate reported by the International Monetary Fund. An alternative conversion factor is applied if the official exchange rate is judged to diverge by an exceptionally large margin from the rate effectively applied to transactions in foreign currencies and traded products. See *GDP (gross domestic product)*.

GDP index One of the three indices on which the human development index is built. It is based on GDP per capita (PPP US$). For details on how the index is calculated, see technical note 1.

GDP per capita (PPP US$) See *GDP (gross domestic product)* and *PPP (purchasing power parity)*.

GDP per capita (US$) GDP (US$) divided by midyear population. See *GDP (US$)*.

GDP per capita annual growth rate Least squares annual growth rate, calculated from constant price GDP per capita in local currency units.

Gender empowerment measure (GEM) A composite index measuring gender inequality in three basic dimensions of empowerment—economic participation and decision-making, political participation and decision-making and power over economic resources. For details on how the index is calculated, see technical note 1.

Gender-related development index (GDI) A composite index measuring average achievement in the three basic dimensions captured in the human development index—a long and healthy life, knowledge and a decent standard of living—adjusted to account for inequalities between men and women. For details on how the index is calculated, see technical note 1.

Gini index Measures the extent to which the distribution of income (or consumption) among individuals or households within a country deviates from a perfectly equal distribution. A Lorenz curve plots the cumulative percentages of total income received against the cumulative number of recipients, starting with the poorest individual or household. The Gini index measures the area between the Lorenz curve and a hypothetical line of absolute equality, expressed as a percentage of the maximum area under the line. A value of 0 represents perfect equality, a value of 100 perfect inequality.

GNI (gross national income) The sum of value added by all resident producers in the economy plus any product taxes (less subsidies) not included in the valuation of output plus net receipts of primary income (compensation of employees and property income) from abroad. Value added is the net output of an industry after adding up all outputs and subtracting intermediate inputs. Data are in current US dollars converted using the World Bank Atlas method.

Grants by NGOs, net Resource transfers by national non-governmental organizations (private non-profit-making agencies) to developing countries or territories identified in part I of the Development Assistance Committee (DAC) list of recipient countries. They are calculated as gross outflows from NGOs minus resource transfers received from the official sector (which are already counted in official development assistance).

Health expenditure per capita (PPP US$) The sum of public and private expenditure (in PPP US$), divided by the population. Health expenditure includes the provision of health services (preventive and curative), family planning activities, nutrition activities and emergency aid designated for health, but excludes the provision of water and sanitation. See *health expenditure, private; health expenditure, public;* and *PPP (purchasing power parity).*

Health expenditure, private Direct household (out of pocket) spending, private insurance, spending by non-profit institutions serving households and direct service payments by private corporations. Together with public health expenditure, it makes up total health expenditure. See *health expenditure per capita (PPP US$)* and *health expenditure, public.*

Health expenditure, public Current and capital spending from government (central and local) budgets,

external borrowings and grants (including donations from international agencies and non-governmental organizations) and social (or compulsory) health insurance funds. Together with private health expenditure, it makes up total health expenditure. See *health expenditure per capita (PPP US$)* and *health expenditure, private.*

HIPC completion point The date at which a country included in the Debt Initiative for Heavily Indebted Poor Countries (HIPCs) successfully completes the key structural reforms agreed on at the HIPC decision point, including developing and implementing a poverty reduction strategy. The country then receives the bulk of its debt relief under the HIPC initiative without further policy conditions.

HIPC decision point The date at which a heavily indebted poor country with an established track record of good performance under adjustment programmes supported by the International Monetary Fund and the World Bank commits, under the Debt Initiative for Heavily Indebted Poor Countries (HIPCs), to undertake additional reforms and to develop and implement a poverty reduction strategy.

HIV/AIDS, people living with The estimated number of people living with HIV/AIDS at the end of the year specified.

HIV prevalence among pregnant women The percentage of pregnant women in the specified age group who are infected with HIV.

Human development index (HDI) A composite index measuring average achievement in three basic dimensions of human development—a long and healthy life, knowledge and a decent standard of living. For details on how the index is calculated, see technical note 1.

Human poverty index (HPI-1) for developing countries A composite index measuring deprivations in the three basic dimensions captured in the human development index—a long and healthy life, knowledge and a decent standard of living. For details on how the index is calculated, see technical note 1.

Human poverty index (HPI-2) for selected OECD countries A composite index measuring deprivations in the three basic dimensions captured in the human development index—a long and healthy life, knowledge and a decent standard of living—and also capturing social exclusion. For details on how the index is calculated, see technical note 1.

Illiteracy rate, adult Calculated as 100 minus the adult literacy rate. See *literacy rate, adult.*

Immunization, one-year-olds fully immunized against measles or tuberculosis One-year-olds injected with an antigen or a serum containing specific antibodies against measles or tuberculosis.

Imports from developing countries admitted free of duties The value of exports of goods (excluding arms) from developing countries that are admitted without a tariff.

Imports of goods and services The value of all goods and other market services received from the rest of the world. Included is the value of merchandise, freight, insurance, transport, travel, royalties, licence fees and other services, such as communication, construction, financial, information, business, personal and government services. Excluded are labour and property income and transfer payments.

Income poverty line, population below The percentage of the population living below the specified poverty line:
- $1 a day—at 1985 international prices (equivalent to $1.08 at 1993 international prices), adjusted for purchasing power parity.
- $2 a day—at 1985 international prices (equivalent to $2.15 at 1993 international prices), adjusted for purchasing power parity.
- $4 a day—at 1990 international prices, adjusted for purchasing power parity.
- $11 a day (per person for a family of three)—at 1994 international prices, adjusted for purchasing power parity.
- National poverty line—the poverty line deemed appropriate for a country by its authorities. National estimates are based on population-weighted subgroup estimates from household surveys.
- 50% of median income—50% of the median adjusted household disposable income.

See *PPP (purchasing power parity).*

Income or consumption, national, share of poorest 20% in The share of income or consumption accruing to the poorest 20% of the population. Data on personal or household income or consumption come from nationally representative household surveys.

Income or consumption, shares of The shares of income or consumption accruing to subgroups of population indicated by deciles or quintiles, based on national household surveys covering various years. Consumption surveys produce results showing lower levels of inequality between poor and rich than do income surveys, as poor people generally consume a greater share of their income. Because data come from surveys covering different years and using different methodologies, comparisons between countries must be made with caution.

Infant mortality rate The probability of dying between birth and exactly one year of age, expressed per 1,000 live births.

Internally displaced people People who are displaced within their own country and to whom the United Nations High Commissioner for Refugees (UNHCR) extends protection or assistance, or both, generally pursuant to a special request by a competent organ of the United Nations.

Internet users People with access to the worldwide network.

Labour force All those employed (including people above a specified age who, during the reference period, were in paid employment, at work, self-employed or with a job but not at work) and unemployed (including people above a specified age who, during the reference period, were without work, currently available for work and seeking work).

Land covered by forest Forest and other wooded land, as defined in the Food and Agriculture Organization's *Global Forest Resources Assessment 2000* (FAO 2001), as a share of the total land area.

Legislators, senior officials and managers, female Women's share of positions defined according to the International Standard Classification of Occupations (ISCO-88) to include legislators, senior government officials, traditional chiefs and heads of villages, senior officials of special interest organizations, corporate managers, directors and chief executives, production and operations department managers and other department and general managers.

Life expectancy at birth The number of years a newborn infant would live if prevailing patterns of age-specific mortality rates at the time of birth were to stay the same throughout the child's life.

Life expectancy index One of the three indices on which the human development index is built. For details on how the index is calculated, see technical note 1.

Literacy rate, adult The percentage of people aged 15 and above who can, with understanding, both read and write a short, simple statement related to their everyday life.

Literacy rate, youth The percentage of people aged 15–24 who can, with understanding, both read and write a short, simple statement related to their everyday life.

Literacy skills, functional, people lacking The share of the population aged 16–65 scoring at level 1 on the prose literacy scale of the International Adult Literacy Survey. Most tasks at this level require the reader to locate a piece of information in the text that is identical to or synonymous with the information given in the directive.

Malaria cases The total number of malaria cases reported to the World Health Organization by countries in which malaria is endemic. Many countries report only laboratory-confirmed cases, but many in Sub-Saharan Africa report clinically diagnosed cases as well.

Malaria prevention, children under five The percentage of children under five sleeping under insecticide-treated bed nets.

Malaria-related mortality rate The total number of deaths caused by malaria per 100,000 people.

Malaria treatment, children under five with fever The percentage of children under five who were ill with fever in the two weeks before the survey and received antimalarial drugs.

Market activities Defined according to the 1993 revised UN System of National Accounts to include employment in establishments, primary production not in establishments, services for income and other production of goods not in establishments. See *non-market activities* and *work time, total.*

Maternal mortality ratio The annual number of deaths of women from pregnancy-related causes per 100,000 live births.

Military expenditure All expenditures of the defence ministry and other ministries on recruiting and training military personnel as well as on construction and purchase of military supplies and equipment. Military assistance is included in the expenditures of the donor country.

Non-market activities Defined according to the 1993 revised UN System of National Accounts to include household maintenance (cleaning, laundry and meal preparation and cleanup), management and shopping for own household; care for children, the sick, the elderly and the disabled in own household; and community services. See *market activities* and *work time, total.*

Official aid Grants or loans that meet the same standards as for official development assistance (ODA) except that recipient countries do not qualify as recipients of ODA. These countries are identified in part II of the Development Assistance Committee (DAC) list of recipient countries, which includes more advanced countries of Central and Eastern Europe, the countries of the former Soviet Union and certain advanced developing countries and territories.

Official development assistance (ODA), net Disbursements of loans made on concessional terms (net of repayments of principal) and grants by official agencies of the members of the Development Assistance Committee (DAC), by multilateral institutions and by non-DAC countries to promote economic development and welfare in countries and territories in part I of the DAC list of aid recipients. It includes loans with a grant element of at least 25% (calculated at a rate of discount of 10%).

Official development assistance (ODA) provided to help build trade capacity ODA directed to activities intended to enhance the ability of the recipient country to formulate and implement a trade development strategy and create an enabling environment for increasing the volume and value added of exports, diversifying export products and markets and increasing foreign investment to generate jobs and trade; stimulate trade by domestic firms and encourage investment in trade-oriented industries; or participate in and benefit from the institutions, negotiations and processes that shape national trade policy and the rules and practices of international commerce.

Official development assistance (ODA) to basic social services ODA directed to basic social services, which include basic education (primary education, early childhood education and basic life skills for youth and adults), basic health (including basic health care, basic health infrastructure, basic nutrition, infectious disease control, health education and health personnel development) and population policies and programmes and reproductive health (population policy and administrative management, reproductive health care, family planning, control of sexually transmitted diseases, including HIV/AIDS, and personnel development for population and reproductive health). Aid to water supply and sanitation is included only if it has a poverty focus.

Official development assistance (ODA) to least developed countries See *official development assistance (ODA), net* and country classifications for least developed countries.

Official development assistance (ODA), untied bilateral ODA for which the associated goods and services may be fully and freely procured in substantially all countries and that is given by one country to another.

Oral rehydration therapy use rate The percentage of all cases of diarrhoea in children under age five in which the child received increased fluids and continued feeding.

Orphans' school attendance rate As reported in household surveys, the proportion of children aged 10–14 who have lost both natural parents and are currently attending school. It is shown as a percentage of the proportion of non-orphaned children of the same age who live with at least one parent and are attending school.

Patents granted to residents Refers to documents issued by a government office that describe an invention and create a legal situation in which the patented invention can normally be exploited (made, used, sold, imported) only by or with the authorization of the patentee. The protection of inventions is generally limited to 20 years from the filing date of the application for the grant of a patent.

Physicians Includes graduates of a faculty or school of medicine who are working in any medical field (including teaching, research and practice).

Population growth rate, annual Refers to the average annual exponential growth rate for the period indicated. See *population, total*.

Population, total Refers to the de facto population, which includes all people actually present in a given area at a given time.

Poverty gap ratio The mean distance below the $1 (1993 PPP US$) a day poverty line, expressed as a percentage of the poverty line. The mean is taken over the entire population, counting the non-poor as having zero poverty gap. The measure reflects the depth of poverty as well as its incidence.

PPP (purchasing power parity) A rate of exchange that accounts for price differences across countries, allowing international comparisons of real output and incomes. At the PPP US$ rate (as used in this Report),

PPP US$1 has the same purchasing power in the domestic economy as $1 has in the United States.

Private flows, other A category combining non-debt-creating portfolio equity investment flows (the sum of country funds, depository receipts and direct purchases of shares by foreign investors), portfolio debt flows (bond issues purchased by foreign investors) and bank and trade-related lending (commercial bank lending and other commercial credits).

Probability at birth of not surviving to a specified age Calculated as 1 minus the probability of surviving to a specified age for a given cohort. See *probability at birth of surviving to a specified age*.

Probability at birth of surviving to a specified age The probability of a newborn infant surviving to a specified age if subject to prevailing patterns of age-specific mortality rates.

Professional and technical workers, female Women's share of positions defined according to the International Standard Classification of Occupations (ISCO-88) to include physical, mathematical and engineering science professionals (and associate professionals), life science and health professionals (and associate professionals), teaching professionals (and associate professionals) and other professionals and associate professionals.

Protected area, as a ratio to surface area Refers to totally or partially protected areas of at least 1,000 hectares that are designated as national parks, natural monuments, nature reserves or wildlife sanctuaries, protected landscapes and seascapes or scientific reserves with limited public access. The data do not include sites protected under local or provincial law.

Refugees People who have fled their country because of a well-founded fear of persecution for reasons of their race, religion, nationality, political opinion or membership in a particular social group and who cannot or do not want to return. *Country of asylum* is the country in which a refugee has filed a claim of asylum but has not yet received a decision or is otherwise registered as an asylum seeker. *Country of origin* refers to the claimant's nationality or country of citizenship.

Research and development expenditures Current and capital expenditures (including overhead) on creative, systematic activity intended to increase the stock of knowledge. Included are fundamental and applied research and experimental development work leading to new devices, products or processes.

Royalties and licence fees, receipts of Receipts by residents from non-residents for the authorized use of intangible, non-produced, non-financial assets and proprietary rights (such as patents, trademarks, copyrights, franchises and industrial processes) and for the use, through licensing agreements, of produced originals of prototypes (such as films and manuscripts). Data are based on the balance of payments.

Sanitation facilities, population with access to improved The percentage of the population with access to adequate excreta disposal facilities, such as a connection to a sewer or septic tank system, a pour-flush latrine, a simple pit latrine or a ventilated improved pit latrine. An excreta disposal system is considered adequate if it is private or shared (but not public) and if it can effectively prevent human, animal and insect contact with excreta.

Science, math and engineering, tertiary students in The share of tertiary students enrolled in natural sciences; engineering; mathematics and computer sciences; architecture and town planning; transport and communications; trade, craft and industrial programmes; and agriculture, forestry and fisheries. See *education levels*.

Scientists and engineers in R&D People trained to work in any field of science who are engaged in professional research and development (R&D) activity. Most such jobs require the completion of tertiary education.

Seats in parliament held by women Refers to seats held by women in a lower or single house or an upper house or senate, where relevant.

Solid fuels, population using The share of the population using solid fuels, which include traditional fuels such as fuel wood, charcoal, bagasse (sugar cane waste) and animal and vegetable wastes.

Tariffs on agricultural products, textiles and clothing from developing countries, average The simple average of all ad valorem tariff rates applied to imports of agricultural products (plant and animal products, including tree crops but excluding timber and fish products), textiles and clothing (including natural and man-made fibres and fabrics and articles of clothing made from them) from developing countries. The tariff rates used are the available ad valorem rates, including most favoured nation (MFN) and non-MFN (largely preferential) rates.

Telephone mainlines Telephone lines connecting a customer's equipment to the public switched telephone network.

Tenure, households with access to secure Households that own or are purchasing their homes, are renting privately or are in social housing or subtenancy.

Terms of trade The ratio of the export price index to the import price index measured relative to a base year. A value of more than 100 means that the price of exports has risen relative to the price of imports.

Tuberculosis cases The total number of tuberculosis cases reported to the World Health Organization. A tuberculosis case is defined as a patient in whom tuberculosis has been bacteriologically confirmed or diagnosed by a clinician.

Tuberculosis cases cured under DOTS The percentage of estimated new infectious tuberculosis cases cured under the directly observed treatment, short course (DOTS) case detection and treatment strategy.

Tuberculosis cases detected under DOTS The percentage of estimated new infectious tuberculosis cases detected (diagnosed in a given period) under the directly observed treatment, short course (DOTS) case detection and treatment strategy.

Tuberculosis-related mortality rate The total number of deaths caused by tuberculosis per 100,000 people. The data are compiled from reports provided at registration of death.

Under-five mortality rate The probability of dying between birth and exactly five years of age, expressed per 1,000 live births.

Under height for age, children under age five Includes moderate and severe stunting, defined as more than two standard deviations below the median height for age of the reference population.

Undernourished people People whose food intake is chronically insufficient to meet their minimum energy requirements.

Under weight for age, children under age five Includes moderate underweight, defined as more than two standard deviations below the median weight for age of the reference population, and severe underweight, defined as more than three standard deviations below the median weight.

Unemployment Refers to all people above a specified age who are not in paid employment or self-employed, but are available for work and have taken specific steps to seek paid employment or self-employment.

Unemployment, long term Unemployment lasting 12 months or longer. See *unemployment*.

Unemployment rate The unemployed divided by the labour force (those employed plus the unemployed).

Unemployment, youth Refers to unemployment between the ages of 15 or 16 and 24, depending on the national definition. See *unemployment*.

Urban population The midyear population of areas classified as urban according to the criteria used by each country, as reported to the United Nations. See *population, total*.

Water source, improved, population without sustainable access to Calculated as 100 minus the percentage of the population with sustainable access to an improved water source. Unimproved sources include vendors, bottled water, tanker trucks and unprotected wells and springs. See *water source, improved, population with sustainable access to*.

Water source, improved, population with sustainable access to The share of the population with reasonable access to any of the following types of water supply for drinking: household connections, public standpipes, boreholes, protected dug wells, protected springs and rainwater collection. *Reasonable access* is defined as the availability of at least 20 litres a person per day from a source within one kilometre of the user's dwelling.

Women in government at ministerial level Defined according to each state's definition of a national executive and may include women serving as ministers and vice ministers and those holding other ministerial positions, including parliamentary secretaries.

Work time, total Time spent on market and non-market activities as defined according to the 1993 revised UN System of National Accounts. See *market activities* and *non-market activities*.

Statistical references

Aten, Bettina, Alan Heston and Robert Summers. 2001. "Penn World Tables 6.0." University of Pennsylvania, Center for International Comparisons, Philadelphia.

———. 2002. "Penn World Tables 6.1." University of Pennsylvania, Center for International Comparisons, Philadelphia.

Birzeit University. 2002. *Palestine Human Development Report 2002*. Ramallah, Occupied Palestinian Territories.

CDIAC (Carbon Dioxide Information Analysis Center). 2003. *Trends: A Compendium of Data on Global Change.* [http://cdiac.esd.ornl.gov/trends/trends.htm]. March 2003.

FAO (Food and Agriculture Organization of the United Nations). 2001. *Global Forest Resources Assessment 2000*. Rome.

Goldschmidt-Clermont, Luisella, and Elisabetta Pagnossin Aligisakis. 1995. "Measures of Unrecorded Economic Activities in Fourteen Countries." Background paper for *Human Development Report 1995*. United Nations Development Programme, Human Development Report Office, New York.

Harvey, Andrew S. 1995. "Market and Non-Market Productive Activity in Less Developed and Developing Countries: Lessons from Time Use." Background paper for *Human Development Report 1995*. United Nations Development Programme, Human Development Report Office, New York.

———. 2001. "National Time Use Data on Market and Non-Market Work by Both Women and Men." Background paper for *Human Development Report 2001*. United Nations Development Programme, Human Development Report Office, New York.

Hijab, Nadia. 2003. "Using Process Indicators to Monitor Maternal Health." Background note for *Human Development Report 2003*. United Nations Development Programme, Human Development Report Office, New York.

IISS (International Institute for Strategic Studies). 2002. *The Military Balance 2002–2003*. Oxford: Oxford University Press.

ILO (International Labour Organization). 2002a. *Estimates and Projections of the Economically Active Population, 1950–2010*. 4th ed., rev. 2. Database. Geneva.

———. 2002b. *Key Indicators of the Labour Market 2001–2002*. [http://kilm.ilo.org/kilm/]. March 2003.

———. 2002c. *Yearbook of Labour Statistics*. Geneva.

———. 2003a. *ILO Database on International Labour Standards (ILOLEX)*. [http://ilolex.ilo.ch:1567/english/index.htm]. February 2003.

———. 2003b. *Laboursta Database*. [http://laborsta.ilo.org]. March 2003.

IPU (Inter-Parliamentary Union). 1995. *Women in Parliaments 1945–1995: A World Statistical Survey*. Geneva.

———. 2001. Correspondence on women in government at the ministerial level. March. Geneva.

———. 2003a. Correspondence on year women received the right to vote and to stand for election and year first woman was elected or appointed to parliament. March. Geneva.

———. 2003b. *Parline Database and World Classification of Women in National Parliaments*. [http://www.ipu.org]. March 2003.

ITU (International Telecommunication Union). 2003a. Correspondence on telephone mainlines, cellular subscribers, Internet users and personal computers. April. Geneva.

———. 2003b. *World Telecommunication Indicators*. Database. Geneva.

LIS (Luxembourg Income Study). 2002. "Population below Income Poverty Line." [http://lisweb.ceps.lu/keyfigures/povertytable.htm]. February 2002.

———. 2003. "Relative Poverty Rates for the Total Population, Children and the Elderly." [http://www.lisproject.org/keyfigures/povertytable.htm]. March 2003.

Mathers, Colin D., Ritu Sadana, Joshua A. Salomon, Christopher J. L. Murray and Alan D. Lopez. 2001. "Healthy Life Expectancy in 191 Countries, 1999." *Lancet* 357 (9269): 1685–91.

Milanovic, Branko. 2002. Correspondence on income, inequality and poverty during the transition from planned to market economy. March. World Bank, Washington, DC.

OECD (Organisation for Economic Co-operation and Development). 2002a. *Economic Outlook*. 2 (72). Paris.

———. 2002b. *Employment Outlook 2002*. Paris.

OECD (Organisation for Economic Co-operation and Development), Development Assistance Committee. 2003a. Correspondence on official development assistance disbursed. February. Paris.

———. 2003b. *DAC Online*. Database. Paris.

OECD (Organisation for Economic Co-operation and Development) and Statistics Canada. 2000. *Literacy in the Information Age: Final Report on the International Adult Literacy Survey*. Paris.

SIPRI (Stockholm International Peace Research Institute). 2001. *SIPRI Yearbook: Armaments, Disarmament and International Security*. Oxford: Oxford University Press.

———. 2003a. Correspondence on military expenditure. March. Stockholm.

———. 2003b. *SIPRI Arms Transfers*. Database. February. Stockholm.

Smeeding, Timothy M. 1997. "Financial Poverty in Developed Countries: The Evidence from the Luxembourg Income Study." In United Nations Development Programme, *Human Development Report 1997 Papers: Poverty and Human Development*. New York.

Smeeding, Timothy M., Lee Rainwater and Gary Burtless. 2002. "United States Poverty in a Cross-National Context." In Sheldon H. Danziger and Robert H. Haveman, eds., *Understanding Poverty*. New York: Russell Sage Foundation; and Cambridge, Mass.: Harvard University Press.

UN (United Nations). 2002a. Correspondence on time use surveys. February. Department of Economic and Social Affairs, Statistics Division, New York.

———. 2002b. *World Urbanization Prospects: The 2001 Revision*. Department of Economic and Social Affairs, Population Division, New York.

———. 2003a. *Millennium Indicators Database*. Department of Economic and Social Affairs, Statistics Division, New York. [http://millenniumindicators.un.org]. March 2003.

———. 2003b. "Multilateral Treaties Deposited with the Secretary-General." [http://untreaty.un.org]. February 2003.

———. 2003c. *United Nations Population Division Database on Contraceptive Use*. March. Department of Economic and Social Affairs, Population Division, New York.

——. 2003d. *World Population Prospects 1950–2050: The 2002 Revision*. Database. Department of Economic and Social Affairs, Population Division, New York.

UNAIDS (Joint United Nations Programme on HIV/AIDS) and WHO (World Health Organization). 2003. Correspondence on adult HIV/AIDS prevalence rates. March. Geneva.

UNAIDS (Joint United Nations Programme on HIV/AIDS). 2002. *Report on the Global HIV/AIDS Epidemic 2002*. Geneva.

UNCTAD (United Nations Conference on Trade and Development). 2001. "Third United Nations Conference on the Least Developed Countries." [http://www.unctad.org/conference/]. April 2002.

UNDP (United Nations Development Programme). 2002. *Bosnia and Herzegovina Human Development Report 2002*. Sarajevo.

UNEP (United Nations Environment Programme) World Conservation Monitoring Centre and IUCN (The World Conservation Union) World Commission on Protected Areas. 2003. *World Database on Protected Areas*. [http://sea.unep-wcmc.org/wdbpa/UN.cfm]. April 2003.

UNESCO (United Nations Educational, Scientific and Cultural Organization). 1997. *International Standard Classification of Education 1997*. [http://portal.unesco.org/uis/TEMPLATE/pdf/isced/ISCED_A.pdf]. March 2003.

——. 1999. *Statistical Yearbook 1999*. Paris.

UNESCO Institute for Statistics. 2001. Correspondence on combined gross enrolment ratio. March. Paris.

——. 2003a. Correspondence on adult and youth literacy rates. January. Montreal.

——. 2003b. Correspondence on combined gross enrolment ratios. March. Montreal.

——. 2003c. Correspondence on education expenditure. February. Montreal.

——. 2003d. Correspondence on gross and net enrolment ratios and children reaching grade 5. February. Montreal.

——. 2003e. "Literacy Assessment and Monitoring Programme." Background note for *Human Development Report 2003*. United Nations Development Programme, Human Development Report Office, New York.

UNFPA (United Nations Population Fund). 2003. "Building Capacity to Ensure the Continuity of Population Censuses." Background note for *Human Development Report 2003*. United Nations Development Programme, Human Development Report Office, New York.

UNHCR (United Nations High Commissioner for Refugees). 2002. *Statistical Yearbook 2001*. Geneva.

UNICEF (United Nations Children's Fund). 2000. *The State of the World's Children 2001*. New York: Oxford University Press.

——. 2003a. Correspondence on infant and under-five mortality rates. January. New York.

——. 2003b. *The State of the World's Children 2003*. New York: Oxford University Press.

UNICEF (United Nations Children's Fund), WHO (World Health Organization) and UNFPA (United Nations Population Fund). 1997. *Guidelines for Monitoring the Availability and Use of Obstetric Services*. New York.

UNICRI (United Nations Interregional Crime and Justice Research Institute). 2002. Correspondence on crime victims. March. Turin.

WHO (World Health Organization). 1994. *Indicators to Monitor Maternal Health Goals: Report of a Technical Working Group, Geneva, 8–12 November 1993*. Geneva.

——. 2002. *World Health Report 2002: Reducing Risks, Promoting Healthy Life*. Geneva.

——. 2003a. Correspondence on cigarette consumption. March. Geneva.

——. 2003b. Correspondence on health expenditure. March. Geneva.

——. 2003c. Correspondence on health personnel. March. Geneva.

——. 2003d. Correspondence on immunization against tuberculosis and measles. March. Geneva.

——. 2003e. *Global Tuberculosis Control: WHO Report 2003*. [http://www.who.int/gtb/publications/globrep/]. March 2003.

——. 2003f. "Measuring Healthy Life Expectancy." Background note for *Human Development Report 2003*. United Nations Development Programme, Human Development Report Office, New York.

——. Forthcoming. *World Health Report 2003*. Geneva.

WIPO (World Intellectual Property Organization). 2003. *Intellectual Property Statistics*. Publication B. Geneva.

World Bank. 2002. *World Development Indicators 2002*. CD-ROM. Washington, DC.

——. 2003a. Correspondence on GDP per capita annual growth rates. March. Washington, DC.

——. 2003b. "HIPC Initiative: Status of Country Cases Considered under the Initiative, March 2003." [http://www.worldbank.org/hipc/progress-to-date/status_table_Mar03.pdf]. March 2003.

——. 2003c. *World Development Indicators 2003*. CD-ROM. Washington, DC.

——. Forthcoming. *Global Development Finance 2004*. Washington, DC.

Classification of countries

Countries in the human development aggregates [a]

High human development
(HDI 0.800 and above)

Argentina	Singapore
Australia	Slovakia
Austria	Slovenia
Bahamas	Spain
Bahrain	Sweden
Barbados	Switzerland
Belarus	Trinidad and Tobago
Belgium	United Arab Emirates
Brunei Darussalam	United Kingdom
Canada	United States
Chile	Uruguay
Costa Rica	*(55 countries or areas)*
Croatia	
Cuba	
Cyprus	
Czech Republic	
Denmark	
Estonia	
Finland	
France	
Germany	
Greece	
Hong Kong, China (SAR)	
Hungary	
Iceland	
Ireland	
Israel	
Italy	
Japan	
Korea, Rep. of	
Kuwait	
Latvia	
Lithuania	
Luxembourg	
Malta	
Mexico	
Netherlands	
New Zealand	
Norway	
Poland	
Portugal	
Qatar	
Saint Kitts and Nevis	
Seychelles	

Medium human development
(HDI 0.500–0.799)

Albania	Macedonia, TFYR
Algeria	Malaysia
Antigua and Barbuda	Maldives
Armenia	Mauritius
Azerbaijan	Moldova, Rep. of
Bangladesh	Mongolia
Belize	Morocco
Bhutan	Myanmar
Bolivia	Namibia
Bosnia and Herzegovina	Nicaragua
Botswana	Occupied Palestinian Territories
Brazil	Oman
Bulgaria	Panama
Cambodia	Papua New Guinea
Cape Verde	Paraguay
China	Peru
Colombia	Philippines
Comoros	Romania
Congo	Russian Federation
Dominica	Saint Lucia
Dominican Republic	Saint Vincent and
Ecuador	the Grenadines
Egypt	Samoa (Western)
El Salvador	São Tomé and Principe
Equatorial Guinea	Saudi Arabia
Fiji	Solomon Islands
Gabon	South Africa
Georgia	Sri Lanka
Ghana	Sudan
Grenada	Suriname
Guatemala	Swaziland
Guyana	Syrian Arab Republic
Honduras	Tajikistan
India	Thailand
Indonesia	Togo
Iran, Islamic Rep. of	Tunisia
Jamaica	Turkey
Jordan	Turkmenistan
Kazakhstan	Ukraine
Kyrgyzstan	Uzbekistan
Lao People's Dem. Rep.	Vanuatu
Lebanon	Venezuela
Lesotho	Viet Nam
Libyan Arab Jamahiriya	*(86 countries or areas)*

Low human development
(HDI below 0.500)

Angola
Benin
Burkina Faso
Burundi
Cameroon
Central African Republic
Chad
Congo, Dem. Rep. of the
Côte d'Ivoire
Djibouti
Eritrea
Ethiopia
Gambia
Guinea
Guinea-Bissau
Haiti
Kenya
Madagascar
Malawi
Mali
Mauritania
Mozambique
Nepal
Niger
Nigeria
Pakistan
Rwanda
Senegal
Sierra Leone
Tanzania, U. Rep. of
Uganda
Yemen
Zambia
Zimbabwe
(34 countries or areas)

---

a. Excludes the following UN member countries for which the HDI cannot be computed: Afghanistan, Andorra, Iraq, Kiribati, the Democratic Republic of Korea, Liberia, Liechtenstein, the Marshall Islands, the Federated States of Micronesia, Monaco, Nauru, Palau, San Marino, Serbia and Montenegro, Somalia, Timor-Leste, Tonga and Tuvalu.

Countries in the income aggregates [a]

High income *(GNI per capita of* *$9,206 or more in 2001)*	*Middle income* *(GNI per capita of* *$746–9,205 in 2001)*		*Low income* *(GNI per capita of* *$745 or less in 2001)*	
Andorra	Albania	Macedonia, TFYR	Afghanistan	Niger
Australia	Algeria	Malaysia	Angola	Nigeria
Austria	Antigua and Barbuda	Maldives	Armenia	Pakistan
Bahamas	Argentina	Malta	Azerbaijan	Papua New Guinea
Bahrain	Barbados	Marshall Islands	Bangladesh	Rwanda
Belgium	Belarus	Mauritius	Benin	São Tomé and Principe
Brunei Darussalam	Belize	Mexico	Bhutan	Senegal
Canada	Bolivia	Micronesia, Fed. Sts.	Burkina Faso	Sierra Leone
Cyprus	Bosnia and Herzegovina	Morocco	Burundi	Solomon Islands
Denmark	Botswana	Namibia	Cambodia	Somalia
Finland	Brazil	Occupied Palestinian Territories	Cameroon	Sudan
France	Bulgaria	Oman	Central African Republic	Tajikistan
Germany	Cape Verde	Palau	Chad	Tanzania, U. Rep. of
Greece	Chile	Panama	Comoros	Timor-Leste
Hong Kong, China (SAR)	China	Paraguay	Congo	Togo
Iceland	Colombia	Peru	Congo, Dem. Rep. of the	Uganda
Ireland	Costa Rica	Philippines	Côte d'Ivoire	Ukraine
Israel	Croatia	Poland	Equatorial Guinea	Uzbekistan
Italy	Cuba	Romania	Eritrea	Viet Nam
Japan	Czech Republic	Russian Federation	Ethiopia	Yemen
Korea, Rep. of	Djibouti	Saint Kitts and Nevis	Gambia	Zambia
Kuwait	Dominica	Saint Lucia	Georgia	Zimbabwe
Liechtenstein	Dominican Republic	Saint Vincent and	Ghana	*(66 countries or areas)*
Luxembourg	Ecuador	the Grenadines	Guinea	
Monaco	Egypt	Samoa (Western)	Guinea-Bissau	
Netherlands	El Salvador	Saudi Arabia	Haiti	
New Zealand	Estonia	Serbia and Montenegro	India	
Norway	Fiji	Seychelles	Indonesia	
Portugal	Gabon	Slovakia	Kenya	
Qatar	Grenada	South Africa	Korea, Dem. Rep. of	
San Marino	Guatemala	Sri Lanka	Kyrgyzstan	
Singapore	Guyana	Suriname	Lao People's Dem. Rep.	
Slovenia	Honduras	Swaziland	Lesotho	
Spain	Hungary	Syrian Arab Republic	Liberia	
Sweden	Iran, Islamic Rep. of	Thailand	Madagascar	
Switzerland	Iraq	Tonga	Malawi	
United Arab Emirates	Jamaica	Trinidad and Tobago	Mali	
United Kingdom	Jordan	Tunisia	Mauritania	
United States	Kazakhstan	Turkey	Moldova, Rep. of	
(39 countries or areas)	Kiribati	Turkmenistan	Mongolia	
	Latvia	Uruguay	Mozambique	
	Lebanon	Vanuatu	Myanmar	
	Libyan Arab Jamahiriya	Venezuela	Nepal	
	Lithuania	*(86 countries or areas)*	Nicaragua	

a. World Bank classification (effective as of 1 July 2002) based on gross national income (GNI) per capita. Excludes Nauru and Tuvalu because of lack of data.

Developing countries

Afghanistan	Honduras	Saint Vincent and	Djibouti	Croatia	Turkey
Algeria	Hong Kong, China (SAR)	the Grenadines	Equatorial Guinea	Czech Republic	United Kingdom
Angola	India	Samoa (Western)	Eritrea	Estonia	United States
Antigua and Barbuda	Indonesia	São Tomé and Principe	Ethiopia	Georgia	*(30 countries or areas)*
Argentina	Iran, Islamic Rep. of	Saudi Arabia	Gambia	Hungary	
Bahamas	Iraq	Senegal	Guinea	Kazakhstan	**High-income**
Bahrain	Jamaica	Seychelles	Guinea-Bissau	Kyrgyzstan	**OECD countries**[a]
Bangladesh	Jordan	Sierra Leone	Haiti	Latvia	Australia
Barbados	Kenya	Singapore	Kiribati	Lithuania	Austria
Belize	Kiribati	Solomon Islands	Lao People's Dem. Rep.	Macedonia, TFYR	Belgium
Benin	Korea, Dem. Rep. of	Somalia	Lesotho	Moldova, Rep. of	Canada
Bhutan	Korea, Rep. of	South Africa	Liberia	Poland	Denmark
Bolivia	Kuwait	Sri Lanka	Madagascar	Romania	Finland
Botswana	Lao People's Dem. Rep.	Sudan	Malawi	Russian Federation	France
Brazil	Lebanon	Suriname	Maldives	Serbia and Montenegro	Germany
Brunei Darussalam	Lesotho	Swaziland	Mali	Slovakia	Greece
Burkina Faso	Liberia	Syrian Arab Republic	Mauritania	Slovenia	Iceland
Burundi	Libyan Arab Jamahiriya	Tanzania, U. Rep. of	Mozambique	Tajikistan	Ireland
Cambodia	Madagascar	Thailand	Myanmar	Turkmenistan	Italy
Cameroon	Malawi	Timor-Leste	Nepal	Ukraine	Japan
Cape Verde	Malaysia	Togo	Niger	Uzbekistan	Korea, Rep. of
Central African Republic	Maldives	Tonga	Rwanda	*(27 countries or areas)*	Luxembourg
Chad	Mali	Trinidad and Tobago	Samoa (Western)		Netherlands
Chile	Marshall Islands	Tunisia	São Tomé and Principe		New Zealand
China	Mauritania	Turkey	Senegal	## OECD	Norway
Colombia	Mauritius	Tuvalu	Sierra Leone		Portugal
Comoros	Mexico	Uganda	Solomon Islands	Australia	Spain
Congo	Micronesia, Fed. Sts.	United Arab Emirates	Somalia	Austria	Sweden
Congo, Dem. Rep. of the	Mongolia	Uruguay	Sudan	Belgium	Switzerland
Costa Rica	Morocco	Vanuatu	Tanzania, U. Rep. of	Canada	United Kingdom
Côte d'Ivoire	Mozambique	Venezuela	Togo	Czech Republic	United States
Cuba	Myanmar	Viet Nam	Tuvalu	Denmark	*(24 countries or areas)*
Cyprus	Namibia	Yemen	Uganda	Finland	
Djibouti	Nauru	Zambia	Vanuatu	France	
Dominica	Nepal	Zimbabwe	Yemen	Germany	
Dominican Republic	Nicaragua	*(137 countries or areas)*	Zambia	Greece	
Ecuador	Niger		*(49 countries or areas)*	Hungary	
Egypt	Nigeria	**Least developed**		Iceland	
El Salvador	Occupied Palestinian	**countries**	## Central and	Ireland	
Equatorial Guinea	Territories	Afghanistan	Eastern Europe	Italy	
Eritrea	Oman	Angola	and the	Japan	
Ethiopia	Pakistan	Bangladesh	Commonwealth	Korea, Rep. of	
Fiji	Palau	Benin	of Independent	Luxembourg	
Gabon	Panama	Bhutan	States (CIS)	Mexico	
Gambia	Papua New Guinea	Burkina Faso		Netherlands	
Ghana	Paraguay	Burundi		New Zealand	
Grenada	Peru	Cambodia	Albania	Norway	
Guatemala	Philippines	Cape Verde	Armenia	Poland	
Guinea	Qatar	Central African Republic	Azerbaijan	Portugal	
Guinea-Bissau	Rwanda	Chad	Belarus	Slovakia	
Guyana	Saint Kitts and Nevis	Comoros	Bosnia and Herzegovina	Spain	
Haiti	Saint Lucia	Congo, Dem. Rep. of the	Bulgaria	Sweden	
				Switzerland	

a. Excludes the Czech Republic, Hungary, Mexico, Poland, Slovakia and Turkey.

Developing countries in the regional aggregates

Arab States

Algeria
Bahrain
Djibouti
Egypt
Iraq
Jordan
Kuwait
Lebanon
Libyan Arab Jamahiriya
Morocco
Occupied Palestinian
  Territories
Oman
Qatar
Saudi Arabia
Somalia
Sudan
Syrian Arab Republic
Tunisia
United Arab Emirates
Yemen
(20 countries or areas)

Asia and the Pacific

East Asia and the Pacific
Brunei Darussalam
Cambodia
China
Fiji
Hong Kong, China (SAR)
Indonesia
Kiribati
Korea, Dem. Rep. of
Korea, Rep. of
Lao People's Dem. Rep.
Malaysia
Marshall Islands
Micronesia, Fed. Sts.
Mongolia
Myanmar
Nauru
Palau
Papua New Guinea
Philippines
Samoa (Western)
Singapore
Solomon Islands
Thailand
Timor-Leste
Tonga
Tuvalu
Vanuatu
Viet Nam
(28 countries or areas)

South Asia
Afghanistan
Bangladesh
Bhutan
India
Iran, Islamic Rep. of
Maldives
Nepal
Pakistan
Sri Lanka
(9 countries or areas)

Latin America and the Caribbean

Antigua and Barbuda
Argentina
Bahamas
Barbados
Belize
Bolivia
Brazil
Chile
Colombia
Costa Rica
Cuba
Dominica
Dominican Republic
Ecuador
El Salvador
Grenada
Guatemala
Guyana
Haiti
Honduras
Jamaica
Mexico
Nicaragua
Panama
Paraguay
Peru
Saint Kitts and Nevis
Saint Lucia
Saint Vincent and
  the Grenadines
Suriname
Trinidad and Tobago
Uruguay
Venezuela
(33 countries or areas)

Southern Europe

Cyprus
Turkey
(2 countries or areas)

Sub-Saharan Africa

Angola
Benin
Botswana
Burkina Faso
Burundi
Cameroon
Cape Verde
Central African Republic
Chad
Comoros
Congo
Congo, Dem. Rep. of the
Côte d'Ivoire
Equatorial Guinea
Eritrea
Ethiopia
Gabon
Gambia
Ghana
Guinea
Guinea-Bissau
Kenya
Lesotho
Liberia
Madagascar
Malawi
Mali
Mauritania
Mauritius
Mozambique
Namibia
Niger
Nigeria
Rwanda
São Tomé and Principe
Senegal
Seychelles
Sierra Leone
South Africa
Swaziland
Tanzania, U. Rep. of
Togo
Uganda
Zambia
Zimbabwe
(45 countries or areas)